Henry Irving: The Actor and his World

———

Henry Irving
By Jules Bastien-Lepage

HENRY IRVING

THE ACTOR AND HIS WORLD

by his grandson
LAURENCE
IRVING

"A great man produces beauty, terror and mirth, and a little man produces cleverness (personality, psychology) instead of beauty, ugliness instead of terror, and jokes instead of mirth."

ROBERT LOUIS STEVENSON

New York
THE MACMILLAN COMPANY
1952

To
H. B. I.
and
L.S.I.

Contents

Contents

PART IV. HENRY IRVING AND ELLEN TERRY

PART V. SIR HENRY IRVING

Illustrations

Illustrations

12

Illustrations

'Three volumes, a stupendous book about a stupendous man, politician and ecclesiastic. As a biography uninteresting, because there are no trivialities which make up existence and banish pomposity.'

Henry Irving on Morley's *Life of Gladstone*

Preface

'Now is the winter of our discontent
Made glorious summer by this sun of York;
And all the clouds that lour'd upon our house
In the deep bosom of the ocean buried.
Now are our brows bound with victorious wreaths;
Our bruised arms hung up for monuments;
Our dreadful marches to delightful measures.
Grim-visag'd war hath smooth'd his wrinkled front;
And now,—instead of mounting barbed steeds,
To fright the souls of fearful adversaries,—
He capers nimbly in a lady's chamber
To the lasc. . . .'

The voice of Henry Irving, recorded for a few seconds upon a primitive cylinder of wax, fades away into the rasping crackle of surface noises. It is strong and deep. His delivery and articulation, in the opinion of those who have studied phonetics, seem faultless and an admirable model for students of acting today. If 'war' is nearer in rhyme to 'far' than to 'for', 'buried' plunges like a leadsman's plummet into unfathomable deeps; the four syllables of 'adversaries' sound like the clipping of horses' hooves along a grassy track. This fragmentary record is all that remains of the living Henry Irving.[1]

For the rest, the brittle cuttings from old newspapers, a hundred or so faded photographs, a gallery of drawings and cartoons of unequal merit, a thousand letters written or received and the little red account books in which were kept the carefully guarded secrets of revenue and expenditure at the Lyceum, must suffice as the raw material of his biography.

[1] In 1903 Irving recorded, in England, Shylock's speech from Act III, Scene I in *The Merchant of Venice,* for the Gramophone and Typewriting Company. A copy of this record is in the private collection of Mr. Roscoe Haley in New York, where it was played recently in a programme of the National Broadcasting Company. The author has not heard it, for there is no copy of it in this country.

15

Preface

'There is this unfortunate thing about the talent of an actor,' wrote Eugène Delacroix; 'after his death it is impossible to establish any comparison between him and his rivals, those who competed with him for applause during his lifetime. Posterity knows nothing of an actor save the reputation which his contemporaries made for him.'

This is only one of many solemn warnings to anybody who has the temerity to attempt to write the life of an actor. It is a task, seemingly, which by ordinary means is foredoomed to failure. 'Irving,' wrote Max Beerbohm, 'is but a memory—to be conjured out of the darkness.' Is sorcery, then, to be the biographer's last resort? Is it possible that by plunging the newspaper cuttings into the top hat of receptive detachment, by covering it with the cloth of sceptical impartiality, and by waving over it the magic wand of filial devotion, there may emerge from it, with the aid of mirrors in which the characters of his friends and enemies are reflected, an authentic presentment, if not of the actor, of the man?

Irving was a mystery to his contemporaries—even to his closest companions. The task of his biographer is to unravel this mystery, to sift the evidence which he soon discovers to be bewilderingly conflicting, and to examine the witnesses who contradict each other so fiercely. The chief witnesses for the defence—his three biographers, Brereton, Stoker and Hatton—individually claimed to be his most intimate companion, yet each in his record hardly refers to the other. Even the witnesses for the prosecution break down under relentless self-examination as the discretion of age extenuates the offences with which they charged the actor in his lifetime. Henry James, querulously critical of Irving in his youth, in his middle years wistfully reflected: 'How . . . can I not lose myself still more in the glory of a time that was to watch the drawn-out procession of Henry Irving's Shakespearian splendours at the transcendent Lyceum?' George Bernard Shaw, whose witty denunciations of Irving seemed at the time to be devastating in their discernment, wrote in the full vigour of his ninety-third year: 'I was never really fair to him, though Ellen [Terry] said that no critic understood him as I did.' Thus the eulogies of Irving's adulators and the animadversions of his detractors must be sprinkled with the salt of dispassionate assessment.

Curiously enough, of the mass of material available to Irving's biographer, the great bulk of professional criticism is not the most informative. As a rule, metropolitan critics judge a piece on its first performance. Actors of temperament are often not at their best on first nights. Irving, who bore the whole burden of artistic and financial

16

responsibility for his productions, often was at his worst—his nervous anxiety accentuating his lack of physical resource. Thus criticisms of his playing a particular part in a revival were often strangely at variance with those of his first appearance in it. Historical dramatic criticism is, in fact, useless unless it can be interpreted in terms of the taste, temper and character of the critic who wrote it. Hazlitt was not immune to personal rancour; Macaulay's literary criticisms must be read by the light of a Whig candle. Thus, William Archer's weakening resistance to Irving's mesmerism is seen to be natural enough now we know that in his later years the translator and champion of Ibsen had an outburst of repressed romanticism when he wrote a first-rate melodrama—*The Green Goddess*. The enthusiastic verbiage of Clement Scott is critical currency only if it is devalued in terms of his personal vanity and pulsating emotion. The poisoned barbs of G.B.S., with which he peppered the flanks of the Lyceosaurus, are patently lethal unless it is appreciated that they were fired by an ambitious and frustrated playwright who was exasperated by such jealousy as only platonic lovers know. Happily the derisive essays on the theatre which he contributed to the *Saturday Review* can be the more enjoyably construed by reference to the copious and revealing glossaries of his later work. When George Sampson began his admirable study of Irving by writing: 'Unless it is understood that Irving is great, there can be no comprehension of his life and art', it is only necessary to turn to his comparative essay on Bach and Shakespeare to realize that this is the pronouncement of a scholarly and analytical observer. So the biographer comes to depend more and more upon the opinions of contemporaries, with whose work, quality and prejudices his readers may be familiar, to reflect the work and quality of Henry Irving. Since there were few great or erudite men of that era who, at one time or another, were not attracted by his magnetism—and in the generous spirit of their time paid their tributes to him on paper—the task has been not to seek for evidence of this kind but to choose from the mass of letters he received those which contained no hint of flattery or self-interest.

Irving has been the subject of much bitter and often fatuous controversy. His biographer should be at pains to avoid being pressed into the ranks of the partisans. There is no excuse for another book about Irving unless it is conceived and written in a spirit of scrupulous objectivity. Less than a month after the actor's death, Shaw wrote to his son, Laurence: '. . . If you write a life of your father, don't make it a vestryman's epitaph. Let us have the truth about the artist the stupendously selfish, self-sacrificing truth. The artist sacrifices everything to his art, beginning with himself. But his art *is* himself; and when the art is the art of acting, the self is both body and soul. Make that your theme, and work it out ruthlessly. . . .' The author has striven to obey this admirable precept. It is for the reader to judge whether Irving's selfishness was as stupendous as Shaw supposed and, if it was, whether he was a greater artist than Shaw was ready to admit.

Many of the characters in the high comedy of Irving's life—for there is more in it of laughter than of tears—later became great men in their own right. There is a danger, as we read of their exchanges with Irving, to attribute to them the opinion, the wisdom and the authority of their maturity. An attempt, therefore, has been made to delineate them as they may have appeared to Irving at the time. One has only to pause to consider the manner and appearance of George Moore in his perky adolescence to realize the need for this transposition. Throughout this book, the eyes through which men and women are perceived are Irving's eyes—as far as it is possible for one man to see with the eyes of another. If occasionally the vision seems a trifle askew, it must be remembered that Irving's pince-nez were seldom horizontal on the bridge of his nose.

Henry Irving was created, indeed he fashioned himself, in the image of his own time. As a young man he was a modernist; towards the end of his life he became a reactionary, refusing to identify himself with the tremendous social and artistic changes which were taking place around him. He never rode in a motor car; he never spoke on the telephone; only with difficulty was he persuaded to pose for the camera in any of his characters. He was perfectly in step with the Victorian procession, a notable and integral figure in the illustrious company which led it. In retrospect, he was as indispensable to that decorous age as its tastes, its manners and its conventions were to his own self-fulfilment.

There may be those who will find it easier to understand Irving if they are able to compare him to men of similar genius and character —though such comparisons can only be superficial. They may, as it were, get a bearing on their point of departure before they are launched in pursuit of him across the turbulent ocean of his life.

Some of his contemporaries found in him, as a man and as an artist, many of the characteristics of Robert Browning. Both men were Romantics who unwittingly hastened the end of the romantic movement. It can be said of both of them that their technique on occasion fell short of their inspiration and that in their great and passionate

moments both had a tendency to become incoherent. There any likeness between them ends. Doctor Jowett said of Browning: 'I had no
idea there was such a perfectly sensible poet in the world.' He meant,
perhaps, that socially Browning's character and behaviour conformed
perfectly to the conventions of the time. He was only a poet north north
west; when he appeared in drawing-rooms, though as a rule he shunned them, he was the very picture of a contented and successful tea-
broker. Irving, whenever he appeared in public or private, was unmistakably the actor. He never lost for a moment the audience-conscious-
ness which was his strongest characteristic. Often it has been said that
he would have risen to eminence in any profession he could have
chosen. In so far that a man, in order to achieve public distinction
of any kind, must have in him something of an actor, this may be true.
Yet it is inconceivable that Irving could have been anything but an
actor. Browning could shed the poet and play the bourgeois man of the
world. Irving, the authentic actor, was incapable, off the stage, of playing anything but himself.

In the opinion of the author, Irving, as an artist, is more closely
comparable to Eugène Delacroix. Both men were almost the last to
learn the academic and traditional processes of their craft; on this firm
foundation they developed theories and methods of startling originality and later themselves were disconcerted by the work of the ardent
disciples whom they had inspired. Delacroix, had he lived to see the
glowing canvases of the Impressionists, who were intoxicated by the
colours in shadow and reflected light which he had been the first to
discover, might have been as unsympathetic towards their splendid
rebellion against tradition as Irving was towards the unmannered
naturalism in acting to which his own rejection of outworn technique
had given birth. Both men were the leaders of a romantic revival and
were imbued with the spirit of the 'new adventure of humanity', pursuing the artistic ideals to which the work of Beethoven, Turner,
Schubert, the pre-Raphaelite brethren and Edgar Allan·Poe seemed to
lead. They were men whose conception of art was one of grandeur
and nobility, and the conduct of whose lives was governed by these
principles. Later generations may see in their work faults in execution
and in their romanticism the artificial respiration of a classical tradition
which was already dead. Yet the sincerity of their purpose was beyond
doubt and their accomplishment was sufficiently great to defy imitation
by their successors.

Recently a veteran playgoer of discernment, who had seen Irving
in most of his great parts, was asked to specify the element that made

him unique among his contemporaries and without parallel in later generations of actors. He answered that, in a life-long experience of the stage, he had reached the conclusion that Irving and Mounet-Sully alone had been capable of inspiring noble emotions in their audiences. To many of the present generation this simple statement may seem meaningless; it is likely to be received with a sceptical raising of the eyebrows or a deprecating smirk. Nobility, as a virtue, is suspect. No actor can inspire in us an emotion of which, if it exists in us at all, we are half ashamed. Perhaps the London playgoers of the late 'sixties believed that, absorbed in commerce and industry, they had outgrown the romanticism from which this conception of nobility springs. Irving's triumph was to have awakened in a society as drab and material as our own a desire to be elevated by entertainment and, having created such an appetite in playgoers of two continents, to have satisfied it for more than thirty years.

'It is the fate of actors,' wrote Irving to a friend in 1891, 'to be judged by echoes which are altogether delusive—when they have passed out of immediate ken, and some fifty years hence some old fool will be saying—there never was an actor like Irving.' For a conscientious biographer to make any such assertion would, indeed, be the height of folly. He would, however, be a fool if, after painful study of Henry Irving's character and achievement, he did not submit to the jury of his readers that here was one of the most remarkable and extraordinary men who ever entered upon the English stage and on his exit could claim justly to be of the company of England's worthies.

Author's Foreword

The reader who is asked to accept this life of Henry Irving as an authoritative work will expect to find it properly documented.

The origin and inspiration of this book was the discovery of the bulk of Irving's incoming correspondence by Mr. Tom Heslewood. Mr. Heslewood, as a young man, was a devotee of the Lyceum and a close friend of Irving's two sons. He became an authority on historical costume and designed a number of theatrical productions and pageants. Having started a theatrical costumier's business, he acquired, after the death of H. B. Irving, what remained of the wardrobe and properties of the Lyceum. Among the many baskets and boxes was a large tin trunk which for several years lay unopened. When Mr. Heslewood wound up his business shortly before the war the trunk was opened and its treasure, nearly a thousand letters addressed to Irving, was disclosed. After the war, having preserved it during the hazardous years, Mr. Heslewood handed over to me the trunk and its contents. For the safe custody of this invaluable material and for the help and advice which he has given me, my gratitude to him is immeasurable.

Though this collection of letters is astonishingly complete—the triviality of many of them is evidence of this—those of one correspondent for which one would look eagerly and expectantly are missing. After Irving's death these letters were examined by his son, Laurence, who told Mr. Heslewood that among them he was surprised to find only one or two from Ellen Terry. Nor, it appears, did Ellen Terry preserve more than a few letters she received from Irving. The absence of such an interchange which might have revealed so vividly the principles and practices that governed this incomparable stage partnership is to be deplored. It is possible that, working in such close association for so many years, written communication between them was unnecessary. Ellen Terry, however, was by nature an incontinent letter-writer and there is evidence that Irving (though, as Toole said, he was 'a Turk' when it came to answering letters) wrote to her a number of letters which have disappeared. I can only conclude that Irving and Ellen Terry, with characteristic if regrettable discretion, destroyed each other's letters when their long partnership came to an end.

In these days when reticence, if revelation has a cash value, is regarded as foolish or eccentric, it is difficult to understand the scruples of our forebears in this respect. Walter Collinson, Irving's devoted valet who served him and later his son Harry for over forty years, kept a diary. After Irving's death, an enterprising publisher offered him a large sum of money for it, whereupon Collinson threw it on the fire. The diary would have contained no scandalous revelations; his action was prompted by a conviction that the sale of it would be a breach of trust. It was my privilege, as a boy and as a young man, to spend many hours in his company and to listen, entranced, to his recitation of reminiscences which were the substance, no doubt more vividly expressed, of the journal he had committed to the flames.

The many hundreds of letters which have been preserved include not only those which express sentiments favourable to the recipient, but many which a vain man would have destroyed had he wished to preserve a false impression of his dignity and infallibility. It is from this quarry that I have mined the material from which I have carved, to the best of my ability, the posthumous effigies of Irving, of his friends and of his enemies. These letters will, in due course, be made available to the public. In the meantime the reader can be assured that neither Irving's nor his correspondents' letters published in this book have been subjected to partisan censorship. I have omitted from them only words or sentences which are irrelevant or the meaning of which is incomprehensible.

The materials for the biography of an actor are, in the main, as transient as his art. The available bibliography consists very largely of theatrical memoirs, most of which are not only marred by the artlessness and pervading egoism of their authors, but, having been designed to please and even to flatter the writer's contemporaries, are scrupulously uncritical. A list of these sources is given at the end of this volume but those who may refer to them are warned that the incidents and anecdotes culled from them frequently have been construed or interpreted in the light of other and more substantial evidence in my possession.

It would serve no purpose to refer the reader to the innumerable newspapers and periodicals which have provided scraps of material—

in many cases the compilers of scrapbooks and collectors of news-paper cuttings having removed the headings which would have identified their source. Whenever possible, I have given the name of the paper from which an article is quoted and of its author in the text.

I believe that this attempt, however inadequate it may be, to recreate the life and work of this great actor, would have been impos-sible had I not had a glimpse, at second hand, of the plays which had been the mainstay of his repertory. When he died, my father, H. B. Irving, felt it his duty to revive such plays as *The Bells*, *The Lyons Mail*, *Charles I*, and *Louis XI*, which constituted in effect his father's residuary estate out of which provision had to be made for his mother. In doing so he stifled to some extent his own original and very con-siderable talent, for he was consummate in modern comedy. Yet those, including Ellen Terry, who were severe and not impartial judges, considered that his performances, technically and visually, were true and sometimes very vivid reflections of his father—though the mag-netism or sorcery in which lay the power and singularity of the father had not been transmitted to his son. I witnessed these performances at an impressionable age. Consequently I have been able to visualise the Lyceum not as in a glass darkly, but clearly as through a filter which excluded only the dynamic rays. Nevertheless, discounting my youthful impressions, I have had constantly to remind myself (as the reader may have to do) that the plays, other than Shakespeare's, in which Irving made his greatest successes, though they make strange reading to later generations, were acceptable to the most cultivated men and women of his own time. When Irving sprang to fame, he had to face the criticism and win the approval of such men as Tennyson, Browning, Whistler, Millais, Gladstone, Chamberlain, Froude, Jowett, Burton, Dewar, Emerson, and the family of Karl Marx—to name only a few who, with their widely differing tastes and standards, formed an imposing and catholic jury from whom he won a favourable verdict in the repeated trials to which for thirty years he submitted himself for their judgment.

The fact that I had seen these plays would have only a limited value had I not been able to supplement my experience by constant reference to Mr. Edward Gordon Craig's incomparable analysis of Irving's genius and method.[1] Many discriminating actors and actresses who had been members of the Lyceum company have assured me that Mr. Craig's book is unique in its penetration and understanding. Mr. Craig was, moreover, the first to discern the significance of Brodribb's

---

[1] *Henry Irving*, by Edward Gordon Craig (J. M. Dent and Sons).

metamorphosis into Irving. For the inspiration I have derived from his book and for the enlightening conversations and correspondence I have enjoyed with Mr. Craig, I owe him a debt which I can hope only to repay in part by recommending those who read this book to regard Mr. Craig's as an indispensable appendix to it.

In the course of time I have heard much talk of Irving by those who served with him. As a young man I sat respectfully on the fringes of groups of many of the leading characters in this book as they puffed out anecdotes like smoke rings in the lounge of the Garrick Club. Few of them passed on without a kindly indulgence of my juvenile cross-examinations. Of all the tutors who instructed me in the subject of my grandfather none was more assiduous or recalled more vividly the image of his hero than the late Sir Seymour Hicks. As a young actor he had attracted the attention and later had won the affection of J. L. Toole, Irving's closest and lifelong friend. He was, therefore, privileged in Irving's eyes. Thus the keen perceptions of a lively young jester, who was close to the Lyceum throne, were transmitted to me in the witty and forceful idiom of his maturity. Seymour Hicks was a superb mimic. Sometimes I have to disabuse myself of the impression that I, too, have sat at the feet of Irving and Toole, indeed of all those whom his mimicry resurrected—Comyns Carr, Mansfield, Wilde, Joseph Knight and Brookfield. Equally am I indebted to the veteran leader of the opposition, the late Mr. George Bernard Shaw, who never failed to answer, copiously and provocatively, any questions I put to him; in fact he showered ammunition upon me and if, occasionally, I have found that it fitted my own gun, I know that he would be the first to forgive me for discharging it, not ungratefully, at the donor.

The tragically early deaths of Irving's sons prevented either of them from carrying out a task which, in every respect, they were better qualified than I am to undertake. It is possible, however, that distance and detachment have enabled me to pull the portrait of my grandfather into the focus of my own and later generations.

The catalogue of my indebtedness would make a volume in itself. When I announced my intention of attempting this work, I received a great many letters from those who had seen Irving act or were anxious to record their impressions of him or their associations with him. Space does not permit me to call the roll of such a legion of contributors, to all of whom I am very much obliged. There are, however, those to whom my especial thanks are due. To the authors and publishers who have given me permission to quote from their books, grateful acknowledgment is made in the Bibliography. For their courtesy, consideration and help I am most grateful to Professor William Van Lennep, the Curator of the Theatre Collection of the Harvard College Library; to Mr. James McManaway, Consultant in Literature and Bibliography of the Folger Shakespeare Library in Washington, and to Mr. Levi Fox, M.A., Librarian to the Shakespeare Memorial Theatre, for allowing me to publish Henry Irving's autograph letters in their possession; to the committee of the Garrick Club for lending me the Fitzgerald collection of Irvingiana; to Mr. Compton Mackenzie for the information he has given me about his grandparents, Hezekiah and Sidney Bateman; to Mrs. Angelo Crevo for her permission to include extracts from her mother's diary; to the Lord Chamberlain's Office for permission to publish letters by the late Sir Ponsonby Fane; to the Curator of the Enthoven Collection at the Victoria and Albert Museum for permission to make use of the valuable notes compiled by Miss Winifred Callwell and her sister on Irving's boyhood in Cornwall; to Mrs. Ellen Robbins for the use of letters written by Irving to her father, H. J. Loveday; to Mrs. Cotterill for her permission to include the letters of her father, L. F. Austin; to my cousin, Miss Irene Stoney, for allowing me to publish the letters relating to Irving's marriage; to Mr. Gerald Lawrence for the gift of Irving's letters to Mrs. James; to Mr. Guy Pollock for the gift of Irving's letters to his grandparents, Sir Frederick and Lady Pollock; to Mrs. Charles Rann Kennedy (Edith Wynne Mathison) for her memories of Irving during the last years of his life and particularly of his last performance.

I have already thanked individually the relatives and executors who have allowed me to publish letters from Irving's correspondents at home. Indebted as I am to Mr. Harold Latham for their discovery, it remains for me to make grateful acknowledgment to those who have made it possible for me to include letters from Irving's American correspondents—namely, those from William Winter to his daughter, Viola Winter Brown; from Edwin Booth to his grandson, Edwin Booth Grossman; from Augustin Daly to his executor, Elizabeth Daly; from Richard Mansfield to Harold Van Doren, his residuary legatee.

Finally I have to thank Mr. A. P. Ryan and Mr. John Parker for their criticism, advice, and invaluable help in reading and correcting the proofs, Miss Jean Scott Rogers for her revision of my manuscript, and my secretary, Mrs. Kay Graham, for her sustained enthusiasm during the two and a half years we worked together on this book.

PART ONE

JOHN BRODRIBB

CHAPTER I

West Country Childhood

———◦≈◦———

Near Somerton, the ancient capital of Somerset, the village of Keinton Mandeville lies along the road to Castle Cary like an exclamation mark, a long straggling street of stone houses detached from the church which stands isolated in a field to the south of it. In the centre of the village, next to 'The Three Castles' inn, there once stood a general store; both the store and the inn were out of all proportion to the village itself, but large enough to meet the needs of the country folk scattered over the rich farming land which lies between Glastonbury and Yeovil.

In 1838 the store was enjoying considerable prosperity and boasted a department employing no less than ten tailors and a travelling salesman, Samuel Brodribb. During January the whole of southern England had been in the grip of a severe frost which, though it had curtailed the salesman's journeys, had given him plenty of time to be with his wife in their home, opposite the store, where she was imminently expecting a baby. This kind of inactivity suited Samuel Brodribb, who was by nature an easygoing and amiable potterer. Yet a more provident or ambitious man in his position, finding himself about to become a father, might have had some misgivings in the face of this added responsibility. A glance, however, at his chubby face, set off with a Newgate fringe and bushy tufts of hair supporting his domed and shiny crown, gave reassurance that he would meet disappointment and adversity with the philosophy of a Micawber.

Born at the turn of the century, Samuel Brodribb was in his thirty-eighth year. The Brodribbs came from Clutton, a village which lies to the north of Keinton Mandeville, where succeeding generations had been tenant farmers since the early eighteenth century and had come finally to rest in Clutton churchyard. Samuel's father, John Brodribb, rented Northend Farm with its substantial homestead and stone barns and acres of rich pasture in the valley to the east of Clutton. He had seven children; only one son remained at Northend, and when he died in 1863 the farm had passed into other hands and the Brodribbs from the records of Clutton. Although four generations of Samuel's forebears had lived and died uneventfully in that neighbourhood, romance had illumined the lives of his cousins, one of whom, William, had in 1783 eloped with the daughter of a neighbouring squire and magistrate. Later William himself became a Justice of the Peace and must have suffered some embarrassment when one of his sons, a solicitor, was deported to Australia for being involved in a poaching affray which had resulted in the death of a gamekeeper. Protesting his innocence, he never returned to England, but became the founder of a distinguished and prolific line of Brodribbs in the country of his forced adoption.

Samuel and his brother, Thomas, left Northend to seek their fortunes in Bristol. Thomas found modest success and fortune with a firm of iron merchants, but Samuel, though apprenticed to a hosier and admitted burgess of the city as a silk mercer in 1826, lost his way along the road of successful hosiery through being lured up fascinating bypaths by a lively and inquisitive interest in almost anything but his work. Travelling salesmanship undoubtedly had its charm, with all its opportunities for collecting interesting facts and impressions; if his excursions were of little profit to his employers, they at least led him to St. Ives, in Cornwall, where he met Mary Behenna.

The Behennas came from Kea, near Truro, where they appear to have enjoyed moderate prosperity, though tantalized by a small fortune which had been left to them by some Spanish relatives, but which now, owing to legal complications, was withheld from them in chancery. Towards the end of the eighteenth century one of these Behennas had moved with his wife to St. Ives, where he acquired a farm at Boskerris. In course of time he drank away his estate, falling into debt to an unscrupulous publican, who, chalking up his customer's account on the door, would resolve these mathematics by taking from time to time a parcel of land in payment until he himself became the owner of Boskerris. No doubt the prodigal behaviour of Behenna led to local speculation as to how, thriftless as he was, he had been able to buy the farm and came to have three daughters of great beauty, who, by reason of their dignified bearing and gracious manner, were said to 'walk like queens', though the fashion of the time discreetly hid a characteristic common to all three; namely, that their queenly torsos were supported by long and spindly legs. Gossip provided the same answer to both questions. It was said that the gift of Boskerris was the price of Behenna's complaisance, and that his wife's lover was the son of one of the largest landowners in the parish of Lelant.

These rumours did not affect the popularity of Sarah, Mary and Victoria Behenna, who managed to earn at once a reputation for gaiety and extravagance and for their devout Methodism. Their piety was, no doubt, a natural reaction to a wastrel father and to a wayward mother, of whom they never spoke.

Sarah Behenna had married Isaac Penberthy, a well-to-do captain of mines, as men of engineering and administrative ability were known in the tin-mining districts of Cornwall. Mary's marriage to a travelling salesman was, by comparison, not much of a match, though Samuel's kindliness and rich fund of anecdotes probably made up for his financial instability. This weakness became all too apparent when the Brodribbs returned to Bristol, and it was perhaps Mary's sturdy common sense which led them to Keinton Mandeville, where, in one of the more spacious houses in the village, they were able to enjoy a measure of comfort on their slender means.

Samuel looked forward to the birth of this child as an object available for constant study and an inexhaustible subject for his diary and scrapbooks. The past year had indeed been an absorbing one; the coronation of the young Queen had competed for space in his scrapbooks with Greenacre, the murderer, whose dismemberment of an elderly lady and subsequent trial and execution had been the theme of street literature and the focus of public interest for many weeks. When news came from the little room on the ground floor of the cottage that Mary had presented him with a son, he no doubt recorded February 6th, 1838, as the happiest day of his life.

The boy was christened John Henry Brodribb. Weighed against the balance of heredity, the child's chances of worldly success seemed small. On his father's side a long line of sturdy but unimaginative Somerset farmers, on his mother's an obscure line of Cornishmen who never appear to have set the Fal on fire. Of material fortune there was none. Moreover, both these branches of his family tree were in process of decay, for William Brodribb, Samuel's eldest brother, shared the fate of Behenna of Boskerris, being forced to sell up Northend Farm and end his days on parish relief. Apart, then, from a reasonable prospect of health and strength, the only other gifts fate had to offer this child were the incalculable qualities he might derive from his grandmother's apocryphal lover. He was, however, twice blessed in his parents: a devoted if ineffective father and a charming, gentle mother, whose devotion would be tempered by a determination to set her son firmly on the narrow path which, to her Methodist outlook, was the only way of life.

The child's first consciousness was the sound of his mother's voice reading from the Bible or, against the undertones of a singing kettle, the murmur of conversation when Mr. Southey, the much beloved minister, came to tea. As soon as his legs, which were unmistakably those of a Behenna, were able to support him, he ran wild among the orchards and fields, filling his lungs with the sea-scented breezes which rolled across the Vale of Avalon from the Bristol Channel. Keinton Mandeville was a perfect playground for a boy who, at three years old, knew the ecstasy of daring himself to venture into the groves of trees which echoed to the eerie cries of guinea fowl roosting in their branches, and had endured the ordeal of being charged by a ram on Mr. Hoddy's farm; in this encounter he suffered a few cuts and bruises, though he gained a lively reaction to personal attack which was to become a life-long characteristic.

In 1842 the prosperity of Somersetshire was on the decline. Land values were falling and many farmers, like William Brodribb, were facing ruin and disaster. Moreover, the household weaving, which had been a staple industry of the county, was losing ground in the face of the competition of Lancashire, where the great mills and their operatives were getting into their stride. In Keinton Mandeville these changes were reflected in the declining trade of the once prosperous store; as business shrank the position of the travelling salesman became less and less secure. The thoughts of Samuel Brodribb turned to Bristol. The railway to London was completed, and the city, which was expanding rapidly, offered chances of more lucrative employment. Anyhow, a burgess would be more at home in his own city; for Samuel, though he might miss his garden and the variety of interests which it afforded him, was bound to confess that to a diarist Keinton Mandeville was a desert.

No doubt Mary Brodribb had foreseen the necessity and approved the wisdom of her husband's choice. But she had no illusions about the difficulties which lay ahead. She knew that, with a growing child to bring up, straitened circumstances and even poverty were supportable in the country where simple food and fresh air were easy to come by; she could foresee as clearly that the hazards and uncertainties of city life, with a husband whose livelihood was precarious, would imperil the decent and healthy upbringing of her child upon which she had set her heart. Her choice was a hard one. With unflinching self-sacrifice,

Samuel Brodribb and 'the Aunts'   Sarah Penberthy

The Inn   Isaac Penberthy's House

HALSETOWN

John Henry Brodribb
1856

and perhaps in the face of Samuel's feckless protests, she made the right decision and, having made it, was never deflected from her purpose. Johnnie must remain in the country. To leave him at Keinton Mandeville with a foster-mother was unthinkable. Her thoughts turned naturally to her sister, Sarah Penberthy, and it was arranged that Johnnie should make his home with her and her two children in Cornwall until she and Samuel were in a position to provide a proper home for him themselves.

The Penberthys lived at Halsetown, a mining village in a fold of the brown hills above St. Ives. Planned and built in 1813 by James Halse, Mayor of St. Ives, to accommodate the men working in the local tin mines, which were then enjoying a period of prosperity, Halsetown was an early experiment in town planning. The grey stone houses, each in its own acre of ground and facing south, were ranged around the chapel, the school and the inn. Behind the village rose a turfy tor littered with smooth grey boulders, while beyond it, to the south, the bleak moors dotted with mine works rose in undulating folds towards the hills above Penzance. In fine weather the prospect was fair enough, but in winter, when the Atlantic gales drove the mist and rain across the narrow peninsula and the long hours of darkness kept folk indoors, the model villagers may well have longed to exchange the enlightened dispersal of Mr. Halse's housing scheme for the crowded back streets of St. Ives.

Where the road to Zennor takes a sharp turn to the south stands the Halsetown inn, and on the opposite corner the most imposing house in the village, which was Johnnie Brodribb's home for nearly ten years. His uncle, Isaac Penberthy, was a bearded, generous-hearted Celtic giant; everything about him was oversized: his temper, his humour and his strength. As a young man he had become the manager of tin mines in Mexico, where a man's life, let alone his fortune, lay in the strength of his hands and the force of his character. Isaac preserved his life and returned to Cornwall with sufficient fortune to marry Sarah Behenna and to become the captain of four tin mines in the neighbourhood of St. Ives. He was a passionate man, given to sudden storms of rage, which died away, as quickly as they had blown up, into gusts of uproarious laughter. Trusted by his employers and respected by his subordinates, he was a romantic figure straight out of the pages of Bret Harte; and his wife, Sarah, adored him. She was possessed of the same rigid principles as her sister, Mary, but, though a strict teetotaller and an ardent Methodist, her convictions were lightened by a lively and tolerant humour, and even her evangelism was on so broad a basis that

33

she did not hesitate to have her children confirmed in the Church of England. This ideally matched couple welcomed their little nephew into their home and embraced him with their own children, John and Kitty. Johnnie Brodribb soon took to his cousins, who were about his own age. Kitty won his unqualified devotion, but his affection for John, a year or two his senior, was tinged with awe and admiration. For John Penberthy had his father's courage and temper and was the acknowledged leader of the many escapades in which his young cousin was his eager companion.

To a child of sensibility and perception, Cornwall, at that time, offered an almost overwhelming variety of impressions and experiences. At his aunt's knee the boy absorbed the daily portion of the Bible, while at the cottage hearths he listened to the credulous whisperings of a people still half enthralled by a fairy mythology. Religious revival contested with lingering paganism for the souls of these Celtic people whose pious expressions in the chapel were periodically relaxed behind the masks and half-forgotten pagan exercises of the guise dancers. On Saturday nights the noisy carousels of the miners in the Halsetown inn flung their challenge against the total abstinence of his own quiet home across the road. The grim hills, weird with monoliths and the fearful enticement of the disused shaft, fell in cataracts of black granite into the cold might of the Atlantic which thundered into the sandy coves. Here he dimly perceived and perhaps never wholly forgot the perfect conduct of a marriage between two strong-willed yet understanding people. One day his uncle returned home unexpectedly and in a towering passion. His wife was out. He stalked into the kitchen and in blind rage began to smash anything he could lay hands on, snapping chairs and tables over his knee as if they were twigs. The children, terrified, fled from his path and hid themselves as best they could in the dark corners of the kitchen, creeping out again only when he was safely on his way back to the mines. When Sarah Penberthy returned she surveyed the wreckage and without comment set to work hanging the fragments on the walls as though they were pictures or pieces of rare china. In the evening she and the children went along the road as usual to meet her husband and, when he came striding along, greeted him in the ordinary way. He put his arm round his wife's waist and led her back to the house. When he saw the relics of his rage hung about the room, he burst into tremendous laughter, in which Sarah joined as loudly; thus in laughter of contrition and forgiveness the episode was forgotten. Isaac had learnt his lesson, for such an incident never occurred again; his nephew had unconsciously acquired a standard of feminine behaviour which few women who came into his life were ever likely to equal.

Once a year his mother came and fetched him for a short visit to Bristol where she and Samuel had made a temporary home on Spring Hill. This entailed an adventurous and even alarming voyage in the small paddle-wheel steam packet which plied between Bristol and St. Ives. His first visit in 1843 coincided with that of the Prince Consort, who came to Bristol to launch Brunel's *Great Britain*, the first iron-built and screw-propelled steamer which had just been completed in the city's shipyards, the forerunner of a long succession of great transatlantic liners. Samuel, probably well-primed with statistics, took his son to the launching, an expedition which would have delighted any boy with a mechanical turn of mind and a natural delight in crowds and brass bands. His son's attention was, however, riveted on Prince Albert's moustache, which filled him with envy. Later, an obliging chemist, to whom the boy confessed his desire to grow such a moustache, sat him on a chair and in a moment conjured a fine growth from the five-year-old upper lip. John Brodribb, now invested with the appearance and dignity of the Prince, walked proudly home, where he suffered his first humiliation and disillusion, for his entrance was greeted with uproarious laughter and his mother, without delay, washed away the magical burnt cork.

When he grew older he was sent to a dame school conducted by a Miss Penberthy in the parlour of a cottage near her namesake's house. The teaching was elementary, but included domestic science, for much of the students' time was spent in helping the mistress with her household chores. He became attached to his teacher, and, once she had taught him to read and write, he was able, by poring over the only books in his aunt's house—the Bible, *Don Quixote* and a collection of ballads—to start a curriculum of self-education which was to occupy the term of his natural life. While his aunt strove with evangelical zeal to direct his mind along paths which might lead him to the Ministry, the door to that other world of the imagination began to open. He had never forgotten the day when, at his father's side, he saw the lion-tamer, Van Amburgh, drive a team of twenty-four horses through the streets of Bristol, and, later, a splendid figure in a leopard skin and cool as ice, enter a den of roaring but intimidated lions. From that moment the guise dancers and the mummers, the cheap-jacks and tumblers in the travelling fairs, and even the oratory of the Minister in the chapel took on a new significance and were observed with rapt attention. As the range of his excursions grew wider, glimpses of new enchantments were revealed. The mining industry was enjoying a period of prosperity; the miners were well-to-do and eager patrons of entertainment. Father Crink, a local impresario, who gave his name to Crink Point in Carbis Bay, where he used to sit and dream away his old age, was not slow to exploit this market. His company of actors, performing in a tent, went from village to village giving rough and ready performances of popular melodrama. Later, he opened an Assembly Room theatre in St. Ives, in which touring companiés from the East played Shakespeare. Many a citizen, experiencing for the first time the startling novelties of *Hamlet*, crept home in terror through the narrow, unlighted and precipitous streets. No doubt all the forces of Methodism were ranged against Father Crink as an envoy of the devil. Nevertheless, such opportunities for self-education were not likely to be neglected by a young student whose adventurous cousin could be counted upon to lead the way to forbidden delights.

In those days travellers and visitors to this part of Cornwall were liable to have a strange and memorable encounter.

In Penzance two little girls, whose family were visiting the town, were chafing at parental restraint which forbade them to visit the beach unescorted, or to speak to anyone without proper introduction. Being children of spirit, they contrived to evade the vigilance of their parents and, while playing on the beach, met a boy of their own age, who confessed that he, too, was a fugitive from the austerities of a nonconformist home. Having found a bond of sympathy, the children met again. Before long the girls found themselves a willing and admiring audience to their new friend, who, with little encouragement, treated them to his repertoire of speeches and declamations. Gaining confidence from their evident appreciation of his talent, he confided to them that his greatest desire was to become an actor, to them an unheard-of and almost scanda'ous ambition. One morning the boy failed to appear and the romantic meeting became a mere memory which was to be revived in strangely different circumstances.

A year or two later, a picnic party, intending to walk to Carbis Bay in St. Ives, were forced to take shelter from the rain near a house above the beach. As evening drew on and the rain showed no sign of stopping, the owner of the house, apologizing for not being able to ask them in, as his wife had just had a baby, offered them the hospitality of an arbour and brought them coats and saffron cake. The company settled down and began to entertain each other with songs and recitations. Gradually they became aware of a strange boy in their midst, who, when his turn came, recited passage after passage from

Shakespeare, until his performance was interrupted by the sound of horses coming down the steep cliff path towards them. The horses drew nearer and nearer until the sound of their hooves ceased as suddenly as it had begun. All were delighted to discover that these sounds came from the Shakespearian reciter, who seemed to be an accomplished ventriloquist. In the early hours of the morning the rain stopped and the tired and dispirited party returned to St. Ives. There they parted from the young ventriloquist; one of them noted with pity that the lad had still a mile or two to trudge before he reached his home in Halsetown.

Sarah Penberthy was not blind to the temptations which beset her nephew. She had sensed the dangers through which she had to guide him if he was to fulfil her cherished hope of his entering the Ministry. Already he had publicly betrayed an antic spirit. Hideously disguised in masks, horns and tails, he and his cousins had appeared at the bedside of an old woman who had for too long persecuted the village children with threats of brimstone and hellfire; she recognized the apparition as a materialization of her own demonology and was too frightened to suspect the unorthodoxy of a devil and his imps who made her pray to heaven for forgiveness for her sins against the children. On another occasion the boy had ridden a donkey through the passages of the Halsetown inn, an escapade which could hardly be excused as a demonstration in favour of total abstinence.

Sarah's task would have been easier if Johnnie had been downright wayward, but it was difficult to understand a boy who, though he showed a leaning to wickednesss in his love of players and play-acting, was, at the same time, as devout a Christian as she could wish. For Mr. Wallington, the minister, was full of reassurances. Rarely had he met a boy who was so attentive and cheerful, so quick in perception and so mature in his responses that, in talking to him, his age was forgotten. Her anxiety, however, was finally allayed when, shortly after his tenth birthday, the lad, during a service, fell into an ecstasy and professed his conversion, the sincerity of which the minister never for a moment doubted. It seemed, indeed, as though her nephew was able to reconcile play-acting and piety and that in time God would reveal to him that, while the former was but a childish aberration, in the latter lay the only hope of grace and salvation.

That year Isaac Penberthy died suddenly in the full vigour of his fifty-sixth year. His death was a tragedy for his devoted family and a calamity for the tin-mining industry, which owed much of its prosperity to his skill and judgment. Two thousand miners attended his funeral, and on that day the mine furnaces of three parishes were cold. Within a year many were quenched, never to be rekindled. Sarah now found herself in straitened circumstances. She could look for no help from her father. Not so long ago a solicitor had come from London and, searching out Behenna, had told him that with his help the Spanish fortune might be rescued from chancery. This meant a journey to London, from which the wretched Behenna shrank. Isaac, hearing of this, offered to escort his father-in-law to the capital. But they got no further than the railway station at Hayle; for, when Isaac suggested that they should share the profits resulting from the expedition, his companion demurred. Isaac flew into a rage and, abandoning his equivocating father-in-law to his chronic poverty and the Spanish fortune to chancery, he returned, no better off, to Halsetown.

She had no doubt that before long her son John would be able to take care of himself; he was soon to imitate his father's early adventures and success in the tin mines of Bolivia. Kitty, until she married, would be of help to her in the house. For Johnnie Brodribb there was no place. His father had, by this time, found work in the City of London, where Mary Brodribb had managed to create a home. Mary, when she heard of her sister's loss, decided that the time had come for Johnnie to rejoin them. There at least he could have proper schooling and the chance of finding employment in some respectable city firm. Johnnie, no doubt, was sorry to leave what had been, in effect, his home. He was never to forget his aunt's kindness or the stern precepts which she had taught him. None the less, when the train brought him to the out-skirts of London, he felt the joy and quickening excitement of one who knows that the journey of his life has started, though its purpose and its goal were not as yet comprehended.

CHAPTER II

The Curtain Rises

I

The Brodribbs occupied the top floor of a house at 68 Old Broad Street. Samuel Brodribb's activities were still rather vague and the source of his modest income was obscure; perhaps by acting as caretakers to the premises below they lived there rent free. Fortune had favoured Johnnie Brodribb by seeing that he had fresh air, sea breezes and all the advantages of country life during his childhood years; now, as he was reaching adolescence, he was lucky to find himself in the most vital square mile in the world, cornered by the Guildhall, Whitechapel, Leadenhall Market and St. Paul's Cathedral, the centre of the world's commerce, a museum of ancient buildings and time-honoured customs, and the nursery of most of the vivid characters who were populating the pages of Charles Dickens's eagerly awaited novels.

As Mary watched her boy adjust himself to the turmoil and restriction of life in a city after the peace and freedom of Cornwall, she knew that she had no cause to regret the sacrifice that she had made. For a boy of eleven he was tall, and, although his hereditary lankiness had earned him the nickname of Spindleshanks among his recent playmates, he was as strong and healthy as she could wish. His face, neither handsome nor plain, was pale and deeply freckled. His eyes were unusually challenging, now bright with interest, now sparkling with a sly humour which suddenly and surprisingly would illumine the serious set of his sensitive mouth. As he seemed to be full of fun and imagination, she attributed the solemnity of his expression to his constant effort to master a pronounced impediment in his speech. If she had been told by her sister of his dangerous interest in play-actors and his love of reciting, she must have marked with something like relief a disability which made it impossible to regard those tendencies as anything more than childish fancies.

39

Anyhow, during the coming year he would have plenty to occupy his mind. It had been arranged that he should go to the City Commercial School, which was conveniently situated nearby, between Lombard Street and Cornhill, in George Yard, at the farther end of which stood the 'George and Vulture' inn, which had sprung into fame some twenty years before as the temporary residence of Mr. Pickwick and Sam Weller. The school was reputed to be the best in the City of London, though the fees were but six pounds a year. The thirty or so pupils had the entire attention of the headmaster, Dr. Pinches, and of his assistants, Mr. John Stone and Mr. Dickens; supernumerary ushers were engaged to teach new fangled subjects like chemistry and shorthand. Dr. Pinches was a kindly man, infinitely patient with the deserving, but swift to wrath if roused by meanness or duplicity. His views on education were advanced for his time; he held that if a boy could write clearly, spell correctly and read aloud with intelligent emphasis, the rest would follow in due course. His appearance illustrated perfectly his character. His round smiling face was haloed by silvering hair; his mouth was small enough to be compressed in disapproval; his voice was clear and strong, his elocution faultless. The academic severity of his black tail coat was relieved by the arrangement of his neckwear, which had a Byronic touch about it.

Johnnie soon found that his mother's choice of a school was one that suited him. Though he found the lessons difficult and Dr. Pinches less easily diverted from his purpose by offers of domestic service than Miss Penberthy, he got along well enough with the other boys. His particular friend was Edward Plumbridge who could be persuaded to return to Old Broad Street to tea and to polish off their homework while his host pored over a volume of Shakespeare—a habit which Edward found less easy to understand than his friend's fondness for the white mice which bred freely in his bedroom. Young Plumbridge was able to make a romantic return of hospitality by entertaining his friend in the warehouse above which his parents lived in Botolph Lane. His father owned a schooner, which would periodically discharge its cargo of nuts from Spain into the cellar where the two boys used to play.

Johnnie, though he disliked the ordinary lessons as much as any normal boy, looked forward eagerly to the elocution class, to which Dr. Pinches attached so much importance that he himself conducted it. The headmaster found in this boy, who studied so earnestly and strove so hard to eradicate his stammer, a pupil worthy of his metal; the boy was overjoyed to find that his ruling passion, hitherto indulged more or less in secret and with a sense of guilt, was now blessed with official approbation. At the end of each term Dr. Pinches held a Speech Day at Sussex Hall in Leadenhall Street, to which parents and friends were invited to hear recitations of Latin verses and English classics by the most promising boys of this class, and to the subsequent prize-giving. Johnnie Brodribb determined to make the most of his first chance to appear in public. By occasionally misappropriating the money which his mother had given him for his lunch, he had been able to buy a few books, among them a copy of *Summer and Winter Hours*, a collection of poems by Henry Glassford Bell, a popular writer of the time with a flair for the macabre and the precursor of Edgar Allan Poe.

Among these verses Johnnie found one which he reckoned would allow him to exercise the full range of his talent. It was entitled 'The Uncle', and began:

> '*He was a man of gloomy mind*
> *And few his converse sought . . .*'

and small wonder, for when this melancholic pinned down his little nephew in conversation, he revealed that on account of his unrequited passion for the boy's mother he had murdered his own brother, and proceeded to prove this startling confession by opening a chest which contained the skeleton of his victim. The sight of these remains, however, proved too much for the uncle, who fell into a delirium and died. Johnnie Brodribb was made of sterner stuff, inured no doubt to scenes of this kind from browsing over the crime cuttings and gruesome woodcuts in his father's scrapbook. He was soon word perfect and, by stubborn practice, had mastered the phrases which affected his stammer. When he rehearsed his piece to Dr. Pinches the effect, though in a way gratifying, was hardly what he expected. The headmaster very wisely decided that this grisly morsel was too strong meat for his prize-giving day and directed the boy to prepare in its place a speech made by the Irish advocate, John Curran, in defence of the patriot, Hamilton Rowan. The speech occupied twenty-five pages of print. Though dramatic enough when punctuated by the applause of the people and the threats of the soldiery in a Dublin court, as a substitute for the pithy horrors of 'The Uncle' it seemed poor stuff for an ambitious reciter. Johnnie relegated Bell's poem to the cupboard of his mind and in the more conventional piece acquitted himself well and to his tutor's satisfaction.

The following term, when Speech Day came round again, he was given the part of Adrastus in Talfourd's tragedy, *Ion*. The wise doctor had not forgotten the boy's daring, if precocious, efforts of the previous term, and his judgment was again rewarded by a carefully prepared and well-delivered performance by his pupil. At the end of the prize-giving the headmaster introduced Johnnie to a friend of his, who, while suffering the boredom that such functions can inflict, had been jerked to attention by the appearance of a boy whose personality and rendering of a difficult part was so much above the average of his fellows that he had asked to meet him. When the boy realized that he was being congratulated by Mr. William Creswick, the famous actor who at that very time was playing Hamlet with great success at the Surrey Theatre, the kindly words of encouragement rekindled the spark which for a year had been dimmed by the stern disapproval which his mother had voiced whenever he had given hint or sign of his inward longing. Now, he realized, was the time, when his bewildered mother had actually seen Dr. Pinches, whose respectability and probity were beyond dispute, present her son to a play-actor with whom he appeared to be on the friendliest terms, to press home the advantage and to insist on being taken to a theatre. Mary Brodribb gave her reluctant permission, making it a condition that the play must be one of Shakespeare's. Since nothing would induce her to enter the abodes of iniquity, it became Samuel's not unwelcome duty to escort his son. So, shortly before Johnnie's twelfth birthday, father and son set out for Sadler's Wells to see the great Mr. Phelps play Hamlet.

2

The London theatre was slowly emerging from a decadence into which it had declined after the death of David Garrick in 1779. From that date until the passing of the Theatre Regulations Act in 1843, actor and dramatist had fought against such heavy and discouraging odds in the exercise of their art that few of the former and none of the latter were able to lift the theatre above the level of vulgar mediocrity. Garrick had been the first man of the theatre in whom were vested the genius of the actor and the flair of the impresario. He was the first to conceive theatrical production in terms of the expression of a single mind. For thirty years as actor and manager he pursued an original policy of which the most novel features were his conception of a performance as a whole and not as an arena in which actors competed for the favour of their audience, his introduction of scenic decoration of a style and quality to match contemporary art and, perhaps the most remarkable of all, his sustained financial success. Of his own particular genius as an actor there was no doubt; such faults as his mutilation of Shakespeare were common to his age and passed unnoticed by his contemporaries. Until his day actors were encumbered and embarrassed by privileged members of the audience who sat upon the stage while the body of the theatre was the concourse of a disorderly and unsavoury rabble. By reforming and disciplining his audience and presenting them with an ensemble which won their approval, Garrick brought to the drama a dignity and order which it had never known. The measure of his genius was his power to fill Drury Lane over a long period with enthusiastic audiences.

It may seem strange that this period of theatrical decadence began with the appearance of an actor of genius and was ended by an Act of Parliament. Garrick had triumphed over a pernicious system introduced by a bureaucratic monarchy which defeated his successors, some of whom were of equal or even greater genius.

In order to exercise some measure of censorship and control over the theatre in a particularly sensitive age, Charles II had granted by royal patent an absolute monopoly of the performance of spoken drama to two theatres royal. Since the early part of the seventeenth century these monopolies were held by Drury Lane Theatre and the Covent Garden Opera House. In 1737 these patents were reinforced by an ill-considered Bill which invested the Lord Chamberlain with unlimited powers of licence and of censorship within the confines of the City of Westminster. Intended to empower the Lord Chamberlain to suppress any illicit play-houses that might spring up, this Act simply added confusion to an already complicated situation and allowed the Lord Chamberlain a dangerous freedom to exercise his personal whims. In 1752 another Act created even greater chaos, for it granted local magistrates discretion to license theatres all over the city on the condition imposed by the Lord Chamberlain, that the premises to which they granted licences were to be used solely for the performance of pantomime, for dancing and for music. Thus the theatre was split irrevocably into the legitimate or monopoly houses where alone the spoken drama could be performed, and the illegitimate or minor houses which were limited to the performance of musical plays or burlettas.

Theatres cannot be filled by legislation. Before long the managers of Drury Lane and Covent Garden found that their monopoly, far from being a source of profit, involved them in increasing loss. The passion of Sarah Siddons, the cold majesty of her brother, John Kemble, the lightning of Kean and the proud grace of Macready had brought these theatres periods of prosperity; but with actors of lesser power these theatres were too large and their overhead expenses too great to reward their backers. The actors, seeking theatres of a size more suitable to their talents, found the smaller houses barred to the spoken drama. While the major issue became a wearisome legal wrangle, the principal sufferers arrived at a compromise; the two patent or monopoly theatres played double bills—the pill of Shakespeare being coated with the sugar of circuses—while in the minor theatres or those licensed by magistrates, earnest actors would perform *Othello* to the accompaniment of a single note struck on a piano at long intervals so that Shakespeare's tragedy qualified as a burletta within the meaning of the Act.

It is not surprising that such a situation gave little encouragement to English dramatists. The early nineteenth century was barren of native drama with the exception of a few romantic works by Byron, Talfourd and Bulwer Lytton. Desperate managers struggled to keep their heads above water by importing plays from Paris, where at that time the theatre was enjoying a period of liveliness. But they had become the lackeys of exacting masters. A new audience had been created by the industrial revolution; democracy was surging into the box office; a democracy, as yet boorish and ill-mannered, which demanded entertainment to its abysmally low taste. Thus, starved of talent, denounced by the clergy and deserted by the world of fashion and intelligence, the English drama looked as though it were on its last legs.

It was generally recognized that the existing laws were devoid both of justice and of common sense; for years, by means of petitions and investigations, the theatres' well-wishers carried on the fight for amendment, only to be defeated by the vested interest of those whose property rights were threatened. At last, in 1832, a number of disgruntled dramatic writers met under the chairmanship of Edward Bulwer Lytton and drafted yet another petition. Bulwer Lytton, as well as being about the only successful dramatist of the day, was a parliamentarian and at that time the member for St. Ives, Huntingdonshire. Through his influence and the energetic backing of Macready, the petition became the Dramatic Performance Bill, which he presented to the House in 1833. Passed by the Commons, rejected by the Lords, bitterly attacked by the Bishop of London, and finally dropped by its despairing sponsors, Bulwer Lytton's Bill did, in fact, carry the day, for, as a result of his importunity, in 1843 the Theatre Regulations Act, granting complete freedom to all theatres, was passed through both Houses without opposition.

At last the scene was set for the restoration of English drama, but there seemed to be no reformer ready to answer his cue. There were playhouses in plenty. Since 1800, those in London had more than doubled their number, from ten to twenty-two; moreover, a large and ever-increasing number of playgoers, avid for entertainment, were ready to acclaim genius and to adjust their tastes. But Acts of Parliament cannot create genius. After years of neglect, no dramatists were forthcoming to exploit their new liberty; while the system of the stock company, or the indifferent local support of a visiting star, which had prevented Kean and Macready from the full development of their genius, still held the stage. Only an actor could restore or advance the prestige of the theatre. Macready, disdainful of his fellow-actors, and contemptuous of his managers, was on the verge of retirement at the height of his powers, leaving the theatre in much the same state as that in which he had found it. For his stalwart advocacy of Bulwer Lytton's petition he had earned the everlasting gratitude of his profession. Only two actors were left upon the scene to take practical advantage of these reforms.

The first was Samuel Phelps. Born in 1804, he started life as a reader on the staff of two London newspapers. He went on the stage in 1828 and won increasing popularity by playing in support of Macready, who had a high opinion of his talent. With Macready he experienced the wretched conditions which the actor had to endure in a theatre which had fallen to such low estate. Being a man of spirit and integrity, he saw 'a glorious vision opening before him of a popular theatre with Shakespeare and the poetic drama'. Phelps was no idle visionary; he set about realizing his dream with practical vigour. Taking over a derelict theatre in North London, he bullied and cajoled a foul-mouthed and unruly audience into a semblance of order and decent behaviour until he won their respect not only by his acting, which, though of the old declamatory style, was of a high order, but by his indomitable courage and determination. Surrounding himself with the best actors he could find, mounting his plays with taste and economy, and showing a sound head for business management, he worked unceasingly until his theatre was recognized by the public as a temple of the classic drama and of all that was best in contemporary plays, and by his fellow-actors as a much needed and long-desired training ground, where newcomers could get sound instruction and practical experience in their profession.

The second was Charles Kean, Edmund's second son, who, with his wife, Ellen Tree, was entering on a long term of management, during which he strove to follow the principles and to revive the glories of Garrick. He began by imitating his father in the great roles of tragedy, but, after every allowance for the handicaps which a son who follows a famous father must always suffer, it was generally admitted that he was but a shadow of his model. Later he was seen at his best in comedy and French romantic melodrama; yet though he strove by engaging an excellent company, by mounting his plays with lavish scenery and costumes of great historical accuracy to win the public favour, he lacked, owing perhaps to chronic adenoids and the repressions of an Etonian education, the quality which makes for greatness or for popular appeal.

It was during Phelps's seventh winter season that Johnnie Brodribb sat at Sadler's Wells, cold with excitement, waiting for the curtain to rise upon the battlements of Elsinore.

3

Only two years had passed since the boy had openly professed to a spiritual conversion in the chapel at Halsetown. That night, at Sadler's Wells, he inwardly underwent a second conversion, as intense and heartfelt as the first. He became confirmed in a faith, hitherto only vaguely understood, which he knew was to be his enduring inspiration. The close succession of one emotional crisis upon the other may have imbued his self-dedication to the art of acting with the almost religious idealism which was to govern his attitude towards the principle and practice of his profession.

He was fortunate in his first experience at the theatre. Phelps was a good, if not a great actor. He was a fine, commanding figure, tall and spare, though a trifle wooden in his movements. His face, with its high forehead above lustreless and close-set eyes, was heavy in repose, yet capable at times of remarkable change and intensity of expression. His ponderous diction in tragedy betrayed his long association with Macready; yet, though of the old school, he was the first to abandon the pernicious custom of making 'points'; namely, in the course of a scene leaving his fellow actors in the shadows and declaiming a popular passage in a manner designed to invite the applause of the audience, thereby reducing the drama to a series of elocutionary juggling acts. He studied his characters in the light of human nature and interpreted them with intelligence and understanding. All in all, he was more successful in comedy than tragedy. His Hamlet, though reckoned to be the best of its time, had not the excellence of his Falstaff, Shallow or

Bottom. His versatility was extraordinary, his company the best that he could muster, and his popularity well-deserved.

Spellbound, the boy watched the much-read story unfold before him. He hung upon the lovely words so clearly spoken, now moved to tears by the gentle pathos of which Phelps was a master, now joining in the uproarious laughter which greeted the actor's broad interpretation of Hamlet's antic disposition, his rallying of Polonius, and his comical exchanges with the gravediggers. The ghost's appearance was, perhaps, a little unconvincing, but he vanished magically––if there could be any deeper magic than the veiled mystery of changing scenes and the breathtaking sword play of the duel. Johnnie was one of an audience of indiscriminating and enthusiastic partisans who rose to their favourite and cheered him to the echo; if from a seat nearby a zealot stood up and roared: 'Where be Charles Kean now?' and his cry was greeted with shouts of derisive laughter, his father was able to explain to him that Mr. Kean was at that very time playing Hamlet at the Princess's Theatre to equally loyal if less numerous adherents. He was thrilled to find the theatre an arena in which deadly rivals contended for popular favour, where loyalties and dislikes were loudly voiced and where the atmosphere before and behind the footlights was charged with excitement and passion.

Johnnie Brodribb was never to forget that night. He was so surfeited with impressions that it took him weeks to assimilate and digest them. Yet, as he did so, he had already begun diligently to plan the future for which he longed and for which, at present in secret, he had determined to prepare himself.

When, during the following March, his brief schooldays came to an end, the Brodribbs sent their son to work as a junior clerk in a firm of lawyers, Messrs. Paterson and Longman, whose office was in Milk Street, Cheapside. Here, under the kindly eye of Mr. Longman, he filled the inkpots, replenished the blotting paper, sharpened quills, manipulated the heavy letter press and looked forward to running messages and taking letters to the post, and to the chance these errands gave him of dawdling through the streets and lingering over the bookstalls. Though he gained a little more freedom and pocket money, the change from school life was hardly for the better. He found the drudgery was much the same and certainly of less variety, while, kind as Mr. Longman was, he missed good Dr. Pinches, who could always be relied upon to lend a ready ear to recitation; the doctor in turn missed his exemplary pupil and for years afterwards would damp the enthusiasm of some budding elocutionist by remarking wistfully, after he had heard a boy's piece: 'Very good, very good, but you should have heard Brodribb do it.' So, for a year, Brodribb had to content himself with private study and lonely rehearsals. He was able to buy a few more books and to make further excursions to Sadler's Wells, where, although the top prices had been raised recently from two to three shillings, even the very poor could for a few pence fight their way into the gallery. The season included a special production of *Timon of Athens*, with its visions of ancient Greece, the diorama showing Alcibiades leading his army on Athens, and with Phelps as the noble Athenian, a part in which he was said to excel even Edmund Kean. There was opportunity, too, to see the great actor as Sir Pertinax MacSycophant in *The Man of the World* and to hear him delight the crowded house with his inimitable Scottish dialect. Once, in the street, Johnnie saw his hero in ordinary clothes and, in wondering curiosity, followed him for some time at a respectful distance. But these were the brighter moments of a dull year.

His mother watched with anxious disapproval his ill-concealed delight in the theatre and the gradual weakening of her authority over him. Money was short, and it was Johnnie upon whom they must all depend for any improvement in their circumstances. Happily an opening for him was found in the offices of Thacker, Spink and Co., East India Merchants of Newgate Street. Here, if he applied himself, he had every chance of making a career in the world of business, and even of journeying to the East, which Samuel knew from his scrapbook to be a place of exotic beauty where rich rewards were to be won. Johnnie accepted the change philosophically—after all, Newgate Street was no farther than Milk Street from Sadler's Wells.

CHAPTER III
Clerical Histrionical

———⊶◦⊷———

I

Either Johnnie Brodribb was peculiarly lucky in those with whom he came into contact during these impressionable years, or the mandarins of Cheapside were conforming unconsciously to the genial characters which were being mirrored for them in the imagination of Charles Dickens. Mr. Thacker might well have been an elder brother of the Cheerybles; he was noble in appearance, courteous in his manner, and venerable in his long silvering hair. Johnnie took to his new employer at once, though he was ready to join his fellow juniors in their guerrilla war against Mr. Blackwell, the senior clerk, whose severity was a necessary foil to his master's leniency. He was quickly accepted by the five or six clerks; two of them, Edward Russell and Charles Ford, became his close friends. These cheerful cockney clerks remarked to each other upon what they called his gentlemanliness, by which they did not mean a self-conscious and assumed gentility but the simplicity and unaffected grace natural to a country boy coming from a home where good manners and high principle were the common change of daily life. By contrast, Brodribb himself was conscious of the roughness of his speech and the shakiness of his grammar; this led him to institute a system by which he and his fellows fined one another for misplaced aspirates or lapses in syntax—a strange discipline to be imposed by the most junior recruit, yet one which they accepted readily and enthusiastically. Far from earning ridicule, his undisguised passion for the theatre aroused sympathetic interest in his two friends, who took an instant liking to this lanky youth, with his black curly hair and the dreamy manner which could so quickly be discarded for a keen and penetrating vivacity. When Mr. Blackwell was out, young Brodribb would create a welcome diversion by reciting to them, earnestly inviting their criticism and listening without offence to their comments on his jerky halting stride and on the still evident imperfections of his speech. For though his body bent over the ledgers and his pen automatically checked the invoices and shipping registers, his thoughts, which were beyond Mr. Blackwell's control, were usually far away dwelling upon the last play he had seen at Sadler's Wells or upon the next which he planned to see. For by now he had realized that in order to study and observe every detail of the performance it was best to have read the play first and to arrive at the theatre as word perfect as the actors. Consequently, as he stalked along the crowded streets on his way to and from his home at midday, the attention of more curious passers-by would be caught by this youth with a pale animated face reciting loudly to himself and oblivious of his eccentricity.

The hours of work were long—nine-thirty to seven—but he always seemed to have a store of unbounded energy when the time came to spend an evening with his new friends through whom he was becoming aware gradually of the wider, teeming life of London beyond the City. He found that recreations and habits, which in his home were regarded as wayward or downright sinful, were the normal pursuits of young men whose characters were beyond reproach. He soon forgot the night not so long ago when, alone and filled with awful doubts, he found his way to the forbidden Adelphi Theatre and in the gallery, expecting the wrath of God to fall upon him at any moment, sat through two blood-thirsty melodramas and an uproarious farce. Now he only remembered the illicit joys of six hours' robust entertainment; in retrospect, his mother's grief and the bitterness of her reproach, when he came home at two in the morning, seemed harsh and unreasonable in the light of the everyday life of other lads of his age. Now he rarely lacked companions and soon found those who loved the theatre as much as he did and were on familiar terms with actors and stage-door-keepers.

One evening Edward Russell took him to his lodgings and introduced his friend to a young man with whom he shared them. His name was Henry Palmer, and he was, like Brodribb, a rebellious junior clerk in the house of Hill and Underwood of Eastcheap. A wealthy aunt had placed him in the firm with a promise of buying him a partnership. Though diligent in his work, young Palmer had no intention of spending his days in the City and used the means with which his aunt provided him to indulge his passion for learning languages. His method was original but effective, and in the pursuit of it Johnnie Brodribb became his constant companion. To learn Italian, Palmer sought out Italians where he could sit among them and hear them talk. This meant journeys to Tichbourne Street, where there was a café frequented by political exiles; to Hammersmith, where the colonies of organ-grinders and plaster-workers were to be found on Saffron Hill; to small Italian restaurants with friendly waiters, and to Italian ships lying in the docks, whose mingled crews could tune his ear to the dialects of Genoa, Naples and Messina. It led them to entrancing evenings in Cremorne Gardens, where they hobnobbed with Signor Buonocorre, the celebrated fire-eater—evenings of adventure and delight, memorable for the scent of garlic and the sour bite of rough wine. Nor was Italian enough. French, too, had to be mastered; the study of it led them into similar, if less colourful haunts, where among other things they learnt much of French criminal laws and at first hand studied the French detective system which at the time was becoming familiar to England through the novels of Gaboriau. In Johnnie Brodribb's romantic eyes, Henry Palmer became Haroun Al Raschid; nor was he far off the mark, for after their ways separated, his friend became the great oriental scholar of his time. It was in these years that Johnnie began to paste into the album of his mind a vast collection of human types and characters which were to become the material of his art.

One night, in Edward Russell's rooms, Palmer suggested an experiment in mesmerism of which recently there had been much talk. Neither Russell nor Brodribb were surprised to discover that their friend possessed this strange power. Rather fearfully, they submitted to his influence; neither was able to exercise control over him. Later Palmer put his powers to practical use. Finding an injured woman lying on a doorstep and in great pain, he rendered her unconscious with such success that she woke up to find herself in a hospital. In Johnnie's mental album this experience had a page all to itself. He had found in Henry Palmer the perfect companion with whom to share his love for the theatre and his abiding curiosity—one for whom nothing was without interest and everything was to be explored.

Johnnie Brodribb had seen enough of the theatre to realize the tremendous physical strain to which actors are put in the course of their work. Characteristically he embodied into his slowly maturing plans a routine designed to fortify and strengthen his naturally good physique. He had always been fond of bathing; now he was often up at five o'clock and walking briskly down Old Broad Street and Gracechurch Street, at that hour strangely quiet and deserted, to the nearest point on the river where he could have a swim. He lacked, unfortunately, what he most needed—adequate food; bread and butter was becoming too constant an item in the diet of a growing boy. It was a hard time, made harder by the diversion of such little money as he had to the purchase of books and theatre tickets.

He spent his summer holiday either with his Aunt Penberthy or with his cousin, Mrs. Wilkins, who lived at Warminster. He grew to find Halsetown a little quiet, for now Isaac had gone, it was not easy for his aunt to make both ends meet. Warminster was very different, and in Mrs. Wilkins he found a kindly confidant and friend, and in her cheerful home a welcome change from the austerities of Old Broad Street. After one of his visits to her he wrote:

'My dear Mrs. Wilkins,

I have been in your debt for some time, but as we are neither of us very punctual in our payments you must please not complain.

You cannot imagine the feelings of a poor pent-up Londoner, on waking on a bright Autumnal morning, the gorgeous sun peering through the window, the lark warbling forth its praise to heaven, and the voices of many children laughing in the street, indeed everything calculated to fill his soul with boundless rapture. He joyfully rises and hastens to complete his toilet, that he may also enjoy the freshness of the glorious morning, hastens downstairs, is saluted by the cheerful faces of the happy household, proceeds along a delightful road, everything smiling with pleasure upon him as if they were all conscious of the beauty around them and shortly comes within sight of the "Old Mill". The very name awakens feelings of pleasure in the heart of everyone, for it is accompanied with thoughts of rural beauty. He arrives at it and is even welcomed by a noble dog, as if he had imbibed the hospitality of his owner, enters the house, and is cordially received by all within, and with an excellent appetite sits down to a magnificent breakfast of Ham and Eggs. The repast is completed, from which he rises with a rather tarnished appetite and consults with a gentleman (the host) on the morning's amusement. It is agreed that they shall spend it in the exciting pleasures of shooting. Fancy his delight in jumping over the hedges and ditches (and, by the by, sometimes jumping in), racing with the dog, laughing with his many companions, or anxiously watching the result of a shot, and joyously bounding after the game, and on they go with hearts light and merry, as if all on earth beside was nought to them. Well, after about 2 hours' sport of this kind, they enter the house of a relation, partaking of the same hospitality as the other portion of his family, and there they are regaled with luncheon and a free orchard. Riding being a luxury he is not indulged with in London, he is provided with a pony (on whose back *he* spent many a *happy* hour, to the *un*happiness of the pony) to carry him home, being a little fatigued by the morning's exertion. They return and after many *very pleasant etcs*. he prepares for the afternoon's fruition.

He proceeds with his fair hostess (who always had the afternoon at her disposal) to a rustic spot, where they are joined by a party of intellectual and happy acquaintances. Picture a circle of 12 sitting in a garden, on a lawn, beside a cottage where

> *The Jessamine clambers in flower o'er the thatch,*
> *And the swallow sings sweet, from its nest in the wall.*

And all around trees and shrubs which partially hide from view a large lake, that shines like crystal through the trees—partaking of that social meal, tea; the innocent jest passing round, a happiness visible on every face. After passing a very merry evening, they return home with hearts light and merry, retire to rest, and are hush'd in the arms of balmy sleep. Such are a very few enjoyments of a country life, and only 1 of our 10 days I passed at Warminster. I hope you will excuse me trespassing on your time so long with this feeble description, for I am sure it must have become tedious to you.

My mother also wishes me to thank you for your kind invitation, but she begs to decline it, as it is impossible for her to leave home this year; she would, tho', be delighted to receive a visit from you, as there are innumerable attractions for London at the present time, one of which is the Crystal Palace. We should all be glad to see you here. Do please try and come. We shall also be happy to see any other branch of your family if they should visit London. . . .

. . . My mother and father, I am happy to say, are in the enjoyment of excellent health and send their very kind regards to yourself and family.

I hope you will excuse this (I'm afraid) incoherent scrawl, but it is a great effort for me to hold my pen, the heat being so oppressive. I never felt it so much as I have during the last week.—Believe me, My dear Mrs. Wilkins, Your sincere friend,

J. H. Brodribb.'

No doubt Mrs. Wilkins enjoyed the reading of this letter as much as Johnnie Brodribb had relished its composition; although it is a rich hash flavoured with Pickwick, seasoned with Pinches and glutinous with the contemporary style of Threadneedle Street, it shows the beginnings of observation and the desire to find an outlet for that observation in self-expression.

About this time the river of British drama, swollen by the fresh spring of the Theatre Regulations Act, was to divide into two channels. At first this diversion was hardly noticeable, the main flood continuing its course while the new effluent seemed but a mere trickle. Yet, as time passed, this new stream, though it lacked the grandeur of the old, gained strength and became itself the main course while the ancient channel shrank and finally dried up. When all but the two monopoly houses were condemned to present only burlettas, a genius arrived upon the scene, who, making a virtue of necessity, created within these limitations an entirely new style of acting. In 1831 Lucia Elizabetta Vestris, an actress and singer of unusual charm, became lessee of the Olympic Theatre, an oasis of gaiety and glitter in the midst of the foulest slums of Drury Lane. Here for ten years she produced and acted in a series of burlettas which established her as the darling of the theatre-going public. Unwittingly she developed a style of comedy acting which, in its naturalness and confidential appeal to the audience, was a striking contrast to the accepted style of which Macready was the best contemporary exponent. In 1835 she married Charles Mathews, junior. This talented young writer and actor, the son of a notable mimic and comedian, through her influence and example, harnessed his own versatile comic genius to the best of the naturalistic French school of comedy and so evolved, after his wife's death, a style of play and performance which paved the way for the elegant domestic, the farcical concubinical, the tragical psychological and the dialectical political drama which was to pervade the British theatre. By 1865 Tom Robertson, a young actor with a gift for writing who had worked as a prompter for Charles Mathews and his wife, was already beginning to formulate a new and realistic style of comedy, with a hopeful eye on the attractive Marie Wilton, who showed signs of refining and developing the art of Vestris; these two, in turn, were being shrewdly eyed by young Squire Bancroft, who was then learning his business as an actor in Liverpool. Bancroft, by employing the playwright and, in 1867, marrying the actress, became the successful actor-manager of the old Prince of Wales Theatre in Tottenham Court Road, where, by producing a series of highly successful cup-and-saucer drawing-room comedies, he began, innocently yet irretrievably, to dig the grave of the romantic drama.

In the meantime the successes of Phelps and the revival of serious interest in the theatre had created a popular taste for amateur acting.

In response to the demand by earnest amateurs for professional instruction and criticism, a number of schools of elocution sprang up in London. Of these the best was the City Elocution Class which had been started by Henry Thomas and his wife, first in a modest way under a railway arch in Fenchurch Street and later in the more spacious Sussex Hall where Dr. Pinches used to hold his Speech Days. Thomas was a great admirer and friend of Charles Mathews, so that his technique and selection of plays leaned towards the modern rather than the traditional style of acting.

It was not long before John Brodribb, one among many stage-struck clerks, presented himself to Mr. Thomas, whose instruction in the best of modern comedy technique would correct the balance of his studies. Mr. Thomas was another of those bright and genial characters who at this time seemed to cross the boy's path with dangerous frequency as though fate was determined to give him an illusory impression of his fellow-men. At the weekly meetings he would preside in the chair, with his buxom wife at his side, listening to the recitations of the members of his class, giving his advice and judgment and inviting his pupils to criticize each other. Now and again he and his wife would take part in a play chosen for rehearsal, which was usually in the Charles Mathews tradition. John Brodribb made a deep impression on Mr. Thomas at his first audition and soon won the admiration and affection of the rest of the class. He was a good deal younger than the average, so that his black schoolboy's suit and deep Eton collar emphasized the spirit and intelligence with which he tackled his work. He was beginning to get the measure of his stammer and succeeded in hiding it entirely from his new fellow-students—only at the cost of hours of patient labour by himself, repeating each difficult syllable slowly, distinctly, and again and again.

When the class moved to Sussex Hall, with its comfortable seating arrangements and a platform supplied with easily adapted screens for scenery, Mr. Thomas and his pupils gave semi-public performances to which, as a matter of business, he invited his friends of the press. At the first of them John Brodribb appeared as Captain Absolute in *The Rivals* and was reported in the *Theatrical Journal* as playing his part 'with intelligent tact and with great credit to Mr. Thomas'. He followed it with a recitation of 'The Last Days of Herculaneum', which caused a critic to overhaul his clichés and to allude to him as 'the young Roscius'. Three months later he won similar praise for his performance in a farce.

This assiduous practice with amateurs was all very well, but it was not enough. In the course of his visits to Sadler's Wells he had made the acquaintance of a leading actor in Phelps's company, William Hoskins, who during the previous autumn had played such parts in the repertoire as Buckingham in *Henry VIII*. Hoskins, who was the son of a Derbyshire landowner, realizing his purposeful sincerity, undertook to give him private tuition. This presented some difficulty, for throughout the day his pupil was imprisoned in the city while he himself was playing nightly at the theatre. It was a measure of their mutual enthusiasm that the young clerk arranged to attend Mr. Hoskins at his house in Middleton Square at eight o'clock every morning, where he had an hour's instruction in elocution and panto-mime. In addition to this he attended regularly a school of arms in Chancery Lane, where he learnt how to fence and to handle the swords and rapiers which to him were the essential furniture of romantic drama. In contrast to the youthful Edmund Kean, whose syllabus of training was arranged by a committee consisting of his Uncle Moses, an aunt and Miss Tidswell, John Brodribb, though in rather better circumstances, had to organize his own theatrical education.

Although by now his purpose must have become evident to his father and mother, he did his best to disarm their prejudices. Whatever Samuel may have thought he kept to himself, for he was utterly dependent upon Mary and obedient to her wishes. In deference to his mother, Johnnie would accompany her to chapel on a Sunday, much as he must have grudged the little time which he could devote to reading and study. That year, shortly before he went on a visit to Cornwall, he writes to Mrs. Wilkins:

68 *Old Broad Street,*
July 29th, 1854.

'My dear Mrs. Wilkins,

. . . Many many thanks for your kindness in inviting me to spend my vacation with you but I am engaged to do so at my Aunt Penberthy's in Cornwall, where I hope to be on August 24th though I am sure I shall not enjoy myself . . . as much as I should at your charming home, which time I always remember with pleasure. . . .

Mr. Binney has received from two of the young men of his con-gregation a very handsome silver inkstand, value £60, as a token of their esteem. You must imagine that he is highly flattered, taking the interest he does in them. . . . My mother and I attend the Albion Chapel, London Wall. The Reverend Mr. Mcfarlane is the Minister and a very superior one he is. He is only twenty-five years old, but exceedingly clever. He often preaches for Mr. Binney (in fact that was where my mother first heard him) who is like a father to him. I have frequently been to his residence. He took me about a month ago to see several of the principal sights in London, such as the Royal Academy, Polytechnic, etc. He has since married one of Mr. Binney's congregation, a Deacon's daughter, who I believe is in every way calculated for a Minister's wife. I have just received an invitation to visit them when I shall have an opportunity of judging for myself. My father still goes to Mr. Binney.

I am still in the same office, though I cannot be comfortable while I remain from half past nine to seven. I am in reality more inclined to rest at the close of the day, than study; however I am obliged to apply (myself) as I know this is my most advantageous time. . . .'

The style is perhaps a trifle precocious for a boy of sixteen, but John Brodribb was growing up in an age of precocity.

A young man of twenty-four, John Millais, who, as a curly-headed youth of seventeen, had won the Gold Medal at the Royal Academy School, was already the established leader of a group of painters fighting for a revival of romanticism and sedulous craftsmanship. Many of these brilliant young men had blossomed in the warmth of encouragement from their cultured parents and from the distinguished men of arts and letters who frequented their homes. It was harder to keep one's eye on the horizon when at the office such abstraction was regarded by Mr. Blackwell as wool-gathering and at home by one's mother as the glimpsing of the gates of hell. As the months passed, his mother's opposition was more clearly voiced. The friends whom he brought home found themselves drawn to one side by this quiet, distressed woman and begged to do all in their power to dissuade her son from going on the stage. Only those who knew him least tried to do so. Such things were hard to bear, for the boy was sensitive enough to long for the affection and encouragement that only a mother can give. But the stern virtues that had led Mary Brodribb to part with her son for ten precious years were now creating a gulf between their mutual understanding, which grew wider as the hour of his decision approached.

During 1855 the members of the Elocution Class decided to take the Soho Theatre in Dean Street, which was available to amateurs and their friends. Mr. Thomas and his pupils played an old costume comedy, *The Honeymoon*, with reasonable success, though Brodribb's performance was not particularly commended. Yet, for the first time, he felt the boards of a stage beneath his feet, and, with dry caking powders, made his face a mask on which to paint the accents of line and colour. He experienced the mystical transformation of doublet and hose and the assumed gallantry of borrowed plumes. Shortly after this, his teacher, Mr. Hoskins, who had decided to try his luck in Australia, invited his pupil, with whose progress he was so delighted, to go with him. Brodribb felt instinctively that his hour had not yet come. Hoskins, understanding the boy's hesitancy, yet convinced that nothing would deflect him from his ultimate purpose, offered to introduce him to the great Phelps. The interview was one which might well have caused a stage-struck youth to lose his head—the ordeal of rehearsing before his hero, almost God-like in his remote impassivity, the blunt but kind criticism and the final crushing yet well-intended advice: 'Sir, do not go on the stage; it is an ill-requited profession.' Something in the boy's bearing, or perhaps an interceding word from Hoskins, led Phelps to reconsider his discouraging admonition. He repeated what he had said, and again the boy made it clear that his advice had fallen upon deaf ears.

'In that case, Sir,' said Samuel Phelps, 'you'd better come here and I'll give you two pounds a week to begin with.'

Two years before, the boy watching *Hamlet* for the first time could not have conjured up this scene even in the most fanciful of moments that come before sleep. Had he been able to do so he would have imagined himself leaping at the offer and snatching greedily this passport to the world of illusion. But Brodribb had his plan and knew that the time was not advantageous. He refused Phelps' generous offer. Hoskins must have watched this scene in mild wonder; he knew how many salted actors would have jumped at the chance, yet it confirmed his estimate of his young friend's quality. Before he sailed for Australia he saw Mrs. Brodribb and tried to console her by prophesying that in time her son would be earning fifty pounds a week. The kindly old actor realized, perhaps, the ineptitude of his consolation. With commendable persistence he wrote a letter of recommendation to Mr. Davis, a provincial theatre manager of repute; this, when they finally parted, he gave to John Brodribb, saying: 'You will go on the stage. When you want an engagement present that letter and you will get one.'

Early in 1856 Mrs. Wilkins received a letter which gave her no hint of the crisis through which its writer was passing.

> 68 *Old Broad Street,*
> *February 17th,* 1856.

'My dear Mrs. Wilkins,

I must first thank you for the paper and book you were kind enough to send me. I was much entertained with both. The former is a very nice journal, and I wish it success; I had no notion that you had one in Warminster, there seems little original in it, but it is a pleasing summary. The critique on the trip to Paris must have been very gratifying to the lecturer, and the lecture exceedingly interesting to you. It is strange what pleasure it gives us to hear or read of places we have visited, although we seldom learn anything new. A correspondent doesn't write much in favour of the intellectuality of your town. What is your opinion concerning it; I don't know (but my knowledge is very limited) of any town, the size of yours, where cultivation of the social and intellectual faculties are more encouraged. I thought you were far advanced. . . .

. . . In reply to your question, I have not yet joined the church in London Wall, and I do not think I shall; perhaps I don't attach enough importance to it. I think it only improves the outward appearance, which, I dare say, strengthens the church in the eyes of men, and is therefore beneficial, but the true joining ties the heart, not the hands; however, if it is necessary, it is a solemn step and requires mature consideration.

The recent opening of Parliament will shortly create intense interest in the English nation. Evangelical and political events of no common order are brewing. The great Evangelical question is with reference to the opening of public exhibitions such as the British Museum, National Gallery and Crystal Palace on Sundays. Dickens's new work[1] (the first number of which had a circulation of 35,000) is written in favour of the opening, and he puts forward in a very ingenious manner (though under a cloak) the advantages arising from such a step. Dickens is a moralist but nothing else. Many Members of Parliament, the leading literary men, and a great mass of the population are in favour of it—on the other hand, petitions by Sunday School teachers & congregations, have been sent, and prayers and sermons are said in opposition to the opening. Much will depend on the issue. The great political question is the establishment of peace;—*much* will depend

[1] *Little Dorrit*

on the issue of *that*. It is very interesting to watch the movements of the different bodies.

"We take no note of time but from its loss."

I was eighteen years old on the 6th instant. . . .
    Believe me to be, my dear Mrs. Wilkins,
                                        Yours very sincerely,
                                            J. H. Brodribb.
P.S. Since I wrote this letter, which I had unfortunately mislaid, the Sunday opening question, as it is called here, has been brought before the House and decided in favour of the opposing party by a great majority.
    What a blessing!
    I have nothing more to say: Goodbye.'

John Brodribb, if he took note of it, certainly was not losing much time. His prose style was losing its youthful flourish; his views and judgments were maturing. Already he manifested an almost morbid admiration for an intellectuality which, he believed, lack of education had denied him. His nonconformist conscience prompted him to support those who opposed Sunday entertainment; yet another instinct may have warned him of a danger which threatened the hard-won rest which the actor, thanks to the Sabbatarians, was able to enjoy.

A few months later his uncle, Thomas Brodribb, gave him a hundred pounds, the proceeds of a paid-up insurance policy. At a critical moment, this windfall provided the means of escape from his office stool and the capital which he needed to equip himself for his new vocation. At last he was able to confide to Edward Russell that he had made up his mind to go on the stage. Shortly afterwards, having got an afternoon's leave of absence, he set off for the West End where he spent some of his legacy and much careful thought in buying an assortment of wigs and properties at the theatrical costumiers of Long Acre and Covent Garden. Returning in the early evening, he found Russell waiting for him in feverish excitement.

'I've got them,' he announced: 'come downstairs and see them!'

In the corner of the room where they worked there was a hinged hatchway through which stores and merchandise could be hoisted from the cellar by a rope and tackle. Russell shinned down the rope while Brodribb, carrying his great parcel, staggered down the stairs. Undoing the packages, he displayed to his friend his newly-acquired treasures. Out came wigs, buckles, lace, feathers, sham jewellery and, last of all, three swords. As he unwrapped each of these weapons he made flourishes and passes with them, lunging at sacks and packing-cases, feeling their balance and testing the temper of their blades, saying: 'This is my court sword—this my fencing sword—aren't they beauties?' It occurred to neither of them that there was anything ridiculous in the fascination which these weapons had for them—weapons now practically obsolete on the battlefield, whose blades would be bent on nothing more heroic than an actor's doublet. They knew that this was no boyish extravagance, for at that time actors had to supply their own properties and accoutrements. John Brodribb had invested a considerable part of his windfall in the tools of his trade—a calculated step in the direction of his goal.

That night, in Old Broad Street, he hung the court sword with its jewelled hilt at the foot of his bed; from time to time he rose and, striking a match, marvelled at his new treasure—the vigil of the play-actor knight before his tinsel arms.

He had refused Phelps' offer because he knew that London was a prize to be won, that his assault upon the capital was not to be attempted until he had perfected himself in the hard school of the provincial stock company. That autumn, before turning his back on commerce and inflicting upon his mother the pain and sorrow which he knew well enough his decision must cause her, he submitted himself to a final test. The recent popularity of schools of elocution had suggested to enterprising theatre owners a way of exploiting the vogue for amateur acting. At certain small theatres managers were ready to put on plays in which amateurs could appear on payment of a fee. Thus the well-to-do tyro who could afford to pay three guineas could command a leading part, while for a few shillings a silent stage-struck gentleman could walk on as a soldier or a reveller.

John Brodribb dipped again into his shrinking capital. Hearing that at the Soho Theatre they were planning an amateur production of *Romeo and Juliet*, he determined to prove himself in a sustained and emotional performance. Making certain that he was first in the field, he put down his three guineas for the part of Romeo.

Having secured the leading part, the matter of billing became one of paramount importance. He knew that if he went on the stage he would have to change his name, and the time had now come for a final decision. Though, at that time, it was common enough for a man or woman entering the theatrical profession to take a stage name— usually to satisfy the sensibility of their outraged families—it was more likely that John Brodribb doubted the effectiveness of such a name as his own on a playbill. For some time past he had considered what name he should adopt and had discussed the matter with his friends. In a letter to Charlie Ford a week or two later he announces his final choice:

'My dear Ford,

I have determined on taking the name of Irving instead of Baringtone and accordingly have ordered fifty cards of Cross which they promised to send to 87 (Newgate Street) tomorrow; please receive them for me.

Kindly get me an inkstand with a screw top the size of the bottom of the enclosed piece of paper and as high *altogether* as that is long. Mordham I think are the best. Blackwell has one on his desk.

I leave here next Monday week; the theatre opens on the following Monday.

Give my kind regards to your mother and look in at the first opportunity.

Sincerely yours,
J. H. B. Irving.'

Baringtone must have been a child of his invention—a mingling of all that stood for success and distinction in the City with the ultimate syllable of the great name of Buckstone, an actor who for the last twenty-five years had shared with Charles Mathews the title of London's most popular comedian. But however often he wrote it boldly in heavy capitals or murmured it to himself, it looked and sounded contrived—a trifle pretentious. In Irving he had united two great influences on his early life; Edward, the evangelist, whose eloquent if unorthodox sermons were much read in his childhood; and Washington, whose *Sketch Book* was among his boyhood's favourite stories. Baringtone—Irving, Irving—Baringtone—no, Irving it should be, and for better or worse let it be splashed in heavy capitals upon the playbills of the Royal Soho Theatre and neatly printed by Cross and Company on fifty visiting cards. It is improbable that he knew of another Irving—Joseph—who was already on the London stage and had a useful start in the race to head the bills. If not the hand of fate, it was, at least, a happy accident which prompted the authentic Irving, christened Henry, to change his name for stage purposes to Joseph when John Brodribb preferred his second name of Henry to prefix the Irving of his adoption.

62

ROYAL SOHO THEATRE

DEAN STREET, OXFORD STREET.

Licensed by the Lord Chamberlain. Lessee, Mr. T. MOWBRAY, 73, Dean-street, Soho-square.

STALLS, 3s. | **DRESS CIRCLE, 2s.** | **PIT, 1s.** | **GALLERY, 6d.**
HALF-PRICE AT NINE O'CLOCK.---Stalls, 2s. | Dress Circle, 1s. | Pit, 6d | Gallery, 3d.

SHAKSPERE'S

ROMEO & JULIET FOR ONE NIGHT ONLY.

FIRST APPEARANCE of Mr. IRVING as ROMEO.

On MONDAY EVENING, AUGUST 11th, 1856,
Will be presented Shakspere's Tragedy of

ROMEO AND JULIET.

Paris,	Mr. FRANKLYN.	Capulet,	Mr. SHIRLEY.
Romeo,			Mr IRVING.
Mercutio,	Mr. JAMES.	Benvolio,	Mr ROOKE.
Tybalt,	Mr. LEO COOPER.	Friar Laurence,	Mr. C. LASCELLES
Friar John,	Mr. HANDS.	Peter,	Mr. MOWBRAY
Apothecary,	Mr. SANDS.	Balthazar,	Mr. HAZELL.
	Lady Capulet,	Miss FLORENCE.	Mrs. HENDERSON.
Juliet,			
Nurse,		Miss HELEN LOVE.	

To conclude with the Screaming Farce of The

DEAD SHOT.

Captain Cannon,	Mr. SHIRLEY.	Frederick,	Mr. C. LASCELLES.
Hector Timid,		Mr. MOWBRAY.	
Mr. Wiseman,	Mr. BLAKELEY.	Officer,	Mr. HAZELL.
Louisa Lovetrick,	Miss HELEN LOVE.	Chatter,	Miss FLORENCE.

On THURSDAY EVENING, AUGUST 14th, 1856,
The Performance will commence with (by particular desire) Shakspere's Tragedy of

MACBETH.

Duncan,	Mr. GRIFFITHS.	Malcolm, Mr. A. NICHOLLS.	Donalbain, Mr. SEYMOUR
Macbeth, }		Generals in the King's Army	{ Mr. LEO COOPER.
Banquo, }			{ Mr. VILLIERS.
Macduff,	Mr. R. KENT.	Physician,	Mr. READ.
Rosse,	Mr. BARTON.	Hecate,	Mr. HAINES.
Lennox,	Mr. R. BENNETT	First Witch,	Mr. J. B. DALE.
Fleance,	Miss NICHOLL.	Second Witch,	Mr. C. G. BROOK.
Seyton,	Mr. HAZELL.	Third Witch,	Mr. HALLAN.
Seyward,	Mr. WENTWORTH.	First Murderer,	Mr. HANDS.
Lady Macbeth,	Miss FLORENCE.	Gentlewoman,	Miss BARTON.

After which, **the Celebrated Transatlantic Dancer.**

Mr. GEORGE ALLEN, HAS KINDLY CONSENTED TO GIVE A NAUTICAL HORNPIPE.

To conclude with the intensely-affecting and pathetic Drama, called,

THERESE,
THE ORPHAN OF GENEVA.

Fontaine,	Mr. C. NICHOLLS.	Picard,	Mr GRIFFITHS
Carwin,		Mr. J. P SCOTT.	
Count,	Mr. FRANKLYN.	Lavigne,	Mr. J. B. DALE.
Therese, (the Orphan,)	Miss LINDSAY.	Countess,	Miss ROSE ANTON.
Bridget,	Miss MAITLAND.	Charlotte,	Miss JESSIE GRAY.

DOORS OPEN AT HALF-PAST SIX, TO COMMENCE AT SEVEN O'CLOCK PRECISELY.

The production of *Romeo and Juliet* was a scratch affair with no rehearsals and with little direction, yet here on a real stage with real footlights and solid scenery he would have to face the most important reality of all—the ordinary paying public and not a conditioned assembly of doting parents and admiring friends. He prepared himself carefully for the ordeal. He studied the text until he was word perfect, modelling his actions and inflexions upon the professional performances which he had watched so intently. His costume was the best that he could hire—red velvet above the waist, white cotton tights below, a black feathered hat upon his head, and on his feet shoes ornamented with blue rosettes. His sword and dagger were from his own treasured collection. His memory of the evening was confused. He lost his way in the scenery, mislaid his dagger, and even his wig; yet, oblivious of his surroundings and undeterred by the clumsiness or hesitancy of the rest of the cast, he succeeded in entering, as best he could, into the soul and character of Romeo. Edward Russell and a few intimate friends were among the audience. He knew them too well to expect flattery or polite comment. All expressed their entire satisfaction with his efforts, which had, indeed, been well received by the rest of the audience. He had stood successfully the self-imposed trial, such as it was. His last doubt was resolved; he had no illusions about the difficulties which lay ahead and was ready to take the plunge.

Yet the most difficult task remained to be done. As gently as he could, yet so firmly as to leave no doubt as to the finality of his decision, he told his parents that he had sent Mr. Hoskins's letter to Mr. Davis, who had replied by offering him an engagement in the stock company of the new Royal Lyceum Theatre, Sunderland. The season was to open at the end of September and he proposed to give notice to Thacker's at once. Perhaps Samuel was secretly pleased and proud of Johnnie's independence and enterprise. Mary Brodribb never found it in her heart to forgive her son; she believed sincerely that inevitably his soul was damned; all that remained was to pray more devoutly than ever that one day he might see the light and that until that time God would protect him from the evils and temptations which surely must assail him. Such were his last memories of home which shortly afterwards he left to seek refuge with some kindly and sympathetic friends near Romford where he could make his plans and dispositions in peace, without fear that his love and respect for his mother might weaken his resolution.

The parting from Thacker's was easier. A row with Mr. Blackwell over his neglecting to see that the supply of postage stamps was

Irving as Hamlet
Manchester 1863

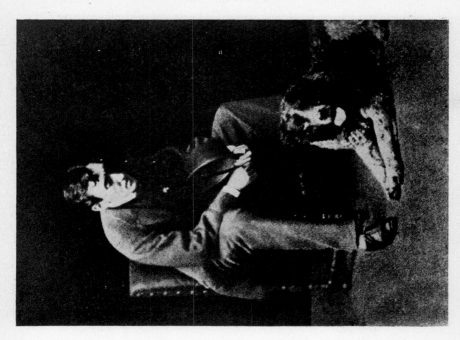

Irving in Liverpool, 1866

Irving in Manchester, 1863

replenished gave him his opportunity. When Mr. Thacker heard that his eccentric but interesting employee had tendered his notice, he summoned him to his office. John Brodribb expected, no doubt, that he would have to endure the usual pained rebukes and gloomy prophecies; the dear old man, however, having dutifully warned him of the temptations which lay ahead, with tears in his eyes dismissed him with a blessing. For the last time Brodribb tidied the desk on which he had boldly carved his now discarded surname. Many years later another stage-struck clerk, A. E. Matthews, would occupy resentfully that same desk. By way of encouragement, Mr. Blackwell, when he heard of Matthew's intention to leave the City for the stage, would explain, not without a certain pride, that this Brodribb, who had left his mark so indelibly on Mr. Thacker's desk, was now the famous Mr. Henry Irving.

Brodribb took a last look round the office where, on the whole, he had been happy enough and had learnt much, for which later he would be grateful. He said goodbye to Edward Russell and to Charlie Ford, who doubted the wisdom of his friend's resolve, and with their cheerful good wishes ringing in his ears, he left the world of ledgers and invoices behind him.

His feelings at this juncture and his profession of faith he expressed in a letter to Mrs. Wilkins:

> *Romford, Essex.*
> *August 18th, 1856.*

'My dear Mrs. Wilkins,

I have left the office I was in at Newgate Street with, I am happy to say, the well wishes of my employers who wished me to remain, and my fellow companions and am staying with some kind friends at Romford, quite free from the smoke and dirt. The change has done and will do me, a great deal of good. The country air and country ale (which I was recommended to take in London, for it is pure) begin to make me look quite ruddy and robust. It is very convenient being able to get to town by train in half an hour and I now and then am obliged to do so.

It would certainly for many reasons have afforded me more pleasure to explore Warminster and dirty Bristol, but I could not leave home for a sufficient time. My mother would have very much liked to visit you, but (always something) we have those dear gentlemen, bricklayers, painters, and plasterers, in the house, who prevent her leaving; my father, too, at such a time, would be quite in a fog without his "rib"—however, I am sure when my Mother leaves home for a holiday, she will spend a short time with you; she is very anxious to come.

Before I left Thacker & Co.'s I had determined to forsake the dull mechanical work of an office and devote my energies to something more intellectual. I knew taking another situation would only be wasting my time, for I have had sufficient experience in the commercial world, and I accordingly told my friends it was my intention to try my fortunes in the Dramatic profession.

They felt it much, and I should be surprised if they did not, for, although they know not what acting is, they know there are many difficulties in the paths of young actors, laborious to surmount. It is the most difficult of arts.

They had foreseen it; they knew I should never rest content with anything else, for I have well weighed the hardships, temptations and toil I should have to undergo; they knew it was no sudden freak of temper, that I did not enter it as too many do, without preparation, and they wisely decided on assisting, not thwarting me, in my future course.

I have £20 to start with, which has bought me many necessary parts of a wardrobe, and I shall begin with a fair stock. The gentleman under whom I took lessons in elocution introduced me by letter to the manager of one of the first provincial theatres, at Newcastle-on-Tyne, and through it, he (the manager) consents to give me a trial at his theatre, at the commencement of the season, in the latter part of September. I accepted it and shall leave London in the middle of next month for "Coaly Tyne".

I played Romeo in Shakespeare's *Romeo and Juliet* at the Soho Theatre here (London) very successfully indeed, and was asked before the curtain at the conclusion. My governor's son was there, was delighted, and came behind and congratulated me heartily after the performance.

As regards the profession which I have chosen I consider it one of the, if not *the*, most intellectual there are.

Actors are created like poets; you can never make one; of course I don't say everybody on the stage is really an actor, there are few. Too many enter it from idle motives and many mistake their calling, but the names of Shakespeare, Garrick, Kemble, Macready and many many others show that they were and are the companions of the master spirits of the ages, and rank as gentlemen and scholars among Royalty and the aristocracy. A person may be as moral and good in that as in any other walk of life. There is much prejudice against it in our circle of society, and that is wearing off as the world grows wiser, but in the higher ones they are considered equals. I have a difficult task before me, and if I succeed, it will be the most fortunate day of my life when I entered it—if I do not (never say fail) there is another field before me elsewhere. I have youth and hope, and relying on a higher power for assistance from temptation and surrounding evils, I hope you and all may never be mistaken in—My dear Mrs. Wilkins, sincerely yours,

J. H. Brodribb.'

There was much to be done before he left for the north. The needs of a junior clerk, living at home and requiring few clothes other than his hard-wearing and sombre suit of office black, were very different from those of a nomadic stock company actor with appearances to keep up, who was unlikely to know, for some time to come, any other home than the bed-sitting-rooms of provincial theatrical lodgings. This meant occasional visits to London and the careful outlay of his dwindling capital in the cheapest market.

At last all was done. On September 11th, with a few pounds in his pocket, with his modest personal luggage and his stage properties, with a screw-top inkpot of the style favoured by Mr. Blackwell, who for all his faults was a sound model for an independent gentleman, Henry Irving set out for Sunderland.

NEW ROYAL LYCEUM THEATRE

Licensed Pursuant to Act of Parliament

Proprietor & Manager, — **Mr. E. D. DAVIS.**

The Erection being completed, the NEW ROYAL LYCEUM THEATRE

WILL BE OPENED

FOR THE RECEPTION OF THE PUBLIC

ON MONDAY EVENING NEXT, SEPT. 29th. 1856.

Mr. DAVIS wishes that his kind Friends and Patrons should themselves judge of the efforts made
for their accommodation rather than be guided by any comments from him, he will therefore
only express his hopes that it will be apparent to all have anxiously he has laboured to redeem
the promise made as to the time of opening.

Architect - - - - - **MR. THOS. MOORE.**
Assistant Architect and Superintendent of Works, - **MR. JOS. POTTS.**
The Decorative Department from the Pencil of **MR. JAS. LINDSAY.**
Executed under his direction by Messrs. SAUNDERS & JOHNSON.
The Masonry by **MESSRS. THOMPSON AND TERRY.**
The Joiner Work by **MR. J. TAYLOR.**
The Gas and other Fittings by Mr. DANNATT and Mr. CLASPER.
The Upholstery by Messrs. ALCOCK, BRYDON, HERRING, &c.
The Painting Work by Mr. ARNISON.

MONDAY EVENING, Sept. 29, 1856

The Season will commence with Sir E. L. BULWER LYTTON's beautiful Play

RICHELIEU

Louis the Thirteenth.....Mr. COURTENAY   Gaston (Duke of Orleans).....Mr. IRVING
The Sieur de Beringhen (a Courtier).....Mr. ALFRED DAVIS
Baradas (Favourite of the King).....Mr. ORVELL   The Chevalier de Mauprat.....Mr. J. C. COWPER
Richelieu, (First Time in Sunderland).....Mr. DAVIS
Father Joseph Mr. FOOTE   Huguet a Spy) Mr. BRUNT   François a Page Miss AGNES MARKHAM
Pages to Richelieu. .... Misses POULSON and MONTAGUE
Pages to the King..... .... Misses MILNER, LEIGH, CARTER
Count de Clermont.....Mr. GIBSON   Captain of Guard.....Mr. WAITE
Gaoler..... Mr. BRODERICK   Governor.....Mr. S. JOHNSON
First Secretary Mr. MASTERS   Second Do. Mr. EDOUIN   Third Do. Mr. MORELLI
Julia de Mortemar (Richelieu's Ward)..... Mrs. ALFRED DAVIS
Marion de Lorme..... Miss DE CLIFFORD

To Conclude with the highly successful New Piece of Oriental Sentimentality, or Sentimental Orientality, extracted from
Dreams of the Arabian Nights, by the indefatigable Visionary, HOO-ZURE-AYAK, and which to be appreciated must be seen,
as the most extravagantly laudatory encomiums must fall immeasurably short of the gigantic merit of

THE ENCHANTED LAKE!

OR THE FISHERMAN AND THE GENIE

Achmet (Autocrat of Bagdad, of imperial splendour and imperious disposition) Mr. S. JOHNSON
Mooney Pacha (his much-abused Vizier) Mr. FOOTE   Abdallah (the Black Enchanter) Mr. MASTERS
Hassan (a Fisherman, who finds out that honesty is the best policy) Mr. ALFRED DAVIS
Monkey (who though at first, a beast," ultimately proves himself "a gentleman") Mr. EDOUIN
Genius of the Bottle..... (who has no connection with the Bottle Imp).....Mr. COURTENAY
Selim..... Cook of the Palace).....Mr. GIBSON
Azor and Azim..... (Two Young Princes).....Mrs. COURTENAY and Miss CARTER
Cooks..... Messrs. BRUNT, IRVING, WAITE, BRODERICK, OWEN
Fatima and Zelica (interesting young Ladies, Daughters of Achmet) Misses OWEN and DE CLIFFORD
Queen of the Peri..... Miss MILNER
Peris..... Misses LEIGH, POULSONS, C. BROCK, B. BROCK, and F. BROCK, &c.

In the Centre of the Burlesque the following SONGS, &c., &c.:—
SONG—"The Lay-sacked Jet,".....Mr. ALFRED DAVIS   SONG and CHORUS—"The fullest times down,".....COOKS.
SONG—"A Piece of Beauty cos,".....Mr. ALFRED DAVIS   SONG and CHORUS—"Hie away,".....THE PERIS.
CHORUS—"Come away my pretty little Peri,".....THE PERIS.   CHORUS—"Try, try,".....CHARACTERS.
SONG—"Waittel a Genius,".....Mr. ALFRED DAVIS   DUET & CHORUS—Spread out our frame,".....THE PERIS.
SONG—"The Lake of the Mountain's surprisingly deep".....CHARACTERS.
DUET—"The Red Rev." - Miss MARKHAM   SONG—"On the Lake's Green Banks,".....Miss MARKHAM.
By Mr. ALFRED DAVIS.   DUO—"Oy tender Banks rendering,".....Miss MARKHAM.
CHORUS—"Have you see a wretched Peri,".....COOKS.   SONG—"Rise from the Waves,".....Miss MARKHAM.
SONG—"Pray Daddy, pray pity your Poor,".....Miss OWEN.   FINALE—"Great to the Crown of all our Wishes,".....Miss MARKHAM and CHORUS.

DANCING BY THE FARNINGHAM SISTERS

Do you know the argument of this play ?   They do beat Joan!—POISON do Joan!!!!
From Shakspeare.   [A long way—F. D.

1.—Here the Peri puzzled their Peri-craniums about a subject, and what an effort of Genius is required to find one.
2.—How Hassan got into a mess with the Genie, and how he ingeniously got out of it.
3.—How Hassan and the Monster fished in the Enchanted Lake, and what were the hot pursuits of the next proceeding.
4.—How the Sultan brought the fish, and how the Cook was embroiled by frying them, together with other matters only related in this history.
5.—How the Sultan and Court watched in the kitchen, and how the fish shewed themselves in common sense.
6.—How the Sultan and Court went a wild-goose chase in the wilderness, and the Mirage they saw there.
7.—How the two Princes were roused from their mountain trance, and how the Black Enchanter took up his abode in rather various quarters than he liked.
8.—Here Oxeg disenchanted the Lake, and with a reduced finale is made.

TUESDAY EVENING, Sept. 30, 1856

The Performances will commence with Sir E. L. Bulwer's celebrated Play of the

LADY OF LYONS!

Claude Melnotte.....Mr. COWPER
Mons. Deschapelles.....Mr. MASTERS   Beauseant.....Mr. ORVELL
Colonel (afterwards Gen. Damas).....Mr. ALFRED DAVIS
Glavis.....Mr. S. JOHNSON   Gaspard.....Mr. COURTENAY
Landlord.....Mr. FOOTE   Servant.....Mr. THOMSON
1st Officer.....Mr. BRUNT   2nd Officer.....Mr. IRVING   3rd Officer.....Mr. F. OWEN
Pauline (the Lady of Lyons).....Miss ADELAIDE BOWRING
Widow Melnotte.....Miss AGNES MARKHAM
Marion.....Miss LEIGH   Janet.....Miss MILNER
Madame Deschapelles.....Mrs. DAVIS

To conclude with the celebrated Burletta written expressly for Mr. DAVIS, entitled

THE ENCHANTED LAKE!

CHARACTERS AS BEFORE.

WEDNESDAY EVENING, OCT. 1.

The Performance will commence with Sir E. L. BULWER's beautiful Play of

RICHELIEU !

CHARACTERS AS BEFORE.

To conclude with the New and Laughable Farce, called

THAT BLESSED BABY ?

Mr. Frank Finnicke.....Mr. COURTENAY   John Thomas.....Mr. S. JOHNSON
First Policeman.....Mr. GIBSON   Second do.....Mr. OWEN
Mrs. Lever.....Miss DE CLIFFORD   Mary Jane.....Miss AGNES MARKHAM

☞ A Numerous and Efficient Orchestra will be provided.

THE PRICES OF ADMISSION WILL BE TO
Private Boxes and Orchestra Stalls.....**2s. 0d.** | Pit.....**1s.**   Second Price,.....**6d.**
Second Price.....**1s. 6d.** | Gallary,.....**6d.**
Centre Boxes.....**2s.**   Second Price.....**1s.** | Second Price.....**3d.**
Second Price commences will same time at which no subject at the termination of an Act will allow.

REFRESHMENTS OF FIRST QUALITY will be provided at the most Reasonable Charges.
RETIRING ROOMS and other accommodations will be found attached to the various parts of the Theatre.

☞ On THURSDAY will be Performed Shakspeare's beautiful Play, THE MERCHANT OF VENICE.
SHYLOCK - - - - MR. F. READ.

Performances to commence at 7 o'clock precisely, and to terminate as nearly as possible at a quarter before 11.

STAGE MANAGER - - **MR. ALFRED DAVIS**

PART TWO

BRODRIBB INTO IRVING

———

'Learning how to do a thing is the doing of it.'

HENRY IRVING.

'. . . In this uncertain world there is nothing more uncertain than the career of an actor. The scene of his life may shift from poverty to comfort almost as quickly as in the stage grooves the cottage gives place to the palace. He has few ties of neighbours or neighbourhood, for

Arab-like his tent is pitched,
And straight again is furled.

Rarely can he reckon upon an engagement of sufficient duration to give him, should sickness or sorrow come upon him, the solace of sympathising friends. An accident may give him the favour of the public, which another accident may snatch as quickly away; and public favour is his daily bread. There are those, too, to whom recognition— if it ever comes—comes so late that, as Ruskin so truly says, the laurel crown so tardily bestowed can only avail to be laid upon their mother's grave. But granted that the actor be one of Fortune's seeming favourites, is it unnatural that even a strong mind might be turned by such a test, or that the prudent economies of private life might be somewhat forgotten in the glamour of the stage? How can the benevolent stage uncle, whose plethoric purse makes life so easy—how can he refuse his last half-crown to an old brother-actor out of an engagement?— for actors are a singularly benevolent race. Or how can a Bassanio who one night has been tossing about 6,000 ducats on Shylock, be expected on the following morning to get to a rehearsal by the third class of an underground railway? He certainly has a great temptation to travel First, and I remember a famous comedian once saying to me—"Sir, when I play Charles Surface, I dine off the liver wing of a chicken, moistened by a bumper of sparkling burgundy." Artistic instincts are frightfully opposed to business habits. I am not speaking of the fortunate London actor in his snug rooms here, his comfortable cottage there, and a handy little sum at his bankers; I am speaking of the poor country actor who, on 25*s*. or 30*s*. a week—when he can get it —to fulfil an engagement has to journey from Aberdeen to Plymouth, who has to play lords, dukes, and electors, and Counts Palatine and dress them all himself; . . . he wants a wig for this, boots, shoes, buckles for that—in short everything that has been worn since clothes were invented—and all this on 25*s*. a week. He must try and look the character he acts, and the more artistic a man's mind is, or the more fastidious his taste, the more he is tempted to be what the thoughtless call extravagant.'

HENRY IRVING.
From a speech at the Royal General
Theatrical Fund dinner.
1st July 1875

CHAPTER IV

The Walking Gentleman : Sunderland

A youth of eighteen, who during the long journey northwards must have visualized the stirring moment of his first arrival at the theatre as a professional actor, might well have regarded the actual event as something of an anticlimax. The New Royal Lyceum Theatre, Sunderland, was indeed so new that it was shrouded in scaffolding and in the possession not of actors but of bricklayers. During the previous year it had been burnt to the ground, a not uncommon disaster in those times. There was so little chance of its completion by September 18th that the opening had been postponed for ten days. Henry Irving's buoyant enthusiasm survived the disappointment. He was soon fully occupied in the business of finding lodgings and meeting Mr. Davis and the other members of the stock company.

The provincial theatre was in a healthier state than that of London. The Lord Chamberlain had never exercised his peculiar authority over provincial playhouses, apart from the theatres royal at Brighton and Windsor. Consequently the spoken drama had flourished more freely outside London, and this freedom to exercise their art had encouraged the great actors to tour the provinces regularly, some of them in fact earning their livelihood and reputation without appearing in London at all. The transport by road or on the primitive railways of supporting companies, stocks of scenery and properties was, however, out of the question. This difficulty was overcome by the creation of a resident stock company in every provincial town which boasted a sizeable theatre. The quality of these stock companies varied, but on the whole they were composed of actors and actresses of great experience and versatility. The princely stars would move alone from town to town and at each theatre would expect to find a supporting company familiar with their repertoire and capable of following their individual actions with the minimum of rehearsals. Sometimes rehearsals were dispensed with altogether; on one such occasion it caused Edmund Kean to warn an actor who, although he had never seen Kean play Sir Giles Over-reach in *A New Way to Pay Old Debts*, considered he need not rehearse with him: 'You had better, Sir, for I shall terrify you!' This system imposed upon the stock company the need of a wide repertoire and gave young actors and actresses a matchless opportunity for the study of characters, plays and the technique of the procession of stars who crossed their stage. The stock company at the Lyceum, Sunder-land, was a good one, and this season was to include visits from such famous players as Miss Charlotte Cushman and Ira Aldridge, the coloured tragedian.

Irving, having found the local hotel beyond his purse, for he was to be paid no salary until he had proved himself useful, carried his books and properties to a cheaper lodging a mile or two beyond the town. This involved a daily walk along the stretch of sands which a few years later were to inspire Lewis Carroll to write 'The Walrus and the Carpenter'. During the first week the company met to rehearse in various rooms and taverns. Among them he found two old veterans, Sam Johnson and Tom Mead, and the leading lady, Miss Glyn, late of the Sadler's Wells Theatre and now on the verge of honourable retirement. Davis himself was an actor and proposed to open the season with Bulwer Lytton's *Richelieu* in which he cast himself to play the Cardinal. The play was in blank verse and was well regarded as a vehicle for a heavy tragedian. The newcomer was lucky enough to be given the part of Gaston, Duke of Orleans, a poor character in himself yet attractive to an actor in that he is upon the stage at the rise and fall of the curtain. By the end of the week the theatre was more or less ready, and in the course of rehearsals Irving learnt to locate the three trap doors used for graves and demons, to avoid the winches which lowered and raised the sky borders, and to beware of the heavy rollered curtain which, if it struck an actor as it descended, would ren-der him insensible and his understudy overjoyed. From the actors who shared his dressing-room he learnt how to make up his face to suit the naked glare of gas footlights. On the evening of September 29th he dressed himself with scrupulous care and in accordance with the period of the play as well as his resources allowed, his stock costume embel-lished with the fineries of his own wardrobe, which included a nobly feathered white hat. His appearance, when the actors assembled on the stage before the rise of the curtain, was noted with admiration and not a little envy. Through the grease-encircled hole in the drop curtain, Mr. Davis, in his Cardinal's robes, assessed the money in the house;

the stage was cleared, the signal was given, and for the first time in the new theatre the drop curtain was rolled up.

The Duke of Orleans, apparently at ease, was reclining upon a fauteuil; his hostess, Marion de Lorme, was at his side, while in the shadows inferior courtiers discreetly revelled. The curtain had hardly reached its zenith when the Duke, raising a goblet, cried—a little haltingly:

'Here's to our enterprise!'

'Hush, Sir!' warned a nearby courtier—needlessly, for the Duke's long speech, which should have followed, had been cut during the rehearsal. In the play the Duke's enterprise comes to nought; he is dismissed contemptuously by Richelieu as the curtain falls upon the last act. If Mr. Davis, as he stood in the wings, noted a strange fervour in the uncertain delivery of those words, it was because 'Our enterprise' was the farewell toast of John Brodribb to Henry Irving.

Richelieu was followed that evening by an oriental pantomime, *The Enchanted Lake*, which had been written for Mr. Davis by a young barrister from Newcastle who had sufficient means to indulge an amateur talent for writing and painting.[1] Irving was one of five cooks and was glad enough of the obscurity which the part afforded him. For he knew that his first attempt had fallen far short of his intention and that the audience were well aware of his shortcomings.

The following evening, as a French officer in *The Lady of Lyons*, he managed to get through his half-dozen lines without difficulty. But a night or two later, when he came upon the stage as Cleomenes in *The Winter's Tale* to describe Leontes' discovery of his daughter, no words came from his lips. His fellow-actors waited in awkward dismay. The prompter groaned his cue in tones that were heard all over the house. Irving was paralysed with horror. Then, with a tremendous effort of will, he managed to blurt out:

'Come to the market-place and I will tell you further!' and, leaving the astonished actors, who knew of no such market-place, to pick up the threads of the play as best they could, he rushed to his dressing-room, angry and ashamed, with the hisses of the audience buzzing in his burning ears. No doubt he deserved the brief hail and farewell of the Sunderland press, who urged him to return to his comfortable home and to abandon any thought of the stage. It is doubtful if the disaster was an attack of stage fright; it was certainly not due to careless preparation; it was more likely that the half-conquered impediment had,

[1] Henry Irving and John Forster Baird, the young barrister, would have been surprised, as they jostled one another during rehearsals, to know that they were to be the joint grandfathers of the author of this book.

in a moment of stress, broken from its secret prison. If that indeed was the cause of his failure, he would not plead it as an excuse. Yet Mr. Davis may have divined his secret. For instead of dismissing the wretched young actor, he stood by him and, together with Sam Johnson and Tom Mead, gave him such firm and practical advice that by degrees his badly shaken confidence was restored. For they were agreed that, with all his shortcomings, the young man had an earnestness of purpose which deserved encouragement. They were, no doubt, surprised when this strange youth, in gratitude for their kindness, said: 'If ever I rise I shall not forget this!' The two old actors, gnarled as they were by lives spent in the ruthless and ungrateful world of the theatre, were even more surprised when, twenty years later, he honoured his promise.

A month later Irving wrote to his friend, Charlie Ford, a letter which though it made no mention of his unpromising start, showed that his faith was still unshaken:

> 14 *Vine Place*,
> *Burrough Road*,
> *Sunderland.*
> *November 24th*, 1856.

'My dear Charlie,

Your patience must be almost exhausted at receiving no reply to your interesting letters—here it is at last.

Little did we think six months ago we should be so distant as we now are from one another or in such opposite occupations. In our happy gossip (to the annoyance of a certain Blackwell gent!) mysterious hints were thrown out of our intention to quit at some time the commercial life, but had not stamps been off and tempers on, it is probable we should have been together still; however, the fates willed otherwise and even circumstances aided to make me what I long had wished to be—an actor.

Well how do you like it? Very much. What do you have to do? Work from 10 in the morning until 1, 2 or 3 the next. But isn't that very tiring? Yes; but at the theatre you are surrounded by cheerful and happy faces who always greet you with a smile and merry word and at home your mind is continually occupied by new study and language. There is no restraint on a laugh or joke, no governor to stop your mouth, no petty subjection to one another, because they are equal—they work for a prize free to all. Macready, Phelps, Kean, were novices once and gained their position by degrees, however aided by genius or talent.

A young aspirant, therefore, has, or ought to have, a special independence of feeling for no-one knows what he may become. Speaking of them as a body, actors are intellectual, rollicking, good-natured, independent, very polite, knowing, eccentric, *short*-haired, *today-care*, class of beings, with one great fault—jealousy. You meet with a few poor blighted looking creatures who, sadly unfit for the stage, have abandoned some good business for it and find their error too late—in fact the majority of them have mistaken their calling.

The leading ladies are superior to the average standard of their sex—the minor ones inferior. The theatre is a nice comfortable place with every comfort; to dress, the ladies occupy one side of the building and the gents the other. The Green Room is next to the stage and where they sit and gossip by a roaring fire during their wait at the rehearsal or performance. All notices are as dear as in London. There is an institution called the Athenaeum, and the best part of it, I think, is the building—very handsome. I saw a board outside a hall of an Elocutionary entertainment to be given by several young gent'n of the town, "Waterloo", "Brutus and Cassius" were among the selections. I thought of old times. How does your beautiful class get on?

I do everything in the bachelor style and enjoy myself alone. There are 2 friends with whom I associate; we sometimes walk together and occasionally meet on Sunday evening after church, to have a quiet cup of coffee. They are intellectual *gentlemen*.

You ask me whether I think Miss Glyn pretty. No; though she might be if it were not for her mouth, but there is a merry lurking smile and intelligent beam of the eye which at once fixes the attention and creates an interest which prettiness never could. I don't know of anything so annoying as a pretty face to look at without expression. It is like a wax strawberry.

> *Tis not a set of features or complexion,*
> *The tincture of the skin that I admire,*
> *Beauty soon grows familiar to the lover,*
> *Fades in his eye and palls upon the sense . . .*

. . . Thank you for the specimen of Routledge's Shakespeare. Some of the illustrations are the most life-like I have seen and valuable for costumes. I think I shall "take it in". My literary expenditure is 4d per week, the *Era* newspaper and the *National Magazine*, a superior periodical; you have seen, I suppose, the capital portrait of Dickens in it. . . .'

Even to his closest friend Henry Irving made no confession of his failures and disappointments, nor did it seem to have occurred to him that he himself might be one of those poor creatures who had mistaken their calling. Though as yet unpaid, and with his resources rapidly dwindling, he decided to stay with Davis until the end of the season. He had no cause to complain of the variety of the parts he undertook. In addition to the steady flow of guest tragedians, Mr. Sims Reeves provided a week of light opera, during which the walking gentleman had to sing and Miss Cushman, who had made theatrical history by acting Romeo to her sister's Juliet, played several of Shakespeare's heroines. It was while rehearsing with this remarkable actress that Irving first learnt the effect that should be got by letting the working of the actor's mind be seen before his tongue gives voice to it. Once, when playing with her in *Guy Mannering*, he had, as Bertram, to give her, as Meg Merrilees, a piece of money; this he did, in the traditional way, by handing her a purse filled with broken crockery, which could be relied upon to give the clink of gold when flung upon the stage in anger or disgust. After the performance Miss Cushman, in the course of other kindly advice, said: 'Instead of giving me that purse, don't you think it would be much more natural if you had taken a number of coins from your pocket and had given me the smallest? This is the way one gives alms to a beggar and it would have added greatly to the realism of the scene.' As the play was only put on for one night he was unable to put her advice into practice—but it was a lesson which he never forgot.

So by singing in opera, dancing in burlesque, and generally making himself useful, he won the regard of his fellow-actors and a salary of twenty-five shillings a week from his manager by the time the season ended with Sam Johnson's benefit and the Christmas pantomime. Though Davis would have liked him to remain in Sunderland, an offer of an engagement at the Theatre Royal, Edinburgh, through the good offices of Tom Mead, who had gone there in November, gave him a welcome chance to leave a town where, though his fellow-actors had shown him nothing but kindness, he had suffered humiliation and despair. He needed a fresh start. What Swinburne later described as his 'plume of pride' could be worn more bravely in new surroundings.

CHAPTER V

The Juvenile Lead : Edinburgh

———◦❉◦———

The Theatre Royal, Edinburgh, had, since 1853, been the headquarters of R. H. Wyndham, a skilful actor and a manager of unusual enterprise and vision. A few years before he had married Rose Saker, the daughter of a low comedian. Being a talented actress with a gift for training children in ballet, she became the perfect partner of his long and successful career. At the end of his life, like a battle-scarred general, he could claim to have had three Edinburgh theatres burnt under him, the Adelphi, the Queen's and finally the Royal. During the previous year he had out-shone Charles Kean with the splendour of his productions of *Henry VIII* and *A Midsummer Night's Dream*.

Irving arrived in Edinburgh towards the end of January 1857. He found a lodging in a tenement in St. James's Square, where he occupied the room in which, a century before, Burns had sat distractedly weighing the claims on his affection of Clarinda M'Lehose and Jean Armour. From the gabled window he could glimpse Princes Street; when, in the misty dusk, day turned almost imperceptibly into night, he watched the squalor and misery of the old town take on a deceptive beauty as the points of yellow light rose high above him until they mingled with the stars. At the theatre he found the stock company rehearsing *Richelieu* in preparation for the appearance of the great Irish tragedian, Barry Sullivan, in the name part. Once more he was allotted the part of the Duke of Orleans; if his enterprise had had something of a false start, perhaps a second and more confident toast to it would be more efficacious. In Barry Sullivan he was able to study an actor of tremendous force whose athletic and graceful physique was matched by his resounding voice, the exercise of which held provincial audiences spellbound; an actor since childhood, without pretensions to culture or a blemish on his private reputation, his face scarred with the constant use of dry, mordant paints, he was the prince of barn-stormers. Having discovered that his method was rather too crude

77

for London audiences, he abandoned the capital and spent his life triumphantly touring the provinces, his salary having by this time mounted to eighty pounds a week. For the first time the young actor was to see a tragedian hold his audience in thrall not so much by art as by the exertion of his forceful personality. Phelps had not used this power—indeed, he did not possess it. In the field of bravura acting Sullivan had no equal in his generation. Irving managed to get through his part on the first night without incurring the disapproval or wrath of this demi-god. For a week he hovered on the fringe of Barry Sullivan's thunder, sedulously studying the gusts and lulls of his tempestuous method. When, as the aged Richelieu, trying to swing his great two-handed sword, Sullivan cried:

> 'With this
>
> *I at Rochelle did hand to hand engage*
> *The stalwart Englisher,—no mongrels, boy,*
> *Those Island mastiffs,—mark the notch—a deep one—*
> *His casque made here,—I shore him to the waist!*
> *A toy—a feather—then!'*

and failing to wield it, let the weapon fall, he seemed indeed an enfeebled Hercules; when for her protection he made the sign of 'the awful circle of our solemn Church' round the head of the heroine, his voice was a miracle of tenderness, swelling suddenly into a threatening roar as he launched 'the curse of R-r-rome!' on her molester.

A day or two later, Irving managed to find time to write to Charlie Ford:

> 30 *St. James's Square,*
> *Edinburgh.*
> *February* 11*th*, 1857.

'My dear Ford,

By the same post I have sent you all the bits I possess defending the stage, (which please preserve) and I can only add go and see—judge for yourself; if then you condemn it, I'll listen to you, but not before— doing so without is passing sentence without proof, witness or trial— anti-English jurisprudence.

My small *experience* tells me earnestly that it is an innocent, intellectual and moral recreation. I will answer your letter soon but don't wait for it before writing again.

With affectionate regards to your mother and self, I am, as ever, very sincerely yours,

Henry.'

This letter was the first shot, a mere affair of outposts, in a skirmish before the battle which he was to fight unceasingly for the next fifty years—a campaign to rout the Philistines and Pharisees who prowled around the theatre.

Thus began an engagement which lasted for two and a half years, first at the Theatre Royal and then, when it was pulled down to make room for the General Post Office, at the rebuilt Queen's Theatre. He found Edinburgh altogether more congenial than Sunderland and hastened to make his report to Mrs. Wilkins:

Edinburgh,
February 23rd, 1857.

'My dear Mrs. Wilkins,

I have as usual mislaid your letter but I think I remember pretty well the contents. I know you took a reasonable and unprejudiced view of my acting desires and gave me your opinion of the dramatic life which (you will be surprised to hear) I had joined before the receipt of your letter.

My theatrical career commenced under the name of Henry Irving on the 29th of September '56 at the opening of the Lyceum Theatre, Sunderland, in Durham, where I remained until the close of the season (a short one) which ended on the 2nd inst. I was considered unusually successful for a first engagement, playing responsible (of course not leading) parts throughout the season. Miss Glyn was with us a fortnight; I thought of the days when I first heard her and how changed our circumstances since then. Through the kind introduction and recommendation of our principal actor I obtained an engagement for "first walking gentleman" (a term given to the line of characters played) at the Theatre Royal, Edinburgh, and opened on the 9th inst. . . .

. . . Sunderland was a very large ship-building, coaly town on the coast, but what can I say of Edinboro'!

It is indeed a city of poetry; I can hardly conceive a more beautiful unity of art and nature, town and country.

Standing on the summit of the castle situate on a hill you see a giant city, consisting of cottages surrounded by trees—buildings of most magnificent design and structure; old dilapidated streets erected centuries ago—new ones vying with Regent Street; village-looking churches—small cathedrals; splendid statues, and one of Scott surpassing, I believe, any other erected; and the whole is surrounded by mountains and valleys seen for miles. The city is full of historical reminiscences of the most interesting kind—the palace of Holyrood, famous for the residence of the unfortunate Mary Stuart and the murder of Rizzio, and very near it is "Jeanie Dean's" cottage—a pretty little house enclosed by trees. I daresay you remember reading of her in *The Heart of Midlothian*—farther on is John Knox's house and many other places of great interest. . . .

. . . I am thankful to say my health is excellent—I take the best exercise and beverage—walking and water.

You kindly invited me to give a reading at your Institution. I considered it a flattering compliment and should have most willingly done so had not my change in life prevented me. Perhaps I may have that pleasure on some future day.

I hope your friends and family are moving healthily along the "bank and shoal of time".

It is needless to tell you I hear continually from my dear father and mother, who are very anxious for my welfare. The devotion of parents and kindness of true friends we never know until separated. I hope you will not allow so long a time to elapse before writing as I have.

My mother and father would unite their very kind regards with, my dear Mrs. Wilkins—

Yours very sincerely,

J. H. Brodribb.

P.S.—When you reply, please direct to—

Mr. H. Irving,

Mrs. Robart's,

17 Elder Street,

Edinboro,

and excuse this disjointed scrawl.'

If his description of those grey weeks in Sunderland was slightly overcoloured, his note of confidence was justified; for he had made so good an impression on the Wyndhams that they had promoted him from walking gentleman to juvenile lead and advanced his salary to thirty shillings a week. Though the salary was small, he found life pleasant enough in the little time he had to spare from almost constant rehearsal and study. The Edinburgh stock company had been so long established that many of its members had been resident with their families in the town for some time. The Wyndhams kept a jealous eye on the credit and reputation of their company so that the actors of Edinburgh were highly respected citizens; so, in making a round of visits to the homes of his friends, the juvenile lead was able to meet all manner of interesting and distinguished people. Irving had cause to be aware of the paternal eye of his manager, for though very soon he left his lodgings in St. James's Square for cheaper accommodation in a temperance hotel, he was apt to be careless of money spent in entertaining his friends or in buying books, an excusable weakness which before long caused the Wyndhams to reprove him for running into debt. His employers became, however, increasingly fond of him and their estimate of his value to them was enhanced when in May, Irving received a letter from Davis inviting him to the Theatre Royal, Newcastle, for the coming season.

Irving very wisely stayed where he was. Among the first of many great personalities to play at the Theatre Royal was Helena Faucit. Coming of a theatrical family, she had won a unique position on the English stage both for her excellence as an actress and for her exemplary character. She had recently married Theodore Martin, an essayist with a turn for poetic drama, and was nearing the end of a career which had been one of continuing success since 1837 when she had joined Macready as his leading lady. In the course of her repertoire, Irving found himself playing Pisanio to her Imogen in *Cymbeline*. This was a longer part than he had yet attempted, and included two or three scenes in which he alone would share the stage with the great actress. Nervous he may have been, yet he had marked a passage which he felt he could turn to good account. At the point where Imogen kneels before Pisanio, her husband's servant, and drawing his sword and thrusting it into his hand, cries:

> '. . . *do his bidding—strike!*
> *Thou mayest be valiant in a better cause,*
> *But now thou seems't a coward . . .*'

Irving put all the strength and passion at his command into the words:

> '*Hence vile instrument*
> *Thou shalt not damn my hand,*'

and flung the sword from him into the wings. He trembled, as for the first time he heard the applause which his own original piece of business and its forcible execution had won from a crowded house. Nor were many of the audience less astonished by this flash of inspired acting by a pale and rather awkward young actor, who until that moment had given an adequate but in no way striking performance. Instead of being intimidated by having to support so great an artist as Miss Faucit with so limited a stock of stagecraft, he had found that he could draw strength and confidence from her genius. At one stroke he had caught the fleeting attention of the critics. Their opinion, on the rare occasions when they noticed him at all, would not always be favourable, but when inevitably sections of the audience countered his modest popularity with hisses or derisive applause, they were ready enough to write in his defence.

Shakespeare, however, was a rare delicacy among the coarser fare with which the Wyndhams had to tickle the palates of the Edinburgh public. During May, in support of Charles Verner, a tragedian of lesser calibre than Sullivan, he played for the first time in *Hamlet* as Horatio and later as Catesby to Verner's Richard III. For the rest of the year he had to make the best he could of the robust rubbish in the triple bills which were changed nightly. At times the pressure of study and rehearsal were almost overwhelming. None the less, he was gaining experience in full measure. The winter season ended on June 1st; this somewhat subtle theatrical solstice was marked by a break of five days which were fully occupied in preparing for the summer season which opened on June 6th and, defying the calendar, lingered on until November. Midsummer was enlivened by the arrival of a young comedian, J. L. Toole, from the Lyceum Theatre, London.

John Lawrence Toole was the son of a renowned City toast master whose stentorian voice had won him fame by praying for silence at the Lord Mayor's elbow by night and as an usher, calling for order by day, in the less convivial surroundings of the Old Bailey. Blazing the trail which Irving followed eight years later, Toole sought recreation from a City wine merchant's office in a school of elocution, appeared as an amateur actor at Sussex Hall, and then, encouraged by Charles Dickens, abandoned commerce for the stage. By 1857 he had become a popular attraction in the theatres of London, Dublin and Edinburgh. Emboldened by this early success, he organized a small company with which he, as star comedian, toured the provinces. This season in Edinburgh was his first engagement of the kind, and the profits from it became the nucleus of his steadily increasing fortune. His leading lady was Louise Keeley, the daughter of two famous comedians Robert and Mary; from infancy she had been rocked in the cradle of burlesque and she was now an accomplished foil to Toole's broad, yet singularly innocent, farcical style. As the principal parts were played by members of the visiting company, Irving reverted to mere walking gentleman and from a respectful distance studied Toole as he grunted and shuffled his way through *Paul Pry* and *London Assurance*. Toole's comic extravagance was a wholesome corrective to the earnest gravity with which up till now the young actor had regarded his vocation. Toole was hardly aware of the diffident and gangling young man who did what he was asked well enough and gave little trouble at rehearsals.

September was a breathless month. On the 7th Irving played a farmer in a farce *'Twas I*, and the Governor in *The Governor's Wife*, while Toole romped boisterously through both plays as a country boy and the Governor's factotum. On the 9th he played Monks in *Oliver Twist*, which was enlivened by Toole, as the Artful Dodger, singing a song, 'The Dodger's Lament', a swan song before he left, with Miss Keeley, to continue his touring vacation. The following night the programme reverted to the popular mixture of national drama, patriotic melodrama and farce. On the 16th Irving had to play Lord Lyndsay in *Mary Queen of Scots*, and Birkie in another national drama, *Cramond Brig*. The following night saw him playing M'Kay in *The Battle of the Inch*, and as Hector Frampton in a farce, *Brother Sandy McDonald*; on the playbills all such farces were hopefully announced as 'laughable', as though implying that it was the actor's fault if they were not. On the 18th he appeared again as M'Kay and as Kenmure in another Highland melodrama, *The Falls of Clyde*. On the 21st he was able for a time to drop his hastily acquired Scottish brogue, when, in the course of a triple bill, he played a Frenchman in *The Lady of Lyons*, and an Italian in *The Hunter of the Alps*—a cosmopolitan sandwich of drama layered with a farce, *The Ladies' Club*, in which he played a Mr. Bookly. Two new farces and a drama, *Therese, the Orphan of Geneva*, were billed for the 22nd, in each of which he had a speaking part. The month's work ended on the 26th when he appeared in an 'interesting' drama, *The Last Man*, as Alfred Fitzfrolic in *The Dancing Barber*, and as Monsieur de Rosembert, Seigneur of the village, in the 'favourite' drama, *The Somnambulist or The White Phantom of the Village*. Thus in thirty days, he had to learn and rehearse seventeen new parts, each of which required a carefully considered make-up and costume and, since he would rather go short of food than of the materials he needed for dressing these parts, constituted a severe drain on his meagre resources.

This exacting programme was by no means exceptional and was the normal routine of a provincial playhouse. There were nights, such as October 16th, for which he had to prepare four parts as diverse as Charles in *Robert Macaire*, a gentleman of title in a farce, *The Irish Tiger*, a Captain of Infantry in a military drama, and the mate of a privateer in a Navy Spectacle, *The Lost Ship or The Man of War's*

Man. By Christmas he was ready for anything; which was as well, for on the last night of the year he appeared as a Colonel of Highlanders, as Sergeant Musqueton in *Gilderoy*, as a farcical private citizen in *Quake, Shake and Simon*, while conserving his energy to curdle the blood of ecstatic children as Scruncher, Captain of the Wolves, in the pantomime, *Little Bo-Peep*. It may have seemed that such plays were unworthy of the attention of an intellectual gentleman—indeed they were so lightly thought of that on the playbills nobody laid claim to their authorship; such a spate of epics, narrating the turgid legends of Scottish military and tribal history, must have kept a team of industrious but anonymous dramatists constantly employed in churning out this highly flavoured fare to satisfy the appetite of patriotic Caledonians. Yet in this simple stuff Henry Irving found all he needed in which to learn the rudiments of his art, to discover the secret that a competent actor can wring laughter and tears from an audience with the crudest of material, and that Scruncher and Horatio equally can possess the God-like power of creating out of a thousand scattered particles a single coherent consciousness which can be played upon like a delicate instrument.

During November Wyndham, threatened by expulsion from the Theatre Royal by the Government, who had now acquired the whole of Shakespeare Square as a site for their palatial post office, had taken the Queen's Theatre, which recently had risen from the ashes of the Old Adelphi. The site had vivid associations for him. As lessee in 1853 he had seen his wife, who had just been confined in an upper part of the theatre, carried with their new-born son to safety as the flames enveloped the stage and auditorium below. Until he had to give up the Royal, Wyndham kept both theatres open, his stock company reinforcing one or the other as necessary. This arrangement gave Irving the chance, as the Earl of Surrey in *Henry VIII*, to support Vandenhoff when, as Wolsey, he gave his farewell performance in Edinburgh. The old actor was then sixty-seven years of age. Irving was able to mark the technique of one who had been taught his business by Edmund Kean during the first decade of the century and who, since then, had not forsaken the style and delivery he had been taught in his youth.

The past year had been one of initiation; this year was to be one of continuing drudgery, rewarding only to one whose course lay clear before him and to whom thirty shillings a week was not so much a fee for services rendered as an interim dividend on the investment of his heart and soul in the calling of his choice. All was for the best in the best of all possible worlds. Snugly ensconced in Abraham's bosom, he sends down to Charlie Ford in his Newgate Street purgatory a comforting word and a few practical hints on escape. He can now afford to look back on Thacker's with wistful tolerance, though he is under no illusion as to his mother's enduring disapproval of his new life:

> 17 *Union Place,*
> *Edinburgh*
> *March 8th,* 1858.

'My dear Ford,
    I am sure you can say

> *Patience,*
> *Of whose soft grace I have her sovereign aid*
> *And rest myself content!—*

or you would not have given me the last interesting letter which I hardly deserve. I thought I was again in 87 gossiping with old chums after a frantic mail day. Remember me to the machines one and all.

I'm sorry you've no prospect at present of anything else. Interest is the stumbling block. You should watch "The Times" as perhaps you do daily; good things are sometimes to be seen. I once answered an advertisement for the "Albion" Insce office and got an answer saying that they had engaged but would keep my note for a future vacancy; I think I lost it by writing a word in the letter twice which I struck out. I was too lazy to re-write it. By the by I found a difficulty in composing a nice letter and got Jemmy who understood those things to do it for me,—my father has copies of two letters I wrote and would give them to you if you think they might be useful. What long talks we used to have about our prospects—oh you won't die at Thackers! I hope we shall spend many more hours and days together. I am very glad that I was at Newgate Street; for I find the great benefit of the commercial insight it gave me,—and had I not been there we should never have met. I am sure you and your mother have been a great solace to mine, and I feel for your sincere friendship a warm affection to you both.

I dare say after the struggle for your next holiday you'll rush to your relations—if you would like a decided change—I should be delighted to see you—a la bachelor—here or elsewhere—wherever I may be. You would be charmed with this spot. I don't think there's another one like it even in Warwickshire. Nothing I can say about myself will be news to you. I like acting more and more. Give my love to your mother.

> With best wishes for your health, happiness and prosperity, I am,
>
> > Yours affectionately,
> >
> > > Henry.'

Toole returned for the summer season, but once again he seems to have taken little heed of the stock walking gentleman. The Edinburgh press, however, had begun to accord Irving a little notice. For the most part the few lines the critics granted him were tributes to his perseverance and to the studied finish of his make-up; his acting was rarely commended; only when he qualified as bad news, which was always news, did the critics defend him in the face of the marked disapproval of the audience. The Edinburgh correspondent of the *Era*, the London Theatrical journal and actor's *vade mecum*, reported: 'Mr. Irving has undoubtedly achieved a success, animated by a sincere devotion to his art as his care and earnestness testify; no doubt he will steadily and successfully fulfil a higher range of parts than he has hitherto done'; and in July he adds: 'In *Marriage, A Lottery* Mr. Irving, as Herbert Manifest, was as usual natural and gentlemanly, tactful in his dress and perfect in his part.' When the pantomime came round once more, he tackled with relish the part of Venoma, the Spiteful Fairy in '*The Sleeping Beauty*', in which he was discovered upon a gridiron lit from below with red lights. His make-up was described by a critic apparently well versed in diabolism, as 'astonishingly correct even to the minutest detail', while even the august *Scotsman* declared him to be 'the model of a spiteful and disagreeable fairy.'

Wyndham often was impressed by the originality and attention to detail which the young actor showed in portraying weird and grotesque characters. As the villain in a burlesque, *The Maid and the Magpie*, he attracted the manager's notice by the use which he made of his hands. In order to give the illusion of having fingers of preternatural length, he had painted dark streaks on the backs of his hands which gave them the appearance of huge bird-like claws; the effect was enhanced when he clutched at things with the tips of his fingers which were constantly curved; at rest, his hands were never closed, but spread out against the black of his voluminous cloak.

The New Year found him well established in the affections of his companions and in the favour of the public, who, though still critical, were impressed by the variety of his carefully studied performances which now ranged from low comedy to heavy lead. When Charles

Dillon, an actor whose playing was described by Dickens as '. . . exactly what acting should be—nature itself', came to the Theatre Royal for a short season, Irving played Claudius to his Hamlet, which had won praise for its originality of conception when seen for the first time in London during the previous year. A week or two later Irving was playing Fag in *The Rivals*.

By now the attention of the whole company, stimulated by the enthusiastic exertions of Mr. and Mrs. Wyndham, was centred upon the gala performance which, on the night of May 25th, was to celebrate the closing of the old theatre. A committee of local gentlemen, friends of the drama, were, with a patriotic fervour peculiar to Scotsmen, making certain that the evening should be of such a character as to recall the glories of the Scottish stage and in particular of the doomed building. Mr. Chambers, the encyclopaedist, was busily at work on a pamphlet which set out the history of the theatre and was to be freely distributed to the audience. Mr. Wyndham, with the help of his panel of local dramatists, had composed a farewell address in rhymed couplets and had planned a copious programme which left no doubt that the last night of the old playhouse would certainly be its longest.

In addition to appearing as Macduff and in the name part in *The Pilot* on the evening preceding these junketings, Irving and two of his friends were deputed by the rest of the company to invest the modest proceeds of a collection to which they had all subscribed in a presentation gift to their much beloved manager and his wife. Thus much time, which could be ill spared from study and rehearsal, was spent in exploring the silversmiths of Prince's Street. At the end of a long and discouraging search they were faced with a choice between a minute cruet stand of pure silver or a tankard of heroic proportions but of electro-plate. Only when the jeweller decided to include in the price the engraving of an appropriate inscription did the committee plump for the tankard, taking an oath as they did so never to reveal its humble elements.

On the long-awaited and ever memorable evening the house was crowded in every part, the boxes bulging with dignitaries and notables of the city. The babble of excited conversation and the rustle of paper as the audience skimmed through Mr. Chambers's pamphlet indicated their excitement and surprise that at last an Edinburgh theatre was to die a natural death. Indeed it was not yet too late and many hearts may have thrilled at the possibility of the traditional conflagration at the eleventh hour. At last the curtain rose on *Masks and Faces*, with Mr. Wyndham as Sir Charles Pomander and Mrs. Wyndham as Peg Woffington. Mr. Irving played Soaper; his delight in the business of lathering Triplet was no less than his pride in being given such a part when even the great Mr. Vandenhoff was content to play Hunsdos. At the close of the comedy Mr. Wyndham came before the curtain and recited his ode. Irving, as he listened to his manager's rich declamation, must have wished that his mother could have heard the words of this kind good man:

> *Still as I strove your kindness to secure*
> *My aim has been to keep your pleasures pure.*
> *And let me hope, in all that I have done,*
> *The Stage has found me no degenerate son.*

The noble sentiments chased through his mind as he prepared himself for the character of Charles in a farce, *His Last Legs*, which on this night of all nights must surely prove laughable. The regular patrons were stirred once more by *Cramond Brig*, their loyal blood tingling in reponse to Mr. Melville's King James, their tears freely flowing while Miss Davies interpolated a little song, 'A Kiss Ahint the Door'. Neither Wyndham nor his juvenile lead appeared in the National Drama which followed, for they were busily preparing the 'Moving Valedictory Sketch', an apotheosis of the Theatre Royal, which included a series of tableaux ranging from Brideswell to Fontainebleau and ending with a pantomimic ensemble. In response to the thunders of applause, the company took call after call. The order of their appearance before the curtain was not without significance. First came Mr. Melville, the leading gentleman, graciously handing forward Miss Sophie Miles, the leading lady; then followed Mr. Lyons, arm-in-arm with young Irving—a generous recognition by an established favourite of the rising popularity and bright prosperity of his junior colleague. The audience responded heartily to this happy gesture and noted with interest and approval Mr. Irving's gentlemanly evening dress with its fashionable note of a cord of gold braid bordering his black waistcoat. When fully assembled, the entire strength of the company—such as it was after so frantic an evening—was devoted to rendering the National Anthem. The citizens of Edinburgh then presented the Wyndhams with a handsome silver tea service, closely followed by the delegates of the company who, nursing their guilty secret, offered up the electro-plated tankard. It was with intense relief that later they heard Mr. Wyndham declare that he preferred the tankard—after all, knowing Mr. Wyndham, they felt sure that if constant use engendered remembrance, they would be more often in his mind than the donors of the tea service.

The first season at the Queen's did not open until June. In order to fill in the time the company made a short tour of the largest Scottish towns, with *Cramond Brig* as their chief attraction. One night in a strange theatre, while having a quick run through the play which included a supper scene, the generous manager provided the company with a genuine meal in place of the usual cardboard properties. The cast included a little girl who had been recruited locally to play the 'neighbour's bairn', an important part in this moving scene. At the end of the meal, when the whisky was being passed round, the pretty, sad-eyed child, to the surprise of the company, asked solemnly if she could have a little of it. While they were all laughing, Irving whispered to her: 'Tomorrow if you want it very much I'll give you a thimbleful.' When they came to play this scene the following evening, the child held out a thimble and reminded him of his half-forgotten promise. He dexterously filled the thimble with whisky, without disturbing the rhythm of the scene, and out of the corner of his eye watched the child turn away from the audience and pour the whisky from her thimble into a little snuff-box, which she sealed with a screw top and hid in the pocket of her dress. This business drew a laugh from those of the audience who had seen it; the manager, delighted with this successful gag, urged its repetition.

'You must do it every night,' he said to the child, qualifying: 'But, my dear, you mustn't drink the whisky—that would never do.'

'Oh, sir, indeed I give you my word I won't,' replied the child, as she ran off the stage.

The piece was played for six nights and each night Irving and the child repeated their pantomime. Curious, he at last asked her who she was and what she did with the whisky. The child's blushing embarrassed silence led him to presume a drunken parent and he questioned her no further. After the fifth performance, by which time he had become attached to this serious little girl, he saw her leave the theatre. He was prompted to follow her. She led him into the poorest quarter of the town where she entered a tumbledown old house and climbed a ramshackle common staircase. On reaching the landing, through an open door, he saw her moving about a squalid, ill-found little room. Before a meagre fire lay a sickly boy, two years her junior, who, when he saw her enter, tried to crawl towards her.

'Oh, sissy,' he whimpered, 'I'm glad you're home; I thought you'd never come.'

The little girl took her brother in her arms and, having gently carried him back to the fireside, kissed him and brought out the snuff-box from her pocket. She lighted a candle and by its feeble glow Irving saw her remove the rags from the boy's rheumatic shoulders and begin to rub the starved little body with the spirit.

'There, Willie,' she said: 'I wish I had more to cure the pain.'

As Irving watched a floor-board creaked under his foot. The child looked up. Her frightened eyes met his. He put his fingers to his lips and tiptoed away. On the stairs he met a drunken man slipping and stumbling as he mounted them. Pushing past Irving, he entered the room where the child was nursing her brother. Irving heard his curses and bemused mutterings and the child's feeble protestations. He went back into the room, where he found the wretch had already flung himself on the bed and was falling into a besotted sleep. With strange dignity the child begged him not to reveal her secret; as gravely he promised to respect her confidence and urged her to ask him for anything she needed. As he turned to go she seized his hands and kissed them.

On the last night of the run, the child looked happier than usual. When the time came for their little piece of business she managed to whisper with pale, trembling lips:

'You need only pretend tonight.'

'Why?' whispered Irving.

'Because he doesn't want it now, he's dead.'

Henry Irving never forgot this; it was his first glimpse of dire poverty and of the supreme courage that can rise above it. He was an impressionable young man and, thereafter, was quick to appreciate the unspoken needs and sorrows of others; moreover, the dignity of this little Scotch girl taught him in the future to keep his own troubles to himself.

Encouraged, perhaps, by his increasing popularity in Edinburgh, he decided to have a managerial flutter on his own account. Enlisting the help of Edward Saker, one of the company and a relative of the Wyndhams, to whom he offered a half share in the enterprise, he engaged a hall at Linlithgow and announced his intention of giving a reading. To this end, for many days, perched on Arthur's seat, he studied and rehearsed Bulwer Lytton's romantic play, *The Lady of Lyons*. Irving and Saker arrived in Linlithgow on the appointed day. They were in high spirits and were further elated by seeing the bills posted on the walls announcing in bold type that 'At eight o'clock precisely, Mr. Henry Irving would read *The Lady of Lyons*'. Over a frugal tea at a nearby hotel they tried to sound the waiter on the probable size of the audience, but could get out of him no more than a non-committal 'Nane cane tell!' Shortly before eight o'clock there were no signs of an eager crowd nor of the doorkeeper of the hall, who appeared to have forgotten that he was required.

The doorkeeper was run to earth, the hall was opened, the gas was lighted and Edward Saker prepared to take the money at the door. The clock struck eight; the time wore on. At half-past eight it became clear to Irving that he must recite the play to his dejected friend and the disinterested doorkeeper or not at all. Finally he and Saker decided to abandon the field, barely scraping together enough money to pay the expenses of the hall and for the printing of the brave but unenticing posters. During the journey in the train to Edinburgh Irving tried to keep their spirits up by reading selections from the play, but it was heavy going, for the unhappy speculation had made a large hole in his hard-won savings. He had learnt, however, that the ripples of fame decrease rapidly as they spread from the centre of disturbance; that it is best to make a very big splash or none at all.

The Queen's opened again on June 25th with a farce, and for the rest of the season 'genteel comedy, juvenile tragedy and touch-and-go farce' were the run of the parts which came his way. Wyndham was delighted at the way his juvenile lead adapted himself to the new policy —if the boy was lucky and industrious he might go far as a low comedian. He seemed equally at home as a comic commercial traveller with a sandy wig, white hat and fawn trousers, as a professional acrobat going through his routine or as a starving poet meeting Queen Bess and convulsing the audience by declaring: ''Tis long since I beheld a sovereign.' He managed to squeeze the laughs out of the most scanty material and earned every penny of his thirty shillings a week. Yet Irving, although he continued to put all he knew into the creation of these trivial characters, was beginning to count the months of his apprenticeship. He had been with the Wyndhams two and a half years and had played over four hundred different parts. He had weaned the Edinburgh audiences from active hostility to amused tolerance— which, in both cases, he admitted he had fairly earned. If he stayed any longer in Edinburgh he would slide gradually into the rut of low comedy; the long-term ambitions of the intellectual gentleman would evaporate in the heady and cheaply won popularity of his parochial successes. Early in August he had had the good fortune to play King James in *Cramond Brig* before the Prince of Wales, who was on a visit to Edinburgh. When he read that his performance had been 'truly noble in heart and speech as a King ought to be' he knew that, though success in comedy was not to be despised, he had within him the power for greater things. The time was advantageous for a change; by a coincidence the opportunity arose for him to effect this change. On August 5th Louise Keeley, who for several seasons had charmed Edinburgh playgoers, took her benefit before leaving the Wyndhams to fulfil an engagement with Augustus Harris at the Princess's Theatre, London. Louise had recently married Montague Williams, a stage-struck ensign of Her Majesty's 41st Regiment, who was to make his last appearance as an amateur actor at his bride's benefit. The benefit programme included *London Assurance*, in which Louise played Grace Harkaway; and a comedietta, in which she was supported by 'Tom Pearce Esq., a distinguished London amateur', whom everybody knew to be young F. C. Burnand, the founder of the New Cambridge Amateur Dramatic Club and the despair of his tutors, who were earnestly bent on his ordination in the Roman Church. Irving played Dazzle in *London Assurance*, a part created by Charles Mathews in the original production. Before Louise and her husband left for London he may have told them of his desire to leave Edinburgh, and they perhaps promised to recommend him to any manager in search of a juvenile lead.

Such promises are easily made and often quickly forgotten. Irving, therefore, was surprised and delighted when, towards the end of the month, he received a letter from Augustus Harris offering him an engagement. Louise had been true to her promise.

Augustus Harris, the son of a well-known impresario, having tried his hand as an actor, was about to embark on his first venture as a manager by taking over the Princess's Theatre from Charles Kean, who for nine years had treated the public to a series of spectacular but uninspired Shakespearian productions, a regime which ended with a public banquet in his honour and a loss of four thousand pounds. Irving found Harris's offer a tempting one; it would bring him before the London public and would allow him to return to his family and friends, vindicated in his intention and independent in pocket. He decided to accept Harris's terms which were based on a three-years contract and to gamble on taking his farewell benefit—for it was always a risk that the popularity of the actor taking his benefit might not be sufficient in terms of cash to balance the overhead cost of the theatre for that night. Perhaps the unrewarded toil of his Linlithgow fiasco prompted him to choose *The Lady of Lyons* as the main piece of the evening and to cast himself for the leading part, Claude Melnotte. Some of his friends may have shaken their heads at such rash presumption in a promising low comedian, for Claude Melnotte was the most popular of romantic lovers.

Irving's estimate of his popularity proved to be correct. On the evening of Tuesday, September 13th, the theatre was packed to capacity and well sprinkled with fashionable patrons. He knew he had the loyal support of his fellow-actors and actresses; nervous as he undoubtedly was when he stepped onto the stage as Claude Melnotte and as the focus of interest in the evening's programme, an encouraging smile from his friend, H. J. Loveday, a violinist in the orchestra, who, for that occasion, occupied the conductor's podium, gave him the additional spur of confidence which he needed. Twice during the play he was called by the friendly and approving house. In the interval between *The Lady of Lyons* and the inevitable farce, in response to further calls, he came before the curtain. The audience were delighted with the modesty and dignity of the young man, whose progress, they felt, owed much to their cautious and discriminating approbation, as he acknowledged the applause which trickled away to an anticipatory hush. Pale, yet complete master of himself, Henry Irving began his first front-of-the-curtain speech—so painfully prepared, so spontaneously delivered:

'Ladies and Gentlemen, I feel I have undertaken rather a difficult task—a task in which I fear I am liable to be charged with either ingratitude or presumption—ingratitude if I go away without saying goodbye to old friends, and presumption for having attempted to do so. Still, I am bound to speak. It is now three years since I first went before the footlights in Sunderland, and a year afterwards I was transplanted to Edinburgh. But I was a long time before I succeeded in giving you satisfaction. [Cries of 'No' and applause.] I was sometimes hissed in this theatre, and I can assure you that thousands of plaudits do not give half so much pleasure as one hiss gives pain, more especially to a young actor. But I am very glad to be able to think that I have won your esteem. [Applause.] I am also very grateful to the newspaper press for the encouragement they have given me and also to the management for the many excellent and suitable parts into which I have been cast. In bidding you farewell in order to fulfil an engagement in a larger sphere in the metropolis, I trust it is not the last time I will have the pleasure of appearing before you. [Applause.] Ladies and gentlemen, I now bid you goodbye.'

The audience, as the young actor bowed and withdrew to the prompt corner, loudly applauded the brevity and engaging frankness of this simple speech. Few of them sensed the curious note of prerogative that ran through it, the acceptance of praise and criticism as the due of an actor with a career before him. Irving could still hear their applause as he sat down before the mirror in his dressing-room and began to remove the make-up from his face. It was easy enough to be flattered by the warmth of his reception—yet how hardly had it been won, how bitter the struggle against discouragement and despair when night after night he had beaten against the wall of their apathy or had had to endure their open hostility. This success, he knew, was only a short downhill slope in the foothills lying between him and the great peaks ahead which he had set himself to climb. This was no moment for self-congratulation; it was the hour for stock-taking. Deceptive illusions must be wiped away with the paint on his face. What did his mirror now reflect? The face of a young man of twenty-one, its natural pallor accentuated by the raven-black hair and by eyes, beneath dark brows, glittering with the exaltation of success. By no ordinary standards could he claim to be good-looking—his features had, no doubt, a certain strength, and individually were well-formed—yet the mask appeared unresolved as though the sculptor, uncertain of his creation, had paused in his work, leaving the modelling fluid and unrefined. Behind the mask was a mind exercised and disciplined by three years of arduous and unremitting toil; a spirit hardened by experience and strengthened in its purpose. The boy, who had left London with nothing but his faith and a parcel of wigs and swords, was returning, a seasoned youth, with a sensible grasp of the rudiments of his craft and a theatrical basket into which now he slowly packed the scrappy components of four hundred and twenty-eight characters—the great cloud of witnesses to the growth of his art and to his painstaking industry. He had reason to hope, as he shut the lid of his basket, that he had come to the end of his novitiate.

CHAPTER VI
London Fiasco

A dauntless young actor, arriving in London in the autumn of 1859, convinced of his genius and confident of his equipment, would have been justified in thinking that the city was his for the taking. The barometer of theatrical art and enterprise had never been lower; only five theatres were open in a city which in Shakespeare's time had boasted at least ten; of these only Sadler's Wells, where Phelps was playing Brutus in *The Fall of Tarquin*, and the Haymarket, where a mediocre production of *As You Like It* was the make-weight for Buckstone's farce, *The Rifle and How to Use It*, had any pretensions to quality. The defences were down and now, if ever, was the time to take the town by storm. Augustus Harris, though an indifferent actor, was a shrewd young impresario; the woeful lack of competition may have spurred him to lease the Princess's Theatre, to redecorate it lavishly and in excellent taste, and to make a bid for the fortune awaiting anyone who could satisfy a theatre-hungry public. His greatest problem was the dearth of dramatists, whose number and talents, as we have seen, had dwindled, owing to neglect and discouragement, to insignificance. The best play he could find with which to open his management was *Ivy Hall*, a pedestrian adaptation by John Oxenford, the dramatic critic of *The Times*, of a play by Octave Feuillet. Owing to a misprint in the advance advertisement it appeared as *Toy Hall*, which cannot have improved its chances of success.

If Harris, as rehearsals proceeded, became gloomy as to his prospects, Henry Irving, the ardent juvenile from the north, was seething with anger and disappointment. Arriving full of hope and ready to give a good account of himself and having, no doubt, drawn a fairly long bow in describing his situation to his family and friends, he found himself with but half a dozen lines in the first of four long acts and no mention of his name on the bills or in the newspaper advertisements. A week

95

after his arrival in London he must have read with bitterness, even if he showed it to his friends with pride, a notice in the *Era* of September 19th:

'We have frequently adverted to the rapid progress Mr. Irving has achieved in his profession by unremitting zeal and study, but on the occasion of his benefit and last appearance, on Tuesday last, he excelled all his previous personations. Some may have deemed it somewhat ambitious that an actor, who has not been quite three years on the stage, should attempt the character of Claude Melnotte in *The Lady of Lyons*, but the finish with which Mr. Irving sustained the part, effectually proved that he had not over-estimated his powers. Thrice was he called in the course of the piece to receive the plaudits of an excellently and fashionably filled house. Mr. Irving took leave of his Edinburgh friends in a most modest speech, and retired amid their encouraging adieux.'

If Edinburgh was satisfied that he had not over-estimated his powers, London was to have little opportunity of judging them. *Ivy Hall* met with the fate it deserved, and his brief appearance in a farce, *The Two Polts*, passed unnoticed. Being modest and persevering, he might have lingered in frustrated obscurity, believing this to be the purgatory through which all young London actors must pass on their way to the stars; but a week or two later he was left in no doubt as to the hopelessness of his position. George Melville, a mediocre actor whom in Edinburgh Irving had succeeded as King James in *Cramond Brig*, arrived at the Princess's to play Hamlet. Irving was cast for Osric— Irving, who had played Claudius with Charles Dillon and Horatio with Wyndham. As the embittered Osric made obeisance to this indifferent Prince of Denmark, who was advised by the London critics to 'eschew unprofitable ambition and to return to the melodramas from whence he sprang,' his pride and tactical sense told him that he must cut his losses. He asked Harris to release him from their contract; Harris, whose own fortunes were in jeopardy, urged Irving to stick to the ship; but Irving, conceding that it was the captain's duty to remain on the sinking vessel, felt that a discontented petty officer was under no such obligation. The contract was annulled.

Though Irving put a bold front on his departure from the Princess's, he knew that he had suffered a severe setback. The kindly commiseration of his friends and the silent acceptance by his mother of the calamities which she had prophesied when he left the sheltered security of Thacker's, were hard for a proud young man to bear. He must even have doubted the wisdom of his decision, when, immediately after he

Irving in 1866

Irving as Bob Gassitt

Irving as Rawdon Scudamore

left the Princess's, Harris retrieved his fortune by presenting Fechter in Victor Hugo's *Ruy Blas* to the British public, who enthusiastically accepted this hybrid tragedian, whose genius and originality overcame the peculiar accent with which he declaimed their language. But Irving had decided to return to the provinces and to stay there until he was offered, by a London manager, an engagement which he considered worthy of his talent and in which he could make his mark. He determined, however, to make a demonstration of force to cover his retreat.

At that time public readings of plays or poetry by actors and elocutionists were a popular form of entertainment—so popular that penny readings attracted large audiences from those who could afford no more than this for their amusements. In the City of London there were several halls where such readings could be given; of these the most patronized were Sussex Hall, to which we have already been introduced, and Crosby Hall, in Bishopsgate, once the home of Richard III, and later of Sir Thomas More, and at this time still unmarred by restoration. Irving, the hope of desperation challenging the ghastly experience of Linlithgow, with the warm support of his old City friends decided to take Crosby Hall and to give his long-prepared reading of *The Lady of Lyons*. His courage was rewarded. The reading which he gave on December 19th, was well attended. The popular critics, E. L. Blanchard and Edmund Yates, were there to deliver judgment, while sprinkled among the audience was a bodyguard of old friends, led by J. L. Toole, who had come with others of the old Edinburgh company to lend their support to his enterprise. Throughout the long play Irving held his audience; indeed towards the climax he reduced them to audible sobs though they recovered sufficiently to call him twice. The critics reported their agreeable surprise that his reading was as effective as his delivery. For the first time a discerning writer perceived 'that finer and indefinite something which proved incontestably and instantaneously that the fire of genius is present in the artist'. Encouraged by this success, Irving gave another reading on February 8th, choosing for his subject Sheridan Knowles's *Virginius*, a herculean task, for the play was in five acts and abounded in strong situations and a variety of characters which gave him every opportunity to display his versatility. The second reading was as successful as the first. Again he held the attention of his audience and won praise for his scholarly interpretation and accomplished technique. His skirmish had been successful; although he had failed to realize the high hopes in which he left Edinburgh, he could withdraw from the capital with dignity knowing that he had made a lasting impression upon those who had heard him.

Irving had not long to wait before he had the offer of an engagement from Edmund Glover of the Theatre Royal, Glasgow. The theatrical world of the north was a small one and was amicably divided between Glover, Wyndham, Davis and Knowles of Manchester, who were always ready to do each other a good turn. Glover was an excellent actor. A little more than a year ago he had come to help his old friend Wyndham with the obsequies of the Theatre Royal, Edinburgh, by playing Triplet in *Masks and Faces* and had, no doubt, good cause to remember the young man who, as Soaper, had lathered him so dexterously. He had made his fortune when, having heard Jenny Lind sing in London, he secured her for a Scottish tour, which brought him a profit of more than three thousand pounds. With this backing he took over the management of the Theatre Royal, Glasgow, with such success that he was able to acquire three more theatres in the neighbourhood. Thus, between managing these and appearing frequently himself in leading parts, his life was full and, as it turned out, all too short. Irving was asked to join him at Easter. Until then he would have had to kick his heels in London but for an unexpected stroke of luck which he hastened to report to Charlie Ford, who had also escaped from Thacker's into the service of H. M. Customs, in a letter of March 2nd:

'My dear Ford,

Very unexpectedly I have engaged for Dublin until I join Glover at Easter.

If you have time to come tomorrow evening I shall be at home and would like to see you and Mrs. Ford.

Affectionately yours,

J. H. B. I.

I have forgotten in this to tell you that I leave on Saturday evening and open on Monday.'

Ford and a few others gathered together at Old Broad Street to wish their friend good luck for his new venture. Dublin was a great place for actors, even if the Queen's was the least reputable of her theatres, whose audiences were famous for their uproariousness. Happily both they and Irving were ignorant of the trap which, already set, he would spring the moment he set foot on the stage of the Queen's. Though Irving was no believer in luck he had two strokes of it at this period of his career. The first was his recent disappointment in London, for, hard as it seemed at the time, it had spared him the risk of failure in a part beyond his powers which were, as yet, very limited; now in Dublin, though in fact the Goddess of Fortune smiled upon him, he had every right to regard her as a malevolent hag.

The Queen's Theatre, Dublin, was managed by Henry Webb, a comedian who understood his larrikin audience and gorged them with programmes which lasted for four hours. During February he had dismissed his juvenile lead, George Vincent, for an act of insubordination. Vincent was the darling of the patrons of the Queen's and of a wife who had enough money to prevent him worrying about re-employment and to allow him to plan his revenge at leisure. The disgruntled actor spent a congenial week or two frequenting the tougher ale houses in the town where he stood treat to all and sundry until, for the outlay of a few pounds, he had recruited a gang of hooligans who were prepared to give his successor a warm reception. In the meantime news came to Webb from London of a young actor called Irving who had won praise for his readings at Crosby Hall. Reckoning that one so far removed from Dublin would be ignorant of local theatrical politics, Webb had engaged Irving who arrived in Dublin on March 5th to play Cassio to T. C. King's Othello. King was an actor of the Barry Sullivan school and was destined to be a great favourite with Dublin audiences. His quality can be gauged from a notice in the *Athenaeum* which described his voice as 'musical, his pronunciation good, and his attitudes all well chosen and expressive'.

Since Cassio had not been one of Vincent's parts, the partisans with sporting discrimination gave the newcomer a fair hearing. But, two nights later, he had hardly set foot upon the stage when there was a questioning shout from the gods in the gallery: 'Is that the omadhaun, Mike?' to which echo came from the other side: 'No, them's the young man's duds—they shove him out later on!' This cryptic reply was the signal for concerted pandemonium. There broke out such a bawling of Irish invectives, such derisive yelling, such whistling and tarryhooting, that the play was brought to a standstill. A day or two later, Irving wrote a temperate account of his ordeal to Toole:

Sunday, Dublin.
79 Great Brunswick St.

'My dear Toole,

I expected a line from you before this, in a strange place everything from home or a friend is a grateful remembrance—but I suppose you've been skipping quarters. . . .

I have plenty of study—but not too much—enough time has been left me to have many jolly hours among the company—who as a body are very good fellows. On Wednesday last, all of us, including Webb—dined at Beggars Bank & a rare spree we had. Pullen was one of our number, I like him very well. When I am introduced to any stranger I immediately mention your name—'tis as good nay better than the weather for it leads to more—Toole is a household word. Last week I made it my business to find out Vincent (who is still in town) to sound his feelings respecting me—& to see how I should be received—we met & he seemed cordial enough—my reason in doing so I will tell you.

You can easily imagine that an ill feeling might be excited against me by Vincent's friends through my sudden appearance & his sudden dismissal—such was not the case on Monday—my Cassio being received with great applause—on Tuesday I did not appear & Wed (nesda)y was an off night—but I made my app(earan)ce on Thursday in Gisippus—in which Vincent had played on Saturday—some of the boys called for Vincent—the same thing continued throughout the piece—less often, although more applauded. I was all right—letter perfect—in the part—upwards of the lengths—therefore was not disconcerted. Since then I played Nicholas Nickleby, Laertes, Florizel —with lots of applause but at times the same diabolical interruption—Webb never attempted to stop it & when I went on last night several of the boys hissed. The house was crowded & I struck while the iron was hot as follows: "Gentlemen, I should be very glad if you would tell me the reason of this disapprobation? (*Great applause mingled w. a few hisses*) I have frequently appeared in England & Scotland & London and Edin. w. applause but among a certain few of the audience here I have been denied the same—I came among you an entire stranger —have endeavoured to please you and really have been treated by some with anything but courtesy." Tremendous applause from all parts of the house—the tables entirely turned on the few roughs—part went splendidly & called at the end.

Of course Vincent having been seen walking about the town, many might imagine I had got him out—& on one of the *Winter's Tale* nights—he actually went into the lower gallery—enough to cause an injurious feeling towards me. He tried to come back—wrote and saw Webb—but no use—& as I am going to Glasgow at Easter, yesterday we engaged Blake to open after the vacation.

Charles Webb opens on Thursday in the *Courier of Lyons*—the two parts usually acted by one person played by the two Webbs. The only notice that has appeared in "Queen's" I sent you. . . . Although the salary would be more here. . . . Mr. Webb told me they were obliged to exclude legitimate comedies and drawing-room pieces here—for the boys would not listen. Fancy, some of the beauties last night wanted Sherton to dance a horn-pipe in *The Winter's Tale* (Oh shade of Avon) & when Webb said, with accompanying voice and saliva, that they might as well ask Mr. Sherton to play Richard III as it was not in the bill (I think that very good) he would not allow the piece to be interrupted—they hissed him every time that he made an exit.

These are two splendid things they said to Miss Parker in Lady Macbeth.

Lady M. (sleeping scene): "All the perfumes of Arabia will not sweeten this little hand."

Gods: "Oh soap & water and be damned to you."

Again

Lady M.: "To bed—to bed—to bed!"

Gods: "Go along ninnie and I'll be after yez."

Goodbye and God bless,

Yours,

Henry Irving.'

Irving's report was by no means highly coloured and certainly was over-optimistic. His speech had only scotched the opposition. Vincent's mercenaries, animated by further rations of whisky and porter, returned to the charge.

The battle lasted for three weeks, the more savage encounters being fought whenever Irving attempted a part in which his displaced predecessor had been particularly popular. At last Webb took a strong line. Police were posted in the gallery and after one night of violent physical combat and wholesale chucking out, order was more or less restored. Webb took the first opportunity of explaining to the more reasonable sections of the house the cause of the disturbance. With that engaging inconsequence which is their nature, the Irish audience, on being told of the conspiracy, recognized the injustice which they had inflicted upon this young foreign actor and immediately were almost as lavish with their applause as they had been with their contumely.

So, for the last few days of his engagement, Irving was able to give Dublin a taste of his quality. In the course of those three tempestuous weeks he had studied and played at least five new parts, which included Laertes and the jeune premier in *The Lyons Mail*. This melodrama, which had been adapted from the French by Charles Reade, was the story of a miscarriage of justice and mistaken identity; here Irving read it for the first time and at once was attracted by its possibilities.

On reflection, he hardly knew how he had managed to hold his own against that continued uproar. It had been an experience such as few actors ever had to endure. It had called on all his reserves of courage and persistence; following upon the blighting disappointment of the London engagement, such a trial might have broken the heart of any young actor. Brodribb might well have succumbed and returned to his ledgers. But in the past three years the armour of Irving had, piece by piece, been forged and riveted. Until now the plating had shone brightly enough, though the metal was still soft and vulnerable; plunged into the boiling oil of Irish antagonism, it had emerged a little dulled but tempered to cold steel. This apparent reverse of fortune was, in fact, a timely blessing. Irving set out for Glasgow no less determined, but with the toughened fibre and blunted sensitivity which he would need if he were to survive the further trials which lay ahead. Vincent, his conspiracy crowned with success, was reinstated at the Queen's and, amid the plaudits of his supporters, sank into unrecorded oblivion.

CHAPTER VII

Theatre Royal, Manchester

Irving arrived in Glasgow on April 7th to find Glover rehearsing a spectacular and topical piece, '*The Indian Revolt, or the Relief of Lucknow*'; it had been written by Glover himself, but was advertised as the work of many authors. Glover had engaged Irving especially to play Prince Jung Bahadour, a part in which he had to compete with a menagerie of professional elephants, camels and bulls. The play proved to be very much to the taste of Glasgow audiences so that for a month the Theatre Royal was pervaded with the musty odours of oriental livestock. Immediately on his arrival, however, Irving had to play, at very short notice, an insignificant part in a Saturday-night attraction, *The Warlock of the Glen*. His pride suffered a further blow when he discovered that on the bills he was announced in both plays as 'Mr. Irwin'.

Glover, though quite a young man, was already a victim of dropsy and was to die before the year was out. Irving realized that a programme of infinite mediocrity stretched out before him. With a sinking heart he tackled conscientiously the poor stuff that was given him to act. He appeared occasionally at Glover's other theatre at Greenock, but only once, when he played Macduff, was he able to make any impression upon Glasgow audiences. Although the dull monotony of the stock plays was for a short time broken by a visit of Charles Mathews, it looked as though he had got into a stagnant backwater. He had a welcome break in May when he was allowed to visit Edinburgh in order to appear in a benefit for his old friend, Edward Saker. Edinburgh had not forgotten him. His success as Captain Popham in a farce, *The Eton Boy*, a few lines of commendation from the press, and the warmth of his reception by old friends, all acted as a much-needed tonic to his self-esteem.

He returned to Glasgow to continue his dispiriting work from which there seemed to be no hope of escape. Yet, on his first visit to Greenock, he met a demure girl of nineteen with a keen sense of humour whose ambition, he discovered, was as lively as his own. The girl was Henrietta Hodson, the daughter of a London publican who had entrusted her to Glover to be trained for the stage. Having started by walking on at Glasgow, she had graduated to Greenock, where she was playing small parts. These two young people recognized each other as kindred spirits and formed an alliance with the object of seeking their fortunes in a more promising field.

At the end of the summer they gave notice to Glover, who was now on the verge of collapse, and together they set out for Manchester. Irving's situation had never been more desperate. When he arrived in Manchester his savings were gone and he possessed no more than the contents of his theatrical basket and the few shillings left in his pocket. He found his way naturally to the 'Printer's Arms', a public house near the Theatre Royal which was a rendezvous for poor actors and the headquarters of the Titans, a 'literary club of convivial character', whose founder and president was Thomas Chambers, the treasurer of the theatre. At all events it was through Chambers' good offices that both Irving and Henrietta Hodson were engaged by John Knowles for the Theatre Royal. Knowles was a remarkable character and about the only theatre manager at that time who had a sound head for business. He was a marble merchant, a connoisseur of antiques and a dealer in pictures; he knew nothing of theatrical art, but was adept at theatre business, having a flair for knowing what pleased the public. Arrogant, overbearing, and as stubborn as a Lancastrian can be, he rarely spoke to actors or actresses in his employment. Though his brusque and brutal manner caused him to be disliked and feared by his employees and business associates, he was said to be a genial and lavish host in his own home. He often lent money to such stars as Buckstone, Dillon and Mathews; since they were all careless and improvident, he was able to extort repayment in the form of engagements at his theatre on terms very advantageous to himself. He did not trouble to disguise his contempt for the press, treating their praise or more frequent abuse of him with equal indifference. Yet, though he attended no rehearsals nor set foot upon his stage, the Theatre Royal, since he took it over in 1842, had been the most prosperous and best-conducted playhouse in the provinces.

Later Knowles rebuilt the theatre in the Italian style and enlarged it to accommodate an audience of two thousand; here, under his patronage and despotic direction, a stock company was formed which was said to be the finest in Great Britain. Thus Irving, although he had accepted an engagement as walking gentleman and a salary little larger than that which he had earned so strenuously in Edinburgh, would be one of a company with far higher standards and would be able to learn much from the procession of great stars who crossed the stage of the Theatre Royal. On September 29th he made his first appearance before the Manchester audience; this was limited to a small part in a farce and to joining the company in singing the National Anthem at the end of the performance; on the following night the farce was dropped from the bill so that he spent the next fortnight rehearsing the part of Faust and swelling the loyal chorus. Irving was soon on good terms with the rest of the company, and by the time *Faust and Marguerite*, a dramatization of Gounod's opera, was produced, he had been elected a member of the Titan Club. Each member of this club had to adopt the name of a Shakespearian character; thus his benefactor, Chambers, was well named Prospero; his stage-manager, Calvert, he learned to address as Hamlet, and Joe Robins, a kindly and genial member of the company, as Dogberry; he himself became Thersites. To address any member of the club during its meeting by his ordinary name entailed the fine of a penny. Irving's choice of the most scurvy cripple in Shakespeare's crowded gallery of characters betrayed his sardonic estimate of his present estate. Among other friendly Titans was Alfred Darbyshire, a young Manchester architect who helped and advised Calvert in mounting Shakesperian productions and was in return allowed to indulge his talent for amateur acting by appearing in the company. Alfred Darbyshire was a nephew of George Bradshaw, the originator of the railway guide. By introducing Irving to his cousin, Christopher Bradshaw, who at the age of fourteen had inherited his father's indispensable and lucrative property, he provided the actor with a life-long friend and, in later years, with a sage and valued adviser in matters of finance.

Irving soon found that Manchester playgoers were more discriminating and the critics more enlightened and consequently more severe than any he had yet encountered. Had not Faust made his final exit down a well in a cloud of smoke and flame, he might have been ignored by the press; as it was, their comment was unfavourable and critical even of his make-up. As the season progressed and the critics came to accept him as a permanent member of the company they began to take him to task for certain mannerisms, the opening bars of a theme that was to be incidental to his theatrical life. 'This young actor,' wrote the critic of the *Examiner*, after seeing him in a comedy, 'possesses many good qualities—nature has done much for him and requires a grateful return. But he is acquiring habits which will ultimately interfere with legitimate progress. Why should he be ambitious to imitate the automaton rather than a graceful or manly bearing? Nature's idea of a gentleman is not that of a modern "swell", with jerking walk and stiff neck and spasmodic elocution. Mr. Irving has a good presence, an intellectual head and eye, a fine sonorous voice, and no slight amount of intelligence. He will be an actor if he has resolution to let nature have more than her own way.'

The seeds of the peculiar gait, which had become a habit and had been criticized in Edinburgh, were sown in the city elocution class where Mr. Thomas had encouraged his pupils, when acting comedy, to adopt the jaunty, jerky stride which his hero, Charles Mathews, employed so successfully. No doubt Irving, when he was forced in Edinburgh to snatch what success he could as a low comedian rather than as a tragedian, turned Thomas's training to good account, but for so long a period that what had been a resource had now become a habit. He was to some extent able to profit by this correction, and to confine this eccentricity of gait to its proper occasions; his elocution, he knew well enough, was open to criticism—since his critics knew nothing of his conquered impediment, it was encouraging to know that they found his voice itself fine and sonorous.

Throughout the first year of his engagement there were few distractions to tempt him from his work; for he had no money to spend on his own entertainment or to join in the kind of convivialities which depend upon each man standing his share. Of the three pounds which was handed to him every Friday night, seventeen and sixpence was posted without fail to his parents—a proud reminder, however ill-spared, that his enterprise still prospered. The balance left him barely enough to live upon. Often he would be forced to ask Mr. Sanderson, the chemist, to allow his bill for make-up materials to run on for a month or more; as often he would have to borrow half a crown from a friend to tide him over until pay night. During that first Christmastide he was fined half a crown by his fellow-Titans. Pleading his inability to pay in cash, he offered the alternative of a ghost story; the offer was accepted and apparently he satisfied his creditors. The Christmas pantomime, *Cinderella*, was unusually successful and was played ninety times including three performances on New Year's Day, 1861. Irving managed to preserve his anonymity as one of the Ugly Sisters, but was billed in the leading part in *George Barnwell*, which was the supporting piece.

Early in the New Year Henrietta Hodson left the Theatre Royal to join a stock company at Bristol, where she found a fourteen-year-old rival, Ellen Terry, who, being one of eleven children in a theatrical family, was no infant phenomenon but a trouper who, from hard necessity, had been on the stage since she was eight years old.

Losing old friends and finding new ones is very much part of an actor's life. Irving found these hard and ill-requited months easier to bear through the kindness and friendship shown him by Charles Calvert and his wife. Calvert had been engaged by Knowles a few years before as leading man and stage-manager of the Theatre Royal with the promise of the management of the new Prince's Theatre which was now nearing completion. Calvert had met his wife in a stock company in Southampton, and since their marriage they had played together in leading parts. Irving and Calvert were mutually attracted, for both of their lives were influenced by deep religious feeling. Calvert was the son of a London merchant, who had given him a good education and had sent him to King's College. While at the university the boy felt that he had a call to enter the Church. A lack of absolute conviction and the arguments of a worldly father led him to become a travelling salesman of straw hats. Through the intervention and encouragement of the Bishop of Oxford, he gave up drumming and entered a Theological College—only to discover the works and teaching of Swedenborg, which disturbed him so much that he abandoned the Church for the stage. He soon became a good actor and developed a flair for production. Once, when Knowles had told him to produce *Hamlet* and had refused to provide him with new scenery or dresses, he conjured from the theatre stock an original Scandinavian mise-en-scène, which was ahead of its time and was praised by the critics.

When Irving had been with the company a short time Knowles, who was not impressed with the new walking gentleman, advised Calvert to get rid of him. Calvert, ignoring this advice, helped Irving with kindly instruction and frank criticism. In their vocational love of the theatre they found a common cause and a subject of conversation for many a long walk on the moors and for suppers after the performance at the Calverts' house where they gossiped over Mrs. Calvert's Irish stew until the fire in the parlour died out, when they retreated to the kitchen and, with their feet upon the fender, continued their talk through the early hours of the morning. Calvert's friendship and wise counsel meant much to Irving in those days when he needed all his sense of dedication and confidence in his own future to support him through the needy and disillusioning present.

Light comedy and farce succeeded each other until April, when Calvert's adaptation of the French play, *La Dame de St Tropez*, was produced and provided a welcome change. In July the company were preparing a series of plays by John Brougham, a comedian who was to win greater fame as a dramatist and had just returned from America, where he had had his first successes as an actor and author. Irving found himself cast for Mr. Dombey, in Brougham's dramatization of Dickens's novel, and with his usual care studied the foibles and prepared the make-up of the elderly city merchant. He was rewarded by reading later, in the *Manchester Guardian*, that he had shown an excellent appreciation of the character. Since the rest of Brougham's plays were evidently written to display the author's powers as an actor, Irving's contribution was a small one, but enough for the press to note a steady improvement in his method. In Brougham he was able to study an actor trained by Vestris and Charles Mathews and an accomplished exponent of their particular style.

October brought the great American actor, Edwin Booth, and a long season of Shakespeare and other classics—a breath of the noble and romantic element of his art which would sustain Irving through succeeding weeks of stifling farce. Edwin Booth was four years older than Irving. He was one of ten children of Junius Brutus Booth, a great tragedian who was comparable to Edmund Kean in his genius, and in the admiration in which he was held by his fellow-countrymen—comparable even in that he, like Kean, had gone to sea as a boy and had served in the British Navy. Junius tried to prevent his son going on the stage, but when Edwin by chance took the place of a defaulter in his company, his son's talent and zeal were so apparent that he became reconciled to the idea. Edwin toured America with his father until 1856, when, having parted from his son in California, Junius died in the cabin of a Mississippi steamboat on his way to New Orleans. Stricken with grief by the loss of a father whom he worshipped, Edwin had gone through a period of drudgery and disappointment similar to that which Irving was now experiencing. Success came to him overnight, when he swept the playgoers of Boston off their feet with his tempestuous portrayal of Sir Giles Overreach in *A New Way to Pay Old Debts*.

He had come to England in 1861 for the first time. For an American actor this was a hazardous expedition. Only twelve years before Macready had gone to the United States when the Americans were still smarting from Dickens's outspoken criticisms. Forrest, the reigning monarch of the New York stage, revived a quarrel with Macready which had begun during his visit to England. He so inflamed the tempers of his partisans that, on the night of Macready's second appearance, they stormed the Astor Place Opera House where the English actor was to play Macbeth. A mêlée ensued involving police, military, partisans and innocent playgoers, over fifty of whom were killed or mutilated. Macready was forced to fly from New York in disguise. This unparalleled outburst of dramatic rivalry overshadowed Anglo-American theatrical relations, which were still further imperilled by the outbreak of the civil war and the growing British prejudice against the North. Booth, like most American actors, was a yankee; yet when he opened at the Haymarket Theatre in September with *The Merchant of Venice* the public received his Shylock warmly enough, though actors and critics were less friendly.

When Booth came to Manchester, Irving for the first time saw the actor of his dreams—or at least a facet of that majestic creature of his imagination. Hitherto nearly all the actors with whom he had worked had got their results by animal, rather than by spiritual, forcefulness. Booth's romantic soul and philosophic mind were reflected in his finely chiselled features and his grave yet graceful bearing. His approach to his art, particularly to his study of Hamlet, was intellectual. Rejecting all the meretricious tricks which were still affected by his contemporaries, he harnessed his fine voice, his flexible technique, and his poetic imagination to a natural interpretation of Shakespeare's characters which he recreated with almost magical sincerity. Irving, well content with such parts as Laertes, Cassio, Malcolm and Orlando, studied with fascinated intent Booth's exalted treatment of Hamlet's mystery and of the conflict between good and evil in the conscience of a soldierly Macbeth. During this season Booth, finding so excellent a supporting company, gave of his best, while Irving relished the happiest and most instructive weeks he had experienced since he became an actor. Booth's visit ended with *A New Way to Pay Old Debts* in which he, too, challenged comparison with Edmund Kean, whom middle-aged playgoers still remembered vividly in this, his greatest part; that they conceded his claim to comparison, in spite of so many inhibiting prejudices, was a tribute to the American actor's genius. At the end of February Booth returned to America. Within three years the honourable position which, by many years of toil and hardship, he had won upon the international stage, was threatened with eclipse. On March 24th, 1865, his brother, John Wilkes, struck down Abraham Lincoln in Ford's Theatre, Washington, and by his bloody act brought misery and death to thousands and came near to ruining his elder brother.

The inspiration of Booth's example was reflected very soon in Irving's work; his steady improvement won him better parts from the management and more encouraging comment from the critics. On April 4th, when he played Claude Melnotte, the *Examiner* remarked that Mr. Irving, 'though one might have considered the part beyond his powers, deserved the applause so liberally bestowed upon him. He delivered many passages with fine feeling and, we have little doubt, surprised many present who have only seen him in characters of less importance'. Four days later he took his benefit, playing in three pieces; his best part was Nicholas in *Nicholas Nickleby*. The rest of the year, except for a Shakespearian season in which G. V. Brooke tore and thundered his way through *Macbeth*, *King John* and *Othello*, was rather an anti-climax. During Brooke's visit the company never had a dull moment, indeed they worked in a state of constant anxiety. The Great Gustavus, as he was called, was given, in the manner of old tragedians, to spending the daylight hours in wandering from one ale-house to another until by the time he arrived at the theatre he was in no condition to face the strain of a long part. One night when he was playing Othello, a part in which, when sober, he excelled, as the curtain was about to rise on the last act he was nowhere to be found. A search was made in the theatre and in nearby taverns, without result. Irving, who was playing Cassio, was told to change his clothes and to go on as the Moor in Brooke's place—no easy assignment for one who prided himself on the thoroughness of his make-up. Thus, for the first time, Irving appeared in a great Shakesperian role before an audience who could have been no less bewildered than himself. When the curtain fell a further search was made and eventually the unconscious form of the missing Othello was found huddled up among the scenery stacked in the wings. Having roused him with difficulty, his fellow-actors escorted the great man back to his lodgings. Not long afterwards Brooke died a hero's death while trying to save the lives of others when the steamship *London* foundered with a loss of 269 lives in the Bay of Biscay on her way to Australia. Dressed in a red Crimean shirt and trousers, he worked at the pumps until they became useless; as the ship sank he was seen leaning against the half-doors of the companion with great composure. To a steward, who was among the last to leave the ship, he said: 'If you succeed in saving yourself, give my farewell to the people of Melbourne'—a perfect curtain line for a Celtic heavy tragedian.

During the autumn an elaborately mounted spectacle, *Peep o' Day*, thronged with supers, perspiring machinists and stage-carpenters, ran for nine weeks, through which Irving, unnoticed, impersonated a Captain Howard. This solid spectacle melted into the gauzes and transformations of the pantomime; Irving ended the old year and saw in the new one as Fergus Graham in Westland Marston's drama, *A Hard Struggle*, which followed the harlequinade.

Christmas came round again with little prospect of good cheer for a poor provincial actor in his lonely lodgings. Irving, therefore, welcomed an invitation from his fellow-Titan, Dogberry, alias Joe Robins, who was little better off than himself, to spend Christmas Day with him and to share his supper. Joe was rich only in his wardrobe; for, when selling his gentlemen's outfitting business which he gave up for the stage, he kept back sufficient of his stock to ensure an adequate supply of haberdashery for the rest of his life. As Irving walked to Joe's house the cold wind bit sharply through his threadbare clothes which had to do duty in winter or summer. When he arrived he could not conceal that he was perishing cold. Before supper Joe, who seemed strangely ill-at-ease, took him up to his bedroom to wash and brush up. There Irving saw, hanging over a chair, a brand-new suit of woollen underclothes—a luxury that he had never been able to afford. As Joe left the room he stuck his head round the door and, in awkward embarrassment, stammered:

'Those clothes, in the chair, old man—upon my word I think you'd better put them on. It's deuced cold for the time of the year, ye know.'

Irving, left alone and overwhelmed by the thoughtful kindness of his friend, went to the chair, and as he fingered the warm texture of this most welcome gift he burst into tears. Charity may discover to those it touches the misery or poverty which they have concealed bravely, even from themselves. Joe Robins passed humbly across the stage, and the world forgot him after he had made his exit; Irving never forgot that Christmas night and was determined that as long as his name was remembered the forgetful world should be reminded of his kindly benefactor.

The New Year found him playing once again the lead in *George Barnwell*. Towards the end of March the company began rehearsals for another lavish production, *Blanche of Nevers*, in which he and Wybert Rousby, a provincial actor of established popularity, were to share the male honours. For this play Knowles had engaged Miss Nellie Moore to play the heroine, thereby introducing a charming actress to Manchester audiences and the first romance into the life of Henry Irving. Having served her apprenticeship in Manchester, she had made her first appearance at the St. James's Theatre, London, while Irving was making his unhappy début in Sunderland. The London audiences and critics were quick to recognize her promise. Nellie had a round, intelligent face, with wide-set eyes, a fair complexion and a mass of golden hair which she wore with a fringe to hide her high forehead. She had a trim figure and on and off the stage had a pleasant and sympathetic personality. She came of a theatrical family; by upbringing and inclination she was a regular churchgoer with a natural leaning towards good works. She was, in fact, the type of actress whom Irving had described so long ago to Charlie Ford as 'superior to the average of her sex'. It was therefore hardly surprising that, in the course of these rehearsals, he fell in love with the sweetest and prettiest girl he had ever met. After the play opened, he would escort her through the streets of Manchester to her home, where he often stayed to supper with her and her mother. Far too poor to consider the possibility of marriage, he was content to enjoy the friendship which she offered readily to him. Her companionship gave him much comfort, and the thought that one day, when his prospects had improved, he might declare his affection and perhaps win hers was an added spur to his ambition.

In May, E. A. Sothern, who, though born in Liverpool, had become one of the leading actors in the United States, came to Manchester with Tom Taylor's comedy, *Our American Cousin*. This indifferent play, which he had performed a thousand times, before he sailed for England in 1861, owed its success entirely to his superb caricature of an inane British nobleman, Lord Dundreary. Irving had no part in this play, but got good notices for his performance in the supporting piece, *My Aunt's Advice*. During this visit Sothern saw in Nellie Moore the perfect casting for Ada Ingot in the play about David Garrick which Tom Robertson was then writing for him.

Spring, however, was in the air and a whole summer was to pass before Nellie had to leave for London. In May, Irving's turn for a benefit came round again, with Walter Montgomery obliging as Hamlet and he himself playing Laertes. In July he got a glimpse of Charles and Ellen Kean, who gave a performance of *The Wife's Secret* before they left for Australia. He decided to spend a short summer holiday in giving readings in nearby towns. He drew no salary when the Theatre Royal was closed; so, in order to keep his head above water, he had to turn his holiday to account. By advertising himself as 'Mr. Henry Irving of the Theatres Royal, Edinburgh, Glasgow and Manchester', by distributing circulars containing the notices of his Crosby Hall recital, and by charging prices which ranged from sixpence to two shillings, he managed to pay his way and to keep himself until the Theatre Royal reopened.

The autumn and winter season, although he was getting more important parts, included too many revivals for his taste, although the critics were becoming more appreciative of his efforts. It was not until April in the New Year that he was able to cut another secure foothold on the slopes which he was trying to scale. Calvert produced *Romeo and Juliet* and decided to give Irving a chance as Mercutio—a testing part in which an actor of spirit and ability can prove himself. This he did to Calvert's satisfaction and to that of the Manchester critics who declared that they had never 'seen Mr. Irving to better advantage, he played the part well'. The following week when Samuel Brodribb scanned the pages of the London *Era* he read that his son 'portrayed the part well and his speech on Queen Mab was loudly applauded; less brusqueness of manner would have improved it'— a comment suggesting a vigorous and natural interpretation to which the writer was not accustomed.

The Theatre Royal company celebrated the tercentenary of Shakespeare's birth on April 23rd. with a series of tableaux and readings by Calvert. Irving was chosen to appear as John Philip Kemble in *Hamlet* after the portrait by Sir Thomas Lawrence. As he posed in the sable cloak and the plumed hat which in Kemble's day was the uniform of the tragedian, a daring plan began to germinate in his mind. His immediate preoccupation, however, was the rehearsal of the part of Hardress Cregan in the Irish melodrama, *The Colleen Bawn*, under the critical eye of its irascible author, Dion Boucicault.

Boucicault, who was born in Dublin, had gone on the stage as a boy of eighteen, and by the time he came of age had written and produced a five-act play, *London Assurance*, at Covent Garden, in which Charles Mathews and Vestris made so outstanding a success that it became a minor classic. In a short time he had established himself as a master of full-blooded melodrama. In 1860, after a visit to America, he took over the Adelphi Theatre in London where for sixteen years he wrote, produced and often acted in a series of plays which made the name Adelphi an adjective as attributive to melodrama as later Aldwych came to be of farce. In *The Colleen Bawn* Boucicault had struck a new reef in the goldmine of Irish genre which was to enrich generations of playwrights, lyricists, baritones and comedians who followed after him. Until his day the Irish were always looked upon, dramatically, as good for a laugh—as sources of comic relief, and the broader the better. Boucicault was the first to discover that, translated into terms of rich sentiment, the domestic life of his native land could wring tears from the toughest audience; in short, he created the Hibernian lachrymatory which has caused the eyes of two continents to stream with copious tears ever since.

Hardress Cregan was one of the best parts Boucicault ever wrote. As a hero charged with murder in the middle of preparations for his wedding and ultimately released when his supposed victim reappears, Irving had plenty of scope to win the sympathies of his audience and the praise of his producer. His Cregan lingered for a long time in the memories of Manchester playgoers; Boucicault, who found fault with the whole company, had no word of praise for the young actor; yet he, too, found the memory of his Manchester Cregan constantly recurring, long after *The Colleen Bawn* had been forgotten in the turmoil of launching his next project. Irving, though depressed by the indifference of a hard taskmaker whom he had done his best to please, found some consolation in the praise he received for his performances in the two plays that followed—*The Merchant's Storye* and a dramatisation of Mrs. Braddon's *Aurora Floyd*. The local press even admitted that he was becoming 'quite a favourite',—a happy augury for his benefit which he was to take on June 20th.

One night, in early June, Mr. W. H. Chippendale, an elderly actor who was on a visit to Birmingham, was entertaining a young friend, Charles Somerset, in the lodgings which they shared. Chippendale had been on the stage for over forty years, in the course of which he had played with all the great actors of his day, including Edmund Kean, Macready and Sullivan. They kept up their conversation until about two o'clock in the morning when, to their surprise, they heard a knock on the street door. Chippendale went downstairs and, drawing the bolts, found a gaunt figure standing on the doorstep. As he became accustomed to the half light, the figure resolved itself into a tall young man, pale and a trifle thin-drawn, whose clothes, though they had a certain distinction and even a touch of dandyism about them, were growing shabby from hard wear. The young man, in a quiet respectful voice, explained that he had seen a light in the upper room which he knew to be Mr. Chippendale's and, though it was late, he hoped that it might be possible to have a word with that gentleman.

'I am the man,' replied Chippendale. 'Who are you?'

'I am an actor,' answered the visitor. 'My name is Irving.'

'An actor?' repeated Chippendale, adding with a gesture of welcome, 'Then by all means come in'.

When they reached Chippendale's room the visitor explained that he was studying the part of Hamlet. Having heard that Mr. Chippendale had played Polonius to Edmund Kean's Hamlet, he had come to Birmingham for the few hours in which he could absent himself from Manchester, to ask him how Kean had played the closet scene. The old actor, recognizing the earnest sincerity of his youthful interrogator, began to describe the performance into which all the fire and imagination of Kean's genius had been poured, causing Hazlitt to speak of it as the greatest commentary ever made on Shakespeare. He recited in vivid terms how Kean, overcoming the first unfavourable reaction of his audience to a Hamlet of such short stature had, by the awe and filial piety of his encounter with the Ghost, by his sublime acceptance of the Ghost's revelation and of the awful mission which it imposed upon him, by his swift transition to forceful urgency as he swore his friends to secrecy, by the fire of his intellect and the exquisite vibrations of his voice, startled London playgoers into realizing how far they had travelled from the genius and fidelity of Garrick and how false and unsatisfying were the soulless ponderabilities of Kemble. Warming to his subject, Chippendale sprang from his chair and rehearsed Kean's successive moods in the closet scene—Hamlet's passionate and indignant indictment of Gertrude; the comparison between his father and uncle illustrated, not with the traditional miniatures or portraits, but in his mind's eye; the gentleness which with he strove to calm the anguish of his mother's mind; the alternating waves of his tenderness and passion, stilled into awed calm by the reappearance of his father's ghost. How much of this—and much more, as Chippendale rekindled the memory of his hero—Irving was able to assimilate even he could not tell. He left the house as dawn was breaking, richly rewarded for the time and money spent upon this intuitive journey. On his return to Manchester he announced that he would play Hamlet for his benefit.

This announcement was greeted by a certain amount of good-humoured chaff from his companions and with sceptical interest by the public. The old clichés about every clown wanting to play the Prince of Denmark were exchanged among those who regarded the twenty-six-year-old leading gentleman as a promising light comedian and nothing more. The company, however, rallied to his cause. Calvert agreed to play the Ghost and his wife to play Ophelia. It may have been Calvert who, wishing to enhance the authenticity of his earlier Scandinavian production, persuaded Irving to wear a blonde wig—though Fechter, in London, had already accustomed his audiences to this startling novelty.

Irving prepared himself for this self-imposed ordeal with quiet confidence. Benefits, as we have seen, could turn out to be forfeits. Failure to attract sufficient public interest could land a young actor, by the time he had paid off the expenses of an inexorable management, in a loss of twenty or thirty pounds. As he went around offering tickets to his friends and soliciting the support of sympathetic patrons, the headshaking and jocular prophecies as to the penalties of his rash audacity told him that at least his showmanship was not at fault, that a crowd will always collect to see a man riding for a fall. In the event, his Hamlet was clearly a patchwork affair; a little of the nature of Dillon, a touch of the gentle dignity of Booth, and a few damp squibs from the fireworks of Edmund Kean, with a gesture or two borrowed from Chippendale himself. On the night, the audience realized that, in an excess of friendly encouragement, they had disconcerted him by the warmth of their applause at his first entrance; Irving was glad enough, however, when at the end of each act they made amends by calling him before the curtain. The press were friendly; if none of the critics thought it necessary to describe in detail the successes or failures of this adventure, they were united in their sober encouragement and in their insistence on his lack of physical and vocal equipment.

The *Examiner*, for instance, declared that:

'. . . the attempt was a bold one but far from being a failure. In the more impassioned passages Mr. Irving wanted power, more from physical, however, than mental deficiency. Where the plaintive predominated—the noted soliloquy, "To be or not to be", for instance—, again in the advice to the Players and the other colloquial passages there was much for commendation—nor should we omit in this estimate the beautiful lines commencing: "What a piece of work is man", the poetry of which was finely appreciated by the actor. On the whole it was a performance which exhibited very considerable intelligence, and conscientious study, and well deserved the warm applause with which it was greeted.'

The *Guardian* adopted a more avuncular tone:

'When a man aims high, it does not always happen that he strikes high. To credit him with the intention, and record regretfully that his achievement does not equal it . . . to say that his personation was not such a success as one could wish for an intelligent and studious man, is simply to add his name to a long list of worthy actors who have done well in other histrionic spheres, even if they have not shone in the highest. A more robust physique than Mr. Irving has is wanted to make a Prince of Denmark, and consequently his voice was unequal to the demands which Hamlet makes upon it. This is a failing which no art can supply. But study can give a greater command over the vocal tones than Mr. Irving displayed; . . . judging by the applause of a full house our estimate of the hero's part was not endorsed by the public. . . .'

The *Courier* was more encouraging and its advice more practical:
'. . . The house knew well Mr. Irving's ability in light drama and scarcely expected an ideal Hamlet from him. It knew beforehand that Mr. Irving was unequal physically to the expression of the highest poetic power—and it therefore judged his efforts by the known strength of the actor as well as by the comparative success which he attained . . . he was best, and perhaps a little too off-hand and easy in ordinary dialogue, and at times, much too hasty for the development of the plot. In the Play scene, he was too impetuous in approaching the King, who ought to rise discomfited by the play, without having its meaning forcibly applied by Hamlet. At other times Mr. Irving found it difficult to avoid the gait and mien of comedy, or rather fell into it from long usage. Such things were to be expected and they are not mentioned disparagingly.'

All three notices betray a previous disbelief in his ability to play the part at all and to remark certain departures from the traditional reading as faults rather than as youthful experiments. None knew better than Irving himself the weaknesses and inadequacies of his performance; none was ever more determined than he that, if art could not supply his failings, industry could and would do so. No doubt he and Calvert sat up late into the night conducting a post-mortem on the dead Prince. Yet Irving knew that, with all his faults, he had held his audience and that his personality had forced from them an attention and appreciation beyond his deserts as an actor. He had been aware of this mysterious and exciting power at his command when he played Claude Melnotte in Edinburgh, during his readings at Crosby Hall, and in the crisis of his recent battle in Dublin. It was the glimmering of understanding that an actor can choose between the exercise or suppression of his personality in the pursuit of his art.

Irving played Hamlet twice more—on the 25th and on the July 9th—though without the support of the Calverts, who were preparing to leave the Theatre Royal and to open in October the now completed Prince's. In spite of the withdrawal of two such popular artists from the cast, both these performances were well attended, the press remarking on the increase of his power and the improvement of his interpretation. During these weeks H. L. Bateman, the American impresario, came to Manchester with his talented daughters, the eldest of whom, Kate, he presented in *Leah*, a biblical tragedy which he had recently produced at the Adelphi, London, with great success. Irving played Joseph—the *Examiner* declaring that they had 'never seen Mr. Irving in a character which suited him so well, or in which he has done better. His make-up was elegant and prepossessing and his acting that of the scholar and gentleman he was intended to represent'. The Batemans' visit was a short one. When the time came for Irving to say goodbye to Hezekiah Linthicum Bateman, whose generous nature combined a florid yet discriminating gift for showmanship with the paternal pride of Vincent Crummles, neither the ebullient manager nor the respectful leading gentleman can have had any idea that, between them, they were to change the course of theatrical history. Once again Irving, having now every right to suppose that he had earned the increasing favour of Manchester playgoers, was chastened by being given a series of inferior parts in the few new plays that went into the bill before the production of the Christmas pantomime. In the autumn, when the theatre had reopened after the summer holidays, Walter Montgomery had returned for a Shakespearian season in the course of which the erstwhile Hamlet had retired gracefully into the skin of Laertes.

Early in the new year a sudden burst of success and acclaim led Irving to hope that at last his years of drudgery were about to be rewarded. On February 18th he was allowed to play Robert Macaire, the whimsical French ruffian whose portrayal had brought fame overnight to the great French actor, Lemaître. It was a short piece, but it gave him a chance to experiment in the subtle mingling of high comedy and cold villainy in a single character. His performance may have been uneven, but to this most difficult aspect of it he succeeded in bringing humour and invention. The *Examiner*, while regretting the lack of robustness to which many excellent Macaires had accustomed them, conceded that 'coolness there was, and effrontery, but not of the devil-may-care sort necessary to throw out the prominent features of Macaire. Thus, the earlier portions of Mr. Irving's acting were most satisfactory, as requiring less energy and greater finish. From those strictures we except the death scene, in which he succeeded in producing a natural and impressive finale. We ought not to omit a hearty recognition of the tact displayed in the dance with the village girls: the fine gentleman in rags changing his one glove from one hand to the other as his partner changed sides, and maintaining his severe politeness to the very close was quite a masterly piece of acting'. The

Guardian, deploring his insuperable natural refinement as a handicap to convincing villainy, was puzzled by this dance with the peasant girl, describing it as 'full of oddity'. Nevertheless, his Macaire was well received and he was about to win even greater popularity in an entirely different métier.

Towards the end of 1864 England had been swept by one of its epidemic fevers of spiritualism. The false prophets on this occasion were the brothers William and Ira Davenport, who had come from the United States with a novel demonstration of the apparently fatuous concern of departed spirits in the entertainment of those they had left behind. They originated the now hackneyed routine of allowing themselves, while sitting in flimsy cabinets of their own design, to be trussed with ropes in such a way as to prevent them reaching a guitar and a tambourine which had been placed in the cabinet beside them. The lights of the hall were then extinguished and, in the course of a minute or two, a twanging of strings and a thumping of tambourines produced what was immediately recognized by the spellbound audience as unearthly music. The lights went up, revealing the brothers still trussed in their cabinet and the instruments lying undisturbed beside them on the floor. From this remarkable manifestation it was concluded that some frustrated shade with musical leanings had, in fact, recrossed the bourne to have a brief strum and to reassure unbelievers that life after death had its charms. In the course of their nation-wide tour, during which the two charlatans had brought false hope to thousands of simple folk, the Davenport brothers came to Manchester. A quasi-religious atmosphere was imparted to their antics by a bogus clergyman, the Reverend Dr. Ferguson, who, with unctuous homilies, reduced the audience to a devotional state of mind which was reckoned to protect the brothers from the scrutiny of sceptics. Manchester, however, proved to be the trio's Waterloo.

Irving, with little enough to engage his attention at the Theatre Royal, went with two fellow-actors, Philip Day and Fred Maccabe, to see this demonstration of occult powers. Irving's lingering methodism was outraged by what he regarded as vulgar blasphemy. His earlier association with Henry Palmer, with whom he had dabbled in mesmerism and such things, prompted him to try to expose the wretched fraud. It was not long before he and his two friends, who were equally convinced that the Davenports were humbugs, were able to devise a way of reproducing all of their ghostly phenomena by trickery. Their task was made easier by the fact that Fred Maccabe was a gifted amateur magician. A rehearsal was given before a few friends in a

Manchester club with such success that they decided to challenge the charlatans in public and to claim the hundred pounds which the rash Dr. Ferguson had offered to anyone who could as successfully invoke the spirits. They engaged the library hall of the Manchester Athenaeum where, on the afternoon of February 5th, there was assembled a large audience who were pleasantly mystified as to what they were in for, and no less intrigued when the leading gentleman from the Theatre Royal came onto the platform and addressed them thus:

'Ladies and gentlemen,—In introducing to you our experiments in what we, perhaps, have ostentatiously called "preternatural philosophy", I propose to explain to you as briefly as possible how this meeting has taken place, and the end we have in view in giving this semi-public séance.

The performance of the Davenport brothers was of a nature to fill some minds with wonderment, some to puzzle and perplex, whilst many, who would not own to either, took to derision and laughter. Three gentlemen, two of whom I shall have the honour of introducing to you, proved exceptions to what appears to have been the rule in the Davenport audiences. They were neither astonished, perplexed nor bewildered, nor did they content themselves by treating the affair with levity, but, in a matter-of-fact way, they said: "Here are effects apparently marvellous; there is no effect without a cause; these things are done somehow. If they are done by a supernatural power, we cannot accomplish the same; but if by a natural power, why, then we can also —if we discover the somehow."

Acting upon this, and beginning with the first axiom of Euclid, that the nearest way from one given point to another is by a straight line, they produced a line and proceeded like two philosophers to experiment. The result was a complete knowledge of the "somehow", and a full discovery of the trick. At a social gathering some ten days ago, a few friends were amused at a burlesque séance à la Davenport, in which I had the rather equivocal honour of impersonating a certain reverend Doctor. The result was so complete a reproduction of all the phenomena, that a committee was formed for the purpose of holding this assembly, in which our object is something more than mere amusement. What do the band of brothers profess to teach? What purpose beyond lining their pockets with money do they desire to obtain? They indignantly decline to be called conjurers; and while not venturing to define what was the precise nature of the occult power they professed to exercise, they wished people to understand that they were in some way connected with spiritualism—that, in their own words, they were producing a new hope to all mankind. So, if we can succeed in destroying the blasphemous pretensions of the unlicensed spirit-dealers, our object will be attained, and this meeting will not have been held in vain. I will assume, as well as I am able, the appearance and manner of the Doctor, and endeavour, as hastily as possible, to introduce him to you as our "media".'

Irving then retired, only to reappear in a minute or two, excellently made up as the Reverend Doctor, and, in perfect imitation of that gentleman's sanctimonious phraseology and delivery, introduced his two friends. Day and Maccabe then skilfully, and unaided by ghosts, performed every trick in the Davenport repertoire, while their friend provided a running commentary in the manner of Ferguson. The exposure was wholly successful. The audience went away delighted and well satisfied that the Davenports stood convicted of an impertinent fraud. The *Manchester Guardian* took up the cause and so advertised the wit and dexterity with which the burlesque had been planned and executed that Irving and his friends were forced to repeat their performance a week later in the Free Trade Hall. By that time the affair had been widely discussed and argued so that, an hour before the doors of the hall were to open, a crowd of the most respectable and influential citizens of Manchester were waiting eagerly for admittance. Once again the audience delighted in the discomfiture of the spiritualists and once more the press were extravagant in their praise of the exponents. Whether or not the Davenports acknowledged their defeat in terms of cash, they were no longer able to impose their deception unchallenged upon the public who, if they persisted in attending the séances, were the victims of their own wilful gullibility. The work begun by these young pioneers was continued by Maskelyne, the famous conjurer. Though they died hard, the Davenports and their associate spirits gave place in due course to other and more ingenious commercial travellers in psychic phenomena.

Irving had enjoyed the whole affair immensely. So, alas, had Knowles who, quick to see the money-making possibilities of this popular turn, told Irving to repeat the performance on the stage of the Theatre Royal. This was a totally unexpected development and involved a matter of principle on which, to the surprise of the manager, the young actor was unshakeable. To Irving, in spite of all the inferior plays which had been put upon that stage and in which he had, perforce, to play, that or any theatre was to him a temple, and the idea of repeating what had been a capital though not wholly frivolous lark on the boards of a playhouse was as unthinkable to him as singing a comic song in a Methodist chapel. He was adamant in his refusal to obey the manager; the manager, who was not accustomed to being crossed and had never valued Irving very highly, made this refusal the excuse for his dismissal. Thus, at the very moment when his stock seemed to stand higher than ever before, he found himself at the end of an engagement which had lasted for over four years; nor had he any immediate prospects of the advancement for which he had toiled so long. In such a situation he would not be able to pick or chose his next engagement. He was now twenty-seven years of age and still a poor man; there comes a point when age overtaking poverty means failure. Calvert sheltered him at the Prince's for a few days, during which he played the Duc de Nemours in *Louis XI*; his performance, the *Examiner* reported, was 'careful, intelligent, well studied throughout; the bedroom scene where the avenger checks his uplifted hand and spares the miserable Monarch's life, was a masterly display of art'.

In view of his difference with Knowles, Irving had no wish to embarrass Calvert with his presence longer than was absolutely necessary. He accepted the first offer of an engagement which came his way—once again from Edinburgh. When his friends—and in this respect he was a rich man—heard of his decision, they organized a benefit for him. Since Knowles was unlikely to offer either of his theatres for the purpose, they took the Free Trade Hall which, on April 12th, was crowded with his admirers and well-wishers. When he appeared to recite an ode which had been written for him by a local poet, he was received with loud and prolonged cheering. The bill included Irving as Jeremy Diddler, an entertainment by Maccabe and, by special request, a repetition of the Davenport burlesque which had been the cause of his departure. The audience showered applause and valedictions upon the young actor, who accepted them with the graceful humility of one who was leaving them for a wider sphere. Yet, though he showed a brave face to his friends, there was bitter despondency in Irving's heart, the weary resignation of the navigator who, knowing that his true course was for the south, must needs run north-east before the winds of adversity ere he could bear up and tack back over the too familiar gulf between him and the port of his desire.

CHAPTER VIII

Provincial Doldrums

After three weeks of unsalaried idleness, Irving left Manchester to join the company at the Prince of Wales's Operetta House, Edinburgh, a grandiloquent name which he knew well enough had been given to an ill-found hall that, in his Theatre Royal days, he had known as the Waterloo Rooms. He arrived in Edinburgh at the end of April, to find that in January the Princess's Theatre, faithful to tradition, had gone up in flames and that consequently, though Wyndham was feverishly building a new one, there was an unusual absence of competition. He had been engaged by Gardiner Coyne, an Irish comedian and vocalist, who was trying his hand at management in the hope, perhaps, of exploiting this temporary dearth of entertainment. His engagement followed that of Master Boulton, a five-year-old prodigy advertised as 'The Infant Roscius', whose diminutive genius had been exercised in what the bills described as 'A Petite Comedy'; Irving was billed to play leading parts in *The Dark Cloud* and *Robert Macaire*. He was well received, particularly in the latter part, by the local press, who were glad to fulfil their earlier prophecies of his success. The correspondent of the *Era* noted that 'An old Edinburgh favourite . . . received a hearty welcome back to the city' and that he played Macaire 'with delicate humour and a tragic dignity which usually are foreign to the character'.

Poorly supported and wretchedly presented, he played to the best of his ability. Notices of this kind were little consolation to an actor who took no pleasure in being a giant among pygmies. The short season ended on May 20th when he took his benefit. After another week with Calvert in Manchester, he found himself unemployed and ready enough to go to Bury where he played Hamlet for two nights, supported by a cast of amateurs which included Alfred Darbyshire, his old friend from Manchester, playing Polonius—a makeshift affair as unsatisfying to his self-esteem as it was to his acute financial need.

From Bury he drifted to Oxford, where, towards the end of August, he joined Mr. T. C. Cooper, another member of the old Theatre Royal company who, during the off season, ran a small theatre in the university town; the leading lady was another old friend, Miss Florence Haydon, whom he had last seen at his benefit in the Free Trade Hall. He stayed with Cooper for a fortnight. The repertoire included the usual melodramas and farces; even when he played Macduff to Cooper's Macbeth, the playgoers of Oxford were chiefly delighted by the length and vigour of the duel in the last act which was prolonged to indulge their incessant cheering. September was almost past; since April his letters to Nellie Moore, who was now an established favourite in Buckstone's company at the Haymarket, had been a melancholy tale of hand-to-mouth engagements, petty successes and periodical unemployment. From Oxford he went to Birmingham. On Tuesday, September 26th, Sothern, who was playing a week at the Prince of Wales's Theatre, was taken ill. Irving was hurriedly engaged to play the hero, Bob Brierly, in *The Ticket of Leave Man*, which was prepared overnight and put into the bill, in place of Sothern, on the Wednesday. This melodrama, adapted from the French by Tom Taylor, introduced a new character in fiction and drama who, by announcing: 'I am Hawkshaw, the detective!', provided successive generations with a catch-phrase and paved the way for Sherlock Holmes. Irving stayed in Birmingham for a month. While playing Laertes he was able to study Fechter's Hamlet, but he got damned by Edgar Pemberton, the local critic and biographer of Sothern, for his own performance.

In October his engagement with the Birmingham company ended with a visit to Liverpool, where they played *The Dark Cloud* at the St. James's Hall. The company disbanded; Irving was stranded in Liverpool. Two weeks of idleness exhausted his resources. During the past year his earnings had amounted to no more than £75, and the tally of his friends who had lent him odd half-crowns to tide him over his recurring financial crises was now as long as it was embarrassing. He had to pocket his pride and to take whatever work he could find. At the beginning of December he sailed to Douglas, Isle of Man, where for three nights he played in comedies and farces with a company of local amateurs. The costs of the journey left little change out of his meagre salary. On his return to Liverpool he was engaged for a week at the Prince of Wales's Theatre to play Archibald Carlisle in *East Lynne* in support of Miss Avonia Jones, the widow of the heroic Gustavus Brooke. Here he found a friend in the stage manager,

Thomas Higgie, whom he had first met at the Princess's Theatre, London, during the brief run of the ill-fated *Ivy Hall*.

At the end of the week Higgie, seeing that Irving was in desperate need, promised to do what he could to help him—though he could hold out no hope of immediate employment. As the year drew to a close Irving, shivering in his dreary lodging, husbanded his few remaining shillings and began to wonder where he should look for a meal when they were spent. His lofty ideals seemed more remote and unattainable than they had been ten years ago when he had set out for Sunderland. He felt that he was losing his sense of direction, that his foothold was insecure, and that he was sliding down a treacherous slope below which there yawned the abyss of failure and humiliation. By now he had lost most of his illusions about himself and his profession. He was bewildered by the turn his fortunes had taken. For a young actor his notices had been reasonably good; he had not entirely failed when he had set himself tasks which were admittedly beyond his powers, and he seemed to have made friends wherever he went or worked. Yet he found himself penniless and frustrated, unable to recognise the causes of his ill-fortune and so to be master of his own fate. That Christmas of 1865, far from being a season of hope and goodwill, sharpened the bitterness of Irving's despair and cheerless poverty.

A fortnight of the New Year had passed before a message from Higgie proved that his friend had been as good as his word. He was to return to the Prince of Wales's Theatre, Liverpool, to play in the dramatisation of another of Miss Braddon's novels, *Only a Clod*. Such notices as he got, while admitting his good qualities as an actor, picked upon his personal mannerisms—' . . . licking his lips, wrinkling his forehead and speaking through his nose'. Mr. Alexander Henderson, the manager of the theatre, told Higgie that he had made a mistake and that he should get rid of Irving; but once again a friendly stage-manager and fellow-actor saved Irving from dismissal. The following week Charles Mathews arrived with his new play, *The Silver Lining*, in which Irving had the part of Arthur Merrivale. Under the eye of his hero of straight comedy, Irving gave of his best. He had not met Mathews since the Glasgow days, but, during this week, a friendship sprang up between them which was to ripen and to end only when the great comedian died. The press acclaimed Irving's performance and, declaring that he shared the honours with Mathews, congratulated him on his 'artistic vividness'.

Sothern followed Mathews with another new play, *The Favourite of Fortune*, which he had just produced in Glasgow. Again Irving had a part which he could embellish with his gift for the sinister; indeed, he seems to have made of it more than the author had intended, for the *Porcupine*, a Liverpool weekly journal, reported that 'in his [Irving's] hands the character is such a perfect study, down even to the minutest detail, that . . . it seemed a pity to expand so much artistic elaboration on a personage of such comparative unimportance . . . he is a remarkable character actor and bestows an amount of attention on every part he plays that nearly always results in the most unquestioned triumph . . . every lineament of face, form and voice, and the thin black moustache gave a ghastly grimness to his smile that might freeze the blood in the veins of anyone over whom the wretch had power'.

In spite of these successes, Irving played only intermittently in farces and burlesques as the season dragged on into the summer. It was now becoming the custom for visiting stars to play their pieces for a week or two. Consequently, an actor in the stock company, if there happened to be no part for him in one of these plays, found himself without work or salary. Irving had his full share of unemployment. Early in July, during one of these periods of idleness, he called at the theatre for his letters and in the hope of hearing of further work; neither were forthcoming.

He lingered outside the stage-door, wondering what next he should do and what future lay in playing trivial parts so occasionally that what he earned in one was consumed in the course of waiting for the next. The brightness and beauty of the summer day accentuated his own depression and uncertainty. He knew that any man as ambitious as himself had to prevail in two fields; the outward struggle for pre-eminence in which he had to compete against his fellow-men on equal terms; the inner struggle to preserve his self-confidence in the face of material hardship and lack of recognition. Both battles were going against him—he was almost on his knees. Any vanity which may have supported him during his earlier trials had long ago evaporated. Only one thing kept him from surrender—a fanatical faith in the art he loved, and loved still in spite of his lack of facility, and the painfully slow progress he had made towards mastering its rudiments. Now there was nothing to fall back upon but the fixed habit of hope and effort. If this failed . . .

As he turned his back on the theatre, the stage-door-keeper hurried out with a letter which he had forgotten to give him. Irving opened it absent-mindedly—it was probably a bill—no—it bore a Manchester post-mark. It was a letter. He took a hasty glance at the signature— Dion Boucicault. The writer was about to produce a play in Manchester in which he believed there was a good part for him. Suddenly the colour of Irving's world was changed. He knew instinctively that this particular crisis was over. He was so certain of it that when he scribbled the reply in the stage-door-keeper's box, he had the presence of mind to accept Boucicault's offer on the condition that, if the play was sufficiently successful in the provinces to justify a London production, he should play the part in town.

In a day or two Irving joined Boucicault for rehearsals at the Prince's Theatre, Manchester. The play was *The Two Lives of Mary Leigh*. It was an unlikely tale of a woman who was prepared to make any sacrifice rather than be torn from her children; pursued by an inescapable past, she is finally hunted down; when exposure is inevitable, she leaves her beloved children rather than let them bear the scars of her infamy. Her persecutor was the unscrupulous Rawdon Scudamore, and it was for this part that Boucicault had secured the Hardress Cregan of his Manchester production of *The Colleen Bawn*. The part suited Irving to perfection—a polished and villainous adventurer. Kate Terry, who though only twenty-two had won a great reputation by acting with Charles Kean and Fechter, was to play Mary Leigh; she had been on the stage since she was a child, when, at the age of seven, she had appeared with Charles Kean before Queen Victoria at Windsor Castle as Arthur in *King John*.

On July 28th Irving returned to Liverpool for one night to play Robert Macaire for his benefit, which was well attended—proving that once again he had won the approbation of a provincial audience, though by now he had learnt how little this meant compared with the favour and patronage of managers. No doubt his popularity was in a measure due to the efforts of Edward Russell, the close friend of his years at Thackers, who was now working in the city as a journalist and well on his way to becoming the dramatic critic and later the editor of the *Liverpool Daily Post*. He was quick to appreciate the development of his friend's talent and delighted to witness his success, but distressed to hear of his misadventures and to recognise all too easily the harshness of his circumstances. Irving was delighted to see Russell again and to rally to his cause a loyal adherent who was to be one of his foremost champions in the years of conflict which lay ahead.

As Macaire, Irving soon had the large audience roaring and stamping with delight at the rich mixture of jocular misery and the tattered macabre of his interpretation. Perhaps it was Russell who wrote: ' . . . but for the accident that the end of the season had come Robert Macaire and Jacques Strop might have played their tragic comedy, their farcical burlesque of a melodrama many nights on the same boards; and the Liverpudlian dramatic world have been the wiser and better for the experience.' Henderson may have regretted his doubts about his leading gentleman, and having missed the chance of playing *Robert Macaire* for a run. But he gave no sign of it. The season ended and with it Irving's provincial purgatory.

The Two Lives of Mary Leigh opened on July 30th and was roundly condemned by the critics for its poor dialogue and far-fetched plot. They were, however, unanimous in their praise of Irving, whose study of Rawdon Scudamore held together the flimsy story. His mastery of technique and evident reserve of power took the house by storm, not only saving an indifferent play from failure but making it into a resounding success. Charles Reade, whose enormous output of plays and novels did not prevent him from dabbling in theatrical management, came to Manchester at Boucicault's invitation and, confirming the latter's high opinion of Irving, immediately offered to put on the play in London. A more attractive proposition came from Miss Louisa Herbert, who was at the height of her successful management at the St. James's Theatre and herself wished to play Mary Leigh. Boucicault closed with Miss Herbert, making it a condition, which she readily accepted, that Irving should play Rawdon Scudamore.

At last, now that the road to London lay clear, Irving could begin to feel the fulfilment of his destiny. Success or failure might await him, but he had chosen his own weapons for the assault. He had a part in which he could not fail to challenge the attention of London playgoers; if he won their acclaim, the years of drudgery and squalid hardship were over. Truth to tell, he had no thought of failure. Before he left Manchester he had to finish his engagement by playing in succession the Ghost in *Hamlet*, Bob Brierly and the leading part as Fouché in *Plot and Passion*, a popular drama based on episodes in the French Directory. He may well have astonished Manchester by following up his Rawdon Scudamore with such an exhibition of versatility; if so, their applause fell upon deaf ears. He was beyond being flattered by the praise or wounded by the obloquy of the north; this was the last they would see of him unless and until he returned in triumph from the south.

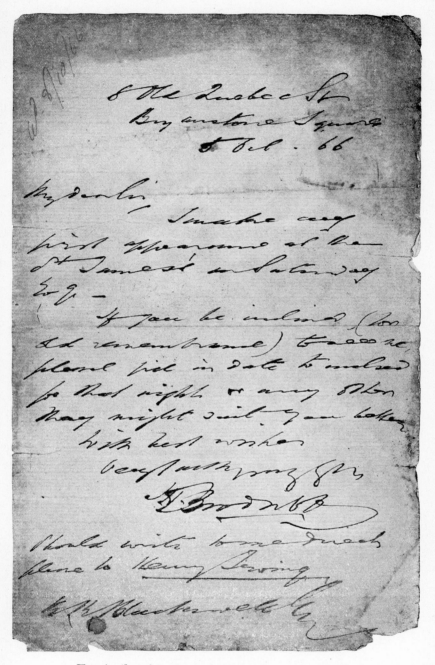

Facsimile of Irving's invitation to Mr. Blackwell

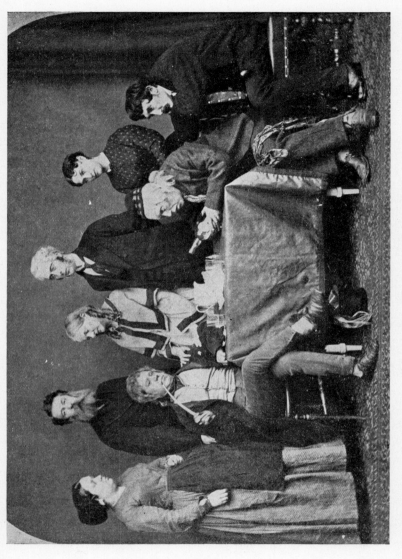

The *Dearer than Life* Company

Charles Wyndham, Mrs. Mellon, John Clayton, Henrietta Hodson

Unknown   J. L. Toole   Lionel Brough   Henry Irving

CHAPTER IX

London Regained

C harles Reade, Dion Boucicault and Tom Taylor formed a literary triumvirate, who, by their staggering energy and prolific output, did much to jerk the moribund English theatre into life. They were the leaders of a school of dramatists who, with indefatigable zest, churned out original farces and melodramas; adapted any French plays they could lay hands on or surreptitiously transcribe from their stalls in the Boulevard du Temple; dramatized other men's novels while fighting for their own copyright against the pirates of America; rushed hither and thither in search of dramatic plunder, actors of talent or money for the production of their plays; made and lost small fortunes, and lived strenuously the lives of authentic bohemians. All three men were scholars of a kind (Reade was Vice President of Magdalen College, Oxford), yet the crude melodramas which formed the bulk of their work were written with the passionate sincerity which is the first requirement of popular success. Reade and Taylor were huge, bearded and irascible—indeed, though they collaborated in writing *Masks and Faces*, they quarrelled before the ink was dry; Boucicault, with the domed head and curly tonsure of a sage, was seething with lurid plots and Irish passion yet was readily moved to sentimental tears. *Masks and Faces* and Boucicault's *London Assurance* were the only works which were to survive their generation; the rest withered before the sparkling realism of Robertson's comedies and the warm glow of the romantic revival. It is remarkable that these ingenuous and sensational plays were acceptable to men and women whose discriminating taste in other directions was beyond dispute. When Dickens, Wilkie Collins and the painter, Augustus Egg, collaborated in writing and in performing for the entertainment of their friends, *The Frozen North*, a highly cultivated audience seems to have enjoyed every minute of this incredibly naïve and artificial confection. The theatre was, to eminent Victorians of that kind, a place apart; a place where they see could great actors and actresses performing to the top of their bent, where they could delight in the ingenuity of the machinist and in the stage pictures of the scene painters—in a world of make-believe where they could surrender themselves to illusion. Real life never got through the stage-door; the audiences left their critical standards in the foyer with their hats and cloaks, only too ready to recapture the enchantment of children with their first toy theatre. The very playbills with their exclamatory typography, magniloquent advertisement and enticing hints of gory scenes and gaudy spectacles were an invitation to a paradise of unreality. To a later generation these unsophisticated plays and uninhibited players must seem as artless as our own mumbled modernities may appear to future playgoers enjoying another romantic revival. Be that as it may, this was the stuff of the London theatre at the end of 1866; few of its devotees were conscious of its absurdity while the most profound critics took Hamlet and Hawkshaw in their stride. John Oxenford, the dramatic critic of *The Times*, wrote or adapted sixty-eight plays to the popular taste, while E. L. Blanchard, the much-loved and genial critic of the *Daily Telegraph*, was, during the autumn of this year, busily writing his twenty-seventh pantomime for the Theatre Royal, Drury Lane, which this year was to be *Number Nip or The Gnome King of the Giant Mountain.* At the Royal Opera House, Covent Garden, the management was getting ready another pantomime of equal splendour. At the Haymarket, Sothern was rehearsing Tom Taylor's *A Lesson for Love*, while Fechter, at the Lyceum, was soon to open with *Rouge et Noir*, a drama which would disclose the evils of gambling and his own charms as a romantic hero. A version of Dickens' *Barnaby Rudge* with a mediocre cast was to be to be seen at the Princess's. This was all the theatre had to offer discriminating play-goers for that autumn and winter season—all except at one other play-house, the Prince of Wales's, where Miss Marie Wilton was playing in Tom Robertson's comedy, *Ours*, to such crowded houses as to suggest that there was a growing public eager for better things.

Irving arrived in London towards the end of September and presented himself to Miss Herbert at the St. James's Theatre. Miss Herbert was at the peak of her long term of management of this theatre which she had taken in 1860. With herself as star, she had enjoyed uninterrupted success for nearly seven years. Undoubtedly she owed this to her talent and personality, which she demonstrated in a wide variety of parts ranging from Lady Audley to Lydia Languish. She was adored and respected by Charles Reade and his friends, who voted her 'a superb creature'; indeed her heavenly beauty and refinement of taste had inspired Rossetti, at the suggestion of Ruskin, to use her as a model for the substantial type of angel which thronged the heavenly courts of his pre-Raphaelite visions.

Rehearsals were begun at once of Boucicault's play, the title of which, by mutual agreement, had been changed to the more striking one of *Hunted Down*. Irving was appointed stage-manager and found himself one of a distinguished company which included Walter Lacy, who had won his spurs in the companies of Vestris and Charles Kean, and Frank Matthews and old Addison, long experienced light and broad comedians. It became apparent very soon that *Hunted Down* could not be prepared by October 6th, the date fixed for the opening. To Irving's dismay, Miss Herbert decided to gain time by putting on *The Belle's Stratagem*. In addition to the disadvantages of the hasty preparation which such a change involved, Irving found himself cast for Doricourt, a part which, although he had played it before, he knew well enough did not suit him—that of a polished man of fashion who only became alive, from Irving's point of view, when he had to affect insanity. It was also slightly disillusioning for a stage-manager who was only too ready to be impressed with the high standards of the metropolitan theatre so long the subject of his dreams, to find himself juggling with a rough and ready fit-up of stock scenery in which an exterior cottage wing had to serve as half of an elegant interior, its rural beauties barely concealed by a portrait conveniently hung upon it. The rehearsals, however, went along smoothly. The old stagers like Walter Lacy were friendly and helpful and full of good advice, feeling it perhaps their duty to modify the rather novel methods of this young provincial actor. During the first day of rehearsal his position as a newcomer had been made easier by the unexpected appearance of Charles Mathews, who had skipped onto the stage and, buttonholing Lacy and the comedian Frank Matthews, had said: 'Ah, Frank me boy, Walter—a moment! My young friend Irving—Frank—Walter! Be kind to him! Goodbye—God bless you!' and with that introduction vanished as suddenly as he had appeared.

The play opened on October 6th. In the earlier scenes Irving felt instinctively that the audience were unimpressed by his Doricourt. They remained cold and indifferent until the mad scene in which Irving exerted every ounce of his skill and personality. At last he felt he had them with him. Nevertheless he was startled when, upon his exit, their applause was so loud and sustained that he had to reappear in the middle of the act and to decline to give the excited audience the

encore which evidently they desired—an extraordinary ovation which
he never failed to get during the rest of the run. The press, on the whole,
reflected the mood of the audience; they were critical of his early and
straightforward scenes, but unanimous in their praise of his effective
coup de théâtre. As things had turned out, he had no cause for anxiety;
his first appearance in a part which he disliked had passed off well
enough. It was on Rawdon Scudamore that he fixed his hopes.

For four weeks before the production of *Hunted Down* Irving's
hands were full. In addition to acting at night and rehearsing the new
play, he was busy with the stage-management of a burlesque which
was to be included in the bill—*Dulcamara, or A Little Duck with
a Big Quack*. The author had been introduced to Mrs. Herbert as a
stage-struck officer in a Highland Militia Regiment. He was, in fact,
a talented young barrister who, in addition to his legal and military
duties, was contributing articles and drawings to the weekly paper, *Fun*;
his name was W. S. Gilbert. Gilbert seemed to be grateful for any
hints he could get from the stage-manager, who was full of praise
for his first dramatic work; after rehearsals he often took Irving back
to his chambers, where they discussed the burlesque and how best
they could make it more effective.

The audience which assembled for the opening night of *Hunted
Down* was unusually distinguished. Perhaps gossip had gone the round
of the clubs that the principal character in Boucicault's new play was
to be a Royal Academician played by Walter Lacy. In a stage box
sat George Eliot with G. H. Lewes, the editor of the *Fortnightly
Review*. Nearby was Lord Lytton, and with him Lord Stanhope,
the progenitor of the National Gallery, whom he had persuaded to
pay one of his rare visits to the theatre. In the stalls, surrounded by
a heavy battery of critics, sat Mr. Blackwell, of Thackers, to whom
Irving had offered a seat—'if you be inclined, for old remembrance,
to see me'. Throughout the audience there was no doubt a buzz of
conjecture about the young actor from Manchester of whom Boucicault
spoke so enthusiastically. Irving could hardly have wished for a more
eclectic jury before whom to submit himself for trial.

At the end of the first act, when he was called before the curtain,
Irving felt that the verdict was not in doubt. As George Eliot turned
to leave her box at the end of the play, which had been well received,
she said to Lewes:

'What do you think of him?'

'In twenty years,' replied Lewes, 'he will be at the head of the
English stage.'

'He is there, I think, already,' murmured the novelist.

After the performance Irving was taken by his new friend Gilbert to the Arundel Club in Salisbury Street, a fashionable resort of artists, critics and men of letters. When he entered the crowded smoking-room, any doubts that he may have had about the morrow's press were dispelled. Introductions invariably led to congratulations, and, if the provincial actor was not entirely at his ease in finding himself the centre of interest of such brilliant company, it was due to his own inability to realize the sudden reversal of his fortunes rather than to any lack of friendliness on their part. His host guided him through groves of literary gentlemen, to the sacred bower where Tom Robertson, in splendid isolation, held a group of critics spellbound with his pungent and cynical conversation. Later, Sir Baldwyn Leighton drew him to one side and introduced him to the great French critic, Schérer, who had been much impressed by his performance. Schérer asked Irving about his childhood and, on hearing of his West Country background, said: 'You may call yourself a son of Somerset, but your temperament and genius, like other things about you, are those of a Celt. You will yet introduce to the stage a churchman such as your Glastonbury reared.'

Strange words to fall upon the ears of a light comedian with a gift for interpreting polished villainy.

If the evening had had a dream-like quality, the next day's newspapers gave him solid satisfaction. The critics not only praised him but—of far greater importance to him—they recognized and approved the novelty of his method. All were agreed upon his freedom from exaggeration or convention and upon his remarkable powers of depicting his feelings by dint of facial expression rather than by the 'blue fire' extravagance of the old school. The *Illustrated Times* went into greater detail:

. . . 'When he is seedy, his seediness is not indicated by preposterous rages or by new trousers with a hole in them; his clothes are clothes that are well—but not too well—worn. In the second act, which shows him under more prosperous circumstances, his prosperity does not take the form of flashy coats, white hat and patent leather boots; he is dressed just as a roué of some taste . . . would dress himself . . . the cool quiet insolence with which he treats his devoted wife—the insolence of a man who is certain of her love, and wishes he were not— is the finest piece of undemonstrative acting that I have seen since I saw Mr. Hare as Prince Perovsky.'

Irving found himself overnight, if not famous, at least a distant comet in the theatrical firmament whose course would in future be watched keenly by critical astronomers. Nothing gave him greater happiness than the delight of his friends in his success. One morning Charles Mathews, having read a bad notice of Irving's performance, left his breakfast table and dashed off to offer his advice and consolation to his young friend. He and Toole made it their business to introduce Irving to their circle of friends. Above all he was able to lay his success at the feet of Nellie Moore and, once again, at the end of the evening's work, to fetch her from the Haymarket and to escort her to her home where he seemed to be as welcome as ever. The Moores were now his neighbours; it was only a short walk from their house off Soho Square to the rooms which he had taken in Old Quebec Street. For the first time for ten years he was able to enjoy a convivial Christmas and to look forward with confidence to the coming year. His parents had left London and had returned to Bristol, where they were living with his Uncle Thomas, the ironmonger, and his two aunts. Samuel had received a steady stream of laudatory cuttings from his son, which he had transcribed proudly in copper-plate handwriting, into a notebook. In January Irving wrote:

January 28th, 1867.

'My dear Father,

On Saturday I will send you £2. I have had very heavy calls this week. It's very annoying and all most distressing to be so worried but it is useless complaining and the matter must be faced and got rid of. I send you this, another batch of papers. You must think them very good. The *Glowworm* is very fine. My part is a great hit and talked of in all circles. Our present bill (by the bye I'll get one and send you) is supposed and said to be the best in London. The first piece is finely acted and the second—the burlesque—is magnificently mounted. I never saw anything to equal it. Business fine. No free admissions *now*. . . .

. . . I have been keeping up the season with parties at C. Mathews, Toole's, Howard Paul's, Bancrofts, etc., who has at last announced his marriage.

I know what might have caused enquiries similar to those you heard of some time ago—but they were premature. I have no engagement or prospect whatever of marriage.

I shall be glad to have a few words from you—it is long since I have heard.

With love to my aunts and Mother,

Affectionately yours,
Henry.'

Money was still short and likely to be so for some time; though the prospect of marriage was remote, the hope of it was strong. For Nellie's affection seemed unchanged and their relative positions in the world of the theatre were restored once more. The seasonal parties presented Irving with new problems.

Shortly before Christmas, he was invited to an evening party by Clement Scott, the dramatic critic of the *Sunday Times*, to whom he had been introduced at the Arundel Club. Scott had been greatly impressed by the natural strength of Irving's acting and believed that he would be the first to break down the artificialities of the old school. He was employed as a junior clerk in the War Office; perhaps it was the distraction of the drama which prevented him raising any higher on the moving staircase of public service. He was rather too emotional to be a judicial critic, but he loved the theatre and devoted columns of erudite comment and florid dissertation to its service. Irving set out for the party in high spirits. Unfortunately he went to the wrong house in Linden Gardens, a mistake which was to have grievous consequences. As the maid was explaining to him his error, a tall, distinguished-looking girl came into the hall. Taking in the situation at a glance, she introduced herself to him—Miss Florence O'Callaghan —adding that she lived there with her mother and sister and that her father, Surgeon-General O'Callaghan, was in India where he had been serving for several years. A keen playgoer and amateur of the theatre, Miss O'Callaghan had recognized the much-discussed actor and very soon discovered that they were both bound for the same party. She invited Irving to escort her to Clement Scott's house. When they arrived it became apparent to Irving that Scott and Miss O'Callaghan were on the friendliest terms. He could not have known that the friendship was so deep as to have inspired Scott to write this handsome girl flirtatious odes, one of which ended:

> And I'll place your dear image high up in my thoughts
> Away from all sorrow and woe
> And pray that the day may be granted me yet
> To guard and protect my loved Flo.

—passable verses perhaps for a junior clerk, but no great shakes for an intellectual critic. Anyhow, neither Scott's verses nor his charms were enough to prevent Miss O'Callaghan falling, then and there, in love with Irving. Of this Irving, whose thoughts were only of Nellie Moore, was blissfully unaware—at least for the time being.

Hunted Down ran till February 8th, and was followed by Holcroft's *Road to Ruin,* in which Irving played a repentant rake. Oxenford, of *The Times,* described his performance in unusual detail:

'Mr. Henry Irving's Harry Dornton is a more than a promising performance by an actor who has only been known to London the last few months, and who has entered a department which stands in need of recruiting. His first appearance supposed to follow many hours of dissipation, when, in a condition vulgarly called "seedy", he lolls about in a fashion half careless, half sulky, is excellently conceived, and his latter scenes are marked by a most accurate delineation of that sort of inebriety which neither brutalizes nor stupefies, but into which some men naturally plunge if they would screw themselves up to the preparation of some desperate act. Against the substantial good qualities of Mr. Irving is to be set off a certain ungainliness of manner which lessens the effect they ought naturally to produce.'

The rest of the press were divided in their opinions, some comparing him to Fechter, others missing a certain elegance of manner as they had done in his Doricourt, but all speaking highly of the stronger passages. The play ran for a month. Already rehearsals had begun of *The Rapid Thaw,* an adaptation from Sardou which was to follow it. About this time, Irving received a letter from Miss O'Callaghan, who, first with messages through Clement Scott and then by direct correspondence, had kept alive the memory of their chance encounter, inviting him and Scott to dine at her mother's house on Sunday evening. In a qualified refusal, sugared with gallantry, he gave his opinion of the part allotted to him in the new play:

'My dear Miss O'Callaghan,
I have had for some weeks past a sword hanging above me and on Sunday (I trust you will be grieved) it must fall. The torture which I have so long delayed and must at last endure, is an evening with a gentle reverential husband and a wife who is "darkly deeply beautifully blue"—at least I fear her stockings are.

Never, with my desire, shall Clementina *alone* enjoy the pleasures offered to us both. A letter to the War Office (odds steel traps and spring guns) will reach him, but perish the thought that the invitation went through me! Envy is a malignant passion and I think I may be reasonably pardoned for refraining to present the poisoned cup to my own lips.

Do not think that I shall fail to see you—no nothing over which I may have control shall prevent that. I'll see you, if but to wish a kind goodnight.

. . . I regret though that Mrs. Frank's information is rather faulty. I shall play the O'Hooligan and I fear it will be my next part. As you appear to take an interest in my theatrical doings, let me assure you that I am sincerely amazed that I have undertaken to enact the lout— as it is. Nay my vanity be pardoned, when I beg you to think that the character will cause me much trouble to impersonate.

. . . I have today had an interview with Fechter, a most flattering offer of engagement—which at present for sundry weighty reasons, of which anon, I have declined.

Entre nous, I beg.

Until Sunday adieu,

Believe me,

Most sincerely yours,

Henry Irving'

The trouble was short-lived for the play, which, with the actors, got a mixed reception, was hurriedly withdrawn. Irving next appeared as Joseph Surface in a hastily prepared production of *The School for Scandal*; the *Illustrated Times* alone commended him for substituting a polished scamp for the hangdog villain of tradition. Probably he had no difficulty in persuading Miss Herbert to allow him to play Robert Macaire in order to fill in time until a drama founded on Ouida's novel, *Idalia*, was ready. Miss Herbert must have had high hopes of this play, for she mounted it lavishly. To give added realism a tank of water was introduced to the setting, which, on the first night, over-flowed. As always with such mishaps, the audience delighted in the discomfiture of the actors; in spite of the inundation, the play had a moderate success. Irving played a ruthless Italian Count; the notices were briefly appreciative of his efforts.

A newcomer, Charles Wyndham, had joined the cast for this play. This handsome young actor seemed to be comparatively well-to-do and, as the owner of a dress suit, brought a certain distinction to the dressing room which Irving had invited him to share. Charles Wyndham was the son of a doctor named Culverwell; though born in this country, he had but recently returned from America, where, after a brief appearance on the New York stage in 1861, he had been serving as a military surgeon with the Southern armies in the Civil War. Irving, since he had appeared in *Hunted Down*, had received a number of letters from an anonymous admirer who complimented him on his work and offered him what was obviously practical criticism and advice; all his attempts to solve this flattering mystery were made in vain. One night, during the run of *Idalia*, Irving came into the dressing-room with a letter in his hand. It was an invitation to a reception given by Mrs. Sartoris, a lady better known as Adelaide Kemble, a niece of the renowned John Philip Kemble, who had herself won fame as an opera singer at Covent Garden. Wyndham was delighted with this social and artistic compliment to his friend and readily agreed to Irving's proposal that he should lend him the dress suit for the occasion.

On arriving at the reception, the slightly abashed young actor was soon put at his ease by his hostess, who confessed that it was she, with the help of Frederick Leighton, the Royal Academician, who had written the anonymous letters. Her son had been at the first night of *Hunted Down* and had insisted upon her going to see the actor who was playing Rawdon Scudamore. Immediately impressed by Irving's talent, and anxious to encourage him, she had adopted a subterfuge which now need no longer hide her confessed admiration nor impede the help and encouragement she was ready to give him if he was ready to accept it. Irving found this all very flattering and agreeable. When he came into the dressing-room on the following night Wyndham asked him how he had got on at the party.

'Oh, all right,' replied Irving. 'It was very pleasant. But,' he continued, 'there was a man there whom I envied—desperately. He entered the room with quiet assurance, greeted Mrs. Sartoris as though he were conferring a favour upon her, and took a seat with a dignity that one might have expected in a duke.'

'Who was he?' asked Wyndham.

'Oh—nobody; a noodle, as it turned out.'

Behind the footlights Irving had already outgrown Brodribb. Robbed of their screening protection, Brodribb was without his armour of self-assurance. That noodle taught him the necessity and possibility of Irving assuming a social self-possession which Brodribb had little chance of acquiring.

Miss Herbert's season ended with the usual round of benefits. Irving, for his own, once more played Rawdon Scudamore. For the first time in his life he looked forward to the end of an engagement, for he had arranged to join his old friend, Edward Saker, in an expedition to Paris; both had been engaged by Sothern, who was taking a company to play *Our American Cousin* at the Théâtre des Italiens, by way of showing the English theatrical flag amidst the other festivities of the Great Exhibition.

CHAPTER X

The Classic Revelation

———❦———

I t is easy to understand that Parisian playgoers were completely
bewildered by the antics of that peculiar and twaddling English
nobleman, Lord Dundreary, although many of them came to
wear the style of whiskers which, thanks to Sothern's make-up,
forever enshrined his name in the English dictionary. The French
critics who had assembled to pity or to condemn were reduced to
helplessness and left the theatre murmuring to each other: 'C'est
étonnant!', their retreat being covered by Napoleon the Third, who,
with an eye on the future, made certain that his applause was as visible
as it was energetic. The English colony were transported; their cheers
and applause were as hearty and indiscriminating as those they would
have accorded to any team of their fellow-countrymen competing in a
foreign capital. At the close of the run, Irving, who was at liberty
until he had to rejoin Miss Herbert for a provincial tour in August,
lingered in Paris. He was able to live in a garret for a few francs a day
and to pay nightly visits to the cheap parts of the theatres. Although
his knowledge of the language was slight, he set himself to study the
French theatre in all its aspects. The effect of this experience on one
who, knowing only the rough-and-tumble methods of his own
country, thought of acting as a fine art, must have been profound
and not a little disturbing.

Here, in Paris, Irving saw for the first time a school of drama,
refined and disciplined by two centuries of unbroken tradition. At
the Comédie Française he discovered a style of play-acting and of
dramatic writing which, with all its superb technical accomplishments,
sprang directly from the genius of Molière. The perfection of dialogue,
of situation, of diction, of gesture and of movement revealed to him
an academic development of the actor's art which laid bare the weaknesses of his own blundering and untutored apprenticeship. In both
countries the State had exercised control over the drama. In England,

this control had been capricious, confused and wholly unconcerned with artistic excellence; in France the royal prerogative had been expressed in terms of enlightened patronage, protection and subsidy. Paradoxically, up to the time of the Revolution there was a deep gulf between the French aristocracy and theatrical artists which was only bridged by amorous liaisons, while actors and actresses at their death were denied the consolations of the Church or burial in hallowed ground. In England an actor of distinction was tolerated and even cultivated by the world of fashion, and he could count, when the time came, upon six feet of consecrated English soil. Thus, at the very time when Mrs. Oldfield, the inexpert yet brilliant Queen of Drury Lane, was being buried in Westminster Abbey, the corpse of Adrienne Lecouvreur, mistress of elaborate art and leader of the Théâtre Français, was being hurried in a cart through the dark streets of Paris to an unknown grave beyond the town. Yet the French theatre, preserving its continuity, blossomed into an exquisite, if artificial flower; while in England actors of great genius had come and gone in a series of unrelated explosions, leaving nothing behind them but a wasteland of confused styles and techniques. It was also apparent that, whereas Molière had founded a school of writing which had been capable of imitation and development by his successors, the genius of Shakespeare was so stupendous that English dramatists either challenged it by feeble imitation or surrendered to it by deliberately lowering their aim.

Thus, as Irving haunted the Comédie Française, he bowed in veneration before the silver-tongued Delaunay, who, with studied periods and melodious emphasis, conveyed the ardour of young love with grace and perfection, though on the eve of his half century, before the rich profundity of Gôt's tragi-comedy, and before the finished by-play between Jean-Baptiste Bressant and Madame Plessy in the most artificial of comedies. He watched with something near jealousy young Coquelin, three years his junior, yet already steeped in the delivery and posture of tradition, free to develop his genius with materials of which he was already a master. Here was a refinement of art to which he knew he could never now attain, an easy mastery of a craft, the feeling for anatomy and sound craftsmanship which underlay the vigorous strokes of original interpretation. No wonder, Irving thought, the crumbs of gait and gesture which, like an eager, hungry sparrow, he had picked up from the older actors as he went along, seemed to his critics to be uncoordinated mannerisms and affectations; no wonder his voice, the uncertain music from a damaged instrument which he had repaired with his own clumsy fingers, must, to those who had been charmed by the mellifluous cadenzas of these Frenchmen, seem coarse, strained and incapable of sustaining a tirade. There was no self-pity in this sudden understanding of the lightness of his equipment and of the limitations of his technical armoury. He was, perhaps, grateful for this revelation of the art which he adored. But such academic triumphs were not for him. Triumph he would, for he knew that within him smouldered the lightning of animal magnetism which, leaping the gap of the proscenium, sent its vital current through the audience, until, returning to its dynamic source, it held actor and audience in the grip of its mystical circuit. If consolation were needed he had but to think of the dying Lemaître, who, though rejected by the Academies, had been the god of the boulevards. He may for a night or two have drawn courage in the theatres from which his own art sprang, the Cluny and the Porte St. Martin, whose melodramas had crossed the Channel, where they were laced with brandy, sugar sweetened, and rebottled to suit the palates of his countrymen. There must be a beginning. Even if his artistic origins were as humble as his parentage and his materials coarse and untrimmed, it lay in his power to raise a temple to his muse in which his successors might find the elements of a tradition.

CHAPTER XI

Villainy and Tragedy

———◦═◦═◦———

Irving, his mind slowly digesting these deep impressions and formulating new resolutions, returned to London and in August set out with Miss Herbert's company for Manchester, where their tour was to begin. Their repertoire included *The Belle's Stratagem*, *School for Scandal*, *She Stoops to Conquer* and Charles Mathews's version of Foote's comedy, *The Liar*. In less than a year he was return-to his old battlegrounds with the hallmark of London approval on a talent which each great city claimed as its own discovery; Irving forbore to remind them that in biting it to test its purity they had come near to swallowing it altogether. Manchester, Dublin, Bath and Bristol welcomed the prodigal with sober praise, all stressing the quiet force and finish of his playing.

The tour ended at Liverpool, where he was invited to remain for a further week to add lustre to the opening of the winter season at the Prince of Wales's Theatre by playing Ashley Merton, another scoundrel, in *Meg's Diversion*, a comedy in the Robertsonian style by H. T. Craven. The *Liverpool Post*, already becoming a stronghold of his partisans under the leadership of his banner-bearer, Edward Russell, found it difficult 'to drive away the impression that there is any role superior to him'; the *Courier* admitted that he had 'fully proved his right to be placed in the first position on the stage as a light character eccentric comedian.' He returned to London well satisfied with the demonstrations he had made of his change of fortune.

He had been engaged to play at the St. James's Theatre in support of an American actor, John Sleeper Clarke, a brother-in-law of Edwin Booth, who was to make his first appearance in London. The light comedies which Clarke had chosen for his début were designed to show off his gifts as an eccentric comedian; in all of them his own part completely dwarfed the rest, Irving's among them. There had been, moreover, a misunderstanding about Irving's salary. He had been engaged to play for his previous salary, which had included an additional remuneration as stage-manager. Finding that he was no longer stage-manager and that his salary had been reduced accordingly, after a month of unrewarding parts and fruitless bargaining, he gave notice and left the theatre. He was beginning to know his own worth and to react sharply to injustices of this kind.

Irving did not have long to wait for an engagement. The short interval of idleness, however, gave him time to face a crisis in his private life. When he and Nellie Moore met again in London, they found that their old affection for one another, which had so nearly blossomed into an engagement, had somehow become tarnished. Both were ambitious, both were the subject of dressing-room gossip, and each may have imagined cause for jealousy of the other. Irving was proud and sensitive. It may have needed only the whisper of some ill-intentioned Iago to make him doubt the loyalty and sincerity of a girl whom, without doubt, he loved deeply to her dying. day. So the affair, such as it was, was broken off. No doubt news of the breach came to the ears of Florence O'Callaghan, probably through their mutual friend, Clement Scott, who had become engaged to George Du Maurier's sister and was glad enough to bring their flirtation to a neat conclusion. Miss O'Callaghan, whose correspondence with Irving had been reciprocated in warm, if formal terms, now made more open advances to him; there was no doubt, at least in the minds of her own family, that she was desperately in love with him. If any spur were needed it was provided by the Surgeon General who, as soon as the news of his daughter's infatuation for an actor had reached him in India, flew into a passion and forbade her to see or to have any communication with Irving for at least a year. Even bad news travelled slowly from India. By the time the interdiction arrived, it only served to add the charm of a clandestine romance to mutual attraction. Nevertheless, Daniel O'Callaghan, even at that extreme range, exercised a stern authority over his family, who would not have dared openly to disobey him.

O'Callaghan, whose Irish forebears had entered the service of the Kings of Spain at the beginning of the previous century and had later returned to Ireland to claim a modest property in County Clare, had entered the Indian Medical Service after a brief experiment in the Royal Navy. He had been at Meerhut at the outbreak of the Indian Mutiny and had become convinced that had his Commanding Officer taken his advice the Mutiny could have been localized and quickly stamped out. In proof of this he published a pamphlet which should have earned him a court martial but seems, on the contrary, to have speeded his promotion to Surgeon General. The O'Callaghans were a good-looking lot. Daniel married Elizabeth Walsh, the sister of 'Handsome Walsh', Master-at-Arms to William IV and Queen Victoria. Elizabeth O'Callaghan was a daughter of her age and position. Her early married life had been spent in India, where both her daughters were born. She was a woman of courage and conviction, beset by false values and social pretensions which she had inculcated in her daughters whom, however, she had endowed with more than average beauty. The serenity of her social horizon was clouded only by the knowledge that her brother-in-law, under the name of Donovan, had opened a phrenologist's establishment in Ludgate Circus, which had become a flourishing concern and excited an embarrassing curiosity in her children. By loyally executing Daniel's instructions and by disparaging the object of Flo's devotion whenever opportunity or gossip gave her the chance, she ensured that, by the end of the year, her daughter's passion would be fully aflame. Irving, now that his romance with Nellie Moore was at an end, was particularly vulnerable to the charms of a beautiful woman of some social position who did not disguise her admiration for him and for his art. Mrs. O'Callaghan's evident reluctance to have a son-in-law who was an actor was a challenge to his pride. So the proud, ambitious Irving (aided and abetted by the forlorn and romantic Brodribb), blind to Florence's shortcomings and seeing her only as the victim of bigoted parents, was all too ready to play the part of the humble suitor pledged to rescue a damsel in distress.

Towards the end of December he received the offer of an engagement from Alfred Wigan. Writing to Flo, he hastened to inform the O'Callaghans of this improvement in his prospects:

'. . . I am famished (it is past four) and that you may read them tonight, I hastily scribble a few lines.

My interview with Alfred the Great resulted in this—that at Christmas there will be an admirable opening (he says) for a leading juvenile actor. He knows nothing of my capabilities but would like to engage me if I were suitable for the above role.

On my merits, I, of course, was dumb, and could only recount the parts in the line he required, which I had played in London with success. "Doricourt", "Harry Dornton" and so on. I wished him to see Mrs. Sartoris—and a friend of his, an author, is going to see me tonight. I needn't tell you that I expressed in no measured terms my dislike for the parts I am now playing, and Wigan expressed himself to be in a similar situation.

Wigan says he should be very glad to accept me and that in a few days I shall hear more. I dare say matters will be settled, and the position, I think, for everyone, first rate.

Jordan is in the field. I nosed him as I went up the stairs in the lobby. Goodbye, my own. Now I revenge myself on the victuals. . . .'

Irving's estimate of his chances proved right. George Jordan, a competent actor in his way, had strayed unwittingly into the path of Irving's destiny, and was tumbled off into perhaps unmerited oblivion.

Alfred Wigan was the nominal lessee of the new and well-appointed Queen's Theatre, which had been built on the site of the St. Martin's Hall, Long Acre, where Dickens had given his readings in the early 'sixties. The Queen's, now the largest theatre in London, except for Drury Lane and the two opera houses, had been built as a speculation by Lionel Lawson of the *Daily Telegraph*, who had leased it to Henry Labouchère, the eccentric journalist and financier. Henry Labouchère was at that time one of the proprietors of the first Liberal daily paper— the *Daily News*—and prospective parliamentary candidate for the Middlesex Division. He installed Alfred Wigan, as nominal lessee and actor-manager—a sensible choice, for Wigan was an excellent actor who, with his wife, had played with Vestris, Kean and Macready and, as manager, had revived the glories of the old Olympic by presenting 'the great little Robson', the prince of burlesque actors, whose success they had shared until Robson's death in 1864. Labouchère's theatrical venture was inspired not so much by love of the drama as by his adoration of Henrietta Hodson, who was to be the leading lady of the new company; on her account he was happy to incur a considerable loss during the term of his management. Henrietta Hodson, with whom Irving had set out from Greenock in search of fame, had thrived in the Bath and Bristol stock companies until she married a solicitor named Pigeon and retired from the stage. Pigeon's early death, however, drove his widow back to the theatre and into the arms of Labouchère whom she married before the end of the year.

Wigan had engaged a first-rate company including, in addition to the lessee's protégée, the heavy tragedian John Ryder, the emotional Carlotta Addison, Irving's old friends, Toole, Wyndham and Brough, and Henrietta's early rival, Ellen Terry. To open the season, Wigan had secured Charles Reade's new play, *The Double Marriage*. The heroine, whose honour and very life are at stake, has given birth to a child whose presence at a critical moment cannot be satisfactorily explained. Her young sister, to save the situation, herself accepts the parentage, which would have been all very well had she not, in the person of Ellen Terry wearing a white directoire gown that made her look an infant herself, and with a heavy cold in the head, come towards the footlights and in passionate tones declaimed: 'It's bine!' This was too much for an already restless audience. The play was laughed off the stage, a débâcle in which Irving had no part. Labby, turning to Charles Reade, who was sharing his box, said:

'They seem to be hissing, Mr. Reade.'

'What of that?' replied Reade. 'If you want to please such a public as this you shouldn't come to me for a play.'

A stop-gap revival of *Still Waters Run Deep* held the stage until *Katherine and Petruchio*, Garrick's version of *The Taming of the Shrew*, could be got ready, with Ellen Terry and Irving in the principal parts. Irving's salary of three pounds a week, which was increased to eight pounds when he took on the duties of stage-manager, was small enough, but it was sufficient compensation to be one of a company of such old friends and such fine actors.

During these rehearsals, Irving had his first experience, and indeed his last, of party politics. Labouchère was standing as one of two Liberal candidates for the Middlesex Division. Early in the campaign he had prejudiced his chances of success by enraging his Tory opponent, Lord George Hamilton, and by conducting a personal quarrel with his fellow Liberal, Lord Enfield. The candidates abused each other vigorously against a background of contending hooligans and prize-fighters, baton charges by the police and vain appeals for order by the sheriff—an affair, in fact, after Labby's own heart. He came out bottom of the poll, but only a thousand votes behind Lord Enfield, who held the seat for the Liberals.

Labby, who was certainly the candidate most popular with the crowd, took Irving with him when he drove in a carriage and four to Brentford to thank his supporters. Having made his speech, he drove through the outlying areas of the constituency where few people knew any of the candidates by sight. Irving, with folded arms, hat pressed over brow, and the picture of baffled defeat and stern resignation, assumed the role of a rejected politician with such success that the crowd, believing him to be the defeated candidate and filled with compassion, took the horses out of the carriage and dragged it back to London. Labby took his cue and played the grateful supporter. At the end of the journey the crowd, deeply touched by the unsuccessful candidate's noble gloom, wrung the hand of Labby's leading gentleman and begged him not to take his defeat too much to heart.

Katherine and Petruchio opened on Boxing Night—a particularly foggy one. Irving and Ellen Terry were neither of them at their best. The piece was only a make-weight for the chief attractions on the bill— Toole in two farces, *Doing for the Best* and *The Birthplace of Podgers*. Toole, no doubt, had been instrumental in getting his friend Irving to the Queen's—not to play Petruchio, but for an important part in a play which had been written especially for him by H. J. Byron and was already in rehearsal. Irving's Petruchio was a failure. The critics complained that he had made the shrew-tamer a good-humoured and rapacious brigand rather than a light-hearted gallant, and they commented severely that in his delivery of blank verse he had much to learn. Irving found little to admire in Ellen Terry except her natural charm. To one whose whole life was centered in his art there was something baffling about this frivolous girl who, for all her talent and early training, had left the stage to be the child wife of an elderly artist and, have left him and returned to the theatre for a year or two, was about to abandon it again for love of an architect. She herself, humiliated and frustrated by the mockery of her marriage to Watts, was longing only for the fulfilment of her womanhood in a domestic life. She, in turn, saw little to admire in Irving, a young actor, with a dull, heavy face, awkwardly self-conscious and lacking the technical proficiency which she had acquired in her cradle. She was, if anything, a little frightened by his fierce application and his earnestness of purpose— as though the forces within him were struggling for liberation. She was touched by his grave courtesy when, always in a hurry to leave the theatre, she accepted his place, which he politely offered her, in the queue lining up to receive salaries on Friday nights. When, at the end of the short run, she left the company, Irving hardly gave her a thought. Determined to retrieve his reputation, he threw himself wholeheartedly into the creation of Bob Gassit, a scoundrel after his own heart and one of the pillars of Toole's new production.

In the part of Michael Garner, that popular comedian was breaking fresh ground. He was trying to portray an honest tradesman, a tender husband and self-sacrificing bread-winner; his son, Charlie, played by Wyndham, his good looks obscured by luxuriant whiskers, was to be led astray by the dissipated Bob Gassit. Irving took immense pains in presenting the vulgar manners and seedy finery for which the character called. His efforts were rewarded by excellent notices in the press which compared him favourably to Mathews, Sothern and Bancroft. He was commended for his careful study of character and for the imaginative bits of business with which he elaborated his part. Perhaps in view of the popularity of Toole and the quality of the company, it gave him most satisfaction to read that his acting reminded one critic 'of the general style that prevails at the Prince of Wales's—that style, it need hardly be said, is the best and represents the most artistic school or mode that is to be found anywhere in London—being founded on that most obvious but most neglected model—nature'. Toole's generous delight in his friend's success was even more rewarding. Indeed it was from this moment that their friendship took the form of a life-long devotion to each other, manifested by the delight of each in the other's triumphs, by endless practical jokes, and by the tender sympathy with which each sustained the other in hours of adversity. Superficially two such inseparable friends could hardly have been less alike. They illustrated perfectly the two categories into which Belloc, many years later, divided the English—Toole the runty and capering, Irving the tall and grave. Toole's laughter and tears were very near the surface; Irving's emotions, as the years went by, were hidden behind a vizor of reserve which was only raised in the company of a few intimate friends such as Toole himself. The common bonds which held them so closely together were their love of the actor's calling and the high sense of duty with which they espoused the cause of the actor and the dignity of his profession.

Irving was beginning to realize that he was happiest in the company of fellow-actors whose humour and sympathies came near to his own. Thus with their arduous rehearsals by day, with the nightly repetition of an agreeable and rewarding part and, between them, the lavish yet miraculously cheap banquets of roast meat which he, Toole and Brough would consume standing side by side at the counter of the ham-and-beef shop at the corner of Russell Street and Bow Street, these weeks at the Queen's were the happiest he had ever known.

Dearer Than Life ran until April, when it was withdrawn to make room for John Oxenford's dramatization of *Oliver Twist*. Irving was cast for Bill Sykes; he was, no doubt, glad to take the shine off his accustomed villainy and to recreate the savage ferocity and dull brutality of a fiendish character who had all but eluded the pen of his creator. Irving must have heard Dickens give his reading of the 'Murder of Nancy', which had often reduced his audiences to hysterics and, by the intensity of its delivery, shortened the novelist's life. Toole miscast himself for the Artful Dodger, Henrietta Hodson played Oliver, and for Nancy another popular and brilliant actress was added to the company—Nellie Moore. This association might have been embarrassing for Irving, were it not for the fact that, where actors and actresses are concerned, personal relationships are left very often with the stage-door-keeper and are not allowed to intrude upon the stage. Irving, who had been appointed stage-manager, had plenty to occupy his mind, but, thanks to old Mrs. Franks, Miss O'Callaghan's grandmother, who was busily undermining her son's authority and acting as courier between the separated couple, his thoughts continued to dwell upon the unobtainable, and were stimulated by frequent correspondence.

Florence, when she heard that Nellie Moore had joined the company at the Queen's, appears to have written, in pardonable anxiety, to her admirer, disparaging the girl whom she knew to be her rival in his affections. His answer was characteristic and should have warned her of the fundamental antithesis of their natures:

'I received both letters today. Although somewhat prepared for the contents of the first, I was, perhaps, a little astonished. It is painful to murmur any fault of those whom we regard and to conceal the wherefore. Say of her to me, Flo, what you will—I willingly accept it, but sayings or opinions of others keep back—especially expressions of condescension. These I cannot endure. They tingle through my veins and cause my blood to circulate at a rate to a phlegmatic man—objectionable.

The end all is that our position is as before. I will do all I can to trust in you. . . .

. . . You did not say whether you liked the "domestic drama" (*Dearer Than Life*). It is a genuine success and my disgusting part will do me much good. I enclose the *Globe* notice (a stupid one by the by) but the critics are unanimous.

Tonight I was called after everyone had *separately* acknowledged a similar compliment—and only the accidental announcement by Ryder, before I could get from my dressing-room, prevented my appearing last night. *Then* I did not anticipate a call—thinking the overwhelming odds in the last scene against Mr. B. G. (Bob Gassett) would overrule any desire the audience might have to see his repulsive carcass.

Byron was in raptures and said things—well to a modest man—distressing. I scrutinized, I thought, every soul in the stalls, but saw no Flo—this a little ruffled me—but had I not imagined mischief was in the wind I should certainly have waited in the lobby—but on Saturday night I foresaw breakers ahead. *Why* God or the Devil alone knows.

I am a "special". Have a staff and badge—have sworn to protect our sovereign lady, the Queen, and can say "Move on" in the heaviest tone of voice. Did a disturbance occur I should say, I think, "Move off". I'm not a boastful man, but I possess a great regard for my personal safety. The only advantage gained by this apparently rash step is that I am only to be called to protect the Queen's Theatre—not the hearths and homes of my native country—for which I don't care a button. As the Queen's is not likely to be in jeopardy I think we have blended loyalty and discretion or discretion and loyalty in rather an admirable manner.

I hope I shall soon hear from you and with all love am ever yours,
Henry.

If you want any seats don't scruple to write for them but, I beg pardon, you won't.'

In London unemployment was widespread and a series of explosions, attributed to Fenian agents, had led to the call for special constables, to which Irving had half-heartedly responded. The Queen's Theatre, however, had not been threatened and, in spite of the prevailing disorder and depression, *Oliver Twist* did better than it deserved. It was a pedestrian adaptation and Toole had not bothered to temper the broad farcicalities of an Artful Dodger, who had delighted provincial playgoers, to the more sophisticated taste of London critics and audiences. The run of three months—until July—owed a great deal to Irving's terrible delineation of Sykes and to the pathos of Nellie Moore's Nancy. Irving was at an age when young actors tend, in searching for a wife, to seek also the perfect complement to his own art —indeed the history of the theatre abounds in such domestic and artistic partnerships, many of which have been lasting and successful. It must, therefore, have been all the more bitter to him to have to share with her the nightly applause and printed acclaim of their collaboration, which both knew to be only transitory. Nellie Moore, who was now only twenty-three, was already recognized as the most promising and attractive actress on the London stage. Irving knew instinctively that he had lost not only the affection of a girl whom he had loved deeply and faithfully for two years but the perfect partner in the career which he had mapped so clearly in his mind.

As usual, towards the end of the run, the dwindling receipts were revived by a series of benefits. On June 1st Irving played Charles Surface in *The School for Scandal* for his own benefit and a few days later he played Cool in *London Assurance* in a performance in aid of the Royal Dramatic College—not, as the name suggests, a school of acting but a foundation on the lines of the Charterhouse to provide lodging for old actors in honourable retirement. The cast on this occasion was a remarkable one, as fine as any that had been mustered since Garrick's day.

SIR HARCOURT COURTLEY . . .	Benjamin Webster.
MAX HARKAWAY	E. P. Addison.
DAZZLE	Charles Mathews.
CHARLES COURTLEY . . .	E. A. Sothern.
DOLLY SPANKER . . .	J. B. Buckstone.
COOL	Henry Irving.
PERT	Mrs. Keeley.
GRACE HARKAWAY . . .	Nellie Moore.
LADY GAY SPANKER . . .	Mrs. Charles Mathews.

To be invited to appear in such company was a measure of the esteem in which Irving was now held by the older members of his profession.

By the end of July, Byron's new play, *The Lancashire Lass*, was ready to go into the bill. The managers of the Queen's who, when it opened, had dedicated themselves so bravely to the cause of high-class comedy and drama, now threw up the sponge of art and surrendered the theatre to catch-penny commercial melodramas of which Byron's play was a turgid example. History was anticipating itself. The London theatre was becoming permeated with a class of entertainment which pandered to the taste of the mass of uneducated playgoers. Avid for sensation and glutted with double bills, they swallowed greedily the same coarse fare with which a hundred years later filmgoers were to be gorged into a satiated torpor. Irving was again cast for a stereotyped desperado—this time a cigar-smoking bush ranger who stroked his heavy moustachios with bloodstained fingers and had to jump through every hoop in the melodramatic routine. He was, however, able to impart an illusion of reality to this crudely drawn villain and, together with the rest of the admirable cast, which had been reinforced with Sam Emery, a fine old character actor, saved the play from the condemnation it deserved. Even Charles Dickens, whose theatrical tastes were robust, found *The Lancashire Lass* rather too much of a good thing. Yet when he described the play to his family round the supper table at home, he said: '. . . But there was a young fellow in the play who sits at the table with Sam Emery and is bullied by him; the young fellow's name is Henry Irving and if he some day doesn't come out as a great actor I know nothing of the art.'

Irving, at the time, knew nothing of Dickens's prophecy. He had to content himself with the *Dispatch*, which reported that '. . . in the last scene, as he, (Irving) lay imploring shelter from his enemies, his mingled terror and exhaustion rose to an unusual point of force'.

At the turn of the year when Irving, for the first time, had good cause to congratulate himself, a tragedy occurred which indirectly overshadowed his whole life. During the first week in January Nellie Moore was taken ill and had to leave the cast. For three weeks she lay hovering between life and death in the house off Soho Square. Irving, deeply anxious for the girl whom he still loved, called to enquire after her and was told by the woman who came to look after her during the day that she had scarlet fever. Finding that Nellie Moore was alone, for her mother and sister were in America, he asked their mutual friend, Laura Hain Friswell, the daughter of the essayist, to call and see what she could do for the sick girl. Miss Friswell did as he asked. On the morning of January 22nd, a fine sunny day, as she was approaching the house, she met Irving coming away from it. His dejected bearing filled her with foreboding. She looked quickly from him to the house and saw with a sinking heart that the blinds were drawn. She tried to persuade herself that they were pulled down to keep the glare of the sun from the sick room, but, when they met, Irving told her that Nellie Moore was dead. He thrust into her hand a bunch of violets which he was carrying. Miss Friswell strove to find words to express her sympathy for him and distress that one so gifted should die so young. Irving took her hand. 'It is not always a misfortune to die young,' he said. To Miss Friswell his words may have sounded strange, for to her and the rest of the world Nellie Moore's death seemed a cruel act of fate. But his remark was not a careless one; death, he suspected, had spared Nellie Moore much unhappiness. Before she died he had discovered that a supposed friend had come between them and, although he had no conclusive evidence, he had good cause to believe that she had suffered grave injury at his hands.

Later, in cold anger, he confronted this man and made it clear to him that although evidence of his guilt had been buried with his victim, suspicion would rest upon him as long as his accuser lived. Toole, fearful for Irving's self-control, was near at hand and never forgot the faces of the two men when they came from the room in which they had faced one another alone. The wound in Brodribb's heart never healed; the armour of Irving was tempered further by this cold shock of personal tragedy.

CHAPTER XII

Comedy and Matrimony

―――◦◦◦―――

I

A few weeks after the death of Nellie Moore the run of *The Lancashire Lass* came to an end. It was followed by another melodrama, *Not Guilty*, which might well have been a parody of its predecessor, for it was such a hotchpotch of villainy and artless situations that it proved intolerable even to the public at whom it was aimed. In March the winter season ended and the company were disbanded. Irving took his benefit on March 19th. For the occasion Wigan revived his old success, *Plot and Passion*, with Sam Emery as Fouché, Toole as a police spy, and Irving as the hero. Much depended on the success of his benefit, for he was struggling to rid himself of a burden of debt which had accumulated during his years of penury—an embarrassment which had come to the ears of Mrs. O'Callaghan and was being exploited by her in her attempts to disillusion her infatuated daughter; but in vain, for, owing to parental obstruction, Florence was more determined than ever to marry Irving. At the same time Irving was now only too ready to seize the chance of domestic happiness which her devotion seemed to offer. On the night of the benefit, through the haze of the footlights, he saw her sitting among the audience. Two days later a letter ran the gauntlet of interception and reached Florence at Linden Gardens:

'. . . Fearing you might now think my silence strange (and sincerely hoping it may cause you no annoyance) I cannot help sending you the result of last Friday.

It was quite satisfactory. Fifty-seven pounds my share. Save and excepting two or three trifles, I am free. I fancy I read your thoughts and the contempt with which you consider the time I have taken to accomplish this—but no thoughts of yours (on this subject) are keener than mine. The past is past.

When I wrote some months ago, I named the end of April as the limit. Let it be. The insurance and all will then be effected and until it is, you had better not, I think, allude to me. I wish to prove how sincere has always been my love and trust; no conditions within my power to prove it have been neglected . . . on Friday I felt unaccountably sad . . . it seemed so strange that the only soul whose praise I cared for, could not give it. As I looked at the seats where you all sat, and not distinguishing any expression, I pictured frowns. I was wrong, I hope. . . . By the bye, how did you like my love-making? The ladies say it was—well, what do you say? . . .'

In April they were allowed to meet. Genuinely convinced of their love for one another, they became engaged. After a final flurry of protest and dark insinuations, Mrs. O'Callaghan struck her flag. It only remained to arrange an exchange of courtesies between the families of the betrothed before announcing the date of the wedding. Of this Irving wrote to his future bride:

'. . . Better few words than none at all. I think by the 8th all might be arranged provided the correspondence or interview with my father were satisfactory.

What crimes, disclosures or horrors may be brought to light I cannot say—I know of none—but surely they cannot have finished with me yet. Your dear mother wrote to me today an exhortation to be candid and reveal any impediment that I might know of "why this man should not" etc.—I really felt ashamed that I knew of none for your Mother's appeal seemed so earnest. Today for the first time I told my father of the coming event—the shadow of which has not, I think, been cast before him.

I carefully avoided attending to the wretched calumnies which have found too credent ears—so that your Mother, if she saw him, might witness his astonishment at anything so disgusting being hinted against his only offspring,—a very fine one too, eh? . . .'

Samuel Brodribb would have to face the onslaught of Mrs. O'Callaghan alone, for by this time Mary Brodribb had faded from the background of Irving's life. The time and circumstances of her death are unrecorded. Her self-sacrifice and stern evangelism had made their contribution to the creation of a genius which she believed to be evil and to be the ruin of her only son.

Irving, even if he was at last free from debt, was painfully aware of his lack of substance as a prospective husband. When he left the Queen's Theatre Fechter, who was on tour in Liverpool, had made him tentative offers of engagement but seemed unable to come to terms. An invitation, therefore, from Toole to join him in a tour of provincial and suburban theatres until June was more than welcome. Toole paid him a generous salary, so much so that he often had to override the objection of parsimonious and sceptical managers. Their repertoire included *Oliver Twist* and *Dot*, a dramatization of *The Cricket on the Hearth* by Boucicault, in which Irving found relief from his habitual villainies in the character of honest John Peerybingle; Toole, moreover, proved as wise as Dr. Pinches in his generation by allowing Irving to recite as a *lever de rideau* that turgid masterpiece 'The Uncle', which for so long had lain pent up in his bosom.

Florence was anxious for the wedding to be as soon as possible. Irving wisely wished to spare his bride the rude transition from the sheltered elegance of Linden Gardens into the rough and tumble of life in theatrical lodgings.

'. . . You see this morning that Fechter goes around by himself. It was settled yesterday. I go on with Toole and we have had a chat about matters. We fill up until the end of June. He wishes to rest in July and after that, if I wish, I could again go on with him. On this I can't, of course, at all determine, but have promised, until the end of June, to remain with him. The only dates fixed at present are—"Standard" until 8th May—Croydon 10th and 11th—travel on Wednesday night and 13, 14 and 15th Newcastle-on Tyne. Then to Glasgow for a week and then work back to Birmingham, probably Manchester and so on— but dates unfixed.

Now my darling, of ourselves. Toole thinks with me that until this scrambling tour is over, we had better wait—what think you? I might then either rest a little or I would endeavour to make some easy engagement, which would I think be more agreeable to each of us—-were we then together, as we might be. I don't see, dearest, how you could rush about here, there and everywhere. 'Twould not be like a regular tour with a fortnight or week at least in a certain place—but tumbling from one town to another which I should certainly not like you to undergo. . . .'

Florence and her family agreed to postpone the wedding until July. After playing at the Standard, Shoreditch and the Surrey Theatre, Irving and Toole left for the provinces. In writing to thank Florence for a gift of slippers he estimated the prospects of a benefit at the Standard.

'. . . All this happiness which has rushed upon me I cannot realize, I had hoped for it, but did hardly dare expect it with so near enjoyment. I seem to tread on the lightest of toes, to which the "slippers" are the veriest lead—this should be seen to and I'll try by wearing something heavier to revisit my native earth.

Concerning the "Standard" benefit (how I hate the word!)—at 12.30 tomorrow I shall know more. A mere trifle we can but each make but believing, as you know I always did, in the wise adage that the sixpences take care of the larger coins (and very kind it is of them to do so)—the merest trifle will be pounced upon by your obedient. . . .'

The benefit must have proved more profitable than he expected. On reaching Birmingham he wrote to her of his future plans and again of his hard won freedom from debt:

Birmingham.

'. . . The London east winds they say are very bitter . . . really the north of England winds have been dreadful. Weather more like Christmas than May. Toole and Brough have succumbed. I myself have alone been cold-proof. . . . Toole opens at the Surrey for a fortnight from June 14th. I may fix this with him. I'm delicate about suggesting it as some weeks ago I was obliged to decline accompanying him in consequence, as I thought, of the Fechter affair. Toole, however, quite understands all this and is very disgusted at the shuffling treatment that I have experienced, and he will I know, if he is not absolutely settled with someone,—ask me to join him. But the proposal I wish to come from him.

Our arrangements for next week are for Gloucester Monday—Worcester Tuesday—Leicester Wednesday and Thursday—Gloucester again I think on Friday. And here on Saturday a monster night when Mr. Irving will appear in his favourite and renowned impersonation of "Robert Macaire" supported by Mr. J. L. Toole as Jacques Strop. On the Sunday following we intend visiting the birthplace of the immortal Bard and should nothing be arranged for the following week we shall, on Monday, start for town.

Don't be nervous about me, dear. I'll not deceive thee. When next we meet I shall "Owe no penny I cannot pay"—the feeling of freedom is really very delightful and accept my best thanks for the extreme interest you have taken in my unfortunate position.

I positively think that when *everything* including the insurance is paid—which I expect will be before we meet—I shall then have sufficient (with I think a little over)—to cover the heavy item of four pounds. Upon my honour these marriages are very expensive things. . . . I have heard from my father—who, poor old man, has been on the qui vive of expectation. I have eased his mind, but tell me when your mother intends going that I may write to him to that effect. I hope your mother is well and less doubtful. . . .'

Throughout the tour Toole and Irving had been in high spirits. They had played to enthusiastic audiences and business had been excellent. While they were at Liverpool, to celebrate their success, they went to dine at a well-known and well-appointed inn at Wavertree. Sitting late over their supper, long after the other guests had gone home to bed, they noticed the unusually fine old silver on tables and sideboard—a collection of which the innkeeper was justly proud. When the time came for them to go, they rang the bell and told the waiter to get the bill. As soon as he left the room they swept up all the silver, put it into the garden through the open window, turned out the gas and hid under the table. After repeated knocking on the door, getting no answer, the waiter came in. When he saw the moonlight streaming through the window into the dark room and upon the empty tables he turned and ran down the passage, shouting: 'Thieves! Thieves!' On the instant, Toole and Irving emerged from under the table, shut the door, recovered the silver, lit the gas and rearranged the tables and sideboard. They had barely finished before the landlord, followed by his family and servants armed with pokers, burst into the room: All they saw were two grave and distinguished-looking gentlemen quietly finishing their cigars and port.

'Do you, sir,' demanded the graver of the two, of the amazed landlord, 'always intrude thus upon gentlemen dining in your hotel?'

This was the first of many such elaborate jokes in which the two friends collaborated—jokes which became legends and were joyfully remembered even by those upon whom they were practised.

With the wedding fixed for July, Irving's prospect of unemployment at the end of the tour was a gloomy one. Since Fechter's offers had failed to materialize, he was forced to accept an engagement with Miss Amy Sedgwick who was looking for a villain for the production of her own play, *All for Money*, at the Haymarket. The play opened on July 12th, but it proved to be a fiasco, though Irving saved one or two encouraging notices from the wreck.

On his return to London he found that Florence, too, was affected by the uncertainty of the future. When they met again something in her manner warned him of an underlying lack of understanding between them which might endanger their happiness. Since it was too late to heed it, he wrote to her insisting on her reassurance:

Margate,
July, 1869.

'My dearest,

I should have called this morning but had to leave by the nine train. If I can at all see you on Friday or Saturday I will—you will know if I do not that the fault is not mine.

The question your mother wrote about was the legality of marrying in the name of Irving—which she—(but I'll enclose her letter.) According to her wish I saw a Solicitor yesterday and have taken out the licence in the name of Brodribb, which he said was imperative. So Mrs. John Henry Brodribb will be the exchange from O'Callaghan— but should we be "fruitful and fructify" as the psalmist puts it—and I sincerely hope that—-well—should we—Irving shall be the name bestowed by the Godfathers and Mothers.

I have been and am now rehearsing—am (as usual you'll say) very tired—and have little time to write. Two other letters I must also send —one to your mother and one to Bradshaw—with a polite request for the 15th.

Toole by the by I think will be with us. I am very anxious that he should.

I hope my dearest with all my soul that when the day is past an end will be put to all reproaches from you or misunderstandings by me.

On Sunday night your manner I though was unsurmountably cold. It was but thought I hope. Nothing I think could so soon dull affection in man or woman as indifference.

You at first lavished on me such love that if I became spoiled—the fault is all your own. But you still love me as you did—don't you my darling? *Answer this.*

Your own
Henry.'

No doubt, as her mood passed, Florence was able to convince herself that she loved this strange man and had overcome her doubts that they could ever arrive at a way of life compatible with each other's tastes and habits.

On July 15th Florence O'Callaghan and John Henry Brodribb were married at the parish church of St. Marylebone. Florence was given away by her brother-in-law, Mr. Morgan. None of Irving's family was present. He had asked his friend, H. J. Montague, a popular actor who was the prototype of the matinee idol, to be his best man; during the previous autumn together they had given a recital of verse and dramatic duologue at the Westbourne Hall, Bayswater. Montague's elegant if eccentric taste in clothes had contributed a good deal to his success as an actor; in his heavily braided black velvet jacket, gay vest and trousers of unorthodox shade and pattern, he held his own among the more soberly dressed friends and relations of the bride. After the ceremony, Irving had the support of his friend, Toole, who bustled into the vestry and signed the register; the other signatories were Mr. Morgan and Mrs. Cross, who, though a close friend of Mrs. O'Callaghan, was regarded by her as socially suspect on account of her husband being in soap. Samuel Brodribb's absence made it possible to put a bold face on his ambiguous profession by describing it, not altogether inaccurately, as that of a gentleman. Irving, in a modest estimation of his métier, entered himself as a comedian. The reception was held at the home of Mr. and Mrs. Frank Matthews, his old friends in Wigan's company.

Three days after the wedding Mrs. Henry Irving had a sharp reminder of the hazards of theatrical life, when *All For Money* came to an abrupt end and its author, belying her title, dismissed the company without paying their last week's salary.

Fortunately, Boucicault was also in need of a villain and he summoned Irving to Drury Lane to add another sinister portrait to his gallery of rogues. The play was *Formosa, or The Railroad to Ruin* and was designed to present with plenty of glitter the life of a prosperous demi-mondaine while, at the same time, pointing a moral which would satisfy the censor without boring the pleasantly scandalized public. Boucicault pulled off this time-honoured trick with such dexterity that the play, though denounced by the press, ran for six months— causing F. B. Chatterton, the manager of Drury Lane, who had striven to keep the Theatre Royal a classical temple, to make his famous answer to the critics who twitted him with putting on such rubbish: 'Shakespeare spelt ruin and Byron bankruptcy.' For Irving, Boucicault spelt solvency, and, though heartily sick of such trashy parts, he was glad of the regular salary it brought him, until Toole returned to

London with plans for the new play. At first it looked as though there might be some difficulty about his leaving an established success, but, thanks to John Hollingshead, Chatterton was persuaded to part with his heavy lead.

Irving was glad to be back again with his old friends whom he joined at the Gaiety Theatre. The play was *Uncle Dick's Darling*, by H. J. Byron; Toole had given him a part in which he could show his quality. In Mr. Chevenix he found a good many of the characteristics of Mr. Dombey whom several years ago he had impersonated so successfully in Manchester—a cold and pompous man of business, something of a parvenu, and a good deal of a snob. His painstaking make-up portrayed what might have been a caricature of Disraeli by Cruikshank and his dress was cleverly dated to suggest the faded elegance of an earlier mode. Toole had a part abounding in humour and pathos which was an ideal foil for Irving. The play opened on December 13th with a flourish; the Prince of Wales was among the audience. Its success was immediate. The critics, welcoming the release of Irving from the shackles of conventional villainy, were as impressed and appreciative of his character study, as were many of his own profession. Yet an indication of the still limited circle of his admirers was to be found in one or two journals which alluded to him as Mr. Irvin or even Mr. Troning. In fact, of the two Irvings, Joseph Irving, the Drury Lane comedian, was better known to the general public. Henry Irving's performance as Mr. Chevenix pulled him out of the rut of melodrama and established him as a character actor of wit and imagination. Dickens, on what must have been nearly his last visit to the theatre, flattered by the demonstration of affection by the audience as he entered the royal box and by the author's obvious indebtedness to his Mr. Dombey, spoke with unstinted praise of the young actor whose talent he had been among the first to recognise. Later he discussed the performance with Edmund Yates, the popular columnist of the *Illustrated Times*, who hastened to report the conversation to Irving:

Good Friday, 1870.

'My dear Irving,

I think you would like to know that when I was dining with Mr. Charles Dickens the other day, he spoke in very high terms of your performance in *Uncle Dick's Darling*. He seemed specially struck with your earnestness and your never forgetting to elaborate, even by small detail, your conception and study of the character. He said, too, that

Irving in 1868

These photographs, pasted back to back, were found in Irving's pocket book after his death

Nellie Moore

Florence O'Callaghan

more than once, you reminded him strongly of my father, and I know that, from Mr. Dickens, it is meant as very high praise.

Sincerely yours,

Edmund Yates.'

Yates, to whom Irving had been introduced by Toole, was to be his loyal champion in the days of controversy which lay ahead. He was the first of the personal gossip writers. His career, in this capacity, began with his expulsion from the Garrick Club for having written an article on Thackeray which the latter considered to be impertinent and to be based on a private conversation which Yates had overheard in those privileged walls; towards the end of his career Yates was sent to prison for libelling the Earl of Lonsdale in gossip culled from the Carlton Club of which he had been made a member. In the years between these well-earned penalties, his pen was always at the service of the theatre in general and of Irving in particular. Clement Scott was full of praise for Mr. Chevenix. He declared that Irving's 'acting was masterly, it showed not only finish but reserve, which to the more discerning showed that more was to come, and all round it was generally admitted that in this character Henry Irving had achieved and obtained emphatic distinction'. Such was the general tone of the press. The play ran until April of the following year. Toole made it, in after years, the keystone of his repertoire, but he confessed that, without Irving as Mr. Chevenix, the play to him was never quite the same.

Irving's success as Chevenix won him a different, if not more prominent, position in the London theatre. He was far more likely to catch the attention of the few managers who were ever on the look-out for exceptional talent in the mediocrity which pervaded the stage at that time. Yet discernment was very necessary, for even at the end of the run Irving's name did not appear in the press advertisements.

2

Three wise young men were the first to hitch their wagon to the new star as he came over the horizon—David James, H. J. Montague and Thomas Thorne, known in the profession as the Jew, the Gent and the Gentile. The trio, pooling their talents and resources, had taken a lease of the Vaudeville Theatre. James was a first-rate comedian. It was probably at Montague's suggestion that the joint managers approached Irving and proposed that he should join them, offering him the same salary as they were to draw themselves—ten pounds a week—a proposal to which Irving readily agreed. The first play to be put into production, *For Love or Money*, offered Irving little scope—a Micawber-like impostor beset with debts and duns—yet, since he himself was dancing on a financial tight-rope with the prospect of an increase in his family responsibilities, he was glad to find immediate employment with a management who professed a desire to aim at modern comedy rather than fustian melodrama. *All For Money* did not prove to be a draw, but for six weeks it was carried along by the success of the supporting burlesque, *Don Carlos or The Infante in Arms*.

Not long after he opened at the Vaudeville Irving received a mysterious invitation from a friend to meet him at an inn in the Strand. When he arrived, he found that his friend had brought another young man whom he introduced as Mr. James Albery. The friend explained that Mr. Albery had abandoned his desk in the family rope-making business in order to devote himself to writing plays, and that he wished to discuss with Mr. Irving his latest work, *Two Roses*. Albery explained that he had written the play to the order of James, Montague and Thorne, but admitted to having been so impressed by Irving's performance as Mr. Chevenix that he had written the chief character to suit him. Knowing, however, that actors were prone to jealousy if they feel that there is a danger of another with a better part stealing the play, he had only sketched in the part of Digby Grant in the hope that Irving would help him to develop it during rehearsals. Irving, protesting out of loyalty to his friends that such subterfuge was unnecessary, allowed Albery to read the play to him and afterwards agreed that if the play was produced he would accept the part and do his best with it. Albery urged him to keep their meeting a secret, and if they should meet again at the Vaudeville to allow himself to be introduced as though to a stranger.

In due course, after these clandestine preliminaries, rehearsals of *Two Roses* were begun. The company was well suited to the play, the dialogue was fresh and up-to-date and the plot contemporary, light and interesting. Mr. Digby Grant, the father of two lovely daughters—*Two Roses*—is a gentleman with a pedigree longer than his purse who, in order to sustain his social position and to command a vestige of the comfort to which he has been accustomed, is compelled to seek the cash and company of his social inferiors. When, unexpectedly, he comes into money, he proceeds to discharge his humble friends with his debts. But his claims to a fortune prove to be unfounded. All that

Irving as Digby Grant

Irving as Digby Grant

he can pocket is his pride amid the rejoicings of his daughters who can now marry the young men they had chosen in their humbler circumstances. It was a slender plot, but in the hands of competent players all the characters sprang to life. Albery was an ardent disciple of Dickens and drew his characters in the style of his master. Digby Grant played conventionally and without humour might have been mildly amusing; moulded by Irving into a 'fidgety, selfish being, self-deluded by social hypocrisy, querulous, scheming and wheedling', he became a masterpiece of pure comedy. For the externals—dress, make-up and tricks of voice and gesture—Irving took as his model a bizarre character, Chevalier Wykoff, whom he had met some time before in the house of James McHenry, an Anglo-American financier. Wykoff was an ageing dandy of the D'Orsay pattern and the agent of Napoleon III who entrusted him with his darkest secrets and, in the last resort, with the dwindling treasures of the Bonapartes which Wykoff succeeded in bringing to England after the disaster of Sedan.

Unfortunately Irving had more to contend with than the creation of Digby Grant. It was becoming apparent that his wife did not share his idea of what an actor's home should be. It was true that she was within a month or so of having a baby and on this account he tried to make every allowance for her unreasonable behaviour. She was beginning to show a capricious temper which, although he had had evidence of it during their engagement, he had tried to humour or to disregard. Already she did not disguise her dislike of his professional friends. He had looked forward to having a home to which he could invite them to supper after the theatre and to sit up with them, until the nervous tension of the evening's work had worn off, gossiping in a way that only actors can fully appreciate. Such simple pleasures she condemned as debaucheries; no doubt their robust talk and uninhibited laughter seemed a trifle barbaric after the artificial dinner-table chat of Linden Gardens. In such an atmosphere of nagging disapproval he found it impossible to concentrate on his work. Rather than risk a quarrel and upsetting his wife at such a time, he hired a cheap lodging in Drury Lane where he could study his part in peace.

Two Roses was produced on June 4th and ran for nearly three hundred nights. The press, with guarded praise, welcomed a comedy that had its roots in ordinary social relationships and actors whose characterizations were based on human observation. Irving's Digby Grant was recommended as one of the best pieces of character acting to be seen on the English stage, masterly in execution and remarkable for the fact that 'he is able to speak the English language like an English gentleman'. Walter Pollock, a shrewd and experienced playgoer, remarked that in Digby Grant, as in Bill Sykes, Irving 'showed the unfaltering touch of true art whereby the horror inspired by the on-fessed ruffian was never thrust beyond endurable limits, while the selfish vanity and unbridled meanness of the adventurer Digby Grant becoming a beggar on horseback were never suffered to pass the just limits of real comedy, as Lamb defines it in the Essays of Elia'. Those, like Mrs. Sartoris, who were watching Irving's progress with sympathetic interest, applauded the fulfilment of the promise which his Chevenix had led them to expect. He was, moreover, encouraged to find that the reception of the play and of his performance by crowded audiences became increasingly enthusiastic as the weeks and months of the unusually long run went by.

The play had barely settled into its stride when the domestic tension which had been the sombre background of those strenuous weeks was broken. On August 5th Florence Irving gave birth to a son. Irving's pride and delight in this event, which he believed would restore the harmony of his home, was expressed in a letter to his friend, Frank Marshall, a young critic and dramatist who had married Ada Cavendish, the leading lady of the *All For Money* company:

Saturday, August 6th, 1870.

'My dear Marshall,

I'm a father! If it comes to that so are you—but nevertheless *I* am.

At 2.40 a.m. on the morning of yesterday, Flo was brought to bed of a fine boy—very like his father. Mrs. Marshall's prophecy was perfectly correct. Give her my kindest regards and tell her I shall be extremely obliged if she would inform me what the *next* will be.

Flo is exceedingly well and happy and as proud of our united efforts as can be.

Ever yours,
Henry Irving.'

As soon as she was convalescent Florence and the baby were sent off to the seaside. Left alone, her gregarious husband had a dangerous taste of the convivial freedom of his bachelor days. H. J. Montague had left the cast of *Two Roses* to undergo an operation; his place had been taken by Lin Rayne, an actor of little experience. On September 7th Irving wrote to James Albery:

'My dear Albery,

. . . Montague is getting on splendidly. By Saturday night he'll be out, I think. He'll return to us, (thank God) about the hundredth night. Lin Rayne is better—but at best the Rain is but Slush. The returns on last Saturday were the *largest* we've, or they've, ever had.

All at home are very well, thank you, I'm the *all* by the by—for the mother and child are at Southend. Come back and we can have long chats.

"Why did I marry?"

Poor Joseph Irving is dead!

It is the Autumn judging by today. It's wretched. I've a fire and still am cold.

"Oh liver, liver, thou shouldst have few sins of thine own to answer for." I'm going to dine with three jolly people and Arthur Sketchley! Three of the jolliest old busybodies you can conceive.

Hope to see you tomorrow. Shall prepare Sweet Epps[1]—for your coming.

Sincerely yours,
Henry Irving.'

The sustained popularity of the play, in spite of the absence of its leading juvenile, was welcome evidence that the public came primarily to see Digby Grant. The death of Joseph Irving, who, though only four years older than Henry, had become the established favourite of a far wider public than his namesake, put an end to the possibility of a confusion of Irvings in the public mind. The brief interlude of unfettered communion with his cronies during Flo's absence made Henry less amenable to the prospect of constraint on her return. Nevertheless, a letter to his father showed that it was his intention, and indeed his earnest desire, to rebuild the shaky edifice of his family life:

September 26th, 1870.

'My dear father,

You will be glad to hear that the baby and his mother are extremely well. They returned from Southend on this day week and benefited by the change. Master Henry is a very fine child—so they say—and I believe he is—and at present, I think, like his mama—if it's possible to detect any likeness in anything so young.

He is to be christened on Tuesday next—as Henry Brodribb Irving—and the reason for this is that as the boy will always be called and

---

[1] Cocoa.

known as Irving—as I am now—it would cause a good deal of unnecessary inconvenience to him in after life had he any other surname. As you said especially should my (as is not at all likely by the way)—money be left to him in the future.

All my present friends will know his name and some future ones might *not*, were his name any other than he might be known by at that time.

A friend of ours—Captain Atkinson—is to be his Godfather. *I* shall be another. Montague returns to us, you'll be glad to hear, today. He is quite well again and does not dread a relapse. . . .

I should think the critiques on *The Two Roses* are the best I've had. Give my best love to my aunts.

> Affectionately yours,
> Henry.'

Not long after this his uncle, Thomas Brodribb, died. He left no will, so that his estate was divided between Samuel and his two sisters. Irving, who was finding it difficult to meet his increasing family expenses, entered into a complicated financial arrangement with his father by which he had the use, at interest, of some of this capital. But it was not enough. He knew now that he was the chief attraction at the Vaudeville and largely responsible for the success of Albery's play. He felt justified, therefore, in asking the triumvirate for an increase in salary of three or four pounds a week. This they refused and, since they were legally within their rights, there was nothing more to be said. Perhaps their shortsightedness was fortunate, for had they increased his salary he would have been prepared to accept from them a long-term contract. Irving felt this rebuff more keenly because his hopes of a happier situation at home had been sadly disappointed. Florence's reasonableness was short-lived; as soon as she had fully recovered from her confinement her ill-temper and mordant tongue made life for both of them intolerable. During October Irving sought refuge with his friend, Montague, until he found rooms for himself in Mount Street. All these things embittered the savour of success which by rights he should have begun to relish. To his father he described his situation:

> 10a *Mount Street*,
> *Grosvenor Square*,
> *December* 23rd, 1870

'My dear Father,

Enclosed is P.O.O. for two pounds which may be useful before Christmas Day which I hope you will all enjoy.

What changes, I wonder, will occur before this time 1871. The last year has been too eventful. My day I spend with Montague who has been a good friend.

From the commencement of the New Year—I see my child once a fortnight. He will be brought to me. It will be useless seeing the dear little fellow oftener *now* for he is but a baby and not at the most interest-ing age. By the way, do you remember on what day he was born?

About making over the hundred to him, we'll arrange by and by. An old friend of mine—has offered to be joint trustee with me—and that I think is a necessity don't you.

We have made no legal separation—nor do I ever intend to. The arrangement is plainly and simply this. As long as I'm in an engage-ment I pay or allow four pounds per week. Should I be ill or dis-engaged the payment ceases till I commence again.

The premium of Insce. on my life (a thousand pounds) my wife pays out of the four pounds.

The mother and daughter are together again and very cosy I dare say they are in their way. Mama has five hundred a year and her child two hundred. . . .'

Early in the New Year Florence came to her husband and begged him to return to her. She promised and, no doubt, sincerely intended to mend her ways; to try, if she could, to put a guard on her temper and her tongue and to make his home more native to Bohemia than to West Kensington. Irving, though he welcomed her contrite surrender, accepted it on his own terms:

'At once disabuse your mind, dear, of any desire of mine to delay our union. I am more than anxious to be with you and our child. My present life has no attraction—although you seem to think it has. It has not.

I feel despite all this 'tis better that we wait till this day fortnight and I'll tell you why.

That I would not go back to any roof save our own you know—enough of that. Your mother resigns on the 25th—and well and good—but why needlessly open a wound, by reminding her that I would not accept two weeks rent from her? 'Tis not my desire to pain—& I'm sure this would. I have made a resolution, which I wish to keep, gently and firmly.

I must be away a great deal for some days to come. I shall have endless trifling worries to attend to, which I'd rather much get rid of before our first meeting.

I shall then have a little extra money and in short what is now un-settled, in every sort of way (I don't mean monetarily) will then be settled and I'm sure dear, 'tis better as I suggest. Our lives will, I hope, be so different to what they were—I do not like to lose the least chance of making them so. I can tell you what I mean, better than I can or have time just now to write, but believe me, dear, I mean, and think it is really for the better.

Concerning, dear, your father. Thought of one who has been so—so very—thoughtless, is hardly necessary. Let us understand one another and what matter all else?

Your affectionate,
Henry'

In writing of this reconciliation to his father, his confidence that all may yet be well is apparent:

10a Mount Street,
Grosvenor Square,
January 24th, 1871.

'My dear Father,

I can't write you a long letter but the contents of this though short are very sweet. You will be delighted to hear that my wife has called upon me, uninvited, and that our married life is to recommence on, I think, a firm and happy footing. I shall not return to "The Grove" but am looking out for suitable apartments for our little family.

Master Henry is a perfect picture of health and beauty. He really is a magnificent fellow. Our piece reached last night its 200th representation and it seems likely to reach its 300th.

You are all well, I sincerely hope. Remember me affectionately to all.'

On March 23rd, the two hundred and ninety-first night of the run, Irving took his benefit. The house was crowded with his supporters and admirers, who gave an enthusiastic welcome to the actor they had come to regard as a grimly humorous comedian. To their surprise, when the curtain fell upon *Two Roses*, after a short interval Irving reappeared in evening dress and announced that he would recite Hood's poem 'The Dream of Eugene Aram'. Then, without scenery or pro-perties to help in creating atmosphere or illusion, he began, not to recite, but to act the ghastly story of the conscience-stricken school-master. He soon had the audience in his power, sweeping them along with the irresistible fury of the poem. He forced them to witness the brutal killing, the panic-stricken attempts of the murderer to hide the body of his victim and to share with him the haunting terror of inescapable justice. At the second climax, when Eugene Aram discovers that

> *A mighty wind had swept the leaves*
> *And still the corse was bare*

the unrestrained applause of an audience seeking relief from almost unbearable tension told him that his bold experiment had succeeded. Suddenly he revealed himself to his public as a tragic actor of such startling power and with such intensity of emotion that the limits of his range seemed to be boundless. The ovation that he received at the end of the performance was echoed in the press. The *Observer* summed up the popular feeling:

'. . . it was such acting as is now seldom seen and the thought must have struck many in the theatre whether, with our little plays and pretty sketches, our dainty realization of every day life, our clever sarcasms, our elegances and sensation drama, we are not losing sight of those great passions, that tragedy of human life, which it belongs to the actor to interpret.'

Irving had first recited 'Eugene Aram' when he was on tour with Toole; he would repeat it hundreds of times in the future in strange places and often with curious effect. But never, as on this night, would the consequences of his efforts be so formidable. For among the audience, as transported as any of them, sat Hezekiah Bateman. He found it difficult to realize that this whirlwind of passion and dynamic force was the young actor who, several years before in Manchester, had played Joseph to his daughter's Leah. Bateman was at a crisis in his own affairs. Having recently returned to England, he had taken a long lease of the Lyceum Theatre which, after having housed a succession of failures, was half derelict and was regarded by a profession, very prone to superstition, as unlucky. Here he proposed to launch his third daughter, Isabel, on a career which he was determined should be as triumphant as that of her elder sister, Kate. Though, as a father, he had a passionate faith in her talent, as a showman he knew that she must have the best support that was available. It was, moreover, his showman's instinct which prompted him, immediately after that memorable evening, to offer Irving the position of leading man in his new venture. It is doubtful if at that time he had any very clear idea of how Irving's talents could best be employed. He had an eye for phenomena and, having found a new one, would delight in its exploitation. Irving had no particular wish to leave Montague and his colleagues and might never have done so had they given him the modest increase in salary for which he asked, for the Lyceum had little attraction as a theatre and Bateman's fanatical promotion of his daughters was a by-word in the profession. The terms, however, that he offered were attractive. By the time the season at the Vaudeville had ended, Irving had agreed to join Bateman in the autumn. Until then the *Two Roses* company would be making an extensive tour in the provinces. Although the tour would bring him to Bristol, Irving could not wait to give his father news of the agreement:

April 20th, 1871.

'My dear Father,

I have received your and my aunt's letters concerning the present you have so kindly sent us, which shall be acknowledged on receipt of the parcel.

My object in writing today is to inform you of the most important business engagement I have ever made—and which I have just concluded.

I have with Bateman (the father of Miss B—of "Leah" notoriety) signed, sealed and delivered a contract by which I am engaged for three years to act at the Lyceum or in any theatre in the United Kingdom—at a weekly salary of Fifteen pounds for the first year—£17 for the second and £19 for the third. The engagement to commence in September next and to be for not less than ten months in each year.

I am engaged as the leading comedian and for character parts of a leading description.

Bateman has become for seven years lessee of the Lyceum. His management commences in Septr. next and everything will be produced in the highest and best manner possible. Now what do you think of this? It is a great advance isn't it? I am in haste and can enlarge no further so goodbye and God bless you all.

Affectionately yours,
Henry.'

Apparently Bateman, in spite of the profound impression which 'Eugene Aram' had made upon him, saw in Irving no greater capacity than an aptitude for character and comedy parts. Probably he thought he was humouring a whim, not uncommon in comedians, when he promised Irving, as a condition of their agreement, to produce (when opportunity arose) a play called *The Bells* in which the actor insisted there was a tragic part well suited to him. The promise given, it was no doubt as quickly forgotten by the impresario; but not by the actor.

Irving had recently made the acquaintance of a solicitor, Leopold Lewis, who had shown him an adaptation which he had made of a French play, *Le Juif Polonais*, by MM. Erckmann-Chatrian. The theme, that of a murderer who escapes the gallows but is destroyed by his own conscience, was developed with more imagination and psychological understanding than were most melodramas of the time and justified the qualification *étude dramatique* which the authors had attached to it, when in 1869 it was first produced at the Théâtre Cluny, with Talien in the leading part. Irving saw at once that it was the perfect vehicle for his peculiar genius and for the style of romantic acting which he sought to make his own. He bought the rights from Lewis and, without departing very much from the original text, helped the author to reshape and to modify the main character of a Swiss burgomaster to suit his own ideas. Lewis had a whole-hearted admiration for Irving and entered with enthusiasm into the collaboration. Bateman may have forgotten that Lewis had previously offered him the play and that he had rejected it. If he recalled this when he gave Irving his promise, he assured himself, no doubt, that his daughter's success would be so sensational that no opportunity to produce plays of which she was not the central figure would ever arise.

Thus Irving set off on his tour well content with the bargain which he had made and happy to think that he would return to a reformed and affectionate wife and to his adored child. His letters to Florence were full of detailed instructions regarding the acquisition and furnishing of their new home. After playing in Leeds and Bradford, he writes from Bristol:

May 27th, 1871.

'My dearest,

I have just within the space of five hours completed three meals—breakfast, dinner and tea—I've the anticipation of a long journey and the Dublin boat—yet, I'm not happy.

The old folks here are very well and the excitement consequent on my arrival has been most intense—there were but two things necessary to drive the aged trio into madness—the sight of you and the sight of our pet.

You really must get his picture taken—society demands it.

One of my aunts has given him (and it'll be sent on) a capital present —a house of bricks—wooden bricks not regular bricks—I can see him seated on a little stool on the drawing-room carpet trying to build his little castles on the floor . . .

Our success last night was extraordinary. . . .'

From Bristol the company sailed for Dublin. *Two Roses* proved to be very much to the taste of Irish playgoers. Among the audiences which thronged the Theatre Royal were a young civil servant and a red-headed boy of sixteen, both of whom were seeing Irving for the first time. The civil servant was Mr. Bram Stoker, who was so put out at finding no word of praise of these accomplished players in the Dublin press that later he himself took to dramatic criticism and so was drawn inevitably into Irving's orbit. The red-headed boy was George Bernard Shaw. Many years after he described the impression that this strange actor, so ill-equipped vocally and physically compared to his hero, Barry Sullivan, made upon him. 'It happened that I saw him first as Digby Grant in *The Two Roses*, a play which seemed new and promising in a dramatically benighted age which produced no considerable playwrights except Robertson, who did not deal in Big Bow-Wow tragedy for male stars. Henry roused in me an interest which did not clash with my estimate of Sullivan; for the two were not up the same street: H.I. in Shakespeare was as unthinkable as Sullivan out of him. I at once picked him out as the actor for me, quite unconsciously; for I did not then know that I was pregnant with the succession to Shakespeare.' Bram Stoker's admiration for Digby Grant was the prelude to a lifetime spent in Irving's service; George Bernard Shaw, though an early admirer, was to become an implacable enemy of Irving and all that he stood for. From Dublin Irving wrote to his wife:

Gresham Hotel.

'. . . I have now shaken off all fatigue from our journey and rehearsals, and begin to feel freshened from the change of scene—that and the bracing air will benefit, I think, me as much as early hours and more rest, will, I hope, you.

I am sorry you didn't visit Marshall (Frank) on Sunday. He is a man of refined sensibility and will, I know, feel hurt at the seeming slight. . . .

. . . our success here is great and as in Bristol the "palpable hit" has been made by me. I think you would like this place—it is dirty . . . but the atmosphere is beautifully clear . . . the streets wide and handsome—the people lively and the environs lovely. Those I have not yet seen, I mean on this visit, and my first stroll will be this afternoon to Phoenix Park, a rendezvous for duels and assignations, which I believe, still flourish—I was told so—from experience I cannot speak.

Decent lodgings are so dear and the difficulty to obtain clean ones so great, that I have resolved to remain here during our stay. Montague and English do the same. I have a fine large bedroom (in which I am now writing) looking onto Sackville Street—which is wider than Regent Street in any part and in it (the bedroom not Sackville Street) is a splendid bath which I luxuriate in at 9.30—my hour for rising. We breakfast together in the coffee room at 10.30 and dine at 4—after which I take my usual "pitch" and so on. The three of us were guests last night at the Dublin Literary Club where we supped and afterwards partook of punch—punch such as your father knows so well how to mix and I may also add enjoy. Of that beverage (ambrosia I think the Irish call it—for they consider it food) I had two tumblers full which I thoroughly enjoyed—for the night was bitterly cold—as even the days are. For May—the middle too—the weather is most unseasonable. Bright but piercingly cold. I've left off nothing and used my thick overcoat.

I'm so glad you intend getting our little darling's picture. The first you have I shall expect to receive and shall want at least six.'

A day or two later he wrote:

'. . . Yesterday we were driven by an Irish gentleman through the county Wicklow and nothing have I seen at all comparable to it. I hope we shall view it some day together. I have never worshipped in any church that gave me the soft, religious, holy calm that God's handiwork gave me yesterday. My heart and eyes were full of tears. We drove on a car through Wicklow to Bray, a town on the coast, and such a coast! We are feted here, I needn't tell you. There is a large supper to be given to us on Thursday next and on Saturday night we were (Montague, English, and I) guests of the Neptune Rowing Club, and a hospitable affair it was. I was discovered to be the image of Robert Emmett and that enhanced my popularity. To certain Irishmen Robert Emmett is second only to J.C.'

This outing was followed shortly by another which inspired him very differently:

'. . . We (Montague, English and other members of the company) made up a party amongst which were three natives, driven by a Dr. Shaw of Trinity College, Dublin, to the Dardle—a divine spot—where we dined al fresco.

A delightful day we had of it, and you'll be surprised to hear—(accusing me, dear, as you sometimes do, of chronic dullness) that I was the life and soul of the party. I astonished myself, I frankly tell you—but I really was in great form.

You dislike practical joking, I know, so do I—sometimes—but English and I yesterday concocted and carried out with genuine success the rarest and best acted little plot that has ever been conceived. It really was most artistic—the spot where it occurred lending a wonderful romance and terror to the whole.

If you would like to know the particulars and will promise me not to be too severe in your judgment—I will—if you think it will amuse— briefly in some letter, describe it. . . .'

Whether or not Florence ever heard the details of this practical joke, it was macabre in conception and thorough in execution. During the picnic their friends noticed that Irving and Montague were not on their usually friendly terms. At one point they drew aside and were heard indulging in bitter altercation. When they returned, Montague made an insulting remark which infuriated Irving and embarrassed the rest of the party, who were at a loss to know the cause of this quarrel. Later, discovering that Irving and Montague were missing, and being fearful that they might have come to blows, the party set out in search of them. At the foot of some rocks they met Irving. He was pale as death and in his bloody hand he grasped an open clasp-knife. He was mumbling incoherently to himself: 'I've done it . . . I told him I would . . . he provoked me!'

One of his fellow-actors, Smale, rushed towards him.

'Back!' warned Irving, menacingly raising the knife.

Now thoroughly alarmed, Smale asked, in God's name, where was Montague.

'There he is—the scoundrel—the false friend!'

Following the direction in which Irving's long finger pointed, they found Montague lying face downward in a tangle of bushes among the rocks, unhurt, but in some danger of apoplexy owing to the handkerchief which he had stuffed into his mouth to stifle his laughter. The comedy was ended. The only casualty was Irving himself who with his customary enthusiasm for make-up and attention to detail had cut his wrist in order to draw the amount of blood necessary to make convincing his appearance as Montague's murderer.

In reply to these letters, Florence, who was going to have another baby, must have written woefully of her own cares and anxieties and critically of the comfort and junketings which he seemed to be enjoying at her expense. Irving did his best to humour her resentment:

Dublin,
May 18th, 1871.

'. . . I know you're inclined to fidget about the future—and by your letter I could plainly see that you were already on tenterhooks concerning it—it is natural to your disposition and I suppose a part of your nature,—but do pray remember this—I am just as anxious on that subject as you are and my only wish is to make you happy and to send you the means to, partly, help you to be so. Don't think I am so unmanly and cowardly as to leave you encumbered with debt and fatten my carcass at the expense of a woman in child. As I told you before I left, and I hope this subject will be respectfully dismissed—every farthing that I can send you I will.

There is one thing, dear, I heartily wish I could do—and that would be to send you home a poplin dress. I have seen some lovely ones—for £5 I could get a beauty—but I have not £5 wherewith to buy it. However, should you in a little time be inclined to have one, I can by writing to a friend here get you one at cost price. I was surprised to see what lovely material poplin seems to be—I prefer its look to the finest silk.

I can hardly wonder at your amazement at my stopping at the Gresham, when I take the matter from your point of view. Did we stay here at hotel charges our salary would hardly get us through the weeks but we do nothing of the sort—we pay so much for board, attendance and everything, and not one penny more. On paying my bill this morning, I find that my week's living has cost me less than one week ever did in Old Quebec Street—dear dear place—in both ways. Now what do you think of that.

However, cheap and luxurious (as you rate it) as this life is—or may be, if properly arranged—I don't like it and in Liverpool, where we open on Monday next, I have taken rooms that Walter Gordon had and in Manchester I shall do the same.

The Two Roses has created in Dublin a theatrical excitement unknown for many years. The dress circle (there are no stalls) which is the largest in any theatre out of London, holds 300 persons (and during our engagement the price has been raised from 4s. to 5s.) and on Saturday night it was crowded and on Friday too, with the elite and fashion of the city. This is here unprecedented. The dress circle, I am told, and sometimes with the most popular stars, is generally empty—comparatively and excepting with Italian opera, which is here a great institution, such audiences as we have had are never drawn to the theatre. You may be inclined, dear, to think I am a little ecstatic. I am not so really. The Dublin Theatre Royal, which is as large and handsome as Drury Lane, has got into sad disrepute and is little patronized by the best people, therefore our success is the more gratifying. Harris, the manager of the theatre, has for years had a monopoly which he has abused—the result of that abuse being that, at last, the monopoly is destroyed and a licence has been granted (after desperate opposition) for a new theatre after the fashion of the "Gaiety" and built by the same architect—which theatre is in the course of construction.

I don't intend, dear, writing a history of the T.R. Dublin, but these one or two facts might, I thought, be amusing. Digby Grant has created a sensation and at night sweeps every part in the piece before it. . . .'

The wretchedness of the lodgings in Manchester which had been recommended by Walter Gordon provide him with little else than a welcome opportunity to contrast his present discomforts with the imagined luxuries of the Gresham Hotel. In order to furnish their new home, Maples must be persuaded to allow them a credit account; chafing at the need for guarantors, he advises Florence how to go about this disagreeable task.

> 5 *Mount Street, Liverpool.*
> *May* 31st, 1871.

'. . . I told you that I had written to Maples. Tomorrow I suppose I shall have a reply. . . . I would refer them as a guarantee of our undoubted probity, respectability and any other ility to Toole and also, I should think, to your father. Toole will, I dare say, be sponsor for me as your father will for his daughter, or daughter's husband . . . it would be wise, dear, if you informed your father before they write to him that we wish him to say he thinks us a trustworthy pair. I hope we shall not again need to bother him or anybody else with such matters—offensive at all times. . . .

. . . My lodgings here are the most dreary and uncomfortable it was ever my lot to occupy on Gordon's recommendation (something must have altered very much since he had these). I booked them for three weeks—worse luck—and I can use the rooms only to breakfast and sleep in—to dine—ye Gods! For Monday afternoon when, very very tired, I ordered a chop as being a light and nutritious meal. Shades of Sheep! Had you but seen, on the removal of the cover, the thing they called a chop!

> *I touched it not*
> *And donned my "pot"*
> *And sought a meal elsewhere!*

I was determined not to be sold again and gave implicit instructions that I should require in this house but one meal a day—breakfast.

"What will you have, sir—chops?"

"No, no! for God's sake no more chops—confine yourself always to this—ham" (on that I thought they couldn't go very wrong)—"ham and tea, put in plenty of tea and pour on it boiling water!"—fair that I thought, they couldn't go very wrong and I was right.

We opened here with our usual success. We closed at Dublin with unusual success. The theatre on Saturday night was a most brilliant sight. I told you, didn't I, that the Lord Lieutenant and Lady Spencer gave their command? I enjoyed the Dublin stay excessively. Much more so than I shall this . . . here I feel comparatively stuffy. . . .

This afternoon's post, just in, has brought the agreement, which I shall sign and send back tonight. So the house is ours for 3 years. There is but one clause in the agreement which you have to sign for me might give you some uneasiness—it is this. The person who signs the agreement must promise not to use number 14 Wharfdale Street as a "residence for a lunatic". No man is bound to incriminate himself therefore I shall, at all hazards, sign the document and get some unobservant person to witness it.'

The arrival of the eagerly awaited photographs of his son helped to brighten even the gloomiest lodgings. He revealed a critical attitude to the photographer's art which was to grow more acute and exacting as the years went by.

June 2nd, 1871.

'. . . the two photographs I have kept, must, I suppose, be considered a success . . . the face especially of the one in which he is lying on his back and not a vestige of an ear to be seen—couldn't be better— I mean more natural.

The expression of the other one I have retained is very jolly. The young gentleman is bolt upright. There is a simplicity though to me, about the picture which, I fancy, must have been taken out of focus. Photographs of the same person taken at the same time are often utterly unlike—and so it seems to me of those in this case. I like the picture very well, but it is not at all the fat, impudent, saucy, young spark of the other picture.

. . . The solemn one enclosed (how like his father!) is the best, most complete photo of the lot, but the expression is absurd—ruined by the mincing and rather idiotic expression of the face and the detestable manner in which the third-rate artist (I said he was third rate) has posed the dear little fellow's hand. Did you ever see anything more unnatural or ungraceful? How odd that in all the pictures his mouth should be so wide apart. . . .'

To his father, who had helped him over many a stile, he wrote frankly of his financial position and rewarded his unfailing help with the pictures of his grandson:

> *Mount Street,*
> *Rodney Street,*
> *Liverpool.*
> *June 6th,* 1871.

'My dear Father,
It is a little more than three weeks since we parted and I don't think a line has passed between us since.

In Dublin our success was very very great as it is here—where we remain during the next week—after which we go on to Manchester—where we also stay three weeks—*not* two, as was originally fixed. I feel much benefited by the changes of air and scene—which I really needed. My reception as Digby Grant has everywhere been great—in fact the greatest in our company.

At home, Flo is rapidly preparing for our moving. We have taken, for three years, a house in West Brompton at £52 10. 0. a year. If you have received the money, which you expected I think early in June—it will be very acceptable. I have already been obliged to scrape together all I could for payments becoming due, and the five or six weeks arrears I owe to you, please deduct before sending the money. There is a good bank here called the Union through which you might send it— but that matters little for any banker can advise you. However, as soon as you possibly can assist me, do—for rent and many things are getting due.

And now my dear Father and my dear aunts, I enclose what I am sure will give you unalloyed delight. Are not the pictures lovely specimens of health, beauty and good nature. Did I extol with sufficient pride the magnificent and noble little fellow before you? Tell me and at length, what you think of your grandson. . . .'

The tour ended on August 19th. Invigorated by his personal success and by the much-needed change of air, happily convinced that he and Florence were to make a fresh start together and with the prospect before him of three years of interesting work which would provide a steady income for them both, he returned to London and presented himself to Colonel Bateman for rehearsals at the Lyceum.

CHAPTER XIII

Bateman and " The Bells "

———◆———

I

In 1870 the Strand formed a bridge between the City of London, where the Victorian nabobs laboured to expand British trade, and West London, where they lived and amused themselves on the proceeds of their business. To the south of this bridge, buttressed by Somerset House and the Adelphi, flowed London river; to the north, within the area enclosed by Lincoln's Inn, New Oxford Street and Charing Cross Road, lay a jungle of narrow streets, decaying tenement houses, disreputable taverns and the dingy shops of second-hand dealers in clothes and books—its dark alleys and unlit lanes haunted by prostitutes and garrotters. On the western fringe of this unsavoury neighbourhood stood a number of playhouses which could be approached in comparative safety by Long Acre or the Strand; of these the largest were the Theatre Royal, Drury Lane, the Royal Opera House, Covent Garden, and the Lyceum. Beyond their glittering façades the dark forest of slum dwellings festered until the Kingsway was driven through the heart of it at the beginning of the present century.

The Lyceum was the third building of that name to occupy the site cornered by Catherine Street and Exeter Street and originally faced the Strand. In 1765 James Payne, the architect, had built there a hall which he intended to be a cultural centre, primarily to house exhibitions of the pictures of the group of artists who were to be the founders of the Royal Academy. When the academicians were granted their Charter and removed themselves to Burlington House, the property fell into less enlightened hands and became an amusement hall offering a variety of attractions ranging from Montgolfier's balloon to shows of waxworks and conjuring. In 1794 Samuel Arnold, the composer, having acquired the premises and converted a part of it into a small theatre, tried to restore its prestige by applying for a licence which the Lord

Chamberlain, under pressure from the patent theatre managers, refused. Condemned to singing and circuses, the Lyceum might have decayed and vanished, as did many theatres of that period, had not Drury Lane in 1809 been destroyed by fire. The homeless patent company sought refuge in the Lyceum and brought with them their licence. Having enlarged and improved their temporary home, they remained there for two years; when the time came for them to return to the Theatre Royal, Arnold's enterprising son pressed home his advantage and persuaded the Lord Chamberlain to let him retain the licence. On the strength of this, Arnold pulled down the ramshackle improvisations, cleared the site, and built a fine theatre which he named the Lyceum, or English Opera House, and opened in January 1816. For fourteen years the new theatre flourished and gained lustre and fame from the procession of great actors and actresses who crossed its stage—Charles Mathews the elder, Edmund Kean, Vestris and Mrs. Keeley. In 1830, unable perhaps to contain the incandescence of such genius, the Lyceum burst into flames which engulfed most of the block which lay between Exeter Street and the Strand.

Arnold, in spite of the heavy loss he had suffered, set about building a bigger and a better theatre. The authorities took advantage of the holocaust by cutting Wellington Street through the ruins, thereby connecting Bow Street directly with the Strand. The New Theatre Royal Lyceum and English Opera House, as it was ponderously called, turned its face eastward so that its pillared portico ennobled the entrance to the new street from the Strand. For a year or two Arnold's new venture prospered and gained distinction by his inviting Frederic Lemaître to the Lyceum, where he astounded London audiences with his Robert Macaire. But thereafter failure followed failure, ruining Arnold, who was forced to give up his position as director, until, in 1844, the Keeleys restored the fortune and reputation of the Lyceum and were followed, after three years, by Charles Mathews junior and Vestris, who for a further eight years enjoyed that peculiar sort of theatrical success which ends in bankruptcy.

After another eight years of alternating successes and disasters, the theatre's glories were restored by Fechter, who, arriving in London from France in 1863, soon won the support and admiration of London playgoers with the originality of his interpretations which, with their realistic style, paved the way for the new school. While Arnold's architectural energies had been confined to the front of the house and to introducing new forms of ventilation for the easier respiration of the audience, the stage of the Lyceum showed little improvement on the

methods and equipment which had been in use since Garrick's day—
a naïve arrangement of wings, drop cloths, sky borders and glaring
footlights which have been perpetuated in the enchanting toy theatres
of Mr. Pollock. Fechter made a clean sweep of all this. He introduced
concealed footlights and semi-solid scenery with interiors roofed with
ceilings which were as revolutionary as his unmannered diction and
restrained gestures. His reign ended in 1867. If he was not a great
creative genius he could be compared justly to a forthright engineer
who, by a series of devastating demolitions, clears the ground upon
which his successors can start to build afresh.

When Bateman took up his lease in 1871, the theatre had, as we have
seen, in the intervening period, ruined several lessees and had earned
a reputation for ill luck. Originally, as its name implied, the Lyceum
had been built as a teaching place; as the years went by its purpose
was forgotten and its name became meaningless. On Monday, August
21st, 1871, a man passed through the stage-door for the first time, who
was to give the old Greek word a new meaning. In the course of
Irving's lifetime the word Lyceum was to become a theatrical adjective
descriptive of a style of dramatic writing and acting—at first laudatory,
then nostalgic and finally, to later generations, suggestive of something
outmoded and faintly ridiculous.

2

When Hezekiah Linthicum Bateman was christened in Baltimore
in 1812, his names celebrated a god-fearing King of Judah with a
flair for public works, and the architect of American state department
procedure—pledges of his father's stern Methodism and patriotism.
His father died while he was a child. His mother, by teaching him her
faith and having him educated to be an engineer, did her best to honour
the pledges made at his christening, but, like Irving, Bateman confounded his parents' hopes by becoming a theatrical manager and
dying in England. At the age of twenty-one he left his home to become
an actor; he played juvenile parts with Booth and Charles Kean, but
had little success. Tall, handsome and taciturn, he was the model of a
Southern gentleman and, though born on the political border-line
of Maryland, his sympathies were always with the South. Later in
life he became known as Colonel Bateman; since he was never a
soldier, this may be taken as a popular tribute to his good looks and
courteous gallantry. Having failed as an actor, he decided to become
a theatrical manager, and when he married Sidney Cowell, the daughter

of an English comedian who had settled in America, he gained at
once a devoted wife and the perfect partner for a showman. Sidney
Bateman was a remarkable woman. In the first years of their married
life she managed to write plays with one hand while she washed the
babies with the other. She bore him eight children, among them Kate,
Isabel and Virginia, on whom she and her husband were able, throughout their lifetime, to concentrate their peculiar gifts of exploitation.
During the civil war the Batemans lived in Brooklyn. When the news
came of Southern disasters, Bateman, in order to conceal his chagrin
from his Northern neighbours, would go into his garden and dig
gloomily until he had regained his composure. Normally he did not
hesitate to give full vent to his explosive rages which, though rare,
were memorable and had earned him in two continents the nickname
'Chained Lightning'. One of his first enterprises as an impresario was
to bring to America Parepa and Bagnoli, the Italian opera singer and
tenor, with a young violinist, Carl Rosa; in so doing he started Carl
Rosa on a career which made the Italian's name synonymous with
opera all over the world. As their three daughters grew up, the Batemans devoted themselves to their dramatic training and presentation;
a fourth daughter, Ellen, who showed great promise, disappointed her
parents by retiring from the stage at the age of fifteen when she married
a Frenchman. Of the other three, Kate alone had the talent and ambition
necessary for a great theatrical career. Isabel and Virginia, who were
rather afraid of their volcanic father and at heart disliked acting,
through being made over-confident as infant prodigies, became un-
teachable as they grew up. Kate, thanks to the shrewd way in which her
parents handled her business and publicity, became famous on both
sides of the Atlantic, particularly for her performance in *Leah*. To
achieve this success for their daughter, the Batemans crossed and
recrossed the Atlantic; sometimes in comfort, sometimes, when money
was short, in great hardship. On one occasion they were forced to
take passage in a small sailing vessel. The ship was delayed by storm,
and after being at sea for over two months food supplies became
exhausted. Mrs. Bateman was worn out and dangerously weak. Bateman kept her alive with regular doses of porter, which he got by
surreptitiously tapping a barrel among the cargo in the hold. His
taciturnity made him a gifted poker player and it was his proud boast
that he had always won the price of his passage money in the course of
a voyage.

When Kate Bateman married George Crowe, her husband took
over the management of her business, thus leaving her father and

mother free to devote themselves to launching Isabel and Virginia on the London stage. When Bateman came to the Lyceum, Virginia had already made her début with her sister, Kate, at the Haymarket. It was for Isabel's début that he had taken the ill-starred theatre and had engaged Irving.

Bateman and Irving took to one another at once. They were quick to recognize each other's qualities and to discover that, among other things, they shared an appetite for punch, cigars, late hours and theatrical yarn spinning. Mrs. Bateman astounded Irving by her driving energy. She wrote or adapted plays and rehearsed her daughters in their parts; she ran the home and was ever at her husband's side in the conduct of his business; in such spare time as she could find she designed and made her own and her children's clothes. The results of her dress-making were dowdy and unbecoming and a constant source of grief to the girls who received no salary but only trifling pocket money on which they were unable to buy dresses for themselves. The Bateman's house in Kensington Gore, with its impromptu readings, its rehearsals and declamations, its early dinners off chops and its late suppers off cold meats and salads, its pregnant silences and thunderous rages, its snipping of scissors and fidgeting fittings, its pervading aroma of cigars and old newspapers and its perpetual unpunctualities, was the apotheosis of theatrical family life in which Irving found himself perfectly at home.

Bateman had chosen for Isabel a play based on a story by George Sand, *La Petite Fadette*, which, having been translated from French into German and from German into English, finally had been rehashed by Mrs. Bateman, and, in the process, Isabel's part had been so padded out and developed that it was really beyond her powers. Irving was to play Landry Barbeau, a lovesick peasant—a part to which he was wholly unsuited and must have made him wonder why the Colonel had ever engaged him. During rehearsals Irving was able to take stock of Isabel, who, for better or worse, was to be his leading lady for an indefinite period. She was seventeen years old and very beautiful; yet in case the audience should fail to appreciate this at once, her mother had interpolated a line for one of her admirers in the play who told her, 'You have lovely eyes and beautiful hair!'; which was perfectly true, particularly as regards her hair, which was brown, lustrous and abundant. Her beauty, however, was of the spiritual kind and her manner serious and thoughtful. She was deeply religious—a high church Episcopalian—and already, but for her father's ambitions for her, she would have become a nun—as she did some time after her

parents' death. Having no desire to be an actress, she lacked spontaneity, and when, with her naturally grave disposition, she tried to
suggest lighthearted gaiety with gestures too carefully cultivated in
early training and a voice which had never lost a certain hardness, she
was unnatural and unconvincing. Her range, therefore, was very
limited and it was unfortunate that her father should have chosen for
her début the part of a mischievous coquette which would reveal her
weaknesses as an actress. Indeed she would be seen at only slightly less
disadvantage than Irving, who could only appear ridiculous lying at
her feet and whispering sentimental platitudes. Bateman was blind to
these things; by the time they became evident to everyone else his
eyes were dazzled by the sumptuous pastoral scenery of Hawes Craven
and the peasant costumes of Alfred Thompson; while his ears, thrum-
ming with the original music of a peasant dance which occupied one
whole act, were deaf to the poverty of the dialogue.

Fanchette was produced on September 11th and was the subject of
reproving finger-wagging rather than outright condemnation by the
critics. Perhaps Bateman had disarmed the harshest of them by putting
on in support of it a laughable farce by Oxenford of *The Times*. Irving
was not as disappointed in the critics as they, expecting something
better after Digby Grant, were in him. Delighted with his new home
and with his prospects at the Lyceum, he wrote to his father:

'. . . the papers I sent assured you that I was not—as you almost seem
to fear—amiss. I was never better but have been very very busy—
rehearsing and since we opened too. The critics, as you may have seen,
are hardly unanimous concerning my playing in *Fanchette*—but that
matters not. Bateman likes it and the public like it—and the piece, I
think, will draw.

Everything is exceedingly comfortable in the theatre and bids fair
to continue so. We are getting settled nicely in our new quarters which
Flo and I like very much. . . .'

And a week later:

'. . . Doctor O'Callaghan has returned to England forever and
yesterday we dined with him and his wife—at a new house they've
taken. He is retired from the service on a pension of £900 a year—so
he's pretty well off. We got on together capitally and he seems a very
good fellow. Flo is very well and very happy and delighted to have
me with her again and seems to have taken a new view of everything.

She is quite an altered woman. Her devotion to our boy is extra-ordinary and a lovely noble-looking fellow he is—the admiration of everybody.

The "benefit" was a big success. I was never so enthusiastically received in my life. I have sent you three papers, the *Era, Observer,* and *Morning Post*—they each contain accounts of the affair and I have also sent you a number of *London Society* containing something about me in connection with Charles Dickens. It's written by Edmund Yates and I want you to cut it out and paste it amongst the other notices. Some day I may need them reprinted.'

The reaction of the returning Surgeon-General must have been as much of a disappointment to his wife as it was a relief and a surprise to Irving. No doubt Mrs. O'Callaghan had counted upon him as a willing ally in constantly calling Flo's attentions to her husband's social and moral shortcomings. To her dismay, Daniel O'Callaghan seemed to be amused by his peculiar son-in-law and showed a distressing tendency to indulge the latter's weakness for punch and to encourage in him the very bad habits which she and Flo had set themselves to cure.

It soon became apparent, after a few nights of *Fanchette*, that the audiences and the applause at the Lyceum were getting thinner and thinner. In vain Bateman, from behind the curtains of the stage-box, shook his fist at the phlegmatic few who stubbornly denied his daughter the ovation she deserved. Disgusted with their lack of judgment, he withdrew Isabel from the cast and hastily prepared a version of Pick-wick which had been adapted for him by James Albery. Irving was to play Jingle, and Albery, though he made a sad mess of the play in general, knew exactly how to write up such a part for Irving, with the result that Alfred Jingle flavoured with Digby Grant dwarfed all the Pickwickians and threw the play off balance. Irving dressed the part with his usual care. With a beaver hat cocked over one eye, a black cutaway coat buttoned tightly below the chest, and the Behenna legs attenuated in tight-fitting overalls, blacker even than his coat, he looked like an impudent cockney crow and all that Dickens could have wished for Jingle. In spite of this his performance lacked the sprightliness his appearance suggested and was praised only as a redeeming feature in a dull evening. E. L. Blanchard went home and wrote in his diary: 'See Albery's version of *Pickwick Papers.* Very bad indeed and I think Bateman must soon give up.'

Bateman would already have done so had not Kate subsidized the Lyceum with the profits of her provincial tour to the extent of three or four hundred pounds a week. The old impresario knew well enough that he could not count indefinitely on his daughter's help. He was faced with defeat and had neither play nor cash ready to stave it off. The moment for which Irving had waited so patiently and confidently had arrived. He reminded Bateman of his promise concerning *The Bells* and suggested that, as there seemed to be no ready alternative, the play should be put at once into rehearsal.

Anyone with experience of theatrical management can appreciate Bateman's hesitancy in falling in with Irving's suggestion. What kind of crazy proposition, he may well have asked himself, is this young actor trying to make me agree to? The chief character? A burgomaster —ridiculous! This lanky comedian as a civic dignitary—and an Alsatian one at that—(and here Bateman would blow out his cheeks and thrust out his stomach to illustrate his point)—whoever heard of such a thing? Besides, another management was putting on a version of the play by Burnand at the Alfred Theatre, Marylebone. Irving countered Bateman's misgivings vigorously and persistently. He knew all about Burnand's adaptation. In place of a criminal who dies as the result of a dream in which he had been forced to confess his crime, the burlesque writer had substituted an innocent and commonplace man who dreams of a crime he might have committed had he not resisted temptation, and lives happily ever after. Such a travesty deserved to fail. As to his own ability to interpret the burgomaster and his conception of the play, had not Bateman engaged him after hearing him recite 'Eugene Aram'? What was that but the portrayal of a haunted conscience, and did he not hold an audience in thrall alone upon a stage bare of scenery or trappings? Bateman, who in his heart adored Irving and had already come to look upon him as a son, gave way to his importunity. To the dismay of the company, who regarded themselves as doomed by this crowning act of folly, *The Bells* was put into rehearsal.

Compared to contemporary plays, the plot of *The Bells* was novel and its treatment considerably more profound than that of the average melodrama. It dealt, among other things, with the very topical subject of mesmerism. Its authors justly could claim to have made the first experiment in psycho-analytical drama, though Freud was as yet an infant, and in the use of the subconscious as an element in human behaviour. The scene was an Alsatian village; the time 1833. A prosperous innkeeper who had become a loved and respected burgomaster is about to give his daughter in marriage to the local chief of police. He alone knows that his prosperity is the result of a murder which he committed fifteen years before. He was faced, at the time, with ruin and with the loss of his inn. One stormy winter's night a Jewish traveller stops at the inn for a meal. The innkeeper, when his guest pays his dues on leaving, sees that he has a girdle of gold. Taking a short cut across the fields, he intercepts the Jew, who is driving a sledge, and murders him. He robs the body and throws it into a lime kiln. The Jew's disappearance becomes a mystery, a riddle that remains unsolved and is finally forgotten. The innkeeper is unsuspected. The illgotten gold brings him success and civic honours. Yet as he gets older and increasingly secure, he becomes haunted by the sound of the sleigh bells for which he had listened so intently on that fatal night. He managed to conceal this obsession from his family and his friends. He believes that when the police officer becomes his son-in-law he will be at last beyond the reach of the law.

One day, while at a fair in the nearby town, he sees a mesmerist who, by putting people in a trance, can make them answer his questions and reveal their inmost secrets. The thought of such a possibility preys upon the mind of the burgomaster. On the night before the wedding he dreams that he is before a court of law. When the cross-examination of the prosecutor has failed to shake him, the judge summons a mesmerist, who, throwing his resisting victim into a trance, makes him re-enact his crime. The burgomaster is found guilty and condemned to be hanged. When, in the morning, his family come to wake him for the wedding, he starts from his sleep and, clawing at an imaginary rope around his neck, he staggers from his bed and, in a paroxysm of half-waking terror, dies in their arms.

In the hands of French actors who had previously played the part, the burgomaster, Mathias, had been portrayed as a callous and remorseless villain upon whom the consequences of the dream, caused primarily by heavy drinking, fall as a just retribution. Irving, when first the play fell into his hands, conceived the character as that of a potentially good man who, in a moment of awful temptation, quickened by the thought of the suffering which his poverty may inflict upon his beloved family, yields to that temptation and commits a crime which he successfully conceals. He lives, however, to curse his immunity as he realizes that death might be preferable to the everlasting torment of his conscience. By his conception, Irving transformed what to others had seemed a conventional melodrama into a criminological study of fearful intensity. Although Irving's idea of the character of Mathias, the burgomaster, was very different from that of the authors of the play, he contrived to put it into effect without appreciably altering the text. In all, he

changed or interpolated about a score of lines, the greater number of
which were alterations of rhythm or of emphasis. For instance, 'It is
simply a jangling in my ears' he altered to "Tis but a jangling in mine
ears'; 'The Rope! The Rope! Cut the rope!' became 'Take the rope
from my neck, take the rope from my neck!' and, throughout, the
word 'Sound' of bells is substituted for the word 'Noise'—nuances
prompted by an actor's sense of dramatic fitness. A virtuoso musician,
taking such liberties with a composer's work as his technique or emotion may dictate, will be praised or condemned, not for his presumption in doing so, but for the results he achieves. Irving, the virtuoso
actor, exercised the same privilege. His claim to it can best be put in
his own words: 'I am the last man to admire a slavish or even an unthinking adherence to the interpretations or acceptance of conditions.
My own conviction is that there are few characters or passages of our
great dramatists which will not repay original study. . . . There is a
natural dramatic fertility in everyone who has the smallest histrionic
gift; so that, as soon as he knows the author's text and obtains self-
possession, and feels at home in a part without being too familiar with
it, the mere automatic action of rehearsing and playing it at once begins
to place the author in new lights and to give the passage being played an
individuality partly independent of, and yet consistent with, and rendering more powerfully visible, the dramatist's conception. It is the vast
power, a good actor has in this way, which has led the French to speak
of creating a part when they mean its being first played; and French
authors are so conscious of the extent and value of this co-operation of
actors' wisdom that they have never objected to the phrase but, on the
contrary, are uniformly lavish in their homage to the artists who have
created on the boards the parts which they themselves have created on
paper.'

Every character Irving portrayed was the subject of deep study and
his performance was the conclusion that he arrived at as a result of this
study. During his day this intellectual approach of the actor to his art
became common practice. As a pioneer he had to bear the brunt of
criticism for shattering the complacency of playgoers who, having
become accustomed to accepting the great characters of classic drama
as tradition had moulded them, were only concerned with the actor's
execution of a part within those limits.

As rehearsals for *The Bells* proceeded, the company became increasingly astonished by Irving's unorthodox approach to the play and
by the decisive clarity with which he directed every inflexion and every
piece of business in their parts and in his own. Typical of this was the

thought and care which he gave to the selection of suitable bells to represent the ghostly echo of the Jew's approaching sleigh. Having chosen the bells, which were mounted in a harness identical with that worn by sleigh horses, he insisted that the crescendo of their approach should be achieved realistically by the ringer starting from the back of the stage and continuing to jangle them until he reached the prompt corner, rather than arriving at the effect in the ordinary way by manipulating them from a fixed point. In a short time the company agreed that they were in the hands either of an eccentric actor or of a producer of genius.

Bateman, having capitulated to Irving's siege, flung himself into the production with his usual vigour. From a trip to Paris he returned with M. Singla, the musical director of the Théâtre Cluny and the composer of the incidental music for the original production, whom he had persuaded to attend rehearsals at the Lyceum. In the painting-rooms of the theatre Hawes Craven, the scenic artist, was hard at work on Alsatian interiors and a fine blackcloth of the view of the village seen through the upstage windows. Costumes, properties and all the mechanical contrivances needed to realise the vision which were essential to the play were put in hand, and no hint of pinchbeck saving was given to those concerned in these preparations. Wherever possible old cloths were repainted and old flats adapted to fit the new scene; but these were sensible makeshifts in a management that had already accumulated a considerable stock of scenery. Whatever Irving needed for his production Bateman saw that he had it. As a result of his two failures, Bateman's resources were nearly exhausted. In desperation he turned for help to James McHenry, the financier at whose house Irving had met his model for Digby Grant. Several years before, the Batemans, during a season in Glasgow, had met McHenry, who was a medical student keenly interested in the theatre. Later they crossed the Atlantic together and during the voyage, which was a stormy one, the impervious Bateman ministered to his seasick friend. In America McHenry gave up medicine for speculation and made a fortune out of his interests in the Lake Erie–New York Railway. He returned to England while *The Bells* was in production and was only too glad to come to the rescue of his old friend. Thus he became one of the contributory forces which kept Irving on his course towards his goal.

Barely a fortnight before the date of production such little faith as the company had in the project was badly shaken when the rival version, under the title of *Paul Zegers, or The Dream of Retribution*, was produced on November 13th at the Alfred Theatre, Marylebone, where it proved to be a dismal failure. Outwardly Irving seemed to be unmoved by this failure, which he had foretold. He pressed on with the rehearsals until he began to see the pattern of his intricate conception taking shape. The responsibility which lay upon him would have been overpowering to a man who for a moment questioned his own ability. However carefully each subsidiary character was rehearsed until timing and inflexions were perfect, the play must stand or fall by his own performance—the one thing he could not, as a producer, see or estimate except in his mind's eye.

Once more his relationship with his wife failed to stand the strain which these weeks of trial had imposed upon it. Florence was going to have another baby. That she, in such circumstances, failed to realize the gravity of the crisis through which he was passing and to provide the sympathetic encouragement that every artist craves was perhaps to be understood; that he failed to appreciate that her apparent indifference to his work and all that it entailed might have been symptomatic of her condition may have been less excusable. It was natural, however, that he should turn more and more to the Bateman family for the invigorating companionship and solicitude which, at the end of the day's work, he so desperately needed. It became his habit to go to supper with them after the theatre. Frequently he stayed the night at Kensington Gore in order to avoid the recrimination which he knew would greet his return home in the early hours of the morning. During the last weeks of rehearsal he rarely saw his wife and every day the chances of their eventual reunion became more and more slender. Irving was too preoccupied to give much thought to anything beyond the approaching first night; Florence, left alone with her mother, had every hour of the day and night in which to brood upon her discontent. No doubt Irving, with unreasoning optimism, imagined that after the first night all would be well. A day or two before the dress rehearsal, he called upon Hain Friswell to ask him and his daughter to escort Florence to the first night and to share the stage box with her. As he was leaving their house, he met Laura on the stairs:

'So, at last!' she greeted him excitedly, 'you are going to act *The Bells!*'

Irving shook his head. 'It may not be a success,' he answered quietly, with a rather sad smile.

The girl gaily predicted a triumph for him. She went up to her father and told him that Mr. Irving seemed a little depressed.

'I can understand that,' said Friswell. 'People are often nervous when they attain their desire. I like him all the better for that.'

The *Two Roses* Company
Irving as Digby Grant

H. L. Bateman

Mrs. Bateman

Isabel Bateman
as Ophelia

On the night of Saturday, November 25th, the audience which assembled at the Lyceum to see the first performance of *The Bells* was neither numerous nor distinguished. When the lights went up after the preliminary farce, *My Turn Next*, the stalls contained a handful of regular patrons, the critics, and a number of gentlemen from the West End clubs who, having heard that the play contained some nonsense about a mesmerist and a murderer, had reluctantly left their dinners with the idea of having a laugh at the expense of the actors. Bateman, depressed by his failure to dress the house, hovered anxiously in the corridors. In the stage box sat Florence with the Hain Friswells; in the opposite box sat Leopold Lewis with Joseph Hatton, an American journalist, who was a friend of Irving. Lewis, who at best was an unbalanced creature, was beside himself with excitement; but for Hatton's calming influence and, at times, his physical restraint, Lewis might have communicated his nervousness to those on the stage. As the house lights were dimmed, only those in these boxes leaned forward eagerly; the rest of the house showed hardly a flicker of interest; the clubmen were prepared for boredom, the critics looked forward gloomily to belabouring half-heartedly the corpse of a play which they had already killed.

The curtain rises on the interior of an Alsatian inn. It is night. There is something unusual about the scene—a warm glow pervades the picture which is low in key and, with its carefully conceived accent of local colour, immediately establishes a certain atmosphere. Outside it is snowing; beyond the windows the white landscape stretches away into the night. An occasional gust of wind suggests an approaching storm. For fifteen minutes the burgomaster's wife, who sits by her spinning wheel near the tall stove, gossips with one or two villagers who are drinking at a table. This overture is well handled, for they are all competent actors; naturally and without undue stress, the elements of the plot are stated. The burgomaster is expected any minute to return from a visit to a nearby town; it is a wild night, the wildest since the night the Polish Jew was murdered fifteen years ago; the burgomaster's daughter and her fiancé, a Captain of Gendarmes, hear the story. At its climax there is a crash of breaking glass which proves to be a kitchen window blown open by the storm; the audience are pleasantly startled by this old, but effective, theatrical trick. This conversation continues until over it is heard the 'hurry' music which rises to a crescendo as the door at the back of the stage is burst open. There stands Mathias, a gaunt figure wearing a fur cap and heavy coat, his fur-gloved hand, which is raised in greeting, holding a heavy horsewhip. Everyone, authors and actors, has skilfully directed each word and gesture towards this moment. Mathias's shout of 'It is I!' catches the climax at its peak and marks the end of a dramatic period. In years to come, Irving's appearance at this point will be greeted by such a storm of sustained applause that at the first sign of its dying he will be forced to break it off with a decisive gesture. On this night, the first of many hundred performances which he would give as Mathias, only a ragged little volley from the two boxes greeted his appearance. He sensed at once that the house was cold and hostile. He accepted the challenge. Mathias is welcomed by his family. They have taken his heavy coat and cap and he sits down in a chair downstage centre and begins to take off his gaiters. Easily and naturally the subordinate characters drop out of focus. Though they are talking to him, the audience is forced to concentrate on his every movement. While he is putting on his shoes, he describes the mesmerist whom he has seen at Ribeauville. As he stoops to adjust the buckles, one of the villagers mentions that the mesmerist can send a man to sleep and make him disclose what weighs upon his conscience. The effect on Mathias of this word 'conscience' is best described by Gordon Craig, who watched the scene many times and has made a penetrating analysis of this all-important moment in the play, for it is now or never that Irving must gain the mastery over his audience:

'Irving was buckling his second shoe, seated, and leaning over it with his two long hands stretched down over the buckles. We suddenly saw these fingers stop their work; the crown of the head suddenly seemed to glitter and become frozen—and then, at the pace of the slowest and most terrified snail, the two hands, still motionless and dead, were seen to be coming up the side of the leg . . . the whole torso of the man, also seeming frozen, was gradually and by an almost imperceptible movement, seen to be drawing up and back, as it would straighten a little and to lean against the back of the chair on which he was seated.'

'Exactly!' Mathias whispers, in such a way that the audience are allowed to share his half-formulated fears.

Mathias recovers himself and tells his daughter there is a present for her in his coat pocket. The scene proceeds. Food and drink is brought in and set out for him on the table. He invites the old villager to join him in a glass of wine. He pours it out, but as he is raising the glass to his lips, one of the company remarks that before he came in they had been talking of the Polish Jew's winter. At the mention of the Jew his movement is interrupted and then, to hide his reaction and to steady himself, very deliberately and delicately he takes an imaginary piece of cork out of his wine. As the villagers prattle on about the Polish Jew, he puts down his glass. The throbbing jingle of sleigh bells is heard but by Mathias and the audience alone, distant at first but becoming louder as the haunted man, bending his terrified gaze upon the audience, communicates to them the horror of his hallucination. Then:

'He moves his head slowly from us—the eyes still somehow with us—and moves it to the right—taking as long as a journey to discover a truth takes. He looks to the faces on the right—nothing. Slowly the head revolves back again, down, and along the tunnels of thought and sorrow and at the end the face and eyes are bent upon those to the left of him . . . utter stillness . . . nothing there either—everyone is concerned with his or her little doings—smoking or knitting or unravelling wool or scraping a plate slowly and silently. A long pause —endless, breaking our hearts, comes down over everything, and on and on go the bells. Puzzled, motionless. . . he glides up to a standing position; never has anyone seen another rising figure which slid slowly up like that. With one arm slightly raised, with sensitive hand speaking of far-off apprehended sounds, he asks, in the voice of some woman who is frightened yet does not wish to frighten those with her:

"Don't you . . . don't you hear the sound of sledgebells on the road?"

"Sledgebells?" grumbles the smoking man; "Sledgebells?" pipes his companion; "Sledgebells?" says the wife—all of them seemingly too sleepy and comfortable to apprehend anything . . . see anything . . . or understand . . . and, as they grumble a negative suddenly he staggers and shivers from his toes to his neck, his jaws begin to chatter; the hair on his forehead, falling over a little, writhes as though it were a nest of little snakes. Everyone is on his feet at once to help:

"Caught a chill". . . . "Let's get him to bed".'

·   ·   ·   ·   ·

The villagers leave the inn; the family go into the kitchen to prepare some mulled wine for him. Left alone, he listens in terror to the continual jangling of the bells. He rushes to the window and, tearing aside the curtains, stares into the empty night. The stage darkens as he staggers to a chair, muttering of giddiness . . . calling on his courage. The bells cease as suddenly as they began. At this relief he turns, only to see towering over him the vision of his act of murder. As the ghostly

Jew standing in his sleigh turns his grey eyes upon his murderer, Mathias gives a cry of terror and falls senseless. The curtain falls.

The perfect illusion of the vision and the actor's coup de théâtre evoke a shout of applause. But it is not sustained. The audience is puzzled. The actor is not called before the curtain. Lewis leaps from his seat and makes for the pass-door to the stage. Throughout the act he had suffered agonies of apprehension. As each cue came for the sound of bells he tugged at his luxuriant red moustache and muttered in hoarse whispers: 'The Bells! Where are they? What the devil are they about?' The sound which terrified the burgomaster brought comfort to the author, who would sink back into his chair with an audible sigh of relief. In his dressing-room, Irving is composed and coldly determined. He knows that success still hangs in the balance but that he had the audience with him for the last five minutes of the act.

The second act is concerned with the festivities on the eve of his daughter's wedding. Now that the guilty secret is out, the audience is able to appreciate keenly the actor's brilliant handling of the burgo-master's appalling mental conflict. 'He is at once,' wrote Oxenford of this passage, 'in two worlds between which there is no link—an outer world which is ever smiling, an inner world which is purgatory. Hence the dreaminess in his manner which accurately represents his frequent transitions from a display of domestic affections to the fearful work of self-communion.'

Here Irving had taken the text and forced it to serve the mood of a man being destroyed by his remorse rather than of a cunning rogue in fear of detection. The audience is moved by his infinite tenderness towards his daughter. When, alone, he counts the gold set aside for his daughter's dowry and finds a coin which came from the Jew's girdle, he picks it out and puts it on one side, murmuring: 'No, no . . . not for them, for me,' as though it was an intolerably heavy burden that he must bear alone. Involuntarily he wipes his fingers, as though wet with blood, upon his coat. When his son-in-law, the gendarme, expounding his theories about the murder of the Jew, comes perilously near the truth, Mathias's kindly indulgence and gentle raillery conceals a pounding heart and a fevered mind from all but the audience.

The frantic Lewis, when he darted behind the scenes after the second act, was able to assure Irving that the audience was with him. Irving, of course, knew that as well as a mesmerist knows when his subject passes into a controlled trance. He felt the calm assurance of a general who, having heard that his troops have turned the enemy's flank, sets in motion the frontal attack which will turn their defeat into a rout. The last act would be entirely in his hands; for twenty minutes, he, whom they knew only as an accomplished comedian, had to hold their attention with a ghastly pantomime. If for a moment his hold weakened, the drama would totter and fall into bathos from which nothing could retrieve it.

The curtain rises on a shallow scene—a small bedroom with a door on the right and opposite to it on the extreme left a curtained alcove containing a bed. Mathias is escorted to his room by his family and friends, all a little exalted by the festivities, the sound of which can still be heard below. After interminable goodnights—which strain the burgomaster's nerves to breaking point, so much is he longing for rest and solitude—they leave him. Taking off his coat, he retires into the alcove; a hand comes through the curtain and puts out the candle. The sound of revelling fades away as, at first an uncertain nebula of lights and shadows, the dim shape of a vast court of justice is revealed as the wall of the bedroom melts away. Three judges in black crêpe and red robes, the only touch of colour in a grim grisaille, sit upon the bench, flanked by advocates and officials of the court. Before them, in the well of the court, is a table upon which lie the ragged blood-stained coat and cap of the murdered Jew. As the scene resolves itself, attention is focused on a figure huddled upon a stool in front of the table. It is Mathias. He is wearing a hooded, full-skirted blouse and gaiters— the clothes he wore on the night of the crime. He is on trial for his life. The president of the court begins his examination. His deadly questioning is parried by Mathias's denials, at first truculent but becoming increasingly hysterical and defiant. The president, unable to shake the prisoner's contradictions, summons the mesmerist and, in spite of Mathias's craven protests and appeals to common justice, hands the prisoner over to him. Mathias's staring eyes are fixed upon the audience. They are the symbols of his resistance, but they droop and close as he passes into a trance. The examination proceeds, but now the prisoner is his own accuser. Step by step, at the bidding of the mesmerist, he re-enacts his crime. In a low, hollow voice, he recalls every detail of the night's horror which is graven deeply on his tortured mind. The Jew has left the inn. Mathias rises from his stool. Now, like a sleepwalker, the wretch begins to mime the pursuit and murder of the Jew—his words recording the conflicting thoughts which pass through his mind. He is crossing the snow-covered field. 'How the dogs howl on Daniel's farm!' The word 'Howl' echoes through the court and with shuddering conviction the audience identify themselves

with the loneliness of the night and of the slayer. For a moment
Mathias, when he reaches the place where he has planned to make his
attack, believes that the Jew has already passed. He thanks God
fervently for his delivery from evil—but the prayer is still on his lips
as the sound of bells announces the Jew's approach. He springs upon
the sleigh and strikes down his victim with a hatchet. The body
tumbles to the road. A flurry of bells suggests the panic flight of the
horse. He fumbles with the body—ah—the girdle—full of gold, quite
full. Bending down, he lifts the cumbrous corpse onto his back and
staggers with it to the lime kiln. As the Jew is consumed in the flames
his eyes linger accusingly on his murderer. Mathias screams and covers
his face with his hands. Exhausted, he sinks onto the stool and is
huddled once more in sleep. At the president's direction the mesmerist
awakens him. Mathias is shown the transcript of his deposition. In
cornered rage and dismay he tears it to pieces. His appeals for justice
and mercy are drowned in the president's solemn pronouncement of
the death sentence. The court dissolves into uncertain shadows which
harden into the severe simplicities of the burgomaster's bedroom. It is
morning—his daughter's wedding day. They are knocking at the door
to wake him. Behind the curtained alcove there is no sign of movement.
The voices outside and the knocking on the door become more urgent.
Blows are struck upon the door which is burst open. As those who have
come to wake him run towards the alcove, Mathias staggers through
the curtain. His face is livid with terror—no make-believe pallor but
waxen features drained of blood. His hands claw at his throat. A thin,
strangled voice forces its way through invisible constrictions. 'Take
the rope from my neck . . . take the rope from my neck!' A strong
man is in his death agony. His unseeing eyes seek pitifully to recognize
the delusions of a dream. The pupils of the eyes roll upwards. The
ghastly mask is petrified and tinted with the greyness of death. The
limbs grow cold. As he falls, his wife catches him in her arms.

3

The curtain fell. For several moments the audience sat in shocked
silence, which was broken by the whispering flurry of attendants as
they removed a lady who had fainted in the stalls. They had witnessed
the violent egress of a soul from a body—hardly able to accept it as an
illusion, such was the appalling physical and spiritual intensity of the
acting. Suddenly the tension was relieved—the mesmerist had broken
his spell. A tumult of cheers and round upon round of applause brought

up the curtain once more. There was Irving, bowing in modest acceptance of their acclaim; there was Lewis, in an ecstasy, wringing the actor's
hand. Another burst of shouting and applause, and there was old
Bateman, leading Irving back onto the stage, beaming all over his
handsome face and patting his friend on the back. The incredible had
happened. Irving's intuition had proved faultless—the fortunes of
the Batemans were saved.

At length the applause died away. The excited chatter which
drowned the orchestra during the interval subsided as the curtain rose
on *Pickwick*. This piece served only to impress upon those who stayed
to see it the contrast between the tragedian who had appalled them as
Mathias and the comedian who now diverted them with his antics as
Jingle. At its conclusion, Irving received another ovation and the
curtain fell for the last time.

In the foyer, the critics jostled each other impatiently as they hurried
to record their impressions of that extraordinary evening. Clement
Scott, who had recently been appointed to the *Daily Telegraph*,
bumped into Dutton Cook of the *Pall Mall Gazette*. The old critic,
who was not much given to eulogy, was full of enthusiasm and praise
for everything he had seen and heard—Irving's performance, the
production and the *mise en scène*. Lord Lytton was loudly voicing his
envy of authors who would be lucky enough to have their plays
interpreted by such an actor. Scott hurried off to write the notice which
he had to submit to J. M. Levy, the founder and proprietor of the
Daily Telegraph, at his home in Gower Street. In the early days of the
paper, Levy, who was an enthusiastic playgoer, had been his own
dramatic critic. He still liked to edit the theatre notices. When first
nights, which he himself usually attended, fell on a Saturday when the
office was closed, he insisted on the critic coming to his house and
discussing what was to be said about the play. That night Levy had
seen *The Bells*; when Scott came to see him after the performance he
greeted him by saying: 'Tonight I have seen a great actor at the
Lyceum—a great actor. There was a poor house. Write about him so
that everyone shall know he is great.'

With such a mandate, Scott was able to give free rein to his own
enthusiasm. A sceptical assistant-editor, when he read the notice,
questioned him about this man Irving and asked if it was wise to write
in such extravagant terms of any actor. Scott quoted his authority.
Meanwhile, in the offices of forty other newspapers and periodicals,
the critics who had been at the Lyceum that night would be writing
in a similar strain.

4

The Lyceum was dark. The last carriages and cabs had clattered away westwards with their cargoes of dumbfounded playgoers in whose ears the sleigh bells still jangled. Irving and his wife drove to the house of the Hain Friswells, who had arranged a small supper party in their honour. Florence had waited in the brougham with growing impatience while her husband received the congratulations of critics and friends who thronged his dressing-room.

First-night parties are hazardous affairs; none can tell whether they will be festive or funereal. Until the curtain falls, the host must remain in doubtful anxiety. All those who sat down to supper at the Hain Friswells were aware of the tremendous risks which had hung over the evening, so that they were overwhelmed with relief and delight in their friend's unquestioned success. The occasion called for champagne. At one end of the table the actor, exhausted but exhilarated, basked in the unstinted praise of those around him as they went over every phase of the performance which had culminated in his triumph. Some of them, however, felt their jubilation curbed by a dissentient; by one who, instead of being the happiest of them all, let in a cold draught of sceptical ill-humour. At the other end of the table Florence held aloof from the celebrations. Eager to get home, she expressed nothing but a querulous anxiety that her husband might be boring the company.

Irving may not have noticed his wife's curious behaviour. In the brougham, as they drove home towards Fulham, he was in the best of spirits. Perhaps he was thinking of his hero, Edmund Kean, who, in the hour of his own hard-won triumph at Drury Lane, exclaimed to his wife, 'Mary, you shall ride in your carriage. . . .' He laid his hand on Florence's arm, saying, 'Well, my dear, we too shall soon have our own carriage and pair!' Florence was no doubt very tired. Incapable of sharing her husband's misfortunes or hopes, she now rebelled against the adulation conceded to him by his friends. Her smouldering and jealous temper lowered her guard on her tongue.

'Are you going on making a fool of yourself like this all your life?' she asked.

They were crossing Hyde Park Corner. Irving told the driver of the brougham to stop. Without a word he got out and left his wife to continue the journey alone. He never returned to his home and he never spoke to her again. He started to walk towards Kensington Gore, where he knew the Bateman family would give him shelter. In that hour the course of his life and his aspect to the world changed.

The night's victory had delivered the English theatre into his hands. Clear of purpose and ruthlessly determined, he knew that the hour had come when, as master of his art and champion of his profession, he could give practical expression to his long-cherished ideals. But he must travel alone. Brodribb, scarred and wounded by the hard years and by the bitterness of estrangement from his mother, his lover and his wife, must in future be invisible and invulnerable to his fellow-men. He would always be Irving's familiar, acquainted with grief and soft of heart, but he would be shielded by the mask and armour of his master. Already, like shifting sands, the very bones and cartilages of John Brodribb's face, the open countenance of a countryman, were resolving into the features of Henry Irving, mobile and serviceable to the actor, yet having the command and dignity natural to a leader and a crusader. Only the mouth was beyond the sculptor's power to change; the tender, almost feminine smile, so endearing to Irving's friends and so disarming to his enemies, was the smile of Brodribb.

PART THREE

HENRY IRVING

———◦◦◦———

' . . . I meditate very often (more than you suppose) on what I saw done by H. I. as metteur-en-scéne (i.e. boss creator of all that goes on on the boards) and in those plays before 1880. "The Bells"—Erckmann—Chatrian had given him their analysis of the whole play, but he had to see it come to life. And *since* then, and since we *saw* it we can say too easily "without Erk—Chat: Where would H. I. have been —for their directions are very exact and copious—good—I allow all that—but ask anyone else except H. I. to attempt to realize what they wrote down and not a man in all Europe but H. I. could have done it. His hovering affectionate CARE for every line uttered, every move made, of everyone in the cast is what distinguished him there—as in every piece he touched afterwards.

Some pieces he loved much more than others—I can allow that— but by jingo! when he did love a piece it began to glow. Oh, not alone his own role—that of course—but everyone's role—and every scene— every bit of scenery and every light—I've used the words "affection" and "love" and they are the only two which are rich enough to say what his thought and touch did. And I would prefer to leave the word *art* and artistry out of it—since I believe that as with some few great artists those things actually never occurred to him.

Expression all the time is what counted and he reached it every time through the affection with which he approached the piece he loved.'

Edward Gordon Craig to the author, May 23rd, 1949.

CHAPTER XIV

Playmaking at the Lyceum

———◆◇◆———

I

On Monday, November 27th, 1871, Henry Irving, at the age of thirty-three, had reached the first stage on the pilgrimage to which he had dedicated himself. The road had been devious and for the most part uphill, but at last he had topped the rise. In twelve arduous years he had played some six hundred and thirty parts. Though he had little material reward to show for his immense labour, the prospect was bright. There appeared to be no obstacle to prevent the full expression of a genius fertilized by study, disciplined by practice, fortified by robust health and held to its course by an infallible sense of direction.

Throughout Sunday he and Bateman awaited with impatience the verdict of the critics. On the Monday morning, with one single and certain note they heralded the appearance of an actor whom they recognized, if not as the saviour of the English theatre, as one who might arrest the course of its decline. The impact of *The Bells*, or of the man whose acting had sustained the play, upon critics and playgoers alike came at a moment when, between the extremes of the postured artificialities of tragedy and the realistic understatement of the new school of comedy, English drama hung lifeless and incapable of rousing deep or noble emotion. Out of a grey, quiescent sky a whirlwind of passion and sincerity had struck the London theatre. Nor was the whirlwind without substance, for all paid tribute to the solid core of accomplished artistry round which it revolved. They had resigned themselves to a period of drama in little, exquisite but unmoving. This newcomer, Henry Irving, reminded them suddenly and surprisingly that the higher drama and the delineation of the greater passions could be portrayed without exaggeration or rant. Only one paper, the *Saturday Review*, qualified its praise; their critic found it difficult to believe that any human creature could wish to see the play a second time. He quoted the

Frenchman's comment on fox-hunting—'I have been!'—a comment which, with its hint of unimaginable horrors, gave an inviting, if false, impression of the play to seekers after sensation. As the weeks went by, the unanimity of the critics was reflected in the response of the public who flocked to the Lyceum and, night after night, acclaimed the actor with undiminishing enthusiasm. 'Have you seen *The Bells*?' became the opening gambit of London conversation; Irving competed with the Tichborne claimant, who was appearing at the Old Bailey, as an inexhaustible subject of speculation and discussion.

Overnight Irving had become a personage who excited the curiosity of the literary and fashionable world. Those who sought his company were surprised to find that a man, whose tragical force had overwhelmed them in the theatre, was gentle and unassuming, with a natural dignity which was a rare attribute among the heavy tragedians of the day. Sir Frederick Pollock, the biographer of Macready, wrote in his diary on April 11th, 1872: 'To the Lyceum. Irving in *The Bells* . . . he came to our box and we then made for the first time the personal acquaintance of a man whose character and good qualities endear him to all who have the advantage of knowing him—generous almost to a fault, considerate, and always studying the good of those with whom he has to do.' Pollock, like many others who met the actor in the hour of his first success, found that their introduction to him was the prelude to a lifelong friendship.

Bateman, overjoyed by this sudden reversal of fortune and fully persuaded that it was the result of his own foresight and faith in Irving, threw himself into the welcome task of exploiting their success with uninhibited zeal. His press advertisements grew longer and more buoyant in tone. The name of George Belmore, his star comedian, hitherto displayed in heavy type, shrank in size, while the name of Henry Irving, in even larger capitals, proclaimed the principal attraction at the Lyceum. Occasionally his American methods of publicity were thought to be in doubtful taste. When the Prince of Wales, proceeding on a state visit to the City, was greeted by a string of golden papier mâché bells hung across the Strand near the Lyceum, he alone seemed to be amused by the Colonel's original welcome. Although several critics warned Bateman that, in allowing Irving to play Jingle after Mathias, he was in danger of flogging a willing horse to exhaustion, his showman's instinct told him otherwise. Indeed, on April 1st he replaced *Pickwick*, in which Belmore had been starred in the title role, by a revival of Kenney's farce, *Raising the Wind*, in which Irving starred as Jeremy Diddler. As the manager foresaw, the audience having been exhausted by the horrors of *The Bells*, delighted in Irving's versatility and in his display of every trick in the comedian's bag as he romped his way through a harlequinade of farcical buffoonery. Irving, who had been long accustomed to such hard and contrasting work, had no complaint to make against the exacting demands of his manager. By the end of April, when *The Bells* had been played for one hundred and fifty nights to crowded houses, Bateman had no very clear idea how

Irving as Jingle

he could exploit Irving's extraordinary popularity in the future. All that he had in mind was to reap the reward of their London success with a tour in the provinces, while his daughter Kate returned to London for a season at the Lyceum. Irving, however, now supremely conscious of his mission and fully aware that he was caught in the floodtide of his affairs, had to decide quickly what his next step was to be.

An actor of genius will always have difficulty in finding original plays to suit his particular gifts; in the face of this difficulty he will have to resist the temptation to fall back exclusively on the classics. The

characters of Shakespeare and Sheridan are to the actor what the son-
atas of Beethoven are to a virtuoso pianist—creations great in themselves, yet forever capable of fresh interpretation by an inspired talent.
As the centuries go by the number of classical plays increases so that
an actor, as for instance a member of the Comédie Française, can with
honour exercise his art for a lifetime without ever creating an original
part by a contemporary playwright. Only once in England had the
supreme genius of playwright and player appeared in the same generation, when Shakespeare and Burbage had collaborated in the creation of
theatrical masterpieces. For the most part, English actors have had to
choose between breaking new ground with the works of untried and
often mediocre contemporary playwrights or of playing for safety in
classic roles of proven popularity. By taking the latter course they risk
only unfavourable comparison with predecessors more talented than
themselves; by indulging in rash experiment they gamble not only
with their reputation but with their hard-won savings. Only actors of
great genius have to make this choice. Excellent and serviceable actors
will fit more readily into the pattern of their time and will earn the
praise of dramatists many of whom abhor the actor of genius and, with
some justification, regard him as a usurper upon the stage which they
wish to use as a dialectical platform.

Henry Irving was an actor of genius, though in the spring of 1872
only a few discerning people had recognised him as such. He had to
find plays in which his genius could develop and expand—and he had
to find them quickly. Shakespeare was his god—a god to be approached
with reverence and humility. He longed, in due time, to play as many
of the great characters of Shakespeare as he deemed his talent and understanding to be worthy of attempting. The time, however, was not
advantageous. Bateman, heedful of Chatterton's dictum, would not
risk what he believed to be certain disaster by backing him to star in a
Shakespearian production, however successful he had been in comedy
or melodrama. For an actor in Irving's position, searching the thin
ranks of English dramatists for a poet who could provide the sinews of
the romantic revival of which he dreamed, the outlook was bleak.
Bulwer Lytton had long ago abandoned poetry for politics. Of the
melodramatists, who were almost consumed by their own prolificacy
and were already half-buried under scenic splendours of their own contriving, Tom Taylor alone had risen above their pervading crudities,
and he was near the end of his life. James Albery had failed to fulfil
the promise of *Two Roses*. Leopold Lewis, intoxicated by success,
was already retiring on Irving's laurels; for him *The Bells* were to

Irving as Mathias
in *The Bells*

Irving as Jingle

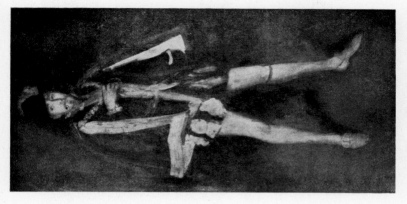

Irving as Philip of Spain
From the picture by
J. M. Whistler

Irving as Hamlet
From a drawing by
Sir Bernard Partridge

Sir Henry Irving as Dubosc in The Lyons Mail

Irving as Dubosc
From a print by James Pryde

ring in and to ring out a life of brief notoriety which ended in a whirl of dissipation and delusion. Robertson, having created 'a minutely modern school of acting' through the medium of the Bancrofts, was already far advanced along a bright metalled road deviating sharply from the romantic glades through which Irving knew his own path lay.

Such was the small company of English playwrights. It was, therefore, with keen and amused interest that Henry Irving regarded an uncouth figure who, at this time, became a frequent visitor to the Bateman's supper table. Above the dreamy eyes of this strange man, a high, intellectual brow ended abruptly in the fringe of a rather unconvincing wig; the lower half of his face being hidden by flowing moustaches and a tangled beard. His clothes looked as though he invariably went to bed in them, his pockets were stuffed with smoking apparatus, the handy gear of an artist and rolls of manuscript; his face, more often than not, was smeared with charcoal or paint; yet, for all this, he wore the unmistakable air of a gentleman. His name was William Gorman Wills, a painter and poet by vocation and a playwright from necessity, whom Bateman had recently engaged at a salary of three hundred a year to be the dramatist at the Lyceum.

Wills was forty-four years old. Ten years ago he had arrived in London from Ireland, torn between the rival claims of poetry and painting; as a poet he had won the Vice-Chancellor's medal at Trinity College, Dublin; as a painter he had made no mark whatever. For several years, on an allowance from his father, he lived in London a life of dilettante bohemianism centred on the Garrick Club and on the Arundel Club where he had his rooms. When his father died, the allowance ceased and he became responsible for the support of his mother. Believing painting to be his true métier, he set himself up in a studio in the Fulham Road where soon he made enough to provide for them both by doing idealized portrait studies in pastel at twenty guineas a time. His barn-like studio became not only the rendezvous of fashionable sitters but the haunt of spongers, beggars and models, who camped upon his dilapidated furniture, ate his meals, and pocketed the money which with absent-minded generosity he gave to anyone who seemed to need it. He looked upon his portraits as a mere means of livelihood. Intermittently and with desperate sincerity he worked upon four great canvases upon which he strove feverishly to realize the romantic visions, barren of art or invention, which haunted his imagination. His portraits brought him a measure of fame and a command to draw Queen Victoria's children at Osborne. When he returned to London he found that royal patronage had increased the number and quality of his clients. He made an effort to play the fashionable portrait painter by engaging a liveried page to attend upon his sitters; but the page soon became infected with the pervading disorder and melted into the background of hangers-on, kittening cats, and a monkey which swung happily from the gas bracket.

Wills found time to write one or two novels, which were commended by his friends at the Arundel Club. They suggested that he should combine his gift for verse and dramatic construction by writing a play. He was introduced to Herman Vezin of the Princess's Theatre, for whom he wrote *The Man o' Airlie*. Vezin produced the play in 1867 and it failed. Encouraged by Westland Marston, Wills, in collaboration with the old dramatist, wrote a gloomy drama, *Broken Spells*, which, again produced by Vezin, was equally unsuccessful. When Vezin heard that Bateman was looking for a play for his daughter Kate, he introduced him to Wills. The Colonel took immediately to this dreamy Irishman, whose appearance conformed perfectly to his idea of a dramatic genius, and commissioned him to make an adaption of the *Medea* of Euripides. Wills managed to satisfy everyone concerned and it was decided that Kate should appear in *Medea in Corinth* at the Lyceum when Irving went on tour.

Wills's greatest charm lay in his simple optimism—anything which he undertook was to be the best which he had ever done. Irving was attracted by his enthusiasm and by his vague absorption in his art, about which there was no affectation. Wills saw in the actor's grave bearing, in his pale ascetic features and in his eyes, which scanned a horizon as distant and insubstantial as his own, the perfect embodiment of the great romantic figures who populated the world of his fertile imagination. Bateman, with a patron's pride, welcomed the signs of harmonious collaboration between his protégés; he saw himself going down to history as the sponsor of the greatest artistic partnership of his age. But the cool wind of commercial reason blew upon his self-content when the actor and the poet suggested that the latter should start immediately upon a play in verse which was to be written round the character of King Charles the First. At first the Colonel was as unable to conceive his Mathias playing a martyr king as he had been to perceive the burgomaster in his Jingle. But before very long Wills's ardour and Irving's quiet self-confidence overcame his doubts. Having agreed to their proposal, he made his own contribution by presiding over their discussions and, by drawing on his vast experience of play carpentry and of the public taste, keeping the poet's feet on the ground in matters of situation and construction. Before Irving and his company left for the provinces in May, Bateman had decided to present *Charles I* at the Lyceum at the end of September, when Kate finished her season with the new *Medea* and the evergreen *Leah*. It is possible that the Colonel agreed to this more readily when they assured him that his daughter Isabel would be perfectly cast in the part of Henrietta Maria.

Before leaving London, Irving wrote to his father:

'My dear Father,

I enclose P.O.O. You have I dare say seen that on 20 May I open in Manchester for 3 weeks. After that I shall probably have a rest for some weeks which I shall not object to.

I am very well indeed—the hard work agrees with me—my health is in capital condition for I've lately been vaccinated—the matter took splendidly—and I've two great scars from the operation but have not experienced the least pain. On Saturday night I rec'd a most distressing letter from the Webbs.[1] They evidently are in a very sad state. But it seems rather hard that I should be solicited (with the heavy expenses that I have) when there are two children able certainly to do something and regularly I should think.

Did I tell you that an oil picture of me in *The Bells* will be in this year's Royal Academy. I have been painted by one of the first artists in London—Mr. Archer.

My domestic matters are progressing in the lawyer's hands—but no signature or definite arrangement has been yet made.

I hope you are well—accept my best love, affectionately yours,

Henry.'

He would have helped the Webbs if he could, but for the moment his heart was larger than his purse; his time and his work he gave freely in such causes. During the run of *The Bells*, he joined several variety artists in giving an entertainment at the Shoreditch town hall in order to raise funds for the widow and children of Henry Thomas, a popular local entertainer. Irving had experienced the charity of actor towards actor which was a theatrical tradition. In following that tradition he was remarkable only in that, as his purse grew heavier and honours were heaped upon him, his concern for those of his companions during his early struggles who had been less fortunate than himself became more acute.

---

[1] Probably Henry Webb and his brother Charles. Henry Webb was manager of the Old Queen's Theatre, Dublin, where Irving made his first and disastrous appearance in Ireland.

The scars of his marriage took longer to heal than those of his vaccination. His second son had been born at the end of December and had been christened Laurence Sidney, after his godfather, Toole, and his godmother, Mrs. Bateman. Toole may have tried to persuade him to attend the christening; he certainly interceded with Florence on his friend's behalf, though not at his invitation. Early in March Irving wrote to his wife of his irrevocable decision:

'. . . I have seen Toole and asked him kindly to leave me to the settlement of my own affairs. Any interference from any quarter is useless for I have determined to live apart from you . . . this course is imperative for my sake and for the sake of those relying on me . . . I sincerely hope that you will not re-open—or attempt to—the causes which have led to our parting. On this subject my mouth for the future will be closed to friend and foe. And now goodbye. I hope you will wish me well as I wish you.'

The separation gave him little satisfaction. Even though he was forced to admit the hopeless incompatibility of himself and his wife, he regretted deeply the estrangement from his children which would be the penalty of his desertion. His responsibilities were indeed heavy. Out of his salary of fifteen pounds a week he gave Florence eight pounds, so that, after deducting his allowance to his father, he was left with about five pounds a week on which to live and to keep up the appearances that the changes in his circumstances demanded. No doubt he did not worry overmuch about money—he had always been careless on that score. It was the sense of failure in his human relationships which had embittered the taste of his recent success. Never, since he left his Aunt Sarah at Halsetown, had he known what it was to have a sympathetic and understanding background, such as only a home can provide. Since his childhood he had longed for this kind of companionship. Yet he seemed doomed to a solitary existence within himself which robbed success of much of its sweetness and made failure harder to bear. For a time he sought to console himself with heavy drinking, but, characteristically, he indulged his self-pity only at the end of the day's work. He found little comfort in these midnight bouts, for, while the Behenna legs were sadly affected, his perceptions remained as acute as ever, so that the burden of his sorrows fell only upon those who had to help him to bed. The Batemans were quick to realize the danger which threatened him and had overwhelmed so many other actors of promise; to combat it, the girls brewed strong beef tea while Henry was at the theatre and, on his return, insisted upon his drinking it, until by degrees the beneficial effects of this innocent stimulant convinced him that alcohol should be a convivial rather than an anodyne resource. Irving owed much to the Batemans, who had taken him into their family circle and had treated him like a son. He could not, however, impose indefinitely upon their generosity. With Mrs. Bateman's help he found furnished rooms in Bruton Street to which he would return at the end of the provincial tour.

The tour was limited to Manchester and Liverpool. In each town he played for three weeks—two weeks of *The Bells* alone and for the last week with *Raising the Wind* added to the bill. In both towns the impression of *The Bells* was as profound and the praise of Irving's Mathias as extravagant as it had been in London. The Liverpool *Courier*, giving up the search for new words of approbation, quoted Lessing on Shakespeare: 'He gives a living picture of all the most minute and secret artifices which by a feeling steals into our souls, of all the stratagems by which every other passion is made subservient to it till it becomes the sole tyrant of our desires and our aversions.' If such comparison with his idol seemed to Irving a trifle fulsome, the general recognition that his effects were the result of study and hard work rather than of inspiration pleased him—coming, as it did, from people among whom he had laboured so long to this end.

Phelps was in Manchester playing Wolsey in Calvert's production of *Henry VIII*. Probably he had no chance to see *The Bells*. No doubt he and Irving met, for they lodged in the same house; though Phelps later spoke warmly of him to Toole, the two actors can have seen little of each other. Phelps, now over seventy, was regular in his habits; retiring to bed immediately on his return from the theatre, he was out and about early in the morning. Irving liked to linger over his supper with a friend and to read in bed for an hour or two in the morning. If Irving respectfully twitted Phelps on having warned him, sixteen years ago, that the stage was an unrequiting profession, the old actor may have signified with a grunt that he stood by what he had said. For this simple man, who had done so much to prepare the way for Irving and others who followed him, who knew no greater happiness than to wander with a friend along the banks of some peaceful trout stream, had to work until, six years later, illness and death ended his last engagement. It is unlikely that Irving, as the grey mists of the unhappy past were dissolving in the rising sun of his success, saw in his boyhood's hero, now aged and burnt out, the proven truth of the earlier admonition.

Irving's old friend, Edward Saker, was manager of the Royal Alexandra Theatre, Liverpool. Saker was pleased and proud to see his friend established as a great and popular actor; Irving must have felt that he had made amends to Saker for the great Linlithgow fiasco, by filling his theatre to capacity during the whole of his engagement.

After a short holiday Irving returned to London. The change of air and scene had done him good; his domestic troubles had fallen into their proper perspective. The provincial audiences, whose esteem he valued, had endorsed London's opinion of *The Bells*. He was eager to get to work on *Charles I*. His confidence in Wills had been increased by the success of *Medea in Corinth*, which would undoubtedly have had a longer run in London had not Kate Bateman been committed to another provincial tour. If he could hold his audiences in a part which called neither for broad caricature nor for the macabre he would be a step further towards the Shakesperian roles on which he had set his heart. He found that it was high time he took a grip of things. Wills was a dilatory worker and needed the spur of praise or penury to make him write a play. Moreover, in Irving's absence, he had begun a large canvas of 'Ophelia and Laertes' which threatened to become a serious distraction. But his poetic muse seemed to thrive on distractions and, to indulge her further, he had acquired a large musical box with a repertoire of operatic airs. Having wound up the instrument and set it going, he would dab happily at 'Ophelia and Laertes' while he dictated blank verse to his young amanuensis, A. C. Calmour.

In a very short time, with the help of Bateman, the play began to take shape. Bateman, from the start, was anxious to avoid politics and urged them to concentrate on the domestic tragedy. At that time, a picture by F. Goodall entitled 'The Happy Days of Charles I', which depicted Charles with his family at Hampton Court, had, as an engraving, enjoyed considerable popularity. Starting with this tableau, they contrived in the first act to show the king's devotion to his family, the queen's hatred and suspicion of the Earl of Moray, a brief glimpse of the king's relationship to the Commons and Huntley's suggestion that he should meet Cromwell. The act would end with the embarkation of the royal party in the state barge. The second act, the meeting between Charles and Cromwell, put them on more dangerous ground. With Irving's insistence that the audience's sympathies must be with the king, with Wills's readiness to give voice to his Irish hatred of Cromwell and with Bateman's impatience of historical truth if it seemed likely to weaken the drama, their confection became such a travesty of characters and facts that, though Irving may have been oblivious of the danger, only a very great actor could save it from disaster. Later a critic, reminding his readers of Lessing's admission that 'the dramatist may deal as freely as he likes with history, provided he doesn't destroy the typical significance of his personages', compared Wills to a traveller who uses a map of the Perthshire Highlands to find his way through the Swiss Alps. In fairness to Wills, Irving and Batemen were his ardent fellow-travellers on this sentimental journey. When plays are written in the theatre by collaborators who know what they are about, they are likely to satisfy the audience and to enrage the historian. It was, no doubt, under such pressure that Shakespeare wrote his fantastic but evidently popular caricature of Joan of Arc. The third act presented more difficulty. The scene was Naseby; the battle at its crisis. Moray's treason, the surrender of the king to Cromwell and his scathing denunciation of the traitor all afforded theatrically effective situations, and plenty of scope for the poet. Wills rose to the occasion. Charles's last words to Moray were perhaps the best in the play:

> *I saw a picture once, by a great Master,*
> *It was an old man's head,*
> *Narrow and evil was its wrinkled front—*
> *Eyes closed and cunning: a dull vulpine smile,*
> *'Twas called a Judas, wide that painter erred;*
> *Judas had eyes like thine, of candid blue,*
> *His skin was smooth, his hair of youthful gold;*
> *Upon his brow shone the white stamp of truth,*
> *And lips, like thine, did give the traitor kiss.*
> *The King, my father, loved thee—at his death*
> *He gave me solemn charge to cherish thee,*
> *And I have kept it to my injury.*
> *It is a score of years since then, my lord—*
> *Hast waited all this time to pay me thus?*

On this note, Wills had intended to end the play. But Bateman would not hear of it; he demanded another domestic scene. By this time the poet and the actor had learnt to respect his showman's instinct. Many alternative endings were considered and rejected. One night, when the problem was still unsolved, they were all supping together at Kensington Gore. It was long after midnight and the Colonel appeared to be dozing in his chair. Suddenly he started from his sleep and cried: 'I've got it! The last act of *Black-Eyed Susan*—prayer-book, chain and all!' He was thinking of the touching scene in Jerrold's old melodrama in which Will, the Jack Tar, unjustly condemned to death by a courtmartial through the evil machinations of the wicked Captain Crosstree, says farewell to his sweetheart, Sue. Irving, who had played Captain Crosstree in his Edinburgh days, followed Bateman's train of thought and interpreted his meaning to Wills, who must have been astonished by this seemingly vulgar irrelevance. In a very short time the act was planned to everyone's satisfaction. It would show the king, on the morning of his execution, taking farewell of his family and hiding from his children the true nature of his last journey; his parting from his wife as the dawn breaks and the recitation of his few personal bequests; the curtain would fall upon his last word, 'Remember', as he turns to gaze upon his queen for the last time before following the guards to the scaffold in Whitehall.

Bateman was now satisfied that he had the ingredients of another success. Under Irving's direction, rehearsals went smoothly ahead. He cannot have been satisfied with the casting of George Belmore for Cromwell. Belmore was a good comedian but had neither the appearance nor the capacity to play a character whose development at the hands of Wills was the play's main hazard. The Colonel held his fire and did not announce the play until a fortnight before its production. Gossip had already promoted the same scepticism of Irving's ability to play a king as had previously ridiculed his idea of playing a burgomaster. Irving knew what he was about and was quite untroubled by any reports of the kind that reached him. The Bateman family noticed in him an unusual lightness of heart; years afterwards Mrs. Bateman recalled that it was the only time that Irving had ever seemed young. Bateman and Irving discovered that they shared a liking for sea fishing. Together with the rest of the family, they made weekend expeditions to Margate. Isabel and Virginia had as little taste for seafaring as they had for acting; but as a filial duty, they put to sea and baited hooks with odious worms for their father and his picturesque friend, who seemed impervious to the wallowings of the rowing boat or to the malaise of the two girls. Once ashore, they soon recovered their spirits and their appetite for the enormous shrimp teas which Mrs. Bateman had prepared in their lodgings for Irving's special delight.

By the middle of September the production of *Charles I* was beginning to take shape. In the scene-painting rooms of the Lyceum Hawes Craven, his head covered with the red bandanna handkerchief which was recognized by his assistants as a signal for close and intensive action, was taking full advantage of the opportunities which the play, and the Colonel's liberal encouragement, offered him. Irving, with all the confidence that his successful direction of *The Bells* had given him, kept a tight hand on the production. With that natural taste and sense of dramatic fitness, which even in his days of apprenticeship had marked his own characterizations, he strove to blend the elements of poetry, design and light into a series of pictures whose harmonies existed only within the frame of a proscenium. The focal point in these pictures was himself—the actor. His conception of the art of the theatre was the creation of a coherent design rigidly held together by the protagonist. To him this was no doubtful theory open to argument or academic discussion. The proof of its validity would be heard at the fall of the curtain on the first performance and would be confirmed nightly in the box-office. It was not an absolute truth but one which had to be reaffirmed by the actor in every role he undertook and could be maintained only by unassailable belief in his own genius. Irving's faith in himself was boundless and so infectious that his fellow-artists surrendered themselves confidently to his direction and fell into the pattern of his design.

During the run of *The Bells* Irving, through an act of kindness on his part, had begun a friendship which meant much to him in the years ahead. The widow of a doctor in Kensington, Mrs. Eleanor James, had written for permission to bring a crippled niece to the Lyceum. She had asked if the girl's chair could be wheeled into the aisle in the stalls. Irving, finding that this was impossible, replied that he would be happy to put the Royal Box at their disposal and invited them to use the private entrance in Burleigh Street. As a token of her gratitude for his consideration and of her admiration for his performance, she sent him a ring. Later Irving called on Mrs. James who, thereafter, was one of several women much older than himself, whose affection he welcomed and upon whose advice on personal matters he depended a good deal. Being entirely outside the world of the theatre, in their company he could drop the guarded reserve which he seldom relaxed in his professional life. A few days before the opening of *Charles I* he wrote to Mrs. James:

'. . . I have been coming to you day by day to offer my regards to you and to thank you also for your luxurious present—but the press of rehearsals has prevented me. If I can possibly call before next Saturday I will—but it's not in my power to say—for we work day and night to complete "Charles". The play is a beautiful one and must I think be successful (I hope you are Conservative) but in these days of odd dramatic taste it is impossible to foretell.

The pleasure of dining with you must be deferred, I fear, some little time. . . . I shall always have a box at your disposal should you like to see "Charles" often.'

To his father he wrote:

'. . . the play was written at my suggestion and the part of Charles—
our martyr king—I, I need hardly tell you, play. You shall come and
see it—you *must*. Costumes, scenery, everything will be beautiful and
the play is a fine one—I think. . . . I have, by the way, a silver snuff
box—sent round from the front on the last night of *The Bells*—in
which I *took* snuff, as I don't take it off the stage, I'll send the box to
you—to use during your lifetime. It's very handsome.

If you can help me (and just as you think best in the matter) to get
clear of these things—I'll send you 30/- instead of 20/-. I wish with
all my soul I could send you 60/- instead but at present I cannot.'

Still hard pressed for money and without financial security of any
kind, Irving with supreme self-confidence and with doubts only of the
play's attraction, was prepared to risk losing the favour of the public
by playing a part for which, in the eyes of his critics and of many of
his supporters, he was ludicrously unsuited.

2

From the moment when, on September 28th, the curtain rose upon
the tableau of Hampton Court there was little doubt of the play's
success—or rather of Irving's success, for it was upon his portrait of
Charles that the play depended. Those who had questioned his ability
to look the part were quickly satisfied. Not only had he outwardly
transformed himself into the twin of Van Dyck's portrait of Charles,
but it was clear that, with his grave and dignified bearing, in his tender
affection for his family, in the fierce disdain with which he denounced
his enemies and in the calm endurance of his own sufferings, he understood the business of kingship. To some it was apparent, in the early
scenes, that Irving was nervous and uncertain of himself. Yet as soon
as he felt that the audience were moved by the play, his nervousness
left him and, as the tragedy unfolded, his Charles grew in stature.
Older theatre-goers found themselves wondering why no actor in
the past had thought of playing this part. As the play proceeded it was
clear that there were to be no dramatic crises, no intrusions of comic
relief—its originality lay in its tranquillity and in the exquisite pathos
of the acting. The audience, few of whom remained dry-eyed, were
blind to everything but the beauty of the production and the grace of
Irving's performance; the verse, however naïve the sentiment or here-
tical the politics it expressed, flowed over them like music. When the

curtain fell on the doomed king's last word, 'Remember!' the applause and cheers were instantaneous. Having recalled Irving several times, the audience shouted for the author. Irving explained that Wills was not in the house but that he would convey to him their favourable verdict. Wills, who shunned publicity of any kind, had stubbornly refused to appear on the stage. Blinded by his own tears, for he was easily moved by his own verse, he had left the theatre. He was well aware that the verdict of the first-night audience was not the final one and that the morning papers might reverse it. He was shrewd enough to know that, however noble and acceptable his Charles had been in Irving's hands, his Cromwell, as portrayed by Belmore, was as provocative a trailing of the coat as ever came out of Dublin.

As it turned out, the opinion of the press was wholly favourable. The critics, to a man, acknowledged Irving's personal triumph. Isabel Bateman's performance as Henrietta Maria was highly praised. In the eyes of her proud father, Irving, now that he had inspired a play which had ensured Isabel's success as well as his own, could do no wrong. Bateman's friends had often criticized him for his persistent exploitation of his daughters and had been struck by a flash of 'chain lightning' for their pains. One of them, old H. J. Byron, who was rehearsing a new play at the Strand Theatre, in a letter to Irving made honourable amends:

September 30th, 1872.

'My dear Irving,

Though I am rather weary of pens and ink I cannot refrain from dropping you a line to express my real delight at your success.

I would also drop a line to Bateman, but possibly he might think it Bunkum. His daughter I thought from the first (when I had the misfortune to speak my mind a little abruptly and perhaps not in very good taste, but I *meant* no harm) was certain to do very well and I am very glad to see *The Times* article on her acting. But of yourself— as one remembering your career from the *first*—Believe me I am charmed. I regret two things—that the play is not mine—and that I cannot see it. Possibly—as they say at the Vic—a day *will* come etc.

Yours sincerely ever,

H. J. Byron.

In due course sharp criticism of Wills's rough handling of Cromwell began to appear in the correspondence columns of the daily press.

Gladstone was Prime Minister, Liberalism was in the air and the author's suggestion that the Protector would have deserted his cause in exchange for the hand in marriage of one of the king's daughters was more than any good Liberal could stand. Wills retaliated with spirit, and a controversy ensued which, cleverly exploited by Bateman, did the play nothing but good. Whenever the audience showed signs of political apathy, the Colonel salted the pit and gallery with a small claque who declared now for Cromwell, now for Charles, with excellent results. The Liberal faction played still further into his hands by promoting the production at the Queen's Theatre of a play entitled *Cromwell*, which was more furiously partisan and a good deal less poetic than Wills's drama. This play failed dismally, and the Puritan cast, though an excellent one, was compelled to surrender unconditionally to the Royalists at the Lyceum. The Colonel, however, was very nearly the victim of his own exuberance. For when, after the play had been running for a month, the Prince and Princess of Wales came to see it, the occasion inspired the factions in the audience, who were fairly evenly matched, to unprecedented cheering and hissing. Fortunately the Royalists appeared to carry the night, but the incident led certain leader writers to call the attention of the Lord Chamberlain to the dangers of playwrights being allowed to engender political heat by playing ducks and drakes with historical facts. Irving had more serious Cromwellian problems on his hands. He realized that Belmore's performance upset the whole balance of the play and weakened the conflict between Cromwell and the king. He insisted, therefore, on replacing him with Henry Forrester, an actor who had been trained by Phelps and was to remain at the Lyceum for many years. When the dust and heat of the controversy had subsided Bateman was able to appreciate the solid worth of their success. He basked in the golden glory of the box-office returns and in the unstinted praise of his acumen and enterprise by distinguished visitors to the Lyceum.

Many years after, Augustus Filon, the French critic, who never forgot Irving's Charles I—'the stately figure with its cold lofty aspect, the look of sadness in the eyes, the lips smiling bitterly under the thin moustache, the pale veined forehead that bore the seal of destiny'—reminded the actor of his visit to the Lyceum when, in 1872, 'I saw you play Charles I. I was sitting then by the side of my dear pupil, the Prince Imperial. The poor boy was all in tears at the farewell scene. Good old Bateman came up to see him and was grandiloquent. I remember to this day his becoming face and his blue coat with brass buttons.' Filon's impression and the Prince Imperial's emotion were shared by the general public who crowded the Lyceum for one hundred and eighty nights.

The success of *Charles I* attracted a new audience to the Lyceum. Henry Irving took his place in the front rank of English actors when Ruskin was the arbiter of artistic taste, when Tennyson was Poet Laureate and when the replicas of Roman and Italian palaces which Leighton and his fellow academicians were building in Fulham and St. John's Wood, bore solid testimony of the esteem in which their peculiar art was held by the intelligentsia and the public. The English drama had lagged behind in the romantic revival which, in the sister arts of painting and poetry, was now in full swing. Every year visitors to the Royal Academy were stirred by vast canvases whose literary message and archaeological accuracy suggested the final tableaux of well-produced plays. Poets were winning their greatest popularity by writing epic verses which, though pleasing enough in print, were most effective as drawing-room recitations. Music, to a lesser degree, conformed to the prevalent romantic taste, though the British public were, on the whole, indifferent to it at a time when 'God Save the Queen' and 'Rule Britannia' gave adequate voice to their hopes and ambitions. None the less, it was the heyday of the sentimental ballad, and even Wills was more widely known as the author of 'I'll Sing Thee Songs of Araby' than as a dramatist. Thus, with Shakespeare under a managerial cloud, and with no choice of entertainment other than the all too robust melodramas and the everyday realisms of the Bancroft school, the public, who sighed over the Pre-Raphaelites and whose dreams were realized by Burne-Jones, found little to satisfy them in the theatre. Suddenly there had appeared at the Lyceum a man who embodied the very spirit of romance, who brought to life the engraved pictures which hung upon their walls and in whose every word and gesture they found their ideal of the long-awaited romantic actor.

It is an all too common mistake for the critics of one period to disparage the art of another in terms of their own imagined enlightenment. Forgetting that their own taste and tenets may be questioned by their successors, they dismiss with contempt those of an earlier generation and the work of the artists who served it. By doing so, they credit both the artist and critics who preceded them with a discernment that most of them were denied. Ruskin, who had been the champion of Turner and had said that Shakespeare was the guide to all that is noblest and truest in English thought, saw in Holman Hunt's 'The Awakening Conscience', ' the perfect union of literature and art'. Sabbatarian England liked her artists to point a moral; her economic expansion and prosperity demanded that their works should be high, wide and handsome. If the Victorian theatre was to take its place with art and literature, the reformation was likely to conform to these principles. Irving's interest in any art but his own was quickened only by its potential effectiveness in the service of the theatre.

Talma, in his essay on the actor's art, wrote that between two persons destined for the stage, one possessing extreme sensibility and the other a profound intelligence, he would, without question, prefer the former. Talma would have preferred Irving. In his life and in his art he was guided solely by his natural instinct for what was right, and by the acute perception which was sharpened by his sensibility. As a boy, he had believed intellectuality to be the most desirable of all attainments. In the intervening years such ambitions were forgotten. He had learnt his art, not by the book, but by rule of thumb; he owed his mastery over it to the exercise of his perception rather than of his intellect, in the academic sense. He had received little education, and none whatever in the humanities. Such culture as he possessed he had picked up as he went along, like a single-handed sailor trying to take soundings as he beats his way up an estuary against wind and tide. His passionate love of Shakespeare was not that of a scholar. He loved him as a divinely inspired actor who, for his fellow-actors, had created characters of gigantic stature and had put into their mouths words of such beauty that, though often his meaning was incomprehensible to the poor creatures who came after him, to declaim them was the summit of their ambition.

At this critical period of Irving's life, when his purpose was clear and the means to achieve it were within his grasp, he had to acquire a sense of artistic values for the proper selection and integration of the work of other artists who would have to contribute to the theatre of his aims. These first two productions had been tentative; yet, after discounting his own contribution, they seemed to have met with the approval of the most cultured men and women of the day. He found, for instance, that Frederick Pollock, who was the friend of Browning, Thackeray and Emerson, and was on intimate terms with many of the members of the Comédie Française, accepted and praised the work of W. G. Wills as readily as that of Bulwer Lytton.

During the run, Helena Faucit wrote to him that her husband, Theodore Martin, 'would tell you how much we admired the Charles I. It is a fine play and finely acted. If *you* were not the hero I should say more but I may say how much I feel that your conception of the character has grown and deepened. You have lived into it and so get within the soul of it. This must be the case in all fine art and thus no first efforts can ever be the best!' Such was the opinion of a scholar who had seen Kean 'plain' and had been chosen by the Queen to write the biography of the Prince Consort.

Irving presumed, therefore, that if Wills could provide him with the material for the expression of his own art he would be acting in accordance with the highest artistic principles if he employed him to write plays for him. From the success of *The Bells* and *Charles I* he took his artistic bearings. He held his course because, in this brief but intensive period of self-education, he believed that, in seeking the guidance and opinion of the best informed people of his time, he had done all that he could to ensure that in matters of taste and aesthetic integrity his theatre would earn the respect and veneration which were accorded to the other arts.

During the last months of the year Irving felt, for the first time, that the ground on which he stood was becoming solid and substantial. To his father, who earlier had offered to lend him a hundred pounds to help him out of his difficulties, he wrote:

'. . . You can do me a very great service by letting me have the money and in case of your being, as you wisely fear, left alone, I'll insure my life for £100 and send you the policy—which I'll keep up myself. In the future I shall give you 30/- a week, and that you can rely on as long as I live—through sickness or any ailment. It is really imperative that the arrears of my wife be all paid off, for until they are, no settlement will she make.

We are doing finely and I've I think a golden harvest in store.'

And a few days later:

'. . . my wife has an appointment with my lawyer either today or tomorrow and then they will settle everything off hand.

I've not time now to write more—"Charles" is going on splendidly and my fortune is made. Think of the position Bateman has placed me in and which I have been able, thank God, to maintain. You must come again when you like and see us in our glory.'

Shortly before Christmas he moved into unfurnished rooms at 15A Grafton Street, which Mrs. Bateman had found for him and were to be his lodgings for nearly thirty years; his home would always be in his theatre. These rooms were at the corner of Bond Street and Grafton Street and were part of the block owned by Messrs. Asprey. Having asked his wife for nothing but his books and his pictures the furnishing of these rooms on his slender income might have taken a long time. His friends, however, came to his aid. To Mrs. James, who had expressed a wish to give him a set of shirt-studs, he suggested frankly a more practical alternative:

'My very dear friend,

You see that at last I've pitched my tent—bedstead. After agonies of doubt and despair at the last moment I took some empty rooms and have since been devoting myself to their fitting up. I'm getting on very well, I think, and have found the novelty of furnishing quite exciting. The attendance in the house is admirable and a great comfort.

And now, like Mr. Cromwell, "I will take the humble boldness" (accepting with delight your exquisite kindness) here to suggest that instead of the studs, would you give me an easy chair or a lounge? Such things are not usually presented as remembrances are they? We'll invent a new method—what say you? I offer no apology. You'd rather, I know, I didn't.

I wish I had known you were at the Lyceum on Saturday. I wonder did your unknown presence have its influence? I thought I acted better than usually—in spite of the dullness of the audience. It was really too bad of you to go alone. However, I'll intercede for your forgiveness.'

At Christmas he wrote to his father:

'. . . I enclose you half of a £5 note—the little extra being enough for a turkey and a bottle of port—which I'm sure the ladies like. Mind it's good. Don't give less than six shillings and none of you'll then be poisoned. I should like to see you all this Christmas—which I hope you'll enjoy. I spend my day with the Batemans—of course.

I yesterday saw my two little ones—and fine fellows they are. The eldest is a regular young Brodribb. The nurse brings them to me—the youngest is just a year old and can't yet walk—but Master Henry is quite a man and I took him to my club[1] where he dined with me in state.

I have a lot of pleasant news in other matters for you. I am surrounded by friends and good wishes, and as far as prosperity, professionally, goes—thank God—no one ever had more. . . .'

There can have been few occasions in the records of London clubs on which a member has entertained his infant son to a Christmas dinner; even if the child's digestion survived the ordeal, the nurse's

[1] Probably the Junior Garrick.

report of it must have caused those at Linden Gardens to dread the little boys' excursions into Bohemia, upon which the law so foolishly insisted.

Christmas Day at Kensington Gore could hardly have been happier. The past year had brought success to all of them; the future seemed full of promise. Irving was keenly sensible of this united family's devotion to him and deeply grateful for their wise and patient ministrations during the dark and troubled months when he had made his home with them. While he and Bateman, in the intervals from feasting, gossiped over their cigars of the past and grew lyrical of the prospects ahead, Mrs. Bateman, thankful for relief from past cares, strummed contentedly upon her guitar. Perhaps, as the evening drew on, the girls played the piano and even persuaded Henry to sit down and sing "'Tis but a Little Faded Flower', an accomplishment which he performed rarely and only in the most intimate company. Before the day was over, he found time to report to his father:

'. . . Bateman—did a very delightful thing last night. Gave me a magnificent watch and chain—the finest that money could procure. A nice Xmas present—what say you? There is an inscription inside—thus:

> *Henry Irving*
> *an outward visible sign*
> *of the*
> *inward spiritual affection*
> *and esteem of his*
> *Friend*
> *H. L. Bateman*
> *Xmas* 1872

The play of *Cromwell*—at the Queen's Theatre last night was a dreadful failure,—another feather in our cap.

Goodbye and God bless you all,

Affectionately yours,
Henry.'

At last Irving seemed to have found a measure of peace; he felt nothing but goodwill towards his fellow-men—even towards his colleagues at the Queen's Theatre, whose misfortune, much as it was to be deplored, was not entirely ungratifying.

CHAPTER XV

The Heir Presumptive : Richelieu

I

There is something grimly fortuitous in the way that the memory of certain villains is kept evergreen by the constant repetition of their crimes in the theatre. Feng, a Jutish prince, committed almost conventional fratricide in order to seize a throne; yet down the centuries his nephew, Hamlet, recites an odious memorial of his villainy which, in his period, was by no means exceptional. Out of a gallery of homicidal Scottish chieftains, Macbeth alone is forever doomed to remind us that crime does not pay. An eighteenth-century schoolmaster in an obscure Yorkshire town was an accomplice in a sordid and commonplace murder; yet, thanks to the poetic genius of Thomas Hood, he is held up to posterity as an awful example of a remorse which, in fact, he never felt. Bulwer Lytton, in a popular novel, gave a fillip to his immortality and now, more than a hundred years after his bones had fallen from a gibbet, he was to be represented to playgoers as an object of pity rather than of revulsion. For, at Bateman's suggestion, Irving and Wills were working on a dramatization of the legend which had long ago, in all but Eugene Aram's name, ceased to bear the remotest resemblance to historical fact. Although *Charles I* was playing to full houses, they had decided to put the new play into the bill before the end of the season.

Wills had retired to Brighton to finish *Eugene Aram*. He had been delayed in Fulham by the loss of his wig which had been removed by his landlady's daughter who had discovered that, by hiding such indispensable articles, she could claim a handsome reward when she rediscovered them for the distracted poet. Wills claimed that in framing the plot of his drama he had based it on tradition. But he came little nearer to the truth than Hood or Bulwer except in so far as he restored Aram's accomplice, Houseman, to his proper place in the story. He did, however, introduce a new character, the parson's daughter, Ruth

226

Meadows, whom the schoolmaster, seeing that his crime had gone undetected for fourteen years, was about to marry. Eugene Aram's agony when, having confessed his guilt to the girl he loved, in abject terror he seeks her pardon before he dies in the churchyard, was designed to give Irving the chance to repeat his success in the last act of *The Bells*. Both parts were studies in remorse; in both plays the murderers believed that they had lived to escape the penalties of their crime. Mathias was the victim of self-accusation, of forces within himself; Eugene Aram, fiercely resisting blackmail and betraying himself only when faced with the grisly evidence of his guilt, succumbed to forces outside himself which exposed his villainy. Mathias, impenitent and calculating, did not hesitate to exploit the proceeds of his crime; Aram, a penitent and conscience-stricken wretch, thought he had found redemption in human faith and love which crumbled away as he put out his hands to grasp them. In this respect the themes of the two plays were entirely different. Eugene Aram was not created in the image of Mathias but as a character in which Irving could present a study of another, and perhaps more subtle, criminal type. Irving had brooded on Hood's poem for several years. He was insistent that Wills's dramatization should incorporate his conception of the schoolmaster's character. If Irving was a hard taskmaster, Wills was a willing and enthusiastic collaborator. From Brighton he wrote:

'My dear Irving,
    I found the point suggested by you, which is no doubt necessary and strong, very difficult. The situation is this—a young fresh girl finds that the lover of her bosom is a murderer. It is a nightmare and must be treated with full colour and truth. Ruth's momentary shrinking in terror from him will give dramatic contrast and value to her after [her] outburst of fidelity and tenderness. Will it do? Five minutes will suffice to write it into its place—which I have indicated pretty clearly.
                                              Yours as ever,
                                                  W. G. Wills.'

Wills had finished the play by the beginning of April and sent it off to Irving:

'. . . I send you *Eugene*. The delay was caused by my having retained two pages by mistake in sending MS. to copyist.
    I want you to notice the use I make of the old passage, "When in the crowded court". In the last scene Ruth—on whose mind the

strange *almost* confession contained in it has made a deep impression—cries out while urging him to confess:

> *If in the felon's dock you stood*
> *And all the crowd stared loathing at you*
> *I am that woman, etc. . . .*

This mortices together the two scenes and makes the great transition natural—I think you'll see what I mean.

I am under some serious embarrassment—so a cheque will be more than welcome.

Yours faithfully, and obliged,
W. G. Wills.'

In appealing to Irving for a cheque, Wills seemed to shrink from a direct approach to the Colonel. Yet a month or two earlier Irving had received a note from his manager which suggested that he was by no means tight-fisted as long as he was getting value for his money:

February 12th, 1873.

'My dear Irving,

As you are now a housekeeper and a nabob generally, I think your income should be slightly increased.

Ever your most affectionately,
H. L. Bateman.'

Irving's income was, in fact, doubled, for Bateman had increased his salary to £30 a week. For the approaching season the salary list at the Lyceum amounted to £83 12s. a week. Forrester got £10 and Miss Pauncefort, who played supporting parts such as Catherine in *The Bells* and Lady Eleanor Davys in *Charles I*, got £6 a week. Isabel Bateman was not included in the list, for the little she got from her father was still in the form of pocket money. Arnott, the property man or machinist, was paid £3 10s., and Irving's dresser, Doody, 30s. a week. Small as Doody's salary was, he contrived to lead a convivial existence on it and often would arrive at the theatre a bit tipsy. As the habit increased, Irving appealed to him, for the sake of his wife and children, to mend his ways. 'I wonder why,' he asked, 'for their sake, you do not reform—besides you look so ridiculous.' Doody, with tears of maudlin vanity in his eyes, protested: 'Ah Sir, they make so much of me!' Doody was devoted to his master, judging the actor's best performance to be those in which he perspired the most.

Wills's financial position was restored, for about this time he invited his friends, among them Irving, to a supper, more formal and of greater substance than the meals he made for his transitory guests and dependants. Wills played the cook and Calmour the scullion. After the first course of cod was finished, Wills called for some fowls and bacon that he had left to stew. But the saucepans were empty; the birds had vanished, having proved too much of a temptation for some hungry model or sponger. Irving left the dispirited party only to return a few minutes later with a parcel containing two gory sheep's heads which he had bought from a nearby butcher. These he proceeded to cook and to serve up to Wills and to his delighted and astonished fellow guests, explaining that he had learnt how to do so when sheep's heads played an important part in the production of *Cramond Brig* at the Theatre Royal, Edinburgh.

Eugene Aram was produced on April 19th. Actor and dramatist had constructed the play on the lines of their early successes—a quiet, idyllic first act, leading to dramatic conflict in the second and ending with what was in effect a prolonged soliloquy which made the success of the play entirely dependent upon Irving's ability to hold his audience. In this he succeeded beyond all doubt. At the end of the play the awed and attentive silence in which the audience had followed the death agonies of Aram was broken by an outburst of cheering and applause, bouquets were showered upon the stage, and when Irving had received his full measure of acclaim there were loud but unrequited calls for the author. Several critics had come to the Lyceum with the intention of chastising Irving for his persistence in idealising crime. Though one of them sardonically remarked that his admitted success in this play opened up to him the boundless range of the entire Newgate Calendar, the rest admitted his unprecedented force as an actor and the tremendous effect of his playing upon the audience. Once again, by delineating the complexities of character in which tenderness and pathos were found lurking in a soul sunk deeply in depravity, he swept critics and public along with him in the storm of his attack. Clement Scott was completely carried away both by the play and by Irving's performance. The cautious Dutton Cook admitted that 'the actor's self-abandonment to the passion of the situation, his powerful display of anguish and despair, were histrionic achievements of real note'.

One critic, Joseph Knight, had certain reservations in the light of which Irving modified his performance. Joseph Knight was at that time dramatic critic of the *Athenaeum,* and in that capacity observed and commented on the career and work of Irving, whom he survived by two years. He was perhaps the most independent and scholarly critic of his time, his judgments being uncoloured by prejudices or disappointments which affected so many of his contemporaries who strove to reconcile unbiased opinions with thwarted dramatic ambitions of their own. He had a wide knowledge and genuine love of the theatre which had prompted him, a year or two earlier, to arrange for the company of the Comédie Française to pay their first visit to London. He realized, as many other critics had done, that Irving exercised his hold over his audiences not only by the power of his personality but by the extraordinary expressiveness of feature and gesture through which, as much as by the force of words, he conveyed the pervading motive of his characterization, so compelling attention to the variety of these expressions at every moment. An actor, once he becomes aware of such unusual powers, is easily tempted into overplaying and upsetting the balance between consummate artistry and exhibitionism. Joseph Knight, having praised Irving's quiet effectiveness and dramatic force in the first two acts of *Eugene Aram*, warned him against artless extravagances and exaggerations which marked the final scene. Irving's ears were not so deafened by shouts of praise that he did not hear this note of warning. In the course of a run of three months these excesses were modified and the methods of achieving effects which had certainly enhanced his reputation were revised and refined.

On the day of the production another conclave had been sitting in judgment on Henry Irving whose verdict had gone against him. Proposed by W. P. Frith and seconded by Toole, his name had come before the committee of the Garrick Club as a candidate for election. It is the custom of the club that members, if they wish, may endorse the page in the candidate's book in which the names of those seeking election are posted. Irving's page was well covered with signatures, including those of Bancroft, Hare and Hollingshead. The Garrick Club had been founded with the object of giving 'actors the opportunity of meeting gentlemen and patrons of the drama on equal terms'. The committee at that particular meeting included no actors—the sole representative of the profession being Mr. A. W. Arnold, the lessee of the Lyceum. Irving was blackballed—but by the gentlemen and not by the players, a fact which, had he known of it, would have softened the blow to his pride. His rejection was the cause of one of those schisms which periodically have rent the club and are a sign of its enduring vitality. The dust of the quarrel between Dickens and

Irving as Eugene Aram

Thackeray over Edmund Yeats had not long settled. Irving's disappointment was eased by a wise and kindly letter from Charles Taylor, the Chairman of the Committee:

> *28 Park Crescent,*
> *Portland Place.*
> *April 21st,* 1873.

'Sir,

I exceedingly regret and at the same time was much astonished at the results of your candidature at the Garrick on Saturday last.

As Trustee and Chairman of the Committee, it is probable that my name would have some weight in the Club—and I shall be much pleased if you will allow me to propose you again as a candidate as soon as the rules of the Club will permit. I am sure my friend Frith will not be offended, and Walter Arnold, who is very nearly the oldest member of the Club, will have great pleasure in seconding you.

Will you not be offended if I take the liberty of saying further (as a man who, in nearly sixty years, has seen much of Clubs) that after all the rejection of a candidate only means that somebody dislikes him —and I suppose you have not the pretension to be liked by everybody. I shall be really sorry (and to speak frankly shall think you ill advised) if you refuse me.

> Faithfully yours,
> Charles Taylor.'

This was followed quickly by a letter of condolence from Anthony Trollope, who, though a member of the committee, had not been present at the meeting:

> *39 Montague Square.*
> *April 24th,* 1873.

'Dear Sir,

I have not the pleasure of being acquainted with you, but perhaps you will allow me, being a stranger, to take the liberty, as a member of the Garrick Club, of expressing my regret that you should not have been elected at the late ballot.

Perhaps, also, you may be willing to allow me, as a man much older than yourself, to say that I think that the caprice of one or two men should not give you personal offence. I am a member of the committee and should you consent to be put up again for nomination I will make it my business to give your candidature what little support may be in my power.

At any rate I trust you will excuse my interference.

Very faithfully yours,
Anthony Trollope.'

The best indication of the sense of outrage which Irving's supporters in the club were enjoying was in a letter from Frederick Sandys, the handsome Pre-Raphaelite, who enjoyed nothing more than a windmill to tilt at or a cause to espouse:

Garrick Club.

'Dear Mr. Irving,

Although I am more or less a stranger, having had the pleasure of meeting you only too seldom, I write to you to give you a truthful—*entirely* truthful—statement of the feeling existing in the Club at your "pilling" on Saturday. It is one of *entire disgust.*

In making this statement pray let me assure you this is not the expression of myself or my own strong feeling of this contemptible committee. I *indeed* convey to you the expression, the universal expression, of the members of the Club—whilst I am writing the few members in the room wish me to make this letter extremely strong—their words being—"that it is a disgrace to the Club". In this I honestly agree.

I hope you will allow yourself to be put up again as soon as possible, when you will certainly come in with flying colours. After this you can remain in the Club or resign with the contempt the Club deserves.

I have to apologize to you for writing this note—for the expression of one's strong feelings is always open to misconstruction—but I feel sure you will not misconstrue the feeling that has "forced" me to write and once more let me assure you my feelings are those of the Club—bad even as it is.

Yours faithfully,
Fredk. Sandys.'

Irving took Charles Taylor's advice and allowed himself to be put up for the club a second time. On the whole the incident was not entirely unpleasing. The vehemence of opinion in his favour by so many distinguished men revealed to him, to an extent which may have surprised him, the esteem and affection in which he was held by many whom he did not count among his friends.

On the last night of the season, July 19th, Irving took his benefit. For this he chose to play *The Bells* in full and the last act of *Charles I*. The reception accorded to him left little doubt that he was now an established favourite and that the policy which he had pursued, with the encouragement and support of Bateman, had been the right one, both for his own development as an artist and for the fortunes of the Lyceum. He had won the favour of the public with three contemporary plays, two of which had been written at his suggestion and, to some extent, contrived under his direction. So far he had not challenged comparison with such famous men as Macready, Phelps or Sullivan by playing any of the parts for which they had become famous. Bateman was impatient that he should do so. When he first heard Irving recite *Eugene Aram*, he had declared that there was the man to play Richelieu. Having let Irving have his fling (and he was the last to deny that it had been very much to his own advantage), he insisted that the time had come for him to assert his supremacy in the much-disputed field of higher drama. Irving was reluctant to do so, particularly in the part of Richelieu, which was so closely associated in the public mind with actors whom only a few years ago he had regarded as demi-gods. When, however, the time came to ring down the curtain on his benefit by responding to the unabated tumult of cheering and stamping with a short speech, Irving expressed the hope 'that the same kindly feeling may be extended to me next season when we re-open in Bulwer's play of *Richelieu*'.

At the end of the London season Irving set off to tour the provinces with *Charles I*. Wherever he went crowded and enthusiastic houses confirmed his acceptance by the provincial public as a romantic actor. His tour included towns in the West Country. From Exeter he wrote to Mrs. James:

'Here I am and just starting off to Plymouth. I've been travelling all night and my time is very limited, having to be in Bristol on Thursday and I am determined to go through Cornwall and visit a few places of my earliest remembrance. . . . I've been to the cathedral this afternoon and a very interesting one it is—but you know what cathedrals are. I shall be glad to get away. Manchester was such a dreadful place. The leaving of it has quite raised my spirits. I hope I shall hear that you're not in London. I'm sure you should shift the scene.'

At the end of August Irving was back in London. He had devoted much time to the study of the part of Richelieu and was ready to face the task of directing the rehearsals of the play. Fortunately Macready's diaries were not available to Irving, for on the night of the first production of *Richelieu* the great actor had written: 'Acted Cardinal Richelieu very nervously; lost my self-possession. . . . How can a person get up such a play and do justice at the same time to such a character? It is not possible.'

In spite of these misgivings Macready made Richelieu one of his most popular roles and his interpretation of the character was firmly implanted in the minds of the playgoers. It was by Macready's standard that Irving's performance would be measured. Bulwer had not been entirely satisfied with Macready's Cardinal; he felt that it lacked roguish humour (what the French call *malice*) or savagery concealed behind a chuckle—*le rire presque gai mais toujours insultant*—suggestions which Macready construed as a vulgar attempt to introduce low farce. The actor had gone to great pains to compare Bulwer's conception of the Cardinal with historical fact and, finding that they had little resemblance, decided that if he was to play it he himself must 'fabricate' the character. To this end he had cut the play ruthlessly and had altered its construction until he felt that it had a measure of theatrical effectiveness. Bulwer, who had written the play in a fortnight, welcomed the actor's criticisms and suggestions; he incorporated them in a revised version which satisfied them both, though they must have been a little disconcerted when their friend, Foster, fell asleep while Macready was reading it to them for the first time.

Irving had not seen Macready play Richelieu. He had seen Phelps, who had played Joseph in the original production, act the part in conscious imitation of his master, yet less gracefully and in a harsher tone than his model. Irving had good cause to remember his early associations with the play and the stentorian senilities of Barry Sullivan's Cardinal, which still seemed to satisfy provincial playgoers. In forming his own conception of the part he strove, as usual, to reconcile a realistic physical portrayal based on natural observation with the sonorous and artificial utterances which the poet puts into the mouths of his characters. He was still experimenting and feeling his way towards the fusion of his original style of acting with the accepted literary form of higher drama. On this account he felt that he was not yet adequately armed to pit himself against the giants. He realized, too, that whereas Macready and Phelps had the support of strong companies, his own, judged by London standards, was comparatively weak.

Bateman, however, was ready to fling down the gauntlet on behalf of his champion and did so with a flourish of archaeological advertisement in the press; the literary and artistic world of London, who for the most part wished Irving well in his venture, eagerly picked it up and, on September 27th, gathered in force at the Lyceum to witness this trial of strength. Lord Lytton, who had said that authors would be lucky to have their plays acted by Irving, had died earlier in the year; thus, by a few months, he missed the opportunity of testing the truth of his assertion. Most of the critics had come to judge Irving with an open mind; but there were others who, bridling at Bateman's growing habit of taking snippets from their reviews and reprinting them in the symposia of eulogy which he issued to the press, were unwilling to provide the manager with such ammunition, if they could help it. Among the audience were several actors of the old school who glumly awaited the outcome of Irving's presumption.

At the outset Irving suffered from the same nervousness and lack of self-possession as Macready. All agreed that his make-up was superb and that his physical portrayal of the ageing Cardinal was faultless. When he was first discovered, as the curtain rose upon the second scene, he was greeted by a roar of welcome such as old first-nighters had not heard for fifty years. In subsequent reports this ovation was variously described as a legitimate tribute to the artist or as the hysterical outburst of an indiscriminating mob; in this violently opposed spirit Irving's entire performance was noted and judged. Those who expected him to adhere to the tradition of Macready were disappointed. As the play proceeded, comparison became increasingly difficult. A clue to the actor's method was found in the course of the third act. While Richelieu is addressing his page, the stage direction, 'patting his locks', is given in the text. Irving, at this point, carelessly rumpled the lad's hair and in so doing was accused of indulging his tricks and mannerisms. There was no doubt, at least on the first night, that in the passages which he attacked with unparalleled vehemence—'vivid outbursts upheaving like volcanic commotions and pouring out words in a boiling torrent, fiery and scathing as lava'—he overtaxed his own power and occasionally became incoherent. Those who revisited the play when the actor was free from the anxiety of a first night found his 'picture of the old Cardinal vigorous and sharply marked and, without over-elaboration, minutely filled in with truthful and significant touches'. When the final curtain fell, the pit and gallery rose and shouted for Irving; in the stalls, against the storm of applause that greeted the actor as he took his call, old Ryder, who had acted with Macready, leapt to his feet and in furious loyalty shouted: 'Mother

Shipton, with trimmings!' He found character study a poor exchange for rounded periods and rich declamation, mistaking subtlety for feebleness.

The notices of the play went into extremes of praise and condemnation. For the first time, Irving found himself the cause of a war of opinion. *The Times* hailed his performance as 'tragic acting in the grandest style'; Clement Scott in the *Observer* condemned it wholeheartedly, finding it either dull or incoherent and punctuated by 'whirlwinds of noise which create applause mainly owing to an irresistible but still unhealthy, excitement'. Dutton Cook dismissed the whole affair contemptuously; Joseph Knight gave it qualified praise but reiterated his warnings against exaggeration. Opinions were evenly divided. None condemned him for attempting the part and few compared him to his predecessors. In later years, whenever he revived *Richelieu*, there was not the same violent diversity of criticism, and the public came to number it among his great performances. After one of these revivals in 1879, Jules Clarétie, the future administrator of the Comédie Française, wrote in the Paris paper, *La Presse*:

'*Richelieu* was the first play in which I saw Mr. Irving in London. Here he is superb. His performance amounts to a resurrection. The great Cardinal, lean, worn, eaten up by ambition, less for himself than for France, is admirably rendered. His gait is jerky, like that of a man shaken by fever; his eye has the depth of a visionary; a hoarse cough preys upon that frail body, which is yet made of steel. When Richelieu appears in the midst of the courtiers, when he flings scorn in the face of the mediocrity who is to succeed him, when he supplicates and adjures the weak Louis XIII, Irving gives that grand figure a striking majesty. And what an artist the tragedian is. I went to see him in his dressing-room after the performance . . . he had before him the three studies by Philippe de Champagne . . . and a photograph of the full-length portrait of the Cardinal by the same painter.'

Such was the judgment of a man steeped in the polished tradition of French pantomime and diction; the groundlings and intelligentsia of London seemed to share his opinion, for *Richelieu* ran for one hundred and twenty nights. Bateman claimed another success for the Lyceum; Irving, having taken stock of these successes, knew that the time had come to embark upon a venture which would surprise even his most loyal supporters.

2

During the run of *Richelieu* Irving was called to Birmingham, where Samuel Brodribb, who was now over seventy, had been taken ill. The old man had lived long enough to see his son justify the distress which his stubborn determination to be an actor had inflicted upon his mother. He recovered sufficiently to return to his two sisters in Bristol where, until he died in 1876, he enjoyed the regard of his neighbours as an authority on theatrical matters and an unfailing source of information about his distinguished son. He was buried beside his brother, Thomas, in a corner of the little graveyard by the Brunswick Congregational Chapel. By their practical help at times when a little money gave Irving liberty of action, these two old nonconformists had played their parts in the history of the English theatre. Upon anyone less robust than Irving these excursions to Birmingham between playing Richelieu twice on Saturdays and the evening performance on Monday, might have imposed a heavy strain. But touring actors were hardened to travel and were able to exact miracles of transportation out of the services of the period. In April Charles Mathews, while on tour, received an invitation from Irving to dine with him in London; he was seventy years old and his reply, though in part facetious, illustrated their hardy indifference to the fatigues of travel:

Jury's Hotel, Dublin.
April 10th, 1874.

'My dear Irving,
  Your letter (received at Glasgow) being dated the 1st of April I thought was a sell, but it has struck me that perhaps, not hearing from me in return, you might fancy I should be with you on Sunday, so I write to say it cannot be. But why not come to *me*? By leaving after the performance tomorrow night you will get here easily at six o'clock on Sunday morning—eat your Sunday dinner quietly with me at 4 o'clock (telegraph by return what you would like) leave by the boat again at seven—travel all night and be in town in time for rehearsal on Monday. What do you say? The trip will do you good—only two nights on the road and the weather so nice—blow you over in no time.
  On second thoughts I shall order on the chance, some Blue Rock oysters and Dublin Bay haddock, some Colcannon and an Irish stew, washed down with Guinness's Stout ad libitum. If that doesn't tempt you nothing will. You need bother yourself with no luggage, as you will not have time to change—perhaps an extra pocket handkerchief

and a bottle of eau de cologne might be advisable in case you should be very sick. I shall be ready with an outside car to meet you at Kingstown—it's better than the railway as, having little time, you must get as much fresh air as possible.

I suppose you couldn't get off playing on Monday night—perhaps Bateman mightn't like it—or else you could come to the theatre here on that evening. They have a small but excellent company and I think you would be pleased.

Faithfully yours,
C. J. Mathews.

Mind—it's the Gaiety I'm at—though if you preferred it there is Charlotte Saunders now playing at the Theatre Royal. But perhaps you've seen her.'

To follow *Richelieu*, Bateman had accepted a play written by Hamilton Aidé, a popular novelist. The drama was based on Balzac's story, *La Grande Bretèche*. The scene of the action was seventeenth-century Spain and its theme was the jealousy of a Spanish Count for his wife and his subsequent remorse on finding that his suspicions of his brother, whom he had ordered to be bricked up in a wall, were unfounded. The story and its treatment were commonplace enough, but, as Count Philip de Miraflore, Irving's romantic appearance and the earnest intensity he gave to the inconsequent passions which the part evoked, imbued it with vitality and a semblance of truth, so that it sustained his popularity and filled the Lyceum until June.

A contrite committee, awed by the outburst of feeling and a candidate's page black with signatures, had elected Irving to the Garrick Club. During April he had given the first of innumerable dinners to his friends which were to become his favourite recreation. Among his guests were Anderson Critchett, a young optical surgeon, Yates, Bancroft and Hare. One of them, Sir Frederick Pollock, recorded that Toole amused them with the tale of his first appearance for two nights at Portsmouth; on his arrival the town was placarded with: MR TOOLE'S FIRST PERFORMANCE IN PORTSMOUTH, and the next day with: MR. TOOLE'S FAREWELL BENEFIT. Bateman capped this with the story of the indolent actor who, being asked at a rehearsal to change his point of exit from a scene, was heard to grumble: 'What—more study!'

Before the end of the season *Charles I* was revived for three weeks and was found by the critics to have improved with age and by John Clayton's performance as Cromwell. Irving took his benefit on June 2nd, for which he played Eugene Aram and Jeremy Diddler; at the end of the performance Bateman announced that he would begin the autumn season with a revival of *The Bells*.

While Irving was carrying *Richelieu* into the camp of his provincial rivals and winning town after town to his cause, in London rumours were spreading that he intended to play Hamlet before the year was out. This was indeed the case. He had persuaded the unwilling Bateman to let him make the supreme appeal to his audiences and to hazard his hard-won reputation on a single throw; if he succeeded in *Hamlet* he would become the undisputed head of his profession; if he failed he would join the over-crowded ranks of competent actors who had come to grief through ill-advised ambition. Bateman's hesitancy was natural. He stood to lose not only his money on a Shakespearian production but the support of the public for the actor who, in the narrower but not unworthy limits of romantic drama and comedy, had filled the depleted coffers of his theatre. Hardened old gambler that he was, he decided to limit his bet to one hundred pounds, which was all that he allowed Irving to spend on mounting the production. Irving, undeterred by the Colonel's evident lack of confidence, accepted this limitation. With a company untried in Shakespeare and a meagre display of costumes and scenery, the whole responsibility and the consequences of his failure would fall upon him. He persuaded Bateman to engage three actors who would leaven the inexperience of the rest of the cast. Old Chippendale, who had initiated him into the mysteries of Kean's Hamlet, for Polonius; Tom Mead for the Ghost, and steady old Henry Compton for the First Gravedigger, a part which he had played intermittently with a variety of Hamlets for nearly forty years. In engaging Mead he fulfilled a promise made seventeen years ago at the Lyceum Theatre, Sunderland; the stammering, tongue-tied boy had risen and had not forgotten.

The provincial tour proved to be an arduous if profitable one. By the middle of September, when it was drawing to a close, Irving's ordeal loomed ominously ahead. From Birmingham he wrote to Mrs. James:

'. . . All thanks for the remembrances received this morning. . . . I am always complaining—but I shall be very glad when the end of this month comes. In Liverpool we changed our plays four times and as that necessitated endless rehearsals, I was pretty sick at the end of the fortnight. *Richelieu* was a singular success there—we ought to have opened with it. I am deep now in the mysteries of *Hamlet*—we shall produce it about the end of October and re-open with some old play . . . at the last moment my man was taken ill—I had to do all my work myself and went to Liverpool without him. He is better now and joined me here—last Monday.

I am a little worried about *Hamlet* of course. He is such a stupendous young man that he awes me—but we're good friends.'

He returned to London to find Bateman more pessimistic than ever. On September 28th the season at the Lyceum opened with *The Bells*; for four weeks Irving rehearsed his company in *Hamlet* by day and played Mathias by night. Bateman was relentless in his economy. The interiors of Elsinore were contrived by placing together a mélange of earlier productions; there was no disguising the fact that Ophelia would be laid to rest in the churchyard of the Reverend Meadows in which Eugene Aram had breathed his last.

CHAPTER XVI

Hamlet : The Accession

'I may not know all Shakespeare but of any play of his which I present on the stage I know more than any man in England.'

HENRY IRVING.

*H*amlet was announced at the Lyceum for October 31st. Three days before, the *Era* published a long article on celebrated Hamlets. Conceding that Garrick and Kean were justly famous for their interpretations, the writer declared that Macready, Charles Kean and Phelps had all failed; their common fault had been a tiresome and lugubrious style; Fechter, intent on breaking with tradition, had worn a blonde wig and had affected a natural bonhomie which was as foreign to the Englishman's idea of princely condescension as the accent with which he spoke his lines. It ended on a note of avuncular patronage, assuring the reader that he could look forward with an impartial mind and earnest interest to the discussion and enjoyment of a Hamlet of 'a young actor and of an intelligent Englishman'. No doubt the young actor noticed that he was expected to fail, but would do so in good company; the intelligent Englishman must have noticed the omission of Edwin Booth in this parade of Hamlets. If during the months of study the reading of any contemporary actor had influenced his own, it was the American actor's philosophical approach to Hamlet's character which had illumined his reflections. The omission of Booth from the pedigree of Hamlets could be taken as a danger signal in that his performance did not merit discussion; on the other hand, it might have been a warning that the public were quite unprepared for the Hamlet that he proposed to show them. Edmund Kean, before his first performance as Shylock at Drury Lane, had retorted to the manager, who was sceptical of his daring innovations: 'Well, Sir, perhaps I may be wrong; but if so the public will put me right.' Irving did not stand to be corrected. His first allegiance was to Shakespeare; his aim was to approximate, for no actor could do more, the truth and beauty of his words and the humanity of his character. He would stand or fall by his conviction; there would be no trimming of these convictions to flatter the popular taste.

The English public never tire of *Hamlet*. Perhaps, regarding themselves as a race apart, they identify themselves with Shakespeare's Prince of Denmark. They see him as a man given to mercy and to the suppression of his own passion, who, deeply averse to the cruelty and violence employed by his fellow-men in the settlement of their personal and political affairs, is forced to take action, gross, violent and abhorrent, in a cause which his essential love of justice and order has made an inescapable duty. Even if this psychological approach to the greatest drama in their language is largely unconscious, English playgoers are ruthlessly critical of actors who attempt its interpretation. While pride prompts them to admit that no actor can wholly fail as Hamlet, the actor whose genius enhances their understanding of Shakespeare's profundity or, by his embodiment of Hamlet, furthers this self-identification, will be enshrined forever among the immortals.

Apparently the public foresaw that a page of theatrical history might be written at the Lyceum Theatre on the night of October 31st. During the afternoon a dense crowd had collected round the pit and gallery door; when the doors opened the theatre very quickly was filled to overflowing. The preliminary farce was endured with impatience. They had come to see Irving; there was nothing else in this revival to excite either interest or curiosity.

The battlements of Elsinore were adequately presented; the sky suggested the approach of dawn and, when Bernardo called attention to it, a star twinkled in its rightful place. The Ghost appeared convincingly out of the mist instead of walking across the front of the stage— effective enough, but Tom Taylor had introduced this novelty when he produced *Hamlet* at the Crystal Palace. The second scene was brightly lit and had a certain architectural but habitable regality. To the sound of harps, the King and Queen entered with a modest retinue, followed by Hamlet, who drew to one side and sat remote from the royal presence. Cordial applause greeted Irving's entrance; then a challenging silence settled on the house—a resisting silence which the actor had to shatter or perish. Irving's unusual appearance gave the audience their first shock of bewilderment. Gone were Hamlet's funereal plumes and trappings of woe and the air of pompous melancholy. Irving was, indeed, dressed in black, relieved only by the gold chain which he wore round his neck, and the cold sparkle of his silver sword hilt and sword belt. But his loose-fitting tunic, deeply skirted and heavily collared with beaver, was such as a young man of action might have ordered to his own design, stylish yet practical, with enough rough swagger about it to give the wearer a sense of well-being. His bearing and manner were those of a young aristocrat in whom grace and self-assurance were modestly combined. There was nothing to distract the attention from the pale face framed in his own raven curls; there was little in the expression of his features to deflect the message of the troubled eyes in whose gaze there lurked the hint of sorrow, dejection and suspicion. The tight-fitting sleeves of his doublet were cut well above the wrist, and the white cuffs, which were turned back upon them, gave freedom of movement to his sensitive and expressive hands.

Hamlet's brief replies to the King and Queen were made quietly, with a touch of cynical impertinence. The audience waited eagerly for the first soliloquy. It was given without affectation or self-pity. The actor seemed to be missing the familiar 'points'. Only his exclamation 'Oh God . . . God!' betrayed the suppression of exasperated grief. The soliloquy was over. What did this quiet understatement, this absence of attack, mean? Scholars were wondering if Irving was striving to fulfil Hazlitt's ideal—the Hamlet who thinks aloud and in whom there is little of the actor. If so, he was playing a dangerous game and so far had not touched the hearts of his audience.

After the entrance of Horatio, Bernardo and Marcellus, Irving's intention became clearer. He chatted with them with an easy familiarity which had no trace of arrogance or condescension—the good manners of a prince well educated in court life by a wise father. Hamlet was presented as a young gentleman, trained to hide his emotions and to regiment his thoughts; a prince on whom scholarship sits lightly, a scholar who has learnt to foreswear abstractions which clash with the conformity his position demands. But in the lines:

> *Would I had met my dearest foe in heaven*
> *Or ever I had seen that day, Horatio*

which he spoke pathetically, he revealed for an instant the depth of his hatred and misery, only to cover it up immediately with a commonplace tribute of a devoted son to his dead father. When Horatio began to speak of the Ghost, his reaction was perfectly studied. Hamlet had enough to trouble him without the freaks of supernature. He seemed, at first, to scarcely heed his friend's words. His 'Saw? Who?' was spoken casually—even irritably. As the significance of their story became clear to him, his interest quickened. 'I will watch tonight' was delivered with intensity and in tones of suppressed excitement—another point thrown away, for traditionally this resolution had been announced with the full diapason of tragic declamation.

When, on the battlements, the Ghost appeared to Hamlet, the audience was further bewildered by the absence of fear in Irving's address to the apparition. Here it was that Betterton's face had blanched, that Garrick had trembled in abject fear and had communicated his fright to his audience. Irving, like Kean, followed the beckoning Ghost with filial confidence, questioned it in almost beseeching terms and hung eagerly upon its answers, as though possessed by a yearning desire to hear the confirmation of his own suspicions. It was, Edward Russell noted, as if to Hamlet this was not *a* ghost but *the* ghost. During the speech, 'Hold, hold, my heart!' Hamlet, for the first time, lost his composure in mounting frenzy and exaltation. When he was rejoined by his friends the frenzy cooled, and out of it his mind was seen to frame the idea of assumed madness. With smooth transition, he tested the nature of his antic disposition upon his friends. Then, to allay their anxiety for him, he fell into the most natural and practical injunctions as to their discretion and, on the words, 'With arms encumbered thus', he took the arm of Horatio and with this gesture ended the scene on a note of friendly assurance, of mutual confidence and of secrets shared.

But whatever Irving, with such restraint, was striving to convey, the audience were at a loss to understand it—or so it seemed, for the curtain fell in chilling silence. Throughout the act they had shown no sign of appreciating this portrait of a man in whose cool veins the virus of vengefulness was slowly spreading. Irving was laying in an underpainting in grisaille; however bold and certain were his strokes, the audience looked in vain for the rich colour to which previous actors, with their *alla prima* methods, had accustomed them.

During the early scenes of the second act, actor and audience remained out of touch with one another. In Hamlet's scene with Polonius, though his assumption of insanity was intellectually perfect and rich in subtle and sardonic humour, his tone was so colloquial and natural that he appeared again and again to miss the traditional points—even though to make his purpose plainer Irving had retained the scene with Rosencrantz and Guildenstern which usually was omitted. In his first scene with the Players he was not the rich patron, the amateur airing his views to bored professionals, but a young prince, who was a connoisseur of the theatre, who found relaxation among artists and who welcomed them as friends. So Irving came to the rogue and peasant slave soliloquy. The audience stirred. Long before he came to the line 'The play's the thing', which earlier Hamlets had delivered as though the idea had struck them like a bolt from heaven, he forced the audience to realize that, while he ruminated, a plan was germinating in his mind. The last lines announced his decision to act upon it and, as the curtain fell, he started to scribble on his tablets notes for the ensnaring speech which he intended to interpolate into 'The Murder of Gonzago'. The audience warmed to this bold innovation; the spell had begun to work upon them. Yet there was little audible evidence of their comprehension. Irving fought against a profound depression caused, not by their apparent indifference, but by the fear that he had fallen below his own ideal.

Yet, in the act interval, an awareness of his purpose seemed to have spread among the audience. During Hamlet's scene with Ophelia Irving knew that at last he had them with him. He came to Ophelia as a lover whose hitherto untamable passion had wilted before the fiercer tumult which overwhelmed his soul. His awful destiny precluded him from the sweet and natural pleasures he had once enjoyed. When he caught sight of the King and Polonius and realized that the girl he loved was their decoy, he was seized by a paroxysm of rage; a torrent of vituperation, the age-old recriminations of man against woman, poured from his lips. In a few lines he had stupefied the audience with a psychological revelation of such power as none of his hearers had ever experienced. Filon described this moment as Irving's Marengo. Had he failed to carry his audience with him at this point his enterprise was doomed. A crash of applause followed his exit, genuine and heartfelt as though it was an atonement for their obtuseness in failing earlier to grasp his intention. Resistance was broken down. Contact was made, and the current of Irving's impulsive energy flowed freely across the footlights. Fortified by the strength he drew from their applause, the actor pressed home the advantage which he had gained and approached the climax of the play scene with vigour unimpaired and with confidence renewed.

The same easy familiarity marked Hamlet's address to the Players. It was noted that his directions to them at no point contradicted the precepts which governed Irving's own performance. Here was an actor as true to Shakespeare's model as to his conception of Hamlet's character. At the beginning of the play scene his words to Horatio, 'I must be idle', forecast his assumption of careless distraction as he lay at Ophelia's feet to watch the jaws of his trap snap upon his victim. Ophelia held in her hand a fan of peacock feathers. Hamlet took it from her, and, playing with it, affected a studied lightness of heart. His reassurance to the King—'No offence i' the world'—was dryly casual. Until the King started from his chair he did not budge from Ophelia's side nor did he betray his keen impatience. Then, with a shrill scream which tore through the noisy confusion of the buzzing court, he leapt from the ground and flung himself into the empty chair from which the King had vanished into the protecting cover of flickering torchlight and shadow. 'Why let the stricken deer go weep' was lost in the wild applause that greeted this *coup de théâtre*. Hamlet swayed from side to side in ecstasy with the success of his stratagem, and then, rising from the chair, began to chant, half crazily:

> *For thou dost know, oh Damon dear,*
> *This realm dismantled was of Jove himself.…*

Sobered by the words, 'And now reigns here,—a very-very— . . .', he seemed to be at a loss for words. He hesitated. Then, looking at the fan in his hand, cried 'Peacock!' and flung the thing away as though, having prompted an idea, it had served its purpose. With this gesture the boyishness of Irving's Hamlet, 'the young man' who, in course of study, had become 'his good friend', pointed the consistency of his conception of the part and, in this climax, rendered it wholly logical and intelligible to his audience, whose thunderous acclamation at the end of the scene showed that they were with him to a man.

At the beginning of the closet scene Irving lost a little ground. As he drove his sword through the arras, his cry, 'Is it the King?' lacked force and failed to express his hope that fate had relieved him of the burden of decision, and had accidentally contrived the murder which he had been steeling himself to commit. But the poignancy and earnestness of Hamlet's scenes with his mother were a further revelation. Dispensing with the customary miniatures or pictures, the portraits of the brothers which he contrasted were imaginary. In the fierce assault upon Gertrude's conscience and in the almost tearful appeal for her penitence, Hamlet threw aside his assumed madness, making her only too aware of his terrible sanity. Studied eloquence and tragic dignity were discarded. A son, exhausted by the intensity of his fierce indictment, knelt and laid his head in the lap of the mother from whom he had learnt and had repeated his childish prayers. As the curtain fell upon the act, the audience was not a little shocked by a reminder of the ruthless barbarity which was Hamlet's background. Irving pulled the corpse of Polonius from behind the arras and started to pull it through the room—though he omitted the brutal 'I'll lug the guts into the neighbour room', and ended the act on 'Thus bad begins and worse remains behind'.

None of the audience had dreamed of such a reading or ever had been made to perceive so clearly the relations between Hamlet and Gertrude. A scene which, until that night, had called for extremes of virtuosity in tragical declamation had, before their eyes, become a deeply moving and intimate reality—a domestic tragedy seen, as it were, through a keyhole. The tension had been as extraordinary as the applause in which the audience sought relief as the curtain fell.

It was now past eleven o'clock. The effects of exertion and anxiety were beginning to tell upon the actor; the audience, too, were becoming exhausted and weaker spirits among them wavered at the thought of the play running beyond midnight when the public houses closed. Isabel Bateman then had her moment of triumph. She played the mad scene with such sincerity and show of original thought that she quelled the restive elements in the audience, rekindled their interest, and had them once more enthralled. The act interval had been cut by half with the result that Swinbourne and Compton played the gravedigger's scene against a background of hammering and shouting as, behind the graveyard cloth, Bateman and Arnott struggled to speed the changes of scene. Compton wisely cut out the traditional business of removing ten waistcoats and Irving was on the stage once more. There was nothing unorthodox in his scene with Laertes. But, having composed his quarrel with him, at the news of the King's wager, he cast aside his melancholy and seemed to have no thought for anything but the sport in hand. He was young Hamlet again and began the fencing bout with a careless zest and a brilliancy of execution which would have delighted the innocent onlooker, but had a ghastly poignancy for the audience who were privy to the plot. Then, in an instant, the fencers were incensed; the change of foils was dexterously contrived and from the lips of the dying Laertes Hamlet heard of the treachery. Leaping upon the King, he held him by the collar of his robe at arm's length and ran him through and through. The vengeance, after all, had come from his hands and by his will but not by his contrivance. He died as the curtain fell upon the valediction: 'The rest is silence'.

It was after midnight. Yet to judge by the sustained tumult of cheers which greeted Irving as he was called and recalled, the audience, though worn out by five and a half hours of intense concentration, had no thought for anything but the expression of their admiration and gratitude to the man who had given them the most human Hamlet they had ever seen. Their instinct had been right, they were lucky to have played their part in the making of theatrical history. In response to shouts for the manager, old Bateman joined Irving on the stage. In a short speech he referred to the working clothes he was wearing, saying that, while he did not apologize for them, he asked their pardon for the noises behind the scenes, for which, in that attire, he had been to some extent responsible. He asked them to forgive him for omitting the farce which should have followed, for it was now Sunday morning. Deeply moved, he added: 'I have done all that man can do. I thank you for your support.'

CHAPTER XVII

Mrs. Bateman Presents

———⊶⊙⊷———

I

Four months later, those who remembered Bateman's words at the end of that memorable evening realized that they had heard his *Nunc dimittis*. The popularity of Irving's Hamlet was such that the play ran for two hundred nights. The Bancrofts at the Prince of Wales's Theatre had, with modern comedies, equalled or exceeded such a run; for a Shakespearian production it was without precedent. Bateman celebrated the hundredth performance by giving a banquet in Irving's honour in the saloon of the theatre. On Sunday, March 21st, Irving gave a supper to Bateman and several of his friends at the Pall Mall restaurant, Haymarket. The proprietor, knowing the nocturnal habits of his guests, had applied for an extension of his licence which the police had refused to grant him. Without warning, while the supper party was at its height, the waiters began to turn out the lights and to clear the tables. The party broke up. Bateman, flying into a passion, after a heated altercation with the proprietor, went home simmering with suppressed rage. On the following morning, while he was dressing, he had a heart attack. For some time he had been threatened with angina pectoris, but characteristically he had said nothing of it to his family or to his friends. He rested all day and in the evening seemed so much better that Isabel went to the theatre without misgiving. Shortly after nine o'clock Mrs. Bateman, who thought that he was sleeping peacefully, found that he was dead. Irving was not told of his friend's death until after the performance. He attended the Colonel's funeral as one of the family. The Lyceum had lost an able and enterprising manager; Irving had lost a much-loved friend and a wise counsellor to whose shrewd judgment and sturdy common sense he owed a great deal. Bateman's words on the first night of *Hamlet* had been the renunciation of a showman; he had lived to sponsor the greatest Hamlet of his time and to set his friend at the head of

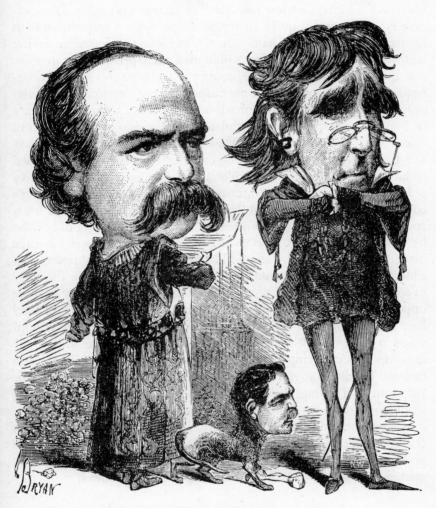

Salvini and Irving: A bone of contention

his profession. There remained, after all, little else that such a man could do.

At the time of Bateman's death the Italian tragedian, Tomasso Salvini, appeared at Drury Lane as Othello. Although he played it in his native tongue, London was quick to acclaim his genius. Mischief-makers were equally quick in trying to promote a quarrel between Irving and Salvini. Immediately after Salvini's first performance, Irving had written to him asking if he would give a day performance in order that English actors and actresses could pay their tributes to him. Chatterton offered Drury Lane for the purpose. A pushing journalist, however, seized this opportunity for self-advertisement. Over his signature he invited a number of actors and actresses to sign a round robin in which Salvini was asked to do what he had already promised to Irving and Chatterton. Irving, though he attended the performance, refused to be a party to such blatant exploitation. The journalist immediately publicized his dissension and intimated that it was on account of Irving's consuming jealousy of Salvini. Irving wrote a short letter to the press stating the facts. 'It was not intended,' he wrote to Lady Pollock, 'to be an absolute reply. I didn't wish the gentleman (heaven save the mark!) even mentioned. I should like everything too, that it was possible to say—said in favour of Salvini—but I should like the folly of comparing our acting exposed. Anything could not possibly be more opposed and each has some especial merit—certainly Salvini's school has. But as the first officer says, "Of that anon". I met Salvini yesterday and very delightful I thought him.' Salvini came to have the same opinion of Irving and the two actors became firm friends. At a farewell luncheon given to Salvini at the Junior Garrick Club, the Italian invited Irving to read, in English, his speech of thanks. The trouble-makers were scotched but by no means killed.

It was not long before Irving realized how deeply the death of Bateman affected his own situation. Lady Pollock, whose love and profound knowledge of the theatre gave weight to her advice on such matters, warned Irving of the difficulties which lay ahead.

> *59 Montague Square.*
> *March 23rd, 1875.*

'My very dear Mr. Irving,

The news of Mr. Bateman's death has shocked me more than I can tell you. You will be a son and a brother in the family, I know, but it cannot be otherwise than a fearful calamity, I ask you as a dear friend to send me one line to say how they are. . . . I love the Batemans;

all of them truly; and I really suffer. Whatever faults he had they were accompanied by many merits and he was a man of force. I hope—having a sincere affection for you—that nothing will induce you to undertake the *management*. Two years of managing and acting together broke down Macready; a great actor has enough in his art; direction of others interferes too much with it.

Affecy. yours,
Juliet Pollock.'

For the time being there was no question of his assuming the management. Mrs. Bateman, who had a tremendous capacity for work and wide experience of theatrical business, considered herself well qualified to take over the control of the Lyceum, as indeed in many respects she was. Irving was her greatest, if not her only asset and it was in her interest to study his wishes about future productions. None the less, Irving's position was that of a salaried actor; his employer was no longer a man of strong character whose judgment and instinct he had learnt to respect, but a woman who was dependent upon him for her livelihood though, by exercising injudicious economies to which women are prone, she could prejudice the quality of his productions and, to some extent, handicap his own career. Bateman had, moreover, been his ardent champion; being adept in the arts of publicity, he knew how, by the judicious handling of critics and paragraphists, to prevent the actor becoming himself embroiled in controversy. Irving's success in *Hamlet* swelled the ranks of his fanatical admirers; it also stimulated his detractors to prepare a counterblast to the chorus of eulogy which, in their view, was unreasonable and unjustified. Indeed there were those who warned the public that Irving was no more than a feat of showmanship—a grotesque comedian palmed off on them by an astute impresario as a tragic actor. At present the murmurings of the opposing faction were scarcely heard. But Irving knew well enough that the greater his success the louder these voices would become, until they would force him to enter the lists and defend himself against attacks which went beyond the bounds of fair comment and prejudiced the dignity of his profession.

In the meantime Mrs. Bateman had no immediate cause for anxiety. The Lyceum was financially sound and had become the rallying point of all who wished to see the English drama rescued from its present plight. The old Chevalier Wykoff, in a letter to Bateman after he had seen *Hamlet*, had expressed the high hopes which the emergence of Irving had raised in the hearts of playgoers:

'My dear Bateman,

I cannot resist sending you a line of congratulation on the triumph of last night. Irving has gone at one bound to the very top of the ladder of fame. His Hamlet is beyond all praise. No higher encomium can be pronounced than that expressed in the familiar phrase of holding "the mirror up to nature"—never, in my time, *never* was Hamlet played so naturally, truthfully and effectively. I confess it—I did not expect so great a performance—you always seemed sanguine which proves you knew Irving's capacity better than I did. It was a great risk on your part for you might have thrown a deep shadow over the rising fame of a promising actor. . . . Now it remains to be seen if Shakespeare so grandly interpreted can hold his ground against opera bouffe and French indecency. We shall soon know "if civilization's a failure, if the Caucasian's played out". For my part I believe the town will go down on its marrow bones to Hamlet the Dane.

The Princess of Wales ought to have been there last night. . . .

Very sincerely yours,

H. Wykoff.'

His fears for civilization and his fellow Caucasians were temporarily allayed; his trust in princes might have been undermined had he known that when the Prince of Wales saw *Hamlet* he had remarked that the only thing worth looking at was Isabel Bateman's face. Within a few months Shakespeare had invaded the stages of three theatres which had been strongholds of burlesque and opera bouffe. The Bancrofts, who kept a weather eye lifted for any change of the theatrical wind, produced *The Merchant of Venice* at the Prince of Wales's Theatre. Edward William Godwin, the architect and early apostle of aestheticism, was engaged to design the scenery and dresses; he was a pioneer in this field, notably in his use of architectural masses as the elements of a stage setting and in his conception of the integration of costumes and scenery by the hand of a master designer. In this respect the Bancrofts were the first to blow the dust and cobwebs off faded scenic contrivance; this breath of fresh air became a gale which, volleying and thundering through the cavernous halls of Adolph Appia and the lofty corridors of Gordon Craig, nearly blew the actor out of his own theatre. Charles Coghlan, who had made his mark in Robertson's comedies, attempted a naturalistic Shylock and failed dismally. Though it was a brave and costly experiment, the understatement which was the key to the whole production was jeered at by the gallery and condemned by the critics. Only Portia won all hearts. There were those among the scanty audiences who could forgive the whole misguided affair for her brilliance and loveliness. Irving was one of them. He found it hard to believe that this exquisite and accomplished actress was the irresponsible and unpunctual girl who, six years ago, had played Katherine to his Petruchio and suddenly had abandoned her profession. The Bancrofts had suffered a heavy reverse, but, having cast Ellen Terry to play Portia, their loss proved to be Irving's infinite gain. There had, however, been a startling element of luck in her restoration to the theatre.

One day, in 1873, Charles Reade, who was hunting in Hertfordshire, jumped a fence and landed in a lane where he found a girl trying to replace a wheel which had come off her dog-cart. To his astonishment he recognized her as Nelly Terry who for six years had been so completely lost to her old friends and admirers that her father had once identified the corpse of an unknown suicide as that of his daughter. Reade soon discovered that she was living a hard but happy life in a house near Harpenden which she shared with Edward Godwin, their two infant children and, at that moment, with a bailiff. Reade knew that her marriage to Watts had ended in a separation. The desiccated painter had been persuaded to doubt his seventeen-year-old wife's fidelity and to suspect her friend Godwin of being her lover. Banished from the house in which her husband was a pampered lodger, Nelly for a time lived miserably with her censorious parents until Godwin, who was ready to marry her, carried her off to Hertfordshire. Watts refused to divorce his wife, so Nelly and her lover made the best of it and, Reade learnt to his surprise, had lived happily together since then in this quiet retreat among incurious neighbours.

Reade told Nelly that it was high time she returned to the theatre. She laughed at the idea. By way of dismissing the subject, she said her price would be forty pounds a week. Reade took her at her word and offered her this salary to play the lead in his new melodrama, *The Wandering Heir*. Reluctantly, Nelly accepted; it seemed the only way of getting rid of the bailiff and of saving their few remaining pieces of furniture. Reade had had a good day's hunting; poaching in Godwin's preserves had given it an added piquancy. Godwin was agreeable to the idea of Nelly returning to the stage. The whole family moved to London and made their home in Bloomsbury. Reade, who knew a good deal about acting, addressed himself to the business of Nelly's rehabilitation as an actress with his usual masterful vigour.

While Trollope was in Australia, Reade, without his permission, had made a hasty adaptation of his novel, *Ralph the Heir*. Trollope was outraged at this infringement of his rights by the man who posed as the champion of copyright, and refused the share of the fees which Reade offered him. This ended their friendship, though for a time they were seen together playing whist at the Garrick Club in hostile silence.

The part of Philippa Chester in *The Wandering Heir* had been created by Mrs. John Wood, who was about to give it up owing to her other commitments. Nelly was the very person to take her place. The part suited her admirably. The secret of her return was well kept. Reade announced that a young actress was returning to the stage after a long period of retirement. When the public recognised the young actress as Ellen Terry, the warmth of their welcome put any lingering idea of retirement out of the head of the renegade. The theatre owed much to Reade's shrewd judgment and perception. The girl, he admitted, was not pretty; yet her queer beauty killed any pretty face that was seen beside it. He had detected the great gifts which were latent in her and, above all, that rare and elusive quality—*le grand art de plaire*. *The Wandering Heir* only ran for a month; but it had served its purpose in bringing the errant actress back to the stage.

2

The run of *Hamlet* ended on June 29th. When all criticism and comment, shorn of fatuous adulation and of the gall of personal enmity, had been digested, Irving had every reason to regard his venture with satisfaction. The wisest and most sober appreciation of his performance had appeared in a pamphlet published by Edward Russell; the briefest condemnation had been the critic Spedding's comment to Edward Fitzgerald—that Irving's Hamlet was 'simply hideous—a monster'. Fitzgerald repeated this to Fanny Kemble, who had not disguised her distaste for Irving's method. As a young man Irving had heard her give a reading of what she called 'Ham-a-lette' and he had decided that if tradition demanded syllabic articulation he had no wish to uphold it. His success had brought him a host of friends and admirers, a measure of financial independence and, if he wished to make use of it, the entry into the close circle of the literary and artistic hierarchy of London. He had struck the first blow to free the theatre of the hypocritical prejudice with which many still regarded it. A friendly bishop, in sending him a word of thanks and kindly

Irving as Louis XI

From a drawing by
Sir Bernard Partridge

Irving as Vanderdecken

Irving in 1876

criticism, wrote: '. . . I must conclude, however, even this criticism, by saying that as I sat back (for I am and was most careful not to startle clerical or even general public opinion by dropping my incognito; opinion in this matter will change but it can't be forced)—as I sat back, I did not see all the actions. I did, however, hear the voice.'

Obviously there was much to be done, but a beginning had been made. At the end of March, Irving took up the cause to which he had determined to devote himself. With the fresh assurance which his success had given him, he opened his campaign and carried the assault into the heart of the enemy's camp. In the Town Hall, Shoreditch, he read a paper at the conference of the Church of England Temperance Society. He criticized strongly the unreasonable attitude of the Church towards the theatre and reminded his audience of the early association between the Church and the drama and of the more recent times when the clergy of the Church of England, during a period of great religious activity, had attended the theatre, had written plays, and had sought the company of actors. He urged the clergy not to denounce the stage from their pulpits but to confine themselves to calling attention to the evils that were allowed to creep into it. If the object of their society was to eradicate the evils of drink, the theatre, he declared, by offering an alternative to the gin palace, deserved their support. 'Gentlemen,' he concluded, 'change your attitude towards the stage and, believe me, the stage will co-operate with your work of faith and labour of love. It will help you in disarming and decimating the forces which make for moral evil, and in implanting and fostering the seeds and energies of moral good.'

About this time he heard that Edward Aveling, whose wife Eleanor was the daughter of Karl Marx, had openly insinuated in Manchester that he and Irving were brothers. Irving, who had met Aveling in his Manchester days, knew that he was an irresponsible rascal. When challenged, Aveling confessed to his folly and apologized to the actor for any annoyance that this foolish gossip may have caused him. A few months later, however, Aveling's father, a congregational minister, publicly denied that his family had any connection with Irving. In reply to Irving's telegram protesting against this unwelcome revival of an incident which he regarded as closed, the Reverend Aveling, by way of apology, wrote:

'. . . the report reached me in an unpleasant form of representation, so that I felt it high time to say something for my own sake—especially as the prominent position I just now occupy gives a greater importance to anything *done by me* or *said of me* than wd have been the case if I had been left, as I heartily wish I had been, to the ordinary comparatively retired position of Congregl Minister.

Right or wrong, the great majority of our people look unfavourably on Theatrical exhibitions; and to not a few it appeared that, if the report of the alleged relationship were true, it identified me with such exhibitions—though I fail to see the logical connection; and I have other reason to believe I was regarded by some as partially compromising them. I, therefore, thought that two or three sentences simply intimating the *truth* wd settle the matter, and render unnecessary any further *correspondence*, of which I have already had enough. . . .'

Irving could hardly have had better evidence of the intransigent attitude of men of religion towards actors or of the strength of the prevailing prejudice which he was determined to break down.

3

Considering how violently Irving's Hamlet had parted from tradition, the actor got off lightly. That same year the Impressionists had held their first exhibition in Paris. It had been greeted with howls of execration. These men of revolutionary vision were denounced by critics and public alike as fumblers who did not know how to paint. The modernist movement had progressed further in painting than in the drama. Irving, in his approach to the art of acting, was the equivalent of Delacroix—a rebel who strove to blend natural truth with romanticism. His struggle against the traditionalists, like the furious war waged by Delacroix against Ingres and the school of David, was preparing the ground for dramatic modernities which even he would not comprehend. At present there were few who questioned Irving's ability to act; he made his audiences accept his modernisms by the force of his personality; when lesser men, such as Coghlan, tried the same thing the public rejected them. It was conceded by those whose theatrical memory went back to Edmund Kean that Irving's Hamlet was second to none in conception, though its execution was open to criticism and argument. A letter from Lady Pollock held up to him a mirror in which he could see his reflection, a dangerously flattering but, on the whole, a true one:

59 Montague Square,
June 30th, 1875.

'My very dear Henry Irving,

You will know without my telling you something of the emotion with which I saw you last night. . . . Twenty-one times I have listened to every inflection and watched every movement of your Hamlet and on every occasion I have gained some new suggestion. As time has gone on I have continued more and more to prize, to admire and to love the art and the artist. I have seen you, in the difficult position of a sudden and immense success, bear yourself as few can do, and I have seen you also strongly resist the malicious attempts of envy to force upon you a foolish rivalry. I have also observed many things of which I need not speak, that have given me experience of a nature and a character worthy of all honour; you have been always what I should wish a son of my own to be . . . and so you will go on . . . you are young; your future may be such as will make you one of the highest reputations in Europe for you have the rare quality of resolution in conquering a fault and of unceasing energy in cultivating a beauty. You have won from your voice deep harmonies such as few believed it to possess and you have almost subdued a tendency which you had to restless, over-elaborated action. In this way you have gained dignity and power. All this you have done under the pressure of a labour which was extraordinary—and now, be proud of it . . . your few words last night had the truth, the grace, the sensibility which I always feel in all you say and do.

Yours most affecty.

Juliet Pollock.'

Irving's only regret was that his old friend Toole had not been there to witness his triumph. The comedian had gone on his first tour to America. With an eye to the future, he had sent Irving reports on the state of the American theatre and on the prospects of English actors in that country. He had found that Fechter was nearing his end—'drinks, they say, and I fear it is true—very much disappoints—breaks engagements and am afraid he's lost—very sad indeed'. He had not met Edwin Booth —'he should have sent his card to me as a stranger—but he don't know manners . . . he's a great favourite . . . wife and Frank saw him play Hamlet and like him very well, though sure they will like you better . . . he makes up privately a good deal like you—his long hair—but he's much shorter than you. I think I shall send him *The Times* notice about you as Hamlet. J. S. Clarke [at whose theatre Toole first appeared in New York] . . . is a humbug—he regularly cheated me about terms, the only management that has—I'll tell you more when we meet'. The press he found 'remarkable and in many respects very degraded . . . in New York quite a blackmail ring. I have not paid nor will I one farthing—they will write up anyone for money—of course there are lots of better men—but the system is terrible and if you once put yourself in their power you are done—because if you don't keep the steam up—lots of actors have paid blackmail like idiots to some of the loafers of the press—men and women you and I know very well—then they are torn to pieces if they discontinue it'. Toole's stubborn honesty and good humour seemed to have won the day. 'Were I alone, I should remain another year—as I am making big way—and in two years should be far more popular than any American comedian. I know at first there is great prejudice against the English but that wears away.'

In August Toole was home again and taking a holiday at Scarborough. 'I am here resting,' he wrote to Irving; 'and hoping you would come and stay here . . . we can have some good boating, fishing, driving, and best of all good talking . . . so many congratulations to give you about Hamlet's success—I want you to act it all to me . . . I have a splendid MOUSTACHE—do come and see it, it wont last long.'

Irving had little thought for boating or fishing; his summer holiday, short as it was, had to be spent in studying *Macbeth*, which Mrs. Bateman had announced for the autumn. He was, no doubt, eager to play the part and was easily persuaded to do so by Mrs. Bateman, who, in casting her daughter Kate for Lady Macbeth, hoped to initiate a theatrical partnership which would rival that of Garrick and Mrs. Siddons. As a piece of showmanship her plan was strategically sound; but she had overlooked the incompatibility of a conventional Lady Macbeth and a Macbeth cast in such an original mould that the actor's already strained resources were not sufficient to execute his novel conception of the part. On the margins of the first pages of his own copy of the play Irving had scribbled—LIAR, TRAITOR, COWARD— and this before Macbeth had met his wife. Such was the estimate of Macbeth's character on which he based his performance. The public had been accustomed to a full-blooded, barbaric villain; Irving's Macbeth was a craven who, though at the outset the poison of murderous ambition is at work in him, shrinks from succeeding crimes to which fear and necessity have driven him until abject terror and remorse make death at the hands of the man he has most injured a welcome consummation. On these lines Irving's study of the part was profound,

MR. HENRY IRVING.

"Now could I drink hot blood, and do such bitter business as the day would quake to look on."—HAMLET, Act III., Sc. 2

and when, thirteen years later, he revived the play, his conception of it was unaltered. For the moment he fell below his ideal. The spasms and hysterias of Mathias and Eugene Aram could not be buckled into the armour of a highland chieftain. It was a pity, for by now there were many who were anxious to see him fail.

Macbeth was produced on September 25th. At the end of the play, the applause, the cheering, the waving of hats and handkerchiefs, suggested a success equal to that of *Hamlet*. Irving, having announced that *Macbeth* would be played for a run, ended his speech with a tribute to his old manager:

'In my pride and pleasure at your approval I cannot but remember the friend whose faith in me was so firm, a friend to whom my triumphs were as dear—aye, dearer, I believe, than had they been his own. The announcement last Autumn that I, a young actor, was thought fitted to attempt *Hamlet* came from a warm and generous heart, and I cannot but deeply feel that he to whose unceasing toil and unswerving energy we owe in great measure the steadfast restoration of the poetic drama to the stage—I cannot but regret that he will never meet me, as he has done on so many occasions, to confirm your approval with affectionate enthusiasm and tears of joy.'

Only Irving's most fanatical devotees, who composed the bulk of the first-night audience, expected him to succeed as Macbeth and resolutely refused to admit that he might have failed. In general the press approved the production, damned Kate Bateman with faint praise, and were sharply divided in their opinions of Irving. His performance satisfied his admirers, embarrassed some of his friends, and delighted those who had always held that he was a flash in the pan. While he was preparing *Hamlet* and *Macbeth* he had sought the advice and help of Mrs. Richard Greville, who, like Lady Pollock, was a student and amateur of the theatre. Sabine Greville was the sister-in-law of Sir Dighton Probyn and a close friend of Carlyle, Tennyson and George Eliot. He may have depended less on her advice than she imagined; but he accepted her criticism, which was frank and carefully considered. After the play had been running for some time, she wrote:

'. . . the last act is an apotheosis . . . nothing can be better, nothing could be better. Every syllable is clear as a bell and knocks at the most callous heart, but you must not drag in the first act. I know what you intend to convey but only a few understand—and you must break up the lines more and let the poetry take care of itself . . . Dr. Linn, who is a Methuselah in his memory, for he still recollects Mrs. Siddons before the O.P. riots, was enchanted . . . indeed he was astonished—he thought all you did very good and some bits quite admirable. He said it was impossible to look the part better. This unbiased good word is well worth having. . . .

I asked Delane—*honestly* his opinion—and remember he really does know Shakespeare—and he said what most struck him was the attention of the audience. . . .'

The editor of *The Times* was able to exercise tact that was denied to Edmund Yates as critic of *The World*. He prepared his friend for the punishment which he felt it his duty to deliver:

> *Lion Mansion,*
> *Brighton.*
> *October 6th,* 1875.

'My dear Irving,

I wish you fully to understand that you will probably have less pain reading the criticism which appears in this week's number of *The World* than I had in writing it. But in issuing the decrees from my little court it is above all things necessary that I should administer justice to the best of my ability, and my praise would be little worth were it given against my judgment.

In order that you may see that there are two sides of the question I enclose, for your private perusal, a note written by my old friend, W. H. Wills, who for a quarter of a century was Dickens' partner and co-editor, and who certainly would not say what he did not mean. Send it back to me when you have read it.

With our united kind regards,

> Yours very sincerely,
> Edmund Yates.'

Perhaps Mr. Wills's remarks took the sting out of Yates's reluctant chastisement. *The World* shared with many other papers the view that the young actor had neither the physique nor the robust vigour required for great tragedy; but since it had not been given to any great actor to excel in all of Shakespeare's leading parts, he need not be unduly discouraged.

Irving was by no means discouraged. *Macbeth* held the stage for eighty nights. The second thoughts of the press were more favourable; they deprecated the comparison of Irving's Macbeth with his Hamlet and, for the most part, held the view that, judged on its own merits, his delineation of the Thane showed considerable genius and great judgment. Irving was still experimenting, and for him adverse criticisms had their value, particularly those of intelligent observers who, unaffected by the partisan bigotries of local conflict, were able to report objectively upon his acting.

Towards the end of 1875 Henry James arrived in London from Paris, and began to contribute unsigned articles on the theatre of London and Paris to American journals and newspapers. Like many Americans he had swallowed the taste and culture of Paris, hook, line and sinker. Surfeited with the grace and finish of the Comédie Française, he approached the London theatre in the frame of mind of a man who, having dined exquisitely at Lapérouse, is forced to eat a cut off the joint with the appropriate vegetables in a London coffee house. 'There is a want of delicacy,' he said, 'in speaking of the first theatre in the world one day and of the London stage the next . . . if you talk about one you forfeit the right to talk about the other.' Henry James explored the London theatres for the first time in the company of Fanny Kemble, whose prejudices were almost as strong as his own. He was as bewildered by Irving's technique (or, as he thought, his lack of it) as he was by the success and popularity the untutored actor had achieved. He strove, however, in his reports to the American paper, *The Nation*, to be scrupulously objective in his criticism of Irving's Macbeth.

'. . . Mr. Irving's acting is, to my mind, not of a kind to provoke enthusiasm, and I can best describe it by saying that it strikes me as the acting of a very superior amateur. If Mr. Irving were somewhat younger, and if there existed in England any such school of dramatic training as the Conservatoire of Paris, any such exemplary stage as the Théatre Français, a discriminating critic might say of him: "Here is an aspirant with the instincts of an artist, and who, with proper instruction, may become an actor." But thanks to the absence of a school and of any formidable competition, success has come easily to Mr. Irving, and he has remained, as the first tragic actor in England, decidedly incomplete and amateurish. His personal gifts—face, figure, voice, enunciation—are rather meagre; his strong points are intellectual. He is ingenious, intelligent, and fanciful; imaginative he can hardly be called, for he signally fails to give their great imaginative value to many of the superb speeches he has to utter. In declamation he is decidedly flat; his voice is without charm, and his utterance without subtlety. But he has thought out his part, after a fashion of his own, very carefully, and the interest of his rendering of it lies in seeing a spare, refined man, of an unhistrionic—of a rather sedentary aspect, and with a thick, un-modulated voice, but with a decided sense of the picturesque, grappling in a deliberate and conscientious manner with a series of great tragic points. This hardly gives an impression of strength, of authority, and it is not for force and natural magic that Mr. Irving's acting is remark-able. He has been much criticized for his conception of his part—for making Macbeth so spiritless a plotter before his crime, and so arrant a coward afterward. But in the text, as he seeks to emphasize it, there is fair warrant for the line he follows. Mr. Irving has great skill in the representation of terror, and it is quite open to him to have thrown into relief this side of his part. His best moment is his rendering of the scene with the bloody daggers—though it must be confessed that this stupendous scene always does much toward acting itself. Mr. Irving, however, is here altogether admirable and his representation of a nature trembling and quaking to its innermost spiritual recesses really excites the imagination. Only a trifle less powerful is his scene with Banquo's ghost at the feast, and the movement with which, exhausted with vain bravado, he muffles his head in his mantle and collapses beside the throne. Mr. Irving has several points in common with Edwin Booth, and belongs to the same general type of actor; but I may say that if, to my thinking, Edwin Booth comes nearer being a man of genius, I find Mr. Irving more comfortable to see.'

At the very moment when controversy was dying down and opinion was turning in Irving's favour, Mrs. Bateman announced that after a short revival of *Hamlet* Mr. Irving would appear as Othello. The opposing faction licked its lips. Apparently the misguided actor was bent upon artistic suicide.

Although the production of *Othello* would give Isabel a chance to distinguish herself as Desdemona (Kate was to play Emilia), Mrs. Bateman might not have put it on if the protracted negotiations with the Poet Laureate for his play, *Queen Mary*, had been concluded. Tennyson's play, the last of a trilogy in which he had portrayed the making of England, had been published during the previous year, the subjects of the other two being *Harold* and *Becket*. Tennyson was sixty-five when he began to write plays. Like many great poets, he knew nothing of the requirements of the commercial stage and had little aptitude for dramatic construction. Bateman had bought an option on the play, though he knew that it would require drastic cutting and reconstructing. Tennyson shrank from handing over his work, which had been praised by Spedding, Froude and Browning, to the sort of rough surgery which it was likely to suffer at the Colonel's hands;

after the death of Bateman he was even less inclined to trust his widow. Irving he knew and liked. After seeing him in *Hamlet*, the poet had said to him: '*Hamlet* is a many-faceted gem, and you have given more facets than anyone I have seen.' He was, therefore, more ready to discuss the alteration of *Queen Mary* with Irving than with anyone else. On October 28th, 1876, he wrote:

'My dear Mr. Irvine [*sic*],

If *Queen Mary* is to be acted and if I am to alter her, I should like as soon as may be to know what the alterations are to be. I have begun other work and I should not like to be interrupted in it a few weeks later, when in the heat of it. So let me know.

I send you Mr. Searle's markings and remarks. I think it's quite worth your while to overlook them, particularly as he told me that his arrangements for the stage were in his day always a success.

I have altered the beginning of the Gate House scene—bringing in the first mention of Wyeth there as you wished—and also some two other passages to please myself. Mind, if Mrs. Bateman doesn't care to have the play acted, neither do I—but if it is to be acted, you must send me my instructions.

Yours ever,
A. Tennyson.'

Tennyson's advisers having agreed with Irving as to the necessary alterations, Mrs. Bateman felt that she must persuade the poet, who was growing impatient, to undertake the work of revision:

Lyceum Theatre,
December 9th, 1876.

'Dear Mr. Tennyson,

After reading over Mr. Searle's commentaries and comparing his suggestions with those formerly proposed by Mr. Knowles, Mr. Irving and yourself last summer, I have thought it best to write and ask if you will undertake the requisite curtailment yourself. It is always an onerous task to propose the alteration of beautiful language but the exigencies of the stage demand that the play be reduced in length and that it may not be longer than *Hamlet* (and it ought to be half an hour shorter) and not fuller of characters, Hamlet being well known to be the *fullest play on the stage*. I should like to receive this acting copy as soon as possible as I propose doing the play at Easter or a little before. You have evidently no confidence in our judgment in the matter and

266

this conviction so crippled my ideas that unless you were to give me instructions to do what I really thought best with the certainty that I would respect your genius too much to do anything that was not demanded by the working of the stage business, I could not undertake it.

As the spurious play has been done in America and has failed *as it well deserves* there is no immediate haste about the contract and I have thought it best to have a clear explanation with you as to the acting play without the formula of law in the matter. With compliments and my respects.

Yours most sincerely,
S. F. Bateman.'

This slightly confused appeal, though it irritated the poet, had the desired effect:

December 14th.

'Dear Mrs. Bateman,

Why do you beat about the bush? If you have repented of your proposal freely made to me in the spring, would it not be better to say so at once? You know very well that I have always said one and the same thing, i.e. "let me know what changes you want making in *Queen Mary* and I will do my best to make them".

Let me moreover remind you that 5th of December has gone by.

Yours most sincerely,
A. Tennyson.'

After this exchange of shots, Tennyson got to work on the play and sent the revised version to Mrs. Bateman in time for its production in the spring.

Early in July Irving had given a reading of scenes from *Othello* and *Hamlet* at the Crystal Palace in aid of a London hospital. He had succeeded in raising laughter and enthusiasm in the staid and genteel folk who frequented such charitable functions. A few days later he received a letter from one of his audience:

Holly Lodge,
July 17th, 1876.

'Dear Mr. Irving,

Familiar as *Hamlet* was to me, I was surprised and delighted with the reading. Some points seemed to me quite unique in reading—a mixture between a market place and a railway station was not the most advantageous position to hear or see poems in but it served perhaps to point the old moral how mind and spirit overweigh materials—I thought you might like to know our impression of a reading so different to *Macbeth*. As a mere reading in which all could follow the story, the drama of *Macbeth* seems to lend itself better in my opinion than *Hamlet*—as a wonderful interpretation or rendering of thoughts without the almost spiritual outside accessories necessary to understand *Hamlet* as a story, your reading would stand quite alone—no reading I have ever heard resembling it. . . .

Yours truly,
Burdett Coutts.'

Angela, Baroness Burdett Coutts, was at that time fifty-two years old. Her lively interest in the arts had led her often to see Irving at the Lyceum; her abiding philanthropy had led her to hear him at the Crystal Palace. His reading had prompted her to begin a correspondence which was the background of a close and intimate friendship between them. Her grandfather was Thomas Coutts, the banker. When she was twenty-three years old his widow left her a vast fortune. No woman had ever been better equipped to undertake the responsibilities of such an inheritance. She had an acute business sense which enabled her to play her part in the management of the bank, in which she was the largest shareholder. She was untiring in her efforts to educate herself and unflagging in social work and charitable enterprises which were remarkable for the prudence and broadmindedness she displayed in their administration. She enlisted the help of many great men of her day in furthering her work among the poor. Dickens had advised her on her private charities and before long Irving became one of her band of almoners. Soon after he received her letter Irving was invited to her house at No. 1 Stratton Street. Here he met her companion, Mrs. Hannah Brown, now an old lady and very nearly blind. Mrs. Brown became deeply attached to Irving and during the few remaining years of her life wrote to him almost daily. At first these letters were in her own hand, but as her sight failed the Baroness wrote them at her dictation. Long before Mrs. Brown met Irving she divined the great future which lay before him. It was for her that the Baroness had rented a box at the Lyceum where together they had seen *Hamlet* thirty times. Irving was touched by the old lady's devotion and rarely passed the house in Stratton Street without calling to see her.

Irving's friendship with the Baroness and the Pollocks pulled him into the orbit of the Dickens family and their wide and amusing circle of friends and relations. Among them was Antonin Roche, who lived with his family in Cadogan Gardens, where, as a professor of French, he conducted a *cours de Français* for fashionable Londoners and their children. The Roches often joined with the children of the late Ignaz Moscheles, who had been a friend and pupil of Beethoven, in giving musical parties to which most of the celebrities in the world of art found their way sooner or later. After one of these parties, two girls, the daughters of Sir Edward Frankland, confided to their diaries their impressions of Henry Irving, whom they had just seen for the first time off the stage. 'Presently,' wrote Sophie, 'we were led into the next room—there by the fireplace stood the great tragedian—a worthy follower of Kemble. His appearance is noble and most striking and a perfect gentleman in manners. The countenance full of changing expression and the absence of any beard at once proclaimed him an actor. I felt almost ready to sink into the ground and *did* sink into an ottoman, but was immediately roused by Mrs. Roches saying to me, "Oh, you've not come to sit down, you must be introduced to Mr. Irving", and so we were introduced to the great man who bowed in a dignified manner to us and shook hands with Percy [her young brother]. Irving, according to our anticipation, was in full evening dress except that he wore a black tie carelessly tied in a bow. A little bunch of violets adorned his coat. He frequently wore a double eye-glass. I expected to see a haggard and emaciated countenance so I was a little surprised to find that this was not at all the case. On the contrary, his face has nothing in the least haggard and has great decision and a very interesting expression. Presently some of the party adjourned to a standing tea, amongst them Mr. Irving leading young Mrs. Moscheles and Mr. Moscheles with Meg [her sister], Miss Liebreich and me. How could I drink any tea or eat sandwiches when Hamlet was standing there, drinking tea and asking people whether they would take some *sherry* or some *claret* and whether custards were ices!! It was quite too much! . . . soon after this Percy had the honour of walking through three rooms with Irving. During this time Percy said: "What a delightful march that is which they played in *Hamlet*. Do you know where I could get it?" Irving: "I don't think it's published but I could get it for you if you like." Of course Percy gratefully declined this kindness. A circle was now formed in the large room in which, no doubt, Irving was the "observed of all observers". Dr. Liebreich sang two Schumann songs and one Mendelssohn with great feeling. Irving clapped! He seemed to be doing his best to be affable and to say a kind word to everyone whom he knew or who was introduced to him. He took

old Mrs. Moscheles' hand into both his and was particularly agreeable
to her. At last dear Meg called our attention to the time and to the fact
that we ought to be going away. So we managed to tear ourselves
away. Percy shook hands with Irving.' Meg, in her diary, recorded
that, in conversation with young Mrs. Roches, Irving had said: 'You
don't know how tired I sometimes feel. I often intend paying some
visits but then I feel so tired that I'm only able to sit down and rest.'
It was not surprising. During December he was playing Macbeth and
rehearsing Hamlet, which was to be revived on New Year's Night.

Earlier in the year there had been some hitch in matters relating to
his separation. To Lady Pollock, in thanking her for the gift of a silver
Caucasian dagger which Byron had presented to Edmund Kean, he wrote:

'. . . the dagger is most beautiful. I shall ever prize it. Yesterday I
had a long talk with Rossi—poor fellow—he was quite pathetic (I
wonder, was it acting?).

You will be a little surprised to hear that I am just going to Sir
Frederick in his chambers. He will probably tell you why. How strange
it would be after all one's prospects in this land, if one had to seek a
home in another. I feel a little pain in my throat when I think of it. . . .'

No doubt Irving was dramatizing his situation, for before very long
Pollock had cleared up the matter satisfactorily. But on Christmas
Eve, when he might have enjoyed a brief respite, he found himself at
the Guildhall police court, with his solicitor, George Lewis, petitioning
the magistrate for a summons against the weekly paper, *Fun*. For some
time past *Fun* had published criticisms of Irving which, increasing
in virulence, now took the form of personal attack. That for which
Irving sought redress was in the form of an open letter addressed to a
Fashionable Tragedian and was signed, 'A Disinterested Observer'.
Evidently the announcement that Irving was to play Othello had stung
the writer into diatribe. While the body of the letter accused him of
having pandered to the lowest passions and debauched the intelligence
of the mob, it was the accusation that Irving had suborned the press
which had forced him to take action. This accusation was contained
in the beginning and the end of the letter:

'*To a Fashionable Tragedian.*
Sir,—I read with regret that it is your intention—as soon as the
present failure at your House can be with dignity withdrawn—to
startle Shakespearian scholars and the public with your conception of

the character of Othello. In the name of that humanity to which, in spite of your transcendent abilities, you cannot avoid belonging, I beseech you, for the sake of order and morality, to abandon the idea. For some years past you have been the prime mover in a series of dramas which, carried by you to the utmost point of realistic ghastliness, have undermined the constitution of society and familiarized the masses with the most loathsome details of crime and bloodshed. With the hireling portion of the Press at your command, you have induced the vulgar and unthinking to consider you a model of histrionic ability and the pioneer of an intellectual and cultured school of dramatic art. . . . You have canonised the cut-throat, you have anointed the assassin. Be content with the ghastly train of butchers you have foistered upon public attention and let your next venture, at least, be innocent of slaughter. If your performance of Othello be trumpeted to the four winds of heaven, by the gang of time-serving reporters in your employ, you will increase the epidemic of wife murder one hundredfold and degrade the national drama a further degree towards the level of the penny dreadful.'

The man who was fighting for the rehabilitation of the theatre in the eyes of the Church and of the public could not afford to let such accusations pass unchallenged. *Fun* had been started as a rival to *Punch*, the first editor having been Thomas Hood, the son of the author of 'Eugene Aram'. Burnand, on his way to *Punch*, had edited it for a time while Gilbert had been a regular contributor of 'Bab Ballads'. In 1876 the editor was Henry Sampson, who later founded the *Referee*. *Fun* could not, therefore, be ignored as a paper of no consequence.

The magistrate, Sir Robert Garden, having read the offending letter, pronounced it a 'scurrilous libel' and granted the summons. On January 4th Sampson and a young journalist, George R. Sims, appeared at the Guidhall police court to answer a charge of having published a malicious and defamatory libel. It was the sort of case in which Londoners delight. The court was crowded and the street outside so thronged with people that Dion Boucicault was unable to fight his way through them in time to give his evidence. Irving, on his arrival, was greeted with cheers, and the warm applause which punctuated his evidence in court made him feel thoroughly at home. After hearing the evidence the magistrate committed the defendant for trial. Young Sims then tendered an apology to Irving 'because if he did not do so he should lose his self-esteem'. On Irving's behalf Lewis accepted this apology and asked that the defendants should be discharged.

Honour had been satisfied, but such distractions were not conducive to the calm study of *Othello*. Moreover, Irving was now aware that a section of the public were ill-disposed towards his attempting the part, regarding it as an impertinent challenge to Salvini. Even Irving's friends doubted his wisdom in thus inviting direct comparison with Salvini; for it was doubtful if any actor had ever excelled in nobility or tigerish passion the great Italian's interpretation of this exacting character. Irving knew well enough what was at stake. In January he wrote to Lady Pollock: '. . . you will be interested to know that we do *Hamlet* until 5 Feb., then *Leah* six nights, then *Othello* on Feb. 14th

> *. . . . . that is the night*
> *That either makes me or undoes me quite.'*

Even so, he was determined to ignore convention and to offer the public an Othello of his own contriving. As few actors had ever wholly succeeded in the part, there was less temptation to seek safety by imitating any one of them. Even Edmund Kean, in Hazlitt's opinion, had only touched the fringes of the part. Irving decided to follow Talma's example in playing down the African aspect of Othello. He therefore modified to bronze the complexion of Othello which, by tradition, had become black, and invited Sir John Tenniel to design for him the clothes and armour of a serving Venetian general. The results were magnificent, but quite out of keeping with the turbans and burnouses which, in the public mind, were essential to Othello's wardrobe. *Othello* was produced on February 14th. Bewildered at the outset by Irving's appearance, his audiences found that, in contrast to Salvini's barbaric passion—beginning in noble repose, wrote Henry James, and spending itself in black insanity—Irving, in his passion, became impotent and in his rages incoherent. 'For nature,' wrote one critic, 'we got exaggeration; for elocution, scolding; for affection, melancholy; and for deportment, tricks. Irving accepted the adverse verdict, but strove, while playing the part, to correct his mistakes. 'I am improving', he wrote to Lady Pollock, 'very much in *Othello*—thanks to you and hardly any other like you'. To her son, Walter, he attributed his failure to 'the fact that they expect to see Othello as something entirely Eastern and mysterious; they've always thought of him in that way and they don't at all understand finding him dressed like other characters in the play. I ought to have thought of that and given up the idea. . . .'

Othello was played for forty-nine performances, which in itself constituted a record, and at the last performance took £136 12s. 6d., which was about two-thirds of the theatre's capacity at that time.

Although his followers were as loyal and as enthusiastic as ever, Irving knew that his comparative failure in *Macbeth* and *Othello* had checked his progress. The production of *Queen Mary* on April 18th gave him a month in an unexacting part in which to consider his situation. *Queen Mary* was a sombre poem rather than a play and was received with respect rather than enthusiasm. Kate Bateman as Mary Tudor and Isabel as Elizabeth held the stage. Irving created a convincing portrait after Titian of the bloodless Philip II and, in the expression of the King's diseased solitude and of the cold concentration of his selfish purpose, his characterization was perfect. He appeared, however, for only a short time towards the end of the play; as far as it went his performance won high praise from Tennyson's intellectual friends, Browning declaring that he 'was very good indeed'. Hallam Tennyson, who took his father to see the play at the beginning of May, wrote to his mother:

> Bath Hotel,
> Arlington Street,
> Piccadilly,
> *May 4th, 1876.*

'My dear mama,

J. H. Butcher and Eleanor and Lionel and the rest of us went last night to *Q. Mary* and enjoyed it—Papa was very much pleased with Irving and Mrs. Crowe's acting and the play seemed to have paid and is to run for the season.

We had a very merry journey up yesterday and in the evening I took Fanny and J.H.B. behind the scenes with papa and Mrs. Greville, and the sight of the actors in undress amused them. Mrs. Bateman gave us a toast of burgundy. Irving told us he took one and a half hours to put on his wig for Philip.

This morning we went to the Academy. Millais' picture of "Over the Hills" is a good picture—much rushland in front—a dark hill—and a peep into a far land. After the Academy Irving had a few minutes conversation with papa about *Q.M.* and I fancy papa will go again tonight for the last act. . . . Mrs. Crowe and Irving are coming to hear Harold tomorrow at eleven o'clock so that we may get back by the late boat —but we will telegraph and you yourself papa insists must dine at 6.30.'

Hallam's estimate of the play's success was a trifle optimistic. On June 17th Mrs. Bateman wrote to Tennyson:

'. . . herewith I beg to enclose a cheque for twenty-three nights' performance of *Queen Mary* at £10 per night—beginning on the 18th of April and terminating on the 13th of May. . . . Had my purse been like that of Fortunatus I should have been only too glad to have kept the play on the boards to the close for the honour of the taste of the British public, the dignity of the stage and the respect due to the greatest English poet. But alas! my poverty was obliged to consent to what my will (and a dogged spirit that strove to resist an unkind opposition on the part of the interested malignants) would have made me reject. And thus the term was twenty-three nights and not, as I had hoped, the end of the season. . . .'

During the run Irving, for the first time, allowed an understudy to play for him in order that he could attend the Royal Academy banquet; but it was a painter excluded from that august company who invited him to sit for his portrait in the character of Philip:

'My dear Irving,

I am greatly distressed at having been prevented at the last moment from seeing you again in your triumph of this evening. I must come very soon—and also I want so much to talk to you. It is hopeless calling for I *never* find you—I have tried before now. Meanwhile *do* look in some afternoon directly at the "Society of British Artists", Suffolk Street—and see my picture of Sarasate—and let that show you what I meant your portrait to be and then arrange with me for a day or two at my new studio.

It is ridiculous that Irving should not be painted—and who else shall paint him!

Always,'

The letter was signed with a cypher which the initiated recognized as a butterfly. Irving agreed to Whistler's proposal, and the portrait proved to be, if not a remarkable likeness, a superb study in black and silver. The sittings were frequently interrupted by the visits of duns, and, although it was spring, the unheated studio chilled the sitter but not the painter, who seemed to be equally impervious to draughts or distraint. Three years later, when Whistler went bankrupt and the house in Tite Street, which Godwin had designed for him, was sold with all his other effects, Irving bought the portrait for thirty pounds.

In June Mrs. Bateman presented a double bill at the Lyceum, *The Bells* and *The Belle's Stratagem*, the latter giving plenty of opportunity to Isabel and Virginia Bateman, with Irving playing Doricourt. Mrs. Bateman's managerial difficulties were not made easier by the contrariness of her daughters; Kate was never happy unless acting, Isabel and Virginia still hated it; Virginia refused to act with Kate, and Kate was jealous of Isabel, who was her mother's favourite. Irving endeared himself to the two younger girls by insisting, now that he was almost one of the family, that they should be more attractively dressed off the stage. With the help of Mrs. James, he took them to a fashionable dressmaker, who relieved Mrs. Bateman of these duties and thus allowed her wholly to devote herself to the management of the theatre. Towards the close of the season there was the usual round of benefits. Irving took his on June 23rd. He chose to play Doricourt and Eugene Aram and the evening was made memorable by the last appearance of Helena Faucit on the London stage. She played the blind Iolanthe in the one-act romantic play, *King René's Daughter*, which Theodore Martin had written for her in 1849 and had led to their betrothal. Irving played Count Tristram. It was barely twenty years since an awkward Pisanio had drawn courage from her Imogen at the Theatre Royal, Edinburgh; the hand that then, on sudden inspiration, had cast away a sword now led her forward to make her farewell curtsey to London playgoers.

About the same time old Buckstone, who had been a pupil of Edmund Kean, was given a benefit at Drury Lane to celebrate twenty-three years of unbroken success at the Haymarket and to acknowledge the public debt to one who had made them laugh for over half a century. *The School for Scandal* was the play and Irving was asked to play Joseph Surface in a cast which included Phelps, Sam Emery, Charles Mathews, Coghlan, Bancroft and Ryder. Buckstone himself played Sir Benjamin Backbite. Though it was a compliment from his elders to be included in such a distinguished company, Irving was curiously ill-at-ease among them. It seemed as though he could not adjust his style to that of these masters of the old school. He was restless; his voice was thin, and at times he was inaudible. There were those among the audience who had looked forward to seeing a great Joseph Surface, and they were disappointed. At future benefits or occasions of this kind Irving was careful to avoid appearing in such a galaxy; though always ready to give his services in a good cause, his contribution was either a recitation by himself or a short piece which could be thoroughly prepared with Toole or some other partner.

The season ended with a performance of *Hamlet*, which may have given it an illusory semblance of success. Self-deception was not one of Irving's failings. The year had begun triumphantly, but since

Bateman's death there had been a marked decline in the fortunes of the Lyceum. During the summer, when Salvini had reappeared in London, the public had been apathetic; they had had enough of *Othello*. Irving realized how dangerously fickle public taste could be; an actor had to be untiring in his efforts to preserve the quality and variety of his performances if he was to retain their favour. His Macbeth and Othello had been too hastily studied and too carelessly presented. Having announced that in the coming season he would play Richard III, Irving applied himself to the preparation of the part with the same intensity that he had devoted to Hamlet.

CHAPTER XVIII

The Actor Manager

———— ❦ ————

I

In the autumn the Lyceum company set off to tour the provinces with *Hamlet*, *Charles I* and *The Bells*. If Irving had begun to feel the chill of adverse criticism in the capital, he was soon thoroughly warmed up by the fire of provincial enthusiasm. 'My success,' he wrote to Mrs. James, 'has been far beyond my expectation—surprising. But *Hamlet* is *the* thing and swamps all else—which makes my work very hard.' Of the seventy-eight performances which the tour entailed, fifty-six were of *Hamlet*. Splendid as his progress had been, he can hardly have been prepared for the extraordinary demonstration which attended his visit to Dublin during September.

Irving opened at the Theatre Royal with *Hamlet*. On the following morning he was invited, unofficially, by the graduates and the undergraduates of Trinity College to receive an address in their dining-hall. This address, endorsed by many signatories including several Fellows of the college, having paid tribute to his three performances, concluded: '. . . throughout your two brief engagements our stage has been a school of true art, a purifier of the passions and a nurse of heroic sentiment; you have even succeeded in commending it to the favour of a portion of society, large and justly influential, who usually hold aloof from the theatre.'

Nothing could have given Irving greater pleasure than this spontaneous act of appreciation. In his reply he formulated the aim which, in success or failure, lay behind all he undertook: 'I believe that this is one of the very rare occasions on which public acknowledgment has been given by an academic body to the efforts of a player . . . I feel not merely personal pride of individual success which you thus avow, but that the far nobler work which I aim at is in truth begun. When I think that you, the upholders of the classic in every age, have thus flung aside the traditions of three centuries, and have acknowledged the true union of poet and actor, my heart swells with a great pride that I should be the recipient of such acknowledgement. I trust with all my soul that the reform which you suggest may ere long be carried out, and that the body to whom is justly entrusted our higher moral education may recognize in the Stage a medium for the accomplishment of such ends. What you have done today is a mighty stride in this direction. . . .'

That same day he read with particular interest a criticism of his Hamlet in the *Dublin Mail*. It was for the most part laudatory, though whenever critical it was outspoken. Whoever had written it had been at pains to analyse Irving's intentions and had himself very definite views on certain aspects of Hamlet's character.

'There is another view,' the writer claimed, 'which Mr. Irving seems to realise by a kind of instinct, but which requires to be more fully and intentionally worked out . . . the great, deep, underlying idea of Hamlet is that of a mystic . . . In the high-strung nerves of the man . . . in the divine delirium of his perfected passion, there is the instinct of the mystic which he has but to render a little plainer, in order that the less susceptible senses of his audience may see and understand.'

Irving expressed a wish to meet this enlightened critic. That night, before the play began, Harris, the manager, brought to Irving's dressing-room a ruddy, bearded gentleman of about thirty with something of the appearance of Sir Francis Drake, whom he introduced as Mr. Bram Stoker. As there was little time for conversation, Irving asked Stoker to join him at supper after the play. Over supper Stoker explained that he was a civil servant who, in the course of duty, was at that time engaged in writing a textbook on *The Duties of Clerks of Petty Sessions*, but by way of recreation wrote articles and dramatic criticisms for the *Mail*. His robust appearance and hearty ebullience did not suggest a clerical bookishness. Irving soon discovered that his new friend had been a redoubtable athlete who, on his way through Dublin University, had won several cups and caps as well as honours in history and mathematics. Irving was naturally attracted by Stoker's emotional enthusiasm, particularly when he talked of the theatre. He was extremely well read and had already written a number of short stories. It appeared, moreover, that he had been the moving spirit behind that morning's ceremony at Trinity College.

A few nights later Irving again asked Stoker to join him at supper, this time in the company of a few friends. After supper, Irving offered to recite 'Eugene Aram'. Perhaps he had some ulterior purpose in doing so, for he exerted himself to such an extent that, at the end, he collapsed, momentarily exhausted. There was a moment's awed silence, and then Bram Stoker, much to the surprise of his friends, burst into hysterics. The effect of his recitation upon Stoker was all that Irving had hoped—as welcome as the effects of the 'Murder of Gonzago' on his uncle were to Hamlet. While Stoker was recovering, he went into his room and returned with a photograph of himself, upon which he had inscribed:

'My dear friend Stoker—God bless you! God bless you!

Henry Irving.

Dublin, December 3rd, 1876.'

Though Stoker did not know it, at that moment the course of his life was changed.

On the night of December 11th the entire theatre was taken over by the university—the stalls and boxes crowded with the leading members of the university and distinguished alumni, while undergraduates thronged the pit and gallery. Irving, when he appeared as Hamlet, had a tremendous reception. The Lord Lieutenant and the Duke of Connaught arrived during the second act, but, happily, the cheers which such a tardy arrival hardly merited were reserved until the interval which followed. Irving was as overwhelmed by the tumult of cheering at the end of the play as he had been by the hooting and hissing which had greeted his first appearance in Dublin. Now he had only to surrender to his audience, which he did with a gracious speech. When he left the theatre he found that the students had gathered outside the stage door in force and had removed the horses from his carriage. With Bram Stoker at his side, Irving was hauled through the streets of Dublin by a team of a hundred students, while those who could not man the ropes crowded round the carriage and kept up a wild uproar of shouting and singing. Up Grafton Street and round St. Stephen's Square, they dragged him to the doors of his hotel. As the crowd filled the Square and swarmed round the carriage, the cheering became more coherent and more directly aimed at the object of their enthusiasm. Irving was quite overcome. Not knowing how to respond adequately to their kindness, he suggested desperately that all should join him in a toast—a gesture which was hastily vetoed by the manager of the hotel and the police who, so far, had been only interested spectators. So, with a wave of his hat and an inaudible 'Good night', he made his way into the hotel. The students dispersed in an orderly manner; indeed their behaviour throughout the evening had been so exemplary that on the Monday morning the following notice was fixed on the college gates:

'At roll call tonight the junior Dean will express his grateful sense of the admirable conduct of the students on Saturday last, at Mr. Irving's reception in Trinity College and subsequently at the performance in the Theatre Royal.'

Later the students of Belfast University took up the challenge. Barry Sullivan, before playing *Richard III* in that town, was escorted to the theatre by students in torchlight procession. After the play a graduate came onto the stage and presented the actor with an address. If these proceedings were less orderly and dignified than those at the rival university, Irving could be no less pleased to have started a vogue for academical acclamation of his profession. In London, Irving had been warned by his patronizing detractors not to set any store by the hysterical praise of the intellectual or well-to-do, and that he must seek his verdict from the ordinary folk in the pit and gallery. Such a spontaneous demonstration of homage by young men of robust taste and of uncertain temper sent him back to London in high spirits, ready to accept adulation or disparagement, the former with due reserve and the latter, however malicious, with the philosophical calm which came naturally in the wake of such a storm of encouraging approbation. He carried away with him a concrete reminder of Dublin's warmheartedness in the form of a long-haired terrier, now his constant companion, which had been given him during this visit and was appropriately named Trin.

During his stay in Dublin, Irving, the Shakespearian missionary, had effected a remarkable conversion. Lord Randolph Churchill had accompanied his father to the gala performance of *Hamlet*. Between the fourth and last act he went round to see Irving in his dressing-room. To the actor's surprise, he asked him how the play ended, confessing that he was not much of a playgoer and that the play was new to him: his appetite apparently whetted by Irving's hasty summary, he returned to his father's box. Later, Irving was invited to spend Sunday at Vice-Regal Lodge. When the time came to say goodbye Lord Randolph Churchill said: 'Mr. Irving, I believe I have to thank you for as great a boon as ever one man conferred on another. I assure you that I knew nothing of Shakespeare and had not seen or read any of his plays. Since that night I have seen *Hamlet* twice and I have read four of the other plays. I feel you have really introduced me to a new world.'

2

The winter season at the Lyceum opened on December 16th with a revival of *Macbeth*, which was hailed defiantly by Lyceum partisans and with reiterated growls by the critics. By day Irving was preparing *Richard III*. During the tour he had enlisted the services of a faithful lieutenant, H. J. Loveday, his old friend who had conducted the orchestra at his first benefit at the Theatre Royal, Edinburgh. Loveday was working in the dual capacity of stage manager and orchestra leader for Edward Saker in Liverpool, but he needed little persuasion to throw in his lot with Irving, who engaged him for the Lyceum as stage manager for *Richard III*. Loveday brought with him to the Lyceum more than his own ability and loyalty. His father had been musical director at Drury Lane during the reign of Edmund Kean. As long as he and his wife, who long survived him, were alive, Irving had at his side trusted and perceptive witnesses who could describe to him Kean's performances with every nuance of gesture and inflection. The baton in Irving's knapsack was beginning to nudge him in the back; quietly and methodically he had begun to enrol his general staff. He also found a place in the cast for R. C. Lyons, another friend of his Edinburgh days with whom he had shared the honours accorded to the leading gentleman at the obsequies of the old Theatre Royal. For the treacherous Lord Stanley he had found a young actor whose appearance was darkly conspiratorial—Mr. A. W. Pinero, who already had a play or two in his portfolio and many more in his mind. With Kate cast for Queen Margaret and Isabel for Lady Anne, Mrs. Bateman recalled with pride how, in 1851, P. T. Barnum had presented her brilliant children in excerpts from *Richard III*—an exhibition of infants so phenomenal that a critic complained that Barnum had inflicted on the public a nuisance by no means proportional to the size of its perpetrators.

Irving had given a great deal of time and thought to the preparation of the text. In 1700 Colley Cibber, with misguided zeal, had rearranged and freely embellished with his own verse Shakespeare's *Richard III*. In his view the original play was unactable. In order to improve its dramatic construction he had interpolated scenes from *Henry V* and from *Henry VI; Part III*. Thereafter Shakespeare's play vanished from the English stage. In 1821 Macready made a half-hearted attempt to prune it of what he called Cibber's fustian trash, but in doing so he fell between two stools, by losing the dramatic effectiveness of Cibber's hotch-potch and failing to recapture the splendour of Shakespeare's original. In any case when, three years before, as Richard III, he established himself as Edmund Kean's only rival, he had used Cibber's tinsel adaptation. Irving, once again, was prepared to take a risk in defence of his principles. Critics might well say that if Cibber was good enough for Garrick and Kean it was good enough for Irving; that Shakespeare's play had not been rejected without good reason. Few playgoers would pretend to be familiar with either text; they would be concerned solely with the actor's ability to entertain them. Irving knew well enough that any innovations which he made would be justified only by his personal success. He was, however, wise enough to know that Shakespeare never failed an actor and that, properly handled, the original play had in it everything which a virtuoso actor needed. In throwing overboard all Cibber's speeches with which his predecessors had won fame he would force the critics, by robbing them of comparative arguments, to judge his performance on its own merits.

Richard III was produced on January 29th, 1877. By the end of the evening he had won back his position as the greatest contemporary exponent of Shakespeare. Hardly one dissentient voice was heard against the concord of praise which welcomed his brave and scholarly vindication of Shakespeare and his subtle impersonation of the Duke of Gloucester. The physical crookedness of Richard he suggested without assuming the deformities of Punch. By the end of the first soliloquy, Irving's intention became clear. He was attempting to restore not only Shakespeare's play but the historical Richard. Here was a prince of ruthless enterprise, reckless in facing the consequences of his acts, capable of exercising a devastating charm of manner which in his lifetime confounded his enemies and at his death moved the citizens of his native York to record in their register that he had been 'piteously slain and murdered to the great heaviness of this city'. Above all, Irving never lost sight of Richard's kingliness. This was particularly evident in the tent scene. Irving discarded the convention of placing Richard and Richmond in inadequate little tents on opposite sides of the stage, from which they might be expected to emerge and to fight it out in bathing costumes. The king's tent filled the stage. A small red lamp on the table gave it its only illumination, and the blood-guilty Plantagenet sat scanning the plans of the morrow's battle array. Presently he put the paper from him, and with a groan of weariness rose, turned, limped his way to the back of the tent, and drew its entrance curtains apart, disclosing a scene steeped in moonlight and a sky glittering with stars. 'I can still see,' wrote H. M.

Walbrook many years after, 'the dark misshapen tragic figure as I saw it that night standing with outstretched arms against the lovely background of the peaceful heavens, and the impression the contrast made is still vividly with me. The whole movement, combined with the poetical setting given to it, made a marvellous commentary on the play. The figure of the king became in that moment a thousand times more tragic than it had been before.'

Tennyson, when he saw the play, asked Irving where he got that Plantagenet look. Anyone less innocent of the theatre than the Laureate would have known that any competent actor could conjure such appearances out of his make-up box. Irving's genius lay in his ability to take Shakespeare's text and, without mutilating it, to bend it to his purpose. It was generally agreed that his interpretation did not violate Shakespeare's portrayal of Richard.

'The literary interest of the Lyceum revival,' wrote a critic, 'was thrown into the shade by Mr. Irving's interpretation of the principal character. The Richard of Shakespeare, with the graces imparted by high breeding, his immense force of character, his utter indifference to ties which ordinarily bind men together, his sensitiveness to the most trifling reflections upon his deformities, his cynical humour and withering sarcasm, seemed to have stepped from the book onto the stage. The conventional Richard since the time of Edmund Kean had been a brusque and rather noisy villain; in Mr. Irving's performance we have the prince, the statesman, and the courtier, who was described by a contemporary as the most enchanting man to be found near the throne.'

Henry James, though he found Irving better fitted for Richard than Macbeth, remained impervious to his hypnotism and scandalized by his methods. His critical integrity had survived even the charms of a supper with Irving at the Garrick Club and the lovely Mrs. Greville's advocacy of Irving as he drove with her through Surrey on visits to Tennyson and to George Eliot. 'It is, of course,' he explained, 'by his picturesqueness that Mr. Irving has made his place; by small ingenuities of "business" and subtleties of action; by doing as a painter does who goes in for colour when he cannot depend upon his drawing. Mr. Irving's colour is sometimes pretty enough; his ingenuities and subtleties are often felicitous; but his picturesqueness, on the whole, strikes me as dry and awkward, and, at the best, where certain essentials are so strikingly absent, these secondary devices lose much of their power. . . . Richard III is of all Shakespeare's parts the one that can perhaps best dispense with declamation, and in which the clever inventions of manner and movement in which Mr. Irving is proficient will carry the actor furthest.'

He had forgotten that neither he nor anyone else at that time had seen Shakespeare's Richard until Irving laid it before them. Nevertheless he condemned unflinchingly Irving's rendering of the whole part —'slowly, draggingly, diffusively, with innumerable pauses and lapses, and without a hint of the rapidity, the intensity and entrain which are needful for carrying off the improbabilities of so explicit and confidential a villain and so melodramatic a hero'. Perhaps, as he thought of Irving, he chuckled over the Paris *Figaro's* description of Manet after the impressionist exhibition at the Hotel Druot—'a cat walking on the keyboard of the piano or a monkey who might have got hold of a box of paints'. Still in search of a reflection of the Comédie Française in London, he sought refuge in the Prince of Wales's Theatre where Madge Robertson (Mrs. Kendal) and Arthur Cecil were playing in an adaptation of Sardou's *Nos Intimes*. Here he found the acting 'very pretty indeed and this little theatre doubtless deserves the praise which is claimed for it, of being the best conducted English stage in the world'.

Irving played Richard for three months, during which he strengthened and refined his performance. It was apparent to those who closely studied his work that on the first nights his strength and his voice began to fail him towards the end of the play. This was, of course, particularly noticeable in plays which reached a violent climax in their final scene. Critics who had commented on this weakness, as they had done in the case of *Richard III*, were baffled when they found, at a subsequent performance or at a revival, that his vocal and physical powers were sustained until the end of the play. His voice, which had always been the most vulnerable part of his equipment, betrayed the fatigue and nervous strain of playing and producing; as he felt it forsaking him he strained physically to recover it and so enervated his powers of attack that, but for the force of his personality, this first-night disability might have proved fatal to his success.

The reception accorded to his Richard assured Irving that his prestige was restored. If the applause of the public and the praise of critics were intangible and capricious rewards of merit, evidence of the esteem in which he was held by his brother actors meant so much the more. After the first night, old Chippendale presented him with the sword which Edmund Kean had used as Richard. From the Baroness came David Garrick's ring in which was mounted a miniature portrait of Shakespeare; she sent it, so ran the inscription, 'in recognition of the gratification derived from his Shakespearian representations; uniting to many characteristics of his great predecessor in histrionic art (whom he is too young to remember) the charm of original thought, giving delineations of new forms of dramatic interest, power, and beauty'.

3

During his first disastrous visit to Dublin Irving had played the *jeune premier* in a melodrama, *The Courier of Lyons*. The dual role of an unmitigated villain and a hero falsely accused had very much appealed to him. Having learnt that one new Shakespearian part in a season was as much as he could handle, he decided to put on this play after *Richard III*. In about 1850 a transcription of the play, *Le Courier de Lyons*, which was being played at the Théâtre de la Gaîté, was brought to England. Charles Reade seized upon it and made an excellent adaptation for Charles Kean. In the course of rough and ready translation the play became *The Courier of Lyons*—which meant nothing at all. Irving, on the advice of Walter Pollock, renamed the play *The Lyons Mail*.

In 1796 a mail van carrying money for Napoleon's troops in Italy was robbed at Lieursaint, a short distance from Paris. The driver and postillion were murdered. Suspicion fell upon Lesurques, a man of commerce, who in due course was guillotined. Later the leader of a gang of robbers, Dubosc, was arrested and executed for a variety of crimes; though the villain stoutly denied it, it was the general opinion that he, in fact, had been the robber of the Lyons Mail. There was considerable circumstantial evidence against Lesurques, whose character was not above reproach, and a slight resemblance between the two men confused the witnesses and the issue. The case remains still a fascinating historical mystery. The family of Lesurques erected a fine monument to him in Père Lachaise and, quite naturally, declared his innocence in a fulsome inscription. The monument caught the eye of MM. Moreau, Siraudin and Delacour and inspired them to write a vivid melodrama in which the gentle and innocent Lesurques, owing to mistaken identity, was found guilty of the crime and only saved from execution by the efforts of his children and the mistress of Dubosc who contrived to bring that callous and engaging blackguard to the guillotine. The original production was famous chiefly for Paulin Menier's terrifying portrayal of Choppard, a drunken horse dealer who was Dubosc's chief lieutenant. Charles Reade's adaptation was well constructed, but at Irving's and Mrs. Bateman's suggestion he made certain alterations and additions and improved upon the version which Charles Kean had played with such success. Irving seized upon *The Lyons Mail* and made it his own; it remained, until the end of his life, one of the most popular pieces in his repertoire. His Lesurques, a blameless and much-loved paterfamilias, baffled by the hideous and meaningless accusation brought against him, was played in the best vein of cumulative tragedy; his Dubosc was a masterpiece of macabre and sardonic humour, a monster of drunken devilry.

The Lyons Mail followed *Richard III* on May 19th and filled the Lyceum until the theatre closed at the end of July. Although the play was well received on the first night, the audience were annoyed by the omission of the usual farce which Mrs. Bateman commendably had tried to eliminate. Although *The Lyons Mail* played for two hours the audience felt cheated of their money's worth. Mrs. Bateman bowed to the storm and added 'A Petite Comedy' to the bill. In doing so, she revived the hopes of young Pinero who had begun to interest Irving in his one-act plays. If the intellectual supporters of the Lyceum accepted Irving's excursion into melodrama with tolerant amusement, the pit and gallery relished it and no one enjoyed the whole affair more than Irving himself. His opponents applauded his good sense in sinking once more to the level where he belonged; his admirers retaliated by declaring that his genius transformed crude melodrama into noble tragedy.

In June, Helena Faucit wrote to Irving:

> *31 Onslow Square.*
> *June 15th, 1877.*

'Dear Mr. Irving,

Can you look in upon us on the 27th? I have not liked to ask you to help me because of your already too great nightly fatigue. What a trial for your voice the assumption of the drunken man's must be! Mr. Martin tells me it is exactly a drunkard's voice. He is especially fond of a good melodrama and enjoyed *The Lyons Mail* immensely. I liked it well enough *"once in a way"*. It is certainly admirably represented. It is the after satisfaction which I miss so much in pieces of the kind. I never can hold the belief that the stage is only for our amusement. I wish you well through the great fatigue which I see lies before you. Believe me most truly yours,

> Helena F. Martin.

P.S. My male assistants in the little reading, which I have been *talked into* giving, will be mostly clergymen. The Reverend Mr. Ainger of the

IRVING-DUBOSC—What! 'Enery? This *is* a treat!
HENRY LESURQUES—Goodness gracious! My old friend, Irving? Delighted!
BOTH—Glad to see you back again in melodrama, old man!

Temple Church has a fine voice and reads Shakespeare extremely well. He is to be the Shylock. I am much wanting a good Bassanio. I asked Canon Duckworth, but he is fully engaged on the 27th. He says, "to his great regret", certainly also to mine for he has a fine manly voice and reads admirably. Not always the case with our clergymen.'

No doubt Irving went to Onslow Square in a missionary spirit; he hoped, by joining in these cloistered Shakespeare readings, to illuminate with the light of his faith the dark ignorance of the clerical mind as regards the theatre. Only Max Beerbohm, whose infant hand, alas, had not yet wielded a pencil, could have done justice to this extraordinary scene. The great actress sternly rehearsing the adoring and earnest clergy, Theodore Martin at hand to prompt and to elucidate the text, and Irving, like Champlain among the Iroquois, discreetly curbing his impatience in the hope of wooing the reverend gentleman from the study to the stalls. These gatherings were not without their embarrassment. Canon Ainger, as far as Irving was concerned, had a guilty past. Before he could encounter the actor in Mrs. Martin's drawing-room certain overtures had to be made:

> 2 *Upper Terrace*,
> *Hampstead.*

'Dear Mr. Irving,

My friend Mrs. Theodore Martin has paid me the high compliment of asking me to take part in a dramatic reading next week at her house, on which occasion she tells me you are to read the part of Bassanio.

Now it would be affectation in me to pretend that you are not aware of my being the author of a criticism upon your Hamlet published some years ago in a magazine (Macmillans), which through the zeal of some well intentioned friends was more talked about than I ever thought or desired it might be. Will you allow me to hope that any differences of opinion on the subject of your delightful art may not serve to prevent our meeting as friends; if, at last, as I hope, there was nothing in the article in question that passed the bounds of friendly criticism. "Thought is free" is a good Shakespearian adage—and I suppose *criticism* is included in this saying. May I add how much I have desired for a long time to make your personal acquaintance. We have, I think, several friends in common . . . believe me dear Mr. Irving,

> Yours very faithfully,
> Alfred Ainger.'

Exterior

Interior

Stage Door

THE ROYAL LYCEUM THEATRE

Bram Stoker

Walter Collinson
From a drawing by
the author

Henry J. Loveday

The offending article was harmless enough. It was mainly a rather peevish deprecation of the critics' indiscriminating praise of Irving's Hamlet and contained a stern admonition to the actor not to let his head be turned by such exuberant and ill-formed commendation. It seemed, however, to lie heavy on the Canon's conscience. Anonymity had not concealed the identity of its author from Irving. The Canon's recantation (for when they met he confessed that he was 'utterly ashamed of it') was accepted. The hatchet was buried and the Canon was converted.

4

The Lyceum season ended on July 31st. Irving played Hamlet at the last performance; in thanking the audience for their continued support, he said he 'was glad that for one season his detractors had left his legs and his voice alone'. The provincial tour, with *Hamlet*, *Richard III* and *The Lyons Mail*, began early in September. Irving, however, had little rest. 'My short holiday,' he wrote to Mrs. James, 'I am keeping at the Lyceum—rehearsing a play for Mrs. Crowe and I only hope she is alive to my sacrifice.' Mrs. Bateman was producing a dramatization of Wilkie Collins's novel, *The Dead Secret*, in which Kate was to have the stage of the Lyceum to herself while Irving and Isabel were away.

Irving made the usual round of the provincial towns on the heels of Barry Sullivan and with Toole following in the wake of his success. Sullivan travelled light, with his swords, with his sparring partner in the stage fights for which he was famous and with, perhaps, a leading lady; he cared nothing for scenery and all he asked from his supporting players were elbow room and cues. Although Irving was attacking the stronghold of the Irish tragedian and playing two parts in which Sullivan was particularly popular, he carried by storm all but one or two citadels, like Manchester, which held out for their old favourite. Here their paths crossed and here, at Irving's invitation, the two stars celebrated their conjunction over Sunday supper.

Sullivan, who was on a farewell tour before going to America, was enjoying something like a royal progress. Arriving in Dublin from Belfast, where he had been treated to a torchlight procession, he was accorded a civic reception and was driven from the station to the Shelbourne Hotel in the Lord Mayor's carriage. But Irving knew that his hold on Dublin was secure. During the run of *The Lyons Mail*, in fulfilment of an earlier promise, he had paid a flying visit to Trinity College, where, on a Monday, he gave readings from Dickens and Shakespeare in their hall. Afterwards he had been chaired by the students, dined by the fellows and escorted by Bram Stoker to the night mail which carried him back to London in time for Tuesday night's performance.

During the tour Irving corresponded with Mrs. Brown almost daily. She was assiduous, through her amanuensis the Baroness, in recommending sights for him to see, patent medicines for his health and in giving him the gossip of the town. From Glasgow, where Mrs. Brown had urged him to visit a captive eagle, he wrote:

'. . . I forgot to tell you yesterday that I had paid a visit to the Bird. In his eerie, a cage about ten feet square, he looked sturdy and desolate. Is he a Scotchman?

Last night I could not resist sending you the telegram for I know how glad you would be to hear the news. I am to do great things here. This is the first Glasgow day, dreary and wet.

How well you signed the paper. I am sure you liked doing so. Friend Critchett's report with such good advice, rejoices me. I always thought we would "drown in a bowl" and we will too, with a right hearty "chorus, John, chorus".

Poor Trin, you will be sorry to hear, has hurt his foot. I took him to the leech today, who said it had been crushed a little. I am afraid some heavy-heeled highlander, or rather *low*lander, has trodden upon him, but he will soon be well again. His spirits are excellent and also his appetite.'

In Manchester he received from Mrs. Brown a bottle of Phynes vinegar—an inhalant for his cough. He seems to have misapplied it for Mrs. Brown wrote in alarm: 'Good gracious. The vinegar is only to smell and that in the extra bottle is only to replenish the sponge in the other bottle—you quite frightened us—did it leave a mark on your face? . . .'

It affected him less adversely than the chill of his reception in Manchester. 'How I shall rejoice to leave this place,' he wrote, 'the enemies are bitter and the friends are freezing. You can hardly think what a comfort Trin is to me'. The companionable Trin soon became the victim of his master's devotion. He lived handsomely on tit-bits from Irving's table. One of these, a chicken bone, lodged in the dog's throat with fatal consequences, and Irving left for Edinburgh alone.

In Edinburgh, although he played to crowded and enthusiastic audiences, Irving once again became embroiled in public controversy. Shortly before he arrived, a pamphlet had been published in Edinburgh and Glasgow called 'The Fashionable Tragedian'. In its twenty-four pages it voiced the pent-up feelings of those who believed that his popular success was a menace to the English theatre. The authors claimed that his diction was execrable, that his mannerisms were grotesque and that his scholarship was a pretence. The case was argued in terms of reasoned abuse and illustrated with a series of derisive woodcuts. The writers, in admitting his inexplicable popularity, and stating in detail the claims that were made in support of his genius, rose above the level of the composers of the previous letter 'To a Fashionable Tragedian'. They professed even to have admired Irving's early work and to have undertaken a painful duty more in sorrow than in anger. In conclusion the lampoon was adorned by a moral—that with proper training the tragedian might have become a tolerable or perhaps a great actor and that the only way to protect the public in future against such imposture was to have a National Theatre and an approved school of acting. The pamphlet took both press and public by surprise. They deprecated publicly the bad taste of its unrestrained invective; in private they chuckled over much of it, particularly over the illustrations.

It soon became known that the authors of the pamphlet were three young Edinburgh men, Robert Lowe, George Halkett and William Archer. Lowe was an insurance clerk with a flair for amateur acting and mimicry; Halkett, too, was in an insurance office though he was already an accomplished draughtsman and caricaturist. Archer was a good deal younger than his two friends; he had taken his degree at the university during the previous year and had done a certain amount of journalism while still an undergraduate. All three men were genuine lovers and students of the theatre, though Archer's knowledge of it, since he had only just returned from a voyage round the world, cannot have been very profound or up to date. Undoubtedly Lowe was the moving spirit, and it was Lowe who, having had some misgivings about his disparagement of Irving in *Richard III*, proposed to publish a second edition in which his strictures would be qualified. But the war of pamphlets was now on and Lowe's second assault was broken up by a vigorous counter-attack. A pamphlet entitled 'A Letter Concerning Mr. Henry Irving' appeared simultaneously in Edinburgh, Glasgow and London. Over the signature 'Yorick', with urbane and good-tempered argument it reasoned with rather than rebuked the authors of 'The Fashionable Tragedian'. Though Yorick professed to have no personal knowledge of the actor, the concluding paragraph of the pamphlet was drafted in Irving's handwriting on a piece of note paper headed 15A Grafton Street:

PRICE SIXPENCE.

THE
FASHIONABLE TRAGEDIAN

A CRITICISM.
WITH TEN ILLUSTRATIONS.

EDINBURGH & GLASGOW:
THOMAS GRAY AND COMPANY.

'And now, Sir, I have nearly done. Perhaps you know the distinguished writer of this pamphlet and his companion who has assisted him in this novel scheme. Perhaps they are both young men who may hereafter look with regret upon their questionable work—if this result should be attained, some unexpected good may yet be done them—I hope so. I beg them, for the sake of any dear or honourable ties they have, to commit to memory and bear in mind these words, "Good breeding lies in human nature and is due from all men towards all men." I am, Sir, yours obediently—Yorick.'

When this pamphlet appeared Lowe's second edition had barely left the hands of the printers. The press, on the whole, ignored Lowe's second thoughts, and several papers which had been amused by the original edition had now gone over to the enemy. Rumours of pending legal action reached the authors, one of whom was about to get married. Rather than risk the heavy loss which even a successful defence would incur, Lowe withdrew such copies as had been issued to the trade. Irving had won the second round of his fight to defend himself and his profession against this kind of defamatory ridicule which passed for fair criticism. He was determined that actors should not be subjected to public personal abuse of a kind which no other profession would tolerate and against which even politicians were able to retaliate in similar terms.

It was, perhaps, natural that at a private dinner in Edinburgh to which Irving had been invited to ask any friends he chose he should have referred to this affair. In a light-hearted way he said that a dramatic critic was a man who required training, culture and experience, but that every profession had its black sheep and—as in this case—the value of dramatic notices written by such people could be estimated by the lowest sums earned in their calling. Several journalists were present and there was a good deal of chaff about the press. When the toast of the press was proposed, it was replied to in grateful terms by a gentleman who, immediately after the dinner was over, wrote an account of it for his paper, in which Irving was represented as having attacked dramatic critics in general. This report was widely circulated and was shown to Irving when he arrived in Dublin. He wrote a letter to the press in which he gave his own account of what had been said and appealed against the injustice of these reports. It was all very tiresome. If he was perpetually to be engaged in a war of pamphlets and *démentis* in his own defence, he would be forced to find a henchman who, skilled in the arts of publicity, could handle these matters for him. Old Bateman would have gone roaring into action at the slightest provocation and given as good as he got. There was something about Bram Stoker which reminded him of the Colonel.

Dublin seemed to appreciate Irving's *Richard III* as highly as his *Hamlet*. During his stay Stoker was constantly in his company, supping with him off hot lobsters at Corless's restaurant or escorting him to wrestling matches in Phoenix Park. Towards the end of the week they supped alone together in Stoker's rooms. Irving then disclosed in guarded terms the difficulties of the situation in which he found himself. The opportunities afforded to him by his success were enormous, yet the debt of gratitude which he owed to Mrs. Bateman made him hesitate to dissolve a partnership which already showed signs of preventing him from making the most of those opportunities. He confided to his new friend that the supporting casts which Mrs. Bateman engaged were inadequate and were becoming the subject of adverse comment by many critics. Moreover, as long as the partnership was continued, he would have to accept Mrs. Bateman's daughters as his leading ladies; Kate alone had any real talent and none of them made any very great appeal to the public. It was possible that before long he would be forced to make a change. Mrs. Bateman was talking of leasing and restoring the Sadler's Wells Theatre; if she did so, her divided interests might prove fatal to his own. If he decided to become his own master, he would need a loyal friend to share the burden of management. Already he was able to leave the details of stage-management in the capable hands of Harry Loveday. A business and front-of-the-house manager was harder to find. Such a post would allow a man of varied talents plenty of scope and was infinitely preferable to the dusty drudgery of the civil service. No more was said; Irving merely ruminated on his recent problems and his future hopes. Stoker, however, thought that by this time he knew his man. When Irving left, he wrote in his diary: London in view!

5

The Lyceum reopened on Boxing Day. For two months Irving rang the changes on *The Bells*, *The Lyons Mail* and *Charles I*, while he was preparing a production of Casimir Delavigne's *Louis XI*. By the time it reached Irving, there was little of Delavigne's work left in the play. Boucicault, seeking fresh inspiration from Comines, Scott and Victor Hugo, rewrote it in blank verse and contrived a happy ending to it for Charles Kean, who, out of very poor material, created one of his greatest successes. In attempting the part Irving invited comparison with Kean but did so with the blessing of Ellen Tree, Kean's widow, who gave him permission to use her husband's version and her advice and help in the course of rehearsal.

Richard III and Louis XI seem to have conducted their lives for the benefit of theatrical posterity. Whatever virtues they may have had have long been forgotten. Their villainies, often apocryphal, have provided such rich material both for dramatists and actors that they are assured of monstrous immortality. On the whole, Louis XI has been the luckier of the two. As long as the English language survives, Richard will be pilloried by the pen of Shakespeare. It is unlikely that Louis will be troubled much by revivals of Delavigne's and Boucicault's travesty of history. As a play it had every fault—unrelieved gloom and a dull first act, in which the principal figures did not appear. It had, however, the supreme virtue of providing a great actor with a subject for subtle characterization. It was a one-man play. It had caused Joseph Knight to wonder if Charles Kean wished to see his company reduced to himself and a ballet. Irving was fully aware of all this. In later years, when he was rehearsing a young actor for the part of the Duc de Nemours, he said: 'Don't search for any hidden meanings—me boy—it's penny plain—ye know—tuppence coloured!' Irving's performance as Louis improved during the thirty years he was to play it, but at the outset it exhibited to perfection one of his many accomplishments. He became inherent in the mind and incarnate in the decrepit body of the old despot and blended them into a stage portrait which was the most elaborate and subtle he ever realized and was admitted to be superior to Kean's by those who had seen them both. He brought to life the Louis of Jean Baffier's statue in Bourges. Most of his mannerisms seemed to vanish or to be absorbed in the whining fear, the querulous rage, and the acutely observed eccentricities of senile regality.

The play opened on March 9th. So eager were the audience for Irving's long-delayed appearance that when, in the first act, a character came upon the stage in a make-up which faintly resembled their hero he was greeted with tremendous yet disconcerting applause. By the end of the second act Irving had completed his illustration of Louis's character—the combination of cruelty, fawning duplicity, fear and hypocrisy lightened with grim humour. Those who remembered Kean and were determined to be faithful to past recollections, soon found their loyalty undermined and their allegiance won over by Irving's more delicate and minutely studied intrepertation. Those who had known Kean personally knew also that this generous-hearted actor, who had no thought but for the advancement of the art he loved, would have delighted in Irving's embellishment of his own creation. The fourth and fifth acts have been best described by Edward Russell in a closely observed study of Irving's performance:

'Act the fourth is far more onerous. Here the King is seen in the solitude of his bed-chamber. Here takes place his extraordinary confession to François de Paule, delivered with great effect in all its blood-chilling frankness and incorrigible impenitence. And here, when the holy father has retired, the monarch is suddenly frozen into abject terror by the appearance of the avenging Nemours. A terrible scene ensues—first of wild pleading for mercy, and then, when Nemours has with contempt and loathing granted the king his life, a fearful paroxysm of rage and hallucination, as the old man, suddenly young again with desperate excitement, rushes up to what he supposes to be the Duc de Nemours, and violently stabs the air until he falls fainting into the arms of those around him—a situation of great power most startlingly enacted. Great as the performance is in every phase, it is grandest in the fifth act where King Louis enters robed and sceptred, with death written in his countenance, and his physique reduced to the lowest stage of feebleness. The skull-cap has been abandoned. Long grey locks stream somewhat wildly on the king's shoulders. His countenance derives a sort of dignity, not seen before, from these changes, though such a figure can never be truly venerable—and also from the absorbing nature of the conflict which Louis wages with visibly declining powers. In this hour of extreme mental exhaustion, deepening momentarily into actual stupefaction and afterwards into coma and then into death, the extraordinary resolution and will of the king still display marvellous power. But never was there such a picture of moving prostration and animated decay. The back of a couch lost hold of for a moment, and the tottering form stumbles forward in a manner which sends a painful start through the whole audience. The sceptre drops, after being used head downwards as a staff, and is forgotten. Then the king is induced to be seated on a couch, and with extraordinary elaborated graduations of insensibility, violently interrupted by spasms of vigour, he gradually loses his consciousness. No physical detail is neglected that can help to realize a sinking of mind and body into annihilating death. The voice and articulation have the weird, half-drunken thickness of paralysis. Even the effect observable in age and sickness of drawing the retreating lips in over the sunken teeth is somewhat simulated. The difficulty of carrying out such a conception of dissolution in a scene in the course of which such matters have to be dealt with as the final sentence of Nemours, and an interview with Coitier, the leech, who comes from a dungeon with the rust of fetters on his wrist, at the summons of the king who sent him there, must be extreme; but Mr. Irving triumphantly surmounts it, and gives a picture of gradual and placid yet horrible death such as we believe has never been achieved before. Perhaps the greatest success of all is the still and silent impassibility into which the king sinks so absolutely that the courtiers and his son suppose it to be death. The actual death is not placid. The king struggles on his feet, and falls forward on a cushion, with his head toward the audience, as the low murmur, "The King is dead, long live the King", proclaims the close of the long, long struggle of a mind that seemed indomitable with the frailties and tortures to which humanity can be a prey, and consoled by none of the assuagements to which the sufferings are most indebted. Such, lit up in the earlier passages by infinite comedy and artistically elevated by several tragic episodes of the highest power, is this famous impersonation.'

The play was well received and ran for three months. The only adverse criticisms were of Irving's levity in accentuating the hypocrisy of Louis' religious devotion; as this was purposely calculated to relieve the pervading gloom of a dull and humourless play, Irving ignored them. Dutton Cook and Joseph Knight were united in their eulogy, and even Henry James admitted that 'Mr. Irving plays his one part very well, and it is probably his most satisfactory creation'. He was, however, quick to qualify his praise:

'In this elaborate, picturesque representation of a grotesque old tyrant, at once passionate and cunning, familiar and ferocious, he has the good fortune that some of his defects positively come to his assistance. He is an incongruous Hamlet or Macbeth, but he is a very consistent Louis XI. The part was a favourite one of Charles Kean, who played it with more delicacy, and, at the same time, (according to my recollection), with more rondeur, as the French say; but certainly, in the actual state of the English stage, there is no actor capable of doing the thing so cleverly or so picturesquely as Mr. Irving—in spite of his always saying "Gaw" for "go", "Naw" for "no," etc. Mr. Irving's eccentricities of utterance, however, are very numerous and on this point the auditor must make a large concession at the outset.'

Henry James spoke of Irving's eccentricity of diction as though it was a natural and incurable defect; others criticized the action of his legs or gait as though it was a physical or nervous disability which could be cured by will power or by exercises. During these formative years the bulk of the adverse criticism of Irving was directed against these faults which were styled mannerisms. Again and again Irving was urged to control or conquer these mannerisms as though they were habits carelessly acquired. Throughout his life Irving strove to refine or improve his art; yet in certain parts these mannerisms were retained until the end. It can be assumed, therefore, that the way in which he spoke or walked upon the stage was as deliberate as everything else he did. Off the stage his mannner was simple and unaffected. It is possible that he found the English spoken by educated men of his day ineffective for his stage purpose. He had been brought up in the West Country and had a natural tendency to short a's and hard o's. 'War' he pronounced as it was spelt, to rhyme with 'far'. Though he could not and did not attempt to impose his dialect on others, no actor in his company was allowed to use the long 'a'—it was forbidden to rhyme grass with farce. Gordon Craig bears witness that 'For good, Irving said god—sight was seyt—stood was stod—smote became smot—hand was often hond, or hend'. And again: 'In *Macbeth* the passage "To trammel up the consequence", became in his mouth "tram-mele up-p the cunsequence", a sharp division of the two m's, a brief stop after the first, second and fourth words.' Rightly or wrongly, he strove to make words convey not only an idea but an emotion. Those who criticized his methods were not the poets or dramatists whose words he spoke or the great audiences who came to his theatre to have their emotions stirred, but those to whom a visit to the theatre was an intellectual exercise rather than an emotional experience. Similarly his gait varied from part to part. Sometimes it was almost a dance; sometimes it was that of a man striding over a ploughed field; sometimes it was as normal as his worst enemies could wish. If in these variations there was a persistent theme, it was the springy step of Charles Mathews's comedy or a lingering tendency to stamp the foot—a legacy of the days of ill-lit stages and competitive acting when a tragedian thus gained the attention of his audience. Whether these mannerisms were admirable qualities or grave defects, there is no doubt that they were an integral part of his technique. At this distance of time it is impossible to imagine their extent or to assess them in terms of later styles. Those who came under his spell accepted them and even doted upon them, those whom he failed to impress found them ridiculous and intolerable. That the former outnumbered the latter was evident. Few great actors have not had their affectations. Posterity can only form an opinion of theatrical style by examining the evidence in the light of the discrimination of witnesses for and against the actor in question. In recording Irving's progress, if the existence of these mannerisms is not constantly reaffirmed, it is because they were an essential part of his armament and he seldom went into action without them.

6

In February of the previous year Irving had given a reading of *Macbeth* in the Birmingham Town Hall in aid of the building of a working men's institute in Perry Bar, now a suburb of Birmingham. On its completion he was elected President, and in March 1878 he was invited to give an address at its opening. Irving never lost an opportunity of spreading his gospel. Though the occasion was a modest one, he prepared his address with great care. He pleaded again the cause of The Stage: 'The Stage, as at its best among us, as it may be in every theatre in the kingdom; as it could be if you, the public, would make it so.' He spoke at length and in the warmest terms of the work which Phelps and Macready had done to restore the theatre in its darkest days. He referred to the 'shafts of malignity' that had been hurled at Macready at the outset of his career. He himself, he admitted, had been the subject of bitter and constant attack. 'I hope,' he said, 'I shall not be thought to be adopting too humble and apologetic a way if I plead for the actors, not merely that their labours have honour but that their lives be regarded with kindly consideration. Their work is hard, intensely laborious— feverish and dangerously exciting. It is all this even when successful. It is often nothing short of heartbreaking when success is missed or sickeningly delayed.' Knowing that Gladstone, whom he had met at No. 1 Stratton Street, did not disguise his love of the theatre and that he numbered among his most ardent followers the most bigoted nonconformists, Irving sent him a copy of this address. Gladstone, owing to his ceaseless attacks on Disraeli's policy following the Russo-Turkish war, was going through a period of extraordinary unpopularity which culminated in an attack upon his London house by a mob of his opponents. Perhaps this made him feel particularly sympathetic towards a profession whose members were exposed nightly to the penalties of popular odium:

March 23rd, 1878.

'My dear Mr. Irving,

I am not sure whether I owe to you the kindness of sending me a copy of your recent address but I cannot in any case omit writing to thank you for that eloquent and weighty and succinct production.

It was a great disappointment to us that you were unable to fulfil your late engagement but I can judge in some measure how many and how imperative are the immediate calls upon you and how you must make it your wholly paramount object to fulfil them.

I wish to impress on you the pleasure we have so largely derived from seeing you act in *The Lyons Mail*, but also to enter tentatively upon that rich and worthy subject of the general position of your profession and of the acted Drama on which your heart is set.

Your own personal place at the head of that profession combined with the feelings you entertain and your faculty of giving effect to them seems to me perhaps to make this an epoch favourable to some practical effort if the necessary convenience can be had.

I hope on some early day you will permit the renewal of our engagement for a meeting.

Very faithfully yours,

W. E. Gladstone.'

Louis XI was followed by a poetic drama, *Vanderdecken*, in which Irving was to play the Flying Dutchman. This subject had been one of Bateman's less happy enthusiasms. Wagner's opera was first heard in London in 1876. The Colonel persuaded Irving that he could make much of the phantom sea captain and commissioned a dilettante artist and litterateur, Percy Fitzgerald, to dramatize the legend. Wills, who was called in to strengthen Fitzgerald's hand and to translate his prose into blank verse, introduced a tedious ballad in the metre and manner of *The Ancient Mariner* which was to be recited by Isabel and described the accursed sailor whom, as the heroine, she believed to be her dream lover. Neither Hawes Craven's Norwegian landscapes nor Arnott's ingenious stage effects could make anything of this gloomy pantomime. Irving had little else to do but to suggest a supernatural being and to look well in the sable cap and rugged dress of a sixteenth-century sea captain. One scene 'was to represent the rolling and curling waves upon a strand. Vanderdecken had been thrown into the sea, knowing that the waves would cast him back again upon the shore alive. After he was cast in from the cliffs there was a prolonged pause; the waters were seen rolling as before, and presently he drifted in upon the sands when he staggered to his feet and looked round with a dazed, confused, and yet victorious expression. This . . . was one of Irving's finest effects. The mechanical part was contrived by a sort of tube three or four feet in diameter which went the whole breadth of the stage. This revolved slowly, and being more or less disguised with painted fringes of water, conveyed the idea. At the proper moment the actor was placed on it and seemed to come from it in a natural fashion'. The play proved less buoyant than its hero and sank slowly with all hands during its brief run of a month. The summer was unusually hot and the whole company in their heavy Norwegian trappings suffered torments of heat which even the hell-bound Dutchman would have found intolerable. Irving's keenest supporters found the play sombre and ponderous and the part quite unworthy of him.

The Bells and the rearrangement of Albery's *Pickwick* saw the season out. Though the latter was renamed *Jingle* and rewritten in order to give Irving opportunity to develop the part to the top of his bent, his public had learnt to expect more from him than this. Though they were cordial enough in their reception of the comedy and as enraptured as ever by *The Bells*, they could not deny that the season had ended on a note of disappointment. Nor were they surprised to hear rumours that, on matters of policy, differences were arising between Irving and Mrs. Bateman which the failure of *Vanderdecken* had brought to a head.

Irving's friends warned him of the risk he was running in appearing in bad plays supported by a mediocre company. Labouchère, during the run of *Louis XI*, had been characteristically outspoken. Earlier in the year he had tempted Irving with the offer of financial support:

'. . . Now suppose I got up a company, with patrons, council of friends of art, etc. etc. Would it be possible to make some arrangement with you by means of which you would act and superintend the production of pieces? The Company is not the difficulty as much as the man—there are lots of people who would subscribe, half from a desire to make money and half from a desire to have a decent national theatre. So far as I am concerned, of course, the company would be bona fide; that is to say, there would be no go between in the form of a "promoter" who would make money, and I would let the theatre (The Queen's) cheap, because on a real lease a person ought to be satisfied with five per cent interest, whereas for some reason best known to those who take theatres, they pay proprietors at the rate of eight or nine per cent on outlay.

I had thought of Phelps, as the man, because he is a kind of God amongst the admirers of William, but you are now in the ascendant and, I suspect, either the Lyceum would cut out the Queen's or the Queen's would cut out the Lyceum.

You make your money, I presume, mainly in the provinces. If you share (after payment of salary) both in London and in the provinces, you make less than if you took a salary in London and took all in the provinces. In a theatre there ought to be a man not a woman, otherwise the completeness of a drama is invariably sacrificed to Miss this or Miss that. Perhaps, however, it might be possible to bring Mrs. Bateman into the combination.

If it occurs to you that you could with profit to yourself work into this scheme, I will call on you at any time you may appoint and have a talk with you for I have got national drama on the brain just now.

Sincerely,

H. Labouchère.'

In May, Labby returned to the charge, this time using flattery to put the spur to Irving's discontent:

10 *Queen Anne's Gate,*
St. James's Park,
Private: *May 27th,* 1878.

'Dear Irving,

I went the other day a second time to see *Louis XI*. Your acting is perfect. I never saw a more complete realization of an historical personage as set forth in a play, for de Vigny's (sic) Louis is not the Louis of history. In former characters there was always something of yourself, but in *Louis XI* you go out entirely of yourself and become the man that you are portraying.

The play has not taken—because it is one of the worst and most undramatic plays ever written and because your company is below criticism. I nearly fled when that barn actor who plays Nemours began declaiming in a red cloak from the depth of his stomach and when the girl responded to this ventriloquist.

Depend upon it, no actor in the world can carry a bad play and a bad company. The better you act, all the worse do the duffers appear —there is a perpetual jarring contrast all through.

I write this because I delight in good acting and because good acting ought not to be smothered by its adjuncts. Without bias a better piece of acting or indeed as good as your *Louis XI* I never saw either on the French, English or German stage.

Sincerely,

H. Labouchère.'

Irving resisted Labby's blandishments. He had no intention of putting himself into the hands of this engaging but mercurial publicist. From a very different quarter circumstances arose which made him face his dilemma and realize the urgent need for him to resolve it. When Irving foreshadowed to Stoker the approach of a crisis which since had been greatly accelerated, he had dwelt entirely upon the professional difficulties which he had to encounter under Mrs. Bateman's management. To these had been added certain personal problems which made his position at the Lyceum unendurable.

Reluctantly and to her own distress of mind, Isabel Bateman had fallen in love with him. She was now only twenty-four years old; she was as devout as ever and already dreamed of seeking refuge from the problems that assailed her by entering religion. Though Irving was fond of her, as indeed he was of the whole family to whom he owed so much, the revelation of her affection for him caused him acute embarrassment. Even had he reciprocated her feelings, he was not free to marry her or anyone else. Isabel realized the hopelessness of the predicament into which she had fallen, yet the more she strove to control or to disguise her love for Irving the more constrained and awkward became her partnership with him on the stage. Her plight was not made easier by the attitude of her mother. Mrs. Bateman, whose thoughts and energy were concentrated wholly upon the theatre, saw nothing but good in her daughter's passion for the most popular actor of the day. It was a pity Irving was not in love with Isabel—he might yet become so; if and when he did, she saw no harm in their living together until such time as his divorce could be arranged.

Isabel, appalled by her mother's amoral expediency, turned for help and guidance to her guardians, Charlotte Yonge and the Vicar of St. Peter's, Eaton Square, who strengthened her resistance against Mrs. Bateman's well-meant worldliness. Torn as she was between the duty she felt towards her mother, who to some extent depended upon her for her livelihood, and the desire to escape from an environment which she detested and an infatuation which she was unable to constrain, she was unfitted temperamentally to be the artistic partner of a man who was regarded by many as the head of his profession. Irving, though he saw no clear way out of this dilemma, decided, as a start, to insist that for the coming season he must be at liberty to engage a leading lady of his own choice, who could give him stronger support and who would bring with her a personal following.

Mrs. Bateman's reply to Irving's letter, which he had worded as delicately as he could, showed that she had guessed already what was in his mind, and with her sturdy common sense had realized that the course he was taking was, from his point of view, the right one.

'. . . Your letter received this morning convinced me that what I *thought I was unjust to you in fancying* was quite true. I must therefore

lose no time in giving you my *business* view of the question. . . .
I am sure your wish to please others has led you to overlook the great
injury it would be to Bella (Isabel) as an actress if she was taken out of
the part of Ophelia. It would be an endorsement signed by you—
the friend of her family and me—her mother—of her entire incom-
petency. I cannot for any selfish consideration lend myself to such an
act of injustice for to do this and retire her from the stage would take
from her the means of a livelihood when I am dead or when my time
at the Lyceum is over. Besides—were I to yield this point it would
only be the forerunner of others *perhaps* as painful. Under these conditions, I think it would be better for our association in business to
end *now*. I am sure for the sake of the past that you will not do anything ungenerous to me and will be glad to meet me in any way you
can. I propose that you take the theatre off my hands from this time
when the last three years commences. I will explain all the details of
just how matters stand and I would propose being afterwards submitted to a person qualified to say on your part that what I ask is
just and right. . . .'

Irving may well have been astonished at her generosity in offering to
surrender to him the lease of the Lyceum which, now that the fortunes
of the theatre had been restored, she could have sold at a profit. This
gesture and the calm and sensible way in which she had faced the
situation was proof, if he needed it, of her deep affection for him.
Although he had no resources of his own nor financial backing of any
kind he did not hesitate to accept her proposition. Perhaps Toole,
whose advice he would have sought, offered his friend such help as
he could. The Baroness gave him every encouragement to strike out
for himself, and Mrs. Brown, when she heard of his decision, insisted
on lending him fifteen hundred pounds, which he reluctantly accepted.
The old lady was failing fast and died a week before the curtain rose
on his adventure which she had discussed with him so eagerly and had
been so anxious to assist. The loan was repaid to her executors within
a few weeks. By the end of July the matter was settled in principle and
only details of business remained to be considered. Throughout the
negotiations Mrs. Bateman manifested a striking unselfishness:

Sunday evening.
'. . . I don't enclose the profit and loss account because I think you
would prefer having Mr. Charman explain it all to you. I will be at
the theatre tomorrow at twelve as I am anxious to be of any use to my

friend in regard to future arrangements. Pray don't think that I wish you to take the theatre off my hands unless you think it would answer your purpose to do so. I wish this to be your only consideration.'

At the end of August Mrs. Bateman issued a statement to the press:

August 31st, 1878.

'Mrs. Bateman begs to announce that her tenancy of the Lyceum Theatre terminates with the present month. For seven years it has been associated with the name she bears. During the three years and a half that the business management has been under her special control, the liberal patronage of the public has enabled her to wind up the affairs of each successive season with a profit. . . . Mrs. Bateman's lease has been transferred to Mr. Henry Irving, to whose attraction as an artist the prosperity of the theatre is entirely attributable, and she confidently hopes that under his care it may attain higher artistic distinction and complete prosperity. In conclusion, Mrs. Bateman ventures to express her gratitude for the kindness and generosity that has enabled her faithfully to carry out all her obligations to the close of her tenancy.'

This single-minded and determined woman had the great but all too rare feminine gift of suddenly and completely renouncing sentiment in favour of realism. For eight years she had done all she could to further Irving's interest and desired above all things that Isabel or Virginia should be the partner of his success. Yet, when it became clear to her that Irving could continue no longer to be a salaried actor under her management, however titular her position, and that her daughters had neither the talent nor the temperament to share the great career which she envisaged for him, she cut her losses and turned to other things. While Irving was on tour she wrote to him a letter which showed how completely she was able to set aside the past and to divert her energies into fresh channels:

9 *Albany Courtyard,*
Piccadilly.
September 21st, 1878.
'. . . As you said you would like to know my plans when decided I write now to tell you that I have bought the lease of Sadler's Wells . . . with the intention of working it as a country theatre—low prices,

pantomime stars or star companies and perhaps a drama production every year. With the exception of the money Arnold is to return I borrow the money for the purchase from the bank and am to get as a business investment the remainder required for the erection of the building but the interest on these amounts and the ground rent will still leave the rent very low and the saloons will almost offset this.

The Theatre is to be very pretty—and is to hold about 2,600 people. The lease is for thirty-four years and I trust with some luck and a great deal of economy and hard work we may be able to make a living and as no special gifts are required for the conduct of such a place that the girls can get a living out of it when I am gone. I was compelled to be rather precipitate about my decision as to buying the place as others were in the field so I concluded the purchase *without advice* but I have since consulted some sharp business men and among them Mr. Valance and they all say it is a good investment. It is so if the fact that I am told I can get the money I require with only the property as a security is any proof that it must have been a bargain. The neighbourhood has much improved—is without a place of amusement and the facilities for getting to Sadler's Wells by trams and omnibuses have greatly increased.

The building cannot be finished before February so we lose the pantomimes this year and I propose doing a drama for the opening, and then stars while it pays to keep open. . . . I have looked at a house near the Foundling Hospital which I think I will take. And now I believe you have all my news. Katie is doing fairly—George and Ginny (Virginia) are with her . . . they are all very well. We read with great pleasure how splendidly all goes with you and that you are not very tired with so many rehearsals, and that you don't neglect wrapping up on these cool evenings—very good for business and delightful for you but rather dangerous for taking cold. . . .

Always yours affectionately,

S. F. Bateman.'

7

Irving set out on a provincial tour, for which he was now wholly responsible, without Isabel. Maude Brennan, who had played leading parts with Barry Sullivan, took her place. Before he left he had made a decision which outweighed all others in its wisdom and importance. While the future of the Lyceum was still under discussion, he received a letter which he was eagerly awaiting:

33 *Longridge Road,*
South Kensington,
July 19*th,* 1878.

'My dear Mr. Irving,

I'm at home all these hot days from 11 to 3 and shall be pleased indeed if you will call any day this or next week—or if you can't come out in the heat, be kind enough to fix your own day and hour (any day but next Tuesday or Monday) letting me know and I'll stay at home to see you.

Yours sincerely,
Ellen Terry.'

Ellen Terry, ever since she had been with Tom Taylor at the first night of *Hamlet*, had taken every opportunity of studying the work of an actor in whom she found perfection. She had stayed with the Bancrofts until 1876, when she had joined John Hare at the Royal Court Theatre. Here, under Hare's severe but able direction, she had played with great success first in a revival of *New Men and Old Acres* and then in the title role as Olivia in Wills's dramatization of Goldsmith's *Vicar of Wakefield*, which owed its success very largely to her spirited and gracious performance and to the charm she exercised upon the public. Lady Pollock told Irving, who had not been able to see *Olivia* himself, that in Ellen Terry he would find the ideal partner for whom he was seeking. Since Ellen Terry's return to the stage, Godwin had deserted her, leaving her the two children whom she adored. Watts at last agreed to divorce her. While she was at the Court Theatre she married Charles Wardell, a young officer of the 66th Regiment who had retired from the army after being wounded in action. Wardell had gone on the stage—taking the name of Kelly. Though his lack of training limited his range as an actor, he played well enough those parts for which his bluff, soldierly manner and kindly nature suited him. Irving, accompanied by Trin's successor, on a stifling afternoon made his way to Longridge Road. Whatever Ellen Terry expected, she greeted a very different man from the raw and awkward young Petruchio who had suffered so deeply from his inability to express himself through his art. She saw at once that 'in ten years he had found himself, and so lost himself—lost . . . much of that stiff, ugly, self-consciousness which had encased him as the shell encases the lobster. His forehead had become more massive, and the very outline of his features had altered. He was a man of the world, whose strenuous fighting now was to be done as a general—not, as hitherto, in the ranks. His manner was very quiet and gentle.'

So quiet and gentle was Irving's manner on this occasion that by the end of the interview Ellen had no very clear idea as to the purpose of his visit. At first he had expressed himself with friendly smiles and embarrassed grunts until his dog, by forgetting his manners, set them both to work with fire irons and hearthbrush and so broke the ice. Irving left the house confident that she had understood and had accepted his proposition. A few days later he wrote to his old headmaster, Dr. Pinches, to whom he turned frequently for advice. '. . . all settled—although lease not signed—mere matter of preparation. Agreement to be signed today . . . how can I thank you, old fellow, for all your kindness in this matter. I am sure you did very much to clear away the briars. . . . I have engaged Ellen Terry—not a bad start—eh?'

Ellen, who had left London to tour the provinces with her husband, was far less clear as to her position.

> *Liverpool,*
> *August 25th,* 1878.

'Dear Mr. Irving,

The Fly is waiting at the door to take us out of this *most horrible place*. My husband will be in London all next week . . . if you will write to me there . . . making me some definite proposition, I will answer you definitely. So far, I think I understand, you wd like me to be with you at the Lyceum next season and will you be good enough to understand that I on my part most earnestly desire to be with you. I hope we shall be able to arrange.

> Yours sincerely,
> Ellen Terry.

P.S. *Dora* has been quite an *extraordinary* success here—Charles Reade being called for and simply *yelled* at! Odd—that it was well acted in London some years ago and failed.'

What they had failed to settle in the parlour was arranged satisfactorily by post. Ellen Terry was engaged for the Lyceum at a salary of forty guineas a week and 'a half clear benefit'. Reade had rescued her from retirement. Bancroft had shown her quality, and Hare had made her a popular favourite. None of these managers had given her security. Ellen had to provide for her two children and to some extent for her husband; forty pounds a week was affluence while it lasted, but a month or two 'at rest' sadly reduced its value as an income. From the day she signed her contract with Irving, her cares vanished. Money, which hitherto had meant no more than the alleviation of nagging debt, henceforward flowed in regularly and abundantly, providing all she could need for herself and for her children. In return she brought Irving her gifts as a great artist and the inestimable blessing of the wise counsel and candid criticism of a friend and fellow-worker. They were about to embark upon an artistic alliance of such brilliance and endurance as the European theatre had never known.

In September, Irving played for a fortnight in Dublin, and during that time Stoker, who was probably aware of it, underwent an intensive period of probation. Irving kept him at his side during performances and rehearsals at the theatre and rarely dined or supped except in his company. He left Dublin without declaring himself, but six weeks later summoned Stoker to Glasgow. At last Irving, having told Stoker that he had taken over the management of the Lyceum, invited him to resign from the civil service and to throw in his lot with him as business or acting manager. Stoker at once accepted his offer. Returning to Dublin, he arranged to divorce himself from 'The Duties of Clerks of Petty Sessions' and settled his domestic affairs, which included his marriage to the lady of his heart.

From Dublin, Irving went to Liverpool. Augustin Daly, who was already the most enterprising impresario in New York, was on his first visit to England and happened to be in the town at the same time. He was the son of a British sea captain and was the same age as Irving; he was a shrewd man of theatrical business with a flair for play carpentry and stage-management in the manner of Bateman and Boucicault. He went to see Irving in *Louis XI* and recorded his impressions in a letter to his brother:

Liverpool,
September 18th, 1878.

'I went last night to see Irving—who is playing at the Alexandra Theatre here; a roomy and convenient but very dingy (almost dirty) place. I could only get a seat on a back bench, or chair, in the 1st balcony—for crowded houses are the rule wherever the great I. appears. The play was *Louis XI*.—a most repulsive character, as you know, for an actor to grapple with; and I fear the great I. did not impress me with his treatment of it. In his frenzy—for it appears to be a frenzy with him,—to be realistic or NATURAL—he descends to the farceur's tricks. The peculiarity of his voice, which we have heard so often referred to, consists of sudden and unexpected and sometimes absurd rises and falls—and I can only compare it to a man speaking half of a long sentence while drawing *in* his breath and letting the other

half fly out while he expels the breath. One of his stage tricks is very
effective but quite unworthy a great artist. He is fond, whenever the
scene permits, of shutting down every light—leaving the stage in
utter darkness, lit only by the solitary lamp or dull fire which may be
in the room; while he has directed from the prompt place or the flies a
closely focused calcium—which shines only and solely upon *his* face
and head; so that you can only see a lot of spectral figures without
expression moving about the scene—and one ghostly lighted face
shining out of the darkness; an expressive face to be sure—but after
all the entirety of the drama disappears and a conjurer-like exhibition
of a sphinx-head wonder takes its place. The enthusiasm was not great
—and perhaps this is not one of the great I.'s best parts. I shall not give
you an opinion about him till I see him again. So far I've only described
him so you may see him as I did.'

Though Daly's first impression of Irving was not a favourable one,
a few months later he offered him a three months' engagement at his
theatre in New York and half the gross receipts with a guarantee of
$500 a performance. Ellen Terry was included in this invitation, but
the rest of the company and the *mise-en-scène* was to be provided by
Daly—an offer which Irving, naturally, refused.

Irving's tour ended at Birmingham in the middle of December, and
thither he summoned Stoker and Ellen Terry. She saw him play Hamlet
on the last night. 'He played,' she wrote, 'I say it without vanity, for
me. We players are not above that weakness if it be a weakness. If
ever anything inspires us to do our best it is the presence in the audience
of some fellow-artist who must in the nature of things know more
completely than anyone what we intend, what we do, what we feel.
Response from such a member of the audience flies across the footlights
to us like a flame.' His Hamlet—wonderful four years ago—became
perfection and she kept the memory of that night fresh and clear in
her mind until she died.

Irving had taken over the lease of the Lyceum in September. When
he returned to London in the middle of December, barely a fortnight
remained in which to organise his staff and to rehearse *Hamlet* for the
opening of his first season as actor-manager. There was much to be
done. The theatre was still in the hands of builders and decorators.
He had commissioned Alfred Darbyshire, his old fellow Titan and
now a distinguished Manchester architect, to undertake extensive
structural and decorative alterations to the Lyceum. The seating of the
stalls and dress circle was made more comfortable and the plain benches

which hitherto accommodated the pit and gallery were provided with backs. The dingy auditorium was repainted in sage green and turquoise blue. The raised ornaments and the figure groups by Bartolozzi, the father of Madame Vestris, were preserved. Hawes Craven, in addition to preparing new scenery for *Hamlet,* had designed and painted a new act drop. The working curtain of green baize was retained. When the house lights were lowered and only the lower part of it was softly illumined by the footlights, this green curtain seemed to fade into infinity—veiling, as Charles Lamb once said, a heaven of the imagination. It was the veil between the world of reality and of make-believe; when it rose the world before and behind the proscenium were blended; the illusory gained substance from the prosaic which in turn reflected something of the glittering imagery of the illusion.

But until that curtain rose everyone, both in front of the house and on the stage, was faced with stern and urgent practicalities. Bram Stoker had to exert all his physical and mental energy in order to master the intricacies of theatre management while dealing with the immediate problems that arose from hour to hour. Loveday and Arnott, when they were not at Irving's side during rehearsals, were busily sorting out from the accumulated stock of the old regime such bits and pieces as could be of service to the new. Irving, the producer, tireless and stern, in seeking the perfection at which he aimed, was a very different man from Irving, the actor, who hitherto could do no more than tactfully influence the performances of the rest of the company. He rehearsed over and over again the first scene on the battlements, striving to impart into each character the individuality, urgency and power which he deemed necessary to 'start the play a living thing'. With infinite care he worked up the procession which preceded his own entrance— the royal yet subdued pageant advancing and dispersing to reveal the sabled, solitary figure of Hamlet, whose spirituality was accented by a subtle dimming of the lights. Ellen Terry watched him work until 'the skin grew tight over his face, until he became livid with fatigue, yet still beautiful'. His labour was eased by the loyalty and trust of his colleagues, for he had assembled round him a fine company of salted actors. Old Chippendale, Forrester, Kyrle Bellew and those stalwart evidences of well kept faith, Sam Johnson and Mead; of the old company, only young Pinero and the veteran Miss Pauncefort remained. Hamilton Clarke, a composer in his own right, had been engaged as a musical director. He had been the organist at Queen's College, Oxford when Irving met him in a Scottish hotel and taking an immediate liking to him, had enlisted him in his train.

Within a week of the first night, the production had taken shape. Irving kept his hand on every detail as the components were completed and fell into their place. Ellen Terry watched these preparations in awe but with increasing misgiving, for as yet Irving had not rehearsed his scenes with her. Her well-intentioned attempt to anticipate his decision as to the clothes Ophelia should wear had taught her a salutary but humiliating lesson. Among others, she had ordered a black dress for the mad scene. Irving, when he heard of it, gravely and diplomatically suggested that white, perhaps, would be more appropriate. Ellen innocently insisted that black would be more original and interesting. Irving made a grunt or two and dropped the subject. Next day, old Walter Lacy, who was helping Irving with the production, tackled her on the subject:

'You didn't really mean that you're going to wear black in the mad scene?'

'Yes I did,' answered Ellen decisively. 'And why not?'

'Why not? My God, madam, there must be only one black figure in this play and that's Hamlet.'

After this rebuff, it took her some little time to summon courage to beard Irving again. But becoming increasingly anxious she spoke to him one day after an orchestra rehearsal:

'I am very nervous,' she said, 'about my first appearance with you. Couldn't we rehearse *our* scenes?'

'*We* shall be all right,' he answered, 'but we're not going to run the risk of being bottled up by a gas man or a fiddler.'

Irving was sensitive to hazards which imperilled his art; material and financial risk he faced with impassivity. When the last dress rehearsal of *Hamlet* was over, his burden of indebtedness was such as might have shaken the nerve of anyone less ready to wear responsibility like a royal robe. Nearly £4,000 had been spent upon the theatre. Another £4,000 had been eaten up by costs of production and rehearsals. In his little leather-bound account book, opposite a 'Receipts page' of virgin whiteness, Bram Stoker cast his account—expenditure £9,369 12s. By the time the curtain rose on *Hamlet* Irving had an overdraft of £12,000 at the London and County Bank for which he had given bills. With no assets other than the combined talents of himself and Ellen Terry and backed only by the invincible faith in his own destiny which had never failed him, he faced his inauguration as sole lessee and manager of the Royal Lyceum Theatre.

PART FOUR

HENRY IRVING
AND ELLEN TERRY

———◦◦◦———

'If one advances confidently in the direction of his dreams, and endeavours to live the life which he has imagined, he will meet with success unexpected in common hours . . .'

THOREAU.

'First lay down your lines; settle what you want to do and do it; the greater opposition the more persevering and courageous you must be; if you are right and strength and life hold out, you must win.'

HENRY IRVING.

CHAPTER XIX

1st Lyceum Season: Hamlet, Claude Melnotte

I

Within a day or two of the announcement of the opening night of the new regime at the Lyceum, every seat in the house was sold. The elect of the artistic and social world of London dressed the elegant parts of the house; a mob of noisy, bright-eyed, intelligent young people thronged the pit and gallery. To Stoker, these illustrious patrons, whom he welcomed on their arrival in the foyer, were the breath of life; Irving, who dismissed them with his blessing from the stage, found that they made him depressed and nervous. He preferred a 'good hearty house who have come to be pleased' and, therefore, was seldom seen at his best on first nights. Yet on this night of December 30th, 1878, he felt that the audience was with him from the rise of the curtain. Their applause, which had been sustained since half-past seven, reached its climax at midnight when, amidst a litter of laurel wreaths and bouquets which had been showered upon the stage, he assured those who clamoured for a speech that 'having worked all his life for the result that the Lyceum had witnessed that night, as long as he was manager of the theatre he would do nothing that was not aimed to elevate his art and to increase the comfort of the public'.

Ellen Terry was not at his side to receive the final acclamation. Overwrought and still feeling that she had not been adequately rehearsed, she was convinced that she had failed. She had left the theatre after the fourth act and in despair was driving up and down the Thames embankment. The newspapers next morning convinced her that her fears were groundless. Irving once said that her genius was fatal to criticism, for it transformed her critics into lovers. The first sight of her as Portia had been their undoing and the chorus of adulation which greeted her Ophelia was the beginning of their long and faithful courtship. They had been enchanted by the charm and tender innocence of her early scenes and agonized by the stark imbecility of Ophelia's derangement. Ellen had been at pains to study insanity at first hand; she had chosen for her model a case of mental vacancy rather than one of maniac frenzy and thus inspired pity rather than horror by her performance. Heads forever wagged in argument about Irving, but in their adoration of Ellen Terry the hearts of the critics beat as one. Familiarity with Irving's Hamlet bred in his most severe judges an added respect and a warmer appreciation. Tennyson, when he saw this production, said: 'I did not think Irving could have improved upon his Hamlet of five years ago; he has done so—he has lifted it to heaven.' Irving and Ellen Terry could not have wished for a more popular coronation as together they entered into their theatrical kingdom with every promise of a long and prosperous reign.

During the hundred nights of the run of *Hamlet* Irving had plenty of opportunity to study the character and artistic resource of this evidently ideal partner whose genius was so complementary to his own. Ellen Terry, when she came to the Lyceum, was ten years younger than Irving; she had been on the stage for twenty-two years and had played eighty-four parts ranging from pantomime to tragedy. Though, like Irving, her impressionable years had been spent in stock companies, her six years' absence from the stage had given her a glimpse of a polite and cultured society. Under the tutelage of Watts she had learnt to appreciate the rudiments of classical art, and as the working companion of Godwin she had become steeped in the advanced aesthetics of her day. She brought to the Lyceum a well developed sense of colour and design and the critical standards of the world of art beyond the theatre. Irving had gained not only a leading lady but a dilettante upon whose judgment he came increasingly to rely.

Though in everything pertaining to their art Irving and Ellen Terry were in perfect harmony, in temperament and character they could hardly have been more diverse. Irving was the epitome of intensity—single-minded, self-centred and self-sufficient. Ellen Terry was essentially extrovert—easily distracted, prone to further anyone's interests but her own, and lacking the power of concentration. Superficially straightforward, frank and impulsive, the real Ellen Terry was an agglomeration of baffling complexities and contradictions. Her features were irregular and ill-matched; yet they made a sum of rare beauty. Her figure had a certain lanky masculinity, yet on the stage she was the picture of feminine grace and charm. Her voice had a husky thickness, yet a whisper of it was heard clearly in the extremities of any theatre. Her eyes, brilliant and expressive on the stage, were weak and delicate—perhaps from working for many months on tracings of Godwin's architectural drawings. Her nature demanded the love of men, yet she was happiest as a mother and as the centre of a domestic circle which included no paterfamilias. Her love affairs, all passion spent, became enduring friendships; her casual friendships 'had the character of innocent love affairs'. She was scornful of pettiness and generous in thought and deed, yet in her train she left a turbulence of small gossip and intrigue. Prodigal of her time, energy and affection, she was provident and careful with her money; parsimonious in ministering to her own comforts, she squandered it only on the projects of her children. She was a God-fearing traditionalist, yet she rebelled against the Church and the social conventions. Unostentatious and careless of her dignity or appearance, she had an air which commanded respect; at an early age she had been nicknamed 'Duchess' by her family. Though she shared Irving's devotion to the art of the theatre and his jealous regard for the dignity of their calling, she harassed her fellow-players with her persistent unpunctuality, not from idleness or caprice, but from an inability to resist the dissipation of her interests. Though she was a mistress of technique and laboured to perfect herself in every part she played, she could, while playing, be overwhelmed by her own emotion. She seldom reached the high standard at which she aimed. Vanity is to some extent a necessary part of an actress's equipment, yet Ellen Terry was less vain than most. With little ambition for herself, she was content to serve as best she could in a company which, under Irving's leadership, seemed to her to be the best the world had to offer. Though she tried to persuade herself that her effects were arrived at through her intellect, her success lay in the exercise of her charm and personality. In this respect the methods of Irving and Ellen Terry were the same, but, whereas Irving laboriously designed a characterization around his personality, Ellen Terry spontaneously superimposed her personality upon the character which she portrayed. 'She played,' her son wrote, 'but one part—herself and when not herself she couldn't play it.'

Ellen Terry very soon made herself at home in the Lyceum, nor was it long before Irving realized that he had introduced an angel into the house, or perhaps a sylph—half angel, half imp. He watched with grave amusement this gay inconsequent creature who slid down the banisters of the staircase leading from her dressing-room, and with such easy transition could one moment be laughing and gossiping in the green-room and the next be bathed in her own tears upon the stage.

He came to understand the inestimable boon of a companion and fellow-worker whose frankly expressed opinions and criticisms he could accept and profit by in the light of their common doctrine. When he asked her if the criticism of his mannerisms was just, she told him plainly of those peculiarities of diction and gait which hampered his self-expression and were in his power to remedy. Years of facetious comments on his legs had made him self-conscious of them and had driven him to disguise their Behenna tenuity with padding. Ellen soon persuaded him that there was nothing wrong with his legs—even though nervousness sometimes constricted their action. The padding was discarded. Finding that Irving tortured himself by waiting, tense and nervous, in the wings for his entrance cue, she persuaded him to stay in his dressing-room calm and relaxed until the call boy summoned him to the stage. In a very short time they arrived at a complete understanding of one another. She submitted herself whole-heartedly to his command and discipline, knowing that he was not an impresario eager to exploit her, but a fellow-artist who was as anxious for her integrity and success as for his own. She could rely upon him to prevent meretricious facility injuring her work—an ever present danger to an artist who could so easily charm the public into laughter and tears. To her, Irving at last unlocked the door of the dark chamber of his introspection and he breathed more freely in the ventilation this accorded him.

After the first night of *Hamlet* H. J. Byron had written:

> *Southern Lodge,*
> *St. Anne's Road,*
> *Brixton.*
> *December 31st, 1878.*

'My dear Irving,

What can anybody write to you but congratulations. Last night was indeed a triumph for you in every way—it was also one for your many friends and though a chap in the pit at my back almost broke the drum of my right ear, I felt inclined to shake hands with him over his enthusiasm, but fancied it might have looked as if we were in league. I have seen much of first night enthusiasm but never anything to approach that of last evening.

Now, old fellow, don't let management worry you—take things easily. The position is a trying one and to a sensitive man frequently a painful and galling one for one meets with so many people who think that kindness means kowtowing and stern justice brutal severity.

You have, however, a clear field and no end of favour and *must* succeed as all who know you wish to see you do. . . .

Yours always,
H. J. Byron.'

No one knew the truth of these words better than Irving or was more keenly aware of the vulnerability of his natural sensitiveness. But Irving's protective armour was now fully forged—his soft heart was protected by an insuperable façade of studied aloofness and caustic humour. Those who served him were soon aware of his natural gifts as an administrator. The first thing he did was to establish an atmosphere of permanence at the Lyceum. Within a month he had created a Provident and Benevolent Fund with himself as trustee and Pinero as secretary. The company were taught to accept discipline not as a means of inflating the ego of those in authority but as a token of respect for the art they practised. Upon the stage absolute silence was the rule during rehearsals and performances; yet everything was done to ensure their comfort in their dressing-rooms and green-rooms. During February old Chippendale had retired from the stage after sixty-eight years' service. Irving gave a benefit of which the entire proceeds, nearly £300, were given to his old friend and tutor. The actor who took his place as Polonius gave Irving an opportunity to test his managerial strength and wisdom. One night, in the third scene of *Hamlet,* a Polonius came upon the stage who was obviously and deplorably drunk. Irving was standing in the wings. He rang down the curtain, sent for the understudy and told the audience that, with their permission, the scene would be repeated from the beginning. The whole company, with the exception of the culprit, were called for noon the following day. On the hour Irving, followed by Stoker and Loveday, came upon the stage. In a few words he rebuked them for failing to report their fellow-actor's condition to the stage-manager, when by doing so they might have saved him from disgrace. He reminded them 'of the loyalty which is due from one craftsman to another . . . and to a manager who has to think for all. By that want of loyalty,' he said, 'in any of its forms, you have helped to ruin your comrade . . . now, my dear friends ·. . . let this be a lesson to us all. We must be loyal to each other and to the honour of our art and our calling'. In the way in which he handled this situation Irving made clear to his subordinates the principles which would govern his conduct of the Lyceum.

By now his life began to take on the pattern which was to govern it throughout his tenure of the Lyceum. By the time his day began, business in Bond Street was in full swing and its western shop fronts were bright with sunlight. At about ten o'clock, Walter Collinson, Irving's valet and dresser, let himself into 15A Grafton Street. Doody, his predecessor, recently had become the victim of his own conviviality. Irving, in an emergency, had asked Clarkson, the wig-maker, for someone to fill the post for the time being. There arrived a wiry, dapper little man with shrewd, kindly eyes veiled behind steel-rimmed spectacles. Walter was an expert wig-maker and had the serene and dignified manner of a craftsman. His looks reminded Ellen Terry of Shakespeare's bust in Stratford Church. There and then he attached himself to Irving with devoted loyalty. When on his master's business, he exercised a certain brusque authority which was respected by everybody in the theatre. He accepted Irving's occasional paroxysms of cold rage with equanimity and carried out his varied duties with quiet dexterity and affectionate zeal. Alone of all men he held the key to Irving's lonely inner life with which he became intimately acquainted and with it he locked within himself the confidences entrusted to him. He had no life outside the situation of his master. He became Irving's fifth limb and his loss at any time would have been crippling. He was a bantam-weight Sancho Panza to his dolorous and much-loved knight.

Irving's room faced north and east. The staircase which led to them was dark and winding. In mounting it, one passed a series of engravings which were only dimly discernible until, upon a landing lit by ruby gas-light, the last was seen to depict the climax of a duel—one swordsman spitting another, to the admiration of two ladies curveting on horse-back in the background. These engravings illustrated the art of fencing—like everything else in the house, they had a practical bearing on Irving's work. When Walter arrived, his master would be still in bed, browsing over a book or a play. The bedroom was sparsely furnished. Over the bed head was a large crucifix, which, oddly enough, Mrs. Bateman had hung there when first she had found him these rooms. On the bedside table stood another crucifix, while beside it, attached to his watch-chain was a small silver one which had been thrown onto the stage by a poor woman in the gallery during a performance of *Hamlet*. The stern theology implanted in him by Sarah Penberthy had left Irving with a strong but undefined sense of religion, or perhaps of religious superstition; his mother would have been torn with doubts as whether these symbols were evidence of piety or popery.

In the adjoining study Walter would make a desultory attempt to tidy up such things as he dared. The sofa, which Mrs. James had given to Irving, seemed to have lost its identity—from the litter which

Ellen Terry as Olivia. Court Theatre, 1876

Irving as Hamlet

From the statue in the Guildhall by E. Onslow Ford, R.A.

covered it, it might have been a wardrobe, a bookcase or a portfolio. Nearby, the top of an inkstand and a bunch of penholders pushing their way up like crocuses through a heap of books and papers suggested the presence of a writing-table. At the foot of the open piano, brown paper cascaded from a stool upon which stood a recently opened parcel of cigars. The floor was so strewn with books that there was little space for walking except where a tiger skin, like a well-worn cricket pitch, was stretched in front of the fire.

The walls of the study were covered with pictures—an engraving of Maclise's 'Play Scene in Hamlet', Delaroche's 'Last Banquet of Girondius' and 'Richelieu in his Barge', a signed photograph of Rossi (a l'Amico Irving), a noble photograph of Dickens taken in New York shortly before his death, medallions of Devrient and Charles Young, and the sketch by Tenniel of the ill-fated Othello costume. By the fireplace hung the silver Circassian dagger which had been given to him by Lady Pollock. There were no portraits or photographs of Irving himself. But at the far end of the room was a frame which had held sketches of him in all his characters and at every stage of their development. For it surrounded a tall looking-glass which reached to the floor. Against it leaned all manner of swords and walking-sticks—swords which had belonged to Edmund Kean and Garrick and those which he had treasured since his Sunderland days. At the theatre Irving had time and patience to rehearse everyone but himself. It was here, before this mirror, that he created his impersonations—where every gesture, movement and expression were tested and refined. On each side of the mirror were slender bookshelves holding folio volumes, ready to hand with their illustrations of costume and of the great actors of the past. This room was in perpetual twilight, for the fleeting sunlight was filtered through curtained windows of stained and leaded glass. Though the dining-room and drawing-room which faced on Bond Street were brighter and conventionally furnished, the place was evidently the haunt of a nocturnal creature whose daylight hours were passed in rest and seclusion.

By eleven o'clock Irving was dressed and on his way to the theatre. Curious admirers (there were usually one or two posted near his front door) were rewarded by seeing the tall spare figure of the actor leave his rooms. It was still early spring, so, always on guard against the cold as against an enemy, he wore a dark heavy overcoat and grey worsted trousers. A black silk scarf fluttered under his chin. Under a very tall silk hat with a brim wider than was the fashion, his long black hair curled naturally over the collar of his coat. He was forty-one years old and at his temples the curls were turning grey. His features were now determined; pale and distinguished, they had left the mould and were those which, for the rest of the century, would be almost as familiar to the public as those of the Queen upon her coinage. Eye-glasses hid the dark dreamy eyes under the bushy and still startlingly black eye-brows. Irving was extremely short-sighted. Normally helpless without his glasses, he seemed to find his way about the stage by instinct; it was Walter's duty, as his master stood in the wings waiting for his cue, to remind him to take them off and to conceal them in his costume. Once tongue tied, still near-sighted and spindle-shanked, he strode down Bond Street, thrusting at the pavement with his cane, his head drooping a little as though in deep thought; and as he passed men and women turned to watch the great actor go by.

Making his way along the Strand, Irving turned up Burleigh Street and let himself into a door at the back of the theatre. It was his private door—the stage-door was in Exeter Street—and led originally through a long narrow passage to the royal boxes. He had taken a room near the stage for his offices. As the passage passed close to this room he had a door cut through the wall which allowed him to reach his office without going through the stage-door. The situation of this office involved a ritual of approach which established the relationship of his two lieutenants, Loveday and Stoker, to their Chief, as they called him, and to one another. The stage—'the sunlit glade in the dark forest', as Craig called it—was the precinct of Loveday, who could reach it quickly and directly from the office. Here Loveday and his Chief enjoyed an intimacy which perhaps only Ellen Terry shared. Stoker's province was the front of the house, and his foothold on the stage was precarious. He could, if necessary, come and speak to Irving on the stage, but to do so would have to go from the office to the front of the house and so to the stage by the normal route—retreating by the way he came.

In the office there were three tables; Irving's was near the door, with Loveday's facing it, and Stoker's to the right of Loveday's in an alcove. Loveday was always dressed formally, in a tail coat, and beside him on the table was his 'Muller-cut-down'[1] and his gloves, which were his uniform during the conduct of rehearsals. His appearance, with his full moustache and soft whiskers, was clerical, and his mannner combined the gentle gravity of a head verger with the quiet authority of an usher. That morning Irving had little time for business, for the company had been called to hear him read through the play. A quick glance

---

[1] The trade name for a low-crowned felt hat named after Frank Muller who in 1864 murdered a city clerk in a train. He inadvertently took his victim's tall hat instead of his own low-crowned beaver. In cutting down this tall hat in order to make it resemble the one he had lost, he provided one of the exhibits which led to his conviction.

through Stoker's figures showed that since the beginning of March the box-office receipts had dropped a little, fluctuating between £150 and £200 a performance. At that time the absolute capacity of the Lyceum was £228, so there was no cause for anxiety. Since it appeared improbable that *Hamlet* would draw the public for more than a hundred nights, Irving had already decided to revive *The Lady of Lyons* after Easter.

In a few minutes Loveday, donning his hat and gloves, led Irving onto the stage. Clapping his hands, he called: 'Clear, please!' and, as Irving settled himself into a chair by the footlights and the company dispersed to wait for their cues, the rehearsal begun. Rehearsals usually kept Irving at the theatre until four o'clock, when he returned to Grafton Street to rest and dine before the evening performance. An hour before the curtain rose he was back at the theatre, where Walter was waiting for him in his dressing-room. A winding staircase of about twenty steps led from a corner of the stage on the O.P. side to a landing onto which Irving's and Ellen Terry's rooms opened. The rest of the cast dressed on the prompt side, above the Green Room; their dressing-rooms were on three or four floors and their relative importance could be gauged by their altitude, the leading players being situated in rooms nearest to the stage. Irving's dressing-room was essentially a workroom. Daylight never found its way through the curtained windows which looked blindly on to Burleigh Street. The cardinal point of the room was the workman's bench, the dressing-table. Around this table, whose clumsy Gothic proportions suggested that it had once been a stage property, hung a constellation of gas lights on adjustable brackets, shielded with shell-like reflectors. This galaxy was poised around a worn and rickety mirror which stood in the centre of the table. This mirror was an old friend to whom his immutable eyes had confided doubts, anxieties and triumphs—for his eyes could not conceal his reflections in their own, however cunningly he could re-fashion and transform with paint the mask in which they were set. For his make-up Irving used water-colours; even when greasepaint became available and popular he adhered to the practice which he had learnt as a youth. On the dressing-table, spread neatly upon a clean linen table-cloth, were the pans and dishes of moistened colour powders which Walter prepared freshly for each performance. The largest pan held the flesh or basic tint which he applied with a sponge. When this mask was dry, he painted upon it with a brush the lines and accents—using blue for shadows, stressing or reshaping bone structure and white for high-lights. Warm tints were rarely used—even to redden the lips. A hare's foot lay handy by a pot of rouge, but this was applied, when all else was done, only to his ears. ('You should try it, me boy,' he once advised a young actor, 'for the ears, ye know—suggests good health.') To the left of the dressing-table an ordinary alarm clock hung upon the wall ticking its warning of the curtain's rise. To the right of the table stood a full-length mirror. A heavy desk near the door, a chair or two and a settee completed the furnishing of the room, one end of which was curtained off to conceal a washing place. On the walls were a few prints or photographs of old friends like Toole or Charles Mathews, and stuck here and there were some of the most recent and grotesque caricatures of himself. Such was the room which, in the course of years, became the ante-chamber of English drama where the acknowledged leader of the theatrical profession received the homage of its devotees.

When the play was over and the last visitors had left his dressing-room, Irving changed and, if he did not go to one or other of his clubs, returned to Grafton Street, where he found a frugal supper waiting for him on the hearth. If he could persuade a friend to return with him to share it—so much the better. 'A little supper—eh?' he would grunt hospitably as he rummaged by the fire. 'Some soup—eh? and a kipper—very good, ye know—kipper!' The dishes were shared over a bottle of champagne, cigars were lit, and he settled down to beguile his companion into keeping him company until the early hours of the morning. For Irving, these were the best hours of the day, but whether of today or tomorrow only he could tell.

2

The Lady of Lyons was produced on April 17th. Probably Irving, in choosing Lytton's already dated play, wished to give Ellen Terry a chance to show her romantic paces as Pauline Deschappelles. It had been, it is true, one of his earliest loves. He revelled in Claude Melnotte's long, fustian speeches and in the opportunities for stage effects that the heroic departure for the wars provided. His army, with banners flying and drums beating—with the correct and more dramatic timbre of French military drums, thanks to the advice of Frederick Pollock—marched past interminably, sustaining the stirring climax as long as the audience chose to keep the curtain rising and falling. The Brigade of Guards, from whom Irving's make-believe armies were recruited, were glad to allow their men to act as supers in London productions and so for an hour or two to be kept out of mischief. The soldiers earned a standard rate of about a shilling an hour, but Irving always paid a little more and so ensured the loyalty and efficiency of his mercenaries.

Helena Faucit, who had created the part of Pauline with Macready in 1838, had written to warn Irving of the play's shortcomings:

'. . . I do not feel so anxious to see this as I have been your other re-productions. I have only once *seen* the play acted and it has not left a pleasant remembrance. The construction is perfect and some of the characters well drawn—but the language is feeble and stilted and so much of it tainted with vulgarity and false sentiment that I was full of amazement in listening to it how such a play could have carried the hearts and souls of audiences with it and moved them to their utmost depths for so long a time and in every country in which I have acted in it. Certainly in this instance I did not see the pride, the anguish, the struggle, the conflict—and without these the play sank to the level of a domestic modern drama. The faulty hero and heroine as depicted by the author had not learned their lesson, accepted their punishment, and through storm and suffering reached their haven of rest, "as after much turmoil the blessed spirit doth in Elysium".

Fechter was the Claude. It is certain in this play Bulwer intended that "The Lady" should give the keynote. If this struck in a minor key it must be very difficult, if not impossible, for the hero to restore the balance. They must work together or all will be out of harmony. I hope you are more fortunate.

I think the critics just now—at least some of them—make such a mistake in what they call real, natural acting . . . they forget that what is real in one person is unreal in another—times and circumstances can elevate common natures. And then there is the reality which is natural to the noble nature and the reality of the commonplace one. The situation may be the same, the words spoken may be the same—the tone and manner will signify the difference. Forgive my boring your patience with my unlucky experience of this play as I saw it represented.

I hope you're not taking too much out of yourself. I thought you looked very weary from the glimpse we had of you in Piccadilly yesterday. No success can compensate for broken health. Be wise in time!'

Irving and Ellen Terry fell into the very trap against which the wise old actress had warned them. Lytton's proud Pauline in Ellen Terry's hands became tender, tearful and coquettish. Irving, knowing that at forty-three he would find it difficult to give a convincing impersonation of a gay, sentimental lover, made Claude a tragic and melancholy figure. Thus they were not only out of harmony with the poet's intention, such as it was, but with each other.

The critics declined to take either of their performances seriously and dismissed the whole affair as a well-appointed frolic which, while it could not enhance their reputation, had not greatly injured it. But Irving's managerial acumen had not betrayed him. He had mounted the play lavishly but with excellent taste. 'Even those,' wrote Clement Scott, 'who are unaffectedly weary of the old-fashioned sentiment of the play, and are bold enough to have formed a very decided opinion on the characteristic of Claude and the pride of Pauline, can gaze contentedly at faultless pictures, at costume raised to the dignity of an art, if occasionally astonishing in its accuracy, and at innumerable graces of arrangement and movement, which please the eye when the ear is out of tune with the passion of the scene.' The public seemed to be delighted with it all and supported it until the end of the season, the receipts comparing favourably with those of *Hamlet*. Having had their fling, neither Irving not Ellen Terry ever appeared in the play again.

Towards the end of the season Irving revived all his earlier successes, in which Ellen Terry was seen for the first time. Her Henrietta Maria and Ruth Meadows were much praised. Henry James, while grudgingly admitting that she was 'the most pleasing and picturesque figure on the English stage,' was bewildered by the same amateurishness and lack of technique which made him impervious to Irving's hypnotism. He was looking forward eagerly to the six weeks' season which the Comédie Française were about to play in London—perhaps when the London public had tasted this exquisite dish they would become more alive to the error of the Lyceum's ways.

The Lyceum season ended on July 26th. Although the French company played to packed and enthusiastic houses at the Gaiety, attendances at the Lyceum were larger than ever. Irving, now well established as the head of his profession, enjoyed enormously playing the host to the members of the Comédie Française. Gôt, Delaunay, Coquelin aîné, Mounet-Sully and Worms were all in London, with Sarah Bernhardt and the other actresses who supported them. Soon after they arrived Lady Pollock, with whom Delaunay was staying, invited Irving to meet the French actor at supper. In reply he wrote:

> 15A Grafton Street,
> Bond Street, W.
> June 8th, 1879.

'My dear Lady Pollock,

I am looking forward to tonight with the greatest pleasure and to meeting Delaunay, my first love as an actor. In him I saw the Romeo of my dreams. He is the rarest artist I ever looked upon. I hope he will like poor Hamlet. It will give me great love and friendship for him if he does. I am sorry we cannot talk together but you must tell me all he says. I wish you could come and see "Eugene Aram". Ophelia is most beautiful again as Ruth.

Believe me, ever yours gratefully and affectionately,

H. Irving.'

After supper, when they were alone together, Delaunay recited de Musset's poem 'Fortunio', to which Irving responded with 'The Dream of Eugene Aram'. Comprehending scarcely a word of each other's recitations, they were, perhaps, able to appreciate all the more keenly the technique and force of their widely dissimilar methods.

Irving was not disappointed in Delaunay, whose heart was as warm as his own. 'I was enchanted,' wrote the French actor a day or two after their meeting, 'dear and honoured colleague, to be with you on Sunday . . . I was very happy to hear you and the emotion you caused me to feel will never be effaced from my memory.' Irving saw one or two of the performances at the Gaiety and put his own theatre at the disposal of the French company. Delauney and Irving may have recognized each other's quality, but old Gôt and Coquelin were as bewildered by the naturalism of the Lyceum style as Irving and Ellen Terry were by the sonorous declamations of the French school. Indeed Coquelin, watching Ellen Terry, murmured to his companions: 'Angèlique, très sympathique, très tendre,' adding, after a glance through his opera glasses: 'Mais c'est charmant: elle a des vrais larmes aux yeux.' Francisque Sarcey, the great French critic who had accompanied his countrymen to London, sought a charitable explanation for his own lack of appreciation of Irving's acting. 'He appears,' he wrote, 'a remarkable actor, notwithstanding a wilful tendency to exaggeration (Bien qu'il donne volontiers dans l'exaggération) possibly in this latter respect he follows the tastes of his audiences whom his instinct judges rather than his own deliberate choice.'

Their artistic disparities did not, however, cloud their personal relationships. Irving gave a supper in a room adjoining his dressing-room at the Lyceum, to which he invited Delaunay and his colleagues and several savants, including Sarcey. Neither hosts nor guests spoke each other's language, but by the end of supper this barrier was down and there was a free, if slightly bizarre, exchange of ideas. When the time came for the party to break up Sarcey was missing. Bram Stoker searched vainly the dim recesses of the darkened stage until at last, led by a rhythmic thumping sound, he found Sarcey dancing and singing in the semi-darkness of a remote passage. One Sunday, a week or two later, Irving invited Delaunay and a few others to drive to Surrey with him on the Dorking coach.' Dear neighbour,' answered Delaunay, 'I will be at the Garrick Club at 11 o'clock. I shall try and be in a good temper and I promise to allow you to forget that we are two great actors . . . .' Mounet Sully, Frederick Pollock and his son, and Percy Fitzgerald made up the party. After lunching in Dorking, they wandered about the country near Box Hill, calling perhaps on Pollock's friend, George Meredith; in the evening they returned to the Garrick Club, where Irving had arranged another supper party for them, happily more bi-lingual than the last so that such tributes as were exchanged could be interpreted clearly to the recipients. Before he returned to Paris, Delaunay wrote:

'. . . Thank you once more for the delightful day you caused me to spend last Sunday. You were cordial, simple and charming as all true and great artists should be. The day will rank among my happiest memories . . . so we shall meet in Paris, as you assure me, and between now and then think over the generous idea of which you have spoken to me—the foundation of a conservatoire and a national theatre—Shakespeare's house. You alone can bring this great idea to a reality. Courage then!

Yours ever,
Delaunay.'

Henry James might well have been scandalized by these junketings and friendly exchanges between those whom he regarded as the enemies and champions of the art he professed to love. Confounded by the London public who seemed to respond as warmly to the art of 'the children of Molière' as to what he regarded at the artlessness of the Lyceum, he would have been aghast had he known that Irving dreamed of perpetuating his heresies in a National School of Acting. But they were dreams and nothing more. Though they recurred often, Irving always awoke with a start at the moment when, behind state subsidy and patronage, there loomed a spectral official who questioned his own policy and authority.

At the final performance of the season, on July 26th, Irving took his benefit, playing scenes from *Richard III*, *Charles I*, *Louis XI*, *Hamlet*, and *Raising the Wind*. If to ring the changes on such a variety of characters was proof, now perhaps superfluous, of his versatility as an actor, the account books of the Lyceum at the end of this first season provided an estimate of his as yet untried managerial capacity. Receipts had amounted to £39,881 against a total expenditure of £32,869, so that his indebtedness had been reduced by about £6,000. These figures allowed for his and Ellen Terry's salaries and for their benefits which had brought them in £250 and £233 respectively. The expenditure covered the cost of two new and handsome productions, *Hamlet* (£1,100) and *The Lady of Lyons* (£1,700), in addition to improvements and additions to earlier stock productions which added a further £1,600. During this period he received the only financial help of his career in the shape of a legacy of £5,000 from Mrs. Brown, which he had paid into the Lyceum Treasury. This sum had been left him, in the words of the Executors, 'in recognition of an unsullied, honest and laboriously won fame and of Mrs. Brown's fervent admiration of the steady and studious perseverance which gained it'. No one would have rejoiced more than she at the great public appreciation of Mr. Irving's first season at the Lyceum.

For a man who but a few months before had been a salaried actor, this change in fortune and situation was remarkable, yet Irving knew that, in striving to maintain it, his most urgent problem would be the discovery of new plays for production. Though his plans were nebulous, he favoured the policy of alternating Shakespeare with modern tragedy or popular melodrama. English drama was in such a poor way that it was difficult to know where to look for new plays of quality. Irving's post brought only too weighty evidence that, though many were anxious to write for the stage, too few writers or poets had taken the trouble to study stage technique. In vain he reminded ambitious writers who came to him for advice that of the three most popular playwrights of the day, Robertson and Byron were actors and Tom Taylor the most adept of stage producers. Tennyson, with his help, was working on two plays, *The Cup* and *Becket*, but neither were ready for production. He had commissioned Wills to make a dramatization of *Rienzi*, and Frank Marshall to write a play, with Robert Emmett, the Irish patriot, as the central figure. He had bought a one-act comedy by Pinero, *Daisy's Escape*, which he had promised to produce during the coming season. In all he had spent about £900 in commissioning new works and, so far, had little to show for it. Nor had his search been a narrow one, for the advice and help of all the distinguished men of letters of the day had been readily available to him. In his farewell speech he announced that he would open the autumn season with Colman's tragedy, *The Iron Chest*, and hinted at a possibility of a production of *Coriolanus*, but apart from assuring his public that his aim was to provide a frequent change of programme, he was unable to specify very clearly what this programme was to be.

3

Owing to previous commitments, Ellen Terry had, while the Lyceum was closed, to tour the provinces with Charles Kelly. Irving wisely decided not to undertake a provincial tour until she was free to go with him. He had arranged to let the theatre for four weeks to Miss Geneviéve Ward, an American actress who had won a considerable name for herself in England. She had studied at the Comédie Française and had played Lady Macbeth at the Porte St. Martin, where, according to a French critic, 'la salle toute entière était suspendueà ses lèvres et frissonait avec elle'. Unfortunately the play she presented at the Lyceum, *Zillah*, failed to inspire *frissons* of any kind in the London public and her season proved a disastrous one. Although Irving let the Lyceum for £150 a week, his own expenses were such that at the end of four weeks he himself was £300 out of pocket. Meanwhile he had been asked by the Baroness Burdett Coutts to go on a cruise to the Mediterranean in the steamer *Walrus* which she had chartered for the summer. The rest of the party was to include Edwin Long, the portrait painter, and Ashmead Bartlett, a young man who helped the Baroness in her philanthropic work and was soon to become her husband. He received his sailing orders the day after the Lyceum closed:

The Walrus,
July 23rd.

'Dear Mr. Irving,
    The Divinity that shapes our ends has shaped them pleasantly and I fixed Wednesday evening or Thursday morning early for you and Mr. Bartlett to join your ship. Our course is changed for Cherbourg and the French coast. Tonight we mean to reach the Isle of Wight. Mr. Bartlett understands. I will only add that G.B.—and G.W.—are singing on the steam engines. The Longs are to join at Weymouth.

Yours sincerely as of old,
Burdett Coutts.'

The *Walrus* was a well-found steam passenger vessel of about eight hundred tons, with auxiliary sails. The Bay of Biscay turned out to be as smooth as a stage cloth and the party reached the Aegean without adventure. It was the first real holiday that Irving had taken since he went on the stage, and, although the comic press had widely pictured the incongruity of the tragedian afloat, he was a good sailor and reaped the full benefit of being completely isolated from work or worry. But Irving was not adept at idleness. By the time *Walrus* arrived at Corfu on the return journey he was becoming impatient for the Lyceum. On August 26th he wrote to Loveday:

> *Corfu (from Yacht 'Walrus')*
> *August 26th, 1879.*

'My dear Loveday,

Yesterday I received your letter with all its good news—especially of yourself. I am glad you are so well.

I hope to be with you on 12th Sept. at the latest—and glad I shall be to get back.

We've had a most delightful time in Spain, Tangiers and Tunis and now we are in Greece or in its Islands—nothing short of fairyland but —oh—it's devilish hot. From here we go to Sorrento—I want to look in at Corsica for Craven's sake. Marseilles for home—I hope to leave on September 10th. Anything that can reach Marseilles up to the 9th—you'd better send to the Post Office there. The 'Era' will be acceptable.

I'm glad you're going well ahead. Craven will have plenty of red handkerchiefs to buy. In the first act of *The Iron Chest* I want *another* scene.

1st Sc.	Rawbold.
2nd Sc.	Hall in "Edwards" *in* 2.
3rd Sc.	Sort of oak wainscot—with cupboard in it—*in* 3.

It is necessary to have this scene because Wilford and Winterton must make natural business in it—to interest the audience properly and this they cannot do unless the place helps them—which a front scene cannot. I fancy part of the second act Eugene Aram might answer the purpose well. By the way the soldier's portrait we had on the wall is exactly the dress for Fitzharding and Barnes might be measured and the dress got on with.

Try and get a *dark* crimson cloth and the older the better. I wonder could an old officer's coat be licked into shape. The hat is important—three-cornered of course. . . . Pinero's piece sounds well. . . . Before *The Bells* we can do *The Boarding School*—what comes after doesn't matter. . . .

I don't think I shall do *The Stranger*—for the present at least. Think of reviving *Othello* and then *Venice Preserved*. The Senate scene will be the Othello one of course, and the principal scene to paint will be the Rialto. We can do the play very well and it's a fine stirring thing.

I hope Ellen Terry is doing well. When can she be back at the earliest? Wake up Clarke about some good entr'acte music for *The Iron Chest* and get him to write some vague and mysterious bits for change of scene. I believe in *The Iron Chest*—but it wants great care taken with it. And now the future I shall leave until I get back and then we can talk it over.

Goodbye, old man,
My love to Stoker,

A few days later Stoker received his preliminary orders for the autumn campaign:

'. . . But now to business. My mind is changed a little about the forthcoming plays and I shall drop out of the list *The Gamester*. On reading it—I don't believe in it. As it will give little trouble to revive after *The Iron Chest* I shall try *Othello* and then *The Stranger—Emmett* perhaps and then *Coriolanus*.

Emmett is good, will act well and I would have played it sooner had the woman's part been better. With that I am much disappointed As soon as you can, learn from Ellen Terry the first Wednesday that she can act with me again. If she can on the 15th of October I shall be glad for I want to announce *Hamlet* in the October programme, and the sooner we can play it the better. Tell her too that I do not mean to do *The Gamester*.

The rehearsals will begin I suppose on the 6th or 8th Sept. I should like everybody *perfect* by the 13th. Till I get back the principal time had better be devoted to the farces and you'd better get the address of Miss Ewell and engage her for three months for *The Boarding School*, Pinero's piece, I hope, has turned out well. By the 13th, too, I should like the music, scenery and properties all ready, so that we can break the neck of *The Iron Chest* before we re-open. I shall rehearse it, I think, in the evening.

Advertisement enclosed, have inserted a fortnight before we open, and put out a few posters—"Mr. Irving in tragedy and drama. September 20th". These won't need renewing.

I'm sorry about Miss Ward. I hope she is doing better now.

My love to Loveday whom, by the way, this letter principally concerns.

Yours ever,
Henry Irving.

You might see Ellen Terry and give her the enclosed. If you do—but only if you do. I shall be glad to get back.'

It is clear that at this time, beyond the revival of *The Iron Chest*, Irving's plans were all too fluid. When he arrived in Venice and, as always, began to absorb impressions which he could turn to account in his theatre, he explored the city, collecting prints and pictures for Hawes Craven with nothing more definite in his mind than a revival of *Othello* or perhaps of *Venice Preserved*. Yet he was haunted by a picturesque figure who had attracted his attention and sympathy in almost every port at which the party had landed in the course of their cruise round the shores of the Eastern Mediterranean. The figure was that of the Levantine Jew, whose romantic appearance and patriarchal dignity against the background of his native landscape was so much at variance with the popular conception of his race which was held by Western Europeans. As the revelation of Venice burst upon him, these two impressions fused in his mind and caused him to consider *The Merchant of Venice*. In his apprentice days he had played Salarino and Bassanio, but the play had made little impression upon him. He knew, by report, that in his own time Charles Kean and Phelps had entertained their public with fine studies of a ranting Shylock whom they represented as a vengeful and malignant usurer consumed with race hatred.

Like *Richard III*, Shakespeare's Shylock had passed through a period of eclipse. About 1570 Stephan Gosson had written a play, *The Jew*, which had been performed at the Bull Theatre. Later, Shakespeare and Marlowe, taking their plot from this common source, had written plays with a Jew as the central character. In *The Jew of Malta* Marlowe had drawn a caricature of a usurer who was a monster of savage cruelty; in *The Merchant of Venice* Shakespeare, profiting by Marlowe's mistakes, had humanised 'the red-haired Jew':

> . . . *which sought the bankrupt Merchants' pound of flesh,*
> *By woman lawyer caught in his own mesh,*

as ran the elegy on Richard Burbage, who had created the part of Shylock. After Burbage's death both plays disappeared and gave place to a comical parody of them, *The Jew of Venice*, which held the stage until Macklin, in 1741, restored Shakespeare's original play to the stage, playing Shylock as a straight villain with a success which even Garrick dared not challenge. Though Macklin wore the red wig which had become the traditional make-up for Shylock, he did not do so for comic effect. Though he may not have been aware of it, it had come to symbolize the red hat which the law of Venice compelled Jews to wear. Edmund Kean made history by wearing a black wig and bringing a touch of nature and human understanding to a performance which outshone Macklin's and was worth, according to Hazlitt, 'a wilderness of monkeys that have aped humanity'. Kean succeeded in mingling paternal anguish with vindictiveness. But Shylock remained a villain, and even Edwin Booth followed his father by depicting him as a 'strongly marked and rather grotesque character'.

Irving studied the play afresh and, as he did so, slowly formulated a new conception of Shylock as the symbol of a persecuted race, a Jewish merchant in some ways more of a gentleman than anyone else in the play, from whom Antonio was unashamed to borrow money and with whose daughter the Christian Lorenzo was ready to elope. Jessica's friendship with Portia did, to some extent, establish her father's social position. Shylock was well read—a devout Hebrew given to quoting the Scriptures. There was little to suggest the snuffling usurer in the man into whose mouth Shakespeare had put some of his finest speeches. Certainly Irving knew of no actor before him who had stumbled on the key to Shylock's alternating dignity and cringing obeisance, his quiet diplomacy which gave way so quickly to bitter satire. He had seen a Jew in Tunis, beside himself over some transaction, tear his hair and his clothes, fling himself upon the sand writhing in rage, and a few minutes later become self-possessed, fawning and full of genuine gratitude for a trifling gift of money. Picturesque in his fury, having regained his composure, the Jew had stalked away with kingly dignity behind his mule team. Why should not Shylock have been of this type—perhaps a Spanish Jew—a proud man, respected on the Rialto, the leader of his synagogue and conscious of his moral superiority to many of the Christians who baited him? As Irving tried to fit this new conception into Shakespeare's text, he realized that the clue to the contradictions in Shylock's character was to be found in the moment when, having struck his bargain with Antonio as something in the nature of a grim jest, his mind becomes clouded by the irresistible temptation to use it as a weapon of revenge. Could Shakespeare's Shylock be so interpreted? Irving, his mind filled with these speculations, and well stored with picturesque details for the production he had begun to visualize, returned to London, where preparations for *The Iron Chest* already were well in hand. The yachting cruise had turned out to be a voyage of discovery and in the stones of Venice Irving had found inspiration which was to turn them into nuggets of gold.

4

As his interest in *The Merchant of Venice* waxed, his enthusiasm for *The Iron Chest* waned. But, for the time being, he kept his new project to himself and tackled his next production as forcefully as ever. It was not a happy choice and he can have considered this dull and sombre play only in the light of the astonishing impression Edmund Kean had made in the part of Sir Edward Mortimer and because, perhaps, its plot recalled the cosy horrors of 'The Uncle'. The young Colman's dramatization of Godwin's novel, *Caleb Williams*, had been produced for the first time in 1796 at Drury Lane with John Philip Kemble as Sir Edward. Kemble's funereal delivery (to which Colman unjustly attributed the failure of his play) might well have interred it in well-merited oblivion. But Edmund Kean, finding the dusty script abandoned on the shelves of Drury Lane, seized upon it and wrought from words and phrases, valueless on the lips of lesser actors, 'the means, point after point and scene after scene, of electrifying his audiences'. Many critics had been of the opinion that in his transition from brutal passion to the agonies of remorse, Kean had excelled his earlier masterpiece, Sir Giles Overreach. Irving was able to incorporate in his study of the homicidal baronet the variety of moods familiar to those who had admired his Mathias, his Philip and his Eugene Aram. But closer acquaintance with the play had revealed its colourless incoherence and the weight of the burden which he had condemned himself to carry.

The autumn season opened on September 20th with a week of *The Bells*. The triple bill ended with Pinero's one act comedy, *Daisy's Escape* in which the author played the lead. The plot was slender—the disillusionment of a girl who had eloped with a rude and ill-tempered bore and her escape from this dilemma—but the dialogue was bright, witty and in the contemporary idiom. Even these early works of Pinero were distinguished by his sense of climax—climax of lines and of situations—a vital dramatic component which he had learnt to reverence during his years in Irving's company. *Daisy's Escape* proved so popular that it remained in the bill for a year, when it was replaced by another of the author's one-act comedies, *Bygones*. Although in 1877 an earlier play of his, *Two Hundred a Year*, had been put on for one performance at the Globe, the Lyceum was Pinero's true cradle both as an actor and as a playwright.

On the night of September 27th the audience endured *The Iron Chest* with respectful attention, and, as always, were appalled and fascinated by Irving's performance. Indeed, the applause at the end of the play tricked the actor, in whom doubt invariably bred defiance, into announcing the play for a run and according it an honoured niche in the Lyceum repertoire. He might well have been misled by the qualified eulogies of the press (even the *Athenaeum* declared his performance 'marvellous, . . . the grimmer aspect of Mr. Irving's powers has never been seen to equal advantage') had not the box-office returns brought sober realization of the play's essential unattractiveness. Ellen Terry returned to the Lyceum by the middle of October when *Hamlet* was played one night a week and on that night the receipts, which had sagged under the weight of *The Iron Chest* to a nightly average of about £110, bounded to over £200. By that time, however, Irving's plans had crystallized.

During his absence in the Mediterranean, certain backstage lumber-rooms which lay behind the armoury of the Lyceum were, at his instruction, being cleared out and redecorated. At the beginning of the century these dark and dusty caverns had been the meeting-place of the Sublime Society of Beefsteaks. Samuel Arnold, the composer and champion of English opera, when he restored the Lyceum, had set aside this part of the theatre as a meeting-place for the society whose membership included Sheridan, Perry (the prolific writer of melodramatic oratorios), Lord Erskine and the Duke of Norfolk. Eating and conversation were the business of the society. No daylight entered these rooms. Above the long dining-table a gridiron was suspended from the ceiling and on the wall was inscribed the society's motto, paraphrased from Horace by Arnold:

Let no one bear beyond this threshold hence
Words utterèd in friendly confidence.

The Beefsteaks sat at table, with their President at the head of it. The first president, the Duke of Norfolk, reigned over them like a despot. He wore the insignia of the Society, a silver gridiron on his breast, and on his head a hat crowned with feathers which had been worn by Garrick. Near the President sat the Bishop, at that time Samuel Arnold, who, when he said grace, put on a mitre which was said to have belonged to Cardinal Gregorio. Nearby sat the other officers, the Recorder, the Secretary, the Laureate, and the Boots, the latter office being the perquisite of the youngest member. Beyond the supper-room, which could seat some thirty members, and in full view of them all, was the kitchen equipped solely with a huge gridiron upon which beefsteaks, the staple diet of the Society, were grilled.

The steaks, cut from the rump, were introduced 'hot and hot' into the dining-room through an aperture in the wall and were laid before the President, who carved for his members delicate and succulent cuts, so that their plates were never overloaded and could be returned for a second or third time. The only vegetable served was a delicious salad in which beetroot predominated. Porter and port slaked the thirst and loosened the tongues of these carnivorous, noble and intellectual gentlemen whose number included those most distinguished in the arts, the law and the medical sciences.

By the time Irving returned, these once famous rooms had been restored to something like their earlier splendour. The Gridiron, though retained as a relic, had been replaced by the most modern of kitchen ranges which was able to provide a greater variety of dishes than the strong meat of the old Society. The walls were hung with the collection of pictures which Irving had begun to acquire. In a recess near the supper table was a large conversation piece by Clint, showing Edmund Kean at the climax of his performance in *A New Way to Pay Old Debts*. Near it was a study which Clint had made for this picture, a superb head of Kean which was believed to be the only portrait for which the volatile actor had ever been persuaded to sit. Among the rest was Whistler's portrait of Irving as Philip and a fine head of the young Napoleon which he had used as a model for his make-up as Claude Melnotte. All was finished, a chef had been installed and the cellar well stocked, when, on a Saturday night shortly after the season began, Irving invited Stoker and Loveday to the first of several hundred suppers which he gave in those rooms. Champagne and brandy were substituted for porter and port, and just as his two henchmen were settling down comfortably to their cigars, Irving with sardonic relish, said quietly, 'I am going to do *The Merchant of Venice*.'

Before they had time to recover from their surprise, for never before had he mentioned the play, he added that he was going to do it at once. Pushing aside plates and glasses and calling for some notepaper, he started then and there to sketch ideas for the production and to tear and bend the paper into rough models of the scenes which he planned to build. When they emerged into the soft light of the early sun which was rising over the Temple, his lieutenants were quite clear as to his intentions but aghast at the idea of having to carry them out in the three weeks which remained before November 1st, on which date he had decided that *The Merchant of Venice* would open. As they parted, Irving said with a smile: 'I think Craven had better get out that—er—red—um—handkerchief.'

5

Rehearsals began at once and followed the usual routine. Irving had already prepared the text from which the parts had to be copied by hand. On the Thursday the company were called to hear him read through the play in the Green Room. After two or three months of intense study he knew exactly what he wanted and how the effects which he had planned were to be realized. Ellen Terry and the company knew, moreover, that at that reading they would hear for the first and last time, before the first night, how Irving would play his own part. He had had a life-long experience of readings of this kind. His characterizations of all the parts made it unnecessary for him to identify the speakers by name. As he read, he indicated roughly the grouping of scenes and the order of processions and crowd movements. At the end of the reading he gave out the parts. The company spent the next day going through the play with Allen, the prompter, checking the transcripted parts for cues or for mistakes. They were not called on Saturdays and Sundays, but were expected during these two days to prepare themselves and to be as word perfect as possible for the first full rehearsal on Monday.

Irving's arrival at rehearsal was eagerly awaited. If he wore a silk hat, which indicated a social engagement of some kind, the company could look forward to a peaceful, if strenuous, day; if he wore a broad-brimmed soft felt hat—they called it his 'storm hat'—they knew they had to look out for squalls and were in for a rough passage. For these early rehearsals mock-up scenes were set and hand properties were furnished as necessary. Each day, one act was taken straight through twice. There was no break for lunch. The company snatched a bite when they could; Irving usually went without it. He was in absolute control of these rehearsals, with Loveday and his assistants at his side to give effect to his orders, to marshal crowds and to attend to the details of stage direction. With infinite patience, though with occasional acerbities, he coached every actor in his part, repeating over and over again word or action until it approximated to the perfection at which he aimed. Ellen Terry would watch despairingly Irving's relentless concentration on this often hopeless task—pitying the actors who, 'when they tried to carry out his instructions were as like him as brass is to gold'. His method had its dangers, for it tended to produce a number of weak imitations of himself; its virtue lay in the unity of conception and execution in his productions for which he took full responsibility and was ready to accept the praise or the blame which they incurred.

CHAPTER XX

2nd Lyceum Season : Shylock

I

Irving, following a precedent created during the recent production of *Hamlet*, had published in advance his acting version of *The Merchant of Venice*. Thus, before the curtain rose, he made his intentions clear to critics and scholars, so that, as the house lights dimmed, their curiosity in this respect had been satisfied, and those whose sensibilities were easily ruffled by any tampering with the original text had got over the worst of their irritation. The cuts he made were few, and, although one or two short scenes had been eliminated or grafted onto others, he had departed from tradition very little in his arrangement of the play. The only casualty was the Prince of Arragon, and he was likely to be missed not so much for himself as for the omission of the speeches which Portia addressed to him. The first glimpse of Ellen Terry, who carried a magnificent dress of gold brocade as though it were made of gossamer, revealed a Portia more mature but no less gay and charming than the one whom most of the audience had seen at the Prince of Wales's.

When Irving entered at the beginning of the third scene his appearance struck the chord that was to be dominant in his interpretation of Shylock. Pale and lean visaged, his wisp of grey beard threaded with streaks of black, he leaned upon a stick, his head slightly bowed, so that normally his glance was upwards and askance. His dress was sober and picturesque; under a dark-brown cloak or gaberdine edged with fur he wore a tunic which reached to his ankles. The sleeves of the tunic were full to the elbow, but tightly fitting over the lower arm, with white cuffs turned back above the wrists. The rusty effect of these garments was offset by a wide sash striped with earthy reds and yellows from which hung a tasselled leather pouch. Gone was the red hat or red wig; in its place he wore a tightly fitting black cap down the front of which ran a bar of yellow suggesting a racial badge. His long grey hair, through which gold earrings occasionally glinted, curled over the collar of his tunic; a black forelock straggled over the high receding forehead. The poise and dignity of his bearing was that of a Levantine Jew, an alien in Venice and therefore more saturated with Judaisms than those of his race who had rubbed shoulders with Europeans. From the outset his manner suggested that Shylock kept his household and himself apart from Western custom and thought—isolated in his habits by choice and force of race.

Irving spoke the opening lines half turned away from Bassanio—his head slightly bent to one side, his eyes looking forward on the ground. He spoke in an even monotone; his voice was subdued and meditative. Previous Shylocks had begun this scene in an aggressive manner. Irving did not. He was deep in thought; his sentences came slowly and haltingly. His Shylock was never impulsive but slow in his planning and dealing, and therefore all the more dangerous. He weighed well the effect of every word which he used before he ventured his money. When Antonio asked for a loan the audience realized that, to Shylock, the idea of a hated Christian being bound to him by contract was a totally new one; one that, in Jewish fashion, he accepted slowly and cautiously. Occasionally, as in his 'Ho, no no . . .' to Bassanio, he used a sneering tone, only to relapse again into his meditative mood. His reply to Bassanio's invitation to dinner was spoken angrily. It acted like a goad and seemed to stimulate his hatred for the particular Christian with whom he was dealing. His anger grew keener and more savage at the beginning of the aside, 'How like a fawning publican he looks. . . .' For a moment he recovered his self-control and then, on the words, 'If I can catch him . . .', his spleen once more got the better of him. At his mention of Tubal the idea of revenge was seen for the first time to overmaster his greed for money. During the Jacob speech, which was spoken with a reverential fervour, he betrayed his conviction that whatever Jacob did was right and just; at 'I cannot tell; I make it breed as fast . . .' he fell into the rasping business-like tones of a modern Jew. Reacting sharply to Antonio's jibe, he turned aside and drew himself up to his full height. The speech 'Signor Antonio, many a time and oft in the Rialto . . .' began quietly, but, increasing in intensity, reached its climax at 'A cur can lend three thousand ducats . . .', which was jerked out in clipped, articulated syllables. After Antonio's reply, suspecting that he had gone too far, his voice took on a fawning tone, soft and quiet. In stipulating the conditions of the bond, at the words 'In merry sport . . .' his face for an instant became pale and haggard at the thought of the grim jest he was about to perpetrate. When, after 'Let the forfeit be nominated . . .' he paused and swept them with a glance, the audience could see in his eyes the dark workings of his mind. Eagerly and rapidly he launched into details—'For an equal pound of your fair flesh to be cut off and taken in what part of your body it pleaseth me . . .'—and here he looked up with wolfish eyes, to see how his victim liked it—a ravenous desire to have it then and there lighting up his face. At the words, 'Oh Father Abraham . . .' he drew apart and tinged his words '. . . muttons, beefs or goats' with a ghastly humour and irony. His exit from the scene, with his cloak flying about him, was almost jaunty and betrayed the ostentatious conceit of a man of his race who has struck a shrewd and hard bargain. The first scene of the second act (Act I, Scene II in the original) introduced Launcelot Gobbo and was ably handled by old Sam Johnson. The last scene of this act was Shylock's house by the bridge. After the elopement of Jessica and Lorenzo, the curtain fell slowly as the maskers, sweeping across the stage, swallowed them up. After a second or two it rose again upon an empty stage. Shylock was seen returning over the bridge. He crossed to his house and, unsuspecting, knocked upon the door. A second and a third knock echoed through the empty house. The curtain fell again as, without word or outward sign, Irving conveyed to the audience Shylock's crushing realization of his daughter's perfidy. This post-script to the scene was Irving's interpolation—for once an improvement upon Shakespeare.

The third act began with the Casket Scene, to which was added an excerpt from the original Act II, Scene I. In the following scene Shylock entered to Salarino and Salanio hurriedly and distractedly; his hair streaming, without a cap, his shirt torn open, he gesticulated wildly at them and was evidently frantic with grief, of which the first outburst was hardly over. 'Let him look to his bond . . .' was said in the calm tone of desperate resolve. At the word 'flesh' his voice rose again to a shriek—'It will feed my revenge. . . .' He threw up his arms only to let them drop, heavy and powerless, at those words which had such deep meaning to him, 'I am a Jew.' The curse was upon him and for a moment crushed him. His scene with Tubal conveyed intense but suppressed suffering. At 'I never felt till now . . .' he beat his breast slowly with his clenched fist. After '. . . she were hears'd at my foot' he paused and, murmuring, 'No no . . .', hid his face in his hands. This momentary emotion affected the next sentence which was spoken in a softer tone, almost a sob. The last sentence was delivered beautifully in a low tremulous voice, full of deep pathos.

At the end of the speech he let his head drop upon his breast. Much of the rest of the scene was spoken in a hissing whisper. When he raised his voice it had the rasp of a file. He contrived to suggest in his delivery of the word 'wilderness' (of monkeys) a vast emptiness, signifying Jessica's life of frivolous and trifling amusement and his contempt for it—an example of his ability to make an effective point out of an apparently insignificant word.

In the Court Scene, Irving gave the finest performance of his life. Loving Hamlet as he did, he considered his own ideal of that character was higher than his performance of it. Probably he was satisfied with his Shylock. In sharp comparison to Edmund Kean (whose mood at the beginning of the scene was one of "exulting joyousness"), Irving was icily and proudly calm. He entered with head uncovered, bowed slightly to the court and moved rather far from the crowd—as far as he could from the herd of Christians. His manner was quiet and dignified. The knife and scales were hidden. During the Duke's speech Shylock's eyes were fixed upon him, though he was turned slightly away from the court. 'I have possessed Your Grace of what I purpose . . .' had a subdued assurance about it. But his tone was deferential as of one anxious to show his respect for the law of Venice. He maintained this attitude towards the Duke, but at any word from Bassanio or Antonio he turned upon them with a contemptuous sneer. After the words, 'If every ducat in six thousand ducats were in six parts and every part a ducat, I would not draw them . . .' he paused before he added very slowly, 'I would have my bond . . .' tapping three times upon his pouch with the knife which he produced for the first time. While Salario's letter was being read, he faced the audience, listening keenly, his eyes drawn towards the reader. As Portia entered and passed by him he scanned her closely and then walked away a few steps, stroking his beard in deep thought. There was a proud ring in his voice as he said, 'Shylock is my name'. During Portia's 'Quality of mercy' speech Irving's eyes never winked. They became fixed with the malevolent gaze which grew in them. His breathing became laboured. At her words, 'It is an attribute to God himself . . .', he raised his eyes, slowly shook his head and murmured, 'No'. 'I crave the law, the penalty and forfeit of my bond . . .' was urged with stubborn monotony. He was perfectly unruffled and stood with head erect. When Bassanio appealed to Portia, Shylock looked about him uneasily, but at Portia's 'It must not be . . .' a look of relief came over his face. Shylock was sure of himself until Portia's entrance and thereafter Irving skilfully worked up an increasing nervousness in the

Jew's manner. He handed over the bond with impatient eagerness and 'An oath in heaven . . .' was uttered with the deep voice of absolute determination. At Portia's 'Bid me tear the bond . . .' he sprang forward with an exclamation of horror to snatch it from her. But this outburst left no trace; the passionless calm returned. So evident was it that no further words could move him that Portia's plea for a surgeon seemed superfluous. Irving's face as he said 'Oh wise and upright judge . . .' wore the same hypocritical look that the audience had seen in his Richard III. At 'Those are the very words . . .' he bent closely over the bond, tracing them with the point of his knife. Eagerly he snatched the scales out of his girdle. His whole attitude now suggested a horrible impatience. He was tensed like an animal before a spring, his elbows back, the knife and scales in his hand. At 'A sentence, come prepare . . .' he leaped forward with a diabolical shriek and a fierce gesture as he bared his arm.

At the end of Portia's verdict he dropped the scales and stood as though mesmerized; when at last he spoke his voice was heavy and thick, though there was still the trace of a sneer in it. Ellen Terry was at her best in this passage, as she always was in scenes which gave an opportunity for a duel between herself and Irving. Shakespeare makes Shylock accept the situation very suddenly, but Irving managed to suggest that Shylock had accepted it with only half his mind—that of the usurer. The other half was still stunned. During Portia's invitation to him to take his pound of flesh with the penalty that it might involve, his lips seemed to be parched and he moistened them constantly with his tongue. His last words came with difficulty and were spoken with unutterable sadness.

During the last minutes of this scene Irving demonstrated his absolute mastery of significant byplay. The whole history of the Jewish race was illustrated in his expression at the bare mention of his turning Christian. At the loathed word (and Antonio purposely gave a long pause) Shylock, who could no longer speak, lifted his head slowly and inclined it backwards over his left shoulder. His eyelids, which hung heavily over his dimmed eyes, were opened to their full and his long, pleading gaze at Antonio showed how bitterly he felt the indignity. Then, as he slowly turned his head, he raised his eyes fervently; his lips murmured incoherent words as his whole body resumed a dreamy, motionless attitude. When Shylock grasped the severity of his sentence, his eyelids became heavy as though he was hardly able to lift them and his eyes became lustreless and vacant. The words 'I am not well . . .' were the plea of a doomed man to be allowed to leave the court and to die in utter loneliness. But Gratiano's ill-timed jibe governed Shylock's exit. He turned. Slowly and steadily the Jew scanned his tormentor from head to foot, his eyes resting on the Italian's face with concentrated scorn. The proud rejection of insult and injustice lit up his face for a moment, enough for the audience to feel a strange relief in knowing that, in that glance, Shylock had triumphed. He inclined his head slightly three times and took three steps towards the door of the court. (Irving had a mystical belief in threefold action.) As he reached the door and put out his hand towards it, he was seized with a crumpling convulsion. It was but a momentary weakness indicated with great subtlety. Then, drawing himself up to his full height once more, Shylock bent his gaze defiantly upon the court and stalked out.

2

At the end of the play Irving and Ellen Terry received an ovation which left no doubt that he had forged a triumphant success out of one of the least popular of Shakespeare's plays. The critics, in their unstinted praise, showed greater unanimity than ever before. Irving's complete departure from tradition gave them a welcome opportunity to dissertate upon earlier Shylocks, and upon Irving's remarkably adroit reconciliation of his own estimate of Shylock with Shakespeare's text. In a short preface to the acting edition of the play he had disclaimed any desire to obscure Shakespeare with elaborate scenic display. But no accusing voice was heard; all were agreed that with the exception of the last scene in Belmont the settings were restrained, imaginative and tasteful. The public needed no second bidding to this feast of entertainment. On the second night the takings were £238 and rarely fell below this figure during the first six months of the run. Pollock, writing to Irving on the morning after the first night, expressed an opinion which was shared by the theatre-going public:

> 59 *Montague Square,*
> *November 2nd,* 1879.

'My dear Irving,

Many and most grateful thanks to you for the great intellectual and visual enjoyment of last night. Certainly never was piece put upon the stage with such surpassing beauty of scenery and costumes. It was a complete success in every way. I think I understand your Shylock;

and it is a most refined and finished study of the part—the last scene not to be improved upon—very fine indeed. In the earlier parts, more intensity might perhaps be given where wanted; more tenderness— in the only tender passage in the character—"I had it of Leah" etc.— less movement in the "Signor Antonio, many a time and oft" etc.— but this is all an affair of light and shade and is sure to come right after one or two performances—so I must crave your pardon for attempting to criticize at all—and especially after having seen only a first night performance. All the best opinions in the house were to the effect that Shylock will be one of your best parts—and I heard no opinion to the contrary—you have got the drawing and colouring of the character quite right—the chiaroscuro will soon get itself properly adjusted.

Portia was, as before, charming, and what one trusts to be her own increased happiness in life seems to tell in the gaiety and buoyancy of her acting. . . .'

Ellen Terry's Portia had delighted all but one or two sour critics who complained that in failing to repress her natural charm or to disguise her striking beauty, her impersonation of an advocate would have deceived nobody. When she had played Portia to Coghlans' turbulent Shylock she had gained her effects by her contrasting quietness. To match Irving's restraint she had to change her conception of the part completely and, in order to create the necessary conflict, to effect a more robust and forward disposition. She, no less than Irving, could accept adverse criticism and profit by it; neither of them, however, could endure the critics who wrote of their mistakes as though they were accidents when these, like their successes, were the outcome of deliberate if misapplied study. The success of *The Merchant of Venice* was a tribute not only to Irving's art as an actor but to his craft as a producer. He had come to the task, so clear in his intention, that in three weeks he had mounted and rehearsed a production which, in its perfection of design, was generally acknowledged rarely to have been surpassed. Considering the scale of the production, its cost—£2,061—was by no means extravagant. Irving, who was careless of money, understood that true economy which could be achieved by clear-sightedness and firmness of purpose.

When the play had been running about a month the Duke, who from his rostrum in the Court Scene was in a favourable position to identify the audience, had told Irving that the great Ruskin was among them. 'Irving,' wrote Ruskin to a friend, 'sent to me to come round after his final discomfiture; and so I went—and made him a pretty little speech. . . .' The Professor was in his sixtieth year. Eighteen years before, in his *Munera Pulveris*, he had used the character of Shylock to illustrate his conviction of the inhumanity of mercenary commerce; he cannot, therefore, have had much sympathy with Irving's interpretation of the Jew. Perhaps on his way home he suspected that his praise had been a trifle fulsome, for on the following morning he wrote:

> *Arthur Severn's,*
> *Herne Hill, S.E.*
> *November 30th,* 1879.

My dear Mr. Irving,

The kind interest you shewed in what I was too awkwardly imperfect in saying when you received me on Friday evening, leads me to write to you with more accuracy and frankness if I can—and may, on what I felt—namely this, that you were a most true and tender and noble actor—but that you had not yet as much love for Shakespeare as for your art, and were therefore not careful enough to be wholly in harmony with his design. . . . I scarcely venture to say more *now*, than that I do not think the greatest actor can ever be seen to full advantage—unless every concurrent or opponent part in the play be at least adequately sustained. Now—and I trust the meritorious actors of the other parts will forgive what I say with pain and in the strictest sense of my duty—your opponent's part of Antonio was not understood by the audience—as it was rendered on Friday evening—still less the brightly opponent part of Bassanio—and though Miss Terry's Portia has obtained so much applause, it greatly surprises me that you have not taught her a grander reading of the part. Portia is chiefly great in her majestic humility (the main sign of her splendid intellect) and—to take only one instance of what I do not doubt to be misinterpretation—the speech, "You see me Lord Bassanio . . .", she would, I am certain, produce its true effect on the audience only if spoken with at least half a dozen yards between her and Bassanio—and with her eyes on the ground through most of the lines.

I am going to look carefully through your reading of the play—but as a painter, I protest against the loss of Arragon. It is like pulling a leaf from a trefoil. I again entreat your patience with me and your trust in my sincere sympathy and admiration.

Believe me, my dear Sir, faithfully and respectfully yours,

J. Ruskin.'

MR. JOHN RUSKIN

CRITICISES MR. HENRY IRVING.

But it was too late. His pretty little speech had found its way into the pages of *The Theatre*, a magazine devoted to 'drama, music and the fine arts', which was edited by Clement Scott. Ruskin was very much put out at having his dressing-room civilities reported as his considered judgment—especially when they were totally at variance with his published opinion. He was not in good health, so he invited a third party, Mr. Laister, to present his views to Irving. Laister wrote to Irving as follows:

> 52 *Lavender Grove*,
> *Dalston, E.*
> *February 9th*, 1880.

'Dear Sir,

Mr. Ruskin writes me on the subject of a paragraph which appeared in *Theatre* magazine for January reporting him to have spoken to you of your representation of Shylock as "noble, tender and true".

As I have not the honour of your personal acquaintance I shall perhaps best further his object if I quote from his letter the passages following:

"I have no doubt that whatever Mr. Irving has stated that I said, I *did* say. But in personal address to an artist to whom one is introduced for the first time, one does not usually say all that may be in one's mind: and if expressions limited, if not even exaggerated by courtesy, be afterwards quoted as a total and carefully expressed criticism, the general reader will be—or may be—easily misled. I did and do much admire Mr. Irving's own acting as Shylock: but I entirely dissent (and indignantly as well as entirely) from his general reading and treatment of the play."

After some general animadversions on modern interpretations of great authors, Mr. Ruskin then informs me that:

"So far as I could in kindness venture I expressed my feelings to this effect in a letter which I wrote to Mr. Irving on the day after I saw the play; and I should be sincerely obliged to him under existing circumstances if he would publish *the whole* of that letter."

You will, I imagine, have no objection to comply with this request. Although giving me directions what to do if the letter is *not* obtainable, my revered correspondent says nothing as to where he would like it printed; he probably leaves that to your choice. It is unnecessary for me to explain at length what are the "existing circumstances" that have led to this request being made. You are probably aware that the Play in question, as revived, has given rise to a vast deal of public teaching, the moral of which Mr. Ruskin and others greatly deplore; and he naturally desires to correct any wrong impression which the unqualified publication of the paragraph in *Theatre* might create.'

Irving turned to Pollock for advice, who drafted the following reply:

'Dear Sir,

I beg to acknowledge the receipt of your letter to me of the 8th of February.

I am at a loss to know in what character you address me, and to understand why Mr. Ruskin, from whose letter to yourself you have made quotations, does not write to me in person, if he has any communication to make to me.

I must, therefore, in all courtesy, decline to enter into correspondence with a stranger and will only add that I am in no way responsible for the paragraph in the *Theatre* magazine, to which attention is called at the commencement of your letter.

I am,
Yours faithfully,
Henry Irving.'

Mr. Laister, having pleaded Ruskin's ill health as an excuse for this triangular correspondence, reminded Irving that all Ruskin asked was a simple yes or no to his request. In conclusion he wrote:

'. . . Pray allow me also to repeat on my own account that the verbal truth of the paragraph in *Theatre* is not disputed by Mr. Ruskin; but that its meaning is—especially in view of the fact that he had written to you quite fully *before* that paragraph appeared. Mr. Ruskin has not said that you are responsible for what appears in *Theatre*—but as he did not supply the paragraph himself he may infer, perhaps, that you did. Further, *if* Mr. Ruskin is under the impression that you are (in one sense) responsible for *Theatre*, he shares it with other people, both private and professional. . . .'

Finally, Ruskin, through Laister, sent to *The Theatre* a recapitulation of his letter to Irving, omitting his criticisms of the rest of the cast, which, in due course, Clement Scott published.

Ruskin's suspicion that Irving was in some way connected with *The Theatre* was not entirely unfounded. Irving, in fact, had been the proprietor of the magazine up to a few weeks before this correspondence. *The Theatre* was originally published as a folio weekly in January 1877. Irving acquired it in August 1878, after which, with reduced format, it was published monthly. As sole proprietor, Irving used it, no doubt, to further his interests and to air his views, until December 1879 when, since it had turned out to be a most unprofitable venture, he handed it over to Clement Scott at a valuation of £1,000, which was never paid, and for a quarter share in future profits, which never materialized. Ten years later, when Clement Scott asked Irving's permission to sell the paper, he wrote:

> Lyceum Theatre.
> October 8th, 1889

'Dear Clement,

I wrote to you I think some time ago—saying that so far as I was concerned you were quite at liberty to get what you could for *The Theatre*—giving up entirely any share that I might have had in it. If you cared I would endorse so much on the deed, if you thought it was necessary. I am glad you are getting something for it. We are all losers by it, I fear. Before I made it over to you I paid £300 to leave it quite clear—and before then—well—I forget, thank God.

> Ever yours,
> H. Irving.'

In acquiring *The Theatre* Irving was pursuing a carefully calculated policy regarding the press which, for some time, he had prosecuted with vigour. When he came to London, dramatic criticism had been at its lowest ebb. It was regarded as the least reputable of journalistic activities. Nearly every dramatic critic was a successful or frustrated playwright. Notices, on the whole, were written in terms either of indiscriminating praise by those who hoped for or enjoyed the favour of theatrical managers, or of scurrilous vituperation by those whom the managers had failed to placate with promises of the purchase of options on their plays. Nearly all were corrupted, if not by the bribe direct, from puff-seeking actors or managers, by too intimate association and traffic with the theatrical profession which coloured their criticism with the pale cast of self-interest. At its best, dramatic criticism was, for the most part, highly coloured reporting; in general it was apathetic to the conditions into which English drama and acting had fallen. Oxenford of *The Times*, who was a prolific playwright and wrote with boyish enthusiasm of nearly everything he saw, was discouraged by Delane, his editor, from enlarging upon the merits or otherwise of any particular actor or actress. Irving had been perfectly instructed by Bateman in the art of handling the more venal sections of the press and, as has been seen in the case of *The Fashionable Tragedian*, was capable of holding his own with those who attacked him out of personal spite or in sincere belief that they were the champions of reform. While studying carefully the criticism of the few whose opinion he valued and respected, in the main he regarded critics and paragraphists with indifference or contempt. He looked upon himself as the public's humble servant. If he was able to win their support and approval without lowering the high standard which he had set himself, he accepted their verdict as that alone worthy of consideration. Directly his popularity with the public was beyond doubt, he exploited with cynical amusement the venality of the press in furthering his aims and in publicising his activities, while striking ruthlessly at those journalists who, by the vulgar or scandalous nature of their comments, undermined his conception of the dignity of the actor's profession.

In time, therefore, he came to divide critics into three categories—the respected and incorruptible, such as Edward Russell, Alfred Watson of the *Standard* and Joseph Knight, whose integrity and love of the theatre was beyond dispute, and with whom he could be on terms of intimate friendship without being suspected of any ulterior motive; the corruptible, who by flattery, entertainment or the purchase of options on their unactable plays could be counted upon to provide him with a measure of dignified publicity and to act as mercenaries in his battles with the third but waning group of those who, impervious to his magnetism or jealous of his success, were ever ready to heave a brick through the windows of the noble edifice which he was labouring to build. Occasionally, while facing and holding at bay professional criticism, he would receive sharp attacks in the rear from Shakespearian scholars, to meet whom, he wrote to Mrs. James, 'I must be in robust health'. These, and members of the clergy who incurred his displeasure, he usually rebuked in the course of some public address. His manipulation of the venal was discreet and urbane; his retaliation to attack was ruthless and persistent. When he bought *The Theatre*, though his activities at the Lyceum, in the lecture hall or on the public platform were fully recorded in its pages, a certain amount of mildly adverse criticism was included in its articles on him which disguised his direct interest in the paper. In handing it over to Clement Scott he virtually made him a gift of the £1,000 which he himself had paid for it, and a potential course of income, retaining in exchange a medium for the expression of his own views and the assurance of favourable comment on himself by Scott in the other spheres in which he wielded the pen of the critic and the columnist. Scott was typical of the theatrical journalist of the early seventies. His industry was tremendous, his discrimination was not profound and his impartiality was open to doubt. His life was entirely devoted to the theatre, but, not contented with the space which the *Daily Telegraph* allowed him to fill with picturesque criticism, he dissipated his energies and to some extent laid himself open to charges of venality in his columns of theatrical gossip elsewhere. He was immensely vain, and on one accasion when Lord Salisbury at the height of his popularity entered the Lyceum and was applauded by the audience, he bowed acknowledgment of what he thought was a tribute to himself. He believed himself to be, and to some extent undoubtedly was, a great power in the world of the theatre. His daily postbag was filled with importunities for favourable mention from actors and managers. Undoubtedly he did something to raise the standard of dramatic criticism but he was the first to fall foul of the younger generation of critics who in 1880 were beginning to make their appearance.

In 1878 William Archer, the forerunner of the new school, arrived in London where he joined the staff of *Figaro*. There he took over the duties of dramatic critic which up till then had been fulfilled by Clement Scott. He wrote over Scott's pseudonym, 'Almaviva', but it must have been apparent to the readers of *Figaro* that Almaviva had undergone a remarkable tergiversation. Archer approached his task with an austerity which surprised his colleagues and those in the world of the theatre who thought, with some justification, that they had got the measure of the press. He had no play in his pocket and he avoided deliberately any social contact with the targets of his criticism. He had no axe to grind but he wielded a bludgeon with which he beat unmercifully those whom he thought were obstructing the progress of the higher drama. The bludgeon was Henrik Ibsen, for whose early plays he was seeking vainly a publisher, let alone a producer, in London. He wrote wittily and fearlessly. Like Henry James, he refused to take the Lyceum as seriously as most of his contemporaries seemed to do and as, indeed, it certainly took itself. Perhaps the knowledge of his partnership in *The Fashionable Tragedian* preceded him to London and the customary invitation to sup with Irving in the Beefsteak Room was withheld. If he had received it, he would certainly have refused it. Irving was soon to feel the sting of this new species of gadfly which he could neither lure with honey nor swat with any of the whisks at his disposal. But for the time being Archer was a voice in the wilderness and his paper a fairly obscure one.

In the autumn of 1878 Samuel Phelps, at the age of seventy-four, had collapsed while playing Cardinal Wolsey at the Imperial Theatre and had died a few weeks later. Shortly after the opening of *The*

Irving as Shylock

"How like a fawning
publican he looks"!

Shylock

Henry Irving: 1889:

Irving as Shylock

Merchant of Venice Irving heard that William Belford, a veteran actor of Phelps' old Sadler's Wells company, had fallen on evil days. With the help of Bancroft, Toole and Hare, he organized a benefit performance for Belford at the Lyceum on the afternoon of December 10th. For the occasion he revived *Two Roses*. Opinions were divided as to whether his Digby Grant had matured or deteriorated with age, though it was rash to draw conclusions from a hastily prepared production of this kind. Even Irving must have been disconcerted when, during the first act, he lost half his moustache and had hastily to remove the other half to restore the balance. Toole and Mrs. Bancroft romped through *The Trial of Pickwick* with the help of many leading actors. Ellen Terry read a eulogy of Belford, written by Clement Scott, which was marred only by an unfortunate reference to the old actor's nocturnal habits. But, if there was any offence to him in the affair, it was soon forgotten when Irving announced that Belford would benefit to the tune of £1,100—enough, as it turned out, to keep him in comparative affluence for the remaining two years of his life. No doubt Irving felt that he had done something to redeem the debt which he owed to those who had made so magical an impression upon him when he was a boy and had kindled the ambition which he had gone so far in fulfilling.

Towards the end of January, some three hundred of Irving's friends received an invitation requesting the pleasure of their company 'At supper in the Theatre at Half past Eleven O'clock on the Evening of Saturday, February the Fourteenth, 1880, to commemorate the One Hundredth representation of *The Merchant of Venice*'. The quality and variety of those who accepted this invitation proved how fast and how far the shy young actor, who had been so ill-at-ease at Mrs. Sartoris's party, had travelled in ten years. The greater part of the company was made up of actors with whom he had worked since he came to London and of companions of his early provincial days. Painters, musicians, dramatists and critics were leavened with a sprinkling of judges, admirals and Members of Parliament, to say nothing of Labby, who represented so many trades and talents. Taking precedence in the role of guests, which sounded like the *dramatis personae* of a Shakesperian tragedy, were the Earls of Dunraven, Fife and Onslow, while the youngest but by no means the least conspicuous guest was an exquisite young graduate of Oxford who for the first time was shedding his effulgence on a London season—Oscar Wilde. Soon after the curtain fell on *The Merchant of Venice* the guests began to assemble in the Beefsteak Room. Here they were received by Irving and Ellen

Terry, who entertained them for a few minutes while, on the stage, Belmont was miraculously transformed into a great scarlet and white pavilion lit by two glittering chandeliers. A banner stretched around the tented walls bore in crimson letters the legend: 'At first and last a hearty welcome'. In no time at all Mr. Gunter's magicians had set out the supper tables and were poised in the wings with a hot five-course supper and cool magnums of Heidsieck 1874. As the guests came down upon the stage and gasped at this transformation they were handed copies of the play bound in vellum and ornamented with gold.

Irving took his place at the head of his table; he was flanked by Lord Londesborough on his left and Lord Houghton on his right. The latter, at Pollock's suggestion, had agreed to propose Irving's health—a seemingly safe choice, for he was renowned as an after-dinner speaker, was himself a minor poet and a dilettante of wide if, uncertain, tastes. Lord Londesborough had every right to his place of honour, for only recently he had demonstrated his enthusiasm for the drama by losing nearly a hundred thousand pounds in backing Boucicault's extraordinary and spectacular musical confection, *Babil and Bijou*, at Covent Garden—his generous subsidies sustaining for a hundred and sixty nights a fiasco which otherwise would have perished within a week. Nothing was spared to promote an atmosphere of genial harmony. An invisible quintet played during supper. When Irving proposed the Queen's health the voices of concealed choir boys sang the National Anthem. The only man who, apparently, was not moved by this concord of sweet sounds was Lord Houghton, whose affections, if not dark as Erebus, were curiously at variance with the atmosphere that these harmonies were designed to promote. When his lordship rose to speak, Irving and his friends no doubt resigned themselves to hearing the brief and conventional tributes for which the occasion called. But, having declared that it was 'a convivial and private meeting', the speaker indulged in a series of ponderous and sarcastic witticisms which, for the most part, were aimed at his host and at many of his fellow guests. Apparently forgetting the century they were celebrating, he deplored the tendency of actors and managers of the day to foster long runs. Having commended actors as a body on the recent improvement in their manners, he assured them that if this was maintained 'families of condition were ready to allow their sons, after a university education, to enter the dramatic profession'. A shudder of embarrassment ran round the tables and the voices of a few bold spirits were raised in protest at this inept patronage. Undeterred and with genial self-assurance, Lord Houghton went on to chide Irving for following the example of some contemporary historians in white-washing and rehabilitating the established villains of the drama, protesting that he for one could not accept Shylock as 'a gentleman of the Hebrew race with the manners of a Rothschild'. Admitting finally that 'there was one character Irving would never pervert and that was his own', he ended by praising him for his wise and considerate management of his theatre and rather belatedly assured his fellow-guests that their grandchildren 'would be proud to find that their progenitors'had been at the Lyceum that night'.

While there were those who found Lord Houghton's speech a welcome change from the usual adulatory platitudes, most of the company did not disguise their irritation with the facetious style and deprecatory tone of his remarks. When he proposed Irving's health, they rose to their feet and with the warmth of their response made it clear that they dissociated themselves from his maladroit address. Though all this had for a moment cast a shadow over the festivities, it enabled Irving to reveal himself to his friends in an altogether new and unexpected light. Taken completely unawares and with any speech he may have prepared rendered useless by the terms in which his health had been proposed, he retaliated for half an hour with a speech which was remarkable for its spontaneity, its good sense and good humour—a performance which surprised those present who had suspected that in the preparation of his speeches and lectures Irving depended on the help of literary hacks. Lord Houghton's remarks, he said, had suggested to him an idea for a new play, *The After-Life of Shylock*, in which even greater sympathy would be solicited for the Jew when he was discovered peddling lemons at Belmont. He vigorously defended his own interpretation of the part, adding that, though people had come from all over the world to see it and expressed their satisfaction with it, only Germans seemed to share Lord Houghton's dislike for it. After justifying his policy of long runs, he concluded: 'Looking round the tables I see men of all stations and of all creeds. Knowing that they are allied by the ties of art and friendship I believe that Shakespeare himself, if he could be present, would rejoice to think that the seed he had sown broadcast three centuries ago had borne such good fruit and that the work which he had done for the sake of art brought fortune in its wake. I cannot say more than by repeating in conclusion his beautiful words:

> '*I count myself in nothing else so happy*
> *As in a soul rememb'ring my good friends.*'

Irving's lively response was greeted with delighted cheers. There were no more speeches. The company broke up into small groups and it was dawn before those who lingered with their host in the Beefsteak Room left the theatre. The evening had been a daring experiment and was certainly the first of its kind in English theatrical history. Any momentary doubts that Irving may have had as to the wisdom of such lavish celebration were dispelled by a leader in the *Daily Telegraph* devoted to the occasion. After amiably disputing most of Lord Houghton's contentions, it continued:

'. . . It is because Mr. Irving is a standing example of care, solicitude and earnest devotion to his art; it is because his success is not based upon the mere passing breath of popular favour, but upon a scholarly style that commends itself to his educated countrymen; it is because when he fails he accepts gracefully the inevitable, and when he succeeds he only pushes forward to stronger and bolder endeavour that his name and fame have grown into public estimation, and that he has been advanced to his distinguished opinion by the unanimous suffrages of his brother artists. It is no ambition to be original, or striking, or eccentric, or a fashionable actor, as it is termed, that called down upon the Lyceum stage the cheers of hundreds of men devoted to literature and art, a large proportion of whom were drawn from the profession which Mr. Irving, by his modesty and his great gifts, has so conspicuously adorned. It is easier to discriminate between the false and the true; and no better chance of doing so can be secured than once more to visit the theatre where Shakespeare has been re-established. It is among the merits of Mr. Irving that he never takes up a part, studies it, succeeds, and lays it down again. He is always studying and ever improving. No one with the power of thought ever saw his *Hamlet* again and again without deriving fresh inspiration and delight, some new idea, and some closer intimacy with the actor's mental process. It is the same in a lesser degree with the Shylock as is the case with all scholars, there is a fascination in the style apart from the actual impression, and as the scenes of Shylock's life pass before the audience one sees more than acting as it is vulgarly known—it is the bearing of an intelligent mind upon a human creation.'

The Merchant of Venice ran for seven months, a record without precedent in the annals of the stage. Towards the end of May Irving announced that for Ellen Terry's benefit he proposed to cut out the last act and in its place put on a new version of *King Rene's Daughter* which had been prepared by Wills and had been renamed *Iolanthe*. Irving was not ideally suited for the part of the romantic Count

Tristan. His purpose in mounting the play, which he did handsomely, was to give Ellen Terry the opportunity of portraying the blind girl whose sight is miraculously restored. F. J. Furnivall, founder of the Shakespearian Society, who was always spoiling for a fight and was at that time having a heated altercation with Swinburne over the conduct of that society, descended on Irving in wrathful indignation:

> 3 *St. George's Sq.,*
> *Primrose Hill,*
> *London N.W.*
> *May 10th,* 1880.

'Dear Mr. Irving,

  I hear with profound regret that *you* are going to have The Merchant played without its fifth act, as a *lever de rideau* to *Iolanthe. Et tu Brute.* Against this damnable barbarism I enter my protest to you first and shall with other Shakespeare men make a public one as soon as I can. May you and your accomplices in this treason, this crime of *lèse-majesté* soon repent and come to a better mind.

> In sorrow and in anger,
> Yours sincerely,
> F. J. Furnivall.'

Irving, who might have been pardoned for thinking that he had earned the gratitude of Shakespearian scholars for the restoration of the play to public favour, protested mildly against the violence of Furnivall's attacks in the press and thereafter ignored them. *Iolanthe* was well received and Ellen Terry much praised for the exquisite tenderness of her performance. It was played with the four acts of *The Merchant of Venice* for the rest of the run and became a very popular feature of the Lyceum repertory. The season ended on July 31st. In the course of it 330,000 people had visited the Lyceum. Receipts had amounted to £59,000 against an expenditure of £49,000, which included the production costs of *The Merchant of Venice* and *Iolanthe*. In such a balance sheet the £600 which had been spent on the famous supper appeared to represent a modest fling. In his farewell speech Irving announced for the coming season, which he would open with *The Corsican Brothers*, a new play by Tennyson, hinting once more at Wills's *Rienzi* and at a production of *Coriolanus* designed by Alma Tadema. He reassured his audience that in spite of innumerable attempts by others to lure her away, he was fortunate enough to have retained the services of Miss Ellen Terry.

The company dispersed. Ellen Terry left for her tour in the provinces with Charles Kelly. Irving and Stoker went for a short holiday to Southsea. On the first day, seeking refuge from the crowds that accosted him wherever he went, Irving took Stoker for a sail in a small boat. The boatman was deaf and neither he nor his passengers heeded the shouting and gesticulating of people on the beach as they headed out to sea; it was assumed to be a further demonstration of the actor's popularity. When they were half a mile from the shore there was a violent explosion as a great column of water rose from the sea so close to them that the boat was nearly overturned by the water which seemed to boil around them. The boatman was frightened into blasphemy. Stoker maintained a studied calm. Irving, readjusting his eyeglasses which had been shaken off his nose by the explosion, regarded with interest the dead fish which floated on the surface in shoals. It appeared that they had sailed into a minefield which was a feature of naval manœuvres which were in progress. Another mine went off, though not as near to them as the first. The boatman implored them to return. Irving lit a cigar. 'Why should we come away?' he asked. 'We are, I take it, about as safe as we can be. The mines here have been fired and we don't know where the others are. Let us stay where we are and enjoy ourselves.' So, for the rest of an afternoon punctuated by the explosion of mines and the thunder of cannon, they lay rolling off Fort Monckton which was being furiously engaged by the guns of H.M.S. *Glatton*. During a lull in the operations they returned to Southsea and later enjoyed watching a spectacular searchlight attack from the esplanade. Having had their baptism of fire, they felt a conscious superiority over the other onlookers. They learned, with some satisfaction, that the mines which had so nearly destroyed them were of the newest pattern, fired remotely by electricity. Britannia no doubt would have wept if with her latest contrivance for ruling the waves she had drowned her favourite tragedian.

CHAPTER XXI

3rd Lyceum Season : Synorix, Iago, Othello

———⊷⊶⊷———

I

'NOTICE/LYCEUM THEATRE. MR. IRVING wishes to announce to the Public that the written applications for booked places for the First Representation of THE CORSICAN BROTHERS so far exceeds the holding capacity of the Theatre that he has been obliged to allot all seats available according to priority of application. The only seats not to be secured by booking for this night are in the Amphitheatre....'

This advertisement, which appeared in the daily press at the beginning of September, indicated that the public supported Irving's policy of alternating Shakespeare with popular melodrama. About the same time, Ruskin, in an address to the Society for Dramatic Reform (the forerunners of an infinity of theatrical busybodies) had said: ' . . . the idea of making money by a theatre and making it educational at the same time, is utterly to be got out of people's heads. You don't make money out of a ship of the line, nor should you out of a church, nor should you out of a college, nor should you out of a theatre.' This was not Irving's view. He considered that the first duty of an actor manager was to make his theatre pay and thereby to win liberty of action to pursue whatever policy he chose. Until the State endowed a National Theatre, Wills, Boucicault and Charles Reade would have to subsidize his experiments in higher drama. Although most of his Shakespearian productions so far had been phenomenally successful, he was not tempted to abandon this policy. No doubt he chose *The Corsican Brothers* (a play which Henry James dismissed as hackneyed and preposterous) because it offered him considerable scope as a producer and because its lack of any part of female interest made it a good stop-gap until Ellen Terry returned to the

Lyceum at the end of the year. The play was an old favourite with
the public; indeed for a quarter of a century, it had been acted to death.
Their eagerness to see him in it was a measure of his hold over them.

In 1660 twin brothers were born into the Tremayne family who lived
near Tavistock. These twins were so attuned in spirit that, however
widely separated, each was instantly aware of how well or ill the other
was faring. Their idiosyncrasy was widely reported in their lifetime;
they perished together at the siege of Newhaven. The fame of their
telepathic accord reached the ears of Alexander Dumas who, trans-
planting the background from Devon to Corsica, made them the heroes
of a short novel. The novel was published in Paris in 1850 and was
dramatised in the same year, Fechter appearing at the Théâtre Histori-
que in the dual role of Louis and Fabien dei Franchi. Boucicault
hastened to adapt it for Charles Kean in whose repertory it became one
of the most popular and profitable pieces. Later Fechter played it in
London but failed to shake the public's allegiance to Kean. Irving used
Kean's version but, whereas the latter had portrayed the brothers as
robust and hot-headed Latins, he invested them with something of the
dreamy introspection of Hamlet—a reasonable conception when the
plot of the play centred round a spectre and a duel. The play had little
to recommend it but its opportunities for the display of rich and imaginative scenic effects—indeed Kean went so far in this respect that a critic
acclaimed him not only as the upholder but the upholsterer of English
drama. Its principal scenes—the Villa dei Franchi, the Opera House in
Paris and a snow-covered forest glade—have been familiar to generations of toy theatre lovers; for it was one of Pollock of Hoxton's great
masterpieces and those who have mounted and cut out his enchanting
sheets and have introduced the ghost of the murdered Louis through a
diminutive trap-door, can claim to have a very fair idea of Irving's
production at the Lyceum.

The third season opened on September 18th. A precedent was
created by presenting, as a curtain raiser to the revival, a new one-act
play by Pinero, *Bygones*, in which the author again took a leading part.
Few critics bothered to comment on the new play but those who did,
praised it. Nor, for Pinero, was this the end of the evening's glory.
Irving had conceived a novel and effective entrance for himself in the
first act of *The Corsican Brothers*. The scene was the interior of the Villa
dei Franchi. By taking in the scene dock, the depth of the Lyceum
stage was increased to more than seventy feet which Hawes Craven had
filled ingeniously with a perspective of vine-covered trellis work leading
to a wicket gate beyond which was seen a panorama of Corsican

mountains. Thus Irving from this distance was able to make a long approach to the stage to the accompaniment of the applause which inevitably greeted his first appearance. Inexplicably, nobody had noticed that Pinero, in a minor role, used the same entrance earlier in the scene or that his dress at a distance suggested a character of some importance. Probably Pinero was fully alive to the possibilities; if so, he had every reason to keep them to himself. In the event, as soon as he hove in sight, the audience took him for their hero and accorded him an ovation which he was able to savour fully as he traversed, slowly to be sure and with perhaps a hint of his Chief's gait, the seventy feet which brought him to the stage and his audience to the recognition of their mistake. This did not, however, temper the warmth of their reception of Irving when he did appear or of the heavy tableau curtains which had been introduced in place of the old rolling act drop. These were of crimson plush and were said to have caused a wail of lament to go up from the footmen of London who calculated that the thousand yards of material which had gone to their making would have provided breeches for five hundred flunkeys. The critics treated the whole affair as an elaborate prelude to a season of better things; they praised the production though they were critical of the costumes. Irving, striving to introduce a new note, had clothed the play in the style and fashion of the D'Orsay epoch, an innovation which was condemned as grotesque and unflattering to the actors. Twenty years later, when the same dresses were used for a revival, Irving was commended, on this account, for his good taste and originality. The notices of his own performance were perfunctory; on the whole he was judged to be too solemn and inert—in fact, too middle-aged to be convincing as a hardy Corsican mountaineer. One critic went so far as to say that as Louis he was better in the spirit than in the flesh. The public, however, were not deterred by these qualifications. *The Corsican Brothers* ran until the end of the year, by which time it had played to a clear profit of £5,000—enough to justify its withdrawal in favour of a nobler work from the pen of the Poet Laureate in which, it was hoped, even Ruskin would discover educational properties.

The Lyceum company had been strengthened and enlived by the engagement of a young actor, William Terriss, who stayed to be Irving's foil for many years. Labby, who often castigated Irving for the weakness of his supporting cast, welcomed the newcomer and complimented him on his performance as the villain, M. de Chateau Renaud. Terriss was naturally cast in the heroic mould. He was known by his friends as Breezy Bill and his early life had been as adventurous as that of any of the heroes of melodrama for which he became famous. His real name was Lewin. He was the son of a barrister who bore a remarkable likeness to Byron; his uncle was George Grote, the Greek historian. He inherited his father's good looks but not his uncle's brains; by turning the former to good account he was never troubled unduly by his deficiency in the latter. His father died when he was three years old and thereafter he stubbornly frustrated any attempt by his guardians to educate him or to start him on a career. He ran away from school, and later, when he was directed into the merchant service, he ran away from sea. Sailing from London in a ship bound for the East, he accompanied it no further than Portsmouth, where a friendly boatman put him ashore. As will be seen, lack of courage was not the cause of these evasions; he seemed to have an incorrigible aversion to committing himself to any permanent form of employment. Drifting on to the stage by way of amateur theatricals, his good looks and self-assurance soon won him an engagement with the Bancrofts at the Prince of Wales's Theatre. He stayed with them only long enough to find a wife with whom he determined to seek his fortune in the Falkland Islands. After leaving Montevideo on the last stage of the voyage, their ship became involved in a collision in the South Atlantic. With all the vigour of poor Gustavus Brooke, and fortunately with happier results, Terriss manned the pumps and, rallying the half hearted crew by his show of courage and cheerful optimism, he was to some extent responsible for the safe arrival of their ship at the Falkland Islands. Here he settled for a time, but in 1871 he and his wife returned to England, perhaps for the sake of their little daughter Ellaline. After playing in a series of melodramas at Drury Lane, in 1878 he joined Hare at the Royal Court Theatre, where he made an immediate success by playing Squire Thornhill to Ellen Terry's Olivia. No doubt she persuaded Irving to engage him for the Lyceum. There were those who may well have thought that his engagement might be a short one. During the dress rehearsal of *The Corsican Brothers*, while fighting a duel with Irving, he noticed that the limelight man was loyally holding the Chief in its beam while he and the rest of the stage were in comparative darkness. Putting up his sword, he said: 'Don't you think, Guv'nor, a few rays of the moon might fall on me—it shines equally, ye know, on the just and the unjust.' Those who stood in awe of Irving waited not for moonbeams but for a thunderbolt to fall upon the presumptuous young actor, but Irving, who detested the sycophants who surrounded inevitably an autocrat like himself, was amused by Terriss's unintimidated self-assertion. He ordered the moonlight to be spread impartially on them both and, thereafter, treated Breezy Bill with a friendly toleration that few of the younger members of the company were privileged to enjoy.

Another newcomer to the stage of the Lyceum was Mr. Gladstone, who paid the first of his many visits behind the scenes during the run of *The Corsican Brothers*. The scene in the foyer of the Opera House was simply but effectively contrived. Tiers of boxes were suggested by painted flats pierced with openings which ran up and down stage; to bring these to life, well-dressed supers, precariously perched on rostrums behind these flats, leaned nonchalantly on the plush ledges of the boxes or peeped from behind half-drawn curtains. Gladstone, who showed intense interest in all he saw, was told that, if he wished, he could sit in one of these boxes from which, provided that he kept out of sight behind the curtains, he could watch the scene at close quarters. For a time he sat there, invisible to the audience and enchanted with the clowns and tumblers who capered about among the masked dancers. But a sudden burst of clapping proved too much for the politician, whose reactions, after all, are similar to those of the actor. Instinctively he leaned forward. The audience, seeing the unmistakable features of the Chancellor of the Exchequer peering at them from the stage, shouted, 'Bravo, Gladstone!' and redoubled their applause. Though Irving never again had the services of so illustrious a super, Gladstone became such a regular visitor behind the scenes that a special seat was provided for him in the prompt corner where, when deafness came upon him, he could follow the plays more easily. Lord Beaconsfield, now a frail old man, came to the Lyceum to see *The Corsican Brothers*. He and his friend Corry, upon whose arm he was leaning, met Stoker in the foyer as they were leaving after the performance. 'Do you think,' asked Corry, 'we could have supper somewhere and ask some of the Coryphées to join us, as we used to do in Paris in the fifties?'

Stoker hastened to explain that the ballet dancers at the Lyceum would be deeply shocked at such a suggestion and that Loveday had been driven frantic in trying to persuade them to overcome their suburban primness in the abandon of a *bal masqué*. Irving was naturally more attracted to Disraeli than to Gladstone. But the serious-minded Liberal was a more fruitful missionary field for the propagation of the gospel of higher drama and the dignity of the acting profession. The Conservatives would be slow to change their view of the theatre as an Arcadia populated with captivating and warm-hearted nymphs who could be lured into 'cabinets particuliers' where their slippers, brimming with champagne, could be raised to the toast of Love, Life and Laughter.

Meanwhile Tennyson's play, *The Cup*, was in rehearsal. In 1879 he had finished *Becket* and had asked Irving to produce it. Irving, though he appreciated at once that the play had great dramatic possibilities and contained an excellent part for himself, declined it. 'He said,' wrote Tennyson, 'that it was magnificent, but it would cost him £3,000 to mount it and he couldn't afford the risk. If well put on the stage it would run for a time and it would bring me credit—but it wouldn't pay.' This excuse, which seemed to satisfy Tennyson, disguised Irving's true and far-sighted intention. The play, though it contained some admirable speeches and some of the poet's best verse, was hopelessly lacking in dramatic construction. Drastic surgery would be necessary to make it fit for the stage. Irving doubted if even he could persuade Tennyson to agree to such radical changes, particularly as Spedding, Browning and George Eliot, who had read it, encouraged the poet to have an exaggerated belief in his skill as a dramatist. Not wishing, however, to lose Tennyson's goodwill or his option on *Becket*, he invited him to write a new and shorter play for the Lyceum.

Tennyson found in Plutarch a story which suited his purpose. In the third century Synorix, a Galatian tyrant, coveting Camma, the stubbornly faithful wife of one of his nobles, orders the assassination of her husband. The widow takes refuge in the temple of Artemis, where she continues to resist the importunities of Synorix. Feigning a willingness to yield, Camma insists that first he must make a libation to the Gods. As a priestess, she comes before the altar with a cup of poisoned wine. Drinking half of it herself, she gives the rest to her would-be seducer. They die together, but not before she has declaimed a prayer of thanksgiving to the Gods for allowing her to avenge her husband. As a plot it was thin and a little trite; nor was it original, for a few years earlier the stately Madame Ristori had played Camma with great success in a play on the same theme by Montanelli. It did, however, lend itself to effective production, and with Ellen Terry as Camma, Terriss as the husband, and Irving as the voluptuous tyrant, it provided them all with good parts.

Early in December, Tennyson gave a reading of the play. His audience consisted of his friend Knowles, the editor of the *Nineteenth Century* and the architect of his house at Aldworth, his son Hallam, Terriss, Ellen Terry and Irving, who sat with Ellen's daughter Edie on his knee, and Charlie, his terrier, at his feet. 'Tennyson, like most poets,' wrote Ellen Terry, 'read in a monotone, rumbling on a low note.

. . . For the women's parts he changed his voice suddenly and climbed up into a key he could not sustain.' This appealed to the irrepressible Edie as a great joke which, to her reproving mother's dismay, Irving seemed to share. The play was too short. Irving suggested alterations and additions to which Tennyson amiably agreed. Hallam acted as mediator. 'Here are all the alterations,' he later wrote to Irving, 'I think them great improvements. Your enthusiasm is infectious and has made us happy. We are grateful for your trouble . . . my father will alter anything—or pray omit any of the lines which you think superfluous. Every amendment has been a real amendment—so please ask for more amendments if you wish for any.' It was a pity that the play was not more substantial, for in its presentation Irving, as a producer, excelled himself. He revelled in the direction of crowd movements and in the devising of the ritual worship of Diana. Ellen Terry, whose nature was devoid of resentment, wrote on Irving's behalf to Godwin asking him to design the dresses and properties and to advise generally on the decoration of the play. Between them Irving, Knowles and Hawes Craven recreated a temple of Artemis. Hawes Craven was suffering from the effects of an accident so the other scenes were entrusted to a young painter, Telbin, whose poetic vision and frank adherence to the schools of Claude and Turner made him the ideal executant of Irving's imaginative conceptions.

The dress rehearsal was on Christmas Eve. Alfred Watson was invited to attend it, a privilege rarely granted to a layman. 'I had supped with Irving,' he wrote, 'a few nights before, and had driven home to his chambers in Grafton Street, he being full of the approaching production, and just before the cab stopped he had begun the recital of one of his speeches. We came to his door, and he continued, not observing that we were at a standstill. The cabman lifted the trap and looked down, apparently desiring to intimate that we had arrived; but Irving did not heed. Presently the trap was raised again, this time the driver keeping it open and listening. I could not help smiling, for he must have thought that his fare was saying extraordinary things, as indeed he was, but we had quite a long sitting before Irving descended, and he kindly asked me if I'd care to see the last rehearsal. He had determined to admit no-one but was good enough to say he would make an exception if I would sit behind the curtain of a box so that my presence might not be detected. *The Cup* was played to the empty house without a pause or correction of any kind, precisely as if spectators had been present, except for the absence of applause and the stir of the audience. From first to last there was no pause, criticism, correction or comment. It was a remarkable experience. When it was all over I found that Toole had been sitting by himself in a box opposite to me, but I had not the least idea of this until we met in Irving's room when the curtain had finally fallen.'

The Cup opened on January 3rd. In spite of all the artistry and money (the production cost £2,370) that had been lavished upon it, it played for so short a time that *The Corsican Brothers* had to be kept in the bill. Criticism of the play was almost disarmed by the popularity and distinction of those who had collaborated in its presentation. That its author was the Poet Laureate and that it was common knowledge that Godwin had had a hand in its preparation ensured the respect of the intellectuals, the admiration of the aesthetes and the discomfiture of the Philistines. Yet in the columns of unstinted praise which was accorded to the actors and scene painters it was possible to detect a note of regret that Tennyson had not written a better and more coherent play. Though the author was disappointed in Irving's Synorix, the critics seemed to be satisfied that he had made the most of the part. Ellen Terry said that as he 'was not able to look like the full-blooded Roman such as we see in long lines in marble at the British Museum, he conceived his own type of the blend of Roman intellect and sensuality with barbarian cruelty and lust. With a pale, pale face, bright red hair, gold armour and a tiger skin, a diabolical expression and very thin crimson lips, Henry looked handsome and sickening at the same time. Trickery was written across his forehead'. Labby, the standard-bearer of the Philistines who apparently enjoyed the evening thoroughly and with great difficulty curbed his enthusiasm, in *Truth* playfully complimented Irving on his showmanship:

'I am inclined to consider Mr. Irving a very practical, hard-headed man of business. He is one of those quiet people who appear to be led, but who invariably have their own way; and besides that, he evidently understands the spirit of the age in which he lives. At a time of affected aestheticism, of rapture and intensity, of sad wall paper and queer dadoes, what a stroke of diplomacy it was to engage Ellen Terry! This graceful and picturesque creature is the high priestess of the enthusiasts. She suits the dreams of the idealists. The age that gave us a Grosvenor Gallery must necessarily adore an Ellen Terry, for she is the embodiment of the aspirations of modern art. With her waving movements and skill in giving life to drapery, she is the actress of all others to harmonize with gold backgrounds and to lounge under blossoming apple trees. The bait held out by Mr. Irving took. The greedy public swallowed it.'

William Archer, who can have had little taste for the cause, acknowledged handsomely the effect of Irving's production, which, he wrote,

was mounted 'with a taste of lavishness positively unexampled. Each
scene was a masterpiece in itself, but the supreme effort was the temple
of Artemis, in which the last act takes place. In the gloom of the background we saw the great Diana of the Ephesians—Artimis Poly-
mastos, the many-breasted mother—looking down upon the forecourt,
with its double row of solid, richly sculptured marble pillars, and its
roof of sandal-wood inlaid with gold. The air was heavy with incense,
and the priestesses moved noiselessly among the sacred lamps. I doubt
if a more elaborate and perfect stage picture of its kind has ever been
seen, and if so certainly not in England. It almost seemed as if stage
decoration could go no further'.

The public, who crowded the Lyceum night after night to see two
such superb productions, had little idea of the man-power, ingenuity
and organization required to handle the complex and swiftly changed
scenery. Under Loveday's expert direction an army of stage hands
man-handled the setting and striking of a sequence of sets which would
have strained the resources of a modern theatre fitted with counter
weights and other labour-saving devices. Percy Fitzgerald described
in detail the major change from the first to the second act of *The Cup*,
for which fifteen minutes was allowed.

'No sooner has the drop scene fallen than men emerge from every
side; the hills and banks, the steps leading down the hill, the massive
pedestal that flanks the entrance to the temple on the right are lifted up
and gradually disappear; the distant landscape mounts slowly into
the air; the long rows of (gas) jets are unfastened and carried away. In
three or four minutes the whole stage is clear. Then are seen
slowly coming down what appear three long, heavy frames or beams.
These are about four feet high and form the pediment or upper portion
of the temple meant to rest on the pillars. Soon busy hands have
joined these three great joists by bolts and fastenings; the signal is
given, and it ascends again. Meanwhile others have been bringing out
from the scene dock the pillars and their bases, ranging them in the
places marked in the ground for them; and as the great beams move
slowly up, they hoist with them the columns attached by ropes which
pass through. In a few moments everything is fitted and falls into its
place with a martial exactness.

We have glimpses in the galleries aloft of men hauling at ropes and
pulleys or turning drums; other men below are bearing in the altars and
steps with the enormous idol at the back, over twenty feet high.
It is worth while looking close at the sound and effective modelling
of the raised classic figures that encircle the lower portion of each

column. They are coloured, too, with that ivory tone which the older marbles acquire. This was all wrought in the property room . . . in papier mache. The great idol now looming solidly at the back is of the same material. It is curious to find that the pillars and their capitals are all constructed literally in the lines of perspective such as would be drawn on a flat surface; they diminish in height as they are farther off, and their top and bottom surfaces are sloped in a converging line. The whole building now stands revealed and complete, some twenty feet high, and round the pillars runs an open space enclosed as it were by the walls. What with the gloom and general mystery the whole would pass, even to those standing quite close, as a very imposing structure . . . when the curtain has fallen on *The Cup* the temple is taken to pieces, reversing the order in which it was put together—the stage is once more clear and the first scene of the Corsican chateau is set.'

The cost of maintaining such a staff was heavy—their salaries alone amounted to nearly £200 a week. In spite of this, when the fourth season ended on April 9th it showed a profit of £8,500.

2

During the previous autumn Edwin Booth had arrived in London to play for a season at the Princess's Theatre. The arrangements for his visit had been made by his brother-in-law, J. S. Clarke, and they could hardly have been worse. The theatre, since the death of Charles Kean, had fallen into decay. The manager, who had no faith in Shakespeare and still less in the drawing power of an American tragedian, was concerned mainly with limiting his liabilities. Booth, an itinerant actor of the old school, was accustomed to working with stock companies and fit-up scenery. Yet he realized at once that Clarke had blundered. 'I have the greatest odds,' he wrote, 'to battle with that an actor ever experienced . . . a deep-rooted love for their (the British public's) idol, who certainly deserves his reward for what he has achieved for the drama here, an unpopular theatre—that is, unpopular with the first class element; for years, a sort of "Bowery" given up to "Drink", "Streets of London", etc., and a sort of "Cheap John" management, with a wretched company, and poorly furnished stage, compared with Irving's superior settings.'

He opened on November 6th with *Hamlet*. He chose this play on the advice of his wife and in the face of warnings of mischief-makers that, in doing so, he would provoke the jealousy of Irving and the antagonism of his supporters. Intelligence of this kind threw Booth on the defensive; at the first performance, his Hamlet, normally gracious and tender, was stern and cold. But he soon thawed when he found that the London public was appreciative and ready to judge him on his merits, that the press was laudatory if slightly patronizing, and that Irving, far from regarding him as a dangerous rival, welcomed him as an old friend and as an honoured master of their art. After *Hamlet*, Booth played Richelieu. At Christmas time he wrote to Irving:

> St. James's Hotel,
> Piccadilly,
> December 23rd.

'Dear Mr. Irving,

I know not how to thank you for your kindly remembrance of me at this time, nor how to reciprocate your courtesy except by my cordial acknowledgement of your gift and the friendly spirit that prompted its presentation.

Oddly enough, the original of this very picture[1] was the subject of conversation, a few evenings since, with some friends who had seen my performance of Richelieu.

Wishing you a long continuance of the triumphs you have won already for our profession, I am sincerely yours,

> Edwin Booth.'

Irving, in due course, received a gift from Booth which he must have valued highly.

> St. James's Hotel,
> February 6th, 1881.

'Dear Mr. Irving,

At last I have succeeded in getting a series of my "Prompt Books" bound for you, which I hope you will stow away in some dark corner of your book case as a mere "stop gap"—for they can be of no use to you. I ask your acceptance of them, however, in kindly remembrance of

> Yours sincerely,
> Edwin Booth.

Have you ever thought of producing Talfourd's *Ion?* I should think the characters of Ion and Adrastus would afford Miss Terry and

---

[1] Probably a photograph or engraving of the portrait of the Cardinal by Philippe de Champagne.

yourself great scope for your best efforts—while the opportunity for scenic effect and costume is very good. I believe the play with your audience would be a great success. When I get through with the *Lear* rehearsals I want to fix a day for a chat with you.

E.B.'

Booth could not have known that Irving probably had been violently prejudiced against *Ion* ever since his schooldays when Dr. Pinches had made him abandon the delectable morbidities of 'The Uncle' in favour of the loquacious speeches of Adrastus. The subject of the chat and its outcome was of deep significance to them both. Although Booth himself had great personal success, particularly as King Lear, the shabby cast and shoddy *mise-en-scène* provided by the pinchbeck management failed to attract the general public whose standards were now set by the Lyceum. 'It is sad,' wrote Helena Faucit to Irving, 'to see how Mr. Booth is surrounded—I hardly know how he gets on at all. . . . ' At the end of March, Booth finished his season playing Shylock and Petruchio; financially it had proved a disappointment. In the course of their conversation Booth told Irving that he would like to give a series of afternoon performances at the Lyceum. Irving readily agreed; but, on reflection, conceived a plan which would be to their mutual advantage and would certainly recoup his friend for the losses which he had sustained at the Princess's. He proposed to put on a production of *Othello* in which he and Booth would play alternately the parts of Othello and Iago with, of course, Ellen Terry as Desdemona. This was to be no makeshift affair. The play was splendidly mounted, and in order to give time for its preparation the first performance was announced for the beginning of May. Booth made only one stipulation— he felt unable to undertake the strain of more than four performances a week. Ten years earlier few leading actors would have dreamed of playing more. Irving, perhaps, unwittingly, had been instrumental in leading the public to expect an actor to give seven or eight performances a week of such exacting roles as Hamlet or Macbeth. He himself lived to regret this and to realize the heavy and destructive strain such an effort threw upon the actor's physical resources. But his own feet were set upon the treadmill; he accepted Booth's limitation and for the remaining four performances played *The Cup* and *The Belle's Stratagem*, which in April had been substituted for *The Corsican Brothers*.

Ellen Terry was at her best as Letitia Hardy; Archer counted it as one of her most exquisite performances. Both she and Irving, to say nothing of the public, found Mrs. Cowley's comedy a refreshing romp after the solemnities of *The Cup* and the strain of *Othello*. For a part in *The Belle's Stratagem* Irving engaged old Henry Howe. He took particular pleasure in having near him veterans of the old school. Howe, who was born in 1812, had been fired with ambition to become an actor by seeing Edmund Kean at Drury Lane. He fulfilled it by taking two engagements. The first was with Macready at Covent Garden, where he remained, playing leading parts, until Macready retired; the second was with Benjamin Webster at the Haymarket, where he played without a break for forty years. He attached himself to Irving with the same loyalty and remained a valuable and much loved member of the Lyceum company until his death in 1896.

Thus Booth came to the Lyceum. But for an earlier negligence on the part of J. S. Clarke the positions of Irving and Booth might have been reversed. In 1871 the theatre had been offered to Booth, who planned to make it his home in London and to appear alternately there and in New York. These negotiations, which were conducted by Clarke, were almost completed when a hitch occurred and Bateman, seizing the advantage, got the lease of the theatre. Booth and Irving must have recalled the disastrous circumstances in which the former's father had played Iago to Edmund Kean's Othello sixty-four years earlier at Drury Lane. Junius Brutus Booth, a Londoner by birth, had modelled himself on Kean to such an extent that for his much praised performance of *Richard III* at Covent Garden he was said 'to have borrowed his predecessor's coat and feathers to appear in on this first and trying occasion'. Booth rashly accepted an offer to play Iago with Kean at Drury Lane. Their partnership was regarded by their partisans more as a bout between heavyweight tragedians than as a dramatic performance. Booth held his own until, as it were, the third round. At the beginning of the third act he seemed for a moment to shrink from the contest, though he quickly recovered himself and joined battle with Kean. 'But,' Barry Cornwall records, 'no sooner did the interest of the story begin, and the passion of the part justify Kean's fervour, than he seemed to expand from the small, quick, resolute figure which had previously been moving about the stage and to assume the vigour and dimensions of a giant. He glared down on the now diminutive Iago; he seized and tossed him aside with frightful and irresistible vehemence. Till then we had seen Othello and Iago as it were together; now the Moor seemed to occupy the stage alone. Up and down, to and fro, he went, pacing about like the chafed lion who has received his fatal hurt, but whose strength is still undiminished. The fury and whirlwind of his passions seemed to have endowed him with a supernatural strength.

His eye was glittering and bloodshot; his veins were swollen, and his whole figure restless and violent. It seemed dangerous to cross his path and death to assault him. There is no doubt that Kean was excited on this occasion, as much as though he had been maddened with wine. The impression which he made on the audience has, perhaps, never been equalled in theatrical annals.' Booth, in the face of such an on-slaught, wisely threw up the sponge and asked to be released from his engagement. Shortly afterwards he quitted England for America to avoid, it was alleged, the consequences of having killed Diavolo Antonio, a celebrated Portuguese slack-wire dancer, in a duel.

No such conflict or deadly rivalry marred the association of the younger Booth and Irving. 'Arrange the order of the programme to suit yourself,' wrote Booth to his host, 'and let me know when you desire me for rehearsal as often as you like and as early. . . . I will be with you Tuesday at 12 o'clock at the theatre. As you suggest, I think it a good idea to try it alone.' For the first time he found himself in a theatre in which everyone, actors and stage staff, worked to one purpose —absolute perfection or to the execution of Irving's wishes which to most of them meant the same thing. At rehearsals Ellen Terry found Booth gentle, apathetic and considerate. ('I shall never make you black. When I take your hand I shall have a corner of my drapery in my hand—that will protect you.') But behind his quiet reserve he was fully alive to all that went on around him.

'Mr. Irving,' he wrote, 'is despotic on the stage. At rehearsal his will is absolute law, whether it concern the entry of a Messenger with a letter, or the reading of a letter by Miss Terry. From first to last he rules the stage with a will of iron, but also with a patience that is marvellous. He sits among his players watching every movement, listening to every word, constantly stopping anyone—Miss Terry as well as the messenger —who does not do exactly right. He rises, explains the fault, and that part of the scene is immediately repeated. His patience holds out against any test. Over and over again the line is recited or a bit of action done, until all is perfect. At the Lyceum one sees the perfection of stage discipline, and in Mr. Irving the perfection of stage patience.'

Booth's apparent apathy was understandable. He was having a hard struggle to play at all—for his wife, who had come with him to England, lay in their rooms in Weymouth Street hovering between life and death with an illness from which she never recovered. Having endured more than his share of suffering and ill-fortune, he had learnt to conceal his wounds from his fellow-men. He once described himself as a man whose life had been passed on picket duty. 'I have been on

Mr. E. BOOTH *(aside)* :—" What does all this tarnation civility mean, I wonder?"

Mr. H. IRVING *(aside)* :—" This move will be certain to pull me through when I visit America."

guard, on the look-out for disasters for which, when they come, I am prepared. Therefore I have seemed, to those who do not know me, callous to the many blows that have been dealt me.' Fate dealt him misfortune and good luck in the same hand. Two years earlier a stage-struck lunatic in the balcony had fired a revolver twice at him when he was playing *Richard II*. The bullets missed their mark. With calm and philosophical courage, he never wavered in his impersonation of the king. Irving and Booth shared many characteristics which inspired in them an unspoken sympathy for one another. They were able to exchange their roles easily and generously on the stage. But in their relative positions Irving's lot was a happier one. Proud and self-reliant men like these two actors find it so much easier to give than to receive. Happy as Booth undoubtedly was during those weeks at the Lyceum, the acceptance of so much kindness and hospitality may well have wounded his pride.

Certain sections of the press did not hesitate to attribute Irving's actions to ignoble motives. His patronage of Booth, it was said, was a subtle self-glorification, designed to curry favour in America against the day when he himself crossed the Atlantic. As yet, apart from rejecting a tentative offer from Wallack during the previous year, Irving had made no plans for such a visit. In view, however, of the turbulent experiences of English actors who had preceded him, he would have been a fool not to do all in his power to promote good will between the English and American theatres, even if in doing so his actions were attributed to self-interest. But attempts to sow discord between himself and Booth failed dismally. For the most part the press applauded their union and credited both actors with a measure of artistic chivalry.

3

Irving and Booth alternately they say
Othello and his Ancient mean to play.
Of our applause, which will be most deserving,
Irving says Booth and Booth (of course) says Irving!

The first performance, with Booth as Othello and Irving as Iago, was on the evening of May 2nd. The London public might well have been wearied of the play, for at Drury Lane another American actor, John M'Cullough, was playing the Moor with Vezin and Isabel Bateman. Although the prices of the more expensive seats at the Lyceum had been doubled, the competition for them had been keen, nor were

the spirits of those who were lucky enough to get them damped by the
downpour of rain through which they had to come to get there. Before
the curtain rose they amused themselves by vigorously hooting Burnand
as he entered the stalls, by way of expressing their disapproval of his
attacks on Irving in *Punch* which even the *Saturday Review* had deplored as being in bad taste. They were also entertained by the ubiquity
of Oscar Wilde who, combining elegance and agility, was seen now
leaning languidly from a box, now chatting in the stalls, and a moment
later figuring prominently in a box opposite to the first. Throughout the
performance the audience maintained a scrupulous loyalty and impartiality in their applause, for there were few who did not welcome this
chance of seeing Booth for the first time in surroundings worthy of his
talent.

Though the criticisms of Booth's Othello bore a strange resemblance
to those of Irving when first he played the part—overstrain, lack of
physical power, and the lapsing of rage into hysteria—he was on the
whole considered to be better than Irving in the part. Ellen Terry found
his playing helpful to her Desdemona. Yet Booth's method would seem
to have put him at a disadvantage against the more modern and
naturalistic technique of his colleagues. His performance, which must
have appeared strangely isolated as he delivered all his lines facing the
audience, was the monologue of a star for whom the performances of
the rest of the company existed only as a figured base. 'We have here,'
wrote Dutton Cook, 'two simply masterly Iagos, two insufficient
Othellos.' This was too great a simplification, but it came near the truth.
Booth's Iago was superb within the limits of tradition. Irving's Iago
was the consummate blending of a daring psychological study with
the illustrative stage-craft of which he was a master. 'The character of
Iago, as understood and presented by these two actors,' wrote a contributor to Macmillan's magazine, 'very clearly marks the distinguishing
quality of their respective styles. The American Iago, clear, cool and
precise, admirably thought out, never deviating a hair's breadth from
the preconceived plan, design and execution marching hand in hand
with ordered steps from the first scene to the last; a performance of
marvellous balance and regularity, polished to the very fingernails.
The Englishman's startling, picturesque, irregular, brilliant—sometimes less brilliant than bizarre—but always fresh and suggestive,
always bearing that peculiar stamp of personality which has so often
saved the actor in his sorest straits.' The writer, keenly as he analysed
the two performances, failed to note the undertone which distinguished
Irving's Iago—the humour which ran like a sparkling seam of gold

through black, relentless rock—'so specious through all his monstrous villainy, that the fact that men are taken in by it is easily comprehensible. Like Satan in Paradise Lost, Iago seems to have said, "Evil, be thou my good" and the only human thing in him is the kind of delight, almost genial, he takes in the success of his own scheme. Cold, concentrated and passionless and with a habit of introspection which seems to guard him against the possibility of error, Iago in Irving's hands is the highest product of the intellectual faculties unrestrained by the moral or the emotional'. Archer, except for the seriousness he attached to the motive for revenge, considered Irving the ideal Iago; to A. B. Walkley he seemed 'daringly Italian or rather better than the Italian, that devil incarnate, an Englishman Italianate'. Ellen Terry never forgot the grapes which, as in the first act he coldly meditated upon murder, he plucked and slowly ate ... 'spitting out the seeds, as if each one represented a worthy virtue to be put out of his mouth as God, according to the Evangelists, puts out the luke-warm virtues.' She counted it a triumph when, as Desdemona makes her appeal to Iago—'Oh good Iago, what shall I do to win my lord again?'—she so moved Irving the man (Irving the actor, with his hands on Desdemona's throat, could mutter 'What's your mother got for supper tonight?') that his eyes became soft and luminous with tears. But her triumph was short-lived. Hardly were his eyes brim full, before Irving the actor, seizing on those tears as handy properties, ostentatiously dashed them away and blew his nose 'softly and with much feeling', conjuring from true emotion the very essence of counterfeit hypocrisy.

Irving's Iago excelled Booth's where intellect was the first requirement. His performance was bejewelled with invention and artifice born of deep study and endless experiment and rejection. There were those among his admirers who felt that on this account he failed occasionally where simplicity was needed. Booth, faithful to tradition, trod firmly the path beaten out for him by his father who himself had followed the track of Kean. Irving, like Kean, having critically examined all that tradition had to offer him, threw it aside and recreated Iago in terms of his own conception. For the first time he played a great Shakespearian role with such excellence that, in praising him, his most fanatical admirers, his sternest critics and his most mischievous enemies found themselves in complete, if uneasy, agreement. It was a pity that Henry James was out of town.

By comparison, perhaps, Irving's Othello was praised beyond its deserts, though he had without doubt modified and refined with constant study his earlier interpretation. When he first played the part, one of his best scenes had been that in which Othello fell, convulsed with epilepsy, at Iago's feet. Out of consideration for Booth he omitted this business; Booth himself, playing Othello, had never used it, and, as Iago, he might have been disconcerted by it. He abandoned subtlety of costume and appeared as a gorgeously apparelled African and blacker than was the custom. One critic wrote that 'in the bed-chamber scene Irving played thoroughly well, making his own painful intensity of feeling manifest without any exertion of voice or action. And when the deed is done and, startled by Emilia's knocking at the door, he stands forth from the curtains of the bed, he presents a figure more dramatically awful than any we have ever witnessed. It gives us particular pleasure to add that this time Mr. Irving could not be charged for a moment with indistinctness of speech. Every line was clearly delivered; and we only hope that Mr. Irving is aware of how much he added in this way to the pleasure of the audience'. Clearly here speaks no partisan. Against this Ellen Terry records that 'he screamed, he ranted, and he raved—lost his voice, was slow where he should have been swift—incoherent where he should have been strong . . . yet night after night he achieved in his speech to the Senate one of the most superb and beautiful bits of acting of his life'. Yet there seems to be no doubt that he fell below his own standard and that, regardless of the praise or blame of critics or the plaudits of the public, he admitted to a failure which he felt very bitterly. 'On the last night', wrote Ellen Terry, 'he rolled up his clothes that he had worn as the Moor, one by one, carefully laying one garment on top of the other, and then, half humorously and very deliberately said: "Never again!" Then he stretched himself with his arms above his head and gave a great sigh of relief.' Into the limbo with his Othello went his Iago—perhaps the finest performance of his life—for unless these two great characters are fairly matched the play falls to the ground and in his lifetime no actor emerged to whom he could subordinate himself as the Ancient. Ellen Terry must have watched his renunciation with wistful regret. Her Desdemona, whose modesty and tenderness had won all hearts, perished with Irving's Othello.

Booth's season at the Lyceum ended on June 17th; at the last performance Irving and Booth gave their services for Ellen Terry's Benefit. It was naturally an occasion for the exchange of compliments, and in a brief speech Irving thanked Booth for his artistic fellowship, his perfect courtesy and his devotion to their common art. It was well known that Booth had set his face against public speaking; indeed, when he was entertained at Delmonico's by a number of distinguished

Americans before he left for England, he remained mute while laudatory speeches were showered upon him—never opening his mouth,
as one reporter said, except to put something into it. That he broke
his vow of silence on that evening was, perhaps, a greater tribute to
Irving than the words he spoke:

'It is, to me, a strange sensation to speak any other words than those
set down for me. Yet I feel that I cannot let an occasion like the present
pass without breaking the silence. It is a pleasant duty to acknowledge
to you the gratification it has been to me to see, nightly, such splendid
audiences as have here assembled. I feel that I owe you a debt of
gratitude for your appreciation of my efforts to please you. My visit
to the Lyceum has been an uninterrupted pleasure. I have to thank my
friend, Mr. Irving, for his generous hospitality, and the talented lady
with whom I have had the honour of playing, for her pleasant companionship and kind assistance. Indeed, to all on the stage, and all
associated with the Lyceum Theatre, my best thanks for the courtesy
and consideration which I have received, are due, and are most heartily
tendered. Believe me, the kind and generous treatment I have received,
from the gentlemen of the press, and from all with whom I have been
associated during this engagement, and the generous reception I have
met with at your hands, must ever be among the pleasantest recollections of my long professional career. I hope to have the pleasure of
appearing before you again, at no distant day. In the meantime I thank
you most heartily, and bid you, for the present, adieu.'

The sincerity of his words was confirmed in a letter he wrote to
William Winter, the senior New York dramatic critic, referring to his
Lyceum engagement. 'Its success is very great in all respects and only
my domestic misery prevents it from being the happiest theatrical
experiment I have ever had. I wish I could do as much for Henry
Irving in America, as he has done for me here.' He did his best. Mrs.
Booth was dying. In order to take her home before it was too late, he
abandoned his plans for a provincial tour and sailed at once for New
York. When he arrived he was, of course, assailed by reporters. To
the *New York Times* he said: '. . . My engagement with Irving was
one of the most agreeable that I ever played. He is one of the most
delightful men I ever met, always obliging, and always kind in every
possible way. He is very popular in London, both socially and professionally, and, I think, deservedly so. He is a very superior actor and
is gifted with a remarkable talent for stage management—two qualifications for the stage which are seldom found united in the same person.
Irving with all his popularity is a very modest man and altogether

charming. If he visits American he will be liked no less for his qualities as a man than for his powers as an actor.'

Both actors had every cause to be satisfied with the outcome of their enterprise. The twenty-one representations of *Othello* had brought £8,258 into the box-office, of which at least a third went to Booth. Irving, even if cynics denied him the warm satisfaction of disinterested altruism, had won for himself an ambassador in the United States.

4

The remaining month of the season was given up to revivals, *Hamlet* being played for a week and Irving and Ellen Terry appearing for the first and last time in a scene from Sheridan Knowles's *The Hunchback* for Irving's benefit on the last night. In his farewell speech he announced *Romeo and Juliet* for the next season and put an end to the prevailing gossip that he had purchased the freehold of the theatre. Although he did not disclose the nature of the negotiations which had given rise to these rumours, Arnold had, in fact, offered to sell him the whole property for £110,000. Irving decided not to buy it—even if he could have raised the money. He obtained, instead, a long lease of the theatre at a rental of £4,500 per annum. No doubt he took the best advice on the matter. Yet in view of the vast sums he was to spend on reconstructing and improving the theatre, there was to come a time when, if he had possessed the freehold, this expenditure would have been an asset instead of an irretrievable loss. But Irving had little cause for pessimism. In spite of the heavy cost of three new and elaborate productions (£9,500) and the handsome sum which Booth had taken to America with him, the third season showed a profit of £10,500. Moreover, after an all too brief holiday, he and Ellen Terry were to set out together on their first tour which the provincial public so eagerly awaited.

Before he left London he presided at the thirty-sixth anniversary Festival of the Royal General Theatrical Fund. In his address, after deprecating the popular idea of the actor as an improvident and irresponsible bohemian, he touched, good-humouredly, on the prospects of young actors of the day compared with his own when he first came to London. 'Then your leading man might be receiving the modest emolument of two guineas per week, with the necessity of providing himself with hats, shoes, tights, and heaven knows what. Many of us present know all about that; but now, forsooth, many a dashing young spark, aping a society drawl and possessing a few well-cut suits of clothes, may obtain his ten guineas (they always ask guineas) or more a week, as a representative of what is called society drama. Why, not fifteen years ago, when I made what was really my first appearance in London at a well-known theatre, I was engaged as a leading actor and stage-manager at a salary of seven pounds a week. I tried for guineas, and they wouldn't give it. Well, I was content and so was my manager; but I firmly believe now, if I were to apply to any London manager for a similar position, that he would give me double that money. Things have so altered.'

'In the practice of our art,' he concluded, 'we win if we can—if we fail we have "only our shame and the odd hits"—and whether we fail or not, the breath of applause or the murmurs of censure, are alike short-lived, and our longest triumphs are almost as brief as either. Our lives are fraught with many temptations, and should be solaced by the thoughtfulness, brightened by the encouragement, and softened by the liberal estimation of the public; for we actors have in charge a trust and a deposit of enormous value, such as no dead hand can treasure. The living voice, the vivid action, the tremulous passion, the animated gesture, the subtle and variously placed suggestion of character and meaning—these alone can make Shakespeare to your children what Shakespeare is to you. Such is our birthright, and such is yours.'

CHAPTER XXII

4th and 5th Lyceum Seasons: Romeo, Benedick

———✦———

I

Irving's hard years of apprenticeship had taught him, if not to respect the taste of provincial audiences, to assess the worth of their capacity to support theatrical enterprise. Although he had not left London for two years, he was confident that his own popularity in the great towns of the United Kingdom was unimpaired; since he last visited them he had joined forces with a partner who had a considerable provincial following of her own. On her last tour with Charles Kelly, Ellen Terry made a great success playing Beatrice in *Much Ado About Nothing*—so great that Irving had decided to produce it at the Lyceum after *Romeo and Juliet*. After this tour Ellen Terry and her husband had parted. She realised that he would not fit into the home which she was trying to make for her children—'one cannot live with a steamroller', she said, thereby indicating that she feared a recurrence of male domination. She had, moreover, failed to save Kelly from his weakness for the bottle, to which he succumbed a few years later. She was, therefore, free to test with Irving the power of their partnership, which had been so remarkably successful in London, to attract the provinces.

There was nothing niggardly about their first sortie. Irving was determined that the whole country should see the Lyceum productions in all their glory. Since his days as a stock company actor, railway transport had vastly improved. He was able to load into a special train the scenery properties and lighting equipment for nine plays, *The Bells, Hamlet, Merchant of Venice, Othello, Charles I, The Cup, Eugene Aram, The Belle's Stratagem* and *Daisy's Escape*—all as complete in every detail as they had been at the Lyceum. His retinue of fifty-four included the players necessary for these productions and the key men in all the departments of stage management. The organisation of this imposing caravan was left to Bram Stoker; it was the kind of work he thoroughly enjoyed and at which he excelled. The burden of supervising the unloading and setting up within a few hours this quantity of scenery in unfamiliar theatres with comparatively untrained stage staffs and of recruiting and rehearsing in each town a regiment of local supers, fell upon Loveday and Arnott, who soon got the measure of these problems.

Such an enterprise was without precedent. Irving carried the theatrical standards of London, which he himself had largely created, through the whole kingdom so that henceforward provincial playgoers would see the best that London had to offer and accordingly could adjust their critical viewpoint. He trained, moreover, a generation of actors who, when they themselves became actor-managers, thought of their public not in terms of a select coterie within the narrow perimeter of the West End, but as the population of the British Isles as a whole, with all its richly varying characteristics of culture, humour and enthusiasm. London came to be the field for experiments which, if successful, were taken to the provinces for the mutual benefit of player and playgoer; in the course of time the procedure has been reversed, the timid West End manager bringing gingerly into London the plays which have been tried out successfully on the provincial dog. Irving's policy got the recognition and support it deserved. The great cities were at once flattered and delighted with what they saw. In Glasgow and Edinburgh, where he played twelve performances in each town, the receipts in each case were over £4,000. These tours were arranged on the basis that Irving took two thirds of the takings. At the end of this first tour his own share amounted to £23,666. Against this were to be set the expenses of conducting such a quantity of men and material around the country—over £17,000. But for sixteen weeks' work the profit was a handsome one and the experience which he had gained had been even more valuable. This was the pattern of Irving's provincial tours which he carried out almost annually until his death. The receipts varied very little, but, as the years went by, mounting expenses steadily reduced the rewards of such exacting toil.

2

When he set out on the tour, Irving had been having a certain amount of trouble over the production of *Two Roses* with which he intended to open his next London season. Of the original company, only David James was available—Montague had died in America and Thorne was in management on his own account. Thorne's old part, Caleb Deecie, was a hard one to fill. Irving was discussing his difficulty with the manager of the Royalty Theatre, Glasgow, when the latter mentioned that in his stock company there was a young actor, hard-working and anxious to get on, who might be the very man Irving needed. In due course Irving was introduced to George Alexander and, as usual, invited him to supper. He was immediately attracted by this good-looking, well-educated and well-spoken young Scotsman who, like himself, had abandoned a city office for the stage. Though he had been an actor for barely two years, he had played with a touring company managed by Tom Robertson, junior, and for a brief season in London with Wilson Barrett at the Court Theatre. Irving offered him the part of Caleb Deecie at a salary of seven guineas a week for six performances. At first Alexander hesitated—he confessed frankly his lack of experience and his conviction that for the time being he should remain in the provinces. But Irving had made up his mind. He appreciated no doubt the sound common sense which lay behind the young actor's diffidence, but soon persuaded him that to come to London was the wisest course.

In Edinburgh he was invited by Sir Alexander Grant to read the opening address of the winter session to the Edinburgh Institution. On November 8th in the Music Hall, choosing his subject 'The Stage As It Is', he reaffirmed his faith in the theatre as an influence for good in a properly constituted society, castigated those whose prejudice and hypocrisy denied to actors the recognition that was accorded to the exponents of the sister arts, and remarked that the fact that he had been asked to address such a discriminating and intellectual body of men was evidence of the great change in the attitude of society towards the theatre which had been wrought in the last fifty years. His points were strongly expressed and well argued; he made no plea or apology for his profession. The speech was widely reported. A leading article in a national daily paper, having quoted him as saying that 'dramatic reformers are very well-meaning people but it was an unwelcome if not an unwarrantable intrusion to come among our people with elaborate advice' declared that the stage might as well organize means of purifying the Church or send its members to distribute tracts among the landed gentry. 'The stage,' it added, 'is very well able to take care of herself and may be left with security in the hands of men like Mr. Irving.'

3

In Irving's absence the Lyceum was once more in the hands of builders and decorators. The great portico was hidden with scaffolding —a sight which led wits who were critical of some of Irving's supporting company, to remark that they were glad to see the sticks were leaving the Lyceum. With a long lease in his pocket and money flowing into the treasury, Irving had decided to take drastic measures to improve the accommodation and amenities of the house. At a cost of £12,000 he increased the capacity of the theatre to £420, though in doing so a little of the elegant symmetry of the old theatre was lost. In clearing out the vast catacombs underneath the stage, the workmen, delving among the accumulated rubbish of half a century, found masses of decayed peacocks' feathers which were proved to be the faded relics of one of Madame Vestris's glittering burlesques. That Irving, on the first night of *Hamlet*, had waved a peacock's feather on a stage whose cellarage was stuffed with such ill-omened plumage, should have ended forever the gloomy superstitions attached to this exquisite bird.

The fourth season opened on Boxing Night. Irving's Digby Grant was relished as much as ever by the critics and by the public, although connoisseurs who remembered the old Vaudeville days found that the play had dated and that Irving, in adjusting his performance to the larger theatre, or perhaps to the demands of his audience, had lost a little of its subtle humour. It was an easy evening for him, the double bill being made up with *The Captain of the Watch*, an old comedy by Planché, in which the lead was played by Terriss. Yet he found the revival stale and uninspiring and confessed as much to Walter Pollock —'they don't care about it and no more do I, so this will be my last appearance in a coat and trouser piece'. Behind this façade of comedy every department in the theatre was absorbed in the earnest preparation of *Romeo and Juliet*.

One Sunday evening Irving came to supper with Walter Pollock and his wife. Usually he brought Ellen Terry with him, but this time he came alone. He discussed with them the task that lay before him. Then he read to them some of Romeo's scenes. 'He read,' wrote Pollock, 'at half tone, yet gave its full force of meaning to every character, and it was evident throughout that his conception of the part of Romeo was instinct with beauty and truth. He indicated fully all the passion, all the moods, all the impulse and all the weakness of the character, and, in a subtle fashion, brought all the movement and

Edwin Booth

Irving in 1881

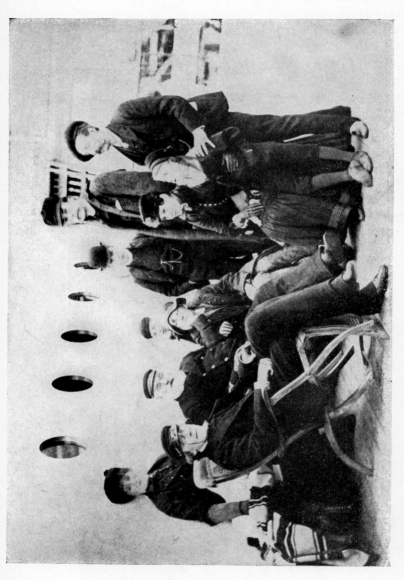

S.S. Arizona Homeward Bound, 1885

Ellen Terry The Captain —— E. Gordon Craig —— L. F. Austin H. J. Loveday
and family

Henry Irving

life of the various scenes before one's mind's eye.' When he had finished, Mrs. Pollock expressed her admiration for his reading and predicted that his Romeo would be a tremendous success. 'No, it won't . . .' said Irving quietly.

'Nonsense. Of course it will be, Crab!' she insisted. (All the Pollocks called him 'Crab', the outcome of jokes about his gait.) 'Don't be silly. You're bound to have a great success.'

'No—that is what I want to make of Romeo. Unluckily I know that on the stage I cannot come anywhere near it—I should like to—but I can't.'

After Irving had left they agreed that if only he could play Romeo as he read it he would set the town ablaze, but in any event he would play Mercutio superbly. And therein lay Irving's dilemma.

He was now forty-four and Ellen Terry only ten years younger. He was not, in his looks or in his manner, a young forty-four; nor, for that matter, had he ever attempted youthfulness successfully on the stage. His Claude Melnotte and Doricourt had had a touch of caricature about them and, as a lover, he had always been moody and masterful. Yet so ardent was his love of Shakespeare that he could not resign himself to the renunciation of the most exquisite and lyrical of his plays. He was well aware of his own physical handicaps and of the criticism which, without any doubt, he would incur for attempting to play Romeo. Ellen Terry, like Irving, was not given to self-deception or blinded by vanity; she shared his misgivings, knowing full well that she was past the age of portraying girlish innocence. Often it was said that she had persuaded Irving to produce *Romeo and Juliet* in order to satisfy her own ambition. There was no truth in this. Nobody ever over-persuaded Irving. If his decision was influenced by any consideration of this kind, it was that he wished to fulfil his ambition for her. No partner in the past had inspired him to produce the play; when the inspiration came, it was at the eleventh hour. Both of them knew that, as the months passed, the disparity between physical reality and their artistic dreams would be accentuated. It was now or never. Irving had seriously considered playing Mercutio. But in all London he could find no actor adequate for Romeo. Terriss attempted it a year or two later with Mary Anderson; he played the part for all he was worth but without a notion as to its meaning—and he failed. So, having weighed the alternative and having coldly assessed the hazards, Irving came to a decision; having done so, he set aside all doubt and set about his task with characteristic determination and whole-heartedness.

4

Once again his first concern was to restore the original text of Shakespeare's play to the stage. In the course of time, *Romeo and Juliet* had suffered the usual mutilations and even the substitution of a happy ending at the hands of unscrupulous players. Garrick had been guilty of subtractions and additions and of contriving a denouement totally at variance with the poet's expressed injunction. Taking the Variorum edition of Furness and the texts of Singer (1826) and Dyce (1857), he prepared a version which came nearer to Shakespeare's original than any which had been seen on the stage since his time. Notably, he restored the prologue and the scenes suggesting Romeo's earlier love for Rosaline, which he regarded as essential to the proper understanding of Romeo's character as the poet had drawn it. Having fulfilled his duty to Shakespeare, he set about what he called 'the illustration, without improvement, of the Italian warmth, life and romance of the enthralling love story'.

It was and will forever be disputed whether Shakespeare, had the resources of the modern stage been at his disposal, would have employed or spurned them. There can be no more idle or unprofitable speculation. He was no lover of the drab and might well have mocked at those who profess to honour him with artificial and self-conscious simplicity. He laughed at the inadequacies and make-shifts of his own theatre through the mouths of Bottom and his mechanicals. If he truly desired 'a Muse of fire, that would ascend the brightest heaven of invention', Irving was his man and he could have had no more devoted or inventive genie. Irving arranged the play in five acts and twenty scenes, whose unparalleled beauty not even the sternest critic disputed. Under his direction, Hawes Craven and Telbin excelled themselves. From the first disclosure of the Market Place of Verona with its well-composed contrast of drenching sunlight and cool refreshing shade, to the ultimate dank gloom of Juliet's vaulted tomb, they designed a succession of pictures which reflected perfectly the dramatic progression of the play.

In the previous May, London playgoers had been startled by the novel use of crowds which the Grand Duke of Saxe-Meiningen's company of actors had employed in their Shakespearian productions at Drury Lane. In *Julius Caesar* and *The Winter's Tale* they had seen the first experiments in the form of theatrical mob management and crowd composition which was to reach perfection thirty years later in Reinhardt's spectacle, *The Miracle*. Irving was quick to see the value of the Saxe-Meiningen method

MR. HAWES CRAVEN.

A HOST OF DELIGHTFUL STAGE PICTURES HE HAS GIVEN US.

and to bend it to his own purpose. These German productions were marred by crudity of colour and occasional lack of restraint. With the help of Alfred Thompson, Irving achieved a balance of colour and movement in his tableaux which brought to the stage the rich harmonies and bold compositions of the Italian masters. As usual, his intentions were not immediately clear to his lieutenant. Having given Loveday a general directive, he left him to knock the crowd scenes into shape. Enthusiasm was never lacking at the Lyceum. The partisans of Capulet and Montague under Loveday's direction warmed to their task and brawled and bickered to the manner born. After a few days, Irving came to a rehearsal to see how Loveday was getting on. Under the eye of their Chief, the actors flogged themselves into a frenzy of factional dispute. Eager bodies of young men rushed about the stage, provoking each other with insulting gestures and baiting each other with cries of 'Have at you—a Montague!'—'Have at you—a Capulet!' Exhausted, they paused, and waited anxiously for a word of praise.

'M'm—yes—very-y gud,' said Irving, with quiet but devastating incisiveness. 'But—er—don't fidget.'

After that he himself took the affair in hand. Patiently and ruthlessly he eradicated the soft, romantic prettiness which until then had been the accepted setting for the story and in its place brought to life a community torn, not by romantic feuds between noble families, but by the mean warfare of contending gangsters. His Verona was a city of fine mansions backing on dark crumbling streets where the stab in the back by an unseen hand was the instrument of revenge and where the medium of vendetta was the assassin's knife rather than chivalrous sword-play between gentlemen. It was a town in which killers were for hire and the discard died without seeing the face of his executioner. Irving clothed the Loop of Chicago in the lush opulence of the Renaissance. Old Sir Julius Benedict, the pupil of Weber, was commissioned to write the incidental music; Mrs. Stirling, another famous veteran of Macready's company, was brought out of her retirement to play the Nurse. If authenticity of atmosphere and stage pictures of masterly design were enough, art and scholarship could do no more. But Irving and Ellen Terry knew well enough that it was upon them that success or failure depended. 'You've got to do all you know with it,' he had told her. The sense of responsibility lay heavily upon them and did not make it any easier for them to pretend a carefree youth which they had long since passed.

Although certain sections of the press had openly ridiculed the mere idea of Irving playing Romeo, the public were prepared to give him a fair trial and stormed the box-office as eagerly as ever. The first night on March 8th, 1882, was attended by the Prince and Princess of Wales. Opposite to them was Florence, who had spent the day at the Central Criminal Court listening to the trial of Dr. Lamson, the poisoner, and now sat in grim but pleasurable anticipation of an adverse verdict on her husband's folly. Irving always sent his wife a box for his first nights. If, as Kean said, the actor makes the boxes his first point of contact with his audience, an insulator in the shape of the implacable Flo may have, to some extent, accounted for the fact that Irving was seldom at his best on these occasions.

The chorus, dressed like Dante, came before the red tableau curtains and gave the audience an optimistic estimate of the length of the evening before them—'the two hours' traffic of our stage'—was spun out to three and a quarter and it was midnight before, dazed with the incomparable pageantry they had witnessed, they staggered to their carriages. Pinero, writing to Irving the next day, expressed the effect the play had had upon most of them: 'I think half-a-dozen visits to the theatre could not do more than justice to the production—its infinite detail and wonderful wealth of colour; but that my one visit has been sufficient to enable me to realize a charm which is quite singular and, I think, ineffaceable.' Even this loyal liegeman refrained from comment on his Chief's performance. Florence, before going to bed, wrote in her diary: 'First night of *Romeo and Juliet* at Lyceum—jolly failure —Irving awfully funny.' Lord Lytton said later: 'He threw the whole force of his mind creatively into every detail of the great play, giving to the vital spirit of it an adequately complete, appropriate and yet original embodiment.' The truth lay somewhere between these extremes. There is no doubt that he failed to convey the appearance or spontaneity of youth and it is hard to imagine a Romeo in whom this is lacking. 'Is it possible,' asked a critic, 'for such a nature to mould itself into an ideal Romeo—for this grave, meditative and at times furiously indignant Hamlet—to put on the impulsiveness, the fresh, spontaneous, youthful ardour of the boy who is Juliet's lover?' It was not only that Irving failed to conform to the handsome hero of commonplace illustration; over-anxious to convey youthfulness in his gestures and actions, he defeated his own aims. Yet in the apothecary scene he was at his very best—in fact, after the death of Mercutio, when the assumption of boyishness was no longer called for, many found him an acceptable Romeo. The critics for the most part were nonplussed. As though intimidated by the thought and imagination which, they acknowledged, had gone into the staging of such a memorable revival, they were non-committal or pronounced Irving's effort as worthy of 'generous appreciation'. Labby would not hear of this. 'I do not know what they mean,' he wrote, apostrophizing Irving in *Truth*. 'I, who am a great admirer of yours, tell you that your rendering of the part is not entitled to any appreciation, generous or otherwise. You simply cannot touch it. This is not your fault, nor indeed, your misfortune; for you are fortunate enough in being able to play many characters better than anyone on the stage. Your fault is that you should not have taken counsel of your friends before attempting to do what they would have told you was a physical impossibility.' He had the temerity to reiterate these views to Ellen Terry. 'I am sorry you don't realize,' she retorted, 'that the worst thing Henry Irving could do, would be better than the best of anyone else.'

In the same terms Ellen Terry's Juliet was damned with faint praise. But she had no harsher critic than herself. She attributed her failure to faulty study at the outset, condemning her interpretation for its lack of 'original impulse'. Though she and Irving found fault with themselves, they sought to sustain each other. 'Beautiful as Portia was,' he wrote to her after the dress rehearsal, 'Juliet leaves her far, far behind. Never anybody acted more exquisitely the part of the performance which I saw from the front. "Hie to high fortune" and "where spirits resort" were simply incomparable . . . your mother looked very radiant last night. I told her how proud she should be, and she was . . . the play will be, I believe, a mighty "go", for the beauty of it is bewildering. I am sure of this for it dumbfounded them all last night. Now you—we—must make our task a delightful one by doing everything possible to make our acting easy and comfortable. We are in for a long run. . . . I have determined not to see a paper for a week—I know they'll cut me up and I don't like it.'

He was right about the length of the run. Henry James, baffled and bemused, peevishly complained that 'the play has thriven mightily and though people are sadly bewildered by what they see and hear in it, they appear to recommend the performance to their friends'. For twenty-four weeks *Romeo and Juliet* played to audiences as large as those that had been attracted to *The Merchant of Venice*. The receipts for the season were £47,912 against an expenditure of £51,883. These heavy costs included nearly £6,500 which had been spent on the fabric of the theatre and £7,500 on the production of the play, a very large sum for that period; they included also the salary of £70 a week which Irving paid himself and of £200 a week which he paid to Ellen Terry— the latter, in effect, being a share in the profits. These statutory salaries remained unchanged throughout the twenty-four years they worked together—except on their American tours, when both of them received a salary of a thousand dollars a week. Considering the risks he had accepted and the generally unfavourable tone of the press, Irving had every reason to be thankful for getting off so lightly. He had got the play out of his system. Romeo, after a brief reappearance to herald the following season, followed Othello into exile. Verona, stored away under a railway arch in South London, faded beneath a layer of dust and dirt until it was dismembered to provide the bones of other scenic splendours.

On the hundredth night of the run, Irving gave another banquet on the tented stage, with perhaps a touch of bravado, for he must have known that the toast to Romeo could not be as whole-hearted as it had been to Shylock. An added illusion had been created by veiling the auditorium with green gauze, in front of which great banks of flowers were planted over the orchestra pit so that those in the marquee looked out upon what appeared to be a moonlit garden. It may have been these inflammable decorations which caused Walter Pollock, as the guests assembled, to ask what would become of that distinguished company in the event of fire. 'You don't suppose', replied Irving darkly to this rather tactless question, 'that I've lost sight of that— do you?—We've taken every—precaution—ye know.' Thereupon, with dramatic emphasis, he described one or two measures he had taken to guard against such an outbreak. Pollock's apprehensions probably were justified and the precautions elaborate only in Irving's lively imagination. Yet such was his hypnotic power that Pollock's vision of a holocaust of roasting artists and men of letters was dispelled; if he gave the matter another thought it was to dwell upon a disaster almost to be desired which Irving, quelling panic with his calm authority, would turn into an amusing mishap. The company were much the same as on a previous occasion, but in the place of Lord Houghton was the Earl of Lytton, whose speech in proposing Irving's health was a model of discretion. He contrived to pay tribute to his host as a reformer and as a producer and even to touch upon the beauties of *Romeo and Juliet* without referring to his performance. The presence of Henry E. Abbey, the American impresario, among the guests gave rise to a good deal of conjecture as to whether it foreshadowed a visit by Irving to the United States in the near future. In responding to Lord Lytton's toast, Irving, after describing the effect upon actors of long runs which, while admitting their economic necessity, he deprecated in principle, continued:

'. . . No matter how enthralling the story, or how fascinating the character, there steals over one at times a weariness almost insupportable. A night or two ago, Sarah Bernhardt, on this stage, was pouring forth ecstatically her delight with our play and, seizing the fair Juliet in her arms exclaimed: "How can you, my dear Madame, act like this night after night?" "I cannot," was fair Juliet's reply, "but you were in front tonight and that inspired me."

Why, I have seen artists come from the stage and cry with sheer fatigue, and regret at not having strength to obey the whip of their intelligence. Now, all this is different when an artist is playing a variety of parts. There is excitement and freshness in the audience which begets the same in the actor, and all of us look with delight upon our provincial trip, when audiences are never crammed with heavy dinners and cynical indifference. "Ladies and Gentlemen," said George Frederick Cooke, "if you don't applaud, I don't act", and applause is well worth the trouble, for the audience gets the full benefit of it. I hope our American cousins, in the autumn of next year, will consider it worth their while to try the experiment by applauding me.'

Thus Irving announced his intention of conquering the new world. Unlike Napoleon, the success of his campaign would, apparently, depend not so much upon the proper victualling of his own little army as on the degree of repletion of the critical forces deployed against him.

5

When the season ended Irving left London for a holiday on the Yorkshire coast. He liked walking and found that the moors and cliffs between Whitby and Filey provided the solitude he needed for rest and reflection. He had worked almost without a break since the summer of 1880 and during these months of intense activity in the theatre much had occurred affecting his situation outside it.

He had received certain honours and compliments which had marked the satisfactory progress of his crusade; in themselves they meant very little to a man whose only ambition was the supremacy of his theatre and the perfection of his art—though no doubt he derived a good deal of sardonic amusement from the capitulation of Society to his subtle manœuvres. He accepted them as due to his profession and to himself at the head of it, like a general in a war of religion, taking the surrender of towns which were ready to embrace the true faith. In February he had become a member of the Athenaeum Club under Rule II by which the committee are free to elect men distinguished in their professions. He was the first actor to be thus honoured. Macready had sought this privilege in vain; ultimately, after being blackballed once, he had been elected to the Club in the ordinary way. During the same month Irving had been commanded, with fifteen other actors, to dine with the Prince of Wales at Marlborough House. Bancroft had sat in the place of honour on the Prince's right hand. Irving always spoke of him as the senior manager—which he was. Yet Bancroft would have been the first to acknowledge that it was Irving who had done most to stimulate the benevolent interest of the Prince in their profession. This Royal gesture made it clear to Victorian society that at last the rogue actor had been freed from vagabondage. It had even been discreetly intimated to Irving by Mr. George Lewis, the solicitor, that His Royal Highness might be pleased to accept an invitation to supper in the Beefsteak Room. His only anxiety, during the month in which these events had enhanced so steadily his prestige, had been when an unwelcome ray of light had fallen upon his inscrutable dealings with the press. Clement Scott, who thrived on altercation, had sued Henry Sampson, the editor of *The Referee*, for libel, an affair in which Irving was in no way concerned. But in the course of the hearing, Irving's late ownership of *The Theatre* was divulged and some pertinent questions were asked about the generous gift he had made of it to Scott. But the news scavengers seem to have overlooked it. Scott was awarded £1,500 damages and the incident was soon forgotten.

His two boys were growing up. He rarely saw them and, when he did, they appeared awkward and embarrassed. Their mother, unforgiving and embittered, never lost an opportunity to hold their father up to ridicule and contempt; it was natural, therefore, that they approached him in a mood of suspicion and hostility. According to Toole, who tried hard to mitigate this estrangement, they were lively and intelligent boys. He had aided and abetted Florence in allowing them to appear with some other children in a charity performance at Wellington Barracks as Charles and Joseph Surface in the Screen scene from *The School for Scandal*. Naturally the occasion inspired a good deal of publicity and gushing praise. Irving cannot have approved of this. He saw very clearly the dangers of putting ideas about acting into their young heads. Being his sons, they would be flattered and encouraged to believe in a talent which perhaps neither possessed. His chief desire was that they should have the educational advantages which he had missed. He had arranged for them to go that summer to Marlborough and, according to Stoker whom he had sent down to reconnoitre, they seemed to be, if not happy, at least enduring the rigours of public school life with cheerful fortitude.

His own circumstances had so altered that he had been able to satisfy a longing to have some sort of home to which he could invite his friends to stay with him. Grafton Street was all very well as a cell for a studious hermit, but it was, in effect, an annexe or dormitory to the Lyceum. A year or so earlier he and a friend were wandering through Brook Green. It was then a decaying village which seemed to have given up the struggle against urbanization, and was waiting passively to be swallowed up by the metropolis which had already begun to engulf Hammersmith. Here they discovered a dilapidated house, standing in its own grounds and approached across grassy but neglected lawns, which was for sale. Its name, 'The Grange', appealed to Irving's romantic nature, although it was, perhaps, a misnomer, for what in fact were two rather spacious cottages knocked into one. On closer inspection they found that, although derelict, the house was well built and had a fine garden shaded with poplar and chestnut trees. Irving bought the lease and spent such leisure as he had in watching its restoration. He supervised the reconstruction of the house and the replanting of the garden with the same pleasure and attention to detail as he devoted to the creations of Hawes Craven at the Lyceum. 'Only,' as he explained to a friend, 'you can smell the scent of flowers and feel the real warmth and life of the real sun at "The Grange".' When all was finished and ready for him to move in, he was able further to indulge his love of dogs. Already he had two terriers who were his constant companions—Charlie, who had been given to him by Ellen Terry, and Fussy, who had been given to Ellen Terry by Fred Archer, the jockey, but, no doubt, on Charlie's recommendation, had abandoned her for Irving. At 'The Grange' he installed an amiable Newfoundland and a bulldog. With these companions, who appear to have got on agreeably enough with each other, Irving spent as much time as he could among his gillie flowers and tulips. It was a simple establishment, the domestic staff consisting solely of the gardener and his wife. Yet his intimate friends looked forward to nothing more than an invitation to 'The Grange'.

The provincial tour of 1881 made it clear to him that, in future, speeches and addresses would be demanded of him wherever he went. He found, moreover, that one of the penalties of success was a swollen postbag. By nature he was, as Toole said, 'a regular Turk about letter-writing', and it was evident that, in view of the approaching American tour, he would have to find a secretary. He had been fortunate in securing the services of Louis Frederick Austin, for some time past an informal secretary to the Baroness Burdett-Coutts, on whose recommendation Irving had engaged him. Rarely can two men have been better suited to each other. Austin was of Irish parentage and, though he had been born in Brooklyn, was a Londoner by temperament and adoption. He had been educated at the Merchant Taylors School, where he developed a love of literature and a natural gift for writing. Gay, witty and amusing, he had already won a reputation as an excellent after-dinner speaker. By the time he joined Irving he had become a regular contributor to various periodicals and revues. Later he wrote the literary page in the *Illustrated London News*, which had been started by George Augustus Sala and in which he was succeeded by G. K. Chesterton. Although he did not disguise his admiration and affection for Irving, he was no sycophant. He spoke his mind fearlessly, and for this, apart from his many other qualities, Irving liked and trusted him. His task was not an easy one. His intimate personal contact with the Chief inspired jealousy and suspicion in those who were ever on the alert if they felt their own interests were at stake. The flummeries of incorrigible time-servers were made to appear ridiculous by this outspoken young man whose apparent lack of awe and respect, as in the case of Terriss, seemed to amuse rather than annoy the great man. No doubt the prestige of being Irving's secretary was very good for Austin; Austin, certainly, was very good for Irving.

All these changes were for the better. In retrospect only one incident had occurred which had left him with an uneasy twinge of conscience. During the run of *The Cup*, in January 1881, old Mrs. Bateman had died. Since she had handed over the Lyceum to Irving, she had struggled vainly to restore the popularity of the Sadler's Wells Theatre. The venture, in which she had sunk all her available capital, had not succeeded. It was, perhaps, inevitable that the close ties between Irving and herself were strained by their contrasting success and failure. Both were surrounded by friends whose loyalty made it incumbent upon them to sow the seed of discord. Irving's adherents were anxious to prove to him that he owed nothing to the Batemans; that, indeed, his association with them had even delayed his triumph. Mrs. Bateman no doubt was persuaded (for Kate had never liked or understood Irving, believing that, but for her financial support, he would never have had his opportunity) that Irving in some way had taken advantage of her and was lacking in gratitude for all that her husband had done for him. Not a few mutual friends had refused to countenance the displacement of Isabel by Ellen Terry; those whose doors were closed to the latter found that their friendship with Irving was ended. Thus gradually he became estranged from the family whose fortunes had been so closely identified with his own and with whom, at a critical period of his life, he had made his home. One winter's night Mrs. Bateman caught a chill while waiting for an omnibus to take her to Sadler's Wells. Pneumonia set in and a few days later this indomitable woman died. Irving called at the house. He was coldly received by Kate, but was allowed to take a last farewell of his old friend. He did not, as he had done when the Colonel died, drive to the funeral as one of the family. For some reason or other he did not go at all. He knew well enough how much he owed to them both. He could not have anything but lasting regret that he had allowed petty professional misunderstandings to come between them, or that he had not made a greater effort to preserve their old friendship for one another. It was too late now. She had died, leaving nothing but the lease of a theatre burdened with debt. Isabel, proud and still longing for the day when she could find peace and fulfilment in a religious order, continued to act until she had paid off her mother's creditors.

Irving was back in London at the end of August for the final rehearsals of *Romeo and Juliet*. There had been one or two changes in the cast. George Alexander had joined the Kendals' company at the St. James's Theatre, and his part, Paris, had been given to a youngster whom Lord Houghton might have described as a cadet of a family of position—Frank Benson. During the previous year there had been a flutter in the academic dove-cots of Oxford University when F. R. Benson (Winchester and New College) announced his intention of performing, with a number of other undergraduates, the Agamemnon of Euripides. This daring and unprecedented proposal actually to perform a work which for centuries had been pastured in the respectable fields of scholarship, raised an issue upon which the university was fairly evenly divided. Many, including Spooner, the Warden of New College, had grave misgivings as to the propriety of such a venture; others, having been assured that the play would be spoken in Greek, were inclined to favour the experiment. Both parties doubted whether Mr. Benson, who had only taken a pass in Mods, had sufficient scholarship to know what he was about. He had, however, recently won the three-mile against Cambridge in the inter-varsity sports and included a number of blues among his fellow-actors. The project would have been so much more questionable if it had been put forward by any of the disciples of Walter Pater such as Mr. Wilde, lately of Magdalen. Mr. Benson was fully aware of his inadequacy and had enlisted the help of all the artists, archaeologists and scholars he could find. He had even dared to approach Dr. Jowett for permission to act the play in Baliol Hall. The Master, who took a more liberal view of the theatre at large than most of his colleagues and found that the cast included a number of his scholars, gave his consent. 'I wish you success', he said, 'above all I hope you will do it well.' Benson, who played Clytemnestra, and his friends, did it as well as they could—so well that as an event it rivalled in popularity the Commem. Ball and the varsity cricket match. Many leading actors and actresses from London came to see them, among them Irving and Ellen Terry.

A few years later it became common knowledge that if a young man raised his head above his peers as a writer or artist, within a very short time he would find himself sitting at Irving's side at supper in the Beefsteak Room. Slightly intoxicated by the glory of the occasion and the Heidsieck '74, he would be conscious of a touch on the shoulder and the voice of his host saying in quiet confidential tones: 'And remember—me boy, if you have anything you think—'m—would do for me—for the Lyceum—ye know—come and see me—ye know— any time.' In due course, Benson and his friends were invited to the Lyceum to see *The Corsican Brothers.* Stoker welcomed them warmly as fellow athletes. Between the acts he took Benson to see Irving in his dressing-room. 'Tough and sinewy,' Benson recorded, 'looked that spare figure in the picturesque Corsican dress. The pale sensitive face wore a wistful, restless expression, modified by lines of playful and sarcastic humour; . . . from under the refined, artistic brows, a pair of piercing yet gentle eyes looked into the heart of men and things. "You young men did splendidly," said Irving with a sigh. 'If only I had had the opportunity in my young days that you have in yours! Why do you not band together in your troupe, work, study and become a company, the like of which this age has not seen? We have the technical skill upon the stage, we have the traditions; the difficulty nowadays is to get a company that has the literary mind and the trained intellectuality that is associated with university students. Should any of you determine to adopt the stage as your profession I shall be only too glad to render you any assistance I can.'

The interview was interrupted by the call boy: ' "Chateau Renaud" just on, your cue for coming, please, Guv'nor.'

Irving was as good as his word. Benson, when he decided to become an actor, asked for and was given a part at the Lyceum. Flushed with amateur success and with his confidence inflated by a smattering of professional tuition, he arrived at the stage-door of the Lyceum for his first rehearsal, seeing himself as the torch-bearer of a new generation of actors who, with their twin gifts of scholarship and athleticism, would enrich the narrow life and fustian art of the theatre. Benson observed the veiled backstage life of the Lyceum with the fresh perception of the uninitiated. The stage-door-keeper, Barry, an Irishman and an old soldier, had acquired, during his years of service at the Lyceum, the verbosity of a Shakespearian clown.

'Come this way,' he said to the young man who explained that he wanted to see Mr. Irving. Pointing to a small crowd of people who were waiting in the passage, he continued: 'They all want to see Mr. Irving. Many in that crowd are Members of Parliament, peers, painters, poets, all the pick of the land; but I've told them that they can't see the Guv'nor this morning. He is busy with an old crony who played with him years ago in stock companies; and I know exactly what'll happen. They will talk of the times when they were glad to receive twenty shillings a week, and not certain of that; they'll talk for two hours, and then the Guv'nor'll get up and he will say, "Fortune has been kinder to me than it has been to you, and if this is any good to you then make use of it for auld lang syne," and he'll slip two tenners into his hand. And he won't care a bit that he's kept the House of Lords and all these swells waiting, as long as he's helped an old brother pro in distress. That's what makes the Guv'nor the big man he is, and that is why he's loved throughout the profession. If you wait for hours, you won't see him.'

The young man explained that he'd been told to attend rehearsal at eleven. 'Och!' exclaimed Barry. 'And why didn't you say so before. You're the young man Mr. Allen has been looking for. Through that door, and you'll see him on the stage.' He found Allen, but before he could introduce himself the prompter said briskly:

'Mr. Benson, I presume? My name's Allen. I will just run through your part; and then you'll be ready to meet the company tomorrow morning. So you're going to take Mr. Alexander's place? He's a young fool to go, and you're jolly lucky to get such a chance . . . now then, we will take the last scene first. You enter left, and strew flowers at the gate that opens out of the tomb onto the stage. Get on with it, please.'

By this time Benson's self-confidence had evaporated. He forgot his words and with them most of his pretensions. Allen took him under his wing and the next day he met the whole company. Rather to his surprise they gave a kindly welcome to this well-to-do amateur who, almost without trial, had been given a part which would have been regarded as a plum by a needy or ambitious professional. There was a sudden hush as Irving came upon the stage, '. . . hardly a greeting to anyone . . . except to Mrs. Stirling whom he kissed on either cheek.' Seeing Benson he gave him a friendly hurried nod. 'Glad to see you— me boy—hope you'll be comfortable.' He passed on and disappeared into his office.

As the rehearsals wore on, Benson was stripped of every shred of his self-esteem as an actor. Almost all he had left was his pride in his skill as a swordsman—in this, by university standards, he knew he excelled anyone at the Lyceum. When the time came to rehearse the duel between Paris and Romeo he assumed the correct stance and faced Irving, confident that at last his quality would be recognized. Irving at a glance took in the situation. Adjusting his glasses, he fell upon the astonished Benson, with one hand seized his foil, hit him over the knuckles with his sword, prodded him in the stomach with his knee, clashed swords once for effect, and muttering 'Die—me boy—die—down—down', elbowed and kneed him into the mouth of the tomb and stood over him brandishing a torch. It was all over in a moment; the polite posturing and dexterous passes of the fencing school had succumbed to the furious onslaught of cut-and-thrust theatrical all-in combat.

Mrs. Kendal, in the course of the scrappy tuition she had given him before he came to the Lyceum, had told Benson that make-up was unnecessary and even hampered facial expression. To the horror of those with whom he shared a dressing-room, he went down to the dress rehearsal properly costumed, but with his handsome face unsullied by paint. As he came off after his first scene he found Bram Stoker waiting for him in the wings. He told Benson sharply that from the front his face looked dirty and that he appeared to be sweating with fear. Benson began to explain that it was a hot night and that he had a theory. The night was cooler than Stoker's temper. He told him to forget his theories and to go and get made up properly like everyone else. By now the crestfallen young man had been rendered into a state of malleability from which it might be possible to mould an actor. He got through the first night without disaster—perhaps better than he knew, for afterwards in his dressing-room he found a note from Ellen Terry: 'Well done for first done.' He became an object of interest to the rest of the company, for, thanks to Ellen Terry's intercession with Irving, he was allowed peculiar privileges such as sitting in the prompt corner where he could take notes of the performances. ('Only,' she begged, 'make your notes afterwards and *not* during the play.') On one occasion he had the innocent temerity to approach the Chief, who between scenes was resting in a chair in the wings. This was an unheard-of breach of etiquette.

'A very beautiful part, that of Romeo,' he confided to Irving, as one scholar to another.

'Yes,' snapped Irving. 'And the odd thing about it is that every damn young fool who's been on the stage two minutes thinks he can play it.' Irving may have been thinking of the three guineas he had paid, as a youth, for the privilege of doing so at the Soho Theatre; it is more likely that his remark was intended to be a chilling rebuff, and as such Benson certainly accepted it. In future when he passed through the stage-door he wrapped his natural self-assurance in a cloak of diffidence. Irving was fully aware of the salutary correction he was undergoing. Later, after a rehearsal, he said : 'You are too modest, Benson— too modest, ye know.' And then peering at him with awful penetration added: 'Or at least—you pretend to be—so.'

Benson was not re-engaged for *Much Ado About Nothing*. The visionary actor-manager and the earnest graduate had shared a curious experience. Irving, perhaps, had begun to wonder whether, for an actor, three years at a university was quite as efficacious as two in the stock company of the Theatre Royal, Edinburgh; Benson's head spun with vertigo as he peered into the gulf that lay between academic theory and the stern, rule-of-thumb method which was the practice at the undeniably successful Lyceum. Neither of them, however, was deflected by this experience from his higher purposes. 'Thank you very much,' Benson had written to Ellen Terry, 'for writing me a word of encouragement. . . . I was much touched at the kindness and sympathy of all the company and their efforts to make the awkward new boy feel at home. . . . I feel doubly grateful to you and Mr. Irving for the light you shed from the lamp of art on life now that I begin to understand the labour and weariness the process of trimming the Lamp entails.'

6

During the first weeks of the fifth season a lightness of heart permeated the dressing and green rooms and even the offices of the Lyceum, such as the older members of the company had never known. For all its apparent successes, the year had brought its anxieties, and the vexations of the Chief were apt to be visited upon his subordinates. Immediately the rehearsals of *Much Ado* began the clouds lifted and discontent vanished before the gaiety and confidence with which Irving and Ellen Terry set about the cantankerous courtship of Beatrice and Benedick. Now that *Othello* and *Romeo and Juliet* had been shelved indefinitely, Irving needed another major Shakespearean production to balance the programme for his forthcoming visit to America. He had, therefore, abandoned for the time being his policy of alternating classical and contemporary drama. *Much Ado* suited his purpose admirably —it would add to his repertoire of Shakespeare and, with its high comedy, would relieve the tragic gloom of most of the other plays he was taking with him. 'The fact is,' he wrote in *Good Words*, 'that Shakespeare is as modern as any playwright of our time. The delightful humour of *Much Ado About Nothing* is as highly relished as the best comedy of our own life and manners.' In this spirit the play was produced. Ellen Terry was on familiar terms with Beatrice. Irving had been studying the play since early July, when he had taken the part of Benedick at one of Helena Faucit's readings at Onslow Square. Ellen Terry was born to play Beatrice. Rejecting entirely any suggestion of the capricious shrew, she was the personification of a 'pleasant spirited lady'—all mirth and audacious mockery—a stranger to melancholy identifying herself absolutely with the part. Since, as Beatrice, she came nearer to playing Ellen Terry than in any other part, Ellen Terry as Beatrice was unrivalled in her own time. As Benedick, Irving found expression for his supreme genius in eccentric comedy. He balanced dry humour and romantic gallantry so perfectly that never for one moment was Benedick in danger of being thought a fool or a serious-minded gentleman, in the manner of Charles Kemble or Macready, whom others could make a fool of. He was the model of chivalrous courtesy to all but Beatrice, who alone provoked him into drawing the rapier of satirical repartee.

The comedy was not so fragile that it could be swamped by sumptuous production. It was mounted handsomely, rivalling *Romeo and Juliet* in its splendour of scene and costume, yet in a gayer and more operatic key. Irving always delighted in the reproduction or adaptation of church ritual for the stage. The church scene allowed him to indulge this predilection. The scene itself was a miracle of illusion— solid structure blending into painted perspectives lit with such subtlety as to suggest an infinity of pillared transepts and vaulted chapels. 'One day,' he told a friend, 'I found in Quaritch's an old black letter volume. It was a work on Italian Ceremonies and it had four large illustrations. I had intended to spend four or five pounds—it cost me eighty. But in it I found a picture of a wedding ceremony which struck me at once as the effect I needed—and which was of the period. It was created by a mass of vergers or javelin men—officers of the church, I should imagine. They were dressed in long robes and each carried a halberd. I pressed these men at once into the service of Shakespeare and his cathedral scene at Messina—Telbin's masterpiece, with its real built-out round pillars thirty feet high, its canopied roof of crimson plush from which hung the golden lamps universally used in Italian cathedrals, its painted canopy overhanging the altar, its great ironwork gates, its altar with cases of flowers and flaming candles rising to a height of eighteen feet, its stained glass windows and statues of saints. It was a great anxiety—we calculated that it would require a wait of twenty minutes to set it. In practice we managed to do it in an act interval of fifteen.' Irving may be suspected, and indeed was often accused, of lusting after spectacle for its own sake. His justification lay in his own words—there was no art or artifice too splendid to be pressed into the service of Shakespeare. When all was done and vast scenes such as this had been set, the stage was plunged in darkness. Then, like a painter, he rediscovered with his brush of light a form here, a detail there, until, softly blending shadow and substance and accentuating significant highlights, he had, as he understood it, done what he could to realize the poet's dream and to create an illusion which would make easier the task of the supreme artist in the theatre—the actor.

The play was produced in five acts and thirteen scenes. All of these, with the exception of the interior of Leonato's house, the garden and the church, were front scenes contrived with nothing more substantial than painted cloths. Yet so perfect was the collaboration between Irving and his scene-painters, who knew exactly how he would light their canvases, that extraordinary illusions of depth and solidity were conjured from one plane to an extent never before realized in the history of stage design.

A gifted and handsome young actor, Johnston Forbes Robertson, was engaged for the part of Claudio. He was a talented painter who had studied under Julian in Paris, but, coming under the spell of Phelps, had abandoned his brushes for the stage. Almost his first appearance had been with Ellen Terry in *The Wandering Heir*. She had thought so little of him as an actor that she had begged him to stick to his painting. During the rehearsals of *Much Ado* she watched him confound her pessimism as he revealed his original and wholly rational estimate of Claudio's character and interpreted it with rare artistry. He, like Benson, was on his way to raising a company of his own. He stayed at the Lyceum only for a season, but long enough to record the church scene in a fine conversation piece which Irving had commissioned him to paint and thereafter had an honoured place on the walls of the Beef-steak Room.

7

At one point in the rehearsals a cloud threatened to darken the sunlit glade, when Irving and Ellen Terry fell out over a matter of artistic principle. Firmly of the opinion that she could not improve upon her earlier Beatrice, she was dismayed to find that Irving's slow, deliberate Benedick forced her to modify the pace and timing of her performance. Her simmering discontent boiled into open rebellion when she discovered that, at the end of the church scene, he proposed to interpolate a gag which, though it had been hallowed by tradition, she had scorned to use in her earlier production. Shakespeare ends his scene with Benedick, as he leaves Beatrice, saying:

. . . as you hear of me, so think of me, Go, comfort your cousin: I must say she is dead, and so farewell.

Many actors before Irving had found that in this climax the great scene lacked vehemence—that Benedick needed, as it were, a more forceful disengagement. It had, therefore, become the custom for Beatrice to repeat:

'Benedick, kill Claudio!'

and for Benedick on his exit to declare:

'As sure as I'm alive I will!'

For a week the struggle continued. Ellen fought hard with every weapon in her armoury—including the 'vraies larmes' which had won Coquelin's admiration. Irving remained quietly obdurate. At last Ellen, protesting that she only wished to shield him from the inevitable recrimination of the Shakespearian scholars, capitulated. Irving may or may not have been right in allowing theatrical expediency to overrule his professed reverence for Shakespeare, but for once Furnivall and his watch dogs were caught napping; no critics detected Irving's fall from grace. No doubt his delivery of the offending line was so forceful that Shakespeare himself might have been persuaded that he had written it.

Much Ado was produced on October 11th and all differences were forgotten in the paean of praise which rose from even the most crusty critic. The audience streamed out of the theatre smacking its lips over the most exquisite confection that the chefs of the Lyceum had yet concocted and with that sense of well-being that came from having been able, at one time, to enjoy a rollicking entertainment and an intellectual recreation. George Augustus Sala hastened to report to Irving the impression the play had made upon his friends:

'It was a Magnificent Performance, complete and (humanly speaking) perfect; and so say all sorts and conditions of men. I was dining at F. de Rothschild's on Thursday and heard what the "swells" had to say. Unanimous and enthusiastic verdict of approval—and so it is wherever I go. Even Hiscius and Spongius (vide Massenger) the habitual carpers and backbiters who *hate* genius simply because it soars beyond their own horizon—which is simply the top of the palings of their own pig-sty—are this time dumbfounded and do not know exactly "where to have you." But let them alone. They will find out something nasty to say, by and by. The well-springs of malignity lie very deep indeed, and are inexhaustible.'

But for once the turgid wells had dried up. Even the *Athenaeum* and the *Academy* vied with each other in praise of Irving's Benedick. '*Much Ado About Nothing*,' cried Joseph Knight, 'must be pronounced the most successful of Irving's Shakespearian revivals—no actor of whom the present generation has any knowledge or preserves any recollection can claim to have so thoroughly entered into the character or charged it with equal vitality . . . it has much fancy and variety and attains distinct intellectual elevation.' 'Mr. Irving,' echoed the critic of the *Academy*, 'was made for Benedick and Benedick for Mr. Irving . . . the element of satire in the part—the conception of the robust humanity boasting its own strength and swayed even while it boasts by the lightest of feminine charms—is much in his own humour. The chivalry of the character suits him . . . and its quiet self-analytical wit. He is excellent in speech and as excellent in by-play.' One critic who felt that Irving's Benedick could not pass unchallenged ('though the challenge is a timid one'), in summing up, aptly described the peculiar radiance which seemed to dazzle Lyceum playgoers who were ready to bask in it and to which those 'too blind to have desire to see' were stubbornly impervious: '. . . for pure enjoyment of a play—or "going to the play" as we say—an evening spent in the society of those beautifully dressed, admirably graceful ladies and gentlemen, in that Lyceum-land where, as in the isle of the lotus eaters it is always afternoon, is perfect. When we leave we have indeed been to the play—not merely looked on at the performance but *been*—to the home of chivalry, romance, ease and wealth, where nothing sordid can ever enter, though malice and all uncharitableness creep in to make it human and to stir those softer emotions without which Paradise itself would not be perfect.'

Several critics commended Irving for giving, in his arrangement of the play, due prominence to the misfortunes of Hero, though in so doing he diverted the attention of the audience from himself and Ellen Terry.

Unwittingly they did him an injustice. Such cuts and transitions in the text of his plays he made, as a rule, with the object of maintaining dramatic tension and continuity of story. If the story was held together entirely by the character which he, the protagonist, was playing—such as Louis XI—other parts were ruthlessly cut and any scenes omitted which, in the absence of the dominating character, might cause the interest of the audience to flag. In the case of *Much Ado*, since the plot centred on the defamation of Hero, it would not have occurred to him to curtail these scenes in order to sharpen the focus on Beatrice and Benedick. The critics nodded in failing to chide him for his inadequate casting and direction of Dogberry and his watchmen. He was careless of his clowns, and had he been sharply criticized for his neglect in this case he would not have fallen into the same error when later he produced *Twelfth Night* with, as he then admitted, far more serious consequences.

Irving knew how important it was that he should advance upon the United States as a conqueror rather than as a suppliant. The news of the extraordinary success of *Much Ado* preceded him and made it clear that he left England in a blaze of glory. The play ran until the beginning of June 1883, when it was withdrawn, although still playing to houses averaging more than £300 a night, in order that he could revive during the remaining two months of the season the plays which he was taking on his American tour. Irving was no impractical dreamer. He had his hands on every detail of the planning and organisation of this vast enterprise. Each production was rehearsed, produced and overhauled before, complete to the most trivial property, it was packed for shipment. In addition to the many tons of scenery required for twelve plays, he was taking a company of nearly a hundred actors, actresses, and stage technicians, including three wig-makers from Clarkson's to maintain the eleven hundred new wigs which plays of such a variety of periods called for.

Irving bade farewell to his London audience on the night of July 28th, when the fifth season ended. As was now the custom, he took his benefit, playing *Eugene Aram* and *The Belle's Stratagem*, while Toole contributed a farce and Sims Reeves a few appropriate ballads to fill the bill. When the curtain fell the theatre was packed from floor to ceiling—it was late and actors from other theatres had hurried round to the Lyceum where they crowded the aisles and gangways. The clamour of applause was deafening. The frantic cheers and undisguised tears of the Victorian audience bordered on hysteria. Irving made a short farewell speech in which he told them that he would be in America for six months and asked them meanwhile to give a friendly welcome to Mr. Lawrence Barrett, who was coming from America to play at the Lyceum in his absence. The curtain fell, and, in response to the thunder of clapping which broke out again and drowned the strains of the band who were playing Auld Lang Syne, it rose once more to disclose Irving and Ellen Terry surrounded by the entire company and stage staff. The tumultuous demonstration of goodwill which this spectacle inspired left no doubt in the minds of those upon the stage that they left London to cross the Atlantic on the floodtide of their success. The wild emotions of the two thousand people who, happily exhausted, dispersed at last into the Strand, were reflected in the cold arithmetic of Stoker's account book. The fifth season showed that receipts exceeded expenditure by £16,000.

Meanwhile, Irving had received a profusion of compliments and tributes from his friends, from the public, and even from royalty, which might have turned a head less level than his own. No banquet celebrated the hundredth night of *Much Ado*, but in May the Prince of Wales had accepted Irving's invitation to sup with him at the Lyceum. Originally it had been intimated that the Prince would like to be entertained in the Beefsteak Room. Irving, however, wished as many as possible of his fellow-actors to share this unprecedented honour; so, with the Prince's permission, supper was laid for fifty on the stage. The Prince, who had been behind the scenes during the run of *The Corsican Brothers* and had astonished the staff with his knowledge of the details of stage management, entered enthusiastically into the deployment of the principal members of the cast who were to appear in this unusual scene. Lord Knollys, his private secretary, wrote:

Marlborough House,
May 4th, 1883.

'Dear Mr. Irving,

The Prince of Wales thinks that the further names which you mentioned to me on Monday will be a decided addition to your supper party.

His Royal Highness will propose that the American minister should sit on his right and that next to him Lord Fife should come. The Duke of Beaufort should sit on your left and Lord Hardwicke next to him.

Yours sincerely,

Francis Knollys.'

and finally, a last-minute correction:

'. . . I think now you'd better put the Duke of Sutherland between the U.S. Minister and Fife.'

In the course of the evening, the Prince told Irving of his interest in the recently founded Royal College of Music and of the need of proper funds to put it on its feet, hinting that a benefit matinée at the Lyceum would further this need and would be an expression of the goodwill of actors towards musicians. Irving readily agreed to put the theatre at their disposal, and the Prince suggested that it would be an excellent opportunity for Irving and Toole to revive *Robert Macaire*, which he had never seen. In spite of the existing pressure of work at the Lyceum, Irving prepared a production of *Robert Macaire* as thoroughly as if it was to be included in his American programme. 'It may interest you,' he wrote to Percy Fitzgerald, 'to see a version of our Macaire and I send a rough proof of the work. You said, I think, that you might have a few bits of business of the immortal Frederic (Lemaître). I never saw that great master, but everything he did would be well worth consideration except perhaps his scaling the boxes and dress circle at the end of the play. I shall make Macaire a ruffian always—sometimes with the touch of a dandy.' The matinée, which included *Iolanthe* with Ellen Terry and excerpts from *Money* by Bancroft and his company, was attended by the Prince and Princess of Wales and made a clear profit of £1,000 for the Royal College. In due course Irving received a warm and friendly letter of thanks for his services over a signature to which was appended the designation 'Chairman'. Irving wrote to Sir George Grove, the Director of the College, thanking him for his courtesy, and adding in reference to the letter: 'By the way, who is our genial friend Mr. Edwards? I do not think I have met him.'

A messenger came post haste from Sir George to point out that the signatory was not Mr. Edwards but Albert Edward, Prince of Wales.

These close associations with the Court gave rise, no doubt, to rumours that Irving was about to be offered a knighthood. The rumours, which of course reached him, were unfounded. An opportunity came for him to dispose of them when a hundred or more British and American actors gave a farewell supper in his honour at the Garrick Club. Bancroft had approached the committee of the club for permission to use the great coffee-room and through their chairman, Lord Glenesk, the committee, in giving their consent, declared that the occasion would be an honour to the club. Thus, surrounded by the portraits of great actors and actresses of the past, Irving, who only ten years earlier had been blackballed by the club, received the homage of all the prominent actors of his day—all but one, for Barry Sullivan had declined Bancroft's invitation 'bluntly and finally . . .

writing that he could not bring himself to acknowledge the justice of the position to which Irving had undoubtedly attained'. For some time past the veteran tragedian had surrendered the capital to Irving and, retiring to the provinces, had successfully maintained his hold on Ireland and Lancashire against all comers. There, with no accessories but his great voice, his still powerful physique and his theatrical basket, and with no expenditure other than his own keep, his revenue steadily accumulated into a considerable private fortune.

In the course of a speech, in which he thanked his friends for their kindness and for the tributes which had been paid to him by Bancroft and others, Irving said: '. . . titles for painters—if you like—they paint at home; for writers—they write at home; for musicians, they compose at home. But the actor acts in the sight of his audience—he wants a fair field and no favours. He acts among his colleagues without whom he is powerless; and to give him any distinction in the playbill which others could not enjoy would be prejudicial to his success and fatal, I believe, to his popularity.'

A few nights earlier, a more public expression of the regard in which his countrymen held him had been given at a banquet in the St. James's Hall where five hundred of the most distinguished men in London (and four hundred of their women folk discreetly hidden in the galleries) wished him godspeed on his journey. Lord Coleridge, the Lord Chief Justice, was in the chair. In proposing Irving's health he paid a sincere and measured tribute to Irving's influence for good upon the English stage in general and in particular to the policy which he had pursued at the Lyceum.

'He has, I believe,' said Lord Coleridge in the course of his speech, 'recognised that in this matter there lies upon him, as upon everyone in his position, a grave responsibility. He has felt, perhaps unconsciously, that the heroic signal of Lord Nelson ought not be confined in its application simply to men of arms, but that England expects every man to do his duty when it lays upon him a duty to do and to do it nobly. Moreover, I believe that what has brought us together tonight, besides that feeling, is the remembrance of the generosity and unselfishness of Mr. Irving's career. He has shown that generosity not only in the parts he has played but in the parts he has not played. He has shown that he did not care to be always the central figure of a surrounding group, in which everyone was to be subordinated to the centre, and in which every actor was to be considered as a foil to the leading part. He has been superior to the selfishness which now and again has interfered with the greatness of some of our best actors and he has had his reward. He has collected around him a set of men who, I believe, are proud to act with him—men whose feeling towards him has added not a little to the brilliant success which his management has achieved; men who feel that they act, not merely under a manager, but under a friend; men who are proud to be his companion, and many of whom have come here tonight to show by their presence that they are so.'

Before the Honourable J. Russell Lowell, the United States Minister, had described the keen anticipation with which his countrymen awaited the arrival of the Lyceum Company, Irving made a brief speech of thanks in which he asserted that for his part the occasion was a tribute, not so much to himself as to the art he was proud to serve:

'Your Lordship,' he concluded, 'has spoken most eloquently of my career. Possessed of a generous mind and a high judicial faculty, your Lordship has been tonight, I fear, more generous than judicial. But if I have in any way deserved commendation, I am proud that it was as an actor that I won it. As the Director of a theatre my experience has been short, but as an actor I have been before the London public for seventeen years; and on one thing I am sure you will all agree— that no actor or manager has ever received from their public more generous, ungrudging encouragement and support . . . the climax of the favour extended to me by my countrymen has been reached tonight. You have set upon me a burden of responsibility—a burden which I gladly and proudly bear. The memory of tonight will be to me a sacred thing—a memory which throughout my life will be ever treasured—a memory which will stimulate me to further endeavour and encourage me to loftier aims.'

The cumulative effect of the public and private compliments which had been showered upon Irving was to provoke a section of the press to lampoon with squibs and caricatures the adulation for him which was condemned as extravagant, hysterical, and often artificially promoted. He was portrayed in *Fun* as a patient and mildly protesting figure being larded with butter and as declining, on account of his numerous engagements, an invitation proffered by the importunate Prince of Wales. Other papers, using transparent pseudonyms, suggested that all these affairs had been organized by his cunning and assiduous henchmen. Neither Irving nor the public paid much attention to this denigration. The public marked the modesty with which he accepted these tokens of their admiration. He had no cause to doubt the sincerity of their applause and good wishes or of the spontaneous evidences of the affection and esteem in which he was held by his friends and his fellow-actors.

He had, moreover, received most welcome evidence that his efforts to secure for his profession the recognition which the State accorded to the sister arts, had not been made in vain.

Lord Coleridge had invited the Prime Minister to the banquet at the St. James's Hall. Gladstone, writing that he regretted his inability to attend, added in his letter:

June 27th, 1883.

'. . . Would it be too audacious to offer Irving a knighthood? Please let this be most secret: for I should have to hold divers consultations before acting.'

Coleridge had already deputed his son, Stephen, among other of the actor's close friends, to find out if Irving would be willing to accept this honour if it were offered to him. Stephen Coleridge recorded in his diary:

'. . . he would not accept it; he said that an actor differed from other artists, musicians and the like, in that he had to appear in person every night appealing directly to the public favour . . . that there was a fellowship among actors of a company that would be impaired by any elevation of one member over another; that his strength as a manager and power as an actor lay far more in the suffrages of the plain folk in the pit than in the patronage, however lofty, of great people; that he knew instinctively that large numbers of these same plain folk would be offended at their simple Henry Irving accepting decorations of a titular kind. He disclaimed any false pride in the matter, he did not affect to despise such an honour and was very grateful to my father for his kind desires.'

Lord Coleridge thereupon reported to Gladstone the result of his tentative enquiry.

1 Sussex Place, W.
St. Peter (i.e. 29 June
1883).

'My dear Mr. Gladstone,

It is most generous & kind of you to have thought of this thing. I had a half intention to get a few names together & memorialize you privately on the subject. But before doing so & before your letter came I took the precaution to sound Irving through a very intimate friend & I found that (I think on the whole wisely) he would not on any account accept it. He thinks that it would be very *ill* taken, instead of well, by

MR. IRVING.—"THE FACT IS, I AM SO PESTERED WITH INVITATIONS TO DINNER, THAT YOU REALLY MUST EXCUSE ME!"

his profession & like a gentleman & true artist as he is he wishes before all things to stand well with his profession & not seem to be put over them. I did this before stirring in the matter because I felt it due to the Queen & to you not to allow an offer to be made of an honour which would not be accepted. So with many & grateful thanks & the thing being an absolute secret so far as you are concerned I suppose it had better now drop—

Yours always truly & gratefully

Coleridge.'

Irving, though convinced that his reasons for declining this offer were sound, had good cause to regard with satisfaction the motives which had prompted the Prime Minister to make it.

The few remaining weeks before he sailed were spent in strenuous work and exacting conviviality. During July he found time to give John Everett Millais some sittings for a portrait which the artist wished to give to the Garrick Club. Millais and Irving had much in common in their characters and predilections and had become close friends. The painter rarely missed a first night at the Lyceum and usually followed up his visits with a letter to Irving expressing his delight in all he had seen and occasionally remarking, with marginal illustrations, on errors or anachronisms which he had detected in costumes or weapons. Millais, too, was pressed for time, for every August he left London for the grouse moor and salmon rivers of his beloved Murthly in Perthshire. Unlike Irving, who neither sought nor enjoyed any recreation from his work and life in the theatre, he delighted in abandoning his studio and the world of fashion for the life of a country gentleman, which he was able to lead in some style on the proceeds of his prodigious industry. Perhaps over-impressed by the number of banquets and receptions in Irving's honour which so recently he had attended, he saw and painted the immaculate and gracious man of distinction—the man who—like himself in the near future—would become the academic dean of a sister art; he failed entirely to portray the actor and the abiding Bohemian. If Irving, perhaps, regarded his friend's handiwork with sly humour, Brodribb certainly was well satisfied with a picture which would display clearly on the walls of the Garrick Club the intellectual gentleman of his early ambition.

At the beginning of September he left London for Glasgow, Edinburgh, and Liverpool, where, staying a fortnight in each town, he tested his organization before leaving for America. In each city he was greeted with crowded houses and civic banquets. During his visit to Glasgow he and Ellen Terry were invited by Sir William Pearce, the chairman of John Elder's Shipyard, to spend a week-end on his palatial steam yacht, the *Lady Torfrida*, which was lying in the Clyde at the Tail of the Bank off Greenock. The party, which included Stoker, was met at Greenock by Sir William, who escorted them to the boat stairs. The night was pitch black and a gale of wind was blowing. They had some difficulty in getting aboard the yacht's dinghy, which, owing to the sea that was running, more than once was nearly stove against the quay. At last they were clear of the harbour with Sir William at the tiller, but once they had left the shelter of the land they felt the full force of the gale and of the heavy seas which threatened to swamp their boat. The crew baled furiously and the guests sat shoulder to shoulder along the weather gunwale, screening the waves which broke upon their backs. The darkness was so intense that Sir William lost his bearings. He ordered several blue flares to be burned and in their lurid light, as Irving no doubt remarked with pleasure, the black waves looked more menacing and their situation more precarious. Irving and Stoker, as in their former marine adventure, chatted away casually and had a calming effect upon the rest of the party who were showing signs of nervousness—with the exception of Ellen Terry, who was rallying her young son, Ted, by cheerful comments on the natural and artificial effects which were varied and fearful. Sir William kept up a boisterous and hearty cheerfulness, but urged Irving and Stoker, in whispered asides, to maintain their stoic calm though their situation was indeed desperate. At last the siren of the *Lady Torfrida* was heard above the roar of the wind, and soon her lights were picked up. The bedraggled and dripping party were unceremoniously hauled aboard and soon recovered their spirits in the bright warmth of the splendid and well-appointed yacht. It had been a near thing. Irving and Stoker may well have wondered if they were fated Jonahs and what further perils lurked in the extended seafaring to which they were committed.

In Edinburgh, Irving, playing Louis XI, opened for the first time the new theatre which had been built by his old manager, Wyndham, in partnership with J. B. Howard, and had been named the Royal Lyceum in honour of Irving and perhaps in acknowledgement of the financial assistance he had given them during its construction. Here, as in Glasgow, he was entertained by the Pen and Pencil Club in the Freemason's Hall where he reaffirmed his affection for a city which he always looked upon as his alma mater. 'When I think of my dreams here,' he told his host, 'some of which have not been wholly unrealized, and when I recall the friendships formed here, some of which have never faltered . . . you will know how dear to me is your noble city.' One or two of the friends of his early days were not there to greet him. Edward Saker had died, and the Alexandra Theatre, Liverpool, was now managed by his wife. It was eighteen years, he reminded those who thronged the theatre on the last night of the season, since he had stood outside the old Prince of Wales's Theatre wondering what he should do next. In Liverpool he had passed the nadir of his transit, but no town, thanks very largely to the loyalty of Edward Russell, had done more to lift him to his present zenith.

He and Ellen Terry, on October 11th, sailed from Liverpool in the *Britannic*; the rest of the company followed in a slower ship, the *City of Rome*. He had time, after a flying visit to London, to spend a day at Knowsley with the Earl of Derby and with Gladstone, who came over to lunch from Hawarden to bid him farewell. On the morning of embarkation, he gave a breakfast to the directors and committee of the Royal General Theatrical Fund, a Pickwickian body composed of about twenty of his closest and most congenial friends, including Toole, who had journeyed from London to see him off. Tremendous crowds gathered on the quay to watch him and Ellen Terry embark. As passengers they enjoyed almost princely privileges. A quarter of the ship's drawing-room had been partitioned off for Ellen Terry's private use, in addition to two cabins which had been knocked into one for her special comfort. Charlie was handed over to the ship's butcher to ensure his proper nourishment.

Irving had said when he took farewell of his Liverpool audience that, like Sir Peter Teazle, they left their characters behind them, but with greater confidence than Sir Peter, that they would be well cared for. As the shores of England receded, he surveyed the English theatrical scene, and felt satisfied that not only his character but his position and fortunes were not likely to suffer in his absence. The London theatre was very much the same as he had found it fifteen years ago. Apart from Bancroft at the Haymarket, the Kendals at the St. James's and the Gilbert and Sullivan operetta at the Savoy, London playgoers had little else to see but melodramas and burlesques of indifferent quality. So far, no rival had lifted his head to challenge his supremacy; nor had any disciple attempted to follow his example by presenting higher drama in the style that prevailed at the Lyceum. The loyalty of his public was unshaken; the press on the whole were well disposed towards him, and his detractors had apparently given up the unequal struggle of proving to him and to his supporters the error of their ways. He may have wondered why, when the position for which he fought so long had been won, and the fruits of victory were there for the picking, he was taking the field on a battleground where so many successful English actors had come to grief. But England's pioneers had always turned westwards to spread their doctrines or to make their fortunes. The time was advantageous and offered Irving a reasonable chance of doing both. The venture certainly was a costly and hazardous one, yet he looked forward confidently to his reception in America whither, as he had recently written to Loveday, 'we don't go for fame but for work and general excellence'.

CHAPTER XXIII

A New World to Conquer

Nobody knew better than Henry Irving that he was crossing the Atlantic, not as a missionary, bringing the light of drama to a stage-starved and backward Republic, but as a foreign tragedian challenging the opinion and criticism of a people who, in the larger cities of the Union, valued and supported an indigenous theatre as thriving and as rich in actors and actresses of talent as that of Great Britain. Since for many years the English-speaking peoples had not produced any considerable playwrights, British and American actors had been forced to use the same material—namely the classics, translations from the French and the works of their native melodramatists. Thus they played to a keenly critical public who could measure coldly an artist essaying, for instance, to play Richelieu, against the stature of four or five brilliant predecessors in the part.

For the last thirty years the stars of the American and English theatre had challenged each other on their home grounds. If their motives for doing so differed at all, it may have been that the Americans sought the endorsement of their triumphs by what they still believed to be the more cultivated audiences of the old world, while the English planned to replenish their treasuries by attracting to themselves some of the legendary wealth of the new. Irving knew that his acting would have to stand comparison with that of Booth and of other popular American tragedians. But, apart from his own performances, he was offering to America a totally fresh conception of theatrical production, hitherto unrealised in that country. As Ellen Terry said, 'they were pioneers, they were new, and to be new was everything in America'.

The American theatre had risen rapidly on the solid foundation laid by the Colonials. Though it had suffered a setback during the War of Independence, its traditions had been preserved by General John

Irving and Ellen Terry
in *Olivia*

Irving in his study
By J. W. H. Bartlett

Burgoyne who had been a friend of Garrick, and himself was a play-wright of some talent; he had even encouraged his troops, when in captivity at Charlottesville, Virginia, to build themselves a theatre for their own entertainment. Three years after the inauguration of Washington as President, an English actor, John Hodgkinson, who had played with Mrs. Siddons and G. F. Cooke, arrived in the United States and rallied round him a number of competent actors and actresses who had recently returned from Jamaica where they had sought refuge during the war. Hodgkinson was the son of a Manchester publican named Meadowcroft, and in England had earned the title of the 'Provincial Garrick'. He enjoyed a brief period of popularity in America before he died in 1805 of yellow fever. By then two young actors, James Fennell and Thomas Cooper, had arrived from England, and were challenging his monopoly of public favour. Fennell, an old Etonian and graduate of Cambridge, founded the star system in America, and was himself the model for so many of his successors—flamboyant in style, by nature generous and affectionate and utterly irresponsible in his private life. Cooper was Irish by birth, and before he was twenty-one was giving immature performances as Hamlet and Macbeth at Drury Lane. He made little mark in London, but in Philadelphia he soon fulfilled his early promise, and, for forty years, was acknowledged to be the leader of the American stage. His acting was uneven, but in its great moments was fired with a reflection of the lightning of Edmund Kean. He died in 1849, by which time J. B. Booth, Edwin Forrest and Charlotte Cushman were attracting increasing numbers of young Americans to their profession. Booth and Forrest developed a declamatory style which was adopted by their disciples and successors; Forrest, less perhaps by his art than by his violent clash with Macready, first focused the attention of the outside world upon the rapidly growing American school of acting.

When Irving set sail for New York the ranks of American stars had swollen and a number of theatrical dynasties—such as the Davenports, Sotherns, Drews and Wallacks—had been founded whose names would illuminate Broadway for several generations and would be found among the pioneers who settled with their cameras in the perpetual noon of California. Irving had long ceased to think of Americans as uncouth and forbidding strangers. Curiously enough, the influences and opportunities which had helped him to become the head of the English stage had been, to a very great extent, American. In Edwin Booth he had seen for the first time an actor of intellectual power; in the hour of his despair, Dion Boucicault (American by habit and adoption) had brought him to London; E. A. Sothern had introduced him to Paris and to the French school of acting; Bateman had enthroned him in the Lyceum. He numbered many leading American actors among his friends. His kindness to Booth, if in the eyes of cynics at home it was tinged with self-interest, was more generously regarded by Booth's compatriots. John McCullough and Lawrence Barrett, second only to Booth in the esteem of the American public, had, when they visited England, been honoured guests in the Beefsteak Room.

Some years before, Toole had sent him a vivid account of the ruthless venality of the American press. As soon as he had decided to tour the United States, Irving made his dispositions to meet this hazard with practised thoroughness. He was determined to be judged on his merits as an actor, and, as far as possible, to avoid any factional disputes. Soon after he came to the Lyceum, he had made a close friend of Joseph Hatton, the London correspondent of the New York *Tribune*. Hatton was a competent journalist, a lover of the theatre and his devoted admirer. Through Hatton, favourable intelligence of Irving reached New York some time before his detractors in England were in the field. Though the standard of dramatic criticism in America had risen since Toole's day, in general it was less polite than in London. There were, however, several critics who compared favourably with Joseph Knight or Clement Scott; of these the recognised leader was William Winter.

Winter was a considerable scholar and learned in the history of the theatre which he adored; he was a talented writer with a gift for turning out emotional odes and sonnets when occasion called for them. He was a loyal friend and an abusive foe—too prone to prejudice to be a very profound critic. In the summer of 1882, he came to England for the first time with Lawrence Barrett. Irving, at the time, was playing Romeo at the Lyceum. Although it was not a part in which the actor was seen at his best, he cast his spell over Winter, who was entranced by everything he saw. After a supper or two in the Beefsteak Room, and after a few days in the company of Hatton, Winter became Irving's liegeman and, if his earlier worship of Edwin Booth caused him to speak of Irving's artistry with certain reservations, his personal attachment to him was deep and lifelong. During this visit Winter, Lawrence Barrett and Irving were fellow-guests at a party given by Wilson Barrett, who was coming to the fore as a romantic actor. Irving, though no doubt he had already made up his mind, invited the company to advise him as to the part in which he should first appear in New York. Barrett suggested *Charles I*, others were for *Hamlet*; Winter insisted on *The Bells*.

'I shall act on my friend's counsel,' said Irving. 'He says that I shall be under great excitement on that night, that my audience will be much excited; that it is best to take advantage of the agitation of that time, and above all to avoid comparison with any established favourite. I shall act Mathias!'

Henceforward Irving, in Winter's eyes, could do no wrong. If by any chance the New York critics were in hostile array, their general had gone over to his camp. To consolidate these gains, he had sent in advance an enterprising young journalist, Austin Brereton, to represent him in New York. L. F. Austin was left behind to hold the Lyceum fort in England. Joseph Hatton, by arrangement with the *Tribune*, would be at his side throughout the tour.

2

The *Britannic* came to anchor off Staten Island in the early hours of October 21st. The sound of her cables running out must have provoked in Irving, hardened as he was to the demands of interviewers and careful as he had been to prepare himself for this moment, the same nervous tension as did the closing bars of an overture on a first night. The journalists were upon him. If he made a false step or created an adverse impression at this first meeting with them, no amount of histrionic genius might prevail in the face of their united disapproval.

Speeding towards the *Britannic* were two vessels—the *Blackbird*, a river steamer in whose dimly lit and smoky saloon was Henry Abbey, the impresario who had arranged the tour, with a number of sleepy and dishevelled reporters; and the *Yosemite*, Colonel Tilden's well-found steam yacht, which had been lent by her owner to Lawrence Barrett in order that, accompanied by W. J. Florence and Winter, he should be the first to greet Irving and Ellen Terry. The *Blackbird*, with thirty Italian musicians, whom Abbey had marshalled on the upper decks, playing 'God Save the Queen', was first alongside the *Britannic*, where, amidships, Irving, pale and smiling, acknowledged the cheers which had greeted his appearance on the main deck. Thereupon the situation became somewhat confused. Hardly had Irving reached the *Blackbird's* deck by way of a plank thrust perilously from her paddle-box, when Lawrence and his party boarded the *Britannic*, having approached her in the yacht's pinnace from the other side. Irving regained the gang-plank and embraced his friends. Bareheaded and clasping hands, the three great actors made a group which moved Winter as one 'of peculiar and touching beauty. Men more intellectual have never graced the stage . . . pale, thin, ascetic, dignified, with dark piercing eyes, thoughtful faces and hair touched with silver. . . . I saw prefigured that cordial union of brotherhood and art which has since been established between the theatres of England and these States'. The tableau dissolved as the Italians, perhaps a little invidiously, burst into 'Hail the Chief!' Florence arranged to transfer Irving and the pressmen to the well-appointed saloon of the *Yosemite*, while Barrett waited to escort Ellen Terry, who in a few minutes boarded the pinnace amid the cheers of her fellow-passengers, her passage to the yacht being accompanied by a rendering of 'Rule Britannia'. In the saloon Irving faced the reporters. Silently they scanned this legendary figure of whom such conflicting accounts had reached them.

'Well, gentlemen.' Irving broke the silence; he lit a cigar and appeared to be thoroughly at ease. No one seemed to wish to start the ball rolling. Florence tried to ease the situation by offering the company champagne.

'. . . and chicken!' added Irving, pointedly. 'That's how we do it in London, they say.'

This reference to current gossip, that he won the praise of critics by filling their stomachs when he failed to turn their heads, was lost upon the robust journalists of the New World where such procedure was regarded as plain common sense.

'Now, gentlemen,' continued Irving good-humouredly. 'Time flies. . . . I have a dread of you. Don't ask me how I like America at present—I shall, I am sure. Meanwhile I place myself at your disposal —don't spare me!'

The interviewers got to work. Already they were pleasantly surprised by their victim's agreeable and unassuming manner. (Ellen Terry called it 'his best Jingle manner . . . full of refinement, bonhomie, elegance and geniality.') They looked in vain for eccentricities which they had been led to expect. There were some pertinent questions as to why he had brought his whole company and all the scenic resources of the Lyceum. He explained that he had done so from an earnest desire to do justice to himself, to the theatre, and to the American public. Inevitably, they asked his opinion of Booth. He evaded the trap, speaking warmly of his association with Booth in London and ignoring the fact that so far no message of welcome had been received from Booth who was acting in Boston. He confessed to his misgiving at having to play in a theatre without pit or gallery—parts of the house to which in England the actor looked for the most lively expression of approval or condemnation. 'The actor needs applause,' he said. 'It is his life and soul when he is on the stage. The enthusiasm of the audience reacts upon him. He gives them back heat for heat. You have no pit . . . your stalls cover the entire floor . . . in England our stalls are appreciative but not demonstrative. Our pit and gallery are both.'

By this time he had the reporters enthralled. In answer to one who asked him what he did for exercise, he replied: 'I act!'

After a pause, with an air of finality, he ventured:

'You—er—must find the work of interviewing very—um—difficult.'

'Sometimes,' came the answer. Laughing and in great good humour with each other, Irving and his inquisitors went on deck. Manhattan was in sight. He had won the first round on points; he had gauged correctly the prejudices and susceptibilities of those Western journalists who had the reputation of being the toughest and least gullible in the world. He had won their regard by his frankness and their respect by his apparent determination to tell them what he chose and no more, making them realise that any attempt on their part to lure him beyond that limit would fail. When he read their reports in the morning he was amazed at the personal details which their public seemed to expect, but he had little cause to complain of the picture of him which they had drawn. If one writer commented on his likeness to young Oscar Wilde—'though more refined and manly'—it was obvious that he intended the strange comparison as a compliment.

3

Only a week elapsed between Irving's arrival in New York and his first appearance on October 29th at the Star Theatre, little enough time to set up and rehearse the seven plays—*The Bells, Charles I, The Belle's Stratagem, Richard III, The Lyons Mail, Louis XI* and *The Merchant of Venice*—which he would present in the order of their original production at the Lyceum. Such time as he could spare from the theatre was spent in accepting the furious hospitality for which New York was already famous. He was the guest of honour at clubs which reflected the character of his own in London—the Lotos with all the boisterous bohemianism of the Savage, and the Century, where, as at the Garrick, men of distinction unbent sedately with artists of proven social reliability. The Lotos, under the chairmanship of Whitelaw

Reid, the proprietor of the *Tribune*, gave him a banquet. The chairman's speech of welcome was warm and friendly, but ended on a note of warning:

'. . . It would not be fair to our distinguished and unsuspicious guest . . . if I did not warn him that all this and much more which he is likely to hear, is said around the dinner-table. Let him not think that he wholly knows us and is fairly naturalised until he has read the papers the morning after his first performance. What they may contain no living man knoweth; but others have sometimes groaned that we accord our guests the same distinguished honour we give our national bird—the turkey—which we first feed and then carve up.'

Irving, replying in an unaffected conversational style which impressed his hearers, threw himself on the mercy of New York's playgoers. 'I am quite sure of this,' he said, 'that no people will go to a theatre with a greater desire to do justice to an actor than you will go to see me on Monday night. If you like me you will express it; if you do not like me, still you will treat me kindly.'

Irving's confident appeal to the fairness and generosity of the American public was made in the face of a situation which must have caused him some uneasiness. The New York theatre was in a state of transition, or rather of migration, as the social centre of Manhattan Island was steadily moving uptown. Until recently the theatres and hotels had been centred round Union and Washington Squares. But the grid of muddy streets and cobbled avenues was spreading northwards, and on the shifting fringes of the old town clapboard shacks were being replaced with imposing houses of brick and stone, the residences of those who now regarded 'down-town' solely as a place of business. Naturally the purveyors of entertainment pursued their public, and the progress of the Wallack family was typical of many. In 1852 James Wallack had taken over Brougham's Lyceum at the corner of Broadway and of Broome Street; in 1861 he built a new theatre (Wallack's), at Broadway and 13th Street, to which his son, Lester, had succeeded in 1864; in 1882, marching with the times, Lester Wallack had built himself a more modern playhouse at Broadway and 30th Street, naming it Wallack's and leasing the old 13th Street theatre, now renamed the Star, to Henry Abbey. The Wallacks were actor-managers; Abbey, a cornet-player in his youth, was an impresario with a taste for musical enterprises; in fact, at the very moment of Irving's arrival, he was in the throes of opening his first season of the new Metropolitan Opera House at Broadway and 39th Street. Irving, therefore, found himself committed to an antiquated theatre in a district no longer fashionable, while further up-town there was formidable competition—Ouida's *Moths* playing to capacity at Wallack's, Ada Rehan and John Drew in *Dollars and Sense* at Daly's, W. J. Florence playing Bob Brierly in *The Ticket of Leave Man* at the Windsor, to say nothing of Madame Nillson in Gounod's *Faust* at the Metropolitan, and several flourishing opera bouffe and vaudeville entertainments.

Such competition Irving readily accepted, but he was not prepared for the operations of speculators in theatre tickets, which looked as though they might bedevil his whole enterprise. The reigning head of this racket was a newsvendor named MacBride. Three days before the iron-barred doors of the Star opened, he picketed the theatre with a small army of men and boys, each of whom was instructed to buy ten season tickets. He paid his henchmen well—boys fifty cents an hour, men five dollars a day, with meals and cigars thrown in. In return for this, they settled down on camp stools, on the stone steps and even upon the window-sills, keeping their watch day and night and effectively forestalling the ordinary public who wished to buy seats. Within an hour or two of the opening of the box-office, MacBride found himself in possession of the equivalent of 3,360 seats for an outlay of $7,200. Thus tickets that he acquired for two dollars he was selling on the first night for ten to fifteen dollars; if the season was as successful as, no doubt, this lover of art fervently hoped, he stood to make $30,000. These manipulations inevitably created confusion at the box office and resulted in a number of seats remaining empty on the first night.

While Irving was making up as Mathias, the news from the front of the house was not very reassuring. A deluge of rain was falling on New York, and the tempers of those who had reached the theatre through a sea of mud in their carriages or had fought their way through the drenching storm on foot, were not improved when they were assailed by MacBride's touts who were hawking the only obtainable seats like bookmakers calling the odds at a race meeting. Among the audience, however, were many distinguished New Yorkers, and Irving was glad to know that in a box with Ellen Terry were his old friends, Felix and Mrs. Moscheles, and young Gilbert Coleridge, the son of the Lord Chief Justice.

Irving had dispensed with the customary martial music with which American audiences were played into their seats. The curtain rose on the Burgomaster's inn, and the company fought against the arrival of late-comers and the constant banging of the doors of the theatre which opened directly onto the street. The pace was slow and the audience inclined to disgruntled apathy until Irving's appearance, which they greeted with a roar of applause. American audiences at first nights were accustomed to reserve their judgment until the end of the piece—consequently at the end of the act there was not enough applause to penetrate behind the curtain.

Young Coleridge hurried round to Irving's dressing-room. He was pacing up and down like a caged lion. '. . . It's a frost, Mr. Coleridge, a damned frost. I'm doing my best, but these Yankees are icebergs, blocks, stone. . . . I might as well play to a churchyard!' Coleridge tried to reassure him, and started to explain the cause of their reticence, but the call boy interrupted him, and Irving went on for the second act. Often he was stimulated by opposition in his audience, real or imaginary, and that night, in Coleridge's opinion, he played *The Bells* better than ever before. At the end of the play the applause was tumultuous, and the calls for a speech loud and insistent. Irving came before the curtain and, on behalf of himself and his company, thanked the audience in a few words, finally expressing the hope 'that our loves may increase even as the days do grow'. Afterwards, Irving and Coleridge escorted Ellen Terry to her hotel. The rain had stopped; the streets were empty. There was no doubt as to the night's success. Ellen Terry was jubilant. She broke into a dance. Arm-in-arm, this strangely assorted trio kept up their 'pas de trois' until they reached the steps of the Dam hotel.

4

With *Charles I*, Irving introduced Ellen Terry to the American public, who were instantly enslaved by her charm; with his sharply contrasting study of Louis XI, he staggered them with his own virtuosity and power of characterization, his portrayal of the old French king proving to be the most popular part in his repertoire. New York capitulated without his having to bring his heavy artillery into action. *Hamlet* was reserved for the assault upon the more intellectual citadel of Philadelphia. The weekly receipts, rising steadily from $15,000 to $22,000, were clear proof of his popular success; for the last week of his engagement the Star Theatre was crammed to capacity. The press notices seemed to be a précis of all that he had read about himself during the past ten years at home. As usual, the critics were divided into three factions. Those, headed by Winter, who hailed his genius with measured eulogies; those who, though conscious of his mannerisms and critical of his eccentricities, were swept away against their better judgment by his manifest power; and those, a small voice in the din of general acclamation, who found him and his company altogether unacceptable. There was ample evidence that the novelty of his method, though it was more alien to American than to English theatrical tradition, was welcomed and appreciated. Even his Shylock, which at first bewildered audiences accustomed to a villainous and declamatory Jew, was soon accepted as a masterpiece.

Gratified as he was by this success, so immediate and so clearly demonstrable to those at home, he was more deeply satisfied by the tributes paid to him by American actors and actresses for whom he gave a special matineé of *Louis XI*. Many of them had played in support of Macready, Forrest, Charles Kean and Salvini. All of them, marvelling at the absolute integrity of his impersonation—the passing of every character through his mind, which was the key to his mystery —conceded that he had won the right to the unique position which, as an artist, he held in his own country, and that as an executant, if not as an elocutionist, he excelled all other actors of his time.

An odd figure, who was described by his enemies as America's greatest actor, was not present at this matinée—Henry Ward Beecher, the pioneer hot gospeller who for forty years had presented to his vast public the drama of hell fire with himself in the rôle of the redeeming fireman. Having won fame and fortune by preaching that such joys as the theatre were of the devil, he was now so mellowed by the scandals and conflicts which assailed him that he had been to see Irving as Louis XI. Subsequently he invited Irving and Ellen Terry to attend on a Sunday his Plymouth church in Brooklyn and afterwards to lunch at his home. Irving, perhaps unaware of Beecher's bizarre career as a revivalist, and always susceptible to any gesture made by the Church towards the stage, had good reason for accepting this invitation. He was curious to meet a man whom he had seen, in his Manchester days, preach the cause of the North to an audience of angry cotton operatives, whose natural sympathies lay with the South, with such persuasive force that they returned to their mills fervent Federalists and eager for the emancipation of the slaves. Irving enjoyed Beecher's sermon (he had recently abandoned hell fire for brotherly love), noting the vigour of his delivery and his undoubted gifts as a comedian. After lunch Beecher entertained them with readings from Shakespeare and on their departure gave Ellen Terry an aquamarine from his collection of precious stones, a predilection which, Irving remarked, he shared with Disraeli. Later, Beecher wrote to Irving: 'I cannot let you go hence without some expression of my gratitude . . . until my seventieth year I had never seen a play in a theatre. It burst upon my ripe old age as June would upon a Greenlander.' Irving, the proselyte, welcomed the conversion of the Plymouth Church. As a rule, he had a keen nose for charlatans. No doubt he recognised in this frail pietist a frustrated actor. If, as he contended, the measure of an actor's talent is to be found in the box-office, Beecher, who single-handed collected forty thousand dollars a year from his congregation, as a draw had no rival on the American stage. The preacher, as his marble-like eyes dwelt upon the imposing figure of the actor whose powerful personality had so recently overwhelmed him, must have thanked God fervently that Irving had never been called to be his rival in the missionary field.

5

Irving's decision to play Hamlet for the first time in Philadelphia was made in the full knowledge that theatrical tradition had deeper roots and dramatic criticism a sharper pen in that city than in any other in America. The rivalry of cities being what it was in the United States, his success in New York would, if anything, tell against him; it was evidence of that success that, as he approached Philadelphia, critics from Boston and other large cities were converging on the cradle of the American theatre. Irving was news; his challenge was accepted.

The outcome was a repetition of earlier triumphs. The audience at the Chestnut Street Theatre, who for the first two acts failed to grasp the intention of an actor who threw away the points and forswore the artificialities to which they were accustomed, were swept off their feet by the climax of the play scene and thereafter sustained the actor with their rapt attention and applause. The staid Philadelphians unprecedently rose and called for Irving and Ellen Terry at the end of the second act; Irving, as was his rule, did not respond to the call. Far from curbing their excitement, his restraint was rewarded by a reception at the end of the play, phenomenal in its enthusiasm and without parallel in Philadelphian stage history. Again the temper of the public was reflected in mounting receipts and ultimate congestion at the box office. As he expected, the press were divided in their opinion of him, though, as he remarked to Hatton: 'It needs a little hostility here and there in the press to give a wholesome flavour to the sweets.' The *Ledger* welcomed 'the most virile, lovable Hamlet that has been seen on the stage . . . he [Irving] realised Goethe's idea of a born prince—gentle, thoughtful, and of a most moral nature, without the strength of nerve to make a hero and overcome by the responsibility put upon him by a vision whose message he alternately accepts and doubts'. Other papers were critical of his Hamlet and Shylock in terms as familiar to him as those in which he had been praised. As usual, if adverse comment was contrary to the verdict of the public it troubled him very little. Of the favourable verdict of American playgoers there could have been no stronger proof than the presentation to him, at a breakfast given in his honour by the Clover Club, of Edwin Forrest's silver watch. This gift clearly symbolised the death of the crude old rivalries and the birth of an international English-speaking theatre in which the English and American stage drew strength and inspiration from each other. Impetuously, in front of a gathering of hard-headed citizens, Irving pressed to his lips the relic venerated by his hosts as that of 'the greatest genius America ever produced on the miming stage', and by himself as a further token that through his art there was a higher purpose to be achieved than the satisfaction of personal ambition. Perhaps it was this impetuous, unashamed betrayal of emotion that endeared him to Americans in all walks of life. Fearful of the cold impenetrable reserve that resisted their approaches to the average Englishman, they responded warmly to one whose expression of feeling was as unrestrained as their own. Irving, having established his ascendancy in the American theatre, left Brodribb free to indulge his simple delight in good fellowship unhampered by the 'lobster shell' into which, of necessity, he retreated at home.

6

In turn, he accepted the surrender of Boston, Baltimore, Chicago, St. Louis, Cincinnati, Columbus, Washington and the larger towns of New England. The applause and honours accorded to him in these cities made up for the trials which he and his caravan endured to reach them. The company set out from New York in a private train of eight coaches including two sixty-foot box cars and a huge gondola carrying their vast impedimenta of scenery and a hundred and fifty stage baskets. But by the time they reached Philadelphia, Irving and his lieutenants realized the impossibility of attempting the tour on such a scale. He therefore abandoned and sent back to New York twenty-seven cloths, eighty flats, sixty wings, twenty set pieces and twelve framed cloths. To make up for this loss he gave orders in advance to carpenters and scene-painters in each city to prepare such scenery as was necessary to fill these gaps and could be contained in the limited stage space of their particular theatres. New York, and Philadelphia alone, therefore, saw the Lyceum productions in their entirety; consequently the favourable verdict of the other cities was won more by the company's acting than by scenic spectacle.

In America at that time actors were expected to play on Christmas Day. Irving, therefore, decided to give the company their Christmas supper in the train during their journey from Boston to Baltimore. Irving delighted in such occasions, but could seldom have presided over a supper table in more curious circumstances, for while he and his guests feasted on oyster pie, cold beef, and jellies, their train was being towed on rafts down the Haarlem River from Jersey City to the Debrosse Street depot of the Pennsylvania railroad. In Jersey City they had had to change trains in the dark and in the first flurries of an approaching blizzard. Irving was much preoccupied with the care of Charlie, who in his surfeited old age was going blind. Ellen Terry's Fussy was able to take care of himself. He had noted Charlie's decrepitude, and was already transferring his affections from his mistress to the inveterate giver of titbits. The full fury of the blizzard hit them on the railway journey to Baltimore. Having been held up by snowdrifts and the general dislocation of traffic, they reached their destination with only four hours to spare, before, in the Academy of Music, the curtain was due to rise on *Louis XI*. Loveday and his staff were undaunted. Somehow the scenery was unloaded, unpacked and set up, while Irving held a rehearsal. At the appointed hour the company played to an audience, whose enthusiasm, though their numbers were small, was indisputable in that they had braved the storm to come to the theatre at all.

At the outset Irving had rejected as an impossibility Abbey's proposal that the company should play the customary one-night stands. As a result, he found he was committed to a wearisome shuttling to and fro over immense distances, as, for instance, from Brooklyn to Chicago, Chicago to Cincinnati, back to Chicago and thence to Toronto. The Irving troupe soon became familiar figures at these widely scattered railroad depots. The Chief, in his astrakhan coat and muller-cut-down, with eye-glasses perched jauntily on an aquiline nose pinched with cold; Ellen Terry, with her top coat of dashing and individual cut, feathered hats and billowing scarves—a model of no particular fashion but of timeless grace; Breezy Bill in his fur coat and tweed cap, the American woman's ideal of an English captain; Tyars, in ulster and tam-o'-shanter, the very picture of a Scottish laird; muffled Mead, whose ponderous stride recalled 'the buried majesty of Denmark'; old Howe, with the glowing face and dapper tweeds of an English country gentleman; Norman Forbes as elegant an ambassador as Savile Row could wish for; and Meredith Ball, the musical director, spectacled, fur-coated and top-hatted—the very embodiment of music and mummery. Seen off duty they were a perfect microcosm of their homeland, as strange and satisfying to citizens of the Middle West as Buffalo Bill, with his cowboys and Indians, were soon to be to Londoners. They certainly had not the appearance of aesthetes. As one theatre manager remarked: 'There is one thing I observe about this company—it walks well; it's the best company on its legs I've ever seen.' To which Irving replied: 'Yes—I engaged them to show me off.'

Vagaries of weather were not their only hazard. For their first journey to Chicago, the president of the Erie Railroad had lent Irving his private train. The crew of the train, to everyone's surprise, were armed. They learned that during Sarah Bernhardt's tour a year or two previously, a band of desperadoes, tempted by her widely reported jewellery, planned to hold up her train. Though this plot had been forestalled, another attempt upon the train was made, and in the ensuing gun fight one of Abbey's agents had been wounded. Irving, however, reached Chicago without misadventure. The still young prairie city welcomed him with youthful enthusiasm in which, for once, the public and the press united. They were the first Americans to see his production of *Much Ado*, and they found the play's gaiety and swift repartee very much to their taste. Their journalists were not lacking in erudition. A twenty-five-year-old critic on the *Tribune* wrote that Irving, who himself inclined towards Talma's theory that an actor should enter into the most tragical situation and terrible of passions as if they were his own, came nearer to Diderot's ideal of the intellectual actor —of penetration but without sensibility—than any actor on the record.

Here Irving found a British subject in distress—if it could be said that his ebullient old friend, George Augustus Sala, was ever distressed. Sala was on a lecture tour. Everywhere his audiences had been sparse, but Chicago seemed completely indifferent to his presence. Irving did what he could to help his friend by buying blocks of seats and enlisting his company to distribute free tickets. But Sala was out of luck, for not only had he to compete with the Lyceum Company but with Mark Twain, who, at the height of his popularity, was lecturing at another hall. Sala, no doubt, was as careless of his own failure as he was delighted at Irving's success, and both were forgotten when, over supper, he regaled Irving with a robust summary of London gossip.

Washington gave Irving a princely welcome. On the last night of the engagement the President, General Chester Arthur, to whom Irving had already been presented, paid a state visit to the National Theatre, where he saw *Louis XI* and *The Belle's Strategem*. Afterwards Irving and Ellen Terry were invited to the White House to meet the members of Arthur's Cabinet and their families at supper. When the rest of the company had left, the President and the actor sat talking together until the early hours of the morning. Arthur was widely read and combined a love of the drama with an aptitude for quotation. Irving studied his genial host with interest. He had been Vice-President to General Garfield, who, two years earlier, had been murdered by a disappointed office-seeker. Before his accession to the Presidency, Arthur himself had been notorious for his jobbery, but, on taking office, he had set about the cleansing of a corrupt administration with fanatical zeal. Perhaps Irving saw in this man in whom responsibility had induced so sudden a metamorphosis, certain characteristics of Thomas à Becket, so long the subject of discussion between himself and Tennyson, though the latter's play on this theme after five years of revision was not yet fit for production.

The tour ended with a return visit to New York and on a gay note, for *Much Ado* was played there for three weeks to crowded and delighted houses.

On the last night he gave a multiple bill, always so popular at the Lyceum, in which he played scenes from *The Merchant of Venice*, *Louis XI*, *Charles I* and *Much Ado*—an indication of American preferences. In his farewell speech he thanked his audience, and indeed all America, for showing 'that no jealous love of your own most admirable actors had prevented you from recognising the earnest purpose of an English company'. He assured them that his own theatre would always be at the disposal of American actors and announced that he and his company would return to the United States in the autumn. He quoted, in illustration of his desire to renew their association, Lincoln's advice to Governor Oglesbie: 'Dick, keep close to the people'—a precept which in fact he himself had always followed. A day or two later he received a letter which rounded off to perfection the extraordinary success and happiness which this visit to the United States had brought him:

42 East 25th Street.
Thursday, April 3rd, 1884.

'My dear Irving,

Will you breakfast with me and a few friends informally some day next week at Delmonico's? Name any day after Tuesday and you will gratify me very much. . . .

I have no doubt this effort of mine to crawl out of my shell will surprise you, but let this not deter you from encouraging it by your acceptance.

Sincerely   yours,
Edwin Booth.'

This gesture, made by the shy, reclusive colleague whom he so much admired, was the most welcome of all the kindnesses and hospitalities which the Americans had showered upon Irving. He managed to keep Booth out of his shell long enough to give a banquet in his honour, at which William Winter recited a farewell ode in eight stanzas, of his own composition, the last of which, if prematurely melancholy, was a fair example of its style and sentiment:

> *And when is said the last farewell,*
> *So solemn and so certain,*
> *And Fate shall strike the prompter's bell*
> *To drop the final curtain,*
> *Be his, whom every muse hath blessed,*
> *That best of earthly closes,*
> *To sink to rest on England's breast,*
> *And sleep beneath her roses.*

Irving had no intention of sinking to rest on England's breast. He was in fighting fettle; a letter to Austin written a week or so earlier was indicative of his liveliness. His comments on the press refer to certain papers—particularly the *Standard*, which at home had only grudgingly admitted his success—and to a Mr. Ranken Towse, who had written a scathing but ill-informed article about him in the *Century:*

> *The Brunswick,*
> *Barnes & Dunklee,*
> *Boston.*
> *Tuesday, March 2nd, 1884.*
> *On the way to Washington.*

'My dear Austin,

Greetings. I have just sent a cable which will surprise you—announcing our return here next September. The seed we have sown I mean to reap—our work has been a revelation and our success beyond precedent.

You have evidently been puzzled by all sorts of reports—and your letters to me seemed quite odd to us here—attending to matters of which we knew nothing,—such for instance as the truthful and con-scientious *Standard* reporter put forward—backed up by his editor. . . .

Thereby hangs a tale not worth telling now—but the end is—our triumph has been complete and the country captured. (It's the devil to write in this jostling car—even for me.)

You were glad to get Ellen Terry's telegram I am sure. She was even better than she ever was in dear old England and has had a glorious and brilliant success. As I told the Boston audience last night—she has "won golden opinions from all sorts of people". . .

Our return visit to Boston, which is just over—was, I believe, the biggest engagement ever played in their huge and beautiful theatre—seven performances realised $24,089—£7,800.

Our return tour will exceed this present one—I am certain—I shall be my own manager and have no middleman. The only trouble we have had has been in travel and we have gone backwards and forwards in the most irritating manner—20 and 30 odd hours, often in the cars. This will be avoided in the future—for I have made a consecutive and easy tour.

The work has been heavy, and what with rehearsals, acting, journeys, interviews and speeches—I have had little spare time.

Speeches by the way remind me of two things—jot down and send me something for the last night in New York and afterwards send me a speech for the Theatrical Fund Dinner—which is just after our return.

Get the books from the Secretary of the Fund (if you have not them) and cull what you can from the different chairmen. I have taken the chair twice—that should be alluded to—also the American tour and the bounteous hospitality of the people—and of course particularly the object of the Fund. The speech will be an important one—for it will be the first I make after my return.

Our return here will, I should think, silence the carpers. Nothing could so prove our success and satisfaction with our venture. It has been a brave fight and bravely won—in spite of Archer and that crew. The public does not endorse Mr. Towse in the *Century*. Towse—Lowse I shall spell it—is the critic in the *New York Evening Post*—a friend of this Montgomery of the *Times*—and one of the critics. Read the *Atlantic Monthly* too—amusing—very. "Personality" is the charm —and all that—and everything but the fact—that the man can *act*—and that the public thinks so.

Hamlet has never been so enthusiastically received in England and it is a bitter pill to certain Americans that any actor but *one*[1] can be accepted in it. . . .

. . . Then hey for the broad Atlantic and the merry shores of old England.

God bless you and yours,
Ever,
H. Irving.'

7

The work had indeed been heavy, and Austin's cheerful help had been sadly missed. In addition to his acting and to the heavy responsibilities of management, Irving had made two or three full-dress speeches in every town he had visited. He attached great importance to these speeches. They were the medium through which he 'kept close to the people' and of his advocacy of his profession. He was no glib rhetorician. All his life he had prepared carefully and learnt by heart even his shortest and apparently most spontaneous speeches. Despising insincerity in any form, these speeches expressed the promptings of his heart and mind at the moment, so that notes which had been prepared for him were often useless. The farewell speech, for example, which he gave in New York, included hardly a word of the painstaking draft which Austin had prepared for him. He reflected that if at times, having commended himself to a dull audience as 'their obliged and humble servant', he had been heard, as soon as the closing curtains hid him from their view, to comment scathingly on their apathy and stupidity—only to smile tenderly upon them as the curtains parted once more, such dissimulation was a necessary duty and as pardonable in him as in a well-disciplined soldier saluting an incompetent general on parade.

He sailed for England at the end of April. Shortly before he left New York he received a letter which helped him to keep these heady successes in their true perspective. It was from his Aunt Sarah Penberthy who was now old and blind, living with her relatives in St. Ives. Before leaving England he had sent Stoker to see how she fared and to provide for her comfort as he could. It was a sad letter, full of sorrow at her daughter's departure for Africa and for her son John's reckless prodigality. But in it she said:

'. . . I think that you will be glad to receive a few lines from your aged aunt as I should be to receive a few lines from your own hand. I am

[1] Edwin Booth.

433

pleased to hear of yours and Miss Terry's success in America. Indeed you seem to be blazing over the wide world like a comet. My daily prayer is that the blessing of God may attend you in all your undertakings, and that in due time you may return to England a happier, a better, and a richer man. . . . '

Certainly a man who had discovered so many new friends, indeed a nation of friends—could count himself happier. Better? Perhaps through playing before so many audiences of such diverse perceptions he had become a better actor and since he believed that an actor's power depended on his integrity, he was perhaps a better man. Richer? A little over $400,000 had been paid by the public to see him, of which he took a half share. When all the costs of this enterprise had been paid there remained a profit of £11,700 to put into the Lyceum treasury. He knew well enough the risks of independent management, particularly on the scale and with the standard which he had taught his public to expect. Now he could foresee that by touring periodically the provinces of England and the United States he could endow the Lyceum so handsomely that he could maintain his ever-increasing establishment and be free to experiment as he chose without undue risk. As for himself, all he needed was enough money to keep himself in modest comfort and to indulge his one recreation—the entertainment of his friends. But for the maintenance of his proud independence and for the realisation of his ambitions, it was everything. In this respect he returned to England a very much richer man.

CHAPTER XXIV

6th Lyceum Season : Malvolio

———◦◦◦———

I

On the night of May 8th Mr. and Mrs. Bancroft were on the point of retiring to bed in their house in Cavendish Square when they heard a loud ringing of the doorbell, followed by the rattle of chains and a drawing of bolts as the servant opened the door. Bancroft ran downstairs, calling to his wife: 'Come down again. . . . I'm sure it's Irving!'

And Irving it was, who had landed in Liverpool that morning and had lost no time in reaching London, where he had dined with J. M. Levy and now sought out his old friend, B. In exchange for a recital of his adventures in America, Bancroft had given him, in his own pontifical way, the gossip of the town. Business had not been good—but the old guard were doing fairly well—the Bancrofts with *The Rivals* at the Haymarket and Toole at his own theatre with *The Upper Crust*. At the Princess's Wilson Barrett was declaiming Wills's *Claudian* in a tremulant baritone and décolleté tunic. At the St. James's, Hare and Kendal were playing in a translation of Ohnet's *Le Maître de Forge*, made by Pinero, who, after a short spell of acting with the Bancrofts, was now wholly devoting himself to playwriting. Wyndham was as popular as ever in *The Great Divorce Case* at the Criterion and at the Globe, a very promising young comedian, C. H. Hawtrey, was acting with W. S. Penley in his own play, *The Private Secretary*. Irving found Bancroft's review of this active theatrical season stimulating; he was less amused to hear that his two sons had again appeared as Charles and Joseph Surface at a bazaar in the Kensington Town Hall.

2

'Mr. Irving has vindicated for his vocation a definite position among the serious arts. He has been accepted in the United States with distinguished honour in virtue of his championship of the right and duty of the dramatic art to be a fine art. The remarkable success he has achieved is a gratifying sign of the willingness of public opinion in America to co-operate with that of England to rescue the stage from the lower level to which it has sometimes sunk.'

Thus on the following morning *The Times* welcomed Irving home. He had every reason to be pleased with the general appreciation of his success in America, though he was sorry to find, when he went down to the Lyceum, that Lawrence Barrett had not shared his good fortune. The American actor had opened with a play translated from the Spanish, *Yorick's Love*. On the first night he had been well received, but the death of the Duke of Albany undoubtedly had a depressing effect on theatrical business and had turned his initial success into failure. He withdrew the play and in its stead put on *Richelieu*; as the Cardinal, he was considered in his own country to be second only to Booth. Irving was distressed at his friend's comparative failure and did all he could to help him, even putting his own bank account at his disposal. On the last night of Barrett's season, Irving gave him the Order of the Garter which Edmund Kean had worn as Richard III. Barrett had appeared at the Lyceum under Abbey's management. On balance, the losses of the impresario in England were handsomely offset by the profits he had made out of Irving in America, particularly as it was generally rumoured that he had a finger in the speculator's pie. That Irving's business affairs were not keenly handled was shown in the Lyceum accounts by a loss of a thousand pounds on Abbey's tenancy. On May 31st, Irving opened his sixth season with a revival for five weeks of *Much Ado*. He and Ellen Terry had a rapturous welcome, and Barrett was much flattered by the cheers which greeted his appearance in Irving's box. At the end of the play Irving warned his audience that, in view of their return to America in the autumn, the season would be a short one, and announced the production of *Twelfth Night*, which was already in rehearsal. Afterwards the stage was crowded with friends and well-wishers, anxious to give him their personal assurance of their delight in his success and safe return.

Irving wished that he had been able to promise his public a new work by a contemporary writer, but he was still harassed by the prevailing dearth of English playwrights—indeed their ragged ranks had been further thinned in his absence by the death of Charles Reade and H. J. Byron. His constant search for new material had had little success, and was becoming increasingly costly. Frank Marshall's *Robert Emmett* had been licked into shape during the previous year, but just as he was about to announce it for production the Irish pot came to the boil once more and the Lord Chamberlain suggested to him that the theme of the piece might prove dangerously inflammatory at such a time Irving abandoned the project and gave the play to Boucicault for production in New York, where, even with the Irish-American element, it proved to be a damp squib. He had given much time and thought to the interpretation of this character, and Marshall had felt the spur of his collaboration. On one occasion when, after supper in the Beefsteak Room, the Chief was discussing the play with Marshall and Stoker and was complaining that one of the scenes lacked a forceful climax, he called the author's attention to an old playbill hanging on the wall. As Marshall turned his back upon him, Irving picked up half a dozen wine glasses and hurled them at the door. There was a shattering explosion. Marshall whipped round, pale with fright.

'What was it,' he gasped. 'I thought someone had thrown a bomb through the window!'

'Exactly,' said Irving quietly, 'that's what the conspirators in Curran's house would have thought when they realised that the fury of the mob to which they had been listening was directed at them. You are now in the rare position, my dear Marshall, of an author who can write of high emotion with experience!'

There remained the industrious Wills. *Rienzi*, to his great sorrow, had been shelved. But Irving was planning a new version of *Faust*, on which Wills had set to work eagerly. 'Your kind letter,' he wrote to his patron, 'was an immense relief and delightfully pointed out what was to do—I went to work at once—in all I quite agree with you. I have lovingly worked up and diversified the character of Meph throughout.' Meph was unlikely to materialise for some time. Meanwhile Burnand and Guy Carleton had been paid advances on two disappointing plays. In all, during the first four years of his management Irving had spent over £3,000 in his fruitless quest for new material. Tennyson, with patient insistence, was urging him to put on *Becket*. But though he had hoped to arrange an actable version of it while he was in America, he had failed to do so, and now the Poet Laureate had decided to publish it as it stood in order to complete, with *Harold* and *Queen Mary*, his trilogy on the struggle between the British people and the Papacy.

Thus Irving found himself with nothing in prospect to offer the public, apart from Shakespeare, but a revival of *Olivia*—Wills's version of Goldsmith's sentimental story, *The Vicar of Wakefield*. Moreover, this play would provide greater opportunity for Ellen Terry than for himself, for Vezin had already created with some success the part of Dr. Primrose.

During June a second and less discreet attempt was made to secure him a knighthood. The first intimation which he had of it was in a letter from Labouchère.

> *House of Commons.*
> *June 4th,* 1884.

'Dear Irving,

I have been preaching to Gladstone through his son the expediency of making you a knight for the last months. G. goes on saying that he will think of it, etc., etc. I think that if Sullivan was made a knight as a compliment to music, you ought to be as a compliment to the drama. Don't say anything about this.

> Yours,
> H. Labouchère.'

No doubt Irving had a good deal to say about it. He had no wish to be lobbied for by Labby of all men, who, in *Truth*, had declared that were he to be told that Shakespeare would never again be acted during the term of his life, he would endure the pronouncement with equanimity. His feelings on the matter would be the same as those of his friend, Canon Ainger, if he had heard that a militant atheist was importuning the Prime Minister to give him a bishopric. It would never do. However, Gladstone, being familiar with Irving's view, was unlikely to heed his son's preachments. The irrepressible Labby took no offence at his friend's refusal to support his well-intentioned representations, for a week or two later he wrote: '. . . Next time you are at the H of C, stand a little to the right in front of Oliver Cromwell's bust, which has just been put up, and you will find it is more like you than anyone else. With a very little get-up you might be it exactly. Why is no play ever written about Oliver?'

Irving was a Royalist at heart and had no wish to get himself up as the Protector. In July, with the matter of the knighthood disposed of, he went down to stay over Sunday with Lord Rosebery at Mentmore, whither he had been bidden to meet the Prince of Wales. Now he could do so with the comfortable feeling that nobody could entertain any suspicions that in moving in such circles he sought favour for himself.

3

Twelfth Night was produced on July 8th, Londoners were enduring a heat wave and those of them who made up the audience at the Lyceum were inclined to be as sultry as the night. Irving had spared no pains to match the decorative beauty of his *Much Ado*—perhaps in this respect he erred in overloading delicate comedy with stage effects. His Malvolio was the outcome of long and original study, for he had never seen the play performed. Phelps had revived the play at Sadler's Wells in 1848; his Malvolio was a masterpiece of make-up and elaborately studied; nevertheless, he did not appear in the part again. Lamb, in his vivid appreciation of Robert Bensley's performance of Malvolio at the end of the eighteenth century, recorded that the actor came near to being the perfect Don Quixote. Many critics drew this parallel in writing of Irving's performance, proving that either he or they had been polishing up their Elia. Undoubtedly Irving interpreted the part in the light of Bensley's conception of a steward whose 'bearing was lofty, a little above his station but probably not much above his deserts'.

Irving must have been bewildered by the contrary opinions his Malvolio provoked. Those critics, who usually handled him harshly, now applauded him, while his adulators hung their heads, embarrassed by their unaccustomed tepidity. For certain, his instinct as a producer had failed him. Afterwards, he confessed to Ellen Terry that he should have engaged three great comedians to play the clowns. As it was, their shortcomings were fatal to the balance of the play, even if the Victorian audience had been ready to be amused by the robust humours of Sir Andrew and Sir Toby.

Ellen Terry should have been, and indeed became, a perfect Viola. But on the first night she was sick with pain from a whitlow in her thumb, had her arm in a sling and was forced to play many of her scenes sitting down. Had not Stoker's brother, a doctor, lanced her thumb during the performance, blood-poisoning might well have caused the loss of her arm.

All these misfortunes and the marked apathy of the audience did not prepare Irving for the demonstration of disapproval which greeted his appearance before the curtain at the end of the play. His speech was interrupted by booing and hissing from the pit and gallery—a sound as painful and unfamiliar to the faithful in the more expensive parts of the house as cat-calls would be to worshippers in a cathedral. For once the gods were demonstrative but not appreciative; the effect upon their humble servant was galvanic. He rounded upon the malcontents and sharply rebuked them, expressing his bewilderment at the presence in his theatre of a strange element which he was at a loss to understand. In defence of his fellow-players, he asked how a company 'of earnest comedians—sober, clean and word-perfect' could fail to have given gratification and pleasure. Though, in his fury, his sense of humour deserted him—for of all men he would have been the last to offer the hygienic or moral excellence of an actor as an excuse for his poor performance—he quelled the rebels and, with his final appeal—'In your smiles we are happy, prithee smile upon us'—he restored the traditional rapture of a Lyceum first night.

Though *Twelfth Night* ran until the end of the limited season, public interest in it steadily waned. Archer, who praised Irving's performance as 'always adequate and sometimes masterly', particularly in those scenes which seemed to puzzle most of his colleagues, put his finger on what was probably the cause of the play's unpopularity. 'Queen Elizabeth,' he wrote, 'is more dead than Queen Anne. The spirit of her age is not alive in the public . . . who are, after all, but the abstract and brief chronicle of the tastes and habits of the times.' Even though the text had to some extent been expurgated, a Victorian audience were unable to relish in public the bawdy innuendos over which they might chuckle in private. Moreover, even the most ardent lovers of Shakespeare can find his clowns, when they are not well played, infinitely boring. The very qualities which made Irving's Malvolio one of his most memorable parts to playgoers of discernment, bewildered the ordinary public to whom comedy and tragedy were two entirely separate things. They delighted in Irving's clowning, but when they found themselves moved to tears by Malvolio's imprisonment, which he rendered tragic and pitiable, they failed to see that it was the very perfection of high comedy.

The comparative failure of *Twelfth Night* had a more serious effect upon Irving's artistic development than was realised at the time. At forty-five he was still a superb comedian, and Ellen Terry was the perfect foil to his style of comedy. A procession of great comic parts lay before him. During the run of *Much Ado*, Walter Pollock had visited him in his dressing-room. On the wall hung a sketch of Irving as Falstaff—complete in every detail except facial make-up. 'Yes,' said Irving, noting his surprise, 'the make-up is wanting, but you'll be satisfied with that when I play the part.' Thereupon 'he became for the moment Falstaff himself; his face seemed to broaden and develop into the very semblance of the fat knight; and he spoke some of Falstaff's words in a deep, rich voice, with a wondrous unctuousness of tone and expression; and, he called up for a brief minute not only Falstaff himself, but with him all the strange company at the Boar's Head'. When he made it clear that he conceived Falstaff, not as a conventional buffoon, but as a decayed gentleman capable of bearing himself as one when occasion demanded, Pollock was of the opinion that his Falstaff might have ranked with his Hamlet in the originality of its conception which was far in advance of his time. It was easy for him to imagine what the actor, who had wrung his heart with sympathy for the absurd but ill-used Malvolio, would make of the shame and chagrin of Sir John when the young king renounced his old fellow-roisterer. But the perplexing reception of *Twelfth Night* made Irving the producer chary of comedy for which Irving the actor had so original a genius. That night, in his dressing-room, he played Falstaff for the first and last time. In jilting the comic muse, he was guilty of a grave breach of promise.

He may well have been led to believe that his most hostile critics had, in his absence, undergone a change of heart. Archer, for example, had published a critical essay, 'Henry Irving, Actor and Manager', which, if not a recantation of the asperities of *The Fashionable Tragedian*, was a far more mellow and considered judgement. He was still severe on Irving's physical shortcomings, and joined issue with Edward Russell, the pamphleteer for the defence, as to the detrimental effect they had upon his acting. He paid, however, an oblique tribute to Irving's intellectual qualities. 'Here,' he wrote, 'we are in his stronghold. It is his face and his brain that have made him what he is, his glittering eye and his restless, inventive intellect. . . . His intellect is strictly that of the executive artist—eager, earnest, rapid and instinctive; rather than logical or profound. When he deals in abstract thought and arguments —in his famous addresses, for instance—his reasoning is often of the weakest; it is in comprehension and illustration of other men's thoughts that he is strong. His place is certainly not the platform but the stage. His intellect is not that of a preacher but of an actor. Edmund Kean read Shakespeare by flashes of lightning; Mr. Irving reads him by the student's midnight oil . . . I cannot myself see that Mr. Irving's peculiar merit as a Shakespearian actor lies in novelty of general conception. Each character certainly comes from his hands something quite different from what his predecessors have accustomed us to; but this arises, I think, more from his marked individuality and the minute attention to detail involved in his method, than from any great originality in conceiving the ground-work of the character. . . . In proportion as a character calls for intellect rather than purely histrionic qualities in its interpreter . . . in precisely the same proportion does Mr. Irving succeed in it. . . . By intellect, he produces the effect of masterful decision of purpose, which saves even his worst parts from the fatal reproach of feebleness. By intellect he makes us forget his negative failings and forgive his positive faults. By intellect, he forces us to respect where we cannot admire him. By intellect, he dominates the stage.'

Archer, so censorious of others who stepped out of their métier, was himself something of an intellectual dark horse. At the time he was sorrowfully chastising Irving and championing the cause of Ibsen, he was, in collaboration with E. V. R. Dibdin (under the pen name, E. V. Ward, which was an anagram of their initials), writing librettos of pantomimes and comic operas for the Theatre Royal, Edinburgh, in the traditional rhymed couplets freely sprinkled with italicised puns. Archer, although he had a pawky sense of humour and a wholesome delight in melodrama and theatricality, was driven by his Calvinistic conscience to exhort the theatre to a higher and more solemn purpose and to castigate, more in sorrow than in anger, those who were deaf to his preaching.

Though his victim was unaware of it, the most bitter of Irving's critics, Henry James, had abandoned temporarily journalism for fiction. It may have seemed to Irving that the battle was won and that the last discordant voice was stilled. At that very moment, however, Archer was signing on a recruit who was destined to be Irving's scourge to the end of his life and from whom death itself would be no escape. In the reading-room of the British Museum, Archer found himself sitting next to a young man whose 'pallid skin and bright red beard' were as contrasting as the books which he was studying—*Das Kapital* and the full score of *Tristan und Isolde*. The conversation of George Bernard Shaw, for that was the name of Archer's neighbour, proved to be as startling as his appearance, and in a very short time Archer was captivated by his voluble and witty companion. Shaw had left Dublin in 1876. He did not find the streets of London paved with gold; had he done so he was more likely to have made an angry protest to the L.C.C. that as a surface it was dangerous and unpractical for pedestrians, than to have mined a pocketful of the stuff for himself. He was already 'dedicated to sociology. Art, in whatever form he chose to use it as a medium of self-expression, would never mean more to him than a sounding-board for his polemics. Already he had made a name for himself among the coagulating Fabians; they welcomed a recruit whose force of argument and flood of loquacity overwhelmed his opponents in debate and his hecklers at public meetings. He wrote novels vigorously but unsuccessfully, and endured the poverty of his circumstances with truculent fortitude. Though he had not yet turned his attention to playwriting, he had arrived in London eager to see how the actor, whose Digby Grant had shown so much promise, was developing. To his dismay, he had

watched Irving, after his success in *The Bells*, 'turn back to the old
Barry Sullivan repertory of mutilated Shakespeare and Bulwer Lytton'.
Irving's defection was exasperating, but, to make matters worse, Ellen
Terry, whose performance in *New Men and Old Acres* at the Royal
Court Theatre in 1876 had convinced him that she was born to be
Irving's partner in 'the new drama which was still in the womb of time
waiting for Ibsen to impregnate it', had been carried off by Irving to
the Lyceum and appeared to be a willing accomplice in his apostasy.
Thus, he saw the two artists whom he had chosen to interpret his as
yet unwritten plays, not only worshipping fustian gods, but becoming
themselves objects of worship to the vast mass of unenlightened playgoers. For the time being he was powerless to give vent to his indignation. Archer, shortly after his meeting with Shaw, was appointed by
Edmund Yates to the staff of *The World*. Anxious to help his impoverished friend and to secure his brilliant talent for the paper, he persuaded
Yates to give Shaw the post of art critic which he himself was vacating
in favour of the drama. He had already had a taste of his friend's uncompromising integrity when, having asked him to make some notes on
art exhibitions which he himself had been unable to obtain, the cheque
which he had sent Shaw in payment of his services was twice returned
with a homily on the depravity of regarding ideas as the negotiable property of the individual. It was not long before Shaw was appointed music
critic of *The World*, a post which he was to enliven for four years and
was the background for the gestation of his plays and the nourishment
of his grievance against the man whom he had chosen to present them.

The season at the Lyceum ended with a week of revivals—*The
Bells*, *Louis XI* and, on the last night, *Richelieu*, the latter causing
Lawrence Barrett to take umbrage in the mistaken belief that Irving
had played it in order to assert his supremacy over him. Irving was
innocent of offence, for he was taking *Richelieu* to America and had
revived it for necessary rehearsal; he was, therefore, quite unable to
understand the cause of Barrett's apparent coolness. He and his public
took leave of each other with every token of warmth and affection.
The unfortunate episodes which had clouded the opening of *Twelfth
Night* were forgotten and forgiven. But, for the first time, the season
showed a loss. Admittedly it was a small one in view of the heavy cost
of the new production (nearly £4,000), which had to be met in the
course of a comparatively short run. Nevertheless it was a timely
hint of the very narrow margin between theatrical profit and loss,
even at the Lyceum, where Fortune had shown herself to be more kind
than most managements had found to be her custom.

4

The second American tour opened on September 30th in Quebec. The *Parisian*, in which the whole company sailed from Liverpool, had battled her way through equinoctial gales. Ellen Terry arrived in Canada more dead than alive. There had been a few changes and additions to the company. George Alexander had taken the place of Bill Terriss, who was staying behind at the Lyceum to play Romeo to Mary Anderson's Juliet. A young newcomer, Martin Harvey, was making himself useful as a juvenile with an earnestness of approach to his work which soon endeared him to his Chief. Sam Emery's daughter, Winifred, had been engaged to understudy Ellen Terry; she was barely of age, but she had been born and bred in a hard theatrical school.

To the outside world the Lyceum troupe appeared to be a united family led by a benevolent patriarch. As in all families, there were, inevitably, internal stresses and strains discreetly hidden from outsiders, which the presence of the forthright Austin, whom Irving had brought with him, aggravated. His sturdy independence and the devoted but unfawning service he gave to his employer, shocked and provoked those who sought to win Irving's favour with their perpetual affirmatives. Stoker and Loveday found it hard to bear Austin's proximity to the throne; the secretary may have betrayed the sense of superiority, social and intellectual, which he felt, however unwarrantably, towards these self-centred theatrical folk. Austin, in his letters to his wife, whom he had left at home, drew an intimate picture of the daily life of the company:

Quebec,
September 30th, 1884.

'. . . No wonder that all the miseries of the sea voyage were soon forgotten or that everybody skipped about in the highest spirits. Henry was in the highest good humour and Ellen seemed to lose the terrible weariness which had nearly quenched the light in her eyes. On Sunday night I dined with Henry, Ellen, Loveday and his wife, and Stoker, and a pleasanter party couldn't have been gathered. I have settled down to an understanding with Stoker and he has become remarkably genial and obliging. . . . You will remember Alexander, he has succeeded Terriss as the leading young man of the company and he is one of the most gentlemanly and unaffected fellows I've ever met. His wife is a perfect lady and their society alone would make the tour a pleasant one. Tonight we give our first performance and then leave by special train

to Montreal where we shall arrive at eight or nine in the morning . . .
the theatre here would make you shriek. It is a cross between a chapel
and a very small concert room and the stage is about half the size of
that of St. George's Hall. The entrance is being washed now, but no
amount of soap and water will repair the broken windows. The kind
of people who play here as a rule are of the least intellectual order—
we found two members of the preceding troupe on the stage—they
were *two hens!*

However, there'll be about £300 in the house tonight, far more
than it has ever held, for our predecessors charged ten cents for
admission and our lowest price is six shillings.'

Later from Montreal:

'. . . The Quebec performance was a great success and was particularly satisfactory as it showed that E.T. had recovered all her old
strength. . . . The engagement here is an enormous success. On the
first night we played *Louis XI* and last night *Much Ado*. The people
crammed the theatre and were wildly enthusiastic. Never have our
people played so well. Henry in particular was never so good in his
life. The effects of the rest he has had are plainly to be seen in his
acting, which is wonderfully fresh and strong. The theatre helps us
much for it is the most perfectly constructed building for sound I
was ever in. But no wonder the company are so good when it is
considered that they are rehearsed half the day. Poor Alexander
especially has an awful grind with so many new parts but he is doing
admirably and will improve every night. Last night there was £500
in the house.'

After a brave start, Ellen Terry collapsed and was forced to stay
behind in Montreal while the rest of the company went on to London
and Hamilton, Ontario; she was able to rejoin them and play again
in Toronto. Winifred Emery played her parts very creditably; much
hung on this girl's future as an actress, for old Sam had abandoned
his wife and children, and she was now the sole support of her
family.

Irving crossed the Canadian border to find the United States in the
throes of a Presidential election—a contingency with which he had
not reckoned when he planned the tour. The campaign was a lively
one, and several novel features had been introduced into the fight.
The Republican, Blaine, had been nominated in place of Irving's

friend, Chester Arthur. Blaine was so notoriously corrupt that those Republicans who had supported Arthur's reforms went over to the Democratic camp and supported the candidature of Grover Cleveland. The hustings were further enlivened by the appearance of a female candidate for the Presidency and by Henry Ward Beecher, who was devoting his zeal and his oratory to Cleveland's cause. Cleveland's opponents were trying to discredit him by disclosing that at an earlier period of his life he had become the father of an illegitimate child— an accusation which he was forced to admit. Perhaps Beecher saw that in championing Cleveland, if the latter was elected, his own widely advertised frailties would be redeemed in the eyes of the public. All this should have been bad for theatrical business. In fact, the receipts in Boston were slightly less than on previous visits, but in New York, where Irving played Hamlet in Booth's stronghold for the first time, they were higher than ever before.

On the first night of *Hamlet*, as Irving, at the end of the Players' scene, leapt onto Claudius's throne, an overheated spirit torch set fire to some draperies. Irving ignored the accident and continued the scene without faltering, but the struggles of the stage staff to quench the fire during the climax of his performance must have broken his spell. A youth in the audience ran in panic up the aisle, but was met by Stoker, who caught him by the throat and sent him back to his seat. A few of the audience wavered, but on the whole they remained calm. The fire was put out and the play proceeded. For all this, Irving's Hamlet made an instant appeal to New Yorkers, as indeed it had to Americans in general. It was a measure of their approval that only one of the critics compared his performance favourably or unfavourably to that of Booth. 'The best Hamlets we have had,' wrote the critic of *The World*,—'Murdoch, Davenport and Booth—were elocutionary triumphs. Mr. Irving's is a pictorial and emotional triumph. It is never lackadaisical or sentimental or sickly, and consequently it has all the asperities and aggressive ruggedness of a distinct individuality . . . Mr. Edwin Booth, who approximates nearer to the *Tribune's* (Winter's) ideal than any other man who ever lived, has but one idea in his performance. It is to look as pretty and to feel as bad as he can. Mr. Booth has so completely filled the American eye in the part . . . that flesh and blood and character look impertinent in the rôle. It is the flesh and blood of Mr. Irving's characterization that offends. Not me. I like it . . . his is the best impersonation of this rôle, intellectually, pictorially and dramatically, that has been presented to us of late years.' For William Winter, 'the night was a golden one while it lasted; and the record of it written in letters of gold will long abide in the pleased and grateful remembrance of this community'. He, too, welcomed the bitterness in Irving's performance, which he found more prominent than the charm, and declared that the public of New York saw 'the cornerstone of his great reputation stand fully disclosed'. The box-office showed that *Twelfth Night* was as popular with Americans as any other piece in the Lyceum repertoire.

The company spent Christmas in the fiery gloom of Pittsburg. Irving, as in the previous year, entertained them all to supper—or would have done had not the kitchen of his hotel utterly failed him. Even the plum pudding which Ellen Terry had brought as a surprise from England had been tainted with camphor in the theatrical basket where it had been hidden. Happily, Irving had taken the precaution of bringing his own cellar with him from England. They dined, therefore, as Ellen Terry said, 'on Henry's wine and Austin's wit'. Austin had been sent back to New York to escort Ellen's son, Teddy, who had arrived with the Coleridges from England, to Pittsburg; he rejoined the company in time to make his contribution to the supper which later he described proudly to his wife:

Pittsburgh,
Christmas Day, 1884.

'. . . We made the night journey from Philadelphia yesterday . . . arriving about midday. I was very weary and found that I had a difficult task before me. The gentlemen of the company had subscribed for a silver tea-service for Ellen Terry. Not a word was said about it that might reach her ears and she knew nothing of our intention till it broke suddenly and *dramatically* upon her. To heighten the surprise, it was suggested that I should write a poem in which every acting member of the company (with the exception of H.I. and one or two of the minor people) should have a verse to be recited at Henry's dinner. Well, in the intervals of pottering about New York I wrote the greater part of this and posted it, but unfortunately the letter didn't reach Pittsburgh in time for the men to receive their parts. So when I arrived I had first to read the thing to them. It was received with a perfect roar of acclamation. I had managed to hit off everyone's foibles so accurately that they all threw themselves into the spirit of the joke with tremendous zest. The parts had to be copied out, three new ones written (including my own) and the whole carried out before dinner, so when the time arrived I was pretty weary. Anything worse than the dinner you can't imagine. There's so little civilization in this town even in the kitchen of the best hotel that the staff was perfectly paralysed by a banquet for 76 people. The intervals between the courses were so long and the food so indifferent that the whole affair would have been a failure but for the simply perfect way in which H.I. played the host. He prevented tedium from obtaining full sway by timely jokes and speeches and was most natural, spontaneous and charming from first to last. Luckily the wine was good and presently everybody began to feel cheerful. Then came the event of the night. Up got Loveday and said the company had met to discuss the next new play. He then recited his verses and every man followed in turn. It was a tremendous hit. Every allusion told and when Stoker began: "I'm in a mortal hurry"—there was a yell of laughter that lasted several moments. That phrase described Stoker to a hair. Well there were 17 of us who held forth in this way, and those not in the secret wondered how it would all end. Both H.I. and E.T. were absolutely in the dark. When I had finished, Katie Brown, one of the girls who play the pages in Portia's Hall in *The Merchant of Venice*, advanced to E.T. and spoke her lines as the present in a case was handed to E.T. across the table. She said the lines with such sweetness, and at the end broke with such a sob, that E.T. was all overcome. The effect was indescribable. E.T's face I shall never forget. The surprise, the pleasure, and the choking emotion made her such a picture as she never has looked on the stage. Then she stood up, with great tears rolling down her cheeks—while Henry tried to conceal his behind his glasses—and said a few broken words more eloquent than any speech. . . . I was delighted by the readiness with which everybody— Stoker excepted—consented to read a little satire on himself. Stoker, of course, resented every joke of mine on *his* personality and was in a rage of jealousy because I had done something so successful. You would be amused by the petty jealousies of this expedition. This contemptible littleness seems to be fostered by the theatrical atmosphere and Alexander is the only actor I ever met who is absolutely free from it. And because he has a finer nature than any of the men with whom he is associated he is made to suffer things which are very hard to bear. . . .'

Poor strenuous Stoker must have suffered torments of jealousy. Irving, who enjoyed pulling the legs of his lieutenants and testing the extremes to which their eager assentations would carry them, got a good deal of sardonic fun out of their rivalries. On one occasion he

Irving as Mephistopheles
From a drawing by Sir Bernard Partridge

Irving as Mephistopheles

From a drawing by Sir Bernard Partridge

himself became the target of Austin's outspokenness, though the latter reported that 'he came out of the encounter with flying colours':

Philadelphia,
February 9th, 1885.

'. . . Henry said to me one day: "Austin, your trouble in life is that you are too sensitive. I should think your wife must find it hard to manage you sometimes. . . ." He was right in the main. He is always telling me that I take life too seriously. Well, I can't stand some of the practices in his profession. And when I find others around him, flattering and scheming, I break out. H. and I had a regular set to in the train the other night and rowed each other for about an hour. Ellen began it by attacking something he had done which she didn't think dignified, —then I made Loveday's hair stand on end by taking the same line much more strongly. Henry said I was a baby—a greenhorn and things of that kind—but I wasn't going to be put down and I know he respects me for it. He has been more friendly than usual ever since. He said I was too truthful to be a man of the world. . . . I had much rather have Irving's respect than be regarded by him as a tool and a sycophant. . . .'

The long train journeys had their lighter moments. From Chicago, Austin wrote:

'. . . the train stopped for twenty minutes to let the company dine. But as there had been a misunderstanding the cupboard was bare. However, in Henry's car seven of us had eaten an excellent lunch. Ellen *would* act as waitress and when I stole Loveday's pie and hid it, she pursued me with a fork. Teddy (Craig) has a little sledge, so when we stopped I took this out in the snow and gave him a ride. Then Ellen came and I pulled her about. Then she would make me sit on the sledge while she acted as a horse! I wonder what the Lyceum stalls would have thought if they could have seen the sight. We couldn't persuade Henry to compromise his dignity by taking a ride. He stood on the steps of the car and gazed at us with a tragic air. Ellen was just like a schoolgirl, every bit as young in feeling as her boy. . . .'

The company played a three weeks' engagement in Boston; towards the end of it Irving was out of the bill for three days. Probably it did the company no harm to have to fend for themselves, and, from Austin's account, they came out of the ordeal pretty well.

'. . . there has been a remarkable novelty in the events of this week. Henry did not play last night; tonight he is still helpless and I am afraid he will not be fit for work again before we open at Brooklyn on Monday. He had a very bad cold, and though this has left him he has got rheumatism in his left leg. This has caused a painful swelling which wanders between the knee and the ankle so that he is unable to stand. There is nothing serious but it's so phenomenal for Henry to be laid up like this that at first there was something like a panic. Last night Alexander played Benedick at very short notice and, except for a few slips, played it very well. Ellen had most of the burden on her shoulders and she rose to the occasion magnificently, rousing the audience to positive enthusiasm. I never saw her play the scene in the cathedral when Beatrice tells Benedick to kill Claudio with such fire and energy. We in the audience were all very nervous at first. Mrs. Alexander ruined her fan by biting it in her excitement, and once or twice she tried to prompt her husband from a box near the stage. It was one of the most interesting evenings of the whole tour, for we sat on tenterhooks, wondering what surprising improvement in the text would come next. The climax was reached when Alexander, at a loss for a word in the last scene, turned to another man and said "What is it?" When he got the word he smiled and went on, and the audience laughed with the utmost sympathy and good nature. Tonight, old Mead— the man with the big voice who plays the Ghost in *Hamlet,* is the Shylock, and as his memory is proverbially eccentric, we expect some entertainment. But he is an excellent actor and will play the part well. . . .

I have been spending part of the evening with Henry, who made half funny, half melancholy attempts to hobble about the room. He thinks he's got rheumatic gout and the idea of gout in a physique like his is so amusing that I laughed. But the poor old boy finds it anything but laughable to lie on a couch all day while the receipts at the theatre suffer from his absence. . . .'

Irving's robust health and unflagging energy were taken so much for granted that this reminder to his people of their dependence upon him was not untimely—the extent of their dependence being registered in the box-office where the nightly receipts fell from $1,900 to $500. Whatever may have been the cause of his indisposition, it vanished as suddenly as it came, so that he was well enough to play to bumper houses for the last two performances before he left for Brooklyn and New York.

The reappearance of Irving in New York, where he played a short season before leaving for England, was made the occasion for a succession of hospitalities in his honour and of tributes to his genius. No wonder, as Austin observed:

New York,
March 27th, 1885.

'. . . Henry is in high good humour today. We were walking up Broadway when he saw some very pretty gloves in a shop, so we went in and he bought a pair for you which I will take over with me . . . his tragic eye lighted on a baby's bodice made of blue silk and he said: "Let's have this too, it'll do for the youngster."

"But it isn't big enough," I said.

"Never mind, it will do for the next!"

And he winked a wicked wink. . . .'

On March 30th Irving, at the invitation of the president of the College, Mr. Eliot, gave a lecture at Harvard University. He chose for his subject, 'The Art of Acting', and prepared, with Austin's help, a long address which, after a short preamble expressing his sense of the occasion, was marshalled under three headings—The Art of Acting, The Practice of the Art, and The Rewards of the Art. In the first he gave a brief summary of the artistic theories of his illustrious predecessors; in the second, he epitomised his own views on the practice of his art which illustrated his intention even if at times it showed that he deviated from his own principles; in concluding his address, he drew attention to the remarkable change in recent years in the situation of the actor and in the public appreciation of his calling. To the young men who thronged the Sanders Theatre he gave two salutary warnings:

'Beware of the loungers of our calling, the camp followers who hang on the skirts of the army, and who inveigle the young into habits that degrade their character and paralyse their ambition. Let your ambition be ever precious to you, and, next to your good name, the jewel of your souls. I care nothing for the actor who is not always anxious to rise to the highest position in his particular walk; but this ideal cannot be cherished by the young man who is induced to fritter away his time and his mind in thoughtless company . . . and I would say, as a last word, to the young men in this assembly who may at any time resolve to enter the dramatic profession, that they ought always to fix their mind on the highest example; that in studying acting they should beware of prejudiced comparisons between this method and that, but learn as much as possible from all; that they should remember that art is as varied as nature, and as little suited to the shackles of the school; and, above all, that they should never forget that excellence in any art is attained only by arduous labour, unswerving purpose, and unfailing discipline. This discipline is, perhaps, the most difficult of all tests, for it involves subordination of the actor's personality in every work which is designed to be a complete and harmonious picture. Dramatic art nowadays is more coherent, systematic and comprehensive than it has sometimes been, and to the student who proposes to fill the place in this system to which his individuality and experience entitle him, and to do his duty faithfully and well, ever striving after greater excellence, and never yielding to the indolence that is often born of popularity—to him I say, with every confidence, that he will choose a career in which, if it does not lead him to fame, he will be sustained by the honourable exercise of some of the best faculties of the human mind.'

The students of Harvard gave Irving a great reception, and a deputation of them escorted him to Boston on his return journey. The preparation of this address had brought the simmering quarrel between Stoker and Austin to the boil. The latter, weary of 'the childish pettiness of the whole atmosphere', was glad to know that this letter which he wrote to his wife from New York was the last report he would make on an expedition to which he had looked forward eagerly but, failing to adjust himself to the peculiar freemasonry of a theatrical company, had found wearisome and exasperating:

New York,
March, 1885.

'. . . I have given him such satisfaction with the address he is to deliver at Harvard University next Monday and with the speech I have written for the farewell banquet on April 6th, that he is more than usually genial just now. I actually made him tearful when I read that speech to him yesterday. I am conceited enough to think that it will make a small sensation—provided he doesn't spoil it. We are always wrangling over little words concerning the meaning and importance of which he has eccentric and not altogether literary ideas. I am chiefly delighted about this business because that idiot Stoker wrote a speech for the same occasion and I was disgusted to find it on the Governor's table. When I read mine to Henry, he said: "Poor old Bram has been trying *his* hand but there isn't an idea in the whole thing." I said: "I should be very much surprised if there was."

The fact is Stoker tells everybody that he writes Henry's speeches and articles, and he wants to have some real basis for this lie. This is why he worried H.I. into putting his name to an article which appeared in the *Fortnightly Review*, a fearful piece of twaddle about American audiences that B.S. was three months in writing. . . . I am not vindictive, as you know, but such colossal humbug as this . . . makes me a little savage. The misfortune is that my position as a *very* private secretary compels me to keep in the background. I cannot tell the truth about my own work for that would not be right. Luckily, I have a faithful friend and ally in Alexander, who knows everybody in London worth knowing and will prick Stoker's bubble effectively.'

Austin's picture of the morbid jealousies which his presence in the company evoked was probably a true one. He failed, however, to differentiate adequately between the extravagant loyalties of Stoker and Loveday. Stoker, inflated with literary and athletic pretensions, worshipped Irving with all the sentimental idolatry of which an Irishman is capable, revelling in the patronage which, as Irving's manager, was at his disposal, and in the opportunities which this position gave him to rub shoulders with the great. This weakness and his emotional impetuosity handicapped him in dealing with Irving's business affairs in a forthright and sensible manner. Irving needed, though he might not have tolerated, a partner of financial and executive ability who would keep a stern check upon the extravagances and irregularities to which a theatrical organisation of his kind was peculiarly prone. Stoker, well-intentioned, vain, impulsive, and inclined to blarneying flattery, was perhaps the only man who could have held his position as Irving's manager for so many years; from him Irving got the service he deserved but at a cost that was no less fatal because it was not immediately apparent. Loveday, on the contrary, was the gentle, self-effacing and adoring friend; infinitely to be trusted and never failing to solve and execute the technical problems which Irving heaped upon him. His domain was the stage and he had no ambitions beyond its confines. If his acquiescence in every word or whim his Chief expressed was something of a joke among the company, it sprang from a lifelong devotion to his friend and from an inherent belief that all he said or did was divinely inspired. In return, Irving treated Loveday with a trust and affection which was never so apparent in his relations with Stoker. While he might have had a shrewder man than Stoker in the front of the house, without Loveday's help he could never have realised all that he contrived upon the stage.

Although the Presidential elections were still in full swing, the company played to phenomenal business during these last weeks in New York. In return for the honours and kindnesses which were showered upon them, Irving and Ellen Terry played the fourth act of *The Merchant of Venice* at a matinée in aid of the Actors' Fund (the equivalent of the Royal General Theatrical Fund at home) in the Academy of Music. On the night of April 6th, three days before he sailed for England, Irving was entertained at a public banquet in his honour, organized by a group of eminent Americans which included Edwin Booth, Oliver Wendell Holmes, Mark Twain and H. H. Furness, the editor of the Variorum edition of Shakespeare's plays. Chester Arthur was prevented by illness from taking the chair and his place was taken by Senator Evarts, who had a wide reputation for the quality and endurance of his oratory. Henry Ward Beecher was among the hosts; now, thoroughly converted, he bore witness to the power for good of a theatre exemplified by Irving's representations. William Winter recited a poetical address longer and richer in sentiment and metaphor than his last. Irving, in taking farewell of this gathering of newly won but firm friends, asked them to believe of him what their distinguished lawyer, Rufus Choate, had said of his fellow-country-men: 'Dearly he loved you, for he was grateful for the open arms with which you welcomed the stranger and sent him onwards and upwards.' It was realised that, in the nature of things, it was unlikely that Irving would be seen again in America for some time, for, except for one short season, he had been absent from the Lyceum for the better part of two years. The abundant evidence of the sincere regard in which America held him, and the warmth of this leave-taking, did much to mollify his regret at leaving a country whose people, at such a time of crisis in their own affairs, had crowded into their theatres to see him act. His decision to arrange and manage his own tour had been richly rewarded. The gross takings had amounted to over £80,000, of which, when all shares and expenses had been paid, there would remain for him a balance of £15,000 clear profit.

CHAPTER XXV

7th Lyceum Season : Dr. Primrose

I

Within a few days of his return to England, Irving began his seventh season at the Lyceum on May 2nd with a revival of *Hamlet*. Once more there was a discordant note in the chorus of rejoicing with which his friends and supporters welcomed his reappearance. He had made a well-intentioned but misguided attempt to do away with pit crowds by making it possible for seats in that part of the house to be booked in advance. No doubt he thought only of the convenience of his patrons whom, every time he entered his private door in Burleigh Street, he saw patiently enduring fatigue and the rigours of the weather while they waited at all hours for the pit doors to open. Oddly enough he had not appreciated the extent of his own popularity and the temptations which the demand for these seats would put in the way of speculators and even of his own staff. A few days before he opened, he received this warning from an unknown friend:

'. . . I have reason to think that a small band of malcontents will be present and should you in any way refer to the new pit arrangements are prepared to give an emphatic negative to it. Should one of their miserable voices reach you it might be as well to be ready for them. It is, perhaps, ridiculous to lay any stress on what they say or do, but the tale is told by them that one man on your staff secured thirteen tickets on Monday morning . . . should anything in the slightest degree mar the harmony of your long looked for return, it would be, to me, doubly painful as your first act has been so generously thoughtful. . . . I am keenly sensible that it is great presumption for so humble a devotee to address you, but, "hearts beat as true in Seven Dials as in Belgravia".'

This warning was no false alarm. At the close of the play, Irving was allowed to express his gratification at being home again and to

455

announce the forthcoming production of *Olivia*. But when he mentioned the new arrangements for the pit, the long pent-up storm burst. At first there was a pandemonium of shouting—those in favour of his proposals trying to drown with 'ayes' the yelling of angry 'no's' by those against them. When the ruder partisans were exhausted, an impromptu but vigorous debate began among the audience to which Irving, smiling and calm as a judge, listened patiently. Having heard them out, and satisfied that his innovation had been a mistake, he fell back upon *Hamlet*. 'So, gentlemen,' he quoted, 'with all my love I do commend me to you; and what so poor a man as Hamlet is may do to express his love and friending to you, God willing shall not lack!' Thus he charmed the malcontents out of their acrimony and restored the harmony of his homecoming. Accepting this public correction, he re-established the law of the survival of the fittest in queues where patience and physical endurance brought their own reward.

During the short run of *Hamlet* Irving betrayed some uneasiness about the steadily rising costs of running his theatre. 'I want you to let me know tonight,' he wrote to Stoker, 'the difference between our present expenses and the lowest to which we got *Hamlet* when I first took the theatre. I have reduced the advertisements. Now or never is our time. If we cannot reduce now, we never shall.'

The answer to his urgent enquiry was that in five years the weekly costs of running *Hamlet* had doubled—from £700 to £1,500—a subtle inflation for which there seemed no single or direct explanation or any particular item in the accounts responsible. Certainly no economies resulted from this inquest. Henceforward, over-burdened with the responsibilities of production and lulled by continuing successes, Irving made no very serious attempt to eradicate the insidious blight which was consuming the fruits of his own labour.

2

On May 27th Wills's *Olivia*, lavishly decorated and with several modifications and additions by the poet's hand, was revived at the Lyceum. Irving had asked Sir Arthur Sullivan to write the incidental music; he accepted the commission with an interesting reservation:

> 1 *Queen's Mansions,*
> *Victoria Street,*
> *March 6th,* 1885.

'. . . I read *Olivia* carefully. . . . I at once came to the conclusion that what music is necessary *in* the piece I would do. But overture and entr'acte involve a great deal of thought and labour which would be thrown away. You cannot get the audience (even on a first night) to consider them as part of the piece and to listen to them . . . consequently it is most ungrateful and disheartening for the composer.'

It was Ellen Terry's evening. Irving relaxed and was content to let her take charge and for the production to be on the lines of her earlier success. Bill Terriss as Squire Thornhill and Norman Forbes as Moses had been with her in the previous production at the Court. Now her two children, Edie and Teddy, were walking on with her for the first time. It was a family affair—'the only comfortable first night at the Lyceum' that Ellen ever had.

Irving's henchmen were not entirely pleased to see their Chief subordinate himself to his leading lady in a part which they considered unworthy of him. Stoker went so far as to voice this opinion and received a modest rebuke. 'My dear fellow,' said Irving, 'it's all right. If I can't play the Vicar to please I shall think I don't know my business as an actor; and that I really think I do.' To Vezin—who created the part of the Vicar—he wrote, when inviting him to the first night: 'Come round and see your daughter; I am only her step-father.'

In fact, Irving found the part of the benign clergyman harder to realise than he supposed. He was not content to follow Vezin's presentment of the conventional heavy father, good as it had been. His own parental experience had been limited to infrequent and embarrassed interviews with his two sons. Consequently his first attempts at fatherly affection were false and awkward. From the mouth of the audacious and unabashed babe, Edie, he received correction.

'Why,' she asked, 'don't you talk as you do to me and Teddy? At home you *are* the Vicar.'

He took the child's advice and managed to confine his personality within the compass of the sweet forbearance and narrow frame of the gentle cleric, to everyone's satisfaction. That he did this with difficulty and that there was some internal conflict between the man and the actor was evident when, after several weeks of unnatural benignity, Irving was heard, as he came off the stage after a particularly moving scene, to mutter to himself: 'Ba-a-a-a-a!'—as though he had had enough of playing the unctuous sheep. Ellen Terry, as she had done in *The Merchant of Venice*, found that Irving took the play at a slower pace and that the Lyceum production suffered from this change of tempo and from over-elaborate scenery which in so large a theatre dwarfed the tender comedy and teacup storms of Goldsmith's story.

But the public seemed to find it all very much to their taste and even Archer was moved by Irving's simple artifices which charmed the rest of the critics to a man:

'Dr. Primrose is one of the parts in which Mr. Irving pays the penalty of that striking personality which is, in a sense, his greatest gift. The Vicar we know and Mr. Irving we know, each so vividly that it takes us some time to fuse the two ideas. Dr. Primrose, wearing the features of Mr. Irving, strikes at first as a quaint incongruity, like one of Mr. Tenniel's cartoons—Micawber with the face of Mr. Gladstone or Hamlet with the forelock of Lord Beaconsfield. Mr. Irving, indeed, is now and then curiously like the received portraits of Sterne, a Divine of a very different stamp from Goldsmith's simple old pastor. But this feeling very quickly wears off. If our preconception of the character differed from Mr. Irving's presentation of it, so much the worse for our preconception. Brought into contact with his exquisite art it rapidly vanishes. Mr. Irving is so clearly the Vicar in the spirit, that we cordially accept him as the Vicar in the flesh. He is altogether a more distinguished personality than Goldsmith imagined, but that is a fault one easily forgives, since it does not make him less simple or less lovable. The performance is full of masterly touches, but the end of the second act stands out from the rest as one of the finest pieces of pathos Mr. Irving has ever compassed. There is nothing more touching even in his *Charles I.* In one or two speeches it seemed to me that his voice was, not too loud, but too deep—otherwise he was perfect.'

During the run of *Olivia*, Irving had direct evidence of the knavery which was infecting almost every department in his theatre. The first scene of *Olivia* was dominated by a realistic apple tree from which hung three of four real apples, ready to be plucked by children who ran off the stage eating them. It was Irving's custom every Saturday to check the accounts. He noticed that the provision of apples for this purpose steadily increased—first a dozen, then a box, and finally a barrel of them, being charged weekly on the property master's account. He could not ignore such flagrant extravagance. Summoning Arnott, the property master, he pointed to the item in the accounts and said: 'I'm—er—glad —er—to see the little Arnotts are fond of ap-ples.' This mild remonstrance may have checked such abuses for a time; but the number of his camp followers steadily grew and before long there were many families who looked to the Lyceum for far more than their dessert.

In June, Irving was invited by Richard Burton and his wife to supper at the Café Royal. He gladly accepted because he hoped to hear, for the first time, the facts about the death of his boyhood friend, Henry

Palmer. After their ways had parted, Palmer, having travelled widely in the Middle East, had become a lecturer in Arabic and Hindustani at Cambridge. When, in 1882, Arabian Egypt had revolted against the Khedive, Palmer was sent on a mission to secure the loyalty of certain Bedouin tribes who could ensure the defence of the Suez Canal against attack by the rebels. He was not the first or the last Englishman to find a deep affinity with the deserts of Arabia and Egypt. Aided by his knowledge of Arabic and a liberal supply of English gold, he was initially successful; having reported to his government, he set out on a second journey through the rebel lines to complete the negotiations. He fell into the hands of a treacherous sheik, who, posing as a friendly guide, led him into an ambush. Palmer was captured and brutally murdered. Burton was sent to bring the murderers to justice. He succeeded in doing so and afterwards brought Palmer's body home, where it was buried in St. Paul's Cathedral. Such was the heroic end of the boy who, by showing Johnnie Brodribb his first glimpse of a romantic world and of the wide horizons that lay beyond the city of London, had played an important part in the actor's haphazard education. Both boys had realised their dreams and ambitions.

Palmer had died in the hour of supreme self-fulfilment. There had been times when Irving had imagined such a quietus to be enviable. Now, when the tide of his success was bearing him along so swiftly, his friend's lonely death seemed to him tragic and premature.

CHAPTER XXVI

8th and 9th Lyceum Seasons :
Mephistopheles

———◆———

I

'Books—£210' was an item of expenditure in the accounts at the end of the seventh season. It marked an intensification in the research upon which Irving had been engaged intermittently for the last five years with a view to producing *Faust* at the Lyceum. Under his close supervision, Wills had been making a free adaptation of Goethe's play; he had succeeded at last in condensing this formidable work into a form presentable in a commercial theatre and, if in doing so much of the literary quality and profundity of the original had been lost, he had, at least, reduced it to a length which could be endured by the ordinary theatre-going public.

Irving, on his return from America, had made up his mind to present the play at the beginning of the winter season. He was naturally tempted to play Mephistopheles; having created so many minor villains, he owed the devil himself his due. As a showman, he knew that the Faust legend made the same appeal to the public as *Hamlet*. Wrapped up in a strong melodramatic story which was capable of entertaining the simplest minds, was an exposition of ethical and mystical truths; even those who were incapable of comprehending the deeper message were unconsciously ennobled by hearing it, while keener intellects could overlook the theatricality of the story as they relished its philosophical content. It is probable that other considerations persuaded him that this was the moment to tackle so vast an undertaking. Wagner had opened his Festival Theatre at Bayreuth in 1876 with his production of *The Ring*. News must have reached Irving of the spectacular scenic effects at which Wagner was aiming and which, in the ensuing years, with the help of his designers, Joukowsky and Bruckner, he had achieved. All that Irving had heard of the production of Parsifal in

1882 must have put him on his mettle as a 'metteur en scène'. As a vehicle for reasserting the supremacy of the Lyceum in the field of stage production, *Faust* could hardly be bettered.

Irving and Wills, as with scissors and paste they did their play carpentry, had the pictorial possibilities of the piece uppermost in their minds. Wills's chatty letters show how ready he was to fall in with Irving's ideas:

'. . . I think I've done the job really well and weirdly—in Meph's onslaught on the witch and simulated fury I have thrown his words into a few swinging verses with sulphur in them. I am *sure* this treatment is right artistically—firstly it gives the same atmosphere as on the Brocken when the witches talk or are addressed—and secondly distinguishes the outburst markedly from that upon Faust and lends a weirdness. I think it will play 10 minutes and is worth doing. . . .'

. . . I now send in the acts complete with the substitute for Twaddle which your copyist can easily copy into the act you have got. Feeling the difficulty of removing the grand set in Act I of German Town and Cathedral with Streets etc.—when followed by a set of Margaret's Room—I have sent you a tavern scene on approval—if adopted by you I must write in a few lines at the end of first scene to correct the sequel. . . . I think I have made a good job of it and given you my best work —as to the terms between us, there never has been any difficulty as you have always been so liberal. . . .'

Wills, singular though his methods were, did his best to be loyal to Goethe and to Irving. It was, as his brother wrote, 'a thankless task. It was not his duty to found a drama upon the poem but out of the poem to make a connected drama . . . the merit of the adaptation is that it is in excellent perspective'. If brevity and theatrical expediency are virtues, Wills deserved some credit for reducing the 1,200 lines which, in Goethe's play, precede the appearance of Mephistopheles, to 60 in his own version, which was ample to prepare the audience for Irving's appearance at the Lyceum. It was not surprising that the obliging poet—with the ruthless actor, with Dr. Anster the English translator of Goethe, with domestic chaos and with chronic insolvency at his elbow—fell between several stools and produced little more than a libretto for an infernal pantomime. Irving had no very great reverence for Goethe. He knew of the travesties of *Macbeth* and *Romeo and Juliet* which Schiller and Goethe had passed off as Shakespeare in their Weimar Theatre. Nor had he any natural sympathy with a poet whose declared intention it had been to rival Shakespeare by creating artificially a national drama in Germany. Irving's attitude to Goethe was very much the same as Gounod's, who, when composing his opera, *Faust*, remarked to his librettist, Jules Barbier: "When literature interferes with music it blunders." Indeed Irving's unscrupulous treatment of Goethe may have been inspired by the composer, for when they met in his dressing-room in 1882 they had found themselves vastly in accord on most subjects.

Several actors had put on versions of *Faust* before him. Lemaître had delighted the audiences of the Porte St. Martin with the lurid version which had been re-adapted by Charles Kean when he appeared with some success as a slightly stunted Mephistopheles. Even in their time, opinion on Goethe's talent as a dramatist was divided. Charles Lamb, in comparing Goethe's to Marlowe's *Faust*, judged the former 'vulgar melodrama'; G. H. Lewes, who found Marlowe's play 'wearisome, vulgar and ill-conceived', admitted that Goethe, in the first part of *Faust*, set 'culture above Passion, and Humour and Literature above emotion', and that the second part was of little interest—'very inferior to the first part in conception and execution . . . an elaborate mistake'. Thus Irving set about this confection of lyrical melodrama and infernal pageantry with none of the guilty feelings of a conscious vandal but with all the zest of an ambitious actor and producer who knew that he was on to a good thing.

The seventh season ended on July 30th. The public had supported *Olivia* loyally, but a heavy production account, swollen by the preliminary expenses of *Faust*, left receipts and expenditure evenly balanced. This did not prevent Irving putting in hand extensive reconstruction of the stage of the Lyceum and the complete redecoration of the auditorium. The last vestiges of Bartolozzi were torn down and an Italian style of ornament and decoration was introduced which survived his tenancy. Frustrated in his attempt to improve by statute the lot of those of who frequented the pit, he was able, with structural alterations, to provide greater comfort and accommodation for his friends in the gallery. In order to make room for the scenic effects which he was planning, the roof over the stage was raised twenty feet so that cloths could be raised out of sight without having to be rolled up. Leaving his theatre in the hands of the builders, Irving set out for Germany in search of local colour. With him he took a congenial party which included Ellen Terry, her children, Joe Comyns Carr and his wife, Alice.

Comyns Carr was ten years younger than Irving. As a young man he had made his mark as an art critic on the *Manchester Guardian*. The sympathy and appreciation which he had shown towards the young aesthetic movement led to his being appointed a director of the Grosvenor Galleries. In 1873 he became dramatic critic of the *Pall Mall Gazette*. Recently Macmillans had made him editor of their new monthly the *English Illustrated Magazine*, with which they hoped to challenge the supremacy of American papers in this field, such as *Harper's* and *Scribner's*. Alice Comyns Carr had been a close friend of Ellen Terry since the latter's day at the Prince of Wales's Theatre; her good taste and her talent for designing costumes for the stage had made Ellen Terry increasingly dependent upon her advice and help. She was a determined Bohemian. Joe Carr had, as it were, brought to their marriage the friendship of senior artists and writers like Burne-Jones and Browning; his wife attracted the younger generation, led by John Sargent and Henry James, to their home, which became famous for good conversation and the artistry of their Bolonnaise cook. Irving's association and friendship with Joe Carr was inevitable. In the crisis of his affairs, this friendship would have adverse repercussions; yet at this time Irving could not have chosen more delightful, witty and cultivated companions than this devoted couple to take with him on his busman's holiday.

The party made Nuremburg their headquarters, but it was in the neighbouring town of Rothenburg that Irving found the architecture and atmosphere he was seeking. Hawes Craven was summoned from London. Together the actor and his scenic artist explored the purlieus of these towns, quarrying ideas and details from this rich mine of mediaevalism. Irving was never happier than when he was buying things—either presents for his friends or additions to his collection of theatrical bric-à-brac. In Nuremburg he indulged his hobby to the full. The shops were crammed with antiquities, among which the whole party, at his instigation, rummaged for appropriate stage properties. Prices were so low and the enthusiasm of the treasure-seekers so great that by the end of their visit crates of furniture, china, authentic costumes and brocades had been dispatched to the Lyceum. Whatever Irving observed or experienced—life in the narrow streets, the crooked timbered houses or the horizon fenced with spires—he assessed subconsciously in terms of its theatrical value or of the effective use to which it could be put at the Lyceum. When one night the party, from the windows of their hotel, were watching a fire which had broken out in the town—flames licking up the old wooden buildings, the river reflecting cascades of sparks as roof after roof collapsed into the incandescence—Irving was heard to murmur: 'What a scene if only one

Faust 304 to 309

RECEIPTS.

DATE.		PLAY.	GROSS RECEIPTS.			DISCOUNT TO AGENTS.			N
			£	s.	d.	£	s.	d.	
1887		Sat. Matinée ...		.	-	-	.	-	
Jany 22	Saturday ...	Faust	294	9	.	3	18	11	2
" 24	Monday ...	do	248	10	.	2	1	10	2
" 25	Tuesday ...	do	257	14	6	2	7	1	2
"	Wed. Matinée ...		.	-	-	-	-	-	
" 26	Wednesday ...	do	267	1	.	3	1	2	2
" 27	Thursday ...	do	273	7	.	1	18	4	2
" 28	Friday ...	do	233	11	6	2	-	10	2
	TOTAL WEEK £		1,574	13	.	15	8	2	1,
	FORWARD ...		34,408	4	.	351	18	11	34,
	TOTAL TO DATE £		35,982	17	.	367	7	1	35,

PROFIT AND LOSS ACCOUNT.	£	s.	d.		
Receipts for week	1,559	4	10	Bills due	
Weekly current expense (A) ...	1,121	.	7		
Profit on Week, not including expenses of production ... £	438	4	3	Amount to Credit advance Booking	7
					7
Total { profit / loss } on season to date £	8,541	3	6	Total Debit · Balance ... £	1

HEATRE.

MR. HENRY IRVING.

ATEMENT.

Week ending Friday, the **28** day of **January** 188**7**

EXPENDITURE.

	EXPENSES (TAKING AVERAGE OF RENT, &c.) A.			EXPENSES (CASH ACTUALLY PAID). B.		
	£	s.	d.	£	s.	d.
Rent / Taxes / Insurance	100	..	..	8	12	11
House Staff	47	19	.	47	19	.
House Expenses	64	13	9	64	13	9
Sundries	11	1	4	11	1	4
Printing	25	13	.	25	13	.
Advertising	77	6	9	77	6	9
Bill Posting	16	1	6	16	1	6
Salaries :—	412	6		412	6	
Supers	27	6		27	6	
Stage Staff	45	-		45		
*Stage Expenses	156	7	3	156	7	3
Gas	28	7	.	28	7	.
Limelight	35	5		35	5	.
Orchestra	73	14	.	73	14	.
Total Working Expenses £	1121	.	7	1030	13	6
†Production Account ...				13	11	.
Expenditure on House ...				8	16	8
Total Week £				1053	1	4
Forward				26 021	5	1
Total to Date ... £				27,074	6	5

Left margin columns:

	£	s.	d.
*			
aint Room ...			
arpenter's Dpt,			
operty ,,			
as ,,			
ardrobe ,,			
£			

	£	s.	d.
†			
LAY :—			
Total £			

	£	s.	d.
Cash in Bank	858	2	8
„ „ Hand	265		
Amount due Library	247	5	5
Amount to Credit ...	4500	.	.
„ Due ...	7,838	.	.
	1,000		
Total Credit . ... £	19,908	8	1

_____ Acting Manager.

4 day of **Feb** 188**7**

night expens = £187

could get it.' He had the subjective outlook of the painter towards the world around him. Sometimes this preoccupation, this seeing everything in terms of the theatre, was queerly manifested. Once when he, Joe Carr and young Teddie Craig had penetrated deeply into the slums of the town, a party of roughs hung threateningly about the prosperous-looking sightseers. Joe Carr, foreseeing an ugly situation, began a strategic withdrawal. Irving stood his ground for a moment and then, assuming the most fearsome posture from his catalogue of grotesque attitudes, advanced upon the hooligans who in terror took to their heels.

The fame of this eccentric, open-handed party of English folk was such that one morning a band played in Irving's honour under the window of his bedroom. This was not the first time that he had been serenaded—the band of the Philadelphia *Evening Call* had similarly saluted him—and no tribute to his popularity gave him greater pleasure. Calling his valet, Walter, he said: 'See that the poor devils have a tankard of beer apiece—and,' he added, 'give them this.' The largesse which Walter distributed was so generous that for the short time that remained of their visit the members of the party were trailed wherever they went by admiring and hopeful crowds.

Before leaving Germany, Irving and Ellen Terry went to Berlin where they were the guests of Ludwig Barnay, who had led the Meiningen Players when, in 1881, they visited London. The German actor's admiration for Irving as an artist was equalled by his affection for him as a host. Himself a product of the cold excellence of a state-aided theatre, in his heart he had envied the artistic freedom which Irving enjoyed at the Lyceum and the warm conviviality of the hours spent at his friend's supper table in 'my much loved Beefsteak Room—in little committee'. Now he had established his independence at his own Berliner Theatre and was free to give, in two special performances of *Julius Caesar* and *The Merchant of Venice*, expression of his regard for his English fellow artists.

2

On his return to London, Irving flung himself into the work of putting into effect the ideas which his travels had inspired and of resolving the mechanical problems which the execution of these ideas entailed. Among other installations which had been completed in his absence was that of a full-sized organ in the deep recesses of the Lyceum stage: this he judged necessary for the accompaniment of the scenes outside Nuremburg Cathedral and of the heavenly choirs which would need all the help they could get if they were to triumph over his devastating diabolism. Loveday was anxious that the Chief immediately on his return should hear the splendid instrument which, with great difficulty, he had fitted into the theatre. Having settled Irving in the stalls, his lieutenants, eager for commendation, grouped themselves around him like Napoleon's marshals. Loveday gave the signal to the organist, already poised at the manuals. Thereupon the theatre echoed to such high-pitched trillings, to such adenoidal tremolos of the vox humana and to such fluty pipings as the organist reckoned would demonstrate effectively his own virtuosity and the celestial resources of the organ. When the recital ended there was an interval of reverent silence as the expectant henchmen strained towards their Chief.

'Well, Guvnor?' asked Loveday.

After another unendurable silence, Irving, already half possessed by the mischievous devil of his own creation, muttered:

'Mm—very gud—very gud. But sounds to me—like an Archbishop —pid-d-ling.'

3

After this organ prelude, the Lyceum community, spurred on by Irving's driving and unremitting energy, laboured day and night to fulfil his exacting demands throughout the short month that remained before December 19th when *Faust* would open the ninth season. Alice Comyns Carr, as designer of the women's costumes, was admitted to the rehearsals. 'It was only now,' she wrote, 'that I realised the existence of two distinct and separate Irvings. Gone was the debonair and cheery holiday companion, and in his place was a ruthless autocrat, who brooked no interference from anyone and was more than a little rough in his handling of everyone in the theatre—except Nell. Irving allowed no one to watch him at work and was ever ready with a flood of bitter satire if anyone accidentally strayed into his vision.'

No one but a ruthless autocrat could have harnessed to his purpose the counterfeit apparitions and the tinsel storms which Irving was brewing at the Lyceum. The angelic visions, the heavenward ascents, the descents into sulphurous infernos, the magical appearances and trap-door vanishings, the lycopodic brimstone, the gauzy treacle, the new-fangled battens of electric lights, the calcium arcs, the sub-stage generation of steam, the daring use of electric fluid (under the personal supervision of Colonel Gouraud—the partner of the great Mr. Edison)—all these ingredients need a firm and practised hand to mingle them discreetly with the work of the scene-painter and to prevent them drowning the words of the poet or overwhelming the actors. As production expenses mounted and more staggering effects of light and atmosphere were attempted, and after endless and costly rehearsals achieved, even Stoker began to doubt the play's chances of success. When Hawes Craven's and Telbin's splendid compositions were set up and appeared to be executed disappointingly in a grey-green monochrome, he wondered if Irving's stage sense had deserted him and dared to say as much. It was, in fact, as sure as ever; though the producer's intention was not fully disclosed until the first dress rehearsal.

Walter Pollock had a privileged seat in the stalls. He watched with amazement Irving's masterly handling of crowds, resulting in the 'seemingly spontaneous impulses which stirred the diabolical crew to wild yet rhythmical movement'. Irving appeared at his side—a towering Mephistopheles clothed from head to foot in vivid scarlet, which was intensified by the cold glitter of his pewter-coloured weapons and their harness. Pollock warmly praised the superb illusions which the producer had created with a grisaille of smoke, light and scenery.

'Very glad you like it,' said Irving. '. . . given a good deal of trouble to it. But—ye know—I can never see it as I should like to. . . .'

'How do you mean?' asked Pollock.

'Why—don't you see . . .' answered Irving, with a touch of impatience and of an artist's natural vanity, 'I want to see the Red Man there—and, of course, I never shall.'

4

Reports, spontaneous and inspired, that some remarkable devilry was afoot at the Lyceum stimulated an unprecedented demand for seats for the first night of *Faust*. The Royal Family had taken a box and it was said that a peer, who had fought for and captured a seat in the gallery, had counted himself lucky. Owing perhaps to Loveday's absence through illness or to the presence of the Prince of Wales behind the scenes through curiosity, the progress of Faust through eleven scenes and innumerable startling effects was not as smooth as it might have been. The enticing visions with which Mephistopheles sought to tempt him failed to materialise, so that the audience watched his spectacular damnation without a very clear idea of the satanic *quid pro quo*. Moreover, as the play proceeded, it was apparent that Faust was wilting under the very real ordeal which he was undergoing. The climax of his sufferings was the duel with Valentine, in which Mephistopheles acted as a not entirely disinterested second. Whenever Faust looked like getting the worst of it, the devil intervened; as his sword disengaged those of the duellers, electric sparks flashed (by courtesy of Colonel Gouraud) with lurid intensity. The swords of the combatants, who wore rubber gloves, were connected by cables to the primitive electric mains, and an effect was produced which was as thrilling for the audience as it was alarming for the actors. Irving presided over this lambent contest with a diabolic relish which was only partly assumed; if by chance the fluid, finding its way through a leak in the rubber gloves, electrified one of his fellow-actors, he covered his discomfiture with yelps of sardonic laughter. It was not surprising that before the end of the play Conway, who was playing Faust, and, anyhow, was on the verge of a serious illness, became increasingly ineffective and appeared to follow his tempter in a daze. But in spite of these shortcomings and the very poor material which had been provided for the actors, the audience was entranced by the awful grandeur and restrained beauty of the scenes and tableaux which successively o'er-topped each other. At the end of the play Irving, in response to an enthusiastic reception, promised to correct the apparent faults and to make such additions and alterations as would ensure its popularity.

Conway's failure as Faust might well have jeopardised the whole vast enterprise. Irving called a rehearsal for the following morning.

'The Company,' wrote Ellen Terry, 'stood about in groups on the stage while Henry walked up and down, speechless but humming a tune occasionally, always a portentous sign with him. The scene set was the Brocken scene, and Conway stood at the top of the slope as far from Henry as he could get! He looked abject. His handsome face was very red, and his eyes full of tears. He was terrified at the thought of what was going to happen. The actor was summoned to the office, and presently Loveday came out and said that Mr. George Alexander would play Faust the following night.'

Alexander had been bitterly disappointed at being cast for Valentine; he had, nevertheless, played the part with dashing brilliance on the previous evening. His success as Faust won him the position in the company which had been held by Terriss. His apprenticeship had been a hard one. He once said that after five or six hours of rehearsal by Irving he would go home almost crying, and that he made up his mind that if ever he had a company of his own he would let them down pretty easy. This was only one of the many lessons in actor-management which he learned in the course of the next three years.

Irving's intuition as a showman had not failed him. Although the inadequacy of the text was plain to all, although Irving's most ardent admirers admitted that his demon teetered dangerously on the edge of pantomime, and although the whole affair offended the genuine and professed students of Goethe, this consummate confection of villainy and piety, of beauty and fearsome hideousness, of claptrap and culture, was the greatest financial success Irving ever had. For many years it was a seemingly inexhaustible source of wealth which subsidised his other more admirable but less rewarding ventures. It would be idle to pretend that he and Ellen Terry did not delight in this histrionic romp. He probably enjoyed every one of the seven hundred appearances he made as Mephistopheles; Ellen Terry, though she thought Irving's part unworthy of him, liked her own as Margaret—'better than any other— outside Shakespeare'. Old Mrs. Stirling wrung the last drop of comedy out of the wet rag of a part which the author had given to Martha. In short, *Faust* was a theatrical concoction into which authors, actors, scenic artists, stage carpenters, property masters and limelight men entered with spirit. As so often happens, the public were infected by their innocent delight in exhibiting their different, but so skilfully co-ordinated, crafts. The wiseacres were baffled by the popularity of a play which seemed barren of intellectual argument or of poetry.

Archer, commenting on a revival of the play a few years later, wrote, fairly enough:

'. . . There is something inspiriting, exhilarating, in great success: the mere spectacle of it warms the cockles of the heart; and he who denies or dissembles the sensation is a hypocrite or a curmudgeon. As for the play—well it really doesn't matter two pins what I think of it. The public . . . thinks differently. Meanwhile, "Goethe in Weimar Sleeps" and, to all appearance, "sleeps well". We do not hear at any rate that his protesting ghost has been seen in Wellington Street. But I do think that Mr. Irving might . . . omit Goethe's name from the programme . . . the dead cannot defend themselves. One can imagine, however, an interesting and animated "Dialogue of the Dead" between the Herr Geheimrath and the late Mr. W. G. Wills—let us hope that the shade of Eckermann is there to report it.'

Henry James re-emerged from his study to rate the whole company for the lack of distinction in their performances. He accused Irving of 'a perversity most singular on the part of a manager to whom the interests of the dramatic art have long appeared so dear . . . saying to himself that he would give great attention to the machinery of the piece,

he omitted to indulge at the same time in this indispensable reflection—
that to prevent the impression of triviality which might easily arise
from an abuse of pantomimic effects, he should take care to put at the
service of a great story a consummate interpretation . . . evidently,
however, Mr. Irving argued in directly the opposite way. It is as if he
had said that he would pile the accessories so high that the rest of the
affair wouldn't matter, it would be regarded so little'.

Henry James must have enjoyed a measure of grim satisfaction when
he read in the papers that Irving literally had been hoist with one of his
accessory petards. Normally, the first scene reached its climax when
Mephistopheles, seizing Faust, bore him upwards in clouds of billowing
steam. One night Irving and Alexander fell off the contrivance that
swept them up into the 'flies'. By great good luck they fell upon the
stage—though upon the brink of an open trap-door. Had they fallen
through the stage into the cellarage, they would have shared a true,
and perhaps more reliable apotheosis, though their evaporation would
have drawn tears rather than applause from their bereaved public.

Irving was quite incapable of presenting any facet of his art to the
public with his tongue in his cheek. That he was in deadly earnest in his
presentation of Goethe's play may have been evidence of his intellectual naïvety but not of his lack of sincerity. The public are not
easily deceived and the first requirement for success in the world of
make-believe is for the actor or author to convince his audiences that
he himself believes absolutely in what he is doing. It was remarkable
that within a few weeks of the opening of *Faust*, playgoers and even
scholars began to persuade themselves that Irving's production had
cultural qualities to which it probably could lay little claim.

5

While in Germany the disciples of Goethe wrung their hands over the
tales which they heard of the English actors' desecration of their native
epic, a party of students from Heidelburg came on pilgrimage to the
Lyceum and went home glorying in what they had seen. The Grand
Duke of Saxe-Meiningen had already decorated Irving with an Order of
his own Court; after he saw *Faust*, having conferred with the Duke of
Edinburgh, he hastily promoted the actor to the Order of the Komthur
Cross of the Second Class of the Ducal Saxon Ernestine House Order;
the only occasion on which Irving wore the insignia of this impressive
decoration was when the Grand Duke supped with him in the Beefsteak
Room. Gladstone wrote to congratulate Irving on his 'remarkable part

in a remarkable whole. . . . I do not know how much time had been given to preparing the mise-en-scène—but had it been ten years it could not have been done better'. Joseph Chamberlain dragged the unwilling John Morley to see *Faust*. '. . . We both,' he wrote 'enjoyed ourselves thoroughly . . . I admired your performance exceedingly and followed your conception of the leading part with the most critical attention. In all the later scenes I sympathise entirely with your presentation of the fiend. Your devil is "vraiment diabolique". In the earlier scenes I am not certain that I follow you with absolute assent. I suppose that it's necessary to avoid too much uniformity lest the general impression should be monotonous. I gather that you admit a frisky side to the Devil's nature. He is a French Devil in this part of the play and chuckles over the mischief he does in his "gaiété de coeur". But is this Goethe's intention? I fancy Mephistopheles is incurably bad . . . in small things as well as great . . . a saturnine wickedness incapable of giving pleasure to its author. . . . Forgive me for boring you with my reflections which I really only send as evidence of the interest which your most thoughtful and intellectual personation has excited.'

John Morley was not a great playgoer, being, he confessed, almost too immersed in work to amuse himself. After a visit to the Lyceum in 1881, he had written: 'I expected to be disgusted by Irving, but his acting in *The Cup* is more absolutely barbarous, outrageous and affronting than anything I ever saw in my theatrical life. *The Corsican Brothers* amused me much more. I loathe Irving but I am very partial to ghost scenes and duels with plenty of sticking in them.' It was not surprising that *Faust* appealed to Morley's simple dramatic tastes.

On the ninety-ninth night of the run, the Abbé Liszt was entertained at the Lyceum. He was now an old man, and such was his popularity that precautions were taken in the theatre to protect him from his admirers which would have been adequate to guard a visiting potentate from determined anarchists. During the entr'acte the orchestra saluted him with his own 'March'. He appeared to enjoy the play, and afterwards had supper with Irving in the Beefsteak Room where he was delighted to find that his host, with characteristic forethought, had provided his favourite dish—lentil pudding, lamb cutlets, and mushrooms in batter. 'H.I. and he,' recorded Stoker in his diary, 'very much alike—seemed old friends as they talked animatedly though knowing but a few words of each other's language—but using much expression and gesticulation.' Among the other guests was Professor Frederick Max Müller, the eminent philologist, whose comments on Irving's Faust summed up, perhaps, all that was to be said from an intellectual point of view for and against the production:

> All Souls College,
> Oxford.
> 18th April, 1886.

'Dear Mr. Irving,

I ought to have thanked you before now for the great treat you gave me—seeing *Faust*, meeting Liszt, and making the acquaintance of Miss Terry. But I am sometimes overwhelmed with work, though my friends say I have nothing to do. Faust always (shakes?) me—I knew every word of it since I was twenty—but the old tragedy remains as new as ever. Everything was magnificent—the scenery most interest-ing—the acting most conscientious. But one has no time to reflect—there is too much that appeals to the eye and then, as you know, the beauty of the German words is gone.

Why should you not try the experiment, before you give up Faust, to take the German text arranged for the stage and have it acted in a good translation . . . you have all that is necessary for the stage, you would only have to learn the true German text and then let people judge and compare the two. Your English arrangement does not bring out the . . . high moral lesson of Faust—people may condemn it, but they should at all events be made to see and understand it. I doubt whether that is possible in your English arrangement.

Meeting Liszt was also full of many reminiscences. I saw him last as a beautiful young man with black hair in a flowing velvet coat with open sleeves—and now—an extinct volcano—with ever so many tourists dancing attendance around him. At all events he ought to have given us one puff of smoke—a few touches on the piano. . . .

> Yours sincerely,
> F. Max Müller.'

If Müller's remarks caused Irving to consider whether, after all, he had treated the great poet a trifle cavalierly, his doubts were soon dis-pelled. Before the year was out an enterprising publisher brought out *The Henry Irving Edition of Goethe's Faust*, with a preface by Henry Morley and a respectful dedication to the actor. The range of Irving's telepathic sorcery was spreading beyond the confines of the Lyceum Theatre.

In March, Professor Müller had been one of the guests at a dinner party in New College, Oxford, which had been given in Irving's honour by one of the college dons, Mr. W. L. Courtney. Among several Heads of Colleges invited to meet Irving was Dr. Jowett, the Master of Baliol. During dinner, Irving, for some time, had endured patiently the gushing account given by a lady sitting next to him of her visit to Oberammergau, of the noble performance and of the deep message of the passion play. At last, when she paused for breath, he interjected quietly:

'It is—mm—so gud—they ought to bring it ·to the Crystal Palace.'

The lady, clearly shocked, repeated Irving's comment to Jowett. There was an anticipatory hush as the whole table waited for the Master to deliver a polite rebuke.

'Why not?' was all he answered.

Jowett and Irving had a good deal in common. Each confessed to W. L. Courtney that they admired the other's 'fine reserve'. Each was in a position to serve the other's purpose and, in doing so, made common cause. Jowett had become Vice-Chancellor of the University in 1882, and ever since his encouragement of Benson and his friends in their production of Agamemnon he had quietly but persistently fostered the revival of drama in Oxford. He had given his official patronage to the Undergraduates' Dramatic Club which had recently been formed under the presidency of Mr. Arthur Bourchier. He had been instrumental in the demolition of the dirty and dilapidated old Victoria Theatre (the only one this seat of learning possessed), and in the building of the New Theatre, the opening of which he attended in his official capacity. That evening in Irving's company prompted him to invite the actor to give an address in the New Examination Hall during June. Irving, sensible of any opportunity which would further his unending crusade, accepted the invitation. He wasted no time in giving Stoker his reasons for doing so with telegraphic clarity:

'. . . A good par. might be made about Oxford. Distinguished compliment paid to H.I. Invitation from Vice Chancellor of Oxford to deliver lecture to University—promised to do so and chosen for subject "Our Old Actors". Coming after invitation from Harvard—great tribute to dramatic art—and if one remembers rightly this is the third university which has recognised etc. etc.—Trinity Col. Dublin being the first etc. etc. If our old friend[1] might care to—or would oblige me by putting something in, it would be of interest to many. Draw up something and ask him.'

The lecture was arranged for the evening of Saturday, June 26th, when, in Irving's absence, the Lyceum would be closed. A week before,

[1] Probably Clement Scott.

he sent Jowett Pollock's *W. C. Macready; Reminiscences and Selections from his Diaries and Letters*. Jowett, in acknowledgement, wrote:

'Dear Mr. Irving,

I write to thank you for your kind present; which I value especially as coming from you. Macready was certainly a great man, though self-conscious and wanting in temper. He has given a very truthful account of himself and has written a most interesting book.

Looking forward greatly to the pleasure of seeing you on Saturday week,

> Believe me,
> Yours very truly,
> B. Jowett.

P.S. I hear that you are likely to have a very large audience.'

Jowett would have preferred the Sheldonian Theatre to be the scene of this unusual occasion; but prejudice against the theatre in general and against actors in particular still ran high in the University and permission to use it was not forthcoming. The New Schools were, however, the Vice-Chancellor's precinct, and there he could do what he liked. Irving, no doubt, marked his host's gift for stage management. Among the party whom the Master of Baliol had invited to stay for the week-end to meet Irving were a Liberal peer, Lord Dalhousie, and the Bishop of Ripon, Edward Boyd-Carpenter, together with their wives. With this irreproachable escort, Irving was conducted to the Schools, and there, to an audience of enthusiastic undergraduates and a number of intimidated dignitaries of the University, he gave his address, now entitled, with less bonhomie but with more befitting dignity, 'Four Great Actors'. It was an unpretentious and, at times, moving address—a public act of hero-worship. He wisely refrained from making his usual claims for recognition of the actor's art. At the outset he warned his audience not to expect any great intellectual profundities. 'I have not,' he said, 'had the advantage—one that very few of the members of my profession in past or even in present times have enjoyed—of a University education. The only Alma Mater I ever knew was the hard stage of a country theatre.' Briefly he surveyed the life and art of Burbage, Betterton, Garrick and Kean. He strove to describe the beauty of their accomplishment, and did not spare his polite audience the ugliness and misery of the midden from which the flower of Kean's genius sprang. Jowett noted with satisfaction the wit and urbanity of Irving's discourse on which the actor, as usual,

had lavished infinite care. When he had finished, Irving was cheered to the echo by the young people in the audience and was presented by Mr. Bourchier with an illuminated address. Then the Vice-Chancellor, in his address to the speaker, made an appeal for a better understanding of the theatre, which may have surprised his colleagues but must have warmed the cockles of the actor's heart.

'. . . The indirect influence of the theatre is very great, and tends to permeate all classes of society, so that the condition of the stage is not a bad index or test of a nation's character. We in England are in part what we have been made by the plays of Shakespeare. Our literature, our manners, our religion, our taste, have to a very great extent been affected by them. And those who, regardless of their own pecuniary loss or gain, have brought back Shakespeare to the English stage, who have restored his plays to their original form, who have quickened in the English peoples the love of his writings and the feelings of his greatness, may be truly considered national benefactors.'

Afterwards the Master's party supped at New College. Irving had been quite long enough on his good behaviour. One of the guests, Alfred Austin, who for years had importuned Irving with an unactable play about Savonarola, had recently vented his impatience with the actor-manager by criticising his policy in a magazine article. He fell inescapably into Irving's web. Irving gleefully described to Ellen Terry his dismemberment of the trapped poet:

'. . . I had supper last night at New College after the affair. Austin was there and I had it out with him—to the delight of all. "Too much decoration"—etc. etc.

I asked him what there was in *Faust* in the matter of appointments, etc. that he would like left out?

Answer: Nothing.

"Too long runs."

"You, sir, are a poet," I said. "Perhaps it may be my privilege some day to produce a play of yours. Would you like it to have a long or a short run?" (Roars of laughter.)

Answer: "Well—er—well, of course, Mr. Irving, you—well—well, a short run, of course, for *art*, but——"

"Now, sir, you're on oath," said I. "Suppose that the fees were rolling in £10 and more a night—would you rather the play were a failure or a success?"

"Well, well, as *you* put it—I must say—er—I would rather my play had a *long* run!"

Austin floored!

He has all his life been writing articles running down good work and crying up the impossible, and I was glad to show him up a bit!

The Vice-Chancellor made a most lovely speech after the address— an eloquent and splendid tribute to the stage.

Bourchier presented the address of the "Undergrads". I never saw a young man in a greater funk—because, I suppose, he had imitated me so often!

From the address:

"We have watched with keen and enthusiastic interest the fine intellectual quality of all these representations from Hamlet to Mephistopheles with which you have enriched the contemporary stage. To your influence we owe deeper knowledge and more reverent study of the master mind of Shakespeare."

All very nice indeed.'

A few days later Irving received a token of appreciation of his address that meant more to him than all the public compliments and printed eulogies it had inspired. Robert Browning sent him the purse of faded green silk which had been found, empty, in Edmund Kean's pocket after his death. 'How can I more worthily place it,' wrote the poet, 'than in your hands, if they will do me the honour to take it, with all respect and regard.'

CHAPTER XXVII

Financial Doubts and Paternal Duties

———◆◆◆———

I

Edward Godwin died on October 6th, 1886. It was twelve years since he and Ellen Terry had drifted apart. After leaving her, he had married Beatrice Philip, who, after a brief widowhood, married his friend, Whistler. Ellen Terry had loved Godwin better than anyone in the world; his children were the axis upon which her life turned. By this time the public had forgotten or perhaps never knew of her years of passionate happiness at Harpenden. Now, if her private life was at all the subject of conjecture or gossip, it was presumed by sentimentalists and cynics that she and Irving were the principals of a conventional theatrical romance. Yet, in the confined, strait-laced and censorious circle of mid-Victorian London society, which opened its doors to them and cultivated their friendship, there seems to have been no hint or supposition that such a liaison existed.

The lives of great artists are inevitably the targets of public curiosity and scrutiny. A popular actor or actress cannot retreat from the lime-lit glare of their professional life into the quiet shade which veils the domestic happiness or the peccadilloes of ordinary folk. Were it not for careless assumptions and innuendoes which have been more widely circulated after their death than before it, the life-long association and partnership of Irving and Ellen Terry would need no further elucidation than the recitation of their work together.

Irving, shortly before he parted from his wife, described himself to her as a phlegmatic man. Perhaps this confessed indifference, this apathy towards his marital obligations, was the true cause of her discontent. The fact was that his thoughts and energies were centred upon his work to the exclusion of all else. 'His art,' wrote Graham Robertson, 'was his life, his soul. He had vowed himself to it by a pact as awful as that between Faust and Mephistopheles; like Peter Schlemil, he had

478

sold his reflection.' The fraction of his life which he spent outside the theatre was passed as host to or in the company of his few intimate friends, and in the mysterious seclusion of his home, to which only Walter Collinson was admitted. Happier in the company of men than of women, he was not a passionate man in the ordinary sense of the word. He formed several intimate friendships with women older than himself whose advice and criticism he welcomed; but in so doing, he strove to satisfy the need he had felt for such companionship since his unhappy alienation from his mother.

At work he was remarkable for his power of cold, sustained concentration rather than for the temperamental paroxysms in which artists of his calibre usually find relief. He was a supreme egoist, which, coupled with his absolute single-mindedness and innate fastidiousness, made him less susceptible to feminine charms than most men. Certainly he adored Ellen Terry with an adoration deeper than that of a self-centred artist for an indispensable and much admired colleague. She was always, to him, 'the Queen of every woman'. He believed, no doubt sincerely, that he loved her and was prepared to sacrifice his jealously guarded independence for her sake. There was a time when he had hoped she might marry him—indeed he pressed her to do so. He may even have bought The Grange with the idea of making it their home. The proof of his love for her was, as he said, that he was not jealous of her—meaning, as she very well knew, not that he might be jealous of any affection she might feel for another man, but of the affection which the Lyceum audience bestowed on her.

Ellen Terry realised the unique nature of their partnership and the miracle of their artistic union. Irving could not marry her unless his wife would agree to divorce him. If, in a moment of reckless passion, Irving had declared his readiness to suffer the indignity of a divorce case in which he would be the guilty party, she had been level-headed enough to count the cost, financially and artistically, of such a scandal— a scandal such as had ruined Edmund Kean. Though she was, in her way, as devoted to Irving as he was to her and was nearer to him than anyone else, except Walter Collinson, she confessed that she never came to know the real Irving and wondered if, after all, anyone knew him. She had a sincere if unorthodox regard for the sanctity of marriage, which to her was far more unethical if it was not firmly based on mutual love and respect, than a temporary attachment if it was. To love a man in this sense one must know him—she had already suffered grievously from submitting herself to men of dominant personality of whom she had no real understanding. Moreover, she was reluctant to introduce so strange and forceful a paterfamilias into the lively family of which she was the undisputed head. Perhaps Irving hoped and believed that when the shadow of Godwin no longer lay between them, she might surrender to his importunity. He owed much to her intuitive wisdom which prevented her from doing so.

There remained the possibility of an ordinary liaison—of a grand passion which, though it might have titillated the vulgar public, would have rendered ridiculous and hypocritical his lifelong advocacy of his profession. For had they formed such a liaison they could not have concealed it from the world. Irving was as jealous of his dignity as he was inept at subtle duplicity; in many ways he retained all his life, as Ellen Terry recorded, something of the innocence of the countryman. She herself moved continually in a cloud of adoring witnesses—her children, her friends who were her devoted servants, and her servants who were her devoted friends. She and Irving would have scorned the indignities which subterfuge would have entailed; anyhow, subterfuge was impossible for two people whose lives, professional or private, were of intense interest to a world-wide public. In the United States alone, where a breath of scandal would have broken the peculiar spell which they exercised over Americans of all classes and creeds, they not only gave no grounds for scandal, but dissipated by their open and scrupulous conduct the romantic legend which the advance agents, rumour and gossip, had diligently spread abroad.

Godwin's death, therefore, marked the crystallization of the conduct of their lives together. The dominant factor in their relationship was their whole-hearted admiration of each other as artists. Bram Stoker wrote of their brotherly affection for one another—but he was wide of the mark. They were at once each other's parent and child. Irving looked upon Ellen Terry as a gifted, irresponsible daughter—adored, spoiled, and often rebuked with unexpected severity; Ellen Terry's love for Irving was that of a mother who had borne a son whose genius filled her with wonder and pride—yet whose stubborn and wilful waywardness called upon all her resources of tact and gentle remonstrance to prevent him hurting himself by his rash decisions and ill-considered actions.

So before long The Grange was sold, and Irving finally gave up all thoughts of having the kind of home which he believed he desired. His awful contract had in it no domestic clause; yet in every other respect the signatory had handsomely fulfilled his undertaking.

Irving as Cardinal Wolsey

Irving as Thomas Becket
From a photograph by Julia Margaret Cameron

2

Faust filled the Lyceum for two seasons. He had gambled £8,000 on its production. By the time he had played Mephistopheles four hundred and ninety-six times he had won back his stake and had made a profit of over £24,000 into the bargain. To relieve the tedium of his record-breaking run, he had staged two productions, each for a single performance as carefully and as extravagantly as he would have done if they were intended for the Lyceum repertory.

In the dark years between 1840, when Bulwer Lytton and Sheridan Knowles had ceased to write for the stage, and 1870, when Irving's successes gave hope and encouragement to poets and serious dramatists, John Westland Marston alone had striven to preserve the continuity of English poetic drama. He was not a great poet, and none of his plays has survived him. But in blowing on the dull embers of English drama, he saved it from being quenched entirely by the flood of importations from Europe. No one owed more to Westland Marston's persistence than Irving; Irving never failed to honour an obligation. For many years the poet had held an honoured place in the literary society of London, earning his living as a critic and as an historian of the English theatre. Recently he had fallen on evil days. The news of his sufferings had reached Irving through Joseph Knight. Irving, glad enough of any distraction after months of repetition of *Faust*, offered at once to arrange a performance for Marston's benefit. His first play, *The Patrician's Daughter*, had been produced by Macready in 1842. Irving decided to present Byron's *Werner*, and himself to play the name part, which was generally agreed to have been Macready's masterpiece. New and elaborate scenery was prepared. Seymour Lucas and Alice Carr designed costumes which were executed by the finest armourers and costumiers in Paris. The play was produced on the afternoon of June 1st, 1887. As a result, a cheque for £928 was handed to the poet by Joseph Knight, a sum mysteriously in excess of the box-office receipts by £100. Westland Marston, who was quite unaware of Irving's intention until he had read the announcement of the matinée in the newspapers, was overwhelmed by this act of remembrance. In writing to Irving he said:

'. . . Your unprecedented goodness has been the means of such help and comfort that when I rise and retire daily I shall have reason to connect the peace and consolation of the day and its freedom from anxiety with your never-to-be-forgotten sympathy and help . . .

the thought that while the beginning of my career was associated with the greatest actor of my youth, my later days have been distinguished by the approval and help of the greatest actor of my age. . . .'

Marston died in 1890. Irving saw that his last lonely years were at least spent in comfort. The legend of his benevolence was beginning to grow, but, apart from Joseph Knight, none knew of the responsibility he assumed for the care of a poet whom he scarcely knew, but to whom he believed himself deeply indebted.

No doubt the occasion disarmed criticism of Irving's *Werner*. The gloom of the play was intensified by the dimly lit production. Ellen Terry described the afternoon as 'A triumphant success due to the genius and admirable industry and devotion of H.I., for it is the dullest play that ever was. He made it intensely interesting'. Irving, who had a weakness for portraying verbose remorse, probably enjoyed himself enormously but, if he had any idea of reviving the piece in America or elsewhere, Ellen Terry certainly talked him out of it. She, equally weary of playing Margaret, had her fling. Irving bought for her the rights of a three-act play, *The Amber Heart*, by A. C. Calmour, Wills's amanuensis, who was less of a poet and even more impoverished than his master. Ellen Terry had chosen the play out of a desire to help the author and for the chance it gave her, as Iolanthe, to exercise her well-known talent for reducing her audience to tears. Irving produced it for her at a matinée on June 7th. By doing so he kept her and the play inside the Lyceum and gave himself, for the first time, the pleasure of seeing her act without him. Among the cast was a young actor, Herbert Beerbohm Tree, in whom this brief and only experience of the Lyceum planted the seeds of twin complexes—an awe which amounted to a fear of Irving and a determination to outshine him as an actor-manager. The same month, Irving gave a benefit performance of *Faust* in aid of a fund to restore the Opéra Comique in Paris which had been destroyed by fire, a performance of *Louis XI* in aid of the Actor's Benevolent Fund, and two performances of *Much Ado*, the first for the benefit of Ellen Terry and the second for Amy Roselle, a popular actress who had started her career with Sothern and Phelps. The eleventh season ended on July 16th when he played Shylock for his own benefit. In his farewell speech, in which he made a number of light-hearted puns on the Mephistophelean theme, he expressed his pleasure in the wide interest in Goethe that the play had awakened in the British public. He also announced that after a short provincial tour in Edinburgh, Glasgow, Manchester and Liverpool, he would make a third visit to America which, though no shorter than his previous ones, would be confined to New York, Philadelphia, Chicago and Boston.

3

Irving's financial position was never stronger than at this moment. He had accumulated about £20,000 of invested capital, his other properties including the rights of many successful plays and the scenery and dresses of his splendid productions. His latest production had been his most successful one and, in spite of the arduous work and heavy responsibilities he had undertaken, his health, though he was nearing his fiftieth year, was unimpaired. He was, in every sense, a first-class life. If ever he intended to shed some of his responsibilities and to capitalize his success in terms of security, now was the time to do it. He alone seemed to realize this. During July, he had asked his friend, W. R. Lawson, who was then establishing, and later became the first editor of the *Financial Times*, to advise him how he could, without losing his independence as a manager, limit his liabilities and leave to others the complexities of his business which were increasing in proportion to his successes. Lawson, whose knowledge of finance and of the City of London was profound, in due course produced two propositions. The first was that a company with a capital of £200,000 should acquire the theatre, his lease and his properties, and should become his landlord. A second suggested that Irving himself should be included in the company's assets and that the shareholders should be entitled to a half share in his profits as manager in addition to receiving 5 per cent on their investment. In this case, the value set on the actor was assessed at a further £50,000 capital issue.

'If,' added Lawson, 'you were to include one or two first-class provincial theatres and work the whole so as to serve for a practical dramatic school, bringing companies and pieces from one to the other— you might ask for half a million. Think it out in this direction.' Lawson suggested that Lord Rosebery should be asked to be the chairman of the Board of Directors (paving the way, as he put it, for the Rothschilds), which might include, among other well-known figures, Alma Tadema and G. A. Sala. He recognized the weaknesses of Irving's apparently prosperous situation, and urged the actor, by taking this step, to turn into money his heavy expenditure on the theatre which he was in danger of losing. Stoker's name was not mentioned in these discussions; nor does he seem to have been aware, at this time, that Irving contemplated turning himself into a company. Irving, therefore, must have considered Lawson's proposals by himself and, in the end, himself rejected the idea of surrendering his independence in exchange for financial security.

Meanwhile he was beginning to realize his responsibilities as a father. His two boys, Harry and Laurence, were now seventeen and sixteen respectively. They had done well at Marlborough. The prizes they had won and the reports he had received from their tutors convinced him that they were taking full advantage of the opportunities he so earnestly desired to give them. The time was near at hand when he would have to decide upon the next stage of their education. The boys, appreciating how much their future lay in the hands of their distinguished father, if he was of a mind to help them, decided to establish direct communication with the man whom for so long their mother had represented to them as a cruel mountebank. 'I never feel satisfied,' wrote young Harry to him, 'in any communication (verbal or otherwise) through a third person, and especially in matters between a father and son.' The long estrangement and suspicion could not be overcome in a moment, but they were soon more at ease with their father, whom they nicknamed 'the Antique'. All went well until, shortly before Irving left for America, Harry wrote to his father saying that he wished to leave Marlborough and to go on the stage. Irving had other plans for his sons. Harry, who seemed to have an aptitude for scholarship, was to go to Oxford; Laurence, who seemed to have a gift for modern languages, was to enter the diplomatic service by way of Paris and St. Petersburg. Irving felt that at all costs the boy had to be discouraged once and for all from following his father in a profession in which, for all his present success, he had so nearly met disaster. Turning for advice to his friend, Edward Pinches, the son of his old headmaster, he showed him the draft of the letter he proposed to send to Harry:

'My dear Harry,

In seeking my advice concerning what you say is your determination to be an actor, you have given me a puzzle, and a grave one.

Knowing the difficulties which beset an actor's career, I had rather you had chosen another walk of life—some calling where there was more certainty of success and where a sedate application to work would ensure an ultimate reward.

This is a very hard time for young actors. There is no school where they can learn their art—where they can get the practice which is absolutely necessary. It is nearly impossible in the present day to get the training that a young man should have who may ever hope to gain distinction upon the stage.

Of course, you aim at the highest, and, unless you reach it, better not have been an actor.

Supposing, now, you were at the Lyceum, and I anxious to push you on. What could I do? How could you begin? By playing a small part in London?—a bad beginning. You must learn the A.B.C. of your work first.

By travelling around the country in some travelling company playing some one part month after month? What could you learn by that?

In my early days, I sometimes played 18 parts in a week—your Romeos, Claude Melnottes . . . and sitting up all night with a wet towel round my head, trying to master the words; and if I had not, as a lad, studied hundreds of the parts I was called suddenly upon to play, I must have broken down.

But I got practice. I learnt my art—for I studied it—the most difficult of all arts to master, and now I am an exceptionally successful actor, whose career it would be dangerous to take as an ordinary example.

And I am obliged to tell you this—and also I am sorry—that my name will be a hindrance to you and not a help, and that it will make your road more thorny.

This *has been ever* the experience of all fathers' sons.

Just for a start-off, perhaps for a month or two, my name might be of a little service. Curiosity would take many to see one—but what's that? A flash in the pan—nothing to weigh against the hard, exacting work of a life-time, when your efforts will be judged solely by your power—your power to satisfy and please the public, an exacting master.

Do not think that my name will help you—believe me, it will not. Nothing can help you but your own, your talent, perseverance and conduct in life.

Now I am not writing this to try and alter your decision, far from that. I know the more I tried to do that, the more resolute you would probably become. But I want you to realize the serious side of your undertaking, and it is indeed momentous—the future career of any young man.

Now to business! You propose as a preliminary to go to Germany and France. For what—for schooling, for the study of languages or what? Do you think you are sufficiently educated in English to start into the world, where every day and in every walk of life education becomes more necessary?

I am curious to know what your real reason for leaving Marlborough is, and would it not be better to stay another year, and show by your industry a promise of a successful future? Education is as beneficial to an artist as to a scholar.

If you are ever to be an actor worth the name, you will need all your knowledge and strength and all your armour for the coming fight.

There is no career where modesty, perseverance, patience, courage and firmness are more essential than to an actor. The pitfalls are great. The weak hopelessly sink and flag. The young man with lots of time upon his hands often becomes spoiled, conceited and indolent, and then all's up.

The theatrical loafer—the poor fellow who at afternoon teas and evening parties thinks he is learning the methods of his art is sure in time to have a rude awakening. Above everything, guard against indolence!

Respect and honour you can always command—if you be an honest worker. Success you cannot—that rests in the womb of time; but there is only one road to success—work, method, discipline. "Deep the oak must sink in earth obscure," etc.

Now what I would advise you to do would be to stay at Marlborough another year. Work earnestly with your heart and soul—then perhaps a year in France under an actor like Got, who would impart to you a serious idea of the task you have before you. Then a course *of English* with a competent master, to speak your language properly and without a cockney accent which provokes upon the stage nothing but ridicule, to read Shakespeare and Milton and the English classics.

During that training of your mind you should also train your body by fencing, drilling, the practice of pantomime and so on.

Then, still almost hopeless of the chance of obtaining the necessary training, supposing you had the necessary gifts to make a fine actor, you might enter your new career with at all events a knowledge of the rudiments necessary to the practice of the art to which you had chosen to devote your life.'

It was a sensible letter. Even if it sprang from a fear that his sons might make fools of themselves, or worse still, of him, Irving's arguments were sound. The letter may have reached the boy in this form or with modifications suggested by Pinches. It had the desired effect.

Harry, for the time being, gave up the idea of becoming an actor, and in due course went up to New College, Oxford, where it had been arranged that his tutor should be his father's friend, W. L. Courtney.

4

The provincial tour ended at Liverpool. Four days later, Irving sailed thence for New York. In the interval he went to Stratford-on-Avon at the invitation of the Mayor, Sir Arthur Hodgson, and of Mr. Charles Flower, through whose energies public interest in Shakespeare's birthplace had at last been awakened. The purpose of his visit was to unveil an imposing monument which had been raised by his friend, W. G. Childs, the proprietor of the *Philadelphia Journal,* to the glory of the Bard. It took the form of an ingenious architectural marriage of a clock and a fountain in the popular Gothic style. It was of granite and it dominated the Rothermarket. If its symbolism as a tribute to Shakespeare was a little obscure, it would be an enduring memorial to its donor. At the monument, in the presence of Mr. Phelps, the American minister, Irving, after reading some verses which Oliver Wendell Holmes had written for the occasion, spoke of Childs's gift as representing 'the common homage of two great peoples to the most famous man of their common race', and hinted that Shakespeare would find the accent and idiom of his language as spoken in the United States more familiar to his ear than the refined articulation of educated Englishmen. At a civic luncheon, having reminded his audience that it was 'the lasting honour of the actor's calling that the Poet of all time was a player', twitted the Mayor and Corporation with the fact that their predecessors had forbidden the performance of Shakespeare's plays in his native town; he added that 'perhaps it was the influence of Shakespeare's memory which induced the Corporation, on one occasion, to pay them the handsome sum of forty shillings to go away'.

5

Faust was as popular in America as it had been at home. By limiting his tour to the four largest cities in the Union, Irving was able to reproduce all the magical effects of the Lyceum production, thanks to the indefatigable energy and resource of Loveday and his staff. The consummate stage-craft and the display of so many original technical devices appealed, very naturally, to a public who found novelty for its own sake infinitely entertaining.

Irving opened in New York during the worst blizzard the city had ever known. Ludwig Barnay, who was to have appeared at another theatre, was so shrivelled and appalled by the cold that he threw up his engagement and returned to Germany as soon as the weather cleared. Irving, hearing of his plight, sent Walter to console him with a bunch of violets which by the time they reached him were frozen as stiff and brittle as porcelain. The Lyceum Company were made of sterner stuff. All of them fought their way to the theatre in the teeth of the storm, though the curtain rose on *Faust* three-quarters of an hour late. Seats had been booked to the tune of $3,500, but only a handful of enthusiasts were in the auditorium; among them were the Mayor of the City, John Drew, and a few fellow-players from Daly's Company. After this tempestuous start, the weather improved and over $100,000 flowed into the box-office during the five weeks of the engagement.

The American critics did not cavil at Irving's treatment of Goethe—indeed, the Goethe Society of New York invited him to address them on the poet's methods of theatre management; nor were they disappointed when Irving made the most of this opportunity to justify his own method of producing Shakespeare. William Winter published a long article asserting that Irving's conception of Mephistopheles transcended that of Goethe, whose Devil, he wrote, 'is magnificent, intellectual and sardonic, but nowhere conveys even a faint suggestion of the Godhead of the glory from which he lapsed . . . this Fiend (Irving's) towering to the loftiest summit of cold intellect, is the embodiment of cruelty, malice and scorn . . . pervaded and interfused with grim humour'. In every city Irving visited, *Faust* played to capacity. There would have been no need for him to vary his programme; but his firm grasp of business or management prompted him to keep his repertory green in the minds of the American public by giving a few performances of his earlier successes.

While he was in New York Irving gave a matinée of *Faust* in aid of a memorial to Henry Ward Beecher, who had died in the previous year. 'The whole affair', wrote Ellen Terry in her diary, 'was the strangest failure. H.I. himself took heaps of tickets, but the house was half empty. The following Saturday—matinée *Faust*—house crammed. Why wouldn't they have come when it was to honour Beecher?' The prophet had long ago sacrificed any claim to be honoured by his own countrymen. Yet he had used these two players well; however equivocal his epitaph may have been, they did their best to commemorate his consideration for them.

When Irving was in Philadelphia he made a point of visiting Walt Whitman. He had first called at Whitman's small, ramshackle home in Mickle Street in 1884, when he had been charmed immediately by the now feeble but still handsome giant of a poet in whom he saw a likeness to Tennyson. Whitman, almost helpless and cared for by a devoted old lady, sat in his great rocking-chair by the fire and traded anecdotes (including an eye-witness account of the assassination of Lincoln) from the rich store of a memory unimpaired, for tales and gossip about the great literary and artistic figures in London, which Irving had in abundance. Stoker, who in his university days had been an ardent admirer of Whitman's verse, had championed the American poet at a time when *Leaves of Grass* was, to most of his contemporaries, incomprehensible or dangerously advanced. He and Irving had, during their previous tour, commissioned St. Gaudens, the sculptor, to make a bust of Whitman. St. Gaudens took casts of Whitman's mask and hands, but a rapid deterioration of the poet's health had made further sittings impossible. Whitman, who could not abide pretention and humbug, as a rule disliked actors; he liked Irving for 'his gentle and unaffected manners and his evident intellectual power and heart'. This was the last time they met. Whitman died four years later. Irving, through Childs, was able to join others in providing Whitman with the modest comforts he needed during his last stricken years.

Few strongholds can have been so heavily defended against the possibly enervating effects of art on its inmates as the United States Military Academy at West Point. Nothing was allowed to impinge upon the monastic routine or to prejudice the stern discipline which the cadets accepted as an intrinsic part of their training. They may well have been 'astonished at their unexpected good fortune' when Colonel Parke, the Superintendent of the Academy, announced that Mr. Henry Irving would bring Miss Ellen Terry and his company from New York to give his cadets and officers a special performance of *The Merchant of Venice*. Irving had visited West Point during his previous tour and had made friends with Colonel Michie, the professor of mathematics, who had been General Grant's Chief Engineer. When he met him again in New York during the present season, he had offered to go up to West Point and to play to those young hand-picked Americans, whose monkish isolation prevented them from coming to see him. The suggestion was so unusual that the matter had to be submitted to the Secretary of State for War in Washington, who, rather to everyone's surprise, agreed to it. So, on March 19th, Irving cancelled the performance at the Star Theatre, New York, and, taking nothing with him but the Company and their costumes, travelled by special train to West Point in the teeth of a blizzard which had played havoc with communications and very nearly frustrated the whole enterprise. 'Of course,' wrote Bram Stoker, 'it was not possible to use scenery in the space available for the performance; so it was arranged that the play should be given as in Shakespeare's time . . . as it happened, the Venetian dress of the sixteenth century was almost the same as the British; so that the costumes now used in the piece were alike to those worn by the audience as well as on the stage at the Globe Theatre in Shakespeare's time. Thus the cadets at West Point saw the play almost identically as Shakespeare himself had seen it.' The whole audience, from Colonel Parke to the most junior student of military logistics, appreciated the imagination, organization and generosity which had made so rare an entertainment possible. 'When the curtain finally fell, there was a pause . . . with one impulse every one of those hundreds of young men, with a thunderous cheer, threw up his cap . . . by the American Articles of War, for a cadet to throw up his cap except at the word of command given by his superior officer, was an act of insubordination punishable with expulsion . . . strange to say not one of the superior officers noticed the fearful breach of discipline . . . they were possibly throwing up their own caps for they were all old West Point men.' Colonel Michie wrote afterwards to a friend:

'. . . You have no idea of the impression Mr. Irving and his people made here with all of us. The cadets were overjoyed, enthusiastic and full of gratitude. . . . Irving's foresight is amazing to me. I am sure he alone could have appreciated the enormous benefit this act of his is bound to be in doing good both to England and America. . . .'

Irving was evidently justified in the claim he made in his brief farewell speech—that 'the joybells are ringing in London tonight because for the first time the British have captured West Point'. A week later he sailed for England. In a little over three months *Faust* had earned him another £9,000.

CHAPTER XXVIII

10th, 11th and 12th Lyceum Seasons : Macbeth, Robert Landry

———————

I

For the first five weeks of his tenth season which opened on April 14th, Irving revived *Faust*. In May he presented a double bill—*The Amber Heart*, with Ellen Terry and George Alexander, and a revival of *Robert Macaire*. He engaged Weedon Grossmith, the brother of George Grossmith who had created several of the leading parts in the Gilbert and Sullivan operas, to play Jacques Strop. Since Irving had played Macaire for a single performance in 1883, W. E. Henley and Robert Louis Stevenson had published a new version of the play. Neither he nor Grossmith preferred it to Lemaître's version, and since he had been at great pains to learn as much of the French actor's original 'business' as he could, he stuck to the original. 'I don't think,' wrote Grossmith, 'the new and aesthetic edition of *Robert Macaire* as good as the old one. I am sure there is only one way of treating it and that was the way you did at the Lyceum.' It was Weedon Grossmith's first appearance at the Lyceum. On the first night he was standing in the wings, sick with nerves, waiting for his cue. He felt a hand on his shoulder. A staccato voice whispered in his ear: 'Not—nervous—are you—me boy?' He looked round and saw Irving at his side—he was smiling and his dark eyes, behind pince-nez incongruous on the nose of Macaire, were bright with encouragement; but Grossmith himself was not trembling as violently as Irving's hand upon his shoulder.

Receptions of plays, with all-star casts, at benefit matinées were always deceiving. Palgrave Simpson, who had seen Lemaître in the part, when asked by Walter Pollock what he thought of Irving by comparison, said: 'I saw Frederick and remember it as vividly as possible; and I think Irving's a decidedly better performance; finer, better put together, more impressive.' The public, however, were not very impressed; the play and the old routines, however perfectly executed, were outdated. Irving had educated his own audiences to a point where they could no longer accept the macabre buffooning which he himself loved so well. The attendances were just good enough to avoid the necessity of a change of bill; the season ended on July 7th and showed a slight loss.

2

Irving needed no reminder of the urgent need to find new plays, or of the fact that even he and Ellen Terry could not fill the Lyceum unless their plays were worthy of them. A day or two before the opening of the past season, he had written to Burnand who, with his eye on the Lyceum, had for some time past been tinkering with a play *The Isle of St. Tropez*, which he had written in collaboration with Montagu Williams in 1860 and was still good for an option or two.

Lyceum Theatre,
April 11th, 1888.

'My dear Burnand,

I am just now thinking more about tonight than anything else, but as you seem anxious I will tell you my prospective plans (as far as I know) and I tell *you* and not the public.

Nothing new this season—autumn tour with *Faust*, Ellen Terry resting, December—*Macbeth*, and afterwards another production on a large scale. The Shakespearian play is a necessity and is expected and must be followed up by something big—which I believe from experience to be a necessity also.

You will say, "Where are we now?" To which I reply—I would like to play *St. Tropez* when I see the time and opportunity to do so successfully—when I feel the time for it has come. My expenses would have to be reduced—our company entirely re-organised and many other circumstances taken into consideration.

If you think it is unreasonable that I should expect you to wait so long, I propose this—that I pay you a certain sum (to be mutually agreed upon) for the extra work you have done on the play (you've already received I forget how much) and to resign my claim and to restore to you the play to be produced where you will. This seems to me very fair and square and will meet your approval I hope.

Yours ever,
Henry Irving.'

Burnand was only one of many authors on whose plays Irving had bought options and to whom he had made advances for work and revision done at his request. So far the search had proved fruitless. The quality of plays produced at this time by other actors and managers did not suggest to him that any outstanding work had slipped through his net. All that he had in preparation was a new version of an old melodrama, *The Dead Heart*, by Walter Pollock, and a dramatization of Sir Walter Scott's *The Bride of Lammermoor* by the now ailing poet, Herman Merivale. Some may have thought that his genius for the macabre might have found expression in a dramatization of Stevenson's recently published novel, *Dr. Jekyll and Mr. Hyde*. The idea may have occurred to him. He had, however, invited the American actor, Richard Mansfield, to appear in this play at the Lyceum during the summer while he was on tour.

Richard Mansfield was of German parentage. He began his stage career in England, but at the age of twenty-eight he went to America, where in a short time he made his mark as a melodramatic actor of some power. He was one of those men who took himself and his work intensely seriously, who lacked sufficient sense of humour to counterbalance his egotism and was continuously involved in misunderstandings and conspiracies of which he believed himself to be the victim. Indeed, Irving's offer of the Lyceum was the outcome of a letter he had received from Mansfield which betrayed a gnawing fear that a rival actor might reach England with another version of Stevenson's novel before him. 'A brute,' wrote Mansfield, 'who has licked my hand and fed on my food and who has been helped from my purse, has set to work and written a new version of *Dr. Jekyll and Mr. Hyde*, and I am very anxious and much worried—he is trying to find somebody to go to England and play it, and I think he will probably succeed. He has all my ideas upon the subject. . . . I have only one hope! That he will not find any cur to match himself. I think I shall go to England and combine pleasure with business and play a summer engagement. . . .' A cur was ready to hand in the shape of another German tragedian, Daniel Bandmann, who was Mansfield's senior as an immigrant and was a popular Shakespearian actor in the United States.

In reply to Irving's apparently unexpected invitation, Mansfield wrote:

> *The Croisic*,
> *26th St. 5th Ave.*,
> *July 13th*, 1888.

'My dear Mr. Irving,
    I have been trying all day yesterday and all day today to write this letter and I think it is about time that I confessed myself unequal to the

task, for I have destroyed great quantities of note paper. I am like the great swearer who lost his load of apples going up a high hill on a hot day with the backboard of the cart loose—"words are inadequate!" What can I say to you? You have sent me a great fortune. You have waved your wand and made me happy. You have done the gentlest, the kindest—but perhaps you *know* what you've done and I needn't tell you; I see you sitting there quietly and smiling. This is very good of you . . . my only thought is that I may do you credit in the matter and hold up my end. . . .

Always yours sincerely and gratefully,

Richard Mansfield.'

Before sailing for England, Mansfield reported to Irving his unsuccessful attempt to get Stevenson's blessing on his enterprise:

'. . . I tried hard to see Stevenson when he was in New York and *once* I found him at home—but his son-in-law or brother-in-law (or something like that) met me at the door and asked me if I had a cold? I confessed I had. Whereupon he regretted I could not see Mr. Stevenson as Mr. Stevenson would never see anybody with a cold, so I took my poor cold home again and didn't see Stevenson.

I am in a state of reflected glory—with a borrowed halo—yours—about me. Everybody says: "When do you open at the Lyceum Theatre, London?" . . . people are much more polite than they used to be—I suppose it will be different if I have to swim home. . . . I have tried to make my Company as strong as possible, without absolutely ruining myself d'avance, and they do all speak the best English to be had in the U.S. The people here like me to take an American company to England —perhaps the people over there won't like it as well. . . .'

Stevenson, quite apart from the sanitary cordon which separated him from the actor who first introduced his work to the stage, was indifferent to the dramatization of his novels, for he did not refer at all to Mansfield in his letters during this period.

Mansfield arrived in England with the turbulent wake which seemed everywhere to follow him, and with Bandmann hot on his heels. He reported to Irving the progress of the rearguard action which he was fighting with Napoleonic energy. His letter gave a vivid picture of the kind of robust feud which had so often enlivened theatrical annals; it was the last flicker of property duelling swords seen in a flash of lycopodium before they were laid aside to rust in a less full-blooded age.

London,
July 26th, 1888.

'My dear Mr. Irving,

I send you copy sent tonight to every newspaper in London, for in addition to the strong legal position we assume, since Messrs. Longman and Green have given us the sole right to the dramatised Dr. Jekyll, I am anxious the Press and the Public should understand that we have a moral one. If (although I can hardly believe it) Mr. Stevenson has thought fit after writing these letters to encourage Messrs. Bandmann and others—"tant pis pour lui!" But as I have said, I hardly believe it.

Mr. Bandmann will be met upon his arrival in Liverpool, (and if not *there* here) by a writ, and he will have his hands very full in order to present *Dr. Jekyll and Mr. Hyde* as he proposes. Mr. Poole (his manager?) showed fight at first, but after consulting with his attorney and after visiting the Lord Chamberlain's office, where he was informed they had grave doubts as to his and Bandmann's license, he submitted quietly and the play was not given tonight. So victory is ours in the *first* round. . . .'

It was largely due to Irving's generosity that Mansfield did not have to swim home. His season was a disastrous one. *Jekyll and Hyde* aroused a flicker of interest, but *A Parisian Romance*, in which, as an epileptic roué, he had taken New York by storm, failed utterly to attract the London first-night audience, who received it 'with the grave solemnity of distrust . . . both play and actor were awarded a firm but respectful negative . . . when the curtain fell there was a faint summons of courteous recognition before the audience departed in solemn silence'. Poor Mansfield: it was not for lack of physical effort that he had failed. One night, after playing *Jekyll and Hyde*, he joined Irving at supper at the Garrick Club. No doubt he dramatized his own exhaustion, telling Irving, as he sank wearily into a chair, that every time he played this dual role he found the physical strain almost unendurable.

'Mm,' said Irving quietly, nodding his head. 'If it's unwholesome—why do it?'

Mansfield's unhappy experience left Irving his creditor for rent unpaid and for a generous loan which he advanced to his stranded colleague to help him home to New York. It also confirmed Irving's distaste and suspicion of contemporary authors whose pathological and realistic horrors seemed to have so much less moral content than the romantic and idealistic villainies which, portrayed by him, seemed to excite and elevate his audiences without giving them offence.

3

Early in September, Irving set out on a provincial tour, with *Faust* once more as his principal attraction. While he was in Manchester, Burnand wrote to him about the case of a stage manager of one of the burlesque houses, whose treatment of chorus girls had caused a scandal which the newspapers, particularly *The Times* and *The Standard*, had not been slow to exploit. Irving was up in arms at once at the idea that this incident should be regarded as a reflection on the theatre as a whole:

> Queen's Hotel,
> Manchester.
> October 27th, 1888.

'My dear Burnand,

I don't see where Mr. Harris comes in. He is surely not the be all and end all of things dramatic. There are blackguards all the world over, but is the influence of any one of 'em enough to tar and feather the whole stage? I hope not. In the first place, no *actor*-manager would keep such a fellow, and if Pettitt and Sims[1] put up with him, more shame to 'em.

We judge every calling by its best representatives. Pettyfogging quacks and hypocrites don't make lawyers, doctors or divines. With a pretty long experience, I have never met with a Mr. Charles Harris, but granted that he exists, how does that affect the art of acting? That is my point. The actor's art is a great art and when suggestions are made of bullying stage-managers and slatternly ballet girls, of masher young men and brainless idiots of women, and that these make up the stage—I say it is unjust and not to the purpose. These do not make up the best of the stage, the stage that we love. Neither Toole, Hare, Kendal, Tree, Bancroft nor Irving and others, are responsible for the abuses of the theatre. There are plenty of theatres where young men and women get excellent apprenticeship and are paid for it too, and learn the rudiments of their art—theatres, where earnest, thorough and artistic work is done —and the majority of theatres in London are, I believe—well conducted.

I would certainly have not bothered about either Moore[2] or Quilter[3] (who by the way was once engaged to the fair Fortescue,[4] and this, perhaps, accounts for his chivalrous attack) had not statements of these

---

[1] Henry Pettitt and George R. Sims, authors of melodramas and burlesques.
[2] George Moore.
[3] Harry Quilter, editor and founder of the short-lived *Universal Review*.
[4] Miss Fortescue, an actress of talent, charm and notorious propriety. She had also been engaged to Lord Garmoyle from whom she got £10,000 damages in an action for breach of promise.

learned pundits been copied all over the country and had not the columns of *The Times* and *The Standard* been open to them. . . . It would not do to let these fellows, without contradiction, attempt to destroy good work that has been accomplished by good workers for many years.

There is another scoundrel at it now, Brenon—. . . and even poor C.S. (Clement Scott) and Mr. Jones (Henry Arthur Jones)—this sort of thing is very catching—have been bewailing the falling off of things theatrical. What rubbish.

But you can put 'em all right—a word or two from you does more good than all the speeches and pamphlets put together . . . you will be sorry to hear that Florrie Toole is laid up in Edinburgh with a desperate attack of gout. Poor dear Johnnie has been terribly anxious about her.

My love at home.

Yours ever,

Henry Irving.

Why don't some of your girls call on Ellen Terry? It would delight her to see them.'

Quilter had employed George Moore to write an article in the *Universal Review* entitled 'Mummer Worship', in which he disparaged acting both as an art and as a profession. If anything aggravated Irving more than an attack of this kind, it was George Moore himself. A few years before, Moore had pestered him with a play about Martin Luther which he had written in collaboration with a man called Lopez. The importunate playwright finally ran Irving to earth while he was breakfasting in an hotel in Liverpool and, sitting down uninvited at the same table, peddled his wares. On this occasion Irving had refused uncompromisingly to have anything to do with Moore or his play. Thereafter Moore sought every opportunity to attack the actor or his work in print. Irving countered this latest attack in a forthright speech to the Edinburgh Pen and Pencil Club, in which he referred indirectly to Moore as a 'flippant lampooner'. Quilter leapt to Moore's defence with a letter to *The Times* in which he wrote: '. . . The present social worship of the stage is a bad thing. The dramatic profession is, generally speaking, a dangerous one for women, an undesirable one for men.' A day or two later Irving made the occasion of his laying the foundation stone of a new theatre in Bolton, the platform for a vigorous retaliation, this time avoiding personal recriminations. Both Irving's speeches were fully reported in *The Times*, which, though in the past it had often criticized him adversely, in a leader, summed up very much in favour of his outspoken correction of those who took advantage of so trivial an incident to denigrate the stage as a whole. The leader ended on a theme with which Irving was all too familiar:

'. . . It is hard upon actors that have thus to be tied to the tap of dramatic authorship which may be copious or scanty, without the least regard for their exigencies. It is grievous for them to feel it in them to be eloquent and moving moralists, and to be given nothing but tawdry truisms to deliver. But this has always been the law of their being; and their art has often shown itself in its greatest perfection by its triumph over the meanness of its materials.'

Irving, however lofty his theatrical ideals may have been, had no prejudice against burlesque or light opera in themselves. Until now the managers of theatres, legitimate and vaudeville, had been, almost without exception, actors or retired actors. This incident heralded a new generation of entrepreneurs, who were in the theatrical business solely for what they could get out of it, and very often lacked the courtesy and consideration with which all but the basest artists treated one another. At the moment, however, the number of these interlopers was inconsiderable.

Having thus given vent to his feelings, Irving went to Paris with Comyns Carr before starting rehearsals of a revival of *Macbeth* with which he had decided to open the coming season. Carr introduced him to the night life of Paris and was amused by the detached and 'half sinister tolerance' with which his friend observed it. One night they were watching in a cabaret a troupe of can-can dancers when one of the girls, greatly daring, flicked off Irving's hat with a high kick of her black-slippered toe. For a moment the dignity which was natural to him and the genial acceptance of the spirit of the place were in conflict. The onlookers, many of whom recognized him, held their breath as they waited to see how he would react to this audacious familiarity. 'When,' wrote Carr, 'he acknowledged with hearty laughter the adroitness of the performer, the Parisians found themselves free to indulge in the amusement which the look upon his grave, pale face had held in check.'

Of all the entertainments Paris had to offer, Irving preferred the Morgue. He liked, in the early morning, to linger there and watch the procession of men and women who filed past the gruesome exhibits. Once he saw a man pass a corpse and return to gaze upon it a second time; this convinced Irving that he was the murderer. Over breakfast at Bignon's he rehearsed to Carr the motive and the method of the crime which his imagination had reconstructed. He returned to London, refreshed and in a proper frame of mind to impersonate the fiend of Scotland.

Ellen Terry had done her best to dissuade him from reappearing in a part in which, when he first played it with the Batemans, he had been fairly roundly condemned. In vain, she suggested *As You Like It, King John, Richard II* and *Julius Caesar* as possible alternatives. He confessed that he would like to play Brutus; '. . . that', he said, 'is the part for the actor because it needs acting, but the actor-manager's part is Anthony—Anthony scores all along the line. Now when the actor and actor-manager fight in a play and when there is no part in it for you, I think it's wiser to leave it alone.'

Irving believed Ellen Terry could play Lady Macbeth. Having set his mind on it, no argument or persuasion shook his resolution. She, conscious of her approaching climacteric, and of the young and sympathetic heroines of Shakespeare she had not yet played, at last surrendered and devoted herself to the conscientious study of the part he had chosen for her. When Irving had studied Macbeth for the first time, Helen Faucit had given him a book which had influenced profoundly his conception of the part. It was an essay on the play by G. Fletcher, which had been published in the *Westminster Review* in 1843. It included a detailed exposition of Mrs. Siddons' views on the character of Lady Macbeth—namely that of a devoted wife who, for love of her husband, seeks to gratify him 'with the eager and passionate sympathy in the great master wish of his own mind'. Irving gave the book to Ellen Terry, who soon discovered a startling discrepancy between Mrs. Siddons' written appreciation of Lady Macbeth and her impersonation of her on the stage, in which her acting was said to have been 'that of a triumphant fiend'. In the margin of the pages Ellen Terry strove to solve this contradiction. 'Yes,' she wrote, 'Shakespeare's Lady Macbeth and Mrs. Siddons' Lady Macbeth are two *distinct* persons and totally different . . . of course as part of a *whole* Shakespeare's is the one which it *wd* be right to try and enact, but as a single, forceful dramatic figure, I believe Mrs. Siddons' was far the most *effective* . . . far finer and probably beyond imitation. I cannot understand why Mrs. Siddons *shd* write *down one* set of ideas upon the subject and carry out a totally different plan. Why? . . . because *one* way is well within her methods and physical presentation.'

At once her way became clear. The doubts that she and her friends may have had about her ability to play the part with conviction were dispelled. She proceeded to persuade herself to do the wrong thing for the right reasons.

'Other actors have done this . . . within my knowledge—a remarkable instance was *Irving*, who played Shylock for sympathy and told me himself (smiling) he *ought* to play him as a ferocity. Again his *Synorix*, the thick lips, gross, natural voluptuaries, as shown—physically—in existing marbles of Roman Emperors, were impossible to him as far as outward appearances went. Yet he so clearly indicated the ——of Synorix that I flamed with outraged modesty and felt one night . . . I could strike him—he licked his lips at me—as if I were a bone and he a beast . . . then Salvini, his Othello . . . he looked like a great Bull, but acted superbly—only he could not *be* it.'

Having thus convinced herself, she put to herself a question, the answer to which she knew perfectly well before she began to study the book.

'Now which of 3 courses—for and against?

1. Make up in every way. In spite of thin lips—build up thick ones. In spite of Roman nose and flashing black eyes—build a nez retroussé and weak, gentle, irresolute eyes—in place of nature's loud voice—low and soft, seductive. Be in fact (I'm afraid) a great actor—deceive audience in to at least *thinking* all this.

2nd Method. Play to the best of one's powers—one's own possibilities. Adapt the part to my own personality with the *knowledge* that sometimes nature *does* freak and put an honest eye into a villain's head.

3rd Method. Don't play at all.'

She took the second and only possible course. Her notes explained her impatience with critics who wrote of her or Irving's failures as mistakes to which little thought or care had been given; they also bore out her son's contention that she could play 'but one part—herself'.

Irving saw no reason for reconsidering his estimate of Macbeth's character. When he had played it first most of the critics had accepted his reading of the part, though they had severely criticized his execution of it. Now, with all the power and mastery of his art which he had gained in the intervening years, he felt confident that he could realize his conception of Macbeth as a barbaric chieftain entirely lacking moral fibre and the courage of his dark convictions. He made one important change in the text. In 1875, unable to reconcile the report of Macbeth's valour in the field with the brutal cowardice of the character which Shakespeare drew in the rest of the play, he cut out the speech of the bleeding sergeant. Now he restored it, feeling, no doubt, that it was within his powers to fulfil more faithfully the poet's intention. With his mind at rest as to his own performance, he was able to devote himself to the presentation of the play; in this he probably came as near perfection as his method and the artistic standards of the time allowed.

Always seeking to bring fresh talents and ideas into the service of the theatre, he commissioned a popular painter, Keeley Halsewelle, to design the scenery. Halsewelle was an accomplished illustrator of romantic books and a landscape painter with much charm of vision. As an associate of the Royal Scottish Academy he could be relied upon to imbue his work with the archaeological accuracy by which Victorian dilettanti set so much store. His preliminary sketches were admirable. Unfortunately, although he was nearing sixty, he expressed the desire to do the actual scene-painting—a formidable undertaking for a man who normally worked on a very small scale and had no experience of handling distemper colours. Several scene-painting frames at Covent Garden were put at his disposal where the cloths and flats were in due course delivered and primed. Time passed and, as repeated enquiries as to his progress met with no response, Stoker himself went to Covent Garden to see how things were going. All that he found were acres of virgin canvas. Halsewelle, appalled by the monstrous task which faced him, had abandoned the field without making as much as a stroke of charcoal or brush upon the snowy surfaces. After this setback, the work was completed by Hawes Craven and a team of painters which included a newcomer, young Joseph Harker. One day Irving came into the painting-room and asked in a quiet but commanding voice for a young man by the name of Harker.

'So you're my old friend Harker's boy, eh?' said Irving, peering at him. 'Well—well! Tell me if there's anything I can do for you. Your father once did me a kindness—many kindnesses in fact, and I have come on purpose to see if I can repay them.'

He led Harker to a corner of the painting-room, where, perched on a table, he chatted to him about his father, William Harker, a popular character actor with whom he had served in the stock company of the old Theatre Royal, Edinburgh. Young Harker told him that it was his ambition to be his own master. After the production of *Macbeth*, with Irving's encouragement, he acquired a scene painting studio and, thereafter, was always able to count on having a handsome share in the designing and painting of the Lyceum productions.

Charles Cattermole designed the costumes, with the exception of Ellen Terry's, which were in the capable hands of Alice Comyns Carr. Sargent later recorded the superb dress in which Lady Macbeth first appeared, a theatrically effective masterpiece, though it was, perhaps, a trifle flattering to the mediaeval milliners of Inverness. The basis of it was a gown of thirteenth-century pattern, crocheted in a yarn of green silk and blue tinsel, which gave the effect of scales. This was 'sewn all over with real green beetle wings and a narrow border in Celtic designs worked out in rubies and diamonds. To this was added a cloak of shot velvet in heather tones, upon which great griffins were embroidered in flame-coloured tinsel'. Irving was very well pleased with this and even more with the blood-red cloak which Alice Carr had designed for Ellen Terry to wear after the murder scene.

'That's a fine splash of colour', Irving told her when he saw it at the first dress rehearsal.

She went home filled with innocent delight in his praise. On the following evening she was a sadder and more Irving-wise woman. Macbeth himself appeared in the red cloak and asked her to contrive a becoming but more discreet garment for his consort.

Sullivan was at work on the incidental music. During the rehearsal an incident occurred which illustrated Irving's ability to get from artists enlisted in the service of his own art not only their best work but that which they themselves recognized as being theatrically perfect. He did not pretend to any very profound knowledge of music, of painting, or, indeed, of literature; but he knew instinctively how to marry these artistic components into a dramatically effective whole. Ellen Terry used to keep the rough drawings which Irving made to indicate his ideas of costume or crowd movements; they showed a grasp of the first principles of design and composition which painters know cannot be acquired by study. Sullivan, like most of the artists who worked for Irving, appreciated his untutored sense of fitness. In answer to a request for certain alarums and trumpets, he wrote: 'How do you wish them done—on the orchestra, or by a single trumpet behind the scenes? I confess a full orchestral flourish in harmony does not seem appropriate. The most characteristic sound would be a trumpet and drum. It is martial, rugged and correct. Please let me know—because if you are of the same opinion, I can write them out in a few minutes at rehearsal.'

This he did; the result was dismissed by Irving as wholly inappropriate—'as music it's very fine—but for our purpose it's no good at all'. Sullivan asked Irving to try and explain what he had in mind. The actor, thereupon, with a combination of rhythmic pantomime and suggestive hummings, strove to convey his idea of what he needed.

Sullivan grasped his meaning which he translated rapidly into musical phrases; when these were rehearsed, he and Irving agreed that they were musically and dramatically right.

4

As the first night approached, Ellen Terry's initial doubts as to her ability to identify herself with Lady Macbeth began to reassail her. Irving, keenly aware of her nervousness and of how much he owed to the aesthetic bridle with which she curbed his bolting imagination, wrote her a letter which put her in good heart:

'. . . Tonight, if possible, the last act. I want to get these great multitudinous scenes over and then we can attack *our* scenes . . . your sensitiveness is so acute that you must suffer sometimes. You are not like anybody else—you see things with such lightning quickness and unerring instinct, that dull fools like myself grow irritable and impatient sometimes. I feel confused when I am thinking of one thing, and disturbed by another. That's all. But I do feel very sorry afterwards when I don't seem to heed what I so much value. . . . I think things are going well, considering the time we've been at it, but I see so much that is wanting and it seems almost impossible to get through properly. "Tonight commence, Mathias. If you sleep, you are lost!" '[1]

Macbeth opened on December 29th. The reception of the play by the critics was all that he expected, by the public it was all that he had hoped. Neither he nor Ellen Terry were whole-heartedly praised or unreservedly condemned for their performances. The character and beauty of the production was unanimously acclaimed. If Irving's stage management erred at all it was in the crepuscular tonality of his stage pictures. Sometimes these effects were in sharp conflict with the text. When Duncan arrived at Macbeth's castle it was deepest night, and he was welcomed in impressive torchlight. Effective as this was, it over-shadowed the exquisite landscape which the poet had painted with the tongues of Duncan and Banquo. Indeed, on one occasion a member of the gallery became so dejected by succeeding scenes of sombre highland gloom that when Birnam Wood was revealed bathed in sunlight he started from his seat and cried: 'Good Old England! Hooray for Good Old England.'

[1] *The Bells.*

There was plenty of stimulating controversy in the press. Labby, in *Truth*, again paid a bantering tribute to what he believed was Irving's subtle but unprincipled showmanship. 'Clever as ever', he wrote, 'alert to catch the shifting straws of public opinion, knowing full well that Miss Ellen Terry is, perhaps, the most popular actress on the stage at the present time, he has persuaded himself that the Lady Macbeth who, thirteen years ago, was a shrew of the most determined type . . . is in reality, the sweetest, most affectionate character that ever drew breath. . . . A *Macbeth* based on recollections of *Eugene Aram*, is now accompanied by an aesthetic Burne Jonesy, Grosvenor Gallery version of Lady Macbeth, who roars as gently as any sucking dove. . . . At the same time it should be stated, in all fairness, that such a magnificent show as the new *Macbeth* has never been seen before. Mr. Irving has proved that he is the first of living stage-managers, a man with a mind to conceive and a head to direct, for all the boasted Shakespearian revivals of Macready, Phelps, and Charles Kean pale before the new Lyceum splendours.' Archer, accepting Irving's conception of Macbeth, conceded that the actor had 'mastered his means more thoroughly than heretofore and keeps a tight rein on those peculiarities of gesture and expression which used to run away with him'. The editor of his paper, Edmund Yates, told a friend: 'Irving was never finer in his life, I doubt if I ever saw him so fine—never fresher—as fresh as though he had come to the arduous task quite free from previous labour.'

Many critics, however, felt that the part taxed too heavily his physical limitations. Irving himself was never conscious of his physical weakness—indeed he imposed upon himself what many might have considered to be unnecessary burdens. During the run of *Macbeth*, a young visitor who was waiting for him in his dressing-room saw the coat of mail which Irving had worn in the first scene lying on the floor. He remarked to Walter that he supposed that it was sham. 'Pick it up,' said Walter. It was so heavy that the visitor could scarcely lift it. Irving believed, perhaps rightly, that gait and carriage were indispensable aids to the true creation of character; that the constricting weight of harness or cut of clothes helped the actor to feel his part. For the same reason, he insisted that hand properties should weigh at least as much as the real thing, thus forcing the actor to handle them with appropriate effort. Irving's apparent physical weakness was in fact induced by nervous strain and was most noticeable on first nights. On the other hand, though he seemed to have inexhaustible reserves of physical and nervous energy, the privations which he had undergone at the outset of his career had left their mark. 'It is strange,' he once remarked as, when rubbing down after a performance, he regarded his lean, bony figure in the mirror, 'how one never entirely makes up for not having had quite enough to eat in one's youth.'

Edward Russell and Comyns Carr rallied to Irving's defence with assertive articles and scholarly pamphlets. The clamour of contending opinions was as effective in attracting and sustaining public interest as a big drum outside a booth in the Place Pigale. A letter from Joseph Chamberlain to Irving reflected once more the gulf between the opinions of doctrinaire critics and those of the average educated play-goer.

> 40 *Princes Gardens,*
> *S.W.*
> *April 7th,* 1889.

'Dear Mr. Irving,

I have to thank you for a delightful evening on Tuesday when Mrs. Chamberlain and myself were immensely interested with the performance of *Macbeth*. I need say nothing of the mise-en-scène which was perfect as usual, but we were especially pleased with the conception of the principal characters. After what I had read in the papers I was prepared for something original but I was doubtful if I should like it—now I can only say that either Miss Terry and you must have altered the presentations since the first performance or else the critics must have been more than usually superficial.

We agreed there was the greatest power as well as delicacy in Miss Terry's rendering of Lady Macbeth. In the scenes of the murder, the banquet, and the sleep-walking she was excellent and in the first two excellently supported. I imagine that the murder scene is for the actor of Macbeth the most difficult and critical in the play for it is here that his character is fully developed. Superstitious, cruel and irresolute, he is quick to see his opportunity and unscrupulous enough to avail himself of it, but he lacks real courage and seeks strength and the confirmation of his purpose from a woman. I assure you that it was an intellectual treat for us to follow your interpretation and I must again thank you for the pleasure you afforded us.

> I am,
> Yours very truly,
> J. Chamberlain.'

5

There were rumours that Ellen Terry, in the face of adverse criticism, was going to give up her part, rumours to which Burnand, in writing to tell Irving that he would have two articles on *Macbeth* in *Punch*, had referred. Irving reassured him:

'My dear Burnand,

Greetings. I shall read with great interest and I am sure pleasure, tomorrow's *Punch*. Of course you are with us—and with the public too.

Ellen Terry has made the hit of her life. She really begins to like her Ladyship and plays it wonderfully. I envy your cottage by the sea— but even Ramsgate has its drawbacks—had you been here you would never have heard about "giving up"—there has been no such stuff in her thoughts.

When the house of Burnand comes back to town we will have a gala night here with beefsteaks afterwards. I hope it will be soon.

Yours ever,

Henry Irving.'

And certainly the public were with Irving. *Macbeth* ran for a hundred and fifty nights and was playing to capacity when the season ended on June 29th, 1889. The production had cost £6,600, but in spite of this the season showed a profit of £5,000. Nevertheless, Irving was still alive to the need for economies. In vain he appealed to one department after another; in every case excellent reasons were given to show that further reduction of expenditure was impossible. An attempt to reduce the size of the orchestra brought a protest from Sullivan which was effectively disarming. He declared that there was not one man too many, and as it was the orchestra sounded lamentably thin owing to its poor accommodation. 'But,' he pleaded, 'as to write the music and to work with you was a labour of love to me, I have borne these disadvantages . . . besides no important saving could be effected—five or six pounds a week at the utmost, and this is hardly worth your while—you, who have such a justly high reputation for splendour and liberality in all your productions.' Always so little to be saved—always so little that saving was not worth while.

One day, while going through the accounts with Toole, he discovered that for years the theatre cleaners had been provided with tea and bread and jam. 'There you are, Johnnie,' he said, 'they're all at it— ten teas—six times a week—at ninepence a head for nine years—add it up—over a thousand pounds.' The Lyceum was reaping a bumper harvest, but the mice were multiplying in the granary.

Early in the New Year he had further cause to regret his benevolence towards Mansfield. The American actor, hoping to redeem his earlier losses and to prove that he was, as he firmly believed, Irving's superior in Shakespeare, took the old Globe Theatre in Newcastle Street and tore himself to tatters in Cibber's version of *Richard III*. He invited Irving to witness his own defeat. After the performance, Irving went round to see Mansfield, whom he found nervously prostrated and in a lather of perspiration. Mansfield prepared to receive the homage of his rival. Irving thumped him heartily on the back. 'Ah—Dick—me boy!' he said. 'I see—mm—your skin—acts—well!'

Mansfield's second venture added nothing to his reputation and a good deal to his debts. The critics were merciless, and of them Clement Scott was not the least outspoken. Mansfield's abiding sense of persecution reached the limits of endurance. During February, Irving received a copy of a letter from Clement Scott to Mansfield:

> 52 *Lincoln's Inn Fields,*
> *W.C.*
> *February 10th, 1889.*

'Dear Mansfield,

I regret I have to write to you on a very disagreeable matter but it is one that affects my personal honour and public character.

I have been informed on authority whose trust I have no right whatever to dispute that you have made the following statement in public and before witnesses not personally known to me:

1. That when you consulted Irving on your arrival in this country as the best thing to be done to secure your success he at once replied "Bribe Scott!"

2. That notwithstanding your letter to me and my letters to you since your appearance at the Lyceum, all of which are produceable—that you have publicly stated that I have asked you a personal favour, tantamount to a bribe, which not having been granted, I have found fault with your public performance and discredited you as an actor. I need hardly say I require a categorical answer to these categorical questions and I may further say that Irving has indignantly denied to my informant that he ever made use of the language ascribed to him or in any way impugned my personal good faith.

> Yours obediently,
> Clement Scott.'

Irving wrote immediately to Mansfield asking for an explanation. At first Mansfield, though admitting that it was not Irving but a certain Mr. Clarke who had made the veiled accusation, stuck to his guns:

> *Westminster Palace Hotel,*
> *Victoria St.,*
> *London S.W.*
> *March, 7th 1889.*

'My dear Irving,

All this bother with Clement Scott is very troublesome just now—very sickening and wearying. As a matter of fact—and I know absolutely nothing about Clement Scott—all my information is derived from Mr. Savile Clarke and from rumour and in one case personal knowledge. I have no time to attend meetings convened with the object of clearing Mr. Scott's character from the mud which other people throw at it. Personally I like Scott—but I dislike his criticism very much—more than that I dislike his manner of loudly exclaiming against a play in the lobby of a Theatre. . . . If Mr. Scott is quite convinced that I have slandered him, or that anything I may have said at any time is *not true*—or has no particle of truth in it—Mr. Scott has his lawful remedy. I have in the face of every kind and sort of provocation endeavoured to treat . . . Mr. Scott with the most forbearing kindness and courtesy and up to the very last have held out the hand of friendship. Should I be called upon I shall tell a very blunt story; but I fear we are all more or less the victims of a little conspiracy by Mr. Savile Clarke.

> Yours always truly,
> Richard Mansfield.'

Mansfield had stirred up muddy waters. The delicately poised traffic between actor-managers and critics of the old school, who with Chinese delicacy traded discreet eulogy for options on their unactable plays, would not withstand the blast of controversy or of legal action. Irving despised the wretched system which was well established when he first came to London. Perhaps he could have put an end to it if he had chosen to do so, but, like most of his fellow-actors, he had taken the line of least resistance. Now he was determined to keep the storm which Mansfield threatened to raise within the bounds, if not of a teacup, of the small theatrical world over which he ruled. A chastened Mansfield replied to Irving's second and more severe letter:

Globe Theatre.

'My dear Irving,

For heaven's sake *what* did I say in my letter to you last night. . . .
I am so rushed—so head over ears in work, that I can hardly be sure
what I write. Poor Scott—I didn't mean *any* unkindness whatever—
when I said whitewashed I meant from the impure blots and stains
that most certainly others have tried to put upon his character. . . .
I have no doubt now that they are lies—although at one time I believed
them. . . . I am very sorry if I have hurt Mr. Scott's feelings—I wish
you had told me my letter was open to misinterpretation—surely you
know—none so well as you—what it is to be in labour with a production even no greater than this. Be assured I am at all times filled
with a desire to do kindly by all—often I am baulked by the damnable
treachery of *my friends*.

Always yours,
Richard Mansfield.'

Adroitly Irving acted as referee, exacting a recantation from Mansfield and a grudging acceptance from Scott, thus preventing the
combatants from coming to blows in public. Like Tweedledum and
Tweedledee, both parties felt that they had been cheated of a con-
frontation which possibly neither of them really desired. Scott, if
he was satisfied that Irving had never implied his venality, felt that
he had failed him as a champion:

52 *Lincoln's Inn Fields,*
6th March, 1899.

'My dear Henry,

I regret for many reasons that you cannot lend me your influence
in this matter in discovering and checking an infamous liar.

If you believe Mansfield you must necessarily be convinced that
Savile Clarke is the most infamous traducer ever known . . . and that
the other witnesses I was prepared to bring forward have proved to
be worse liars than Piggott. If we had all met we should have arrived
at the truth. Mansfield treats it in an impudent spirit. He first traduces
one—and then laughs. This may be the American form of chivalry—
it is not mine. And you leave me powerless and defenceless when you
could help me.

Yours,
C. S.'

For the time being calm was restored and honour was satisfied. The game of puffing and play-peddling went on undisturbed. Irving was relieved, no doubt, when he got a letter from this turbulent tragedian in which he announced his return to America and suggested that Irving could quickly recover his debt if he allowed him to arrange another American tour on his behalf for which he would take a share in the profits.

Irving showed the letter to Ellen Terry, who wrote across the bottom: 'impudent fellow'. Irving, though often provoked, refused to quarrel with him and the debt was paid five years later.

6

It was amusing, in the middle of all these boring and embarrassing altercations, to hear from Toole of a rival production of *Macbeth*. He wrote as he talked—a breathless grunting of terse phrases, hyphenated by a murmuring buzz as of a thousand asthmatic bees.

> *Rome,*
> *Tuesday, March 26th,* 1889.
>
> 'My dear Harry,
> Just a line to tell you I'm alive and running all over the place—got here last night—have been today to the Coliseum—that *is* a place—marvellous—opens your eyes—very grand—not a touch of low comedy about it—same St. Peter's—quite the proper place for tragedians only—you'll have to come here—had five days at Geneva—most interesting old palaces—Monte Carlo—nine days—beautiful place—lots of people we know there—saw Macbeth opera—such a lark—the Macbeth—great fat fellow—good robust tenor singer—when Banquo came up trap with a bunch of gauze on his head to denote that he was a ghost—Macbeth fell flat on his back and got a roar of laughter—piece miserably mounted—the usual two chairs etc.—Lady Macbeth came in with a letter and rushed into a little ballad—how I wished I was at the Lyceum seeing Ellen and Henry . . . hope you're doing well.
>
> With love,
> Yours sincerely,
> J. L. Toole.'

That winter, Sargent was painting Ellen Terry as Lady Macbeth in her beetle-wing dress. When Irving came to his studio to see the picture, Sargent told Ellen Terry that he had the head of a saint and asked her to persuade him to sit for his portrait. Irving was an unwilling and impatient sitter, but in the end he agreed to do so. Sargent, in spite of his initial enthusiasm, was baffled; the subtle mingling of Brodribb and Irving eluded him. In the end the picture was a brilliantly executed but superficial study of Irving 'with white face, tired eyes, holes in the cheeks and boredom in every line'. Ellen Terry's picture, after being shown at the New Gallery where it promoted lively discussion, was hung in a place of honour in the Beefsteak Room. Irving's portrait, after being exhibited in the Royal Academy (Mr. Punch described it as 'Hedly Irvil wi' such a bad cold id is 'ead'), was hidden away in a cupboard in Grafton Street. The only painter who succeeded in transmitting something of the essential Irving to canvas was Jules Bastien Lepage, who painted him in 1880. His brush discovered the simple rusticity behind the mask of aesthetic refinement, the shrewd humour lurking in the dreamy eyes of the visionary, the characteristic angularity of a vital and arresting pose, the romantic set of conventional attire and, above all, the tender smile flickering over the deceiving gentleness of a determined mouth—the smile which had been the inspiration and the despair of Sargent. It was a masterly portrait which Irving liked little better than Sargent's. A man likes to see himself as he hopes he appears to others; in this respect Irving infinitely preferred Millais's portrait to either of them.

Bernard Partridge who, as a young man under the name of Gould, was an actor in the Lyceum Company, made innumerable drawings of Irving in and out of character and, with Hawes Craven, illustrated the souvenir programmes of many productions. His intimate friendship with Irving, his training as an actor and his superb draughtsmanship enabled him to hand down to posterity a faithful and invaluable record of Irving's appearances as an actor and of his skill as a metteur-en-scène.

On April 6th, Irving received a letter from Sir Dighton Probyn, secretary to the Prince of Wales, concerning arrangements for a supper in the Beefsteak Room after Easter which His Royal Highness was 'really looking forward to'; it concluded:

Sandringham
Norfolk

'Private and Confidential.

The Queen is coming here on a visit to the Prince and Princess of Wales on Tuesday, the 23rd of this month—Tell me *honestly* whether in the event of the Prince of Wales hinting at such an idea, you could manage to act anything here on the evening of Wednesday the 24th before Her Majesty. You will remember that some years ago when the Queen was coming here, but prevented by an accident from doing so, that you then were coming down to act before Her Majesty. . . .'

The Prince of Wales did more than hint. A summons came and Irving readily answered it. From Shakespeare's day until the accession of Queen Victoria the Court preferred to go to the theatre rather than bring the theatre to the Court, with the exception of George III, who liked Mrs. Siddons to come and to recite to him passages for which she was famous. Queen Victoria and Prince Albert, though on several occasions in Macready's time they attended performances at Drury Lane and Covent Garden, had returned to the practice of Queen Elizabeth and James I, by establishing the 'Windsor Theatricals', with Charles Kean as their Master of Ceremonies. When the Prince Consort died all such entertainments were suspended; but Irving had heard first hand accounts of these performances, in which any actor or actress of note took part, such as old Phelps, Charles Mathews, and Buckstone. That he should be invited to revive this custom was, no doubt, personally gratifying; but, as he said, he looked upon the honour primarily as one 'in which we all share—we, the actors of the time,—it reflects all round. It is a tribute to the stage which is not merely individual—it is collective.'

The performance was arranged for April 24th. The Prince asked Irving to play *The Bells* in full and the trial scene from *The Merchant of Venice*. A stage with a proscenium opening of eighteen feet was erected in a room which had recently been added to Sandringham to house the trophies with which the Prince had returned from his visit to India. New scenery to fit this limited space was built and painted, for which Irving paid out of his own pocket while the Lyceum accounts bore the expense of suspending *Macbeth* for three performances. The combined retinues of the Queen and the Prince made a large audience. The Queen directed that they should applaud as they wished—which they did, enthusiastically, as Stoker noted, 'within the bounds of decorum'. The Queen had seen no dramatic entertainment of any kind since 1861, except a performance by a company of London actors of a comedy by Burnand which, in 1881, the Prince of Wales had induced her to attend at Abergeldie Castle.

The impact upon Her Majesty of this utterly new and realistic style of acting must have been tremendous. Though she thanked very

Irving as King Lear
From a drawing by Sir Bernard Partridge

Irving on holiday in Boscastle

From photographs by W. Graham Robertson

graciously Irving and Ellen Terry for their performances and presented them with souvenirs of their visit, she was, in fact, a little bewildered by what she had seen. The Prince bestowed the players handsomely; his equerries entertained the company, while Irving and Ellen Terry, after their audience with the Queen, joined the royal guests at supper. In the early hours of the morning the whole company were on their way back to London, well pleased with their reception and with the thought that, in a modest way, they had made theatrical history. In one respect this Command Performance had differed from previous ones. Charles Kean's company had been paid out of the Privy Purse—he himself suggesting the scale of salaries and acting as paymaster. This worked very smoothly until the actor's managerial duties were taken over by a business agent whose bureaucratic methods soon upset the sensitive players, one of whom, whose services as a comedian were rated low in the official scale, was so indignant at the pittance he received that he gave it to charity as a gift from himself and the Queen. Irving was determined to avoid trouble of this kind and to establish a precedent for the sake of those actors who in the future might be honoured by Royal patronage. He stipulated that, with the exception of the transport of his company to and from Windsor, he himself should bear the whole cost of the performance.

The eleventh season ended in June. During the last week Irving gave a benefit performance for the Actors' Benevolent Fund in which Coquelin aîné took part, thereby putting an end to rumours that these two great actors were at loggerheads with one another. Before Coquelin, at the suggestion of the Prince of Wales, had played in London for the first time in 1888, he had written an article in *Harper's Magazine* in which he had criticized Irving's technique or lack of it. Irving had rebuked Coquelin in the *Nineteenth Century*, not for any offence he had given him but in defence of the principle that it was an unpardonable breach of taste for one artist publicly to criticize another. Later Coquelin unwisely challenged Irving by playing *The Bells* in London. Coquelin's Mathias was a genial innkeeper who, having eluded the police with cunning and relish, died of *la soif de vin blanc*. Though undoubtedly he played the part superbly and with the perfection of comedy technique, Coquelin failed to raise the play above its inherent mediocrity—indeed Henry James, in his adulatory appreciation of the French actor, did not mention *The Bells* among his notable performances. Mayer, the impresario who arranged Coquelin's season in London, brought the two actors together at a supper to which Toole and Bancroft were also invited. Their duel in public had engendered a mutual respect which, when they met, soon blossomed into understanding; they argued fiercely, the vehemence of their gestures making up for their ignorance of each other's language. After that evening Coquelin was admitted into the fellowship of the Beefsteak Room, where, in the years to come, he was a frequent and welcome guest. The French actor celebrated this reconciliation by appearing at this benefit matinée and later, when he republished the offending article in the *Revue Illustrée*, by removing from it all the criticisms he had made of Irving.

7

While the Lyceum was closed, with Irving's blessing and permission to use any of the theatre's stock of scenery and costumes, some of the company, under the leadership of Haviland and Martin Harvey, toured the country with *Othello* and *The Lady of Lyons*. Irving's holiday was a short one, for he had decided to reopen the Lyceum at the end of September with an elaborate revival of *The Dead Heart*.

This melodrama by Watts Philips, written against the background of the French Revolution, had been produced at the Adelphi in 1859. Ben Webster, as the hero, Robert Landry, had had one of his greatest successes; Toole had provided the comic relief. Even the staid *Athenaeum* had declared that Webster's performance 'stands in the present day alone . . . there is no London actor who can compete with it in its rough strength and its intense feeling'. The theme was one of revenge and self-sacrifice; the plot was well contrived. Before the revolution, Landry, a Parisian sculptor, and the young Count de St. Valéry, were both in love with Catherine Duval. The villain, the Abbé Latour, a power at Court, incites the young count to abduct Catherine and, with a *lettre de cachet*, secures Landry's imprisonment in the Bastille. Landry, unaware of Latour's conspiracy, believes that Catherine was faithless to him; Catherine, believing Landry to be dead, marries the young Count who himself dies shortly afterwards, leaving her with their son. Eighteen years later the Bastille is stormed. Among the released prisoners is Landry, a bearded wreck, half blinded by the daylight into which he has emerged from the darkness of his cell. In time he becomes a powerful member of the Convention and revenges himself upon Latour and Catherine's now grown-up son by throwing them into prison. Later he sends for Latour and forces him to fight a duel in which the Abbé is killed. The young Count is condemned, with many other aristocrats, to the guillotine. Landry, by chance, meets Catherine outside the prison. He hears for the first time that her husband had tried to obtain his release from the Bastille but had been told by Latour that he was dead. Landry promises to save her son. He does so by taking the boy's place in the tumbril and dies on the scaffold.

The *dénouement* of the play resembled that of Dickens's *Tale of Two Cities*. Indeed this new production revived the old charges of plagiarism against the author. In fact, the play was written three years before the novel; in any case, the plot was dignified by age. The dialogue of the original play was hopelessly dated, particularly in its crude comedy, so Irving had commissioned Walter Pollock to rewrite it. Pollock did his best, but the play remained essentially one of action and situation, relying upon its actors to bring it to life. It gave Irving plenty of scope for imposing stage pictures and for the exercise of his genius for handling crowds. As Robert Landry he had ample opportunity to indulge the appetite which gave him so keen a delight in melodrama—the ability to hold an audience spellbound by long passages of virtuoso acting almost unaided by dialogue. Irving brought Bancroft out of his recent retirement to play the Abbé Latour. The negotiations between the two actor-managers were a model of tact, dignity and grace. 'Irving,' wrote Bancroft, 'flattered me by saying that unless I would appear with him as the Abbé Latour, he would not carry out the play. I tried to persuade him to let me undertake the part as a labour of love, but he would not listen to the proposal. After a long talk—neither of us looking at the other, but each gazing separately at different angles into the street—he said that I must content him by being specially engaged on terms which at least were settled. The money, which I arranged with the Treasurer should be paid in bank notes, was regularly put aside by me into the drawer of my desk. My income was fixed and ample . . . and so eventually I gave a thousand pounds to the "Darkest England" scheme . . . founded by General Booth.'

Ellen Terry would have rebelled against playing another, if more sympathetic matron, but by casting Gordon Craig as the young Count St. Valéry, Irving appealed to her strong maternal instinct and, as usual, had his own way. While at work on the play he wrote to her:

'I am full of the French Revolution, and could pass an examination. In our play, at the taking of the Bastille, we must have a starving crowd —hungry, eager, cadaverous faces. If that can be well carried out, the effect will be very terrible and the contrast to the other crowd (the red and fat crowd—the blood-gorged ones, who look as if they'd all been drinking wine—*red* wine as Dickens says)—would be striking. . . . It's tiresome stuff to read, because it depends so much on situations. I've been touching the book up though, and improved it here and there, I think.

A letter this morning from the illustrious — — offering me his prompt book at look at. . . . I think I shall borrow the treasure. Why not? Of course he will say that he has produced the play and all that sort of thing; but what does that matter, if one can only get one hint out of it?

The longer we live, the more we see that if we only do our own work thoroughly well, we can be independent of everything else or anything that may be said. . . . I see in Landry a good deal of Manette —that same vacant gaze into years gone by when he crouched in his dungeon nursing his wrongs. . . .

I shall send you another book soon to put any of your alterations and additions in. I have added a lot of little things with a few lines for you—very good, I think, though I say it as shouldn't—I know you'll laugh! They are, perhaps, not startlingly original, but better than the original, anyhow! Here they are—last act!

"Ah, Robert, pity me. By the recollections of our youth, I implore you to save my boy!" (*Now* for 'em!)

"If my voice recalls a tone that ever fell sweetly upon your ear, have pity on me! If the past is not a blank, if you once loved, have pity on me!" (Bravo!)

Now I call that very good, and if the "If" and the "pitys" don't bring down the house, well it's a pity! I pity the pittites?

. . . I've just been copying out my part in an account book—a little more handy to put in one's pocket. It's really very short, but difficult to act, though, and so is yours. I like this "piling up" sort of acting, and I am sure you will, when you play the part. It's restful. *The Bells* is that sort of thing.'

All this, commented Ellen Terry, was to put her into conceit with her own part.

8

While Irving was engrossed in rehearsals news was brought to him that in a burlesque, *Ruy Blas*, at the Gaiety, Fred Leslie, an admirable and very popular comedian, was giving an imitation of him, in which he was represented in female attire. Leslie was a brilliant mimic, and caricatures of this kind were among his most popular turns. Irving, no doubt, should have gone himself to see the performance. At any other time he might have done so; as it was, he accepted the reports of his friends and fellow-actors—Weedon Grossmith, for instance, wrote: '. . . had I paid for my seat I should have felt strongly inclined to hiss at a disgusting exhibition I witnessed at the Gaiety last Saturday.' Irving wrote a sharp letter to Leslie and demanded that he should withdraw the offending burlesque. George Edwardes, the manager, piqued that the protest had not been addressed to him, told Leslie to ignore it. Irving had neither time nor patience to argue the matter. He reported it to the Lord Chamberlain's office. The Comptroller, Sir Ponsonby Fane, wrote to Lord Lathom:

'. . . You will see by enclosed we have trouble about the Gaiety and Irving. I have told H——[1] to tell Edwardes, Gaiety manager, that unless the "offensive personality" is stopped, his licence would not be renewed. It is a strong measure and will cause an infernal row, but I see nothing else to do. I go to London tomorrow and will try to see Edwardes and make him reasonable. Meantime perhaps you will send me a telegram to the office if you can suggest any other course.'

Lord Lathom approved of his action. Edwardes at first was defiant; in an interview in the press he protested that Lord Lathom was guilty of a breach of duty for taking action on the *ex parte* statement of a personal friend. Sir Ponsonby Fane exercised forceful tact and made a further report:

Lord Chamberlain's Office,
St. James's Palace.
September 30th, 1889.

'My dear Lathom,

I have been interviewing the Managers all day long and have just finished them off.

I spoke to many of them about Irving and Edwardes and the general sympathy is with the former—more particularly as to the "bad form" of Edwardes in not withdrawing the offensive entertainment when complained [to]. But they all say that Irving is very "sensitive". He told me that he had no objection to be being burlesqued but objected to being made a disgusting and ridiculous figure which was in no sense a burlesque.

Edwardes declared it was quite a harmless skit and that lots of people had asked him to put them on the stage in that fashion. He apologized

[1] The clerk.

for a paragraph which he said was quite inaccurate, in which he accused the L.C. of having been biased by his friendship for Irving. The whole thing will drop now and do good. . . .

Yours very sincerely,

J. Ponsonby Fane.'

George Edwardes accepted defeat. This was not the first time that the Lord Chamberlain had to remind him of the clause in his licence that expressly forbade the representation of living persons on the stage; not long before he had been told to withdraw a similar burlesque of Gladstone. The affair was a nine-days wonder. The press, on the whole, while admitting that Irving had ample personal and legal grounds to justify the action he had taken, implied that he had been a trifle high-handed and over-sensitive in the matter. It was, after all, a Pyrrhic victory. A few nights later Fred Leslie reappeared in ballet skirts, his completely bald and masked head wrapped in folds of gauze; by silent mimicry of Irving's gait and gesture he got the last laugh and louder applause than he had done for his original misdemeanour.

9

The Dead Heart was produced on September 28th and was played a hundred and eighty three times during the season. At first it was as popular as *Macbeth*, but towards the end of the run public interest, which showed signs of waning, had to be stimulated by revivals of *Olivia* and other favourite pieces of the Lyceum repertory. The play was received by the critics in good part. It was full-blooded melodrama produced in a full-blooded way and with impeccable taste. Some complained of Ellen Terry's lack of opportunity. She considered her sacrifice was very well rewarded by the favourable reception of her son's début. Bancroft, if his style deviated occasionally from the salons of the Bourbons to the drawing-rooms of Tom Robertson, was made welcome at the Lyceum by everyone. If the play did not add to Irving's laurels as an actor, it enhanced his reputation for stage-management. Yet he had moments which those who saw the play never forgot—as, for instance, the scene following Landry's release from the Bastille, which Edward Russell recorded in detail:

'. . . When prisoner after prisoner had been brought out, tottering, ragged and blear-eyed, a figure nobler, more striking, but bearing, if possible, worse signs of suffering than any, is supported across the bridge and down to the centre of the stage. Some of Landry's old friends recognize him in this forlorn, long-bearded, peak-faced man, gazing or trying to gaze (for the light nearly blinds him) vacantly into space. At first he makes no effort to recall himself. When at length he seems to aim at framing words it is with lips that seem smitten with paralysis and in a voice raucous with prison damps and tremulous from disuse. This living picture is a most masterly one, and will be remembered as Mr.. Irving's most intense and profound achievement in physiognomical and psychological assumption. The acting is so great that there seems to be none. The vitality of the worn, wan man is evident enough; but his visage is marred, and his soul is in the suspense of an irresistible overmastering torpor. In the meshes of thoughts gradually shaping into weird remembrances as he submits scarcely conscious to the questioning of his long-forgotten friends—during the slow, slow filing of the fetters that have rusted to his limbs undisturbed for years and years—the prematurely old man faintly moves and stretches as it were the tardily recovering faculties of his mind. His face is a miraculous study of perfectly true dormant and yet surviving consciousness. At long last . . . the strange figure does become self-responsible and self-responsive. It is the name of Catherine, pronounced by his old Bruin friend, the gruff Legrand, that really and completely awakes the mind, the bright and flashing mind that still inhabits this extraordinary Job-like tenement of wrecked and racked humanity. Almost with screams of freedom, he rises and half staggers, half is carried away, from the scene of his liberation, into the thickening, crowding, embarrassing activities of his newly arisen life from the dead . . . let me suggest one measure of the great actor's truly colossal and also truly minute power . . . let this scene, if no other, be read before going to the theatre. Let the spectator do his best to elaborate and heighten it from the mere skeleton the text affords. Then, after making his own poor effort, let him see Henry Irving dead and alive again, lost and found, by the long but not weary process of the action which supreme truth to life and nature and the human spirit—yes, and the human physique, too—have taught him. It will then be understood what the art of the actor can achieve in the grandest crisis of artistic opportunity. . . .'

The duel between Landry and the Abbé, which was fought with sabres, never failed to excite the audience; had they been aware of the real hazards of this fight they might well have become hysterical. Both Irving and Bancroft were extremely short-sighted and practically blind without their glasses. Both were accomplished swordsmen, and Irving, to add realism and suspense to the struggle, had told Bancroft to lay on as he wished and that he would look after himself. Thus, had they known it, playgoers had the unique experience of seeing two partially blind men furiously engaged in a combat in which everything was left to chance but the issue. 'The conjunction of the two actors,' wrote a critic, 'gave the artistic climax of the evening. They rose upon one another as though each would scale the other and over-top him and did it so quietly and composedly . . . that not until the act was over did the audience realize what admiring terror had been roused.' There were some who found Irving and Bancroft more entertaining in action than when engaged in exchange of dialogue. Alice Meynell wrote that '. . . the two men used echoes of one another's voice, then out-paused each other. It was a contest so determined, so unrelaxed, so deadly, so inveterate that you might have slept between the encounters. You did sleep. These men were strong and knew what they wanted. It is tremendous to watch the struggle of such resolves. They had their purpose in their grasp, their teeth were set, their will was iron. They were foot to foot'. If indeed this contest was a nightly occurrence, those members of the audience who appreciated its finer points were able to act as umpires and, unlike the duel with the sabres, the issue of which was predetermined, would judge for themselves who was the winner.

One night, after they had taken their calls, Irving put his arm on Bancroft's shoulder as they walked from the stage. 'What a big name,' he said; 'you might have made for yourself had you never come across those Robertson plays—what a pity—for your sake—for no actor can be remembered long who does not appear in classical drama.' This oblique compliment might have offended an actor less composed than Bancroft. He admired Irving, but he did not envy him his success. There he was, three years younger than Irving, comfortably retired and, being a man of prudent and careful habits, with many years of enjoyable life ahead of him in a respectable and distinguished social circle. On the other hand, Irving did not envy Bancroft his retirement. Yet he may have envied his thrift and business acumen which prompted him, every day of his life, to call at his bankers where he was handed a slip of paper which contained the precise statement of his account.

10

Though the production of *The Dead Heart* was well timed to celebrate the centenary of the capture of the Bastille, the Republican background of the play may have prejudiced its popularity at a time when Great Britain was torn by strikes and violent industrial disputes. This was reflected in a letter which Irving received from J. A Froude:

'. . . the Play itself has great merits—one especially that it requires no previous knowledge. The situations are clear throughout. The last scene is well constructed to disguise the horror. I expected a fiercer intonation of the Marseillaise; historically it was sung with a fury of enthusiasm but this, too, you doubtless have well considered—excessive passion might imply too much sympathy with the Revolution.'

Irving was at heart a Liberal, but he held himself aloof from politics unless they concerned affairs of the theatre. When, in 1890, the London County Council threatened to impose a stamp duty on theatre tickets, he reminded them sharply of the benefits which the public derive 'from well conducted theatres—many of which in civilised countries are heavily subsidised by the State, and of the inordinate expenses which in our own country have brought monetary disaster upon such managers as Kemble, Macready, Charles Kean and Phelps'. Yet when Lady Pollock asked him to sign a tribute to Pasteur from representative Englishmen, he replied:

'I think I would rather not add my name to the Pasteur testimonial— for either socially or politically to associate myself with any movement in which party feeling runs high—is, I have found to my cost, a reckless proceeding. Punch, you know, should have neither feelings nor politics in public—certainly I have a horror of vivisection, greatly as I admire the genius of Pasteur.'

His social life reflected his impartiality. Though he was a member of six clubs, he rarely used any of them except the Garrick, where the variety of its members was as diverse as their opinions and conversation. In the following March he was elected to the Marlborough Club —proposed by its founder, the Prince of Wales, and seconded by the Duke of Fife. Any political tint that the blue limelight of the Marlborough Club might have thrown upon him was offset by the pink glow of his membership of the Reform; the cloak of decorum which might become him at the Athenaeum was discarded in the vestibules of the Savage and the Green Room. He could not be said to belong to any club or coterie. Even at the Garrick, where members who supped there swarmed, as it were, instinctively on him, he seemed to preside over rather than to be part of their fellowship. 'In some undefined way,' wrote W. L. Courtney, 'he conveyed the impression that he stood apart —that his personality moved in a sphere of its own, and that though in bodily presence he was there, the spiritual part of the man was wandering elsewhere—in worlds unrealised.' It was, therefore, all the more devasting when his attention focused upon anyone who was given to mundane pretension. One night Richard Harding Davis, an adventurous war correspondent with an excess of panache, was brought there as a guest. He entered the coffee-room in a fur-lined overcoat, which he took off and flung to a waiter. On his dress coat he wore several medals.

'Eh! Ah!' said Irving, looking up as they were introduced and pointing to these decorations. '. . . and where—mm—did you get them —eh—swimming?'

II

During the past year he had made the critical transition into middle-age. Yet at fifty-one he had no reason to regard this climacteric as the overture to a decline. His health was unimpaired; it was true that earlier in the year, after a convivial supper party, his old friend, Joe Knight, had sounded a note of warning: '. . . you did not look quite fit on Sunday and pleasant as the occasion was, I was glad to see you retire. You must take, my dear good friend, great care of yourself for every reason. I want you to look quite yourself. Of course, we had an enchanting evening. . . . I, however, begin to fear such, delightful as they are.' But *Macbeth* had been a production with unusual anxiety and the playing of him more exacting than any part he had undertaken for some time. On the other hand, in all his years at the Lyceum he had only once been out of the bill on account of illness. His last two productions had been his most ambitious and by no means the least profitable; his hold over his public had never been stronger. He had celebrated his fiftieth year by taking under royal licence the name of John Henry Brodribb Irving—a proof of his sincerity in refusing hitherto to accept any titles or honours which could only have been borne by Brodribb.

The year had seen the publication of the last of eight volumes comprising *The Henry Irving Shakespeare*. In 1887 Irving and his friend, Frank Marshall, had conceived the idea of presenting to the public in a popular form the plays of Shakespeare with notes and commentaries based upon the recent researches of Furnivall and Furness. Irving had become very friendly with Furness in America and had enlisted his help in this project which Blackie's had undertaken to publish. Each play was introduced by its literary and stage history and was followed by copious textual notes. The work was profusely illustrated by Gordon Browne, whose black and white drawings helped the reader to form some idea of costume and dramatic action. Irving did a good deal more than to give his name to the edition. He indicated in the margin not only those cuts which in his opinion were essential for the production of the plays in the commercial theatre, but a more drastic revision for public readings or for performances by those whose resources of time, money and cast, were very limited. In so doing he exposed himself to the attacks of those who accused him of mutilating Shakespeare; on the other hand, he left proof for posterity that his cuts were not a work of vandalism by an egotistical actor-manager, but a conscientious adaptation which studied the tastes of the squeamish Victorian audience and made it possible to present the plays within the limits of the theatrical habits and conventions which, for better or worse, prevailed at that time.

Frank Marshall worshipped Irving; during their many years of friendship he owed much to his ready help in times of stress, which ill-health and domestic anxiety caused all too frequently. Yet he dealt forthrightly with his benefactor in the preparation of this work, as two of his letters to Irving clearly showed:

'. . . I feel—I do not know whether you do—such a horror of anything like puffing or seeming to puff you in this edition. I am so afraid of giving them a chance to say that I have buttered you in the introduction. Some day I shall be able to write about your Othello as I feel, but I thought it best to keep silence in this introduction.'

And again:

'. . . You will quite understand why I avoided saying much about the Lyceum *Macbeth*. I hope you approve my reticence. I need not say, as far as I am concerned, I could say a great deal more, but I think it better not to say too much about your productions lest the Krickets should say I am glorifying you too much.'

Marshall had been working against time, for his health was failing rapidly and, to Irving's great sorrow, he died before his task was completed. The last volume, to which Professor Edward Dowden, of Trinity College, Dublin, contributed a general introduction and a 'Life of Shakespeare', was seen through the press by Arthur Symons.

In his prefatory note Irving wrote: 'Frank Marshall was a friend of my life. We were brought together and linked by the golden bond of a common love for the great Englishman whose work he endeavoured worthily to set forth; and from the hour we first met our friendship ripened till in all the world I had no warmer friend.'

Robert Browning died in December, 1889. Though he had not been an intimate friend, Irving wrote to Lady Pollock: 'I feel his loss almost personal, for his sympathy and appreciation of one's work was among the highest spots of a hard working life."

12

The season ended in May. During June he and Ellen Terry toured the provinces together, giving readings of *Macbeth*, which he had adapted for the purpose, with an orchestral accompaniment of Sullivan's music. Irving had always enjoyed giving readings, at which he excelled. Like Dickens, he was able, single-handed, to hold the attention of large audiences and to induce in them transports of horror and pity. This tour was, perhaps, an experiment to test the possibility of solving, by such means, the economic problems which sooner or later must overtake him. Like Barry Sullivan, he might insure against his old age by touring the country with nothing but a reading desk, dispensing with the enormous retinue that every year seemed to consume an increasing proportion of his receipts. Strangely enough, Ellen Terry's participation in these readings made them less rather than more effective. She entered into them with enthusiasm and perhaps gave a better rendering of the part of Lady Macbeth than she had done on the stage. On the other hand, the introduction of music may have destroyed the unity which had distinguished readings given by Irving alone. Whatever the cause, the experiment was not as satisfying to themselves or to the public as they had hoped, and it was never repeated. They wound up their short tour with a recital at the St. James's Hall. To this the clergy of every Anglican creed and denomination flocked with clear consciences; some of them may have been persuaded that, after all, the theatre was not entirely an instrument of the devil. There may even have been a few Roman Catholic priests among them, though Cardinal Manning, in whose character and appearance many saw a resemblance to Irving, had forbidden priests to attend dramatic performances of any kind in their own dioceses. After this, the Lyceum company played *The Bells* and *Louis XI* for a fortnight at the Grand Theatre, Islington, before Irving and Ellen Terry went on holiday, he to Lowestoft and she to Winchelsea. The Lyceum had been let to Augustin Daly, the American impresario, who was introducing his star, Ada Rehan, to English audiences.

13

For some time past Daly had pressed Irving to let him bring his company to the Lyceum; for one reason or another, Irving had rejected his proposal. There was much in Daly that Irving might have admired or at least appreciated. His theatre in New York was famous for its careful and elaborate productions and for the high standard of playing by his stock company which he ruled with iron discipline. John Drew was an admirable romantic and comedy actor; Ada Rehan, who made her début in New York in 1879, was an actress of extraordinary natural charms, who, by this time, had perfected herself in the technique of comedy. The fact was, Irving did not like Daly. He had done his best to do so. When Daly brought his company to England, in 1886, Irving had given a supper in their honour and later had invited Daly and Ada Rehan to meet the Prince of Wales in the Beefsteak Room. He had even, as a parting present, given Daly a bull-pup; in honour of the donor the dog was named Mephisto and it lived up to it, so that everyone except its master, whom it adored, was glad when it died. Irving and Daly shared a whole-hearted devotion to the theatre, though their tastes and their manners were utterly different. Daly once complained to Booth that Irving never repaid calls of ceremony, to which Booth replied that Irving had never called on him or on anyone else. Though both men were stern autocrats in the theatre, Daly found it difficult to unbend in private, whereas it was natural to Irving to shed his autocratic severity when, so to speak, he was off duty.

At last Labby undertook to persuade Irving that in inviting Daly to the Lyceum he would be furthering the well-beloved cause of Shakespeare.

Ada Rehan had recently played Katherine in *The Taming of the Shrew* and Rosalind in *As You Like It* in New York with well-merited success. Irving had reluctantly given way. Daly started his season with a farcical comedy which failed to attract the London public. On the opening night, at the end of the play, Daly had, as a critic said, 'judiciously resisted the demands of the injudicious for a speech'. A second farce fared no better. *The Taming of the Shrew* was an immediate success, and in *As You Like It* Ada Rehan's Rosalind established her firmly in the affections of the English public. During the season John Hare invited several of the company to a supper in their honour at the Garrick

Club. Daly refused to come on the grounds that the invitations had been sent directly to the actors concerned and had not been submitted to him. Perhaps this incident explained the fundamental incompatibility of himself and Irving.

From Lowestoft, where he was studying the part of Edgar and working on the production of *Ravenswood*, Irving wrote a letter to Ellen Terry, which made clear his attitude towards his tenants:

July 25th, 1890.

'. . . I hope that you are resting and like the place. I don't think you can rest much with a lot of people about you but the air will revive you like magic.

This place will suit me very well—it's quiet, unfashionable and unlovely. That's not exactly a recommendation but it keeps a lot away. . . . Hatton is coming to spend the Sunday . . . he was at Daly's the other night and Clementina[1] too, and of course, Winter too. I told Winter that you meant to write to him. I should do so, but they're false, false all round—I felt it with an instinct passing prophecy. I was glad you were not there—it wasn't worth it.

When I went into the office—our office—the Labbys were there . . . and some American reporters, I think. They seemed all over the place—the reporters I mean. "Well, Irving," said Labby (I saw little Hetty[2] grinning like a Cheshire cat), "you're happy now that Daly's doing Shakespeare." "Of course," said I, "Daly is faithful to the tradition of the house and in presenting the finest performance of Shakespeare the world has ever seen!" God forgive me—and the subject dropped with "Yes, yes, of course, of course, of course." A good shut up, wasn't it, and done in the lightest manner.

I'm not brown yet but soon shall be—the dark Edgar. A long walk with him today, he's a fine fellow—but too young for me, I fear, and Hamlet too. The Trees and Barretts are youngsters now and have the monopoly of the sweet princes. I wonder if "flights of angels" sing those two gentlemen to their rest. I don't believe it. . . .

I want to get to Winchelsea, my Nell, and be by you. It *is* dull here, upon my word—but I'll walk it off and stick to my work or perish in the attempt, though it's a pretty hard struggle. . . .'

Irving was extremely allergic to two-faced humbugs; anybody he suspected of this was 'false'. His few close friends he trusted implicitly,

---

[1] Clement Scott.
[2] Mrs. Labouchere, Henrietta Hodson.

but as he grew older he found that life had sharpened his suspicions of his fellow-men until few at one time or another were not labelled with the stigma of Iago.

14

Towards the end of his holiday Irving joined Ellen Terry at Winchelsea, where she had rented a cottage from the Comyns Carrs who had led the Bohemian invasion of the Ancient Town. Ellen Terry loved the country. Few playgoers would have dreamed that the gentle actress who, at the Lyceum, melted them to tears with her pitiable femininity, would frequently, after the performance on Saturday night, jump into a pony trap and drive herself through slumbering Surrey and Sussex in order to reach Winchelsea by daybreak. As a rule, Irving liked to idle away his holiday, but there he spent much of his time exploring the countryside with Ellen, Edie and the dogs in the trap. 'We drove to Cliff End,' she wrote in her diary. 'Henry got the old pony along at a spanking rate—but I had to seize the reins now and again to save us from sudden death.' One afternoon at Tenterden Irving saw in a shop window a bill announcing a performance of Clowe's Marionettes for that evening. He sought out the proprietor and, hearing that his takings on a good night were five pounds, asked if he could give a special show in the afternoon for that sum. The proprietor readily agreed. 'Henry and I,' wrote Ellen, 'and Edie and Fussy sat in solemn state in the empty tent and watched the show which was most ingenious and clever.' Mr. Clowe, no doubt, savoured the appreciation of a fellow showman and his leading lady, whose patronage, thereafter, was proudly advertised on his handbills.

CHAPTER XXIX

13th, 14th and 15th Lyceum Seasons: Ravenswood, Wolsey, King Lear, Becket

---

I

Ravenswood, adapted by Herman Merivale from Scott's *Bride of Lammermoor*, was a tedious and gloomy play. Irving had been brooding over it for seven years. He and Merivale had been faithful to Scott, but not to the theatre. Stoker, when Irving first read him the play, wrote in his diary: 'Play very fine. Literature noble. H. I. had cut quite one half out.' The residue left an unbalanced play with all the parts, except Edgar, weakly conceived and, as a result, poorly played. Ellen Terry, as Lucy Ashton, had her moments, though the adaptors had robbed Lucy of her greatest scene—her insane murder of Bucklaw in their marriage chamber—her madness was merely hinted at in a pale reflection of Ophelia. The whole affair was a woeful example of the folly of attempting to adapt a novel of unusual length for the stage. Situations which were acceptable in print, when enacted, came dangerously near bathos. Edgar, while he is fighting a duel with Sir William Ashton in the library of Ravenswood, hears Lucy's cries as she is being pursued by a mad bull. He snatches a gun from a rack. 'Is it charged?' he asks Sir William. 'Yes, yes,' answers Sir William, who ought to have known better. Edgar fires through the window and bags the bull. 'There is no cause for fear,' he cries. Lucy's life was saved, but the reverence of the Lyceum audience was severely strained—indeed, on the first night the scene produced a titter of derisive laughter. Alexander Mackenzie, who had composed the incidental music, had been inspired to add realism to this scene by a blare of trombones which he thought might suggest the bellowing of the dying bull. After the play, he apologized to Irving for having heightened the absurdity of the scene. 'Never mind, Mackenzie,' said Irving, 'I got the best laugh in the piece.'

528

Earlier Mackenzie had been pleasantly surprised by the Chief's willingness to readjust his own ideas if any of his colleagues had anything better to suggest. In his score he had accompanied the death of Edgar and Lucy with a triumphant exposition of the love motive. Irving, who had planned to bathe the final scene in cold moonlight—indicating misery, failed to grasp the composer's meaning. Mackenzie explained that, whereas in *Faust* the lovers had been severed, in *Ravenswood* they were united by death. Irving seemed unconvinced, but on the following morning Mackenzie received a reassuring note:

> *Lyceum Theatre,*
> *February 15th, 1890.*
>
> 'Dear Mackenzie,
>   You were right after all. Faust lives and I hope gets up to heaven in the second part.—Edgar and Lucy, I am sure, go together.
>   At all events your music will certainly send them there—and the moonlight—on the sea—I shall change to the breaking of the rising sun.
>   Sincerely yours,
>   Henry Irving.'

Irving, as he realized, was too old to play the romantic lover. When he faced the audience he forced them to accept an illusion of youth; but when he turned, his back betrayed his age. Nevertheless, Weedon Grossmith told a friend that if young actors wanted to know how a lover should be *played* they should go to *Ravenswood*. Irving, conscious, no doubt, of his own and the play's deficiencies, mounted and produced it to perfection. Daly, when he took the theatre, had installed electric stage lighting. Irving had observed its effect, and as soon as Daly had departed he threw it out; for the subtleties of lighting of which he was such a master, gas was the only medium. The last act revealed one glowing pastiche of Turner after another and culminated in a magnificently executed picture of sunset over the quicksands, the accent of Edgar's black-plumed cap marking where they had engulfed him.

One of the reasons which prompted Irving to risk the production of *Ravenswood* was Loveday's illness. For some time past they had been planning a spectacular production of *Henry VIII*. This, according to Irving's policy, should have followed *The Dead Heart*, but without his friend at his side such a formidable undertaking would have been impossible.

Ravenswood opened on September 20th. The play was well received by a distinguished audience. Even during the intervals they were entertained or scandalized by unaccustomed brawling in the stalls. During the first interval, Oscar Wilde's brother, Willie, fell to argument and then to blows with an American gentleman, both parties fighting a running engagement as they left the theatre to bring the matter to a conclusion outside. During the ensuing act, a Mr. Brett audibly and adversely criticized the performance. When the curtain fell, he was roundly rebuked by Joseph Hatton, who was sitting behind him. Mr. Brett received these admonitions by shouting 'Blackguard! Snob!' at Mr. Hatton, who retaliated by hitting his opponent smartly over the head with his opera hat; whereupon Mr. Brett, as it were, drew his, but before their opera hats could be crossed in this original duel, the combatants were separated by Mr. Samuel French, the publisher.

During the run of *Ravenswood* an incident occurred which showed the acute sense of rhythm and accuracy of timing which distinguished Irving's work as a producer and as an actor. One night Ellen Terry came off the stage after a scene which she had ended with a burst of almost hysterical laughter. Irving was waiting for her in the wings, 'evidently', she told her young friend, Graham Robertson, 'much annoyed.

"Why did you alter the laugh?" he asked. "It put me out altogether. I was waiting for you to finish."

"I laughed as usual," said Ellen Terry.

"No you didn't," said Irving. "You always say Ha-ha—seventeen times. You only said it fourteen times tonight." '

She had been quite unconscious of the unvarying repetition of Ha-has; she thought it was a matter of luck; but during rehearsal Irving, no doubt, had impressed upon her subconscious the exact measure of her laughter, limited by the tempo and rhythm of the whole scene.

Such was Irving's hold over his public, *Ravenswood* was played to houses crowded as ever until the middle of December. In November he wrote to Loveday:

'My dear Loveday,

I was rejoiced to hear the good news this morning that you were so much better. I am sure that your suffering must have been very great. What do you think of going away for a week or two? Now would be the time, wouldn't it, when all going smoothly.

That was a sad business last night—that poor fellow just getting out of the stalls in time to die. It was some kidney trouble they said. Rather a grim affair. He was laid out in the property room and about midnight the coroner's people took him away.

What weather—May not November! I'm sorry to think now that the story of Jameson is a true one. His wife's account in *The Times* today confirms it.

Ever, old fellow, yours,

Henry.'

Irving's political awareness at this time may have been due to Gladstone's frequent visits to the Lyceum. He seemed to enjoy *Ravenswood*. His chair in the O.P. corner had been upholstered, velvet curtains were arranged to protect him from draught and dust, and a stage hand was detailed to see that the roller curtain did not fall upon the Prime Minister's head. Gladstone always made a point of being in his place 'before they began to tune the fiddles'. He was constantly in Irving's dressing-room, where Stoker's presence stimulated melancholy discussion of Parnell's hours of trial. 'How goes it?' wrote Irving to Loveday a week or two later. 'I hope you are improving . . . everything goes on steadily. A sort of even mediocrity in the business. About the middle of January I shall produce *Much Ado* . . . the *Liberator* is engrossing attention—his manifesto is the finest since Iago—and will make the Unionists the most powerful body in the country.'

At Christmas-time he had been surprised by the delivery at Grafton Street of the carcasses of two frozen sheep and a live kangaroo. These proved to be tokens of affection from Toole, who was at the time enjoying a successful tour in Australia. His immediate reaction was to send these rather embarrassing gifts round to the Lyceum. The following day the sheep were sent as a Christmas present to the Costermongers Club in the Mile End Road. The kangaroo, having survived a night without damage to itself or to the theatre, was presented to the Zoological Gardens. There it survived for many years, deriving a certain theatrical glamour from the brass plate on its cage which described it as the joint gift of J. L. Toole and Henry Irving.

Towards the end of the year receipts at the Lyceum had begun to fall. Reports from other theatres showed that business was deteriorating everywhere. One night Ricarde-Seaver, a financier, was one of a party in the Beefsteak Room. Stoker asked him if he could account for these signs of depression. For the first time he and Irving heard of Baring's impending failure. Obviously *Ravenswood* was not the fare to cheer an audience seeking distraction from the real and pervading gloom of the outside world. It was on this account that Irving revived *Much Ado* on January 5th when business began to improve again. The season was one of Irving's longest—ten months. It included revivals of most of his earlier successes, among them *The Corsican Brothers* and, for Ellen Terry's sake, *Nance Oldfield*. Irving's production of *The Corsican Brothers* seemed as fresh and elegant as it had in 1880; yet, since he was now old enough to be the father of the dei Franchi twins, and Gladstone was no longer available as a supernumerary, the play had lost a little of its old glamour. But all the labour that such a heavy repertory entailed was scantily rewarded by a profit of barely £4,000. Considering that the production of *Ravenswood* had been paid for out of the proceeds of Daly's tenancy, the season could only be regarded as having been moderately successful. On the night of May 2nd the Lyceum had been closed to enable Irving to attend the Royal Academy banquet. 'It is my intention,' Sir Frederick Leighton, the President, had written to him, 'to substitute for the toast of "Music and Literature"—this time "Music and the Drama"—a toast I have long wished to give . . . both I and the Council much wish that on this, the first occasion that is being toasted at Burlington House, the response should be entrusted to you, who hold so conspicuous a position in your profession, and who will grace the duty so well.' So, on the arm of Irving, the Tragic Muse, with her unblemished Sisters, was the guest of the Academicians and received the homage of the Church, the Stage and the Armed Forces. Her eldest sister, Terpsichore, was still regarded as an incorrigible demi-mondaine—indeed, even Irving would have raised his black eyebrows if she had appeared at the Banquet escorted by George Edwardes. But hard-headed George Edwardes would not have closed his theatre at the cost of two or three hundred pounds to indulge in such quixotic gallantries.

2

During the year Irving may have been taken aback by several incidents which were the outcome of his own missionary zeal. The status and self respect of the actor had been so improved that in the preceding February, Benson and another young actor, Robert Courtneidge, had convened a meeting in Manchester which resulted in the formation of the Actors' Association. One of the main objects of this body was to protect members of their profession against the increasing danger of 'bogus managers'—or absconding impresarios who left their companies penniless and stranded in the middle of a tour. Benson asked Irving's blessing on their enterprise. At first Irving hesitated—surely the bogus manager was too rare a beast to justify a step that seemed so dangerously republican? Hardly had the report of this first meeting been published when an actor wrote to the press denouncing one of the sponsors of the Association as a manager who had once left him high and dry and still owed him his salary. The public wrangling that followed this assertion did not add to the dignity of the profession or to the prestige of the Association. Irving stepped in, accepted the presidency and offered Benson the Lyceum for his first official meeting, thereby lending weight and authority to their deliberations.

Nevertheless, the subtle changes which were overtaking his profession were a little baffling. When he had invited Tree to meet the Prince of Wales to supper in the Beefsteak Room, the former's letter of acceptance had been surely a trifle flippant:

> *Haymarket Theatre,*
> *May 23rd, 1891.*
>
> 'My dear Irving,
> My wife and I will be delighted to come to you on Tuesday night— we have no deep-rooted aversion to Princes, though the etiquette towards Serene Highnesses has occasionally caused me a sleepless night. It is, however, only through stress of this kind that one emerges a man of the world. . . .
>
> > Yours sincerely,
> > H. Beerbohm Tree.'

Did he, wondered Irving, take for granted the actor's hard-won social emancipation, or was he the eternal vagabond, cocking a snook at patronage.

The Church, which until now had accepted Irving's reiterated rebukes for her attitude towards the theatre in silence or had professed an apologetic willingness to be as broad-minded as public opinion would allow, suddenly found her voice. From several pulpits bold young preachers challenged Irving's vindication of the stage as a force for good, declaring roundly that historically it had been the most demoralizing influence with which the Church ever had to contend. Turning to account the journalistic stratagems which Mr. Stead had used so effectively, one of these zealous preachers, the Reverend Stratton of St. Helen's, Lancashire, sent his sermon to the press, in whose columns the questions he raised were hotly debated. By this time there were plenty of men and women eager to champion Irving's cause. When in November he lectured to the Philosophical Institute of Edinburgh on 'The Art of Acting'[1], he contented himself by remarking that 'the theatre as a whole is never below average moral sense of its time'. To this moderate pronouncement the *Methodist Times* replied:

[1] *see appendix.*

'If the modern drama were the ideal and elevated and glorious thing which Mr. Irving imagined at Edinburgh, the attitude of the Christian churches would be altered. But what is the use of ignoring ugly facts? Everybody knows that there is only too much ground for Mr. Stratton's denunciation. It is inevitable that Christian ministers should fix their attention very largely upon the terrible evils that have hitherto been identified with the theatre. If so attractive and powerful an institution could be saved from the horrible evils which have always been associated with it, and made the vehicle of innocent recreation and elevated instruction which its advocates describe, we are sure that no one would rejoice more than the young minister who has so bravely and eloquently denounced existing evils.'

Irving was concerned primarily with the message of the theatre rather than with the morals of those who played in it. After all, as Stoker pointed out, statistics showed that after revivalist meetings illegitimate births increased. The Church had far better attack the morbid and unwholesome plays of Ibsen than rake over the sins and shortcomings of players who did not pretend to be better or worse than their fellow-men.

There had been a flicker of lightning on the otherwise clear horizon, which the pilot of the Lyceum had not recognized as a sign of stormy weather ahead. A pamphlet had been brought to his notice entitled *The Quintessence of Ibsenism*, written, he understood, by the music critic of his friend Edmund Yates's paper, *The World*. He could not follow the author, George Bernard Shaw, into the labyrinth of argument which set out to prove that the crude reality of plays written by a rebel against the social conventions of his time was truly idealistic, while the pursuit of beauty and nobility, ideals which Irving had always kept before him, was nothing but an attempt to hide from inescapable truths in a pretty jungle of romantic self-delusion. When, however, Mr. Shaw publicly declared that actors and actresses of established reputation were not sufficiently educated to play Ibsen, he felt it his duty as publicly to defend them. He took the opportunity at a banquet given in his honour by the Liverpool Philomathic Society, to put Mr. Shaw in his place once and for all:

'I have lately read in the polite language of the writer of a book about what is called Ibsenism, that our finished actors and actresses cannot play Ibsen because they are ignoramuses. I thought that some of our younger actresses had played Ibsen rather well, though this, it seems, is because they are novices in art but experienced in what is called the political and social movement. Outside this mysterious movement you find "inevitably sentimental actresses" we are told, who are quite good enough for Shakespeare but not educated enough for Ibsen. I understand from this authority that one of the qualifications for playing Ibsen is to have no fear of making yourself "acutely ridiculous" and I can easily believe that this exponent of Ibsen is not troubled by that kind of trepidation; but if the "inevitably sentimental actress" in Shakespeare should be a Helen Faucit or an Ellen Terry, I think that most of you will be satisfied with her capacity for the finest achievement of her art. It is certainly a ludicrous pretension that the fitness to play Shakespeare disqualifies an artist for embodying the creations of some dramatist who is supposed to represent a political anti-social movement. I do not know whether the Ibsen drama would obtain any permanent standing on our stage, but it is a comfort to find that, in the opinion of the author I have quoted, Shakespeare will not be entirely extinguished.'

Irving was bound to admit that, thanks to William Archer's persistent advertisement, Ibsen was in the air and it was hard to know who would next catch the infection. Janet Achurch, an earnest and hard-working actress who seemed always to be in financial difficulty, had asked him for money to sustain her and her husband, Charles Charrington, in a comedy, *Clever Alice*, at the Novelty Theatre. He had sent her £100, only to discover that she and Eleanor Marx Aveling were conspiring to produce Ibsen. She asked him to come and see *A Doll's House*. He went. 'If that's the sort of thing she wants to play she'd better play it somewhere else,' was the only comment he made to Graham Robertson. He felt that in some way he had been accessory to her folly and was glad to hear that she was leaving with her husband for a tour in Australia.

Meanwhile, although the flow of prophylactic drama from Scandinavia seemed inexhaustible, his own efforts to find or to inspire the kind of plays he needed for the Lyceum were ill-rewarded. He had cast his net wide. Thomas Hardy had sent him an adaptation of one of his novels—eager for his opinion but realizing that 'there was too much actuality in it for the romantic Lyceum, and it is therefore all the more kind of you to consider it so carefully'. Hardy was right; but Irving found that the lack of a dominating character for himself to play was a graver fault than the play's realism. Oscar Wilde had pressed him to put on *The Duchess of Padua*, which Lawrence Barrett had produced under the title *Guido Ferranti* in New York. '. . . The name of the author being concealed,' wrote Wilde, 'it achieved . . . immense success which of course pleased me very much as it was entirely on its own merits . . . at Barrett's request I acknowledged authorship by cabling my thanks to the public for their reception of my play. Now, of course, you are the one artist in England who can produce poetic blank verse drama and as I have pointed out in this month's *Fortnightly*, you have created in the theatre-going public both taste and temperament, so that there is an audience for a poet inside a theatre though there is no, or but a small audience for a poet outside the

J. L. Toole, J. Comyns Carr, H. Beerbohm Tree and Oscar Wilde
at the hearing of the Parnell Commission.

theatre.' Wilde was over-hasty in his gratitude and self-revelation to the American public. The play ran three weeks. Irving had shown it to a friend who remarked that Oscar had certainly read *The Merchant of Venice.* 'I expect so,' agreed Irving, 'and apparently thought little of it.'

Earlier in the year he had become interested in a young Scottish journalist who, at supper at the Garrick Club, had expressed a keen desire to write for the theatre. Irving encouraged him, and, as usual, invited the young man, whose name was James Barrie, to send him anything he wrote which he thought might be appropriate to the Lyceum. Disregarding Irving's qualification, in a short time he sent him a burlesque called *Ibsen's Ghost.* Irving sent the play and introduced the author to Toole, urging him to produce it. Toole acted on his friend's advice and not long afterwards received a full-length farce from Barrie called *The House Boat*. Again at Irving's instigation he bought the play, retitled it *Walker, London* and with it had instant and lasting success. Irving was delighted at Toole's good fortune, though he hoped one day to get a play out of Barrie for the Lyceum, where at the moment the cupboard was bare of promising material.

The difficulty of finding plays and playwrights who understood his needs made Irving doubly grieved to know that poor, uncouth Wills was broken in health and lay near to death in Guy's Hospital. For some time past he had, at Irving's instigation, been writing a play on the Arthurian legend. To the end he worked in an atmosphere of conspiracy and unfailing optimism. His letters to Irving about *King Arthur* were echoes of Bateman's supper table and the enthusiasms of *Charles I*.

'. . . I never see an allusion to the play but I feel a cold sweat lest my idea of the fourth act should get out and be stolen by some playwright shark.

Arthur has been to me an inexpressible labour of love. I have given it infinite thought and care. . . .'

And in what was perhaps his last letter to Irving:

'. . . Do read Arthur as soon as you can as my mind is unsettled— I do not think I ever did better work but your opinion, of course, is the question.'

He died in the following December. Perhaps Irving had not the heart to answer this question and so to darken his old friend's last hours with shattered hopes. For Wills's *King Arthur* would not do. The new generation of playgoers were not so easily enchanted by his simple sentiments and tinsel verbiage. No one regretted this change of taste more than Irving.

3

While Irving was preparing for his autumn tour in the provinces, which began at the Grand Theatre, Islington, he wrote to Mrs. James:

15a Grafton Street,
September 15th, 1891.

'My dear friend,
I am truly sorry to hear that you have been unwell—and pray that the demon influenza has left you unhurt. I escaped, I think, but

something malign was hovering near me last season, for I felt depressed and ill, with no special cause. Perhaps it was that my work was very exacting, for our change of bill kept me in the theatre by day—and night.

I wish I could see you now and have a long time with you—but I must wait, I fear, till I come back in December to tell you all my plans. Every day I am at Islington now, rehearsing for our tour and for the pieces here and expect after the going and coming I have little time left—unluckily, too, leaving to go to Canterbury on Wednesday.

Henry The Eighth will I think delight you. It will be a great thing.

You know that Harry makes his first appearance on Saturday at the Garrick Theatre under Hare's management? I wonder would you be able to see him—I should like to send you places if it were possible that you are going out. Harry and Laurence have both determined to be actors and although I am sorry for the poor boys (Harry would have made his mark at the Bar)—it is impossible to oppose them and I am anxious to further their interests in every way. Laurence is feeling his way in the country in young Benson's company. . . .

Affectionately yours,

Henry Irving.'

Irving's apparent resignation to his sons' decisions concealed an inward and bitter disappointment. Harry had done well at Oxford, where his success with the O.U.D.S. and the wearing of a white bowler hat had made him a popular and notable figure. He had played Decius Brutus in *Julius Caesar* and the title roles in Browning's *Strafford* and Shakespeare's *King John*; in doing so he won the praise of his friends and the flattery of his father's enemies. He received an offer from Mrs. Langtry to join her at the St. James's at a salary of £12 a week, which he wisely refused. His tutors had expected him to get a First in History, but owing to these distractions he got only a Second, though he was already well advanced with a biography of Judge Jeffries which was remarkable for its maturity and cynical wit. When he came down from Oxford his father's friend, Hare, had offered him a leading part in a revival of Robertson's *School* at the Garrick Theatre. Such a prospect, approved if not blessed by his father, seemed infinitely preferable to the drudgery of taking a Law examination. It was with mixed feelings that Irving heard and read of Harry's woeful failure. The critics found him stilted and ultra priggish; their references to his parentage fulfilled the prophecy in the letter he had received from his father at Marlborough. After a second and perhaps more promising appearance in Grundy's *A Fool's Paradise*, his engagement with Hare ended. Dispirited by this experience and by lack of offers from else-where, he left the stage and started to read for the Bar. His father's influence, reluctantly exercised, had put him in a position as false as the prejudice which his father's name had excited in his critics. Laurence had returned from Russia with a thorough knowledge of the language and a deep reverence for Tolstoy, whose disciple he became for the rest of his life. Though he had every qualification for the foreign service, he lacked the private income which was as necessary as scholar-ship. For all his apparent success, Irving was not able to settle on his son a large enough sum to give him the necessary independence. He was, therefore, forced to accept Laurence's choice of an alter-native career. He was able to save him from making the same mistake as his brother by sending him to the nearest thing he could find to the stock company of his own early days. Laurence joined the Benson company, among whom he was billed as Mr. Lawrence. Thus, though his introspection and dreamy speculation may have set him apart from his hearty and athletic companions, he was able quietly to assimilate the rudiments of his art without exciting comparison with the illustrious Antique.

The purpose of Irving's visit to Canterbury was to unveil a memorial to Christopher Marlowe which had been designed by Onslow Ford and had been erected in the Butter Market. He had undertaken to do so at the earnest request of Edmund Gosse and he had suggested that Gosse should write some verses for the occasion. Gosse modestly demurred, writing that 'his friend, Mr. Swinburne, would expect to be asked first; if you will give me leave to do so I will write and propose it to him in your name'. Swinburne's reply was misapprehensive and laconic:

'Dear Gosse,
    If Irving wishes to recite my published verses on the Marlowe Memorial I have no objection to his doing so.
                                    Yours sincerely,
                                        A. C. Swinburne.'

In the event, Irving, not inappropriately, recited a few lines of Marlowe's verse and delivered a eulogy on the poet in which he skil-fully avoided referring to the fact that his plays were no longer performed on his native stage. The occasion, however, provided a pleasant entertainment for the people of Canterbury, though few of

MR. HENRY IRVING PLACES HIS SON UNDER THE CARE OF DR. JOHN HARE.

them had any very clear idea as to whom they were doing honour. As Irving was leaving, a citizen asked him if the widow had been present at the ceremony. When Irving explained that Marlowe was a poet who had been dead these three hundred years, the man confessed that he thought the monument had been raised to Marwood, the famous and extant public hangman. If the man was disappointed, the incident was the highlight of Irving's afternoon.

Towards the middle of December, Irving returned to London from his provincial tour which had added £6,000 to his treasury. He needed every penny of this to meet the enormous and rapidly increasing costs of his production of *Henry VIII*. He knew that the play was little more than a chronicle and, by custom, an excuse for pageantry; he had determined to honour it at the Lyceum with a pageant such as had never before been seen. When Burbage first produced it at the Globe, the stage cannon, fired in honour of the Princess Elizabeth, set fire to the thatched roof of the theatre, which was burnt to the ground; it was rumoured that Irving's reckless expenditure on the play might well consume the Lyceum.

His enemies hinted that he was caught in his own toils, that having debauched his public's taste for spectacle, he must ever go one better in extravagant display. This was not so. His present prodigality was to some extent a symptom of his ability to get inside the skin of the man he was to portray. Imbued with the infectious pomp of Wolsey, he was assuming his habit of princely liberality.

A symptom of this assumption was his treatment of a young musician, Edward German, whom he had commissioned to write the dances and incidental music. When German, whose work had given him great satisfaction, sent in his bill, it was returned to him endorsed in Irving's hand: 'This account needs revising.' The next day, German, in dismay, called on Irving and protested that for the work entailed the sum he asked was not unreasonable. 'My dear German,' said Irving, 'I paid Sullivan double the amount for music not comparable in my opinion to yours. Please amend your account as a favour to me with that fact in mind.'

Yet there was method in his apparently mad extravagance. He perceived that the characters of those who motivated the events the play chronicled, were as integral a part of the English Renaissance as figures in a tapestry; that, torn from their background (designed in conceit, lush in texture, and even a little vulgar), they would be as incomplete as a Tudor tapestry mottled with patches of threadbare canvas—the ghosts of unstitched kings and queens and prelates. He was determined, by enlisting the help of artists expert in design and archaeology, to re-create this background; to gain his purpose he was ready to squander his fortune with the proud munificence of the upstart Cardinal himself. Alma Tadema was engaged to supervise the work of Hawes Craven and his team of painters; Seymour Lucas and Alice Comyns Carr construed the exquisite records of Holbein in terms of the theatre. Rudolf Lehman, the painter, lent him a cardinal's robe of the period. To match its weight and texture, a silk was specially woven and sent to Rome to be dyed an authentic red. Rome failed, but a rosy dye, more theatrically effective, was produced in England. Fifty years afterwards a playgoer recalled that one of her most vivid memories of this production was the premonitory swish of silk that heralded Irving's entrances.

To fortify a play lacking in dramatic cohesion Irving had mustered a strong cast. Forbes-Robertson returned to the Lyceum as Buckingham, Terriss found an outlet for his robustiousness as Henry the Eighth, while Ellen Terry, as Queen Katherine, was well supported by a talented newcomer, Violet Vanbrugh, as Anne Boleyn. The production inspired learned commentary and preliminary speculation in the press. High hopes were raised in the minds of the public and of scholars; neither were disappointed.

Henry VIII opened on January 5th, 1892, and was welcomed by a chorus of praise and delight. Irving's purpose, nobly achieved, was perfectly understood and, for once, no critic decried his rich upholstery of Shakespeare, whose text, owing to the shortness of the play, suffered few excisions. He had not underestimated the hunger of the people of Victorian England for the colour and pageantry that the sombre styles and conventions of their daily life denied them. 'The plain truth is,' wrote the critic of the St. James's Gazette, 'that for a good number of average modern Britons this is about the noblest kind of artistic pleasure that they are capable of appreciating . . .' there are some pleasures at once universal and not unrefined—the appetite for bright colours and lively action, for sonorous music and poetical rhetoric is as natural as it is blameless and it is one which ought to be indulged whenever the chance occurs. In other countries this taste is catered for by the Church and by the State. We practise an aestheticism on the cheap—or, as Pericles put it, we continue the love of the Beautiful with a due regard for economy. We do not vote public money for the shows that are to delight the people. We leave them to pay their money at the box-office of the theatre—the only place apparently where in our climate and under our social conditions, the "colour sense" and the sense that delights in moving masses of figures can be fully satisfied.'

Irving played Wolsey with such force and insight that he dominated the play even when he was absent from the stage. Though not his greatest part, it was the most perfect in study and execution that he had yet played. Hardly a critic accorded him anything but unqualified praise. Though its range was necessarily limited, his physical and intellectual aptitude for the part enabled him perfectly to portray the assured pride of a crafty cardinal at the height of his power and the extremes of 'mental torture which arises from the vague dread of impending calamity'. Ellen Terry said that Henry's pride as Cardinal Wolsey seemed to eat him. Of his last scene the often censorious critic of the *Saturday Review* wrote:

'. . . Mr. Irving rises to the highest expression of histrionic art. With his hands affectionately resting on the head of the only human being who still loves him and feels for him in his misery, he utters his words of wisdom and regret with a depth of feeling and a conviction which never admits a doubt as to the sincerity of his rather sudden conversion. With an intensity rarely exhibited on our stage, as he sits in lonely grandeur in his chair, Mr. Irving depicts with surpassing effectiveness the soul struggle which rends the heart and intellect of the great statesman who now, in his disgrace, remembers perhaps for the first time that he is a Christian priest. . . . No wonder if after an exhibition of such art as that displayed throughout the whole of this trying scene, when the curtain at last slowly descended on the retreating form of the humbled and sorrowing man, the deeply moved audience insisted on its being lifted again and again.'

Irving's Wolsey induced several unbelievers of long standing to conversion and penitence. Before the production Robert Lowe and William Archer had collaborated in an article which, after tracing the play's history, encouraged the public to expect 'a somewhat loftier view of the famous churchman' than Charles Kean or Phelps had taken. Archer was as warm as his colleagues in praising Irving both as actor and stage-manager. Lowe was moved to timely expiation. 'You will see,' he wrote to Irving, calling attention to certain articles he had written in praise of Shakespearian productions at the Lyceum, 'that I have said a few words of implied regret for a certain notorious pamphlet[1]—one of the sins of my youth.' Several critics saw in Irving's Wolsey a physical and characteristic likeness to Cardinal Manning—a topical comparison inspired no doubt by Manning's death a week

[1] *The Fashionable Tragedian.*

after the production. Not all those who made this comparison did so as forcefully as Sir Robert Peel, a picturesque Tory who had just suffered a political eclipse as complete as Wolsey's through allying himself to the cause of Irish Home Rule:

9 *Spring Gardens*,
March 18*th*, 1892.

'My Lord Cardinal,

and under the spell of last evening's representation it is impossible to address you otherwise, I must thank Your Grace for giving me the opportunity of seeing the performance under such favourable circumstances. The stage effect was really admirable; the blond and blithesome King excellently well portrayed and in the sweet delineation of her character there was a tendency and a dignity worthy of a queen, and if I may make bold to add Your Grace just looked what Wilberforce once said of Manning, "the very incarnation of evil".

I am Your Grace's humble and obliged servant,

Robert Peel.'

4

The malign depression which Irving had felt in the autumn was deepened by personal anxiety which marked the turn of the year. Toole had returned from Australia a sick man. While he had been there he had written racy accounts to Irving of his success and had tempted him with promises of glittering rewards that were his for the taking if he would venture so far afield. Irving had missed his friend and now was sad to find him, on his return, tired and dispirited— the early symptoms, perhaps, of his painful and tragic decline.

During the third performance of *Henry VIII* news was brought to him that Laurence, who was in Belfast with the Benson company, had been wounded by the accidental discharge of a pistol and that his condition was critical. Harry, on hearing this news, had come from the Garrick Theatre to the Lyceum where he found his father looking pinched and aged. Later reports were more reassuring, though the circumstances of the accident were mysterious and therefore disturbing. It appeared that Laurence had returned in the afternoon from a rehearsal to his lodgings with a fellow-actor, Hippisley, with whom he shared them. He and his friend had agreed to study their words until tea-time and they went to their separate rooms. Shortly afterwards Hippisley heard a loud report and, running to Laurence's room, found him writhing on the bed in great pain from a wound in

George Bernard Shaw: Man of Destiny

From a drawing by Sir William Rothenstein

Henry Irving: Man of Distinction
From a drawing by Sir Max Beerbohm

his chest which was bleeding profusely. A revolver lay upon the floor. In a short time three doctors arrived; they found that the bullet had entered the chest, had passed through the lung and had lodged in the muscles of the back. No satisfactory explanation of the accident was forthcoming. The pistol was of foreign make; Laurence was said to have been in the habit of carrying it since his travels in Russia. Absent-minded and hopelessly unpractical, he was the last person in the world to be trusted with fire-arms which were a far greater danger to himself than to any imaginary assailant. It was assumed that the pistol had gone off while he was examining it; there was, of course, the possibility that he had tried to take his own life, but there seemed to be no motive whatever for his doing so, unless too deep drinking at the wells of Tolstoy and Dostoievsky had affected his mind. Outwardly, he had shown no sign of abnormal melancholy, in fact he was very much liked by the rest of the company for his cheerful and unassuming manners. Irving sent his own doctor to report on the boy's condition; his mother had gone to Belfast as soon as the news of the accident had reached her. There was nothing more to be done. In a month or two Laurence was well enough to make his first appearance in London at Toole's theatre in Pinero's old part in *Daisy's Escape* and later as Andrew M'Phail in *Walker, London*.

Harry's failure at the Garrick and Laurence's unlucky accident were setbacks to the closer understanding which Irving so earnestly desired to establish with his sons. Though they had grown to admire their father, their sense of failure, of which he had warned them, made them more reserved and suspicious in their approach to him. Irving may have wondered if they were envious of the favoured position which Ellen Terry's son seemed to occupy at the Lyceum, where he had just added to his earlier successes by his performance as Cromwell. It was hard, no doubt, for them to realize that, having no parental responsibility for young Craig, he was indifferent to the harm this early preferment, at his mother's request, might do him; whereas he cared far too much for his own sons to watch them being spoilt by the flattery and favouritism they were bound to encounter in his own theatre.

Not long before, he had told William Winter of his regret that he saw so little of them. 'They say,' he wrote, 'we see ourselves in our children. I have not realized that—I always had and have to fight my way—theirs has been too smooth. They are both clever and have good prospects—if they will only strive to reach them.' Irving had smoothed the way not only for his sons but for his whole profession; the scene of his own early struggles had been struck and could not artificially be reconstructed. It remained to be seen whether genius or talented mediocrity would flourish in the refined and cultivated theatre which he had laboured to create.

5

Henry VIII played to packed houses throughout the fourteenth season which ended on July 30th. During May, Irving had revived *Richelieu*, thus inviting comparison of his twin portraits of political churchmen. Though the public were under the impression that this had been one of the Lyceum's most successful and splendid seasons, the accounts at the end of it showed a loss of £4,000. The cost of the production, nearly £12,000, was hard enough to recover; the weekly running costs, which averaged about £1,800, were crippling. These figures were disturbing. Irving had decided to produce *King Lear* early in the following season. Though the initial cost would be far less, he could not hope to reduce substantially the steadily rising running costs and the risks of *Lear* as regards both his ability to play the part and its popularity with the public were infinitely greater.

During April, Irving gave evidence before the Select Committee of the House of Commons, which was enquiring into the licensing of theatres and music halls. At about the same time, William Archer and his friends of the Independent Theatre Society opened their campaign, with a salvo of satire and ridicule, for the abolishing of the censorship of plays by the Lord Chamberlain. Irving, before the Committee, made it clear that he and his colleagues would be jealous of any interference with the prestige given by a licence coming from the representative of the Crown, and opposed the granting of licences to perform stage plays in music halls which he described as 'taverns which had obtained licences for music and dancing'. He defended the existing censorship, although two of his plays, *Robert Emmett* and *Mahomet*, on which he had spent a considerable sum of money, had been abandoned on the advice of the Lord Chamberlain that their performance would be politically undesirable. He realized the absolute protection against police or private legal action which the Lord Chamberlain's censorship, exercised beyond the sphere of private influence or party strife, gave to theatre managers who, under a lesser authority, would be ever at the mercy of energetic cranks or of powerful religious or political associations.

On July 6th, Irving was out of the bill. He had gone to Dublin, in company with Alma Tadema and Leighton, to have conferred upon him by the provost of Trinity College the degree of Doctor of Letters, 'which, I suppose they have made me,' he wrote to Burnand, 'owing to my vast correspondence'. When those who had received their degrees emerged from the Examination Hall into the Quadrangle Irving was picked up and borne upon the shoulders of the cheering students to the steps of the dining-hall, where he was called upon to make a speech. For this he was unprepared, but he was able to satisfy his audience with a few lighthearted words. He had, however, prepared very carefully a speech which he proposed to deliver that evening at the Tercentenary banquet. It was, after all, the first occasion when an actor had been given an academic degree by any university. Owing, however, to a misunderstanding, Drama was mute at this feast. Leighton was called upon to respond to the toast of the Arts; unaware that as President of the Royal Academy he was the official mouthpiece of the Arts of Great Britain, he confined himself to the subject of painting. There was no toast to the Drama to which Irving naturally would have responded. The Dublin press, stimulated no doubt by Stoker, who had accompanied Irving to his old college, were quick to resent this apparent slight to their darling actor. The Faculty was embarrassed. News of this pother reached England and the ears of Leighton, who wrote at once:

> *2 Holland Park House,*
> *July 19th, 1892.*

'Dear Irving,
    A rumour reaches me that ill feeling has been created amongst some members of your profession because I did not include your name in my response at Dublin the other day; I should be greatly concerned if any such feeling were really entertained and pained if you shared it in any degree and thought me capable of wittingly putting a slight on so old a friend as you are and a man of so much distinction. . . . I trust that my feeling in regard to Drama is too well known to you to permit of your harbouring any resentment in this matter—for no one I am sure received more sincere pleasure from the ovation you received at Trin. Col. than

> Yours always,
> Fred Leighton.'

Irving at once gave Leighton absolution, though he was determined that in future his art should not be bundled into the portmanteau of Burlington House. The Lyceum closed, the London season was at an end. Leighton, increasingly weary of the tiresome and enervating duties which his position in society imposed upon him, sought refuge in his lonely cottage at the foot of the cliffs near Whitby where, in monastic isolation, he found peace and recreation by the sea's edge. Irving went west to Boscastle to rest and relax among the fisherfolk of Cornwall. But in his pocket was a much-pencilled copy of *King Lear*, and in his mind's eye the stage of the Lyceum seldom was wholly obscured by this much-needed change of scene. He had been there but a few days, stretching his legs along the cliffs towards Tintagel and putting to sea to fish or watch the seals in the caves beyond the harbour, when he wrote to Ellen Terry to say how surprised he was to find himself, at his time of life, having to *study* a Shakespearian part—for hitherto those that he had played, including Hamlet, he had known all his life. He made no bones about the difficulties of playing Lear, commenting shrewdly on those passages in the play in which he was likely to succeed and those in which he would find difficulty or even fail. He had, in fact, been studying the part since January. 'This,' wrote Ellen Terry in her diary, 'is what only a great man would do at such a moment in the hottest blush of success. No swelled head— only fervent endeavour to do better work. The fools hardly conceive what he is.'

Graham Robertson joined him for a few days at Boscastle. Rarely can a more curiously assorted couple have been seen striding over the turf-carpeted cliffs. The gaunt, lanky and taciturn actor, dressed like a game-keeper in loosely fitting and full-skirted tweeds, his muller-cut-down perched over his right eye against the wind; at his side the fragile, volatile and gay young painter whose almost tubular elegance Sargent was at that time recording on perhaps his finest canvas; and at their heels a no less incongruous couple—the rather portly, self-indulgent and essentially cockney fox-terrier, Fussy, with the chic, well-groomed and cosmopolitan poodle, Mouton. Graham Robertson always remembered an incident which perfectly illustrated Irving's jack-daw habit of mind—never missing a trifle to add to his actor's hoard:

'Once, during a walk, when we were discussing some totally different subject—probably dogs—he stopped and, gazing fixedly at me, demanded, "Where am I going to get that feather from?"

"Feather?"

"Yes. *You* know—when I say 'This feather stirs, she lives'. What am I doing with a feather in my hand? Where did it come from? Did you ever see Lear acted?"

"No," said I.

"That's a pity; you might have remembered. I saw in a book that Macready used to pluck the feather out of Edgar's helmet, but I can't do that."

"Why not?" I enquired.

"Why not? Why if I started plucking feathers out of Terriss the whole house would roar. What *can* I do?"

We sat down and became gradually aware of feathers, quantities of feathers lying about on the grass.

"Here are feathers," said Irving slowly. "Any amount of 'em—and the scene is by the sea—just like this. I'll have a feather tacked to the stage-cloth just where I kneel beside Cordelia; then I can pick it up and—there I am."

He gathered up a few feathers thoughtfully. Next day I found him near the same spot, his handkerchief full of feathers.

"I'm going to keep them and use them in Lear," he said, displaying his take. "I shall like to feel they were picked up by the sea—real sea-birds' feathers."

"Ye-es," I said, regretfully, "but you know, those are all *hen's* feathers. They've blown out of that yard—somebody has been plucking a fowl."

"Ah," said Irving, with one of his curious staccato grunts, and emptied his handkerchief. The feathers had lost their powers of inspiration—why could I not have held my tongue?'

Towards the end of his holiday, Irving, hearing that in the village lived an authentic witch, sought her out in the tiny white-washed cottage to which he had been directed. After all, in his childhood, witchcraft had been as tangible as Wesleyanism; and had not he, as a boy, twisted the tail of the Halsetown Hecate. Getting no response to his knock on the door, he opened it and peered into the gloom. Gradually he discerned a pair of eyes fixed upon him, and then the crooked figure, not of a witch, but of a wrinkled old woman of great age who, when awkwardly he questioned her, disclaimed all know- of witchcraft and spells—adding that if she had any she would have used it to cure her crippled husband who had lain for several years, like a dead man, in the garret. Abashed and ashamed of his curiosity, Irving was glad when a buxom woman, her daughter, came in and asked him to share their tea. Soon they all became friends while Fussy and the witch's cat sat amiably by the hearth. He stayed long enough to discover that the old woman's supernatural powers lay in her ability to keep the home together on four shillings a week. He left, realizing that witches, like so many other things, had changed since he was a boy. On the other hand, the witch's faith in human nature was restored when, at Christmas-time, a large hamper from London was delivered at her cottage and when later she found that in hard times the village doctor was able to help her from a small fund which Irving had left with him before he returned to London.

6

The fifteenth season opened in September with a week of *The Bells*, followed by five weeks of *Henry VIII*, during which Irving rehearsed *King Lear*. Once more he took infinite pains in the creation of atmosphere and period, striving to picture, with the aid of Ford Madox Brown, barbaric Britons camping, as it were, in the crumbling ruins of the Roman occupation. Bit by bit, effects as fine as any he had yet obtained took shape upon the stage. Ignoring Charles Lamb's warning that *King Lear* was too titanic a play to be contained in the theatre and the tragedy so calamitous that it must overwhelm the puny thunder of a stage storm, Irving brought all his accumulated knowledge of stagecraft to the task of refuting this argument.

Irving, sooner or later, had to play *Lear*. Since Shakespeare's day every tragedian of any consequence had played it, and most of them had come out of the ordeal with credit. It was a part through which the great declamatory actors could roar with fine effect. To temper the rantings of the mad old king, of the distracted patriarch, with tenderness and subtlety, was a task which few actors attempted. Of those, only Edmund Kean had been sublime. Lear was his noblest creation; the part in which the flame of his genius burned its brightest in the hour before it was quenched in the flood of calumny and bitterness which overwhelmed him. Hazlitt on the subject could be ignored, for his critical faculty had become atrophied by prejudice and pique. Irving must have studied very carefully Dr. Doran's description of Kean's performance which had appeared in *Blackwood's Magazine*. He may have noted the passage: 'His warmest bursts of passion never removed him beyond the weakness of age; his violence was that of the spirit, not of the frame; it had words and looks of fire, but none of the tempestuous agitation which, had his skill been less consummate than it was, would have revealed strength of body and youth of mind.' It was in restraint and pathos that Kean's Lear excelled all others; in Phelps Irving had seen a reflection of this interpretation.

King Lear opened on November 10th. When Irving first appeared, looking like one of Michelangelo's prophets and magnificently robed, there was a strange stir among the audience as though his perfect embodiment of their mental conception of the character was the promise of fulfilment of their highest hopes. So the more crushing was their disappointment. One of his greatest admirers, Henry Arthur Jones, wrote that on this night he was 'slow, laboured, mannered, uninspired, screechy, forcibly feeble, failing chiefly where all representations of Lear fail'. Irving seemed to fling away all restraint, yet in agitation strength eluded him and he was smothered by the monstrous tempests of his own contriving. When he came before the curtain at the end of the play, Irving said to his audience, who were weary and baffled by three hours of inaudibility and incoherence: 'If our humble efforts have been able to suggest to anyone here assembled one of the countless beauties of this titanic work, we have indeed been amply repaid'; a voice from the auditorium cried, more in sorrow than in anger: 'Why didn't you speak like that before?' A murmur of assent ran through the house. The audience melted away, bewildered by what they had seen and had not heard. A critic asked his colleagues: 'Now who's going to tell the truth about this?'

Behind the curtain, Irving turned to Ellen Terry and asked what the man had meant—had he, indeed, been inaudible? In great distress, she told him that she had not heard a word he said from start to finish. Why, he asked, had she not told him this at the beginning. She reminded him that when, during the dress rehearsal on the previous night, she had offered some criticism, he had rebuked her and had told her that she had put him out of temper with his part. Yet he knew very well one of the causes of his failure. He, like Macready, had made the mistake of assuming a characteristic voice. This had thrown too great a strain upon his weakest organ so that first the assumed voice and then his natural one had completely broken down.

If the critics had returned five nights later when Graham Robertson, who had witnessed the disaster on the first night, saw a new Lear, 'magnificent and terrible in its pathos', the truth might have been told. But it was too late. Their theme was one of wistful regret; their censures restrained, their praises faint. From the wreckage of his performance they were able to salvage his last scenes with Cordelia and his most moving death for commendation. All paid a tribute to his earnestness of purpose and to the majesty of his failure. The actor-manager had many hazards to face—not the least was that, although labouring under the strain of managerial effort and responsibility, it was on his first performance that he was always judged and that this judgment was recorded in the annals of theatre history. Irving accepted the risk.

He was the last man to deceive himself with excuses or to seek consolation in self-pity. His Lear had failed. He believed that he had put into it the best of which he was capable; the depth of his disappointment was measured in terms of the months of labour which had gone to its creation.

7

On the night of November 26th, when Irving returned to his dressing-room after the first act, he found upon his table a statuette in clay of himself as Mathias—Mathias awe-stricken, tensed, his head tilted to catch the sound of ghostly bells, the Jew's bag of gold clasped in his hand. It was the work of Onslow Ford and was later cast in bronze. On its base was inscribed:

LYCEUM THEATRE, 25th NOVEMBER, 1892
Presented by his comrades of the
LYCEUM THEATRE
On the 21st Anniversary of his First
Appearance in *The Bells*
25th November, 1871
25th November, 1892

This token of his people's affection and of the coming of age of his genius made present failure seem of less consequence and future prospects bright with the knowledge that he was secure in their loyalty and fellow-feeling.

8

Lear was kept on until the end of January. At first full houses tempted Irving, ever an optimist, to write to Brereton that 'the play goes triumphantly and is perhaps the most marked success ever in the Lyceum. The audiences are most enthusiastic'. But this enthusiasm was short-lived and the receipts gradually dwindled until the margin of profit grew dangerously small.

After the last performance of *Lear*, Irving gave a supper in the Beefsteak Room to a few close friends; Toole and a young friend of his, Seymour Hicks, a promising comedian and playwright, were among the guests. He was amused by young Hicks, whose sprightly humour and warmth of heart reminded him of Charles Mathews; one day he said as much to Hicks, who obviously was flattered and delighted at being compared to a man of such legendary charm. He gave the young man time to relish his esteem before he added: 'You see, he wore the same shape of collars as you do.' Nevertheless, from that day, Hicks was Irving's man.

The party broke up at seven o'clock in the morning. Irving drove Toole home and an hour later was sitting on the end of his friend's bed, finishing his cigar. At eight o'clock he left, reminding Toole and Hicks that they were to meet him at Waterloo Station at eleven o'clock that same Sunday morning, whence they would travel to Box Hill and to lunch with George Meredith. At the appointed hour Toole and Hicks, more dead than alive, found Irving waiting for them, debonair and incredibly fresh for a man who had given two performances of Lear, had sat up all night and had snatched barely two hours' sleep in the morning. Meredith was now a full-grown and roaring literary lion; his weary guests were perhaps only too glad to sit back and let his high-pitched, energetic conversation flow over them. At one point Irving intervened to ask his host what he thought of the young actresses of the day.

'What do I think of them, Irving? Not very much. Most of them are vulgar young women who laugh from their stomachs.'

Irving refused to be drawn into a discussion on the anatomy of laughter. After leaving Meredith, Irving and his friends, having dined together at the inn at Burford Bridge, returned to London. While they were waiting on the country platform, a party of youths, recognizing the unmistakable figure of the actor whose still dark curls were copious beneath the brim of his curvilinear top hat, began first to comment loudly on his appearance and then to chant a popular song of the period, 'Get Your Hair Cut!' For a minute or so Irving endured their impertinence, his face blanched with anger. Then he advanced upon them. Towering over them, striking them with the thunderbolts of his furious regard (for his eyes could be terrible in rage), he paused with perfect timing before he rapped out:

'Merry fellers, aren't yer. Well . . . get your tongues cut.'

He turned on his heel. Perhaps they had seen the awful expression which had dried up the terror-stricken Pinero when Macbeth beckoned to him as 2nd Murderer and asked for news of Fleance. The merry fellows were struck dumb. On them had been vented all the bitterness and anger of defeat which for weeks had been generating within the steel walls of Irving's studied composure and reserve.

CHAPTER XXX

16th and 17th Lyceum Seasons :
King Arthur, Corporal Brewster, Don Quixote

I

Lord Tennyson had died on October 5th, 1892, a month before the production of *King Lear*. Up to the last his thoughts turned constantly to Irving and to his long-discussed and much-revised play, *Becket*. It was twelve years since he had finished it when Irving, eager as he had been to put on a piece by the Laureate, had said that the estimated running costs (£150 a night) involved too great a risk. Times had changed since then and now Irving would have been glad to keep these costs down to twice that amount. It was not, however, a change in his financial outlook which had led Irving to cheer Tennyson's last hours with the promise that at last his play would be put on at the Lyceum. In 1879 Hallam Tennyson had written to Irving that 'My father feels that so many alterations are needed to fit *Becket* for the stage that he would rather not publish it first and he would sooner that these alterations should be made for you under your guidance than of others'. Whether it was because Irving had been unable to make a satisfactory adaptation or had found that the cutting and reconstruction were more drastic than he dared ask the poet to make, by 1890 the play was no nearer to production. In 1891 Tennyson accepted an offer for the rights of the play from Lawrence Barrett; Irving had agreed to this, and was considering producing another play of his, *The Foresters*. In 1891 Barrett died before signing the contract for *Becket*, and Irving decided that *The Foresters*, although it was already in rehearsal, would not at that time appeal to his public. A less philosophical poet must have been exasperated with these procrastinations and misfortunes. Irving now had an opportunity to study Barrett's version of *Becket*, which gave him a clue as to how to set about its rearrangement. In 1892 Stoker was sent to Freshwater to discuss the matter further. He outlined the necessary changes to Tennyson, who was ill and not unnaturally a little fretful.

'Irving may do what he pleases with it,' he said, perhaps weary of the whole thing.

'In that case, Lord Tennyson,' said Stoker, as though the poet's concession removed the only obstacle, 'Irving will do the play within a year.'

Irving was true to his word. A few days before Tennyson's death Stoker came to see him with Irving's version. The cuts were deep enough to wound the most long-suffering poet, but Tennyson, having recovered from the shock, indicated his approval and resignation. Having pleaded for the restoration of one of his favourite characters who had fallen to Irving's scissors, he dismissed Stoker with his blessing and with a new speech which Irving had asked him to put into the mouth of Becket. When the end was near, Tennyson asked his doctor for news of *Becket*. Having been reassured, he said: 'It will be successful on the stage with Irving. . . . I suppose I shall never see it?'

'I fear not,' replied the doctor.

The dying poet sighed, adding after a pause, 'with a flash of the old pugnacity which had always so impressed Irving: "I can trust Irving—Irving will do me justice" '.

Irving's ultimate possession of the play was to some extent fortuitous. He owed much to Tennyson's stubborn faith in him—a faith which, in spite of all these delays and disappointments, was richly rewarded. Tennyson probably cared more that his play should be worthily presented to the public than that he himself should see it. He had not been a great playgoer. Like many poets, he flirted with drama as a means of expression, but did not bother to study the requirements of the stage. This was a pity, for much of his verse had the authentic ring of the theatre.

As soon as the failure of *Lear* was apparent, Irving pressed on with the preparation of *Becket*. Tennyson's conception of Becket's character gave Irving the opportunity to portray a prelate utterly distinct from his Wolsey and Richelieu—a statesman and soldier transformed by preferment and revelation into a saint and martyr. The poet had done little to elucidate the process of this conversion. In the prologue Becket is the Chancellor, 'flush as May'; at the beginning of the first act he is filled already with the exaltation of theocracy. Thus it fell to the actor to make this transfiguration credible and dramatic. While Irving was studying the part he had at his side the antipathetic essay on Becket by J. A. Froude, whose forceful prose and open hostility to the mediaeval church might have caused him to doubt the sincerity and question the motives of the archbishop's antagonism to the king. He was, however, proof against Froude's anti-clericalism, and he used the book only as an aid to stage-management, underlining with heavy pencil the vivid descriptions of the meetings at Northampton and Montmirail, and scrawling in the margins notes of such theatrically effective details as— 'Becket—monk—always in tears', 'Earl of Cornwall—old', 'Leicester— hunch back', and so forth. For the rest he seemed perfectly to understand what Bryce had seen so clearly when he read the play—'the influence on commerce of the conception of the Church, blending with his own haughty spirit and sanctifying it to his own conscience'. For all Irving's labours with scissors and paste, the play remained loosely constructed and episodic; yet as rehearsals went on Irving seemed 'to tighten it and gather it round him as a rich becoming robe for his superb embodiment of the Archbishop'. Upon Ellen Terry fell the almost impossible task of breathing life into the scenes in which Rosamund de Clifford had been introduced with a naïvety and irrelevancy which were unworthy of the major theme.

Irving, although he was uncertain that the play would appeal to the general public ('dealing as it did,' said *The Times*, 'with the question of ecclesiastical jurisdiction than which nothing could well be more inherently undramatic'), mounted it as handsomely as he could in his desire to honour the poet so recently buried in Westminster Abbey. With Tennyson's warm approval, he had engaged Dr. C. Villiers Stanford to write the music. Stanford had already written oratorios on several of Tennyson's poems, notably 'The Ballad of the Revenge', and his knowledge of church music fitted him admirably to mingle the theatrical and the Gregorian in an effective accompaniment to the play.

Becket was produced on February 6th, 1893, Irving's fifty-fifth birthday. Its reception by the first night audience was rapturous. Here was a new Irving, shorn of mannerisms, clear of diction and moved, it seemed, by an inspiration akin to that which had sustained the man whom was he impersonating. Though the scenery and crowd compositions were as imaginative and masterly as ever, though Terriss played Henry Plantagenet with his usual robust force, though Ellen Terry contrived to lighten the essentially masculine conflict with Rosamund's tenderness, though Genevieve Ward made what little she could of Eleanor's absurdities, all were dwarfed beside the simple grandeur of Irving's Becket. He seemed to lift a romantic poem to the level of tragedy, supplanting pagan finality with a Christian consummation, no less inexorable and tragic in its climax. After each act Irving was called again and again. At the end of the play, in response to storms of applause and to birthday good wishes shouted from the pit, Irving made a very brief speech in which he said that 'it had been for him and for his whole company a very great labour of love to add one more laurel wreath to the brow of the Master, who was so lately with them'.

Certainly since Irving first came to London no play had been received with such unanimous approval. Most of the critics had read the published version, and their notices betrayed their surprise that out of such dramatically unpromising material Irving could have hewn such a strong and gripping tragedy, though all were agreed upon the beauty and nobility of Tennyson's verse. For once they were able to bear witness to a miracle which very occasionally is wrought in the theatre when the intention and expression of a great poet or playwright are realized absolutely in the personality and performance of an actor of genius. William Archer took to task his colleague on the *Pall Mall Gazette* who attributed Irving's success in *Becket* to the fact that it was a melodramatic part in which 'the acting is more important than the thing acted'. 'This is, I think,' wrote Archer, 'unjust both to the poet and the actor. They have co-operated in the strict sense of the word, in a character-creation of remarkable beauty. It cannot be called tragic, but melodramatic still less. How about poetic? I think that is the word that meets the occasion; and, in the slang of the day, it is good enough for me.' Archer flung up his cap with the rest of the critics. He had always been stern and uncompromising in his criticism of Irving; therefore his analysis of this performance explained more clearly than anyone else's the conjunction of forces which enabled Irving to affect so deeply those who saw him in a play which lived only as long as he was able to interpret it:

'It is difficult to analyse the impression produced by Mr. Irving's Becket, and decide how much of it is due to artistic intention and effort, how much to mere physical aptitude. The latter element is undoubtedly of great importance. It would be almost impossible for Mr. Irving to fail in an ascetic, a sacerdotal character. His cast of countenance, his expression, his manner, are all prelatical in the highest degree. Nature designed him for a prince of the church; he would have played the spectacular side of the character to perfection, and I do not think that the diplomatic function would have suffered at his hands. Thus a part of his success of Becket lay in his mere personality, and is to be accounted to him for (artistic) righteousness only in so far as that very personality is a work of deliberate art. Every self-conscious human being is his or her own creator to a certain extent; and this is specially true of actors in general, and of Mr. Irving in particular. But there is much more than his mere personality in Mr. Irving's Becket; there is imagination, there is composition, there is—pray, Mr. Printer indulge me with characters adequate to so startling an averment—there is DICTION. If the actor had relied on his personality alone, and played the part simply as he could not help playing it, there would have been nothing except details of costume to distinguish it from his Wolsey. As it is, the two men are clearly individualised—one may almost say sharply contrasted. Wolsey was above all a statesman priest; Becket is the hero priest. Craft, policy, personal ambition, love of power, were the ruling forces in the Cardinal; the Archbishop was animated by an intense, simple-minded, almost fanatical devotion to the Church, untainted by either subtlety or self-seeking. This may or may not be the Becket of history; it is certainly the Becket of Tennyson, whom Mr. Irving embodies with infinite sympathy, fidelity and charm. Truth to tell, he is no great genius, this Thomas of Canterbury. He impresses us by force of character—by courage and single-mindedness—rather than by vigour of intellect. . . .

. . . In the three or four really vital scenes of the play, Tennyson has sketched a noble and touching figure, assigning to him many noble and touching speeches, full of the true Tennysonian melody. The history may be bad, the dramatic quality, even of these three or four scenes, is none of the highest—but the writing is exquisite. And to this exquisite writing Mr. Irving does ample, almost perfect, justice. Oh, the difference between his diction in *Becket* and in *Lear*. Here he gives us— or at any rate gave us on the first night—clear-cut, beautiful English speech in smooth flowing, delicately cadenced, poetic periods. Many of his lines and sequences of lines were a joy to the ear—one regretted the evanescence of their charm. . . . Mr. Irving shows himself acutely sensitive to the polish and refinement of the verse, delivering it with a smoothness I have never hitherto known him to attain. And let him not imagine that, because this beauty of diction is not consciously recognised by the majority of the audience, it is therefore a thing of no importance. Beauty is beauty, and ugliness is ugliness, however little we may think of analysing or docketing them; and because only a few members of an audience can put into words their sense in the presence or absence of the given quality in a performance, it by no means follows that the others do not *feel* it. If Mr. Irving had *spoken* Lear, especially in the latter scenes, as beautifully as he speaks Becket, we—well, we might have had longer to wait for this production.'

Irving sincerely desired to please and to satisfy Tennyson. A letter, therefore, from Hallam Tennyson meant a good deal more to him than the laudatory published criticism:

> Farringford,
> Freshwater,
> Isle-of-Wight.
> *February 9th*, 1893.

'My dear Mr. Irving,

As more than one dramatic critic has said—*Becket* is a great play: and yours is a noble piece of acting, fine in conception and in execution. Ellen Terry cd not play more beautifully or be more inspired as Rosamund; Genevieve Ward is a powerful element. The putting on of the play and the way in which each individual actor appreciates his part are truly delightful. We are most grateful for all the care and munificence of the production. May you have all the success that you desire.

> Yours very truly,
> Tennyson.

Pray assure your company of our heartfelt thanks. I need not attempt to express my feelings on your touching words at the close.'

Irving told Mrs. Walter Pollock that no play or character had influenced him as much as *Becket*. When she asked him if this excluded older plays and greater poets, he reiterated his belief. 'You know,' said Mrs. Pollock, 'that people talk of your having made the play.'

'No, no,' he protested, 'the play made me. It changed my whole view of life.'

Irving was no poseur. Yet ever since that night when Brodribb went to Mrs. Sartoris's reception in his friend Wyndham's dress suit, he had adopted a pose which, in time, became Irving. Perhaps the mystery of Irving, which even Ellen Terry never penetrated, lay in his ability to be three different Irvings, each of which was authentic. The raffish and companionable Irving, known only by his closest friends; the stern, autocratic yet lovable Chief—the actor-general in the field who made his rankers believe that they were members of a *corps d'élite*, the Irving of the Lyceum; and Irving, the figure-head of his profession, courteous, condescending and reticent, wearing his 'plume of pride'. It was this third aspect of Irving which underwent a subtle change after the production of *Becket*. His manner became slightly pontifical, though without a hint of pomposity. 'This pontifical manner,' wrote Henry Arthur Jones, 'was effective . . . as an assertion of individuality and superiority, while it commanded a much higher and worthier respect and admiration.

It would be made the chief instrument of compassing a nobler ambition . . . as the years passed by, this manner grew more natural and easy to him and it was more often blended with a lofty and winning sweetness and graciousness that easily and softly united with it.'

Unquestionably in *Becket*, Irving established a closer affinity with his public than in any other piece he played; he promoted, in a sense, a spiritual rather than emotional exhilaration in his audience. As Becket he never stooped to play upon their emotions; his rendering of the part was most remarkable for its superb restraint and for the awful serenity of its repressed passion. Thus he came, like Becket, to regard the Augustinian habit which he assumed as the vestment of an officiating priest. Never having forgotten the stern religious precepts of Aunt Penberthy, having striven all his life to wring from the Church a benediction on his art, he persuaded himself that in the performance of Becket, spanning the gulf between Church and Stage, he and his audience united in an act of worship. Irving was a simple man; he could have arrived at this make-believe state of grace in all sincerity, without being suspected for one moment of unctuous humbug.

Walter Pollock, who, like his mother and father, saw Irving plain— the 'Crab' in their domestic circle—came to plumb the depths of the actor's feeling for this play. One night, not long after its production, at supper in the Beefsteak Room, Irving recited Becket's lines beginning: 'There was a little fair-haired Norman maid . . .'—as always, apparently enraptured by them. When he had finished, he said that he doubted if there was anything in Shakespeare to be preferred to them. Pollock was startled to realize that the actor whom he so much revered was capable of such literary irreverence. Accustomed to speaking plainly at Irving's table, he leant forward to challenge what he believed to be a gross overestimate of Tennyson's worth. One of Irving's lieutenants laid a hand upon his arm. 'Don't,' he said. 'Of course I understand your impulse— but you don't know how he feels about this play.' Pollock remained sceptical, but held his peace. Later, when he became aware of the love and sense of mission that the play inspired in Irving, he remembered with gratitude that restraining gesture.

Even after the triumphant first night, Irving, underrating the popular appeal of *Becket*, played *Lear* once a week until the discrepancy in the receipts of these plays made clear that the old king was better dead and buried with Othello and Romeo. In March Irving was summoned to Windsor by Queen Victoria to give a performance of the play by 'her noble Poet Laureate' in the Waterloo Chamber. Once again a production in miniature had to be prepared, and once again the costs of the

Command Performance were borne entirely by the actor-manager. The occasion was the visit of the Empress Frederick of Germany to her mother, who recorded her impressions of Irving in her diary:

March 18*th,* 1893

WINDSOR CASTLE:

Bertie arrived; and he and Louise dined with us four[1] and afterwards Tennyson's play, *Thomas à Becket* was performed in the Waterloo Gallery. Irving acted well and with much dignity but his enunciation is not very distinct, especially when he gets excited.

Ellen Terry as Rosamund was perfect, so graceful and full of feeling and so young-looking in her lovely light dress, quite wonderfully so for she is forty-six!!

The last scene, when Becket refuses to fly and defies his murderers, is very fine and his death and the way he falls down the steps, very striking. The language is very beautiful and so is the incidental music, expressly composed by Stanford.

The performance was over by 12 and we (expecting Vicky, who was much interested) went to the drawing room, all the visitors passing by, after which Irving and Ellen Terry came in. I spoke to them and told them how pleased I was. She is very tall, pleasing and ladylike.'

Becket was probably a good deal more to the Queen's taste than the terrors of *The Bells* or the paroxysms of Shylock. 'It is a very noble play' she told Irving. 'What a pity that old Tennyson did not live to see it. It would have delighted him as it has delighted Us.' Irving's enunciation suffered, as usual, from the nervous strain imposed by the constriction of space and the quality of his audience. The Queen treated the players with every consideration, and had invited Hallam and Lady Tennyson to see the play and to spend the week-end in the castle. She had gladdened Stoker's heart, already bursting with loyalty, by permitting him to send a long despatch to the press after the performance, putting the telegraph office in the castle at his disposal and insisting that the charges were met from the privy purse.

Becket played to crowded and enthusiastic houses until the end of June. The last month of the season was spent in reviving and over-hauling the most popular pieces of the Lyceum repertoire in preparation for the fourth visit to America in the autumn. This was planned to cover a wider field than any previous tour in the United States; the

[1] The Queen, Princess Beatrice, Prince Henry of Battenburg and the Empress Frederick.

Lyceum expeditionary force now numbered eighty-two, the presentation of *Becket* making it necessary to take a chorus master, a harpist and an organist in addition to Meredith Ball, the musical director. It was now vitally necessary to replenish the empty coffers of the Lyceum. The sixteenth season had shown a further loss of £4,000. Against this, Irving had acquired in *Becket* a valuable addition to his repertoire. Assessed in purely worldly terms, the value of *Becket* to Irving was incalculable. Like *The Bells* and *The Merchant of Venice*, it was the kind of breadwinning play upon which every actor-manager had to depend. 'Without one under you,' wrote C. E. Montague, 'the life of brave experiment in the theatre is the high trapeze without the net. They are enterprise's policy of insurance, art's tax-gatherers, like Goldsmith's Natural History.'

2

Directly the Lyceum closed, Irving, with Ellen Terry, her daughter and the Lovedays, left for Canada, where they enjoyed a well-earned holiday until the beginning of September, when they met the rest of the company in San Francisco. The old plays sufficed in the West where Irving had never been seen before. The company worked its way back through Portland, Seattle, Tacoma and Minneapolis, making one and three-night stands. *Becket* was played in America for the first time in St. Paul, Minnesota. A five-week engagement in Chicago coincided with the opening of the World Fair. The population of the town had swollen to 700,000 and on three or four nights the receipts at the Columbia Theatre were over $4,000. At the end of the fourth week, the Mayor of Chicago was murdered, but neither this characteristic tragedy nor the public funeral which followed it had a very depressing effect on theatrical business.

Arriving in New York to open Abbey's new theatre with *Becket*, three days of the engagement were lost owing to the theatre being still in the hands of the decorators. The opening night, when it came, was a gala affair; the receipts amounted to over $6,000. It was hardly surprising, though a trifle disappointing, that *Henry VIII* proved to be the least attractive of the pieces Irving played in New York. Royal succession and reformation were not subjects which were likely to appeal in a Republican city with a large Roman Catholic population. The ingredient in the melting pot which nourished the New York theatre was indicated by the fact that Irving's Shylock was still the most popular of his impersonations.

Two friends and fellow-players of long standing were missing from the New York scene. Lawrence Barrett had died in harness in 1891, and Edwin Booth had passed away in the seclusion of his bedroom at the Players Club two months before Irving began his tour.

After the New Year, Irving played for four weeks in Boston, whither, after making shorter sorties to Philadelphia, Washington and the larger cities in Canada, he returned for a week in March, which ended the tour. Once more he was invited to address the students at Harvard. He chose as the theme of a rather informal talk, Individuality and Self-sufficiency, subjects on which he was perfectly instructed. As usual, the young folk gave him a tremendous reception, and in the evening they and the members of the Faculty thronged the Tremont Theatre to see *Nance Oldfield* and *The Bells*. Afterwards, by way of celebrating the occasion, a deputation of students presented him with a gold medal. Their gesture was more symbolic than they realized. In six months, the transfusion of American gold into the wasted reserves of the Lyceum repaired the losses of two unsuccessful seasons and gave Irving financial strength to provide the new and costly production which his public at home now expected from him. The tour showed a profit of £24,330. As long as he could depend upon the new world and the provinces at home to provide this subsidy, the economics of the Lyceum were sound, even though, for all his labour, it seemed impossible to make any substantial provision for himself.

One of the happiest features of the tour had been the delight with which the American audiences had welcomed Ellen Terry in *Nance Oldfield* which made up the double bill with *The Bells*. All too rarely was she seen in comedy, in which she was incomparable. As Nance Oldfield she had the stage to herself for an hour, and she made the most of it; a less level-headed or modest actress would have been intoxicated by the laughter and applause which her charm and magnetism seemed to excite so easily. Perhaps Irving should have realized that to feel no jealousy of the public's infatuation for her was not enough. More than half her life as an actress had gone by, and of late the parts she had been given at the Lyceum allowed her no more than a limited exercise of her talents. Her single-handed success in *Nance Oldfield* might have made her vulnerable to those who were only too ready to sow in her the seeds of discontent. Irving, devoted as he was to his partner and foremost among her admirers as an actress, was blind to this danger. Yet already a red and provocative fox was sharpening his teeth preparatory to nibbling at the vines of the Lyceum.

3

Irving embarked for England with his whole company on the *Majestic*. During the voyage he kept them busy with preliminary readings and rehearsals of *King Arthur*. He had long been determined to have a play on this subject. Dissatisfied with Wills's attempt, he had asked Comyns Carr, after the poet's death, to lick it into shape. Carr could make nothing of it, but offered to write Irving a new play which he had read to him shortly before he left for America. The reading had been interrupted by loud snores. The author, naturally alarmed, was relieved to see that Irving and Ellen Terry were awake. Fussy was the critic. Irving, however, was not entirely satisfied. While he was in America, he gave the manuscript to William Winter for his opinion; in thanking him for it, he wrote: 'Your notes on *Arthur* are of inestimable value and confirm my own opinion that our play is somewhat languid and lacks ginger. Surprising how thoroughly and quickly you get to the heart of the thing and I could but regret as I read your comments that I not often have such a mentor by my side.' His regret was only wistful; he knew that the task of Irving's mentor would be about as thankless as that of Job's comforter. Carr's blank verse was a good deal better than Wills's, and his construction of the play, though it lacked action, was sound. In order to avoid too direct a comparison with Tennyson, he had gone to Malory for his inspiration; but as Archer wrote later, though no doubt he went to Malory it was hard to discover what he had brought away from him. Often Irving had hammered success out of less promising material; he had already invited Burne-Jones and Sullivan to provide the necessary ginger or, perhaps, the gilt on the Arthurian gingerbread. Anyhow, for the moment, it was the only play he had in his locker.

Another relic of Wills was a full-length play on Don Quixote, which Irving had commissioned six years before. As it had the same weaknesses as *King Arthur*, Irving applied the same remedy. While he was in America he had asked J. I. C. Clarke, a successful New York playwright, to overhaul it, with the result that he had brought away with him an entirely new play on this theme, which only confirmed his suspicion that Cervantes' comedy was too subtle and episodic to provide material for a full-length piece. Not long after the production of *Walker, London*, Barrie had sent him a comedy, *The Professor's Love Story*, which seemed, on first reading, to have possibilities. Irving wrote Barrie a letter which showed his eagerness to encourage young writers and his straightforward dealings in the matter of fees.

August 13th, 1892.

'Dear Mr. Barrie,

The comedy is delightful, like everything you write, and will act, I believe, deliciously. I am not quite fixed about the future but would offer you £100 to let me keep the play for six months and then either forfeit the money or add £400 to the purchase. That is, £500 to include all rights or £6 a night to you whenever or wherever the play should be acted, all rights to be vested in me. This seems a fair proposal —and at all events near enough to consideration. If I should have the good fortune to get the play back I should at once have it printed— —privately of course. I agree with you about Lucy in the last act for if Ellen Terry played it I would like it to be a great comedy part. The "Professor" I know will be a great friend of mine. You have a re- markable way of getting your characters off—always a difficulty with playwrights and players.'

On further acquaintance the "Professor" seemed to shrink in stature; his adventures, however charming, were too trifling to satisfy the demands of a Lyceum audience. Irving forfeited his rights, which were taken up by E. S. Willard. He produced the play during Irving's absence in America; it proved to be, in Archer's opinion, 'a mere patchwork of little mechanical devices, irrelevant anecdotes, wheezes and comic business'. Playwrights seemed to be working in miniature; not one was, apparently, inspired to express himself on the heroic canvas the Lyceum had to offer.

Irving began his seventeenth season in the middle of April with a revival of *Faust*, which, with a few performances of *Becket*, filled the bill until the end of July. By that time he had played Mephistopheles six hundred and sixty times. The short season ended with two perform- ances of *The Merchant of Venice*, the last of which raised over £300 for the struggling Actors' Association.

Before he left on a provincial tour in September, the preparations for *King Arthur* were well in hand. It was unfortunate that the author had put himself, for the time being, in Irving's purgatory for the "false". While he had been away, Carr, having entered into theatrical manage- ment, had lured his son, Harry, who had just been called to the Bar, from the Temple to the Comedy Theatre. Irving was angry because he felt that Carr knew perfectly well how anxious he was for his son to succeed as a barrister, and because he had been given once again parts beyond his powers and had been doomed, consequently, to a second failure. He went, on his return, with Carr to *Sowing the Wind*

in which Harry was playing Lord Petworth, but afterwards left
the theatre without going round to see him. Harry was wise enough, if
not to return to the law, to leave London in order to equip himself for
the profession he had chosen by joining Ben Greet, in whose ramshackle
Shakespearian company he found the training he needed and, ultimately, his wife.

Irving's provincial tour followed the usual pattern—bumper houses,
public and private banquets, speeches, addresses, and the great labour of
an almost nightly change of bill. At the Walsall Literary Institute, he
spoke for the first time of the need for municipal theatres. He drew
attention to the vast funds provided by private individuals for the
endowment of schools of painting and music, and to the comparative
neglect of his own art in this respect. It is doubtful if he had a very
clear idea of the kind of theatre which ought to be subsidized by private
or public funds. He certainly did not cite as an example the only-semi-
endowed theatre that existed at that time—the Independent Theatre
Society, where the production of plays which were unlikely to appeal
to the general public, was financed by private subscription. He would
have been the last to suggest that public money should be used to
nourish the school of Ibsen.

Wherever he played it, *Becket* created a deep impression. At Bristol
he tried out a new one-act play by Arthur Conan Doyle, *A Story of
Waterloo*; it was a study of the last hours of Corporal Gregory Brewster,
a veteran of Waterloo whose wandering thoughts ever returned to the
great day when he had fought under the eye of Wellington. Doyle had
sent him the play in 1892; out of his short story, *The Straggler of
Waterloo*, he had contrived a well-constructed sketch in which humour
and pathos were perfectly blended. It gave Irving an opportunity to
build up a character study of great virtuosity. Many of the London
critics came to Bristol to see him, and returned with news of another
small but exquisite addition to the Irving portrait gallery. During the
tour he modelled and refined his performance until it ranked with his
Louis XI as a presentment of senility in which the vivid and staccato
recollections of the past burst like rocks through the babbling torrent
of second childhood.

The end of the year was clouded by his anxiety for Toole, who was
also touring the provinces, but was in no condition to endure such a
strain. 'At it hard just now,' wrote Irving to his friend, 'day and night.
I'm just home on this blessed Sabbath from four hours in the shop.'
After suggesting they should help Miss Le Thière, who had played with
him in *Hunted Down* and was now living in poverty and distress, he

added, 'I would give ten years of my life to keep you from this tour.' Enjoying, as he had said, prosperity beyond his deserts and deep satisfaction of artistic fulfilment, ten years was little to give out of a future which seemed limitless in time and opportunity.

4

King Arthur was produced on January 12th. Under Irving's hand the arts and sentiments, which distinguished mid-Victorian England, reached their apotheosis in the theatre, springing together into glorious life at the very moment when new artistic ideas and intellectual forces were getting ready to sweep them impatiently into the dustbin of discarded aesthetic principles. Burne-Jones's ethereal and bloodless heroes were clothed in the substantial flesh of the Lyceum Company; he saw his vision of a landscape, half earthly, half celestial, realized in three dimensions by Hawes Craven and Harker. Comyns Carr's workmanlike libretto—an idyll, as it were, of Freshwater and Kelmscott—was set to Sullivan's operatic music, with sonorous and mellifluous recitatives by Irving as Arthur and Forbes-Robertson as Lancelot. The eternal triangle was gently delineated in sorrowful iambics—soothing the public by calling Excalibur almost for the last time Excalibur, before the spade became all too familiar as a bloody shovel. All hearts but one were melted—even Archer's, who welcomed Irving's latest enterprise as a 'splendid pageant and well-built folk play . . . in producing such a work Mr. Irving is putting his opportunities and resources to a worthy use. In the historic or legendary pageant play he seems to have found the formula best suited to the present stage of his career'.

Irving was the Arthur of his admirers' dreams and perfectly embodied the Arthur of Tennyson (though perhaps less of a prig) for those who knew not Irving.

The results had not been achieved without a good deal of give and take on the part of the distinguished collaborators. Burne-Jones had had no previous experience of the theatre; Hawes-Craven and Harker had never been called upon to execute exactly the designs of another artist. Whereas the latter were accustomed to Irving's imperious demands and ruthless alterations, Burne-Jones was at times put out by Irving's seemingly capricious modifications to his design. When at the dress rehearsal he saw a parody of the Merlin he had designed, he stood up to Irving and ultimately had his own way. Irving's nerves, already taut with the night's anxieties, reacted sharply to a skirmish of this kind. It was unfortunate that shortly afterwards Sullivan, who, in the orchestra, was enduring with growing impatience an interminable wait during a change of scene behind the lowered curtain, tapped loudly on the music stand with his baton and shouted: 'Well—what are we waiting for—Irving, are you ready?'

The green curtain parted. Arthur, in his black Gothic armour, stalked slowly down to the footlights. For a moment or two he peered at the composer over the pince-nez perched askew on the thin bridge of his nose. 'Ready,' snapped Irving. 'Ready—for *what?*'

In the world of the theatre success is balm to frayed nerves and a great composer of differences. 'I don't wish you to think,' wrote Sullivan the next day, 'that I consider the music of such importance as to make it unduly prominent. But I do want you to believe that the interest which I take in the musical portion of your venture is inspired by a strong feeling of personal affection for yourself. My most fervent wishes for tonight's success. . . . ' Burne-Jones's reconciliation was characteristically warm-hearted:

> *The Grange,*
> *49 Northend Road,*
> *West Kensington.*

'My beloved Irving,

Here is a little final suggestion for an amended Merlin, but I will make any changes you think well—if strange writing comes on his borders and breast he will look magical enough.

You look glorious but I am sorry for the spike that came in your way —that I could have put right quickly if I had seen a "proof sheet" of the armour. . . . I could have explained it to the armourer in a moment. For the rest it is a beautiful pageant.

I CAN'T BEAR to have the credit of that work of clothing an army —my sketches and suggestions were no more than hints and clumsy workmen or unintelligent could have made all absurd. All have put their hearts into it.

Some of the faces under the helmets I did not design—some artist with a morbid love of variety is responsible for these—but I was happy and delighted and am always,

> Your affectionate,
>
> E. B. J.'

The first-night audience had been even more scintillating than usual. After the performance, Irving waited to receive his guests at the now customary gathering on the stage. Graham Robertson was among the first to arrive. Irving had recently heard of an oil which was said to be a cure for canine rheumatism. He had ordered two bottles and had sent one to his young friend, for Mouton, like Fussy, was a victim of his master's indulgence.

'Distinguished guests', wrote Graham Robertson, 'were thronging up—each must have a word and a smile—but as I slipped past, he stopped me with a gesture and carried on a conversation under great difficulties which shaped it more or less thus:

"Did you—how d'you do—get the seal oil?"

I nodded.

"Did it—how are you?—glad you were able to come—didn't it?"

I was able to supply the missing word and nodded still more violently.

"Yes, it *did*, something awful . . . didn't yours?"

"Awful—yes—wonderful play—so glad you were pleased—you wouldn't rub *that* stuff—*how* d'you do—into your dog's leg, would you?" '

The reverence and praise which was accorded to *King Arthur* and the immediate registration of its popularity in the box-office made Irving all the more astonished and irritated by the notice of the play in the *Saturday Review*, whose critic seemed to have a heart impervious to the romantic charms of the Lyceum. The notice was particularly galling in that the critic's witty praise of such crumbs of excellence as he could find only accentuated the ridicule which he heaped upon the whole confection. The target of these shafts was Irving, though the path of their flight was given illusory deflections—a word of praise for his momentary flashes of genius, a paragraph of withering contempt for Comyns Carr's hireling verses, and a handsome tribute to Forbes-Robertson's Lancelot. 'But how am I,' wrote the critic, 'to praise this deed when my own art of literature is left shabby and ashamed amid the triumph of the arts of the painter and actor? I sometimes wonder where Mr. Irving will go to when he dies—whether he will dare to claim, as a master artist, to walk where he may any day meet Shakespeare whom he has mutilated, Goethe whom he has travestied, and the nameless creator of the hero-king out of whose mouth he has uttered jobbing verses. For in poetry Mr. Comyns Carr is frankly a jobber and nothing else. There is one scene in the play in which Mr. Irving rises to the height of his art and impersonates, with the noblest feeling, and the most sensitive refinement of execution, the King Arthur of all our imaginations in the moment when he learns that his wife loves his friend instead of himself. And all the time, whilst the voice, the gesture, the emotion expressed, are those of the hero-king, the talk is the talk of an angry and jealous coster-monger, exalted by the abject submission of the other parties to a transport of magnanimity in refraining from reviling his wife and punching her lover's head.'

This banter, though no doubt exasperating, made very little impression on Irving's armour which by now made him more or less proof against personal attack. His assailant, well aware of this, shot a final bolt which pierced the only chink in his victim's harness:

'. . . As to Miss Ellen Terry, it was the old story, a born actress of real women's parts condemned to figure as a mere artist's model in costume plays which, from the woman's point of view, are foolish flatteries written by gentlemen for gentlemen. It is pathetic to see Miss Terry snatching at some fleeting touch of nature in her part, and playing it not only to perfection, but often with a parting caress that brings it beyond that for an instant as she relinquishes it, very loth, and passes on to the next length of arid sham-feminine twaddle in blank-verse, which she pumps out in little rhythmic strokes in a desperate and all too obvious effort to make music of it. I should prove myself void of the true critic's passion if I could pass with polite common-places over what seems to me a heartless waste of an exquisite talent. What a theatre for a woman of genius to be attached to! Obsolete tomfooleries like *Robert Macaire*, schoolgirl charades like *Nance Oldfield*, blank verse by Wills, Comyns-Carr, and Calmour, with intervals of hashed Shakespeare; and all the time a stream of splendid women's parts pouring from the Ibsen volcano and minor craters, and being snapped up by the rising generation. Strange, under these circumstances, that it is Mr. Irving and not Miss Terry who feels the want of a municipal theatre. He has certainly done his best to make every one else feel it.'

The marksman knew that he had inflicted a deep wound to which salt could be regularly applied. The article was signed—G.B.S.

Irving did not need these initials, which so rudely intruded upon the habitual anonymity of the *Saturday Review*, to identify his new adversary. Bernard Shaw had already provoked him with *The Quintessence of Ibsenism*. As long as this uncouth Irishman, who dared to write frivolously about Shakespeare, confined his critical activities to music, the less attention given to him the better. It would be harder to ignore him now that he was on the rampage in the theatre, for which he had so little respect that, according to reports, he refused to fulfil his duties in the uniform dress suit of the critic, and on one occasion, when a manager had looked askance at his bizarre mufti, had threatened to adjudicate a play in his shirt-sleeves. Irving noted, however, that Shaw, like most of his colleagues, had a play in his pocket; indeed, three of his plays had already been produced by the Independent Theatre Society with such little success that even his friend, William Archer, had done his best to convince him that he was no dramatist. Perhaps, like others before him, he would attack the Lyceum until the manager realized that his goodwill was worth an option or two. In short, Shaw differed from his kind only in the violence of his political opinions; since he seemed to share them with that inveterate sponger, Edward Aveling, he could be dismissed as an eccentric and even disreputable addition to the critics' circle. Such, if he considered him at all, was Irving's estimate of Bernard Shaw. Shaw, on the other hand, was obsessed by Irving as the symbol of an outworn romanticism which had to be swept aside if he and Ibsen were to have a voice in the theatre. Irving was an Ogre and the Lyceum his Castle, in which the gifted Ellen Terry languished as a damsel in distress. Like a hero of the romances which he despised, G.B.S. was scrambling up the beanstalk of the *Saturday Review*, with his pen between his teeth, acting in a melodrama of his own contriving in which the villain and the heroine were as yet blissfully ignorant of the parts they were expected to play.

Shaw had written about music for a livelihood; Corno di Bassetto had no intention of becoming a virtuoso on the Basset Horn. He became a dramatic critic as a means to an end, accepting Frank Harris's invitation to the *Saturday Review* with the alacrity of a military genius with an eye for country, seizing an unoccupied strategic position. He no longer found it necessary to seek anonymity in a trumpet when he had reached a position from which he was determined to blow his own. Now he was engaged in a literary operation of war—'a siege laid to the theatre of the XIXth Century by an author who had to cut his way into it at the point of the pen and throw some of its defenders into the moat'. Shaw had, as it were, been born and bred to music; he had to pick up the technique of play-writing as he went joyously along. The critical method which he applied to music would suffice in the theatre— namely, to startle his readers to attention by demolishing their contemporary idols with a series of hilarious explosions. He had championed Wagner by disparaging Brahms and mocking at Paderewski; now he would force the public to listen to Ibsen and himself by decrying Shakespeare and ridiculing Irving.

Having set up his artillery, Shaw had fired a ranging shot at Sidney Grundy's *Slaves of the Ring*, a salute of blank in honour of Henry James's *Guy Domville*, which his fellow-critics had already shot to pieces, a few air bursts over Oscar Wilde's *An Ideal Husband*, and then, having warmed to his task, had let fly with everything he had at *King Arthur*. A less exuberant marksman might have been discouraged by his inability to observe the effects of his broadside on his target. A desire for accurate intelligence on this score may have prompted him to start a pillar-box flirtation with Ellen Terry, although his avowed purpose in doing so was to destroy her belief in Irving and so to lure her from the Lyceum. There is evidence that his hardboiled iconoclasm was not as whole-hearted as he supposed, for some of his letters to her were the expression of arrested calf-love; moreover, at that very moment, he was putting the finishing touches to a one-act play, *The Man of Destiny*, which he claimed to have written expressly for the theatrical partnership he was trying to disintegrate. Indeed, the futile scrimmage between these two great men was a tragi-comedy unworthy of either of them, and, since Shaw continued to worry the bone in public long after Irving had dropped it disdainfully, he had only himself to blame if posterity cast him for the part of the Clown.

Irving and Shaw were, in fact, allies marching towards the same objective. Irving might have been expected to grasp the hand of the man who wrote of the members of his profession 'that they had a deeper claim to be considered, not merely actors and actresses but men and women, not hired buffoons and posturers, however indulged, but hierophants of a cult as eternal and sacred as any professed religion in the world'. Shaw, had he not been blinded by his own combative egoism, might have respected Irving as the actor who had created an audience in the theatre of an intellectual calibre which enabled them, when the lights of the Lyceum were dimmed, to appreciate and support the new school of dramatists for whom he had, indirectly, prepared the way. Instead, Shaw, as he advanced, wasted his ammunition by taking pot shots at his fellow-campaigner, while Irving was unable to recognize his friend through the smoke of his own discharge. It is perhaps doubtful whether, had they reached their objective together, they would ever have agreed as to which of them should occupy it.

5

During the production of *King Arthur*, Irving must have dwelt upon the paradoxical situation in which the Knights of Painting and Music were working in the acknowledged Academy of Drama under the direction of the master-actor on whom no official recognition had as yet been bestowed by a society based upon a system of titular awards. It was true that twelve years ago he himself had declined the honour of a knighthood. Perhaps the time had come to make it clear that his earlier rejection of this honour had been a personal one and should not be taken as a sign that the actor's services to the nation should be denied the recognition that was awarded to painters and composers. Irving found himself in something of a dilemma. He desired no preferment or distinction for himself; no title could add to his stature as an artist or as a citizen of the world. Yet, if he insisted that his profession was as entitled to these rewards as any other and the justice of his claim was admitted, inevitably the accolade must fall upon himself. Fully aware that, though his friends would appreciate the sense of duty which prompted him to take action, his enemies would ascribe it to a desire for personal advancement, he seized the opportunity of an invitation to address the Royal Institution of Great Britain to make public his views on the matter. Choosing as his subject 'Acting, An Art', he came straight to the point:

'My immediate purpose is not so much to deal with the existing classification of the Fine Arts as to add to the recognised number one other, the Art of Acting—that little art which Voltaire spoke of as "the most beautiful, the most difficult, the most rare". The claim that I make is a purely technical one, for the thing itself has long ago been done. The great bulk of thinking—and unthinking—people accept acting as one of the Arts; it is merely for a formal and official recognition of the fact that I ask. The people, who are the students of life, have learned their lesson, and perhaps the professors should now learn it also. In the face of the widespread influence of the stage today and its place in the thoughts and hearts of the people, it would seem about as necessary to vindicate acting as an art as it would be to justify the existence of the air we breathe or the sunshine which makes life joyous; but when we find that the records are deficient, we should, I think, endeavour to have them completed. . . . Official recognition of anything worthy is a good, or at least a useful thing. It is a part, and an important part, of the economy of the State; if it is not, of what use are titles and distinctions, names, ribbons, badges, offices, in fact the titular and sumptuary ways of distinction? Systems and courts, titles and offices, have all their part in a complex and organised civilisation, and no man and no calling is particularly pleased at being compelled to remain outside a closed door.'

He then pressed his claim by reminding his audience once again of the range of aesthetic appreciation and the variety of gifts which the actor needed to bring to life so many other arts in the exercise of his own. 'Acting may be evanescent,' he concluded, 'it may work in the media of common nature, it may be mimetic like other arts, it may not create, any more than does the astronomer and the naturalist, but it can live and can add to the sum of human knowledge in the ever varying study of man's nature by man and its work can, like six out of the seven wonders of the world, exist as a great memory.'

The speech was widely reported. That it provoked no public discussion suggested the tacit acceptance in principle of the wisdom and justice of his arguments. Shaw noted the operative passage and stored it away as a shot in his locker, where it lay rusting until he had to rummage for ammunition after Irving's death.

6

In the course of the seventeenth season *King Arthur* was played a hundred and five times. During March, when Irving was out of the bill for a week or two with influenza, the receipts dropped considerably, but the last performances, like the first, were played to capacity. In the middle of the season Forbes-Robertson left the Lyceum to play with Mrs. Patrick Campbell in Pinero's *The Notorious Mrs. Ebbsmith* at the Garrick. In reply to Irving's telegram of good wishes for his first night, he wrote:

22 *Bedford Square.*

'My dear "Arthur",

Your kind telegram cheered me up very much last night and sent me on to the stage to face an uphill game with a better heart. But what a contrast—Lancelot and the limp wretch I am playing now. My mind goes back to our farewell on Saturday night. My short stay with you has been so delightful to me. But indeed my three engagements at the Lyceum have been the bright sunny spots in my stage life. I do not think you can have any idea what a pleasure it has been to me to act with you, to take up the tone and movement of the scene with you, to play into your hands as best I might. All this has been a labour of love. Circumstances may never permit me to act with you again, but at least I have some delightful memories in connection with you to look back to.

Ever yours truly,

Johnston Forbes-Robertson.

March 14th, '95.'

At the beginning of May, Irving appeared for the first time at the Lyceum in *A Story of Waterloo*. To make up a bill which included Pinero's first one-act play, *Bygones*, he produced what he called *A*

Chapter from Don Quixote; it consisted of two scenes which he had contrived out of the first act of Wills's play and to which he had added interpolations of his own culled from Cervantes.

The play presented a casting problem in the part of Rosinante. It was Loveday's pride that he had never failed to meet his Chief's most extravagant demands. With his usual energy and efficiency he set about finding an emaciated horse with stage experience. As the dress rehearsal grew nearer, Irving made anxious enquiries about his mount. Loveday assured him that he had found the very animal in the North of England. On the morning of the dress rehearsal he told Irving with evident relief that the horse had arrived at Euston. Unfortunately, as the skeletal beast was led stumbling through the streets, it caught the eye of the police, who impounded it, condemned it to the knacker's yard, and issued a summons against its callous owners. Now desperate, Loveday produced a robust and well-covered horse who was a veteran of the London stage. It was led before Irving, ghastly with counterfeit ribs and bones which the property master had striven to suggest with paint. Irving, only half satisfied by this unconvincing substitute, asked its owner if it was trained for the theatre. The man assured him that it was; in fact it had recently supported Mr. Tree in a play and had given every satisfaction, though he had to admit that now and again a passing flatulence had caused it to break wind.

'Mm,' said Irving, now warming to the animal. 'A bit of a critic, eh?'

Those critics who had seen Irving's Corporal Brewster at Bristol noted how he had strengthened and refined his interpretation during the intervening months. His Don Quixote was disappointing. Though, as everyone had foreseen, his physical presentation of Cervantes' hero was perfect, he strove too hard to distract attention from the poverty of the text with extravagantly comic business. This was the more aggravating, even to his greatest admirers, because when he fell upon his knees in prayer before his ill-fitting, junk-yard armour, he suddenly wrung their hearts as he had done as Malvolio. He revealed to them, as A. B. Walkley wrote: 'A noble spirit, however distraught, filled with the solemnity of his mission.' He played Don Quixote because, for so many years, his friends had pressed him to do so; in the event, only those who had never read Cervantes were able to derive much satisfaction from this amorphous charade. The critics, for the most part, warmly applauded Corporal Brewster and dismissed the Don with a caution. W. L. Courtney, who had left Oxford to join the editorial staff of the *Daily Telegraph*, wrote to Irving that his performance in *A Story of Waterloo* had made upon him 'a lasting impression—a memory of mingled pleasure and pain, such as I have not experienced since I saw Salvini act "Othello" and Eleanora Duse "La Dame Aux Camellias". The whole impersonation took one by the throat, as it were, it was absolutely vital and convincing'. Yet the taste of the public was sharply reflected in the box-office. The receipts for *King Arthur*, which was played twice a week, were double those of this alternative programme.

An excess of zeal in Irving's partisans led them to write that Conan Doyle's play only existed in what Irving made of it. This was only partly true. The author recorded that he had sobbed as he wrote it, that every nuance and detail of business he had indicated in the text and that he had been moved by an amateur performance by a real corporal almost as much as he had been by Irving. Irving had been the first to appreciate the masterly detail with which Doyle had drawn his characters; as proof of this, having bought the play, he altered nothing but the title. He had, however, made the part his own, and few who saw him in it ever forgot the truth and human understanding of his portrayal of the old soldier. These extravagant eulogies provoked Shaw into revealing the substance of his antipathy for the Lyceum and all it stood for. He was shrewd enough to diagnose Irving's antics in *Don Quixote* as a blowing off of steam after months of repression as Wolsey, Becket and King Arthur. He even sympathised with him—admitting that he, too, 'had something of the aboriginal need for an occasional carnival in him'. But for Corporal Brewster he had neither sympathy nor mercy. Under the headline, 'Mr. Irving Takes Paregoric', he wrote:

'Anyone who consults recent visitors to the Lyceum, or who seeks for information in the Press as to the merits of Mr. Conan Doyle's *Story of Waterloo,* will in nineteen cases out of twenty learn that the piece is a trifle, raised into importance by the marvellous acting of Mr. Irving as Corporal Gregory Brewster. As a matter of fact, the entire effect is contrived by the author, and is due to him alone. There is absolutely no acting in it—none whatever. There is make-up in it, and a little cheap and simple mimicry which Mr. Irving does indifferently because he is neither apt nor observant as a mimic of doddering old men, and because his finely cultivated voice and diction again and again rebel against the indignity of the Corporal's squeakings and mumblings and vulgarities of pronunciation. But all the rest is an illusion, produced by the machinery of "a good acting play", by which is always meant a play that requires from the performers no qualifications beyond a plausible appearance and a little experience and address in stage business. . . .'

Laurence Irving

G Bernard Shaw. phot.
circa 1902 or 3

Laurence Irving

Irving and a friend at Margate

Shaw, having dissected very wittily the performance with the heartlessness of a small boy dismembering a fly and with the cold objectivity which would have shattered any theatrical illusion, concluded:

'Every old actor into whose hands this article falls will understand perfectly from my description how the whole thing is done, and will wish that he could get such press notices through a little hobbling and piping, and a few bits of mechanical business with a pipe, a carbine and two chairs. The whole performance does not involve one gesture, one line, one thought outside the commonest routine of automatic stage illusion. What, I wonder, must Mr. Irving, who of course knows this better than anyone else, feel when he finds this pitiful little handful of hackneyed stage tricks received exactly as if it were a crowning instance of his most difficult and finest art? No doubt he expected and intended that the public, on being touched and pleased by machinery, should imagine that they were being touched and pleased by the acting. . . .'

Thus he betrayed his deep jealousy of the actor as an original artist and an ignorance of the impulses which govern the actor's practice of his art as deep as that of which he accused Irving as regards literature. He liked actors well enough as long as they were content to follow the directions of a puppet-dangling playwright. Bravura acting left him unmoved; he was unable to comprehend what Irving described as the actor's power 'to arouse the intelligence by the vibrations and modulations of organized sound'. He was constitutionally immune to the spell which an actor of genius can, with the poorest literary material, cast upon his audience; his allergy to the world of romantic illusion upon which the curtain of the Lyceum rose was incurable. His insusceptibility to the forces which have sustained the art of acting through centuries, often barren of dramatic literature, was as inherent as Irving's inability to understand the new generation of playwrights who would use the stage as a platform for the dissemination of their social and political doctrines.

7

On Friday, May 24th, two letters were delivered to Irving at Grafton Street. One was from Lord Rosebery, telling him that the Queen had conferred on him the honour of knighthood in personal recognition and for his services to art; the other was a note of congratulation from the Prince of Wales. Irving summoned Stoker, who found him much moved, and together they drove to Ellen Terry's house to tell her the news. On the following morning his name appeared among the list of new knights in the birthday honours. This time no official enquiry had been made as to his willingness to accept this title. Lord Rosebery had succeeded Gladstone as Prime Minister during the previous year. For a long time he had been on very friendly terms with Irving and was, perhaps, familiar with his wishes in this respect. On the other hand, the fact that official action had been taken so soon after Irving's speech at the Royal Institution suggested that at the time he made it Irving was unaware of the Prime Minister's intention.

'It seemed,' wrote Stoker, 'as if the whole world rejoiced at the honour to Irving. The letters and telegrams kept coming literally in hundreds during the next two days and cables constantly arrived from America, Australia, Canada, India and from nearly all the countries in Europe.' No warmer congratulations were received than those from Coquelin, Mounet-Sully, Sarah Bernhardt and their fellow-actors and actresses in Paris. It was not surprising, for, in that hour, players the world over were conscious of a perceptible change of circumstance; for the first time in the history of their ancient calling one of their number had been honoured by his State. They felt that he had lifted from their shoulders the burden of contumely and prejudice which to a greater or lesser degree each one of them had to bear in the exercise of their profession. On that Saturday afternoon a packed house gave Irving an ovation when he appeared as King Arthur; in the evening a thinner audience gave an even more enthusiastic demonstration of their approval and affection. At one point Irving, as Don Quixote, said: 'Knighthood sits like a halo round my head.' To which his housekeeper replied: 'But, master, you have never been knighted.' Naturally this was a signal for a storm of laughter and cheers. The audience were in no mood to let Irving go without a speech in which he thanked them 'for the appreciation they had shown of the honour conferred through him upon the calling to which he had devoted his life'.

The press all over the world were unanimous in acclaiming this long-delayed recognition of the stage as a social force and in their personal congratulations. Shaw was strangely silent on the subject of Irving's knighthood; perhaps William Archer's generous allusion to it took the wind out of his billowing sails:

The New Budget.
30th May, 1895.

'We may congratulate ourselves rather than Sir Henry Irving on his having at last won for his profession that official honour which carries such weight in the estimation of the British public . . . certainly

Puritanism has received no more decisive facer for many a day than this public recognition of the worthiness and utility of the actor's calling. In a sense, of course, it is a personal triumph for Mr. Irving. There is about his whole individuality a certain native distinction to which many great actors of the past could lay no claim. He has long been recognized as a man of such essential and, so to speak, inward dignity, that no outward dignity could possibly mis-become him. But we may be sure that Mr. Irving himself values more than his personal triumph the victory gained for his profession. It is not as an individual exception but simply as the foremost representative of a great art, that he will wear for many a year (we may trust) his well-won knighthood.'

It had been a strange week for Londoners who were concerned with the arts. Irving's knighthood had been announced on the day that Oscar Wilde was convicted at the Old Bailey. This official exaltation of an actor put a damper on the carmagnole with which the Philistines were celebrating the degradation of a man of letters. Irving must have felt a profound contempt for the members of his profession who were riding to Lord Queensberry's hounds. Irving did not know Wilde very well, though his sons delighted in his company and in his gentle wit. A veiled lady, generally believed to be Ellen Terry, had left a bouquet of violets with a message of sympathy at Wilde's home where, in dazed resignation, he was spending the interval between the two trials; the violets suggest that Irving and Ellen Terry were partners in this kindly gesture. Two years later, when Charles Ricketts went to meet Wilde on his release from prison, among the few messages of encouragement which he brought with him was one from Irving. Wilde had an almost childish love of the theatre—the romantic candle-lit theatre that Irving had created—though his own work ushered in the new school of sophisticated comedy. No doubt Irving was grateful to Wilde for not having involved in any way the all too vulnerable world of the theatre in his own calamity.

Irving was summoned to Windsor to receive his knighthood on July 18th. The intervening weeks were spent in the rehearsal and production of the repertoire which he had planned to take to America in the autumn. He could not have foreseen, when he arranged this tour, that he would land in New York as Sir Henry Irving; but he knew very well that nowhere did such honours excite greater interest and enthusiasm than in a republic where titular distinctions are officially disdained.

On the morning of July 18th Max Beerbohm was crossing the road opposite Marble Arch. 'A brougham passed me,' he wrote. 'It contained

Irving, evidently on his way to Paddington. Irving in his most pre-latical mood had always a touch,—a trace here and there—of the old bohemian. But as I caught sight of him on this occasion—a great occasion, naturally, in his career . . . he was the old bohemian and nothing else. His hat was tilted at more than his usual angle and his long cigar seemed longer than ever; and on his face was a look of such ruminant sly fun as I have never seen equalled. I had but a moment's glimpse of him; but that was enough to show me the soul of a comedian revelling in the part he was about to play—of a comedy philosopher revelling in a foolish world. I was sure that when he alighted on the platform of Paddington his bearing would be more than ever grave and stately with even the usual touch of bohemianism obliterated now in honour of the honour that was to befall him.

Apart from his genuine kindness and his grace and magnetism it was this sense that he was always playing a part that he preserved always, for almost everyone, a certain barrier of mystery—that made Irving so fascinating a figure. That day, when I saw him on his way to Windsor and tried to imagine just what impression he would make on Queen Victoria, I found myself thinking of the impression made there by Disraeli; and I fancied that the two impressions might be rather similar. . . .'

Max Beerbohm's conjecture was not wide of the mark. Normally the Queen, on these occasions, said no more than the traditional words of the ceremony. As she laid the sword on Irving's shoulder she added: 'I am very, very pleased.'

On the following day the actors and actresses of London and as many as were able to get there from the provinces gathered in the Lyceum to witness the presentation to Irving of a congratulatory address signed by more than four thousand members of his profession. They filled the auditorium, while on the stage Irving faced the committee of his colleagues and friends who had organized this impressive tribute. Bancroft was in the chair. After describing the signatures on the address as 'a personal roll call of the British stage . . . the names of the survivors who have done honour to our calling in the past, the names of those who are its most distinguished ornaments now, and the names of those whose destinies lie in the future', he unveiled the gold and crystal casket which had been designed by Johnston Forbes-Robertson to contain this roll. He then read the address which had been written by Pinero. 'It is certain,' he concluded, 'that today every member of our craft is benefited and advanced by the distinction you have so justly gained; and we believe that the debt of gratitude due to you will be acknowledged as fully by posterity as it is by ourselves, your contemporaries. For the history of the theatre will enduringly chronicle your achievements and tradition will fondly render an account of your personal qualities; and so, from generation to generation, the English actor will be reminded that his position in the public regard is founded in no small degree upon the pre-eminence of your career, and upon the nobility, dignity and sweetness of your private character.'

As the cheers of hundreds of his fellow-players rang in his ears, Irving knew that this was the sublime moment of his life, the memory of which neither the successes nor the disappointments which lay ahead could dim. In his reply, he stressed once more that the honour had been conferred rather on their art than on himself. His final words were a simple expression of the deep significance which their action had for him. 'In olden times,' he said, 'our Britons showed their appreciation of a comrade by lifting him on their shoulders and I cannot but feel, and feel it with an unspeakable pride, that you, my brothers in our art, have lifted me on your shields. There is no more honour to come into the life of a man so raised. It puts upon him a new and grave responsibility which I accept with hope and fear—a pledge to work with a more strenuous endeavour for the well-being of our calling and for the honour of our art.'

Perhaps his thoughts turned to the day when as a boy he had stood before Samuel Phelps and had heard the old actor, from the bitterness of his experience, try to dissuade him from going on the stage. Whatever shortcomings he might have as an artist, however far he had fallen below the ideal at which he aimed, he had ensured that never again could a veteran actor, faced with an ardent, stage-struck youth, refer to his calling as an ill-requited profession.

8

The seventeenth season ended on July 27th. It was known that more than a year would elapse before Irving would be seen again at the Lyceum, and the leave-takings were correspondingly emotional. Irving, though in fact his plans were very indefinite, announced that on his return he would produce *Coriolanus*, a new play by Pinero, and Sardou's *Madame Sans-Gêne*. Only the latter was in active preparation. His choice must have been governed by a desire to see Ellen Terry triumph in a part which Réjane had made famous, for he would find it hard to button himself into the tunic of Napoleon. After the performance, in the presence of a great company of his friends gathered together on the stage, the Lord Mayor of Dublin presented him with an address written by Dr. Edward Dowden, which conveyed congratulations on his knighthood from his adherents in that most faithful city.

At the end of August Irving sailed for New York with Ellen Terry and a party of friends. His short holiday in England had been spent with Toole, at Margate. He planned to take a longer one in the Adirondacks before he joined his company in Montreal in the middle of September. Before he left England he wrote to Mrs. James, who was in Cornwall:

'We sail tomorrow and my heart will be with you.

You're having a pleasant holiday I hope. . . . I know Boscastle— a beautiful spot—close to the Atlantic. I shall think of you when crossing. There is every prospect of a good time for us and I hope this is my last visit. God bless you, my dear friend.

Ever yours,

Henry Irving.'

PART V
SIR HENRY IRVING

As an actor, and as a manager, he had his faults; and these faults were obvious. But as a personality he was flawless—armed at all points in an impenetrable and darkly gleaming armour of his own design. 'The Knight from Nowhere' was the title of a little book of Pre-Raphaelite poems that I once read. I always thought of Irving as the Knight from Nowhere.

SIR MAX BEERBOHM
from 'Around Theatres'.

CHAPTER XXXI

18th Lyceum Season : Iachimo, Richard III, Napoleon

———❧———

I

In the Adirondacks Irving found the rest and quiet he needed before setting out on a gruelling tour which, in the belief that it was his last, he had planned to range from Montreal to New Orleans. 'Have begun well,' he wrote to Ellen Terry, who was in New York, '—glorious day and two hours' walk. W(inter?) tells me I must get out in the morning and out in the sun which sets about 4. W. is quite a guide about here. It's very high—magnificent views and pure, fine air. Hotel very comfortable and extremely quiet.'

It was about this time that Irving acquired the habit of committing aphorisms, memoranda and drafts of letters as they occurred to him to small notebooks, which he carried in his pocket. While on this holiday he was trying evidently to convince himself of the merits of *Coriolanus*, for he wrote: '*Coriolanus*—a play not familiar to the public. Seems to be impression that it is a declamatory play—but really not —compared to many of Sh'ksp's tragedies. It is realistic and absolutely natural in expression. John Kemble—the piping, asthmatical John— was, I read, of all actors the most renowned Coriolanus—the greatest Roman of them all—Macready and others failing from a too robustious performance of the part and rendering. The comedy of *Coriolanus* is delicious.'

Nevertheless when he reached New York, after five successful weeks in Montreal, Toronto and Boston, he had abandoned the idea and had decided that *Cymbeline* was to be his next production at the Lyceum. *Cymbeline* was no more familiar than *Coriolanus* to the public, few of whom remembered Helen Faucit's Imogen at Drury Lane in 1864, which was the last production of any account. No doubt he was prompted to choose it by a desire to give Ellen Terry her head as

Imogen; in casting himself as Iachimo he would have to be content with a couple of effective scenes. Apparently Ellen Terry was not deterred from impersonating 'divineness no elder than a boy' by her age; after all, Helen Faucit had been nearly fifty when Henry Morley wrote that 'Imogen, the most beautiful of Shakespeare's female characters, is that in which this lady seems most to delight and to excel'. The play would give him more scope as a producer than *Coriolanus*, though its straggling plot or confusion of plots presented formidable problems in cutting and adapting it to the requirements of the Lyceum. As soon as he arrived in New York, Irving enlisted the help of William Winter in this difficult task.

2

Irving had often to contend with political crises during his American tours. This visit coincided with President Cleveland's stern reminder to the British Government, who were disputing the boundary between Venezuela and British Guiana, of his determination to adhere to the Monroe doctrine. The situation had inspired one of those waves of anti-English sentiment which periodically sweep through the United States. Irving did all he could to allay this feeling, not only for business reasons but because he had a sincere desire to strengthen the friendship and understanding between the English-speaking peoples. His recent knighthood and the new plays he had brought were enough to excite interest and to confound prejudice. At first the American press were a trifle disappointed that he insisted on being billed as plain Henry Irving. Soon they recognized and appreciated the democratic principle which prompted his desire not to be distinguished from his fellow-players by anything but the quality of his acting. *King Arthur* proved to be immensely popular, perhaps for the very reason which Irving, by a happy inspiration, was able to exploit. In St. Louis, when at the end of a performance the audience called for a speech, Irving thanked them 'for the appreciation of this effort to illustrate an old world legend', adding, after an effective pause, '—*your* old-world legend'. This reminder of common ancestry was widely reported and applauded, but it was only incidental to the policy of fostering Anglo-American fellowship which Irving pursued wherever he went.

During the tour *Cymbeline* passed to and fro between Irving and Winter in various stages of dismemberment and with it indications of the rigours which the company were enduring. From Baltimore he assured Winter that he was 'the most practical editor I've met.

Splendid time in Philadelphia. Found the sunny south (I suppose Baltimore is in the south) nothing but snow and ice—suffering from terrible cold and neuralgia'. He had good reason to cherish pleasant memories of Philadelphia, where he had received the sort of tribute which he prized above all others. Eleanora Duse was appearing at another theatre. One day he received a letter from her, signed by all the Italian members of her company, expressing their gratitude to him and to Ellen Terry 'for having revealed to the minds of aliens, through your great talent, and by the proud flights of your genius, the sweet idioms of Shakespeare'. In reply he wrote:

'My dear Madame Duse,

I cannot tell you with what surprise and delight I received, before leaving Philadelphia, the most affectionate letter from you and your Dramatic Company. To have such a commendation of our efforts is indeed a delight to Ellen Terry and myself and we can only thank you again and again for your sympathy, your appreciation and your most sweet courtesy to us. It has been a great happiness to me to meet your encouragement and help. With respect and devotion, believe me, ever sincerely yours,

Henry Irving.'

Having exchanged salutes like stately ships meeting in a foreign port, these two great artists parted company—Irving's heart aglow with satisfaction which fortified him against the chills of Baltimore.

At the turn of the year, on the return journey from New Orleans to Memphis, Irving's special train had to be diverted from the Mississippi Valley where the tracks for most of the way were two or three feet under water—almost up to the fire-box of the engine, which could only travel at a snail's pace. The crossing of the Mississippi was particularly perilous, for the floods, pouring over the bridge, made it impossible to see if sections of it had been swept away.

In Cincinnati, Irving suffered an irreparable loss in the death of Henry Howe. By this time the old actor, now in his eighty-fourth year, was perhaps something of a hazard as a member of the cast. But since old Mrs. Loveday had died in 1893, he had become the last link with the theatrical past which Irving loved so dearly to revive in gossip and anecdote. Howe had been the sole surviving eye-witness of Edmund Kean's *Richard III*, and no doubt his lively memory had during those last weeks been called upon for recollections of Chatterton's production of *Cymbeline* at Drury Lane. In April, Irving was back in Boston. 'You have also, I suppose,' he wrote to Winter, 'been suffering from the heat. It was terrible—95 in the shade and with *Macbeth* upon me also—Ye Gods! Here it is better—though summer, not spring, coming so quickly on our eight months' hard work, is a little trying. I have made a splendid beginning with *The Lyons Mail*. I am much indebted to you for your notes (on *Cymbeline*) and I am cutting and cutting more and more.'

If the Lyceum company found these changes of climate and of temperature hard to endure, the warmth of their reception wherever they went varied as little as the round of interviews, receptions, complimentary banquets, lectures, and the exchanges of after-dinner oratory which had characterized previous tours. Irving sailed from New York at the end of May. On reaching Liverpool, he made a five-week tour of the northern towns before disbanding his company for a short holiday. He seemed none the worse for the strain which a tour lasting nearly a year, with so large a repertoire, must have imposed. Yet the balance sheet showed a comparatively meagre return for this great labour, however deep the satisfaction which Irving, as an artist, had derived from playing to vast and enthusiastic audiences. The American public had paid £116,500 to see him, of which his own share was £75,735; but the expenses had been staggering—nearly £70,000 —so that a profit of barely £6,000 was all that remained after seven months' strenuous work. This would keep the wolf from the stage-door, but it seemed that the beast's appetite, however regularly it was fed, became heartier year by year.

3

News had reached Irving in America of Harry's engagement to Dorothea Baird, a young actress who had recently won the hearts of London playgoers by her performance as Trilby in Tree's production of the play based on du Maurier's novel. He had reached England in time for the wedding, but probably he was thankful that his tour prevented him from attending it or from having to make other excuses for his absence. His wife, who was now deriving a certain grim satisfaction from being Lady Irving, would be a prominent participant in the ceremony—as she had every right to be. He had not seen her for twenty-five years and he felt that his son's wedding was hardly the occasion for such a highly charged and hazardous reunion. In a letter to his future daughter-in-law he wrote:

THE LATE MR. HENRY HOWE AND SIR HENRY IRVING.

(AN INCIDENT AT THE LAST DRAMATIC FUND DINNER)

July 6th, 1896.

'. . . I shall be sorry not to be with you on what, I hope, will be the most auspicious day of your lives. Never mind, we'll make up for it by and by and be together as our days do grow. Much as I should like to be present, circumstances made it impossible.

I am told that brides like sometimes to wear their favourite flower— tell me yours and wear mine . . . my heart will be with you. . . . I think I shall try Bamborough (for his holiday). It is not far from Edinburgh and I shall go on from there. They say, as you do, that it is a beautiful spot and quiet, and that's what I want—without a soul.

Affectionately yours,

Henry Irving.'

The young couple were spending their honeymoon at Bamborough, on the coast of Northumberland, and he was proposing to join them there for a few days when his tour ended. In the meantime, he had to be in London to confer with Alma Tadema, whom he had commissioned to design the costumes and settings for *Cymbeline*, and to deal with several matters connected with the purchase of new plays. His hopes of a play from Pinero had not been fulfilled. At the moment, Sardou seemed to be the only dramatist who was capable of turning out a piece of the scale and structure necessary for the Lyceum. Irving had already acquired the English rights of *Madame Sans-Gêne* and had commissioned a new play about Robespierre. Sardou, who commanded higher fees than any contemporary playwright, had a keen head for business. His envoy, whom he had sent to negotiate with Irving, assured the actor that 'M. Sardou has the whole play on Robespierre in his head, act by act, and would have only to write it down when he has come to an agreement with you'. The terms finally agreed upon were £500 on receipt of the scenario, £500 on receipt of the play, and a further £1,000 if Irving, within a month of the production, decided to take it to America; in addition to these advances the author was to have five per cent of the gross takings. 'This, in the main,' wrote Irving, 'is more than it seems if you compare our business with ordinary business, as since we cannot, with our vast expenses, afford to play to mediocre business . . . the result of percentage on our takings is more than ordinary.' These negotiations were considerably less involved than those which were proceeding for the rights of a one-act play by George Bernard Shaw.

In November of the preceding year Shaw had finished *The Man of Destiny*. The theme, not a particularly original one at a time when

Réjane was playing *Madame Sans-Gêne* all over the world, was a verbose encounter between the young General Bonaparte and a Strange Lady during the campaign of 1796. At the climax of the play, Napoleon had to deliver a satirical diatribe against the English which would have warmed the heart of any Irishman. Even Shaw's mischievous imagination must have boggled at the idea of Henry Irving, in a theatre dedicated to the expression of noble sentiments, chastising the starched and straitlaced Victorian audience with the words: '. . . There is nothing so bad or so good that you will not find Englishmen doing it, but you will never find an Englishman in the wrong. He does everything on principle. He fights you on patriotic principles; he robs you on business principles; he enslaves you on Imperial principles; he bullies you on manly principles; he supports his King on loyal principles and cuts off his King's head on Republican principles.'

The play was prefaced by a character study of the young Napoleon, who apparently had much in common with the middle-aged Shaw, and a none too brief chronicle of the Franco-Italian war; the text was peppered with stage directions and with niggling advice to the players. The author appeared to be ignorant of the business of production or the conduct of rehearsals by a competent actor-manager, let alone by Irving himself. 'What is a Lyceum rehearsal like?' he asked in a letter to Ellen Terry several months later. 'Does H.I. work out all the business at home or does the prompter take it down as it turns up and work out in rehearsing?' He seemed to be unable to credit Irving with the professional integrity which he so volubly claimed for himself. Shaw sent the play to Ellen Terry while she was in America; she had reported that 'H.I. quite loves it and will do it finely', though she warned him that 'it was always difficult to fit a one-act play into the Lyceum bill'. Though Irving may have loved the play at first sight, he did not discuss the purchase of it until he returned to England. Already Shaw was convinced that if he bought the play, he would do so in the hope of corrupting the critic who had written it; he warned Irving that he could have the play only on his own terms—performance guaranteed and payment only on performance. Like a middle-aged spinster preoccupied with preserving a virginity upon which nobody had designs, Shaw flourished his incorruptibility in Irving's face. No doubt Irving had no higher opinion of Shaw, the critic, than of most of his colleagues and would have waited with sardonic interest to see if an option had an emollient effect on his abrasive notices. Nevertheless, in July, ignoring Shaw's demands, he offered him the same terms as Conan Doyle had accepted for *A Story of Waterloo*; seeing that at that time Doyle was already famous as the creator of Sherlock Holmes, they seemed to be generous enough for a comparatively unknown author.

Shaw's correspondence with Ellen Terry, which until these negotiations began had been sporadic, now became an almost daily exchange in which he stimulated his amused agent to put a spur to Irving's hesitancy and applied a goad to her own discontent. Irving, having indulged Ellen Terry's whim, probably forgot about Shaw and his play. A sharp reminder came in an ultimatum from Shaw in which he made three proposals: alternatively that Irving should accept unconditionally his original terms, that he should amuse himself with the play until he was tired of it, or that the author would make him a present of it if he instantly produced the works of Ibsen. This was too much. Irving went on his holiday wondering what had induced Ellen to concern herself with such an eccentric protégé.

4

From Bamborough Irving wrote to Toole:

Victoria Hotel,
Bamborough.
August 7th, 1896.

'My dear Toole,

A cheery letter from Lowne—we shall meet during the few days that you are in London. I shall be back about the 20th. He says you're in Scarborough on the 31st. One could wish the holiday had been longer—for your last was a very long season—but one thing I am sure will be better—playing the old things instead of the new ones.

Parkinson[1] was here for a few days and went driving and fishing, and caught a few excellent sprats which we took home and had for dinner. And who do you think are here now—the young bride and groom. They are very happy—God bless 'em, and the more I see of her the more *our* opinion is confirmed.

I shall try and get to North Berwick for a week to finish off work. N.B. is difficult to get in to I hear, and full of golfers. . . . I greatly look forward to seeing you, when we will talk over our late doings. All love and affection, my dear Toole,

Henry Irving

Ellen is in Winchelsea and greatly rested, and her eyes much better.'

[1] Joseph Parkinson, at that time chairman of the Reform Club.

Ellen Terry needed all the rest she could get. Rehearsals of *Cymbeline* began at the end of August. Her prolific correspondent now turned his attention to coaching her in the part of Imogen, proposing cuts in her speeches and threatening vengeance if *Cymbeline* was not to his taste. She managed to hold her own with her self-appointed tutor and to work as loyally as ever with Irving towards their common purpose. It was hardly surprising that on the eve of the production, when her indefatigable pen-friend wrote that he must 'go to bed betimes to be prepared for the slaughter of *Cymbeline*', she could find in herself 'no inspiration, no softness, no sadness ever. . . . I feel nothing . . . my head is tired. I can't care, can't think, can't feel.'

Cymbeline was produced on September 22nd. 'Well,' wrote Irving to Winter, 'we are launched and pretty stiff work it has been. At it day and night for the whole season but the result has been triumphant.'

The reception of this little-known play justified to some extent what Irving must have known to be a risky experiment. Ellen Terry, in spite of her misgivings, charmed everybody with her Imogen. Irving, by playing Iachimo and trimming other parts to disguise the inherent inadequacy of his own, upset the balance of the play; but the critics were indulgent. 'Sir Henry's Iachimo,' wrote Archer, 'is not a slight thing at all. He is a subtle, tenebrous, deadly creature, beside whom Posthumus, in the person of Mr. Frank Cooper, is a very slight thing indeed. But his acting is extremely artistic, both in what he does and in what he refrains from doing. He seemed to me, in fact, to refrain almost too sternly from the cheap by-play of the commonplace villain. There were times, for instance, in the scene with Imogen, when his show of moral earnestness almost took me in for the moment. It is a nice question whether it be not an over-refinement, a super subtlety, to let the audience forget that he is playing a part within a part.'

Shaw dismissed the play as stagey trash, trounced most of the cast, rhapsodized on Ellen Terry and found 'that this Iachimo was quite fresh and novel to me. I witnessed it with unqualified delight; it was no vulgar bagful of "points", but a true impersonation, unbroken in its life current from end to end, varied on the surface with the finest comedy and without a single lapse in the sustained beauty of its execution'.

Shaw's criticism was just and discerning, but in order to pad himself out to fill the part of the Incorruptible, he made out to Ellen Terry that it was all very ferocious and provocative. For Irving had summoned him to conference; perhaps he took these words of praise as a signal that after all an option would be acceptable. 'I shall see him,' wrote Shaw, 'with the Saturday article (which he will get up at five in the morning to read) up to the hilt in his heart. Unfortunately he will have the satisfaction of getting the better of me in personal inter- course. In correspondence I can always maintain an iron consistency, in conversation I shall get interested in *him* and forget all about the importance of my rubbishy little play. . . .' When Irving had announced his forthcoming production of *Madame Sans-Gêne*, Shaw realized that with two Napoleons in the field the chances of his own candidate were dwindling. He had, therefore, taken the offensive:

> 29 *Fitzroy Square*,
> *W*.
> *September* 23rd, 1896.

'Dear Sir Henry Irving,
    May I take it that your announcement of Sardou's Napoleon dis- poses of mine as far as the Lyceum is concerned and that I am free to submit the piece, for the first time, in other quarters?
    After your very kind expression of interest in the play, I do not like to act in the matter without a final word from you.
> Yours sincerely
> G. Bernard Shaw.'

Irving's answer had been an invitation to talk over the matter. What occurred at this encounter, probably one of the strangest in theatrical history, will never be known. Ellen Terry intended to be present, but her courage failed her when she reached the door of Irving's office. 'Heard your voice,' she wrote to Shaw, 'and then skedaddled home again full tilt and, oh, I was laughing. . . .' Oddly enough, neither Shaw nor Irving seem ever to have confided to Ellen Terry the gist of their conversation. Years afterwards Shaw wrote to Laurence: 'Your father did not like me, partly in consequence of an interview at which I demagnetized him (quite unintentionally) and made him uncomfortable. . . . But I was much too conceited to be unfriendly; and if he had only had your extra inch or two across the forehead, we should have got on excellently.'

5

Irving's managerial intuition had not failed him. He had predicted to Ellen Terry that *Cymbeline* would play to capacity for ten weeks (its running costs demanded no less), which it did. Yet after seventy-two performances it had failed to recover its cost of production. At the beginning of December, while *Richard III* was in rehearsal, Irving played *The Bells* two or three times to bolster up the flagging receipts. One of these performances was on November 25th—the twenty-fifth anniversary of its original production. Irving played Mathias as vigorously and terrifyingly as ever. He did not allow the occasion to pass without reminding his audience of the debt he owed old Bateman. When the curtain fell for the last time he turned to find his whole company and the staff of the theatre assembled on the stage. In their midst was Alfred Gilbert, the designer of the great silver bell nearly two feet high and in the style of Cellini, which was presented to Irving as a memento of the occasion. Gilbert had designed it as a labour of love and as a token of his own admiration for Irving; everyone in the theatre had contributed to the casting of it; round it ran the inscription: 'Honour to Irving. Through the love of his comrades. I ring through the ages.'

Irving was deeply touched by this token of the continuing loyalty and affection of his company after all those years. He had been a hard master, insistent on discipline, relentless in rehearsal and often merciless in his withering sarcasm; but, like all good commanders, he asked of them no more than he gave himself, and they knew that if any of them were in trouble of any kind they could look to him as a sympathetic and generous friend. Among them were several needy actors, mostly companions of his earlier days who drew their salaries in return for nominal services, while his list of pensioners grew year by year. Yet there were inward and scarcely visible signs of stresses and discordances which were at variance with this outward and visible demonstration of their unity and grace.

Inevitably cliques and factions had begun to disrupt this unity; the principals in one Green Room became the subject of whispering gossip and partisan arguments among the junior players in the other. Tongues had begun to wag over Ellen Terry's undisguised partiality for Frank Cooper. Cooper had played Laertes to her Ophelia when she first came to the Lyceum, and now, after a long absence, he had rejoined the company to play Mordred in *King Arthur*. Lena Ashwell was playing Elaine and was a newcomer to the Lyceum. She had been deeply distressed to discover an undercurrent of petty rivalries and conspiracies in what she looked upon as a hallowed temple of the art in which she was so earnest an initiate. One night Irving, in the wings, found her in tears. 'Is there anything I can do?' he asked, adding by way of kindly consolation, 'You know—we were born crying.'

Later, even Shaw got wind of this affair; there was a hint of platonic jealousy in his quizzing of Ellen for her attachment to Cooper: 'Quite a pretty, amiable-looking, chubby fellow off the stage, with a complexion as charming as wig paste. Perhaps it *is* wig paste. Why can't he be taught to act? Has he *NO* intelligence?' Irving, of course, was fully aware of all this and no doubt annoyed by it in so far as it affected the morale of his company. He gave no hint of his irritation until one day, during the rehearsals of *Cymbeline*, Cooper, in an excess of zeal nourished by his embarrassment and by his Chief's frigid taciturnity, asked his approval of a certain piece of business. Irving strode up to him, seared him with his terrifying glare and rapped out: 'Write to me!' Cooper remained in the company; he was one of Ellen's many foibles —arriving late at the theatre, giggling on the stage, forgetting her words, and Bernard Shaw—which Irving overlooked on account of the affection and admiration he bore her.

6

Aunt Penberthy had likened her nephew to 'a comet blazing over the wide world'. During the night of December 19th, 1896, that comet, flashing upwards on its determined orbit, burned for a few hours with peculiar lustre at its zenith. The first night of *Richard III* set Irving on the peak of his achievement. Ellen Terry, it was true, was not playing with him. During the run of *Cymbeline* she had been far from well and was suffering from a recurrence of her old eye trouble. The women's parts in *Richard III* were not of much account, so that she was able to follow her doctor's advice to take a cure in Germany before she began rehearsals for her strenuous part in *Madame Sans-Gêne*. The house was crowded with those old enough to remember Irving's earlier production, who whetted the appetites of the younger generation of playgoers with vivid assurances of the treat that was in store for them. Perhaps it was the old story of first-night nerves and physical exhaustion; whatever the cause, Irving's performance did not come up to their expectations. His first Richard had been what Archer called one of his 'grotesque, diabolic' impersonations; that night he allowed grotesqueness to get the upper hand and, in so doing, failed to express Richard's subtle hypocrisy. At times he seemed, as it were, to throw his arm round the shoulders of the audience and, with an evil leer, to make them party to his ghastly conspiracy, with the cynical detachment of a monstrous chorus—thereby undermining any sympathy that the audience might have had for Richard's victims. His diction was perfect, even to Archer's 'syllabically punctilious ear'. He tended to trip the rhythm of the piece with over-long pauses which weakened his grip upon the audience and gave them time to reef their emotions to meet the storms of his intensity. Nevertheless the old spell was as potent as ever; if the elderly wagged their heads during the intervals over sage comparisons, the young, to whom Irving's interpretations and the restored text were a revelation, carried away with them a lasting impression of incomparable acting and production. J. F. Nisbet, the critic of *The Times*, spoke for them:

'Irving's personality happens to be peculiarly rich in the elements of the weird, the sinister, the sardonic, the grimly humorous, the keenly intellectual; and any character into which these qualities can be introduced by him remains indelibly stamped upon the mind as a great creation. As a compendium of the Irving personality, I am not sure that Richard does not excel in considerable measure both Louis XI and Mephistopheles. The new Richard holds the spectator as securely with his glittering eye as ever did the Ancient Mariner; and a curious effect, which I have never seen before remarked at the Lyceum, where so high a standard of excellence is maintained, is that in the presence of this colossal Plantagenet villain all the other dramatis personae are dwarfed to nothingness. Absolutely Irving's Richard is the most Satanic character I have ever seen on the stage.'

Henry James was there. He was still immune to Irving's sorcery—he confessed that he found a first night at the Lyceum, with its excess of Irvingism, hard to bear—yet in his comparative analysis of Irving's two Richards there were signs that his resistance was weakening:

'. . . Sir Henry Irving's Richard III is not his first playing of the part, but it is his first presentation of the piece. Upwards of twenty years ago it was produced at the Lyceum by the management immediately preceding his own, and was then one of the successes which presumably determined him to take over the theatre from failing hands. His Richard of those days, as I remember it, strikingly showed his gifts, but he has had the artistic patience, all these years, to leave the character alone. His gifts have not changed, though they have visibly developed, and his power to use them has matured. His present creation has the benefit of this maturity, though I seem to remember that even the earlier one, when so much of his reputation was still to come, had that element of "authority" which is a note by itself in an actor's effect, independent of the particular case, and almost as distinguishable in what he does worst as in what he does best. What Sir Henry Irving does best, as happens in this instance, is exactly what he does with Richard—makes, for the setting, a big, brave general picture, and then, for the figure, plays on the chord of the sinister-sardonic, flowered over as vividly as may be with the elegant-grotesque. No figure could have more of this livid complexion and Gothic angularity than, singly and simply seen, the monster drawn by Shakespeare. Singly and simply—in this light —Sir Henry Irving sees him, and makes him, very obvious yet very distinguished, hold the Lyceum stage with any of his predecessors.'

After the performance, five hundred guests thronged the stage, pressing round Irving to exchange congratulations for a word of welcome. It was midnight before the last of them left the theatre. The strain of playing and the exhilaration of applause combined, as always, to coil the springs of Irving's nerves; rest or sleep were out of the question until the springs relaxed. With his friend, Professor James Dewar, Irving went on to the Garrick Club, where he joined the usual Saturday-night gathering at supper. In the early hours of the morning they walked together to Dewar's rooms at the Royal Institute in Albemarle Street, where for a time they sat smoking and talking—as usual, about the theatre. When Irving decided to go home, Dewar walked with him to Grafton Street; over another cigar they continued their conversation. It was dawn before they parted. Irving was relaxed and ready for sleep. It was his habit, however late, to take a bath before going to bed. On his way up the narrow stairs he slipped and struck his knee against a chest which stood upon the landing. He managed to reach his bedroom, but at the cost of aggravating the injury. The next morning Walter found him in considerable pain and unable to move his leg. He sent for a surgeon. Irving had ruptured the ligatures of his knee cap and would be unable to play for some weeks.

7

For the first time in his life Irving found himself an invalid—disabled, idle and cut off from his theatre and his work. This sudden interruption of the rhythm of his working life emphasized an exhaustion which was more significant than the local injury. He once wrote that the first condition of success was that a man should be a good animal. He owed much to the unimpaired physical and nervous resources which he had inherited from his West Country forebears; but he had overdrawn heavily on these reserves. This accident ushered in the inevitable day of reckoning. Seymour Lucas, in a message of condolence, wrote that he had heard from the doctor that 'your enforced rest probably saved you from an illness—as he could see that you were much overwrought'. Rest was an indulgence which gave Irving no pleasure. How could a man rest knowing that while he lay helpless the structure which he had laboured to build was rocking on its foundations?

He was by nature a buoyant optimist. He had never reckoned with the possibility of ill health coming between him and his work. Now that it was forcibly impressed upon him, the realization that he was subject to the ills of ordinary men was made keener by disturbing news he had received of Toole, whom a mutual friend had seen recently in Birmingham:

'. . . I supped with him and all idea of discussing his retirement had left my mind. So long as he will and can go on there is no fear of his public deserting him. . . . But the lethargy, almost verging on coma, which affected him after leaving the stage, cut our evening short and showed me that my view was only too correct. He is suffering from serious brain change which will not be long in asserting itself effectively. But after all it is better to be struck down in harness than out of it. . . .'

Poor Toole: better indeed—it was the only tolerable end for an actor. The musician, the painter and the man of letters could mitigate enforced retirement by the gentle exercise or contemplation of their art. For the actor, denied his stage, the warm limelight and the music of applause, sickness or retirement must be unendurable purgatory.

Yet on Christmas Eve, when Toole, Hatton and Professor McHardy, the oculist, gathered round Irving's bedside, they found him cheerful and resigned. McHardy, a formidable raconteur with the persistence and resource of Scheherazade, told story after story to entertain the invalid. Occasionally Irving smiled at the story-teller and patted his hand encouragingly, but at last, in the middle of a racy anecdote, he fell asleep. The bells were ringing in Christmas Day as Toole and his companions left the homely bedroom and tiptoed down the dark stairs.

For a week the Lyceum was closed. Ellen Terry would not be back from Germany until the end of January. As a stop-gap Stoker revived *Cymbeline*, with Julia Arthur as Imogen, but the play which, with Irving and Ellen Terry, drew £200 a performance, now brought barely a quarter of that sum into the box-office. Irving decided to cut his losses and to close the theatre for three weeks. On Ellen Terry's return they tried *Cymbeline* again, but with little better results. A revival of *Olivia* kept the theatre open, running at a slight loss, until the end of February; by then the accounts showed a loss of £10,000 on the season.

A week after the accident, a notice by Shaw of *Richard III* was published in the *Saturday Review*, which shocked Irving's henchmen. In their opinion, it implied that their Chief had, on the first night, been under the influence of drink. In fact, Shaw had not written or intended to write anything of the kind. In general the criticism was fair, though he pounced severely on any weaknesses which he could detect. This was the offending passage:

'. . . As to Sir Henry Irving's own performance, I am not prepared to judge it, in point of execution, by what he did on the first night. He was best in the Court scenes; in the heavy single-handed scenes which Cibber loved, he was not, as it seemed to me, answering his helm satisfactorily; and he was occasionally a little out of temper with his own nervous condition. He made some odd slips in the text, notably by repeatedly substituting "you" for "I"—for instance, "Shine out fair sun, till you have bought a glass." Once he inadvertently electrified the house by very unexpectedly asking Miss Milton to get further up the stage in the blank verse and penetrating tones of Richard. In the tent and battle scenes his exhaustion was too genuine to be quite acceptable as part of the play. The fight was, perhaps, a relief to his feelings; but to me the spectacle of Mr. Cooper pretending to pass his sword three times through Richard's body as if a man could be as easily run through as a cuttle fish, was neither credible nor impressive. The attempt to make a stage combat look as imposing as Hazlitt's description of the death of Edmund Kean's Richard reads, is hopeless. If Kean were to return to life and do the combat for us, we should very likely find it as absurd as his habit of lying down on a sofa when he was too tired or too drunk to keep his feet during the final scene.'

It was an indication of the hysteria which prevailed among Irving's lieutenants that the association in their minds of Irving's nervousness and Kean's inebriation should have made them spring so loyally to such unfortunate conclusions. The idea of Irving being drunk on the stage of the Lyceum was as ludicrous and improbable as that of a Dean reeling up the nave of his cathedral, particularly to those who had worked closely with him for so many years. Gordon Craig, who had seen as much of him as any of the company in the theatre and out of it, saw him 'intoxicated' but once: '. . . after eating a small steak and drinking nothing. It was about two in the morning and it was in the Beefsteak Room; and there he lay back in his chair, saying very little, dog tired after a nine hours semi-dress rehearsal. . . . I watched him and wondered what was the matter; that was all that was the matter—dog tired.' If Irving read the notice, he ignored it.

At 15A Grafton Street, Walter was kept busy answering enquiries as to his master's health and admitting privileged visitors to see the invalid; Irving, however, became increasingly impatient of his enforced and unnatural idleness. Ellen Terry took advantage of his immobility by reading to him the first two acts of *John Gabriel Borkman*; he read the third to her. 'What a play!' he commented, with an inflection that left no doubt as to his opinion of it. To his notebook he confided: 'Threadworms and leeches are an interesting study; but they have no interest to me.' Perhaps it was her next proposal that she should bring Shaw to visit him that hastened his convalescence.

8

On January 9th he wrote to Mrs. James: 'I am just off to Sevenoaks. They think the change of air will do me good—my leg is bound up— not to be examined for another week—and the doctors think that I had better get some fresh air in the meantime. All is going well—but it is a slow business . . . they are working along surely at the Lyceum— preparing for the future which I think will be brilliant. . . .'

A month later, he was well enough to go and see Vezin and Ellen Terry in *Olivia*. Shaw, in his criticism of it, showed an indecent relish of Irving's absence; he remarked that 'the company, not supporting but supported by Mr. Vezin and Miss Terry—thereby reverting to the true artistic relation between the principal parts and the minor ones—appeared to greater advantage'. As a critic he displayed an inhuman disregard of his own interests; since Irving was essentially human, this notice only added to his resentment against the writer and lessened the chances of *The Man of Destiny* being produced at the Lyceum.

Irving, when he reappeared as Richard at the end of February, was greeted by a great shout of welcome. At the end of the play, characteristically he made no reference to his own misfortune, only asking the audiences to join him in good wishes to Ellen Terry for her birthday. He received assurances from all manner of people of his success in the part. Mrs. Asquith, writing to ask if she might take his private box, wrote: '. . . Mrs. P. Campbell, Mr. Balfour, Mr. Asquith and I want to see it so much. Lots of my friends say it is the finest bit of acting they ever saw—your presentation of Richard. I am still on the sofa, getting over my confinement, but hope to be strong enough to see a morning performance. . . .' Helen Faucit, comparing his performance favourably to his earlier one, added to her praise a word

of warning: '. . . most heartily I congratulate you upon the whole-
ness of your treatment of Richard—but it is, as you make it, a very
fatiguing character to personate and I say, pray spare yourself and
never attempt it more than twice a week. We have thought much of
you during the trying time of your late illness—and although you
may have recovered from it, yet to keep your health would advise you
not too freely taxing it. . . .'

These were wise and kindly words, but it was impossible for Irving
to heed them. For *Richard* was not attracting large enough audiences
to pay his way. So, in addition to playing this exacting part six times
a week, Irving was rehearsing *Madame Sans-Gêne*, which he hoped
might prove more to the taste of a public in Jubilee mood.

Julia Arthur, who was playing Lady Anne, had left the cast. She
had become a little temperamental—a luxury in which, at the Lyceum,
only Ellen Terry was allowed to indulge. Lena Ashwell took her place.
For the first time she was able to play a sustained scene with Irving
and to appreciate the precision of movement and timing which
characterized his method. In the wooing scene, he told her never to be
beyond arm's length from him; when she discovered that every time
Lady Anne wavered in her hatred of Richard, a bell tolled off-stage,
the whole mood and meaning of the scene became clear to her.

Irving was disappointed to find that Ellen Terry, for whom he had
bought Sardou's play, became more and more out of temper with her
part as rehearsals went on. Perhaps it was because her tiresome family
and the man Shaw were constantly discouraging her. She was having
her usual difficulty in learning her words and had not fully mastered
them by the first night.

Madame Sans-Gêne was produced on April 10th. Ellen Terry noted
in her diary that she 'acted courageously and fairly well; extraordinary
success'. Though her estimate of her own playing was probably a
modest one, her hopes for the play were over-sanguine. Inevitably
her performance invited comparison with Réjane, and, considering
the bias of the English public in favour of an artist of any nationality
but their own, she came very creditably out of the ordeal. Irving's
Napoleon, on the other hand, received only luke-warm praise. He
was too tall and the part was too short. Though he contrived a masterpiece of make-up and managed to dwarf himself by the ingenious use
of over life-size furniture and properties, the illusion he gave of
Napoleon, though remarkable at the rise of the curtain, evaporated
as the play went on. 'It seems to me,' wrote Ellen Terry, 'as if I were
watching Napoleon trying to imitate H.I. and I find myself immensely

interested and amused in the watching.' The feelings of the public were, perhaps, best expressed by the Prince of Wales, who, when he received Irving in his box during the performance, said: 'Sir Henry—you should not play Napoleon. Wellington perhaps—but not Napoleon.'

Hurst, the box-office manager of the Lyceum, probably under orders from Stoker, made a half-hearted attempt to refuse the critic

of the *Saturday Review* seats for the first night. Shaw threatened to gain entry either with a ticket or at the point of a revolver. 'He capitulated,' wrote Shaw to Ellen Terry, 'and gave me a stall, but said it was very hard on the Guvnor to have the likes of me representing the papers, when everyone knew it was only Miss Terry I came to see.' Shaw's article, when it appeared, dissected her performance—praise and reproof alternating with lofty scorn of a part unworthy of her talents. He gave Irving a friendly pat on the back as though he had come through a successful audition for *The Man of Destiny*. A few days later, having heard belatedly of the construction Irving's friends and family had put upon his criticism of *Richard III*, he wrote him a letter which brought their negotiations to an abrupt conclusion:

29 *Fitzroy Square,*
April 29th, 1897.

'Dear Sir Henry Irving,

The murder is out! They tell me that you consider that my criticism of *Richard III* implied about you what it said about Kean. I reply flatly that it *didn't*: if I had thought so, I'd have said so bluntly or else said nothing at all. Such a construction never occurred to me, and was certainly not conveyed to any of the people who spoke to me about the article. Now that the thing is suggested to me I can see that if you had that sort of reputation the article might have been misunderstood; but who told you that you had? You underrate your immunity.

I am sorry that the article should have caused you any uneasiness; but my vanity as a critic is severely wounded by your very cheap estimate of the sort of work I do. If you knew the trouble your performances give me—you are in some ways the most difficult subject a critic can tackle, and quite the most exasperating for an author-critic —you would be astonished at my patience and amiability.

At all events, however strongly you may still resent the article, (which I stand by to the uttermost comma—especially the part about Shakespeare) don't resent it on *that* score. I never dreamt of such a thing.

Yours sincerely,
George Bernard Shaw.'

Irving's reply included these words:

'. . . You are absolutely wrong in your polite insinuation of the cat out of the bag—as I had not the privilege of reading your criticism— as you call it—of Richard. I never read a criticism of yours in my life. I have read lots of your droll, amusing, irrelevant and sometimes impertinent pages, but criticism containing judgment and sympathy I have never seen by your pen.'

With a whoop of joy, Shaw tucked up the coat-tails he had been trailing for so many weeks, rolled up his sleeves, and sailed into the attack:

29 *Fitzroy Square,*
May 10*th,* 1897.

'Dear Sir Henry Irving,

Now that we are beginning to deal seriously, we shall get this matter settled fast enough.

Here is the position. I don't want you to play the *Man of Destiny* if you don't like. Only, you mustn't suppress it; you must either take it or leave it. And, if you elect to leave it, you must play fairly to my public position, as I have played loyally all through to yours. The public have been suddenly informed that the reports that you had accepted a play of mine were false, and that what has really happened is that I have sent in a play to the Lyceum and had it rejected. The "Era" hastens to rub this in vigorously; and though a certain London letter-writer explains that you have changed your mind, he adds that you have paid me a handsome compliment and made me a handsome present—in other words, that you have bought the critic of the *Saturday Review* and had him cheap. Such a presentation of the case, if uncontradicted, will disgrace both of us professionally; and sooner than leave the least whiff of it in the air, I will give London another version in a style that will secure its eager attention. But the contradiction ought to come, not from me but from you; and if it does take the shape of an emphatic public statement that the play will be produced, and an implied dignified rebuke to the tattlers, then we must at once concert some explanation of the abandonment of the play that will be entirely creditable to both of us, and which will leave me instantly free to deal with the play in other quarters.

I suggest the following plan. Forbes-Robertson has just written to me about a project of ours which I shall have to discuss with him this week . . . well, he and Mrs. Campbell can play *The Man of Destiny* for me well enough—I should have suggested it to them before but for those prior claims which you are at present so irreverently playing pitch and toss with. Now, if you want to get rid of the play in a highly effective and Charlemagnanimous manner, let me arrange the transfer with Forbes and flood next Sunday's papers with "The Truth About the M. of D." to wit, that the latest instance of your well-known interest in the fortunes of your younger colleagues, especially your old lieutenant F.R., is that you are handing over my play to him with my reluctant consent, and that this is the foundation of all the rumours.

If you can think of anything better than this, let me know. But the thing must be settled at once—fate is peremptory. The public is listening; and if we don't seize the moment to speak, we shall not get the chance again. If you don't move, I shall. Weathercocks are steady in a storm and I'll supply a raging one if necessary.

I should waste your time and save my own if I called to talk. I am an expert at that too, and can talk your head off and Stoker's as well, with half the trouble it gives me to write to you. Ask Cyril Maude.

I beg you to let me have your final decision or indecision at once. In a week Forbes will have left town and my press powder will be getting damp. A reply by return will reach me here; but I shall probably go down to Dorking by some train in the forenoon. Address: Lotus, Tower Hill.

In haste, haste, post haste—what the devil possessed you to worry me at this busy time with this storm in a tea-cup?

Yours sincerely,
G. Bernard Shaw.'

A day or two later Shaw received his manuscript, returned by Stoker with a curt note of rejection, and a letter from Irving in his own hand.

'His reply,' wrote Shaw, 'which had a slip in grammar and touched and reconciled me by its sincerity, amounted to "For God's sake let me alone". And I did.' His whirling arms fell limply to his side. He gave a whimper of frustration in a letter to Ellen Terry: '. . . I have tried to make the best of him; but there is no best. I have suddenly given him up and now it is all over.' It was the cry of a child whose favourite toy had been taken away. *The Man of Destiny* now seemed 'a silly little play'—the succulent bone of contention had lost its flavour. Ellen Terry, weary of nursing two fractious children, administered a final smack to the one whom she now suspected of trying only to annoy because it teased the other. 'Don't pity H.,' she wrote to Shaw; 'he thinks he has quite got the best of it in recent altercations. The fact is he don't think the whole thing matters much. I do, and I'm angry with you . . . what I cared for more than for you or H.— or the parts, was the Play—and now—well, go your way.'

So two men who, in their different ways, wrought lasting changes in the English theatre, turned their backs upon each other. Though both were inspired by a vision of theatrical reformation, they were as irreconcilable as devout Christians of different denominations—Irving orthodox and established; Shaw the dissenter to whom the candles and incense of the Lyceum were anathema. Irving was too old to tolerate a man who, in his opinion, was old enough to know better than to behave with such eccentric impudence. Once he remarked that

Shaw was disrespectful to dignitaries—meaning the hierarchy, social, political and professional who were the ornaments which crowned the structure of Victorian society. However false they may have appeared to later generations, these were the social values he had acquired in his boyhood; to become a man of distinction, with all the obligations and responsibilities that such a position incurred, was an ambition worthy of attainment. Shaw's irreverence shocked and bewildered him. Though happily he was unaware of it, ominous cracks were appearing in the foundations of the social fabric which he so much revered; Shaw, rambling through the vaults, had found the cracks and was driving wedges into them with all his might.

Irving's rejection of *The Man of Destiny* did Shaw little harm—indeed, as Ellen Terry said, it was probably of use to him as an advertisement. Irving, on the other hand, suffered more than he realized from Shaw's unrelenting attacks on the Lyceum and insidious destruction of Ellen Terry's faith in him. It was curious that at about that time both men suffered a similar injury to their legs. Irving struggled to his feet to face the hard years of declining fortune. Shaw hobbled into the arms of an Irish heiress and lived happily ever afterwards. Had he met with her or the accident a few months earlier, he might never have become a dramatic critic—for journalism meant nothing to him but a means of livelihood. The loss to dramatic criticism would have been irreparable. The relief to Irving, who told Laurence that he would cheerfully have paid Shaw's funeral expenses at any time, would have been incalculable.

9

Actor-managers invariably sought for explanations of poor business in natural or social phenomena, real or imagined. It was reasonable to suppose that the counter-attractions of the Jubilee celebrations rather than the unpopularity of *Madame Sans-Gêne* accounted for the comparatively poor attendances at the Lyceum; at least they were better than at any other theatre in London. Irving felt it incumbent upon him to contribute to the occasion. On the afternoon of June 25th, at his invitation and with Royal Assent, two thousand Colonial troops marched from Chelsea Barracks to the Lyceum, where, with the visiting Colonial premiers and Indian princes, they saw him play *Waterloo* and *The Bells*. Even the duskiest soldiers were stirred by the simple patriotism of Corporal Brewster, though many of them may have wondered at the agonies of Mathias as a form of white man's Voodoo. In spite of the fact that Irving, rather rashly, stood unlimited treat to his guests in the bars of the theatre, the troops returned to their barracks in good order, supporting and concealing from the cheering public their only casualties—two drummer boys who, from an excess of brandy and soda, had lost the use of their legs. Earlier in the season, on May 31st, at the invitation of Dean Farrer, and in spite of the disapproval of Ellen Terry, he had given a reading of *Becket* in the Chapter House of Canterbury Cathedral for the benefit of its Restoration Fund. Within a few yards of the scene of Becket's martyrdom, for an hour and a half he held enthralled a large audience which included many from London and elsewhere eager to be present on such a unique occasion.

A fortnight later, he unveiled the statue of Mrs. Siddons on Paddington Green which had been placed there largely through the energies of the Shakespeare Reading Society. He was the first president of this society, which had been founded in 1875 by students of University College, London, to promote interest in the study of Shakespeare and the literature of his period. Later, this society had become the instrument of William Poel in his tireless efforts to present the plays of Shakespeare uncut and without the changes of scene and the interminable act intervals which wrought such havoc with their continuity and rhythm. Up to this time his presentations had been limited to platform recitals by a company wearing conventional evening dress. Poel admired Irving as a man and as an actor, but abhorred him as a producer; Irving respected Poel's earnestness of purpose but was alive to the shortcomings of his method. 'It is the fashion' he would warn a newcomer to the Lyceum whose declamation was impeccable, 'to be a platform reciter—there are many and good ones. You have all the qualities for platform recitals—but, if you want to be an *actor*, you must above all acquire character. Now, me boy, get into your part. Live it and do not merely recite the lines.'

Nevertheless, he had presided over a public lunch at which it had been announced that the members of the society, under the direction of William Poel, would give a performance of *Macbeth* at the St. Georges Hall in aid of the Siddons fund. It was the first time they had ventured from the platform to the stage or had abandoned their tail coats for actors' costumes. Lady Macbeth was to be played by a platform reciter whom this occasion would transmute into an actress— Miss Lillah McCarthy. She was presented to Irving, who kissed her hand, smiled, and wished her success. With Irving's support, an adequate sum was raised and the first public monument to a member of his profession was erected—'. . . striking proof,' as he said when

Homage to the Antique

H. B. Irving

Dorothea Baird   Laurence Irving

Irving and the Lyceum Company
in *Robespierre*

he unveiled it, 'of an enlightened tolerance which would have surprised most people in Sarah Siddons' lifetime'.

These public functions provided some distraction from the grim picture presented by the accounts of the Lyceum, which at the end of the season in July showed a loss of £10,000. Owing to the elaborate precautions taken by Stoker to ensure that the financial position of the theatre was known only to himself and to Irving, no hint of these losses reached the outside world. Stoker, no doubt, would have felt less anxiety if Irving, who showed no signs of reaping the reward that awaited him if he chose to tour America and the provinces with his old successes, had not seemed to be faltering in his judgment of what were likely to prove new ones.

Two new plays were on the stocks: *Peter the Great*, written for him by Laurence, and *The Medicine Man*, by H. D. Traill and Robert Hichens, a curious collaboration, inspired by Irving, between an academic journalist of the old school and a literary rebel with a novel or two to his credit who had succeeded Shaw as musical critic on *The World*. He had invited them to provide him with a Monte Cristo story in modern dress—that of a man of wealth using his power for purposes of revenge. The authors pointed out that 'the millionaire has been vulgarized and now stinks of the stock market and the financial newspapers'; as an alternative they proposed that Irving should impersonate 'a scientific enquirer who, to the outer world, and in other people's drawing-rooms, should be merely a brain specialist or what not, but secretly, in his consulting-room, is a cold-blooded experimentalist using his patients in the spirit in which a vivisector uses his rabbits'. On this singularly unpromising theme, with Irving's blessing, Traill and Hichens were hard at work. If Irving was thinking of returning to coat-and-trouser melodrama of this kind, it was strange that he had recently declined Conan Doyle's offer to write him a play round the now widely known and popular figure of Sherlock Holmes.

10

During the run of *King Arthur*, Irving had asked Forbes-Robertson why he had never attempted *Hamlet*. Forbes-Robertson confessed that it was the ambition of his life to do so, though he feared that such an ambition in a man of his age might be considered egotistical.

'My boy,' said Irving, taking him by the hand, 'don't piano students pound away at Beethoven long before they are able to master the technical difficulties?—not because they are egotistical about their ability but because they feel the beauty of the music. A young actor need not feel egotistical when he aspires to play Hamlet. Go ahead! Play it.'

Forbes-Robertson had now decided to take his Chief's advice; the latter, when he heard of this decision, offered him the Lyceum at a nominal rental of £140 a week until he returned from a provincial tour in December—throwing in for full measure the loan of his scenery properties and costumes. 'I am not here', Irving once remarked, 'to collect money.' He certainly scorned the idea of profiting by the lease of his theatre to his fellow-actors.

On September 11th Forbes-Robertson played Hamlet for the first time. His interpretation was instantly acclaimed as the finest of his generation. The mantle of Irving fell upon him—for such was Irving's reverence for Shakespeare's supreme work that he had decided never to play it again now that he lacked the mental and physical alertness of youth which he believed the part demanded of the actor.

'On the morning after the first night,' wrote Forbes-Robertson, 'while going through some of the scenes with the company, Irving sent me word that he would like to see me. . . . I found him seated at a table on which were several morning papers spread before him. He banged the papers with his open hand, and said: "Well, you've done it." I was very much played out, and had sunk into a chair on the other side of the table, but his cheering words, uttered while that wonderful smile played over his face, put new life into me. "Yes," he repeated, "you've done it, and now you must go and play Hamlet all over the world." We had a long talk. As we moved together towards the door, he opened it, then placing his hand upon my shoulder said: "Well—the readiness is all".'

II

Irving spent his holiday at Cromer where he was joined by Laurence, who brought with him the script of *Peter the Great*. As a Russian scholar, Laurence was well qualified to write on this subject; he had, however, become steeped in Slavonic melancholy and resisted any attempt by his father to introduce a grain of humour or his appeals to bring the play to a less gloomy conclusion. Irving had already produced a one-act play by his son in Chicago. The first stage-direction 'Enter a chorus of lepers', set the tone of the piece. Ellen Terry thought highly of it, and herself, much to Shaw's disgust, appeared as a leper—but only for half a dozen performances. Laurence, earnestly desirous to obey the dictates of Art and the Antique, sat in silence while his father rehearsed the play, scene by scene; he interrupted only to press the claims of a divine actress for the part of the heroine—Ethel Barrymore, with whom he was deeply in love, as indeed were several of his contemporaries.

Irving had not been at Cromer very long before he received an invitation to tea from Mrs. Aria, who, with her younger daughter, was staying at a hotel in Sherringham. He remembered her very well as his partner at a supper given by Walter Ellis, the proprietor of the *Court Circular*, when he had been much amused by her direct manner and her dry wit; she had, moreover, in the name of all her race, thanked him for his interpretation of Shylock. Together, he and Laurence drove over to see her. The tea-party was the overture to a close and light-hearted friendship which animated the holidays of his later years. Mrs. Aria was a journalist—a diarist of gossip and fashion for weekly papers, notably *Truth*. Her father, despairing of providing for his large family as an artist, set up a photographer's studio in Bruton Street. She was instructed at a day school to which most of the distinguished Jewish families sent their children; she was educated by the conversation of Labby, Wilde, George Moore and their satellites, which she had absorbed in the house of her brother, James (Owen Hall), who made his money in law and librettos and dissipated it at race meetings and Romano's. Her sister, Julia, was soon to become famous as the novelist, Frank Danby. Mrs. Aria's marriage was short-lived. 'Nothing,' she said of her husband, 'in his life became him so well as his leaving me for South Africa five years after I had driven with him from the Synagogue to hear his first rapture expressed in "I wonder what has won the Lincoln handicap?" '

Irving found in Eliza Aria a humour and temperament perfectly complementary to his own. Impatient of sentimentality, mordant in criticism of humbugs, generous in her praise of the authentic, she combined a gift for intelligent listening with that of flippant and witty interjection—attributes which egotistical men admire in women above all others. She was, as Shaw wrote in answer to Ellen Terry's rather anxious enquiries, 'a good sort'. Never very strong, she turned her delicacy to account by cultivating a studied helplessness which proved so attractive that in later years she became the Recamier of Regent's Park—rarely leaving a chaise-longue round which literary tigers like Courtney, Wells, Arnold Bennett and George Moore purred in happy competition. She was a mirror, attractively ornamented in the Edwardian style, in which writers and artists saw the most flattering reflections of themselves. She was superbly selfish in the assurance of her own comfort and exacting in the claims she made upon her female friends and relations; she made no demands upon her male retinue, whom she treated as equals and spared the tedium of commonplace coquetries.

For the rest of their stay in Norfolk she accompanied Irving and his son in their carriage drives through the country; by the end of it she surrendered him lightly to his theatre, for which he was already impatient, intuitively certain that this was the first of many rambling holidays they would spend in each other's company.

CHAPTER XXXII

19th Lyceum Season : Peter the Great, Dr. Tregenna, Robespierre

———◦∞◦———

I

The handsome profits of the autumn tour, with *Madame Sans-Gêne* as the principal piece, very nearly restored the balance of the Lyceum accounts—sufficiently at least to satisfy Irving, who was always ready to put a blind eye to the economic telescope. Aided and abetted by Ellen Terry, Laurence, who had joined the company, persuaded him not only to cast Ethel Barrymore for Euphrosine in *Peter the Great*, but to take her on tour to play the burgomaster's daughter in *The Bells*; thus, encouraged by her brother, Jack, who was at Cambridge, he was able to conduct his wooing and the rehearsals of his play at the same time.

In Manchester, Fussy met his death from causes natural after years of gross indulgence by his master. 'A carpenter,' wrote Ellen Terry, 'had thrown down his coat with a ham sandwich in the pocket, over an open trap in the stage. Fussy, nosing and nudging after the sandwich, fell through and was killed instantly. When they brought up the dog after the performance, every man took his hat off. . . . Henry was not told until the end of the play.' The following day Irving carried the corpulent little remains up to London and buried them in the dogs' cemetery in Hyde Park. 'Irving loved his dog,' said Ellen Terry, 'almost as much as his rehearsals.' That was about the measure of it. His Boswells attributed to him a maudlin attachment to his pets which was quite foreign to his nature; most of them ignored a tragedy which, five days later, deeply shocked him and his whole company.

On the night of December 16th, William Terriss was murdered outside the stage-door of the Adelphi Theatre in Maiden Lane. A half-crazy small-part actor with an imagined grievance stabbed him in the back as he was entering the theatre for the evening performance. The news reached Irving at Bradford. His grief at the untimely loss of one of the oldest members of his company (Terriss had written only a few weeks before asking if he could return to the Lyceum) was sharpened with anger; his bitterness found expression in his reference to the murderer —'they will find some excuse to get him off—mad or something. Terriss was an actor—his murderer will not be executed'. His forecast was right, though there were strong legal grounds for committing the assassin to Broadmoor. In the meantime Irving met the situation in a way that characterized all his actions. First he asked, through the appropriate channels, if he might bear to Terriss's widow a message of condolence from the Queen—a request which was immediately granted. Then having fulfilled a duty which fell to him as head of his profession, he was prompted by his own tenderness of heart, by his loyalty to his dead friend and by his unerring divination of the public mind, to an action which could only be appreciated in the light of the social conventions of the time.

Terriss had died in the arms of Jessie Millward, an actress who had played with him for fifteen years and was his devoted companion. Her position was such in the eyes of society as to preclude her presence at her lover's funeral. On the morning of the funeral Irving came to her flat. In his hands, he carried a bunch of violets. He brought her a message of condolence from the Prince of Wales and asked if he might escort her to the funeral. 'There was not a member of the theatrical world,' wrote Mrs. Aria, 'in the crowd which followed the murdered man to his resting-place, who did not fall in worshipful admiration of Irving when they noted the tenderness which went to his shepherding.' He looked pale and care-worn in the raw December air. After the funeral Jessie Millward collapsed. For several nights Irving, after he left the theatre, went and sat with her for an hour or so urging her not to surrender to her grief, but to seek relief in work. He persuaded her to go abroad, and in her absence entered into a conspiracy with Frohman which resulted in her returning before 'long to the stage in New York.

In May a third distraction contained an element of comedy. Clement Scott, intoxicated by the power, real or imaginary, he wielded as the arbiter of theatrical success or failure, had committed professional suicide. For years he had sat at his desk, opening letters which solicited favourable mention in his columns from almost every member of the theatrical profession. His friendship was courted; his hostility was feared. Neither he nor his supplicants realized that the tide of dramatic criticism had swept on, leaving him and critics of his type isolated on little islands of self-importance. It was ten years since *The Times* had decided that its criticisms should be written for the public rather than for managers and actors, and had astonished and offended the fraternity by appointing an able member of its staff, innocent of theatrical tradition and Green Room gossip, to judge plays and players solely on their merits. Other reputable papers followed this example; Mr. Puff, at a ripe old age, went into retirement. In the course of an interview by the representative of a magazine, *Great Thoughts*, Scott had been struck by a singularly unhappy one. Speaking of the stage as a career for a woman, he said: '. . . I do not see how she is to escape contamination in one form or another. There is no school on earth so bad for the formation of character, or that so readily, so quickly draws out all that is bad in man and woman as the stage . . . I marvel at any mother who allows her daughter to take up a theatrical career; still more am I astonished that any man should calmly endure his wife to become an actress, unaccompanied by himself. He must either be a fool or a knave.'

These were strange words from a man whose wife was striving to get an engagement as a professional actress and, presumably, himself had no intention of abandoning the critic's desk to protect her on the boards. If Scott had struck an attitude on a pedestal of dynamite and had himself lit the fuse, the result could not have been more spectacular. In a moment, those who had licked his boots were snapping at his heels. The theatrical profession and the public clamoured for his dismissal and for unqualified recantation. In the midst of this hubbub stood two calm but most embarrassed men—Irving and Sir Edward Lawson. Irving as head of his profession was called upon to lead the assault on Scott; Sir Edward Lawson, as Scott's employer, was necessarily the instrument of revenge, but fortunately he was on holiday in France. The article, it might be supposed, would enrage the man who for so long had defended the honour of the stage. Lawson and his father had been the best friends the Victorian theatre ever had, and the sturdiest supporters of Irving in his crusade. But Irving's anger against Scott was cooled by his contempt for the sycophants and time-servers who now clamoured for the ruin of a man who had at least paid for their flattery with puffs. As the representative of the Council of the Actors' Association, he was compelled to see Le Sage, the editor of the *Daily Telegraph*, and to convey to him the view of his colleagues. He had urged them to be moderate; but even he failed to control the storm. A few days later he received a letter from Lawson which ended:

'. . . I hasten then to inform you that Clement Scott has placed his resignation in my hands and that I have expressed my opinion that there is only one honourable course for him to pursue—absolute apology and retraction. Frankly I am convinced that when he thus grievously erred, he was not master of himself physically or mentally. But that scarcely affects the issue. He who has wronged you ought to endeavour to repair the harm he has done. I earnestly believe the great profession of which you are the titular head, is strong enough and wise enough not to imagine that its stature and well-being can in any way be affected by the campaign initiated against it by *Great Thoughts*. But I fully comprehend the general desire strongly to resent the attack made on it by one who has, throughout a long career, done much to advance its welfare and prosperity. . . .'

Scott published an abject apology and retired to the Continent. From Hyères he wrote to Irving:

'God bless you, old friend, for your loyal and affectionate champion-ship in an hour of very dark trouble for me and the noble woman I am proud to call my wife. I did an idiotic thing but I was dragged into it when I was sick, ill, racked with pain and quite demoralised. That is no excuse I know but it may serve as some mitigation of my punishment. God knows I have suffered enough these last five weeks. Hell can have no more tortures for me than I have endured night and day. If I have to go under I am sure I shall retain your friendship and affection and if I leave the theatre and am seen no more there I must go to the desk and write my story of the stage with all its ups and downs from the time you were introduced to me at the War Office in the dear old Charlie Mathews days. I wish that Wyndham could be as generous as Hare and your dear self. I shall never forget it. Don't answer this. I cannot bear it. I am very down. God bless you. Your old friend,

Clement Scott.'

Nobody had relished Scott's article more than Flo, who eagerly collected any snippets of stage scandal she could find. Probably her thoughts turned to the night, so many years ago, when she had es-corted the shy young actor who had lost his way to Scott's house; she may have derived some satisfaction from the fact that retribution had at last overtaken the man who indirectly had been the cause of her abiding bitterness.

2

All these events had taken place against the background of the final dress-rehearsals of *Peter the Great* which opened on January 1st, 1898.

No critic accused Irving of parental folly in producing a play written by his son. For so young a man it was a remarkable piece of writing, containing fine and imaginative passages, but it was an epic poem rather than a play, and it was lacking in action or humour. Irving had never been very successful in portraying physical power; now he was quite unable to convey the bull strength of the Czar against a ground-base of barbaric tumult. In the effort to do so he fell into his old manner-isms. Yet the collaboration in itself had been rewarding. In hammering out a play about a brutish father's contempt and cruelty towards his weak idealistic son, he and his own son finally bridged the gulf of estrangement which for so long had separated them from one another. Laurence and the Antique emerged from the testing ordeal without a shadow of difference falling between them. On the morrow of the pro-duction Laurence wrote to his father:

'. . . I came to see you today but found you resting. It is impossible to tell you how grand your performance was and what overpowering impression was made on the minds of all who saw it. I can't tell you how full my heart was and is of admiration and gratitude. I hope the play won't require much cutting—like most authors I am foolishly fond of my words—foolishly fond of them, and I think with closer playing, which is sure to come with familiarity, some twenty minutes can be saved. But I know you love the play as much as I do, you couldn't have given such a performance if you hadn't. Your exquisite judgment has guided the play safely into harbour so far and I can rely on it implicitly.

Best love. "My father is great. I am proud to be his son."

Laurence.'

His optimism was not entirely unjustified. He himself had a good press. Shaw reviewed the play twice—the first on reading it and later when he had seen it. He wrote encouragingly of the play, but could not resist the Mephistophelean temptation of playing off the son against the father. 'This is the moment,' he wrote to Ellen Terry, 'to play for Laurence and not for the Lyceum, which has had its innings and made its name already.' He could not turn Laurence's head, which was already swimming with exhilaration. On the night of the visit of the Prince and Princess of Wales to the Lyceum, Irving had lost his voice and was unable to play. Laurence took his place. He rose to the occasion, sufficiently at least for the Prince to compliment him with a quotation from the play—'Emperors don't have sons, they have successors.' Shaw was in front and thought his acting very bad. '. . . as author of the piece he tried to do everything he wanted Peter to do, instead of like a cunning old actor, simply picking out what he himself could do.' Yet at the same time he marked down Laurence as the creator of his half-fashioned Captain Brassbound. And there were extenuating circumstances. After half a dozen proposals, Laurence had become engaged to Ethel Barrymore. His cup of happiness was full even if nightly the chests of the Lyceum became emptier and emptier. *Peter the Great* and the author's engagement were both short lived. The play was withdrawn after thirty-eight performances in favour of the old repertory.

3

On the night of February 18th Irving suffered a second misfortune, more crippling and disastrous than the first. He was the first theatrical manager to be faced with the problem of finding storage space for the vast bulk of scenery and properties which he had accumulated over a period of twenty years. It was difficult to warehouse, economically and safely, valuable and perishable property made up for the most part of painted cloths thirty feet high, even when they were rolled on battens forty-two feet wide, and framed pieces of similar proportions which were vulnerable to damage by damp, by awkward handling or by careless packing. Moreover, this great stock had to be easy of access, for productions were constantly being taken in and out of store as they were needed for the repertory. At last, ideal premises were found in two arches under the Chatham and Dover railway at a point in Southwark where they carried the track high above the streets below. Here, readily accessible, yet sufficiently isolated from neighbouring buildings to obviate contagious risk of fire, the mass of Lyceum scenery was lodged. Indeed the risk seemed so small that Stoker had insured the contents for only £10,000, which recently Irving, searching for economies which he could directly put into effect, had reduced to £6,000. In the early hours of the morning of February 18th Stoker received a message from Bow Street police station that the stores were on fire. By the time he reached Southwark the two arches were like fiercely glowing ovens. The contents were utterly consumed and the fire brigade were concerned only to contain the blaze. By the time the news reached Irving, his entire stock-in-trade—the coinage of his brain as a metteur-en-scène— was a black and smoking heap of ashes. Two hundred and sixty scenes—the settings for forty-four plays—had been destroyed. Nor was this simply a holocaust of wood and canvas. Acres of the original and irreplaceable work of the greatest scenic artists of the day were now no more than calcined pigments powdering the charcoal ruins.

Such was the material loss to be set against the paltry recompense of insurance. Irving had spent over £30,000 on these productions; twice that sum and an incalculable length of time would be needed to reproduce them. Far greater was the extinction of a policy upon which, as his working life was drawing to a close, he had every right to rely. Most of these plays had been popular successes; many of them had been taken off when their drawing-power had shown no signs of waning. He had looked forward to a time when, calling a halt to the search for new material and to the heavy expenditure on new productions, he could fill his theatre and make some provision for his retirement by reviving these pieces—already mounted and rehearsed—with no great expenditure of money or of his own declining nervous and physical energy. He woke on that Feburary morning to find himself stripped of the resources upon which his hopes of retrenchment and recoupment were founded. His temperament enabled him to accept success or ill-fortune with equanimity—at least so it seemed to those around him. His only comment on this disaster was that he thought the fire might have been caused by a spark of the moral indignation of those playgoers who insisted that to produce plays without scenery was the highest development of the simple life.

4

These sombre months were brightened momentarily by a conquest, an honour and a reconciliation. In May the Roman Catholic Church for the first time acknowledged, if a trifle obliquely, his services to the drama. Cardinal Vaughan, overruling the scruples of his colleagues still imbued with the uncompromising attitude of his predecessor towards the theatre, invited Irving to lecture on the character of Macbeth at his own house in aid of the Catholic Social Union. Irving accepted; though the Cardinal, in his speech of thanks, gave no indication of any change of heart of his Church towards the stage, he had every right to feel that he had broken her icy disapproval of his profession. After his lecture he recited *Eugene Aram*. Cardinal Vaughan afterwards assured him that anyone planning murder could not bring himself to the act after his guest's rendering of Hood's poem. Though this was flattering to Irving, his chances of exercising this restraint were not very great. In June the University of Cambridge conferred upon him the degree of Doctor of Letters. His discourse was dryly humorous; to the young men, who as usual gave him a boisterous reception, he appeared debonair and blessed with all the world had to offer. Earlier, as the result of a promise he had made to Virginia Bateman to recite at a bazaar, he received a letter which was as unexpected as it was welcome. It began with a few words of thanks for his sympathy for the particular cause and ended:

'. . . As I am writing may I tell you that every feeling of bitterness about the past has entirely faded from my mind and my thoughts of you are only kind ones. I never had any bitterness on my account or because of what I suffered. I always felt myself reponsible for that, not you; it was on mother's account that I found it so very hard to feel kindly. But time teaches us all a great deal and perhaps one's own failures to live as we would wish to live teach us even more, and I hope from my own shortcomings I have learnt some measure of sympathy for others. I have not seen you for seventeen years, but I should be glad to meet you again and hear your voice reciting. I know you won't think I want an engagement or money or anything else. I want nothing but to hold out the olive branch.

Believe me,
Yours sincerely,
Isabel Bateman.'

His conscience as regard the Batemans had never been entirely clear; Isabel's generous absolution of his past shortcomings did much to lighten his present anxieties and forebodings. This letter was her *nunc dimittis*. A few months later she found the peace for which she had waited so long in the Anglican Community of St. Mary the Virgin, at Wantage.[1]

The public and critics had shown an amiable indulgence towards *Peter the Great*—there was enough in the relationship between the author and actor to attract the curious, even though their numbers were inadequate. For *The Medicine Man* they had neither curiosity nor tolerance. It was roundly condemned or ridiculed. Irving knew that he had nobody to blame but himself; he believed in his part which was as long as it was preposterous. He had devoted as much care to the preparation and rehearsal of it as ever. Hichens, in generously accepting the responsibility for its failure, wrote: 'Any good there is in it you put there.' Yet Irving had, in a sense, betrayed the authors by persuading them that plays, lacking inspiration or ideas, could be contrived by methods now

---

[1] Isabel Bateman received the Habit in January 1899. In 1920 she became Mother General of the Order. She died in 1934.

long outmoded. *The Medicine Man* was withdrawn after twenty-four performances. Irving was still able to stage *Louis XI*, *The Bells*, and *The Merchant of Venice*, which, with *Madame Sans-Gêne*, kept the theatre open until the end of June.

Among the audience, on the last night of the season, was M. Georges Bourdon who until recently had been the stage director of the Odéon Theatre, Paris, and now, on behalf of the Minister of Fine Arts, was studying theatre organisation and management in England. In recording his impressions of that evening,[1] M. Bourdon manifested the fundamental difference, in their appreciation of the art of acting, between French and English playgoers.

'M. Irving . . . was playing *The Merchant of Venice*. . . . Shylock does not appear in the last scene. At the end of the play, hardly had the curtain fallen, when Irving came before the front scene . . . and advanced gravely towards the centre of the stage. He had stripped off the beard and wig of Shylock and appeared in a dress suit and white tie; his noble head, with its broad brow and deep set eyes, framed by his long silver hair. Applause. With the urbanity of a convivial gentleman presiding over a gathering of his friends, he made, in simple phrases and in a conversational tone, a genial and distinguished speech which delighted his audience, now on its feet to a man. He spoke for some time—thanking the English public for their continued support, announcing the end of the season, the coming appearance (at the Lyceum) of M. Coquelin in the celebrated *Cyrano de Bergerac* by Rostand, and the tour which he himself was about to make in the English provinces. In conclusion, he outlined his programme for the following year—first of all Macbeth, then a new play which M. Sardou had written specially for him, and other new pieces; he ended by expressing his good wishes to his loyal public and assuring them of his lively gratitude. Loud applause. He bowed. He led forward by the hand Ellen Terry who had been waiting in the wings—and that was all.

We had taken part in a family gathering which, by its very nature, overcame our prejudices. Is not this flagrant identification of a man's personality with his performance as an actor, strange and a little disconcerting to us who come to the theatre with so strong a desire for illusion and with emotions so ready to be stirred that we demand above all that the actor should forget himself and make us forget that he is other than the hero whom he has created in our imagination. What should we say of a Phèdre who, rising from the dead, tells us that she

[1] Georges Bourdon, *Les Théâtres Anglais*. Paris, 1903.

is going to play L'Aiglon or of an Oedipus who confides to us that he is going to appear as the bard in the adventures of *Les Cadets de Gascogne*?[1] What are we to think of a Shylock announcing that M. Sardou has written a new piece for him? But here I must quote the words of a friend who wisely warned me that he who makes too many comparisons is a bad critic. And, without doubt, it is we who are at fault in being so surprised, since things of this kind please the English.'

Evidently, like Henry James, Bourdon was scandalised by Irving's exploitation of his personality; Irving, on the other hand, felt equally strongly that it was incongruous for a character of his creation to bow in acknowledgement of applause for his creator. There was much to be said for both these points of view. Like Henry James, Bourdon failed to remark the admirable eclecticism of English theatre-goers who, having cheered Irving's naturalistic Shylock to the echo would, a week or two later, as warmly applaud Coquelin's classic portrayal of Cyrano.

Irving had little time to brood upon the trials and disasters which beset him before he set out on the provincial tour, the proceeds of which were already pledged owing to a loss of £6,000 on the past season. The tour began disappointingly in the suburbs of London. The company had to contend with caprices of weather and their fellow-men; the account-books recorded 'intense heat and water famine', 'tram strike', and indications of a rebellious musical director who perhaps refused to play on account of the heat—all preparing the reader for the miserable profit of £122 in the first three weeks. A month's break enabled Irving to have a short holiday at Cromer before setting out for the provinces. At the beginning of October the company went to Glasgow after a week in Edinburgh. Irving had arranged on the Sunday to lunch with Lord Rosebery at Dalmeny and to follow them to Glasgow in the evening. On his way to the train, picking his way through mud and puddles in the dark approaches from Prince's Street to the new, but as yet incomplete, railway station, he got his feet wet. He was always lightly shod—his shoes were like those of a dancer or tight-rope walker. The journey was cold; there was no heat in the carriage. On the following Thursday night, just before the curtain rose on the second act of *Madame Sans-Gêne*, he summoned Stoker to his dressing-room, where he was sitting down dressed for his part. When Stoker came in he said: 'I think there must be something wrong with me. Every breath is like a sword stab. I don't think I ought to be

[1] A serial story of the tushery type, popular at that time in Paris.

suffering like this without seeing someone.' Stoker saw that he was really ill and suggested that he should dismiss the audience. Irving would not hear of it. 'I shall be able to get through all right,' he said, 'but when I've seen a doctor we may have to make some change for tomorrow. . . .' The doctor arrived during the last act, but he could not see his patient until the end of the play. Then, seeing that Irving was dangerously ill, he hurried him off to his hotel.

Irving was found to be suffering from pneumonia and pleurisy. Before he passed into the semi-oblivion of alternating pain and delirium, he sent a note to Loveday:

'. . . If there is anything to say tonight and tomorrow night—and there will be until next week, I should if I were you try Stoker on the stump. He's good with them lungs of his and would do anything you asked him.

I am taking a heavy sleeping draught tonight and hope it will do me good.

Not the least chance for next week. We mustn't have any of our *actors* making speeches.'

The company continued the tour without him, playing to sparse and disappointed audiences. By the end of it the profits, so urgently needed, and so confidently counted upon, had dwindled to a mere £500. Stoker acted wisely and promptly. He let the Lyceum for the approaching season and made arrangements for a provincial tour in the spring, with plays which would throw no great strain on Irving. *Robespierre* would have to wait. As he made these plans, he waited anxiously for news from Glasgow as Irving approached his crisis.

5

All his life Irving had been conscious of the force of threefold emphasis. Within a year three catastrophes had befallen him. The first eliminated his capital resources; the second destroyed his stock-in-trade; the third undermined the health he needed to recover his fortunes. He survived the crisis of his disease, and in the winter gloom of a Glasgow hotel faced the tedium of slow recovery. Stoker, when the immediate danger was passed, went up to see him. He found him looking very old and weak—his hollow cheeks and cadaverous jowl bearded with white bristles; his nose, like that of the dying Falstaff, was 'as sharp as a pen'. Walter was in tears and would not trust himself to go with Stoker into the sickroom for fear of upsetting his beloved master. The burden of caring for the sick man had fallen upon him; Irving, being quite unused to feminine care, would not allow the two nurses who had been engaged to do more for him than their medical duties made necessary. The elder of them wrote to Dorothea, his daughter-in-law: 'I am pleased to say he's had another good day. . . . I was not to go on duty till 2 p.m. so was dressing leisurely when Walter came to my door to say Sir Henry wanted me when I was ready. . . . I was told he wanted me to sponge him all over, as he thought Nurse Thornton was too young! Hard upon me, n'est-ce pas?'

At the beginning of December he was well enough to leave Glasgow for Bournemouth, where he had arranged to complete his convalescence. He broke the journey in London where he found waiting for him an offer of practical help from his 'faithful and affectionate' Pinero:

'. . . if I can be of any service to you in helping you to rehearse your new production—no matter what shape it may assume. It would be a pure labour of love for me, to fag for you. I can lick an act or two, or the whole of them, into shape and then leave them for your imprimation. Anything to save you from unnecessary exertion. I am handy at drilling, and at the arrangement of movement—thanks, in no small degree, to my recollection of my service in your theatre.'

From Bournemouth Irving replied:

The Bath Hotel,
Bournemouth.
December 1898.

'My dear Pinero,
How good you are and how truly kind is your suggestion. Such a help as yours would, under some conditions, be of inestimable value, but my present intention is to produce no more new work for some time—but to travel—to realise and not to speculate. . . .'

Within a few days these sensible resolutions were broken. Early in the New Year, while Irving was still low in spirit and comparatively infirm of purpose, his friend, Joe Comyns Carr, came down to see him, and put before him a proposition which, at such a time, was dangerously attractive. Carr had guessed, if he did not know, that Irving's financial position was a desperate one. On behalf of a syndicate composed of himself and his two brothers (one a solicitor, the other a financier) he offered to relieve Irving of all financial responsibility in return for his services and the transfer to the syndicate of his interests in the Lyceum. On the face of it the proposal was both opportune and practicable. In general it was similar to that which Lawson had suggested to Irving a few years previously. In brief, it comprised an offer to float a public company—the Lyceum Theatre Company—which would take over the remaining eight years' lease of the theatre and such furniture and fittings as were Irving's property; in addition, Irving was to fulfil an annual engagement of at least one hundred performances at the Lyceum on sharing terms with the company; he was to bear 60 per cent of the cost of new productions, to pay all stage expenses and half the cost of advertising and to guarantee to play on tour, in England or America, at least for four months every year—a quarter of the profits of these tours being handed over to the company. In return Irving was to receive £26,000 in cash and £12,500 in shares in the company which, he was told, would issue to the public £100,000 of Preference and £70,000 of Ordinary Shares. To a sick and almost penniless actor, whose livelihood depended upon his own exertions, this was a tempting offer. For the first time in his life Irving felt the need of financial help and of relief from the anxieties of business. To tide him over his illness he had been forced to borrow money from one or two friends who readily had offered him their help. He had sold the most valuable of his theatrical books and prints, the collection of which had been his life-long and only hobby; they fetched nearly £1,300, which enabled him to pay off his immediate debts.

He summoned Loveday and Stoker to Bournemouth, outlined to them these proposals and, to Stoker's dismay, told him that he had tentatively accepted them. Stoker was leaving for New York in a few days to make arrangements with Frohman for an American tour. Both he and Loveday tried to dissuade Irving from coming to an immediate decision, but they soon realized that already he had made up his mind. It was only possible for them to suggest a modification of the terms to his advantage. Stoker insisted that he should not, as had been suggested, be a director of the company or be implicated in it in any way beyond the sale of his property and services. Later, at a joint conference with Carr, it was agreed that the company should pay him the nominal weekly salary of £70 which hitherto had always been charged to the accounts of his provincial tours. When Stoker returned from America, the contracts had been drawn up and signed, the company had issued its prospectus and the shares had been bought up eagerly by the public. He was further dismayed to find that, owing to the issue of £120,000

Mortgage Debentures to the free-holders of the theatre, the capital issue had risen to £290,000 and that Irving had allowed his name to appear on the prospectus as 'Dramatic Adviser'.

As Irving regained his strength certain persistent symptoms caused, though nobody had detected it, by a discharge from the wound in his lung that had not healed, continued to distress him. As his health improved he may have regretted the hasty surrender of his independence and of the inevitable division of the loyalty of his associates between himself and the company. He was not a man to admit he had made a mistake. Yet the knowledge that he had done so in the face of Stoker's earnest opposition—to say nothing of Stoker's natural pique at his Chief's disregard—clouded a little their relationship to one another. A hint of these divided responsibilities and sharp misunderstandings lay in a letter which Irving wrote to Stoker when he was back at the Lyceum and rehearsing *Robespierre*:

April 4th, 1899.

'. . . There has been the most astounding, stupid mistake about the Sunday papers, which have no advertisements. Tell them in future to show *me* an advt. list—which I will supervise—in fact it is *you* who ought to make advts. for which I am reponsible for biggest share. At all events you must *revise*.

I thought it was understood that you should look it over. As it is now we have destroyed six notices in the papers with a very big circulation —one omitting to notice play at all.

I hope you're all right and not tired out.'

Laurence had translated Sardou's play for his father and was at his side to ease the burden of rehearsals. Earlier in the year he had given, in Manchester, a performance of Justice Shallow of which the *Manchester Guardian* wrote: '. . . you might go to the theatre regularly for twenty years without seeing so singular a piece of creative imagination by an actor of a minor or middle-aged part.' A few critics in London had noted his growing power as an actor when, for a few performances, he had played the author in *Hedda Gabler*. At the time Ellen Terry had written to him:

'. . . Admirable—my dear Laurence—very impressive—Don't put so much white on your upper lip (*this is a detail*) for it spoils the face's expression . . . . I am reading *Robespierre*! ! *Second act tremendous*. First act (it appears to *me*) the lovely *Cart* scene is thrown away by coming to an end too soon. Good God—MY part ! ! ! ! ! (but that is a detail!) (And don't speak about it to ANYONE) (DISCRETION! !) Your Catherine before a dozen "Clarisse"-es's—Well! Well! Shall we meet at the Lewis's tomorrow? I hope so.

Affect'tly yours,

E. T.'

Too many of her recent parts had been mere details—or so Shaw had persuaded her to believe. The truth was that she was reaching an age at which any actress had difficulty in finding leading parts to suit her. She had shown Irving Shaw's *Caesar and Cleopatra*. Of all Shaw's characters Caesar, in the length and conception of the part, would have fitted him perfectly. He refused to play it or to give his real reason for rejecting it. Shaw was less gallant. 'I don't want you to do Cleopatra,' he wrote to Ellen Terry. 'She is an animal—a bad lot. Yours is a beneficent personality.' The inference was not lost upon her. Irving would have contrived to fit her into any new play he produced—indeed it would have been a condition of his accepting it. But such parts as she could play were bound, in her eye, to be inadequate. Yet all Shaw had to offer her was a caricature of herself as Lady Cicely Waynflete; when she looked into the mirror he held up to her she did not at first care for the reflection. Her loyalty to Irving was sorely tried; the bonds which held her to him and to the Lyceum were weakening. During his illness she had toured the provinces with Frank Cooper. Now she returned to find herself a member of Sir Henry Irving's Travelling Company (for that in effect it had become), appearing for a season at a Lyceum owned by a limited liability company. Dispirited, deeply distressed for Irving, yet exasperated by his 'naughtiness', uncertain of herself and of her future, listlessly she strove to learn her wretched part and to apply herself to the tumultuous rehearsals.

The well-made piece was the pride of the Parisian dramatic workshops. Sardou was the most skilled among their carpenters. Yet he had reached the age when his artifice had outrun his inspiration. The alchemy of play writing had yielded its secret; a masterpiece could be produced by mathematics. 'An unwritten play,' he said, 'always appeared to him as a kind of philosophical equation from which the unknown term had to be disengaged—once the formula for this was found, the piece followed itself.' *Robespierre* was the first play he had written expressly for Irving. The formulae and logarithms were consulted, the slide rules of plot and situation were applied, but the eyes of the mathematician were growing dim and an equation or two were missed. The result was an example of what Shaw called Sardoodledum, if not at its worst, at something less than its old effectiveness. He did, however, provide Irving with a part worthy of his powers, one with which he could identify himself mentally and physically—the prerequisite of sincere interpretation. He had given Irving the opportunity to portray every aspect of Robespierre's many-sided character—the doctrinaire, the autocrat, the conspirator, the peacock, the poet, and the martyr patriot. He gave him the physical metamorphoses in which the master of make-up and illusion delighted. He gave the supreme stage-director a storm of turbulent action to ride. All these things Irving, with the sense of crisis in his affairs, seized with both hands and bent to his purpose. The first night of *Robespierre*, on April 15th, was the last of its kind to have the glitter and emotion of an authentic Lyceum premiere. There was a demonstration of genuine rejoicing in Irving's restoration to health. There was enthusiastic applause for his performance with all its signs of the old fire and subtlety; the audience as yet were not sufficiently aware of the change in the regime to be sensible of fading glamour. Ellen Terry was noticeably uncertain of her words; this was not an expression of her dissatisfaction with her part, but the first symptoms of steadily deteriorating powers of memory and concentration. Though the period of the play inevitably called to mind *The Dead Heart*, the situations were sufficiently blood-curdling and the handling of crowds in the scenes of the Convention so masterly that the public, stimulated by a favourable press, flocked to see it. Indeed there seemed to be every prospect of an artistic and financial success, comparable to that of any of Irving's earlier triumphs. In a week or two, however, the flaws in his contractual obligation to the Lyceum company became apparent. He was, as will be remembered, responsible for the greater part of the production and for all the stage expenses. With a cast of seventy players and the heavy initial expenditure on scenery, these amounted to over £1,000 a week. His share of the gross takings, which were greater than they had been for several seasons past, rarely exceeded and often fell below this sum. Thus by the end of the season he himself had lost about £4,000, less the nominal salary upon which Stoker had so wisely insisted. The company, on the other hand, made a handsome profit which promoted a wholly false sense of security in the minds of the shareholders.

The inequity of his position was not at once apparent to Irving, who had more immediate difficulties to overcome. In writing to condole with Loveday, who had been ill for some time, he gave a hint of his own infirmity:

May 9th, 1899.

'My dear Loveday,

It was a true pleasure to get your letter and to feel that you're getting back your lost strength. And dear Mrs. Loveday. She, I hear, has had a very painful time—all very sad. If the spring ever comes again it ought to do us all good. Since Thursday I've been fighting off an attack of influenza, crawling out of bed to work and from work to bed again.

I wonder do you escape the east winds at Brighton? They are really very trying here and have given many a very rough time. . . . When you are running through I shall hope to see you—but you must not return too soon and try and get a good long rest. You know all about the success—which is as great as ever—perhaps greater—but I mean to discontinue the "mornings"— the work is far too exacting.

I shall not bother you with "shop"—but Fillery (the machinist) had decided, he says, not to go to America, having a "little house—little pigs" and which he would not like to leave and thinks of setting up a little shop on his own account—taking commissions, etc. and we are on the look-out for a good man who will learn the ropes of *Robespierre* and I shall take besides the *Merchant—Bells—Nance Oldfield* and *Waterloo*—and that's all.

Robespierre of course will be principal attraction. Shall hope to see you soon. God bless you both and my best love to both.

Yours,

H. I.'

A day or two later he was out of the bill; once again Laurence took his place. His illness had left him with a chronic inflammation of his throat. Seeking relief from a condition particularly trying to an actor, he went to a doctor, who, in the course of his examination, allowed a steel instrument seven inches long to slip, apparently irretrievably, down his patient's gullet. The wretched doctor urged an immediate visit to a specialist. Irving, however, had another appointment and insisted on keeping it. Later, in a violent fit of coughing, he regurgitated the instrument and returned it to its owner with a double fee and a note begging him not to suffer any undue remorse on his account. Other medical advisers suggested a more practical remedy—that he should move from the perpetual twilight of Grafton Street to a sunnier flat which was found for him in 17 Stratton Street. The move and the disposal of bric-à-brac collected over a period of twenty-seven years was a formidable undertaking. The comparatively simple task of settling him into Grafton Street had been done by Mrs. Bateman; the removal to Stratton Street was carried out by Mrs. Aria and Walter with Irving's active, if unintentional, obstruction. 'Having ordained,' wrote Mrs. Aria, 'that crimson was to be the dominant note of his new dwelling, and this being faithfully applied to the walls of the spacious entrance to the corridor and to the carpet, he cared about no other details than the righteous bestowal of Whistler's and Sargent's pictures and the proper fittings for his innumerable bookshelves . . . he would wander towards a pile of volumes in the corner, and extracting one, would ignore the prevailing chaos, pushing all intruding parcels onto the floor while he sat at the far end of the super-sized sofa and read, his long finger marked his place when he looked up sharply resentful should an unpacker venture to dump, to his disturbance, or a carpenter presume to hammer a nail.'

In the end, the migration for the most part had to be effected when Irving was safely at work at the Lyceum.

He was well enough in July to pay a flying visit to Glasgow, where he received the degree of Doctor of Laws. His address of thanks voiced the amused reflection of a man who on his first appearance in that city had been announced as Mr. Irwin and whose name, forty years after, wards, had become a household word throughout a kingdom united at least in bestowing upon him the academic awards of three of its principal universities. No wonder that he remarked to a young actor who was smarting from an adverse criticism: '*Good* God, my boy—they talked about my legs for ten years—now they talk about my head.'

6

In September, Irving and his company took to the road with *Robespierre* and the three productions which the fire had spared. A long and arduous journey stretched ahead of them which would not end until the following April—a five-week tour in the provinces, followed by six months in the United States and a further nine weeks in the provinces on their return. In Manchester, before he left England, he was invited by his friend, Judge Parry, to attend a session of the County Court. Parry soon found that every defendant instinctively addressed himself, not to the judge, but to the actor at his side on the bench. When suitors had heard his judgment they instinctively looked to Irving for his endorsement, which was indicated by a genial bow. Parry entertained him to lunch, but discouraged him from returning to the bench, saying that he was glad to see him starring anywhere in the world but not in the

Manchester County Court. Irving once tried to explain to a friend the reason for the interest and curiosity he excited wherever he went: '. . . You see, there are a great many illustrated papers, and other people cut their hair.'

He could have no clearer proof of the enduring affection and admiration which the people of America and Canada felt for him than was demonstrated in the box-offices of the thirty towns in which he and his company played. The receipts, amounting to £111,000, were almost identical to those of his previous tour, which had been of the same duration though he had travelled with twelve productions as opposed to five in the present one. How much was saved in money, let alone in wear and tear to himself, was shown in the profits which were nearly four times as great— his own share, after the Lyceum company had taken theirs, was £24,000. It had been hardly earned, though the strain of responsibility had been lessened by having Laurence with him and ready to take his place if the American winter proved too much for him. In fact, he was never out of the bill, though in Chicago he was far from well. To William Winter, who was ageing fast and anxious for his ailing son, he wrote:

> *The Auditorium Hotel,*
> *February 16th, 1900.*

'My dear Winter,

You are one of the bravest and kindest of men—you are brave enough to bear your great burden or burdens, for you have more than should be. Poor boy! There's hope that the change may work his salvation—with all my heart I hope so, for your sake and for all. . . . I wish I could do something for him.

We shall be back in New York for a fortnight from 12 March. Come and stay with us for a few days . . . we can talk things over then— many things.

We are trudging along as usual and I have been down for a week with a cold in my head and a sty in my eye—inconvenient—but would supply, I should think, a little local colour to the appearance of the Incorruptible. He is very popular with Chicago audiences. My impression is that Maximillien had a sty in each eye and that another would add to the realism of his impersonation.

I sent to Philadelphia for the capsules which it was kind and thoughtful of you to suggest and the doctor here has recommended a cod liver oil emulsion which I take consistently three times a day—so be prepared when we meet to encounter a stalwart. . . .

All thanks for the cuttings—yours are always delightful reading.

I read Laurence your "Holy Sappho", a remarkable piece of English and scathing. . . .

If my wishes and blessing can bring to you and yours health and happiness, you have both, old friend and true friend—dear friend.

I love you and as ever,

Yours,

Henry Irving.'

Winter, dramatizing his own infirmity, was convinced that when he said farewell to Irving in New York it was for the last time; Irving's counterfeit presentment of his own robust health added strength to this conviction. Their parting was emotional. As Irving's liner steamed out to sea it took on, for Winter, an Arthurian magic to which his romantic soul surrendered with ecstasy, finding expression in a letter which pursued Irving across the Atlantic:

Home,
Tuesday, May 22nd, 1900.

'Dear Henry,

It is impossible for me to express the sense of bereavement that came upon me after I left you at the ship. The shadow had been impending all the time and it fell darkly at last. I cannot shake off the dread that we are not to meet again.

I made for my island as soon as we parted. Your ship was passing the Liberty statue as my boat left the dock, and so I followed you down the bay, about half a mile astern. There was something very sadly impressive in the *inexorable* way in which the great ship sped seawards. and left us behind. . . . Off Robins Bay light-house a vast rain-cloud hung low in the heavens and the smoke of your steamer rose and seemed to mingle with its drift. The scene was wild and very desolate. I lost sight of the ship when I landed. It was then raining heavily. By the time I reached the top of the hill your ship had passed the fort and I suppose you went to sea in a storm. . . .

I don't think that you quite realize how much you have endeared yourself, not only to me but to many others; and how much you represent to many hearts all that is lovely and noble in life.

God be with you and guard you. If we meet again we shall be glad. If not, I hope I shall not be forgotten. Nothing that I have ever said can half express my affection. In all ways I have tried to stand by you and, whatever may be the vicissitudes of fortune, I want you to feel that by me at least your splendid nature and your glorious purposes are understood. . . .

Ever yours,
William Winter.'

Premonitions fulfilled are eagerly recorded; those without consequence are conveniently forgotten. Winter's forebodings were unsubstantiated—at least in so far as his own death was not the cause of their final parting. If their next meeting was something of an anticlimax after such a moving valediction, Irving had enjoyed the rare satisfaction of a man who has read his own premature but flattering obituaries.

7

During the American tour Irving and Ellen Terry had openly discussed the prospect of ending their professional partnership. They were still good friends. She, perhaps, in justification of her own waning faith and patience, felt at times that he no longer cared for her. '. . . I can only *guess* at it, for he is exactly the same sweet-mannered person he was when I felt so certain Henry loved me. We have not met for years now, except before other people, when my conduct exactly matches his. All my own fault. It is I am changed not he.' He was less adept than she at dissimulation. The last two years had had their effect upon his outward bearing; a shield of cynicism concealed his bruised pride; an affectation of republicanism, the refuge of the dethroned autocrat, tempered his austerity. He evaded a difficult decision and was more tolerant of the incompetence of others. In short, he was a sick man.

When they returned to England, Ellen Terry proposed that, after playing one more season at the Lyceum, she should make a farewell tour lasting two years on her own account. Then, having made provision for her old age, she would retire to the country. Irving at first seemed agreeable to this plan—not by any means guilelessly— but later he asked her to postpone it and to tour once more with him in the autumn. '. . . I appear to be of strange *use* to H.,' she wrote to Shaw, 'and I have always thought to be *useful, really* useful, to any one person is rather fine and satisfactory.' It was evident that Irving would not scruple to use every subtle inducement to keep her at his side. Shaw seemed equally reluctant to 'give up' Irving. For some time past *Captain Brassbound's Conversion* had been the subject of a second conspiracy between the author and Ellen Terry—he would have

633

accepted Irving as Brassbound if that had to be the price of her playing Lady Cicely. They trailed the play under Irving's pince-nez, but he failed to understand it. 'It is like a comic opera,' he said. When, before sailing for America, she had given a copyright performance of the play in Liverpool with Laurence and other members of the Lyceum company, he did not go to see it.

Though he himself had no taste for the modernists, he was ready to defend them against any outside attack in which they were used as a stick to beat the theatre in general. When the Presbyterian politician, Samuel Smith, quoting the opinions of the outcast Clement Scott, sent him a pamphlet in which he denounced immoral plays and players, Irving sharply rebuked him:

Lyceum Theatre,
July 18th, 1900.

'Dear Mr. Smith,

I beg to thank you for your letter of the 13th instant . . . to rely on such evidence seems to me to be ministering, however unwittingly, to those unworthy prejudices which have for so long hindered the public appreciation of the art of the theatre—prejudices which I believe to be far more injurious to the moral life of a nation than the influence of any individual plays you can select for censure. For myself I know of none that deserve the terms of reprobation you have seen fit to employ and I find in our modern theatre so much more to welcome than to condemn, that I should feel myself ill at ease in using any influence that I possess to denounce the little that may still stand in need of amendment.

I return the letter you so kindly sent me and if such statements concerning certain plays are true, my reverence for the bible is not diminished because of the grossness of some of its pages.

I have the honour to be,

Yours faithfully,
Henry Irving.'

Irving fulfilled his obligation to the Lyceum company by appearing there for a short season in *Olivia* and other old favourites at no great profit to the company and at a slight loss to himself. While he was enjoying a much-needed rest at Crowborough news came of the devastation of Galveston, Texas, by a hurricane. Colonel Tom Ochiltree, the head of the American Press Union, appealed to him for help. At once he offered to organize a benefit performance in aid of the

stricken town; but a letter to Loveday showed that he understood the
need to husband his own strength:

'. . . The Honourable Tom Ochiltree is at the Carlton Hotel. I wish
you could see him and talk the matter over of this Galveston affair.
Afraid not much chance of my appearing—have been obliged to
decline so many other requests of the same sort—in fact am away from
London—but am heart and soul with the cause and anxious to do
everything or anything. . . .'

The benefit performance was given at Drury Lane on October 16th.
As usual, every actor and actress in London offered their services; but
generous as actors are, they can be jealous of their place in the bill.
In this case nobody volunteered to fill the unpopular first turn in the
variety programme. The matter was settled by Irving reluctantly
undertaking to open the proceedings with a recitation of *The Dream of
Eugene Aram* and to provide the penultimate turn with *Waterloo*—
Charles Wyndham and Lewis Waller having agreed, very sensibly,
to wind up the matinée with a scene from *Still Waters Run Deep*. As
a result a cheque for $6,085 was sent to Governor Sayers of Texas,
and Irving started out on his autumn provincial tour less rested than
he might have been. By December Ellen Terry was reporting to Shaw:
'. . . Henry is very ill, and it is necessary now that he should obey
doctors orders and go south. He is splendid—but he must give in
and he knows it.' He knew it, but now he felt the spur of need. His
share of the tour's profit was £3,500—little enough to meet the cost
of the new production which he had undertaken to present in April at
the Lyceum.

Four projects had been under consideration for some time. A new
play on Charles IX, an English version of *Cyrano de Bergerac*, *Richard
II* and *Coriolanus*. Ellen Terry had condemned *Charles IX* to well-
merited death; Coquelin had played Cyrano with great success at the
Lyceum, and Irving was wiser than to challenge the French actor in
a part he had made his own; he had prepared versions of *Richard II*
and *Coriolanus*, and elaborate productions of them had been designed
by Edwin Abbey and Alma Tadema respectively. He realized that he
was now too old to play Richard. His collaboration with Abbey had
brought out the best in both of them, and gave every promise of a
fine and most artistic Shakespearian production. He proposed to make
a gift of it to his son, Harry, who one day, he hoped, would play the
part. Abbey, up to this time, had not asked for any fee. Yet when he

heard of Irving's intention, he generously refused an offer for the work he had done from a rival actor-manager. *Coriolanus*, therefore, alone remained possible, with all its legendary unpopularity. Volumnia was a part which Ellen Terry could not spurn. In January, in the gloom of London in mourning for Queen Victoria, with even the gas-lights half-dimmed in the crêpe-hung streets, Irving worked with Loveday and Alma Tadema to put the preparation of scenery and costumes in train, so that they would be ready when he returned from another trudge through the provinces.

CHAPTER XXXIII

Pompes Funèbres : Coriolanus

I

At the turn of the century, the theatrical conditions which prevailed while Irving conquered and finally dominated the London stage had gone forever. Now he had to face vigorous competition not only from rival actor-managers, but from new styles of entertainment. The public still looked upon him affectionately as the grand old man of the theatre—but they no longer gravitated instinctively to the box-office of the Lyceum. Whereas when he came to London there had been only seven or eight theatres of repute, of which three had been the permanent homes of popular actors, now no less than fourteen offered a variety of first-class entertainment. Tree, at His Majesty's, was acknowledged to be his heir-apparent in the Shakespearian field; Wyndham was firmly established at the Criterion; his own graduates, Alexander, Harvey and Forbes-Robertson, had companies and theatres of their own, and their work was of a quality at which he himself had taught them to aim. There seemed to be playwrights galore to supply everyone's needs but his own. Pinero, Barrie and Henry Arthur Jones were producing play after play as much to the taste of the public as of the actors they served.

The greatest threat to these legitimate rivals and to himself were the musical plays with which George Edwardes was beginning to lure the public from the more serious forms of entertainment which, for so long, had been their only resource. At Daly's and at the Gaiety Theatre there could be seen a bright conjunction of light comedy and musical numbers which was clever enough to appeal to the older generation of intelligent playgoers whom Irving had attracted to the theatre; these musical comedies also provided the ideal entertainment to which young men could escort their feminine friends and relations who were already enjoying a foretaste of their emancipation. In addition to the attractions that these gay pieces presented on the stage, the stage-doors of the Gaiety and Daly's were becoming the happy hunting-grounds of the *jeunesse dorée*. At the close of the performance, young men, like elegant penguins—their gloved hands clutching a bouquet, their elbows pressing their opera-hats to their sides—would, under the stern eye of the stage-door keeper, eagerly await the appearance of a flounced vision which a note, carried by a commissionaire during the interval, had engaged either for the rest of the evening or for a lifetime. Many an heir to an ancient and perhaps enervated line, in search of an amusing supper companion, found himself married to a robust and lovely member of the chorus who set the sap stirring in the withered family tree. Irving, remembering that in the past he had won over to Shakespeare and the higher drama a public giddy with burlesques and French comedies, resented this revival of frivolities which were causing the defection of playgoers from the legitimate stage. The failure of *Coriolanus* added to his rancour.

While the play was in rehearsal he received a message of encourage ment from a source strange to anyone less gregarious than himself:

The cabmen's shelter,
Waterloo Station.
April 13th, 1901.

'Dear Sir Henry,
We beg to wish you, Miss Ellen Terry and your company every unqualified success in your production of *Coriolanus*, and that at the close of the season you may have every reason to congratulate yourself both from a physical and also a financial point of view. Believe us to be, yours very truly,

Thos. Ryan.
(pro—the London Jehu's here)'

London cab-drivers had every reason to regard him as their patron saint. It was his habit to set his own value on services rendered to him by his fellow-men—these values were often at variance with contemporary commercial practice. If a cabby drove him safely and goodnaturedly from the Garrick Club to Grafton Street, invariably he paid him half a sovereign. One night an honest cabby called him back, thinking that he had been over-paid in error.

'What's that? eh?' said Irving. 'Half-a-sovereign?—mm—consider yourself lucky—me man—that it wasn't a sovereign.'

Though good wishes of this kind may have persuaded him that *Coriolanus* had the ingredients of popular success, he failed to persuade the public that their traditional suspicion of its dullness was unfounded. Tadema's admirable settings and the inspired handling of the crowd scenes were unable to disguise the fact that Irving and Ellen Terry were sadly miscast. As in his Lear, Irving was handicapped by an elaborate make-up which obscured his expression and therefore weakened his hold over the audience. After thirty-three performances to thinning houses, *Coriolanus* was withdrawn—to be played only once more, on the last night of the season. Ellen Terry noted that then 'H.I. for the first time played Coriolanus beautifully. He discarded the disfiguring beard of the warrior he had worn during the run and now that one could see his face all was well . . . even an actor of Henry Irving's calibre hardly begins to play an immense part like Coriolanus for what it is worth until he has been playing it for fifty nights'.

2

A holiday, however short, revived Irving's spirits even if it could do little to improve his health. Wherever he went, the warm greetings and out-thrust autograph books reassured him that however empty were the stalls of the Lyceum, the hearts of the people were as full as ever of affection for him. He had no false modesty, and did not feign to deprecate these popular demonstrations. He was never happier than among the Bank Holiday crowds on Yarmouth sands or when stalking through the streets of Stratford-on-Avon with a suite of curious Americans on his heels. He liked to gossip with cheap-jacks and gipsies or to talk seriously with fair proprietors, as one manager to another, showing a genuine interest in their hazards and problems and in the state of their trade at that particular moment. The puppet proprietor at Tenterden was not the only travelling showman to enjoy his patronage. Once, at Whitby, he found a circus in distress, with every prospect of doing very poor business. Seeking out the manager, he ordered a bespeak performance and invited George du Maurier and other visitors to attend it. Smalley, the representative of the *New York Tribune*, brought a young American friend who accepted the ring-master's challenge to ride a bucking horse, and to everybody's delight succeeded in keeping himself in the saddle. The circus, as a result of this réclame, left the town richer than when it arrived. On this holiday he escorted the reluctant Mrs. Aria to the shrines of Stratford, which, with the exception of the church, she found 'a mausoleum to be mistrusted'.

And so on to Wales, where even on the slopes of Snowdon he was assailed by his admirers—as close to the people as ever.

During the short provincial tour before he sailed again to the United States, he made an excursion which would have tried a man in robust health. Leaving Leeds after the evening performance, he travelled to Winchester, where the next day he gave a reading of *Becket* in Castle Hall for the benefit of King Alfred's millenary celebrations, and left immediately to rejoin his company that night.

The seventh American tour was no less arduous than the previous one, but it was no less successful—his own share of the profits was about £12,000. On the eve of his return to England he gave the Trask lecture at Princeton University. His subject was 'Shakespeare and Bacon', and in the course of it he made a shrewd guess at the origins of the controversy:

'. . . Some people, I believe, are spiritually comforted by the notion that the plays which they misread at home but would on no account see enacted, were written not by a vagabond player who stole a deer in his hot youth, and kept company with Bardolph's nose, but by a statesman, a philosopher, and a judge, who was convicted of taking money from suitors, and degraded in his old age. I make no complaint of this singular frame of mind, for its lack of clarity touches not only Shakespeare and his fellow-actors, men like Burbage and Edward Alleyn on whose fame there is no reproach; it gathers under one comprehensive anathema a whole society of distinguished men in all ranks of life, poets and patrons, courtiers and critics. . . .'

He was back in England in time for rehearsals of *Faust* with which in April he opened his twenty-fifth season. Cecilia Loftus was engaged to play Marguerite—a part which Ellen Terry undeniably had outgrown. Irving hoped, however, to persuade her to play with him in other of the old pieces later in the season. In a reply to a letter from Stoker making this proposal she wrote:

> *Tower Cottage,*
> *Winchelsea.*
> *May 18th, 1902.*

'Dear Bram,

Your writing was *most beautiful*—clear as—clear! Thanks for your letter.

1. The present season for *me* please begins when *I begin to act*, on the 7th June and not on the 31st May. (I don't want salary when I don't give services! Many thanks all the same.)

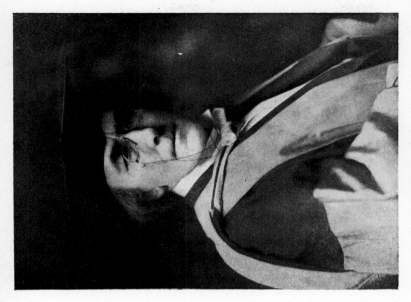

Doctor of Letters

Irving and Fussie

Irving in *Dante*

2. I will join Sir Henry on the twelve weeks tour (beginning in Birmingham 22nd September) acting two or six times a week (as Sir Henry may desire) at half my usual touring salary—that is to say at £100 per week.

3. I cannot decide at present about the further ahead tour (January 1903). What you call my "*own repertoire parts*" seem to have dwindled down to 2. Portia and Henrietta Maria—haven't they, unless we played *Macbeth*, *Much Ado*, *The Cup*, or a few things of the kind. However, there is no particular hurry about 1903 and I shall see H.I. soon. Yes thanks, I'm having a good rest, but oh . . . the cold.'

Shortly after his return Irving caught a chill while unveiling a memorial window to D'Oyley Carte in the Chapel Royal, Savoy. He was, therefore, in no condition to attend Tree's first banquet on the stage of His Majesty's to celebrate the success of Stephen Phillips' *Ulysses*; yet, fearing that his absence might be misinterpreted (for he managed to carry on with his rehearsals), he went. Towards four o'clock in the morning, he was one of half a dozen lingering guests. He sat stiffly at the head of the table; his face had a ghastly waxen pallor which accentuated the feverish glitter in his eyes. From fatigue and from the unavailing stimulus of champagne he had become more or less incoherent, his grunted ruminations were interrupted with paroxysms of coughing. Tree, anxious for his guest, felt that he should have an escort on his journey home. He asked the youngest actor present, Gerald Lawrence, to undertake this duty; but Lawrence, who had never met Irving before, demurred—fearing that the implication that such an escort was needed might have embarrassing consequences. Finally, Tree himself offered to drop Irving at Stratton Street on his way home. Dawn was breaking as they parted in the cab. In the half light, Tree saw the man he so much admired yet feared, supporting himself by the railings with one hand, the other sawing the air with a splendid gesture of farewell.

'The Oriflamme!' cried Irving, tragically and with unexpected clarity, as the cab moved away. 'The Oriflamme! We must keep—the Oriflamme—burning brightly . . . !'

The Oriflamme, no doubt, was to him a symbol of all that he had laboured to create, which he now feared was threatened with extinction. He had disconcerting powers of recovery which left him with a very shrewd idea of the amusing story which his host would make of the incident. A day or two later a mutual friend spoke to him of Tree.

'Ah—eh—a gud fellow,' commented Irving. 'A very—mm—gud fellow,' adding with a rueful nod, '. . . A pity he—er—drinks.'

3

Soon after he had reached England he had discovered that the Lyceum company and the theatre itself, as far as he was concerned, was doomed. The London County Council had embarked on a rigorous inspection of theatres and a strict enforcement of safety regulations and precautions against fire. There was no doubt that in most theatres, including the Lyceum, these reforms were already overdue. In the case of the Lyceum the alterations upon which the authorities insisted would involve the lessees (not the freeholder) in an expenditure of £20,000. Although Irving had earned the company nearly £30,000 and, as a result of the only suggestion he ever made as Dramatic Adviser, William Gillette in *Sherlock Holmes* had earned them a handsome profit, the whole over-capitalized concern built on the quivering sands of theatrical specula-tion was bankrupt. The ultimatum of the London County Council forced the company, whose capital had been eaten up and whose shares were practically worthless, to close the theatre at the end of Irving's season and to call in the Receiver. Perhaps Irving felt this more deeply than all the other misfortunes that befell him—not on his own account, but because he felt in some way responsible for the losses suffered by the shareholders, many of whom might have invested in the company because of their faith in him. In fact he was guiltless. He had, as Stoker said, 'received in all for his property, lease, goodwill, fixtures, furniture, the use of his stock of scenery and properties and a fourth of his profits elsewhere, £39,000 paid as follows: Cash £26,800, Shares £12,500. He repaid by his work £29,000 in cash. The shares which he received proved valueless. He gave, in fact, his property and £2,500 for nothing —and he lost about two years of his working life.' Nevertheless the revelation of the company's bankruptcy mortified and angered Irving. 'You think I don't know you've been robbing me,' he said bitterly at a meeting of the promoters, 'but I *do*.' He was not prepared to surrender the theatre, to which he had given so much of his life, without a struggle. At this time he wrote to Loveday:

> 17 *Stratton St.,*
> *Piccadilly.*
> *Monday evening—just off.*

'My dear Loveday,

Mr. Chas. Scotter, Director of S. W. Ry.—with whom I was dining last night—says it should be seriously considered—as do many who joined the Company on the inducement of my name—whether it would not be well to do something for the shareholders' sake, for my own sake, and for the preservation of the theatre.

If certain liabilities of the Company could be wiped off—Company newly constructed, a sum of £50,000 subscribed—County Council alterations made—with certificate of finality for certain period—theatre redecorated and brought up-to-date—and an *invitation* to me to undertake management—I should be inclined to accept it under certain conditions which we have already talked over—and the more inclined if we could baffle the pack of daylight robbers. I feel it now to be my duty. Show this to Stoker.

H. I.'

But though he knew where his duty lay, it was impossible to raise further capital. There were those who blamed the rich and influential friends who for so many years had enjoyed his art and his hospitality, for making no effort to preserve what had become a national institution. Yet with the evidence of past figures before them and the evidently failing strength and judgment of the man upon whom all hope of success depended, it was difficult to see what good further endowment could do. Several did all they could to help Irving personally—though it was not easy to offer financial aid to so proud a man. His affairs were in the hands of Alfred Rothschild, who never failed to tide him over difficult periods with loans on which no interest was charged. In spite of all this, the last season was played through without any one other than those immediately concerned realizing that the days of Irving's reign at the Lyceum were numbered.

As far as the public were concerned, the greatest surprise was to see Ellen Terry's name on the bills of Tree's His Majesty's Theatre and on those of the Lyceum at the same time. Tree's hunger for the throne that Irving occupied was well-known; this apparent capture of his Queen seemed to herald the deposition of the reigning monarch. Earlier in the year Tree had asked her to play Mistress Page in a revival of *The Merry Wives of Windsor*; having no illusions that he was Irving's equal as an actor, he surrounded himself with the best supporting cast he could find. In this case Oscar Asche and Mrs. Kendal as Mr. and Mrs. Ford, Ellen Terry as Mistress Page, and his wife, Maud Tree, as Ann Page, were engaged to play with his balloon of a Falstaff. Ellen Terry faithfully asked Irving's permission, which he gave on condition that she played with him at the Lyceum at matinées of *Charles I* and *The Merchant of Venice*. On her first night he sent her a telegram: 'Heaven give you many many merry days and nights.' But later, as he drove past

His Majesty's in a cab and glanced at the bills—MISS ELLEN
TERRY—MRS. KENDAL—MRS. TREE—he was heard to mutter:
'Mm—three little—meds, (maids) eh?—three—little meds.'

4

With the spring, London had thrown off the trappings of woe and
at the beginning of June had begun to bedeck herself for the Coronation
of Edward VII. Irving, in the past, had done much to recall to the
theatre the intellectual and middle-class public and to overcome their
old prejudices against his profession. It is doubtful if he could have
done so had he not, at the very outset of his campaign, had the private
encouragement and public approval of Albert Edward, Prince of Wales.
By the courteous entertainment of actors at his own table and by the
gracious acceptance of their hospitality in return, the Prince had endorsed Irving's claims for his profession and had indicated to a society
prone to trim its opinions to those of the Court that actors were no
longer to be considered as being beyond the pale of respectability. His
patronage was the expression of a genuine love of the theatre. He was
equally at home and at his ease in Toole's dressing-room or behind the
scenes of the Lyceum, discussing technicalities with the master machinist.
Above all, he appreciated and admired Irving's simple loyalty and integrity, rightly assessing his value to the Kingdom over which he
would ultimately reign. Irving knew how much he owed to the friendly
gestures and sage advice which had been extended to him from Marlborough House. Now, if ever, was the moment to give public expression
to his gratitude. That the enthronement of his patron and his own
dethronement happened to coincide was not to be deplored but rather
to be welcomed as an excuse for according the Lyceum obsequies of
unparalleled splendour.

Already Rajahs, Sultans, Tribal Chiefs and Potentates of every
shade and degree were converging on London from the furthest corners
of the Empire. Irving, as usual, considered them in terms of the
Lyceum. Here was material for a noble and glittering assembly such as
had never been seen on the Lyceum or on any other stage. Heedless of
his empty purse, disregarding the need to make provision for his old age,
he wrote to the Lord Chamberlain to ask if a gala performance, followed by a reception on the stage of the visiting princes and their suites,
would be acceptable to His Majesty. The King not only welcomed the
idea but instantly directed the Indian and Colonial Offices to see that
these plans were effectively set in motion. The date decreed by the

authorities for the entertainment was July 3rd. Thus, as far as the public was concerned, Irving would surrender his sovereignty of the Lyceum on July 19th, not in the sombre twilight of chagrin and bankruptcy, but in a radiance which would typify and even surpass the past splendours of his long and illustrious reign.

On June 26th, owing to the King's sudden illness, the Coronation was postponed. Those, however, who were responsible for the entertainment of so many distinguished visitors were instructed officially to fulfil the engagements they had made. So on the night of July 3rd, Irving played *Waterloo* and *The Bells* to a resplendent and heterogeneous audience which at the end of the performance surged into the corridors and foyers of the Lyceum where they waited until Stoker's magical transformation of the stage and the auditorium was completed.

At his command, regiments of carpenters gutted the stalls and pit, hurling the seats into carts waiting at the exits; a tornado of cleaners swept up behind them and on their heels upholsterers laid a field of crimson carpet. While sappers bridged the orchestra with an imposing staircase, the florists planted a jungle of palms, exotic flowers and shrubs which would make the most equatorial chieftain feel at home. In a trice the stage was cleared of scenery and properties, and the vast naked walls hung with scarlet draperies. Great chandeliers were hoisted aloft, and over the proscenium glowed a monstrous Union Jack surmounted by a crown in coloured electric lights (electricity was convenient for nonsense of this kind). Meanwhile, perhaps to Stoker's special delight, a posse of detectives rummaged every corner of the theatre for anarchists and, having drawn a disappointing blank, posted themselves at the entrances to see that among the guests there were no thieves tempted to pluck a ruby from a passing turban or diamonds from the jewel-studded Rajahs, some of whom were said to be worth half a million as they stood. This transformation seemed to have been instantaneous. In fact, only forty minutes had elapsed when Irving took his stand, with a son to the right and left of him, to receive the thousand guests who filed in through three entrances. In no time at all, the Night became Arabian—Rajahs and Sultans rivalling each other in the splendour of their retinues. Irving on these occasions was master of everything and everyone but himself. He was never quite able to assume an impersonal formality. As he grasped the hand of a Ranee, he would catch sight of an old actor he had known in Manchester and, breaking the ranks, would single him out for a greeting of unceremonious warmth. In order to keep him, as it were, on the saluting base, Lord Aberdeen and the Premier of New Zealand assumed the duties of bodyguard and prevented him straying from his post.

When the last of that great assembly, probably the most remarkable which up to that time had ever assembled under any one roof in London, had drifted away, when the detectives and the caterers had departed, Irving, his sons, Austin and Bram Stoker were left alone in the crimson void. They sat upon the empty stage telling not sad stories of the death of a great enterprise but recalling the triumphs of a glorious past. They all knew that the days of the Lyceum's glory were numbered and that 'the sun-lit clearing in the dark forest' would echo no more to the light clapping of the Chief's hands and to his quiet command—'Very good—yes—yes—begin the piece!' as the company settled down to rehearsal. It was six in the morning when, as they prepared to leave, Irving pronounced his verdict on his own genius: 'I am going to say something I have never said before. I know none of you will misunderstand me. Looking back on my life's work and attempting—in all humility—to appraise it—I feel certain of one thing— mine is the only great Shylock.'

The season ended on July 19th, with a matinée of *The Merchant of Venice*. For the last time Irving led Ellen Terry forward by the hand to acknowledge the applause of a Lyceum audience. The eyes of the public's 'respectful, loyal and loving servant' were glistening with tears. He knew that their partnership was nearing its end; if the Lyceum had to perish, it was as well that it should not survive their parting. She was no less moved. 'I shall never be in this theatre again' she said to him after their last curtain call: 'I feel it . . . I know it.' The audience filed out, happily ignorant of the deeper significance of the occasion. That afternoon, Irving made his final exit from the theatre which he had first entered so confidently thirty-one years ago.

5

Hospitality of such oriental magnificence could only be returned adequately by the Viceroy of India— as it would have been, had Irving been able to accept Lord's Curzon's invitation to the coming Durbar at Dehli. 'If you should feel,' wrote Curzon, 'the slightest inclination to come, a wire of one word, "Coming," will ensure you the best accommodation that we can provide as well as the heartiest reception.' It was, however, urgently necessary for Irving, after such a burst of prodigal extravagance, to gather in the golden provincial harvest. It was a grim struggle. Racked as he was with coughing and at times so weak as hardly to be able to stand, his disabilities seemed to leave him as he stepped upon the stage, so that he appeared to play his old parts with undiminished power. He began to depend to some extent on stimulants. In the old days, Dubosc, as he reeled about the garret gloating over the imminent execution of Lesurques, pulled at a bottle of sugar and water; now Walter saw that the bottle contained burnt brandy to accelerate the beating of his master's weakening heart. There were unexpected calls upon his small reserve of strength. The King was convalescent and was entertaining his cousin, the Kaiser, at Sandringham. Irving was commanded to entertain the royal guests on November 14th, with a performance of *Waterloo*. He was playing on that date in Belfast. By employing special steamers and trains at heavy expense to himself, he found that he could obey the Royal command without disappointing his audiences for more than one evening.

Leaving Belfast after the evening performance on the 13th, he landed at Liverpool in the early morning. A special train was waiting to take him to Sandringham, where he arrived at 6 p.m. Having played before the King and the Emperor after dinner, he caught a return train to Liverpool at midnight. As, in the early hours of the morning, the rest of the little party were leaving the train, Irving beckoned the station-master into his carriage. He asked him to send a telegram which he had written. It was to Toole.

'My dear old friend—I am on the road back to Belfast after having played before His Majesty at Sandringham. The King enquired very kindly after you and reminded me that it was just about 26 years ago since he first saw you in *Uncle Dick's Darling*. He also wishes me to give you his kind wishes for your birthday.'

His own fatigue was forgotten in his desire to cheer his old friend. There was still a sea voyage of a hundred and fifty miles between himself and the theatre in Belfast, which he reached ultimately at five o'clock in the afternoon. When Mephistopheles stepped upon the stage he was greeted with a cheer. He deserved it. The employment of the blackest arts hardly could have accelerated this phenomenal journey, nor could any magic repair the damage that such strains were inflicting upon a man grievously sick.

6

Irving returned to London at the end of the year to find that his son, Harry, had come to swift maturity as an actor, with a personal success comparable to his own sudden graduation from stereotyped villainy to the high comedy of his Digby Grant. After several years' service with Alexander at the St. James's Theatre, where he had made a name for himself as a portrayer of polished villains like Rupert of Hentzau, he had been engaged by Frohman to play the title role in Barrie's *The Admirable Crichton*. His performance was among the most memorable of a brilliant theatrical decade. The play ran for over three hundred nights, and by the end of that time his position as a leading actor of the younger generation was assured. Between Irving and his elder son there was still a certain constraint which no longer embarrassed his association with Laurence. Harry was in nature much akin to his father; proud, independent, unemotional and apt to be suspicious of his fellow-men. When he went on the stage he had not chosen the comparatively smooth path of service in his father's company. As an actor he was a modern—adept in the restrained technique which was displacing the broad flamboyance of the old school to which Laurence still affection-ately clung. Whereas Laurence's literary gifts found expression in the theatre, Harry had already made a name for himself as a biographer and essayist. His *Life of Judge Jeffreys* was a scholarly and witty, if not an entirely convincing, vindication of the notorious Lord Chief Justice; his collection of *Studies of French Criminals*, published in 1901, was remarkable for its dispassionate and objective scrutiny of the work-ing of the criminal mind which, in later years, characterized his prefaces to several of the *Notable British Trials*. It was perhaps this natural affinity which made Harry and his father uneasy in each other's com-pany. They met and supped together often enough; sometimes on Sun-days they drove together into the country, and as the brougham rattled along the road to Box Hill or climbed towards Hampstead, Irving would exchange his vivid memories of the trial of Thurtell and Weare for Harry's grim minutiae of the crimes of the Abbé Bruneau and of Madame Weiss. Irving went to see *The Admirable Crichton*. Harry nervously awaited his verdict. When they met after the play, his father seemed ready to talk about anything other than the performance.

'Barrie—M'yes—charming piece,' he said at last. '—fantastic comedy —Irene Vanbrugh . . . excellent.'

Then after a dreadful pause he added:

'Do you—er—*like* acting, me boy?'

And that was all. Proud as he undoubtedly was of his son's success, he could not bring himself to praise a style so foreign to his own.

CHAPTER XXXIV

Valedictory : Dante

—————

I

Now that the doors of the Lyceum were closed to him, Irving, at the invitation of Arthur Collins, had arranged to present a new production at the Theatre Royal, Drury Lane, in April. Indomitable but wilfully deaf to the warnings of his friends and advisers, he threw all his limited financial resources into a venture as splendid and extravagant in conception as any he had undertaken. He did so in order to retain his supremacy as a producer, knowing full well that the risks were as great as they were unnecessary. As an actor, he could have rested on his evergreen laurels; he could, as he told Laurence, 'turn up in any town in England with a bottle of water and a tumbler and walk away with £200'—a lack-lustre security which appealed to him as little as the prospect of peace after Tilsit had done to Napoleon. Many years ago he had asked Tennyson to write him a play about Dante, to whom he knew and was often told that he bore a striking resemblance. Tennyson had demurred. '. . . A fine subject! But where is the Dante to write it?' was his wise and modest excuse. Sardou, to whom Irving now turned for a play on this long-cherished theme, had no such inhibitions. He set to work and, for a handsome fee, produced a piece in thirteen scenes as unendurable as the inferno itself and as formless as primordial chaos. Laurence undertook the translation and adaptation of the text, but try as he would it seemed to offer his father nothing but the part of a rhapsodic Cook conducting a one-man infernal tour. The only resemblance it bore to the *Divine Comedy* was its utter lack of humour. Neither he nor anyone else, however, were able to deflect Irving from his disastrous purpose.

He assembled a cast of fifty players and a small army of damned spirits and supernumerary mortals. In addition to the difficulty of having to adjust himself to work in a strange theatre, Irving had to endure the presence of Moreau, Sardou's friend and agent, who had

649

come over from Paris to advise on the production. For a few days he exercised great patience, but at last he called his son aside.

'Tell me, Laurence,' he asked his interpreter. 'What is—mm—the French for—bloody fool . . . eh—ah? Well—tell him he is one and that he can go back to France.'

Moreau was tactfully persuaded to withdraw. Acres of scenery had been built and painted in Paris. All of it reached Drury Lane safely; much of it was discarded in rehearsal. A vast moving panorama, a triumph of mechanics, was designed to roll past Dante and Virgil to give the illusion of one of their interminable journeys. At the first experiment the machinery jammed and the landscape remained immobile. For a whole day Irving, in his storm hat, sat in silence watching the frantic efforts of the engineers to coax their contraption into life. At last he could stand it no longer. He sprang to his feet and, flinging his hat into the orchestra, gave a scream of rage.

'They can take it away and burn it,' he cried. 'Do they think I'm a damned showman?'

Irving, though comparatively careless of financial risks, never, if he could help it, took one which might mar the artistry of his production. As in this case, he did not hesitate to discard an unreliable contrivance even if the experiment had cost him several hundred pounds.

When Irving read the play to the company, few of them had the remotest idea of what it was all about, though Stoker recorded that he 'read it wonderfully well. Adumbrated every character'. Stoker, however, had his misgivings. Anticipating the bewilderment of the audience, a sixpenny booklet was prepared for sale in the theatre: *Some Explanatory Notes by an Italian Student*. At an early stage, he warned his Chief that he could not stand the loss which the failure of such a play might incur. 'My dear fellow,' answered Irving, 'a play like this beats Monte Carlo as a hazard. Whatever one may do—about losing—you certainly can't win—unless you play high!' The incorrigible punter seemed to be enjoying his last fling. His stake was over £12,000.

Dante was produced on April 30th. Even if it had been a great success, the loss would have been heavy. It was not an absolute failure. Now and again, the public, watching a piece of profound and unintelligible nonsense, persuade themselves that it has an intellectual and subtle content beyond their understanding and is therefore worthy of their attention and respect. In such a spirit the audiences at Drury Lane took some pleasure in the succession of spectacular scenic effects and the appearance of Irving in a rust-red robe embodying to perfection their idea of Dante. Here and there were to be found those for whom the play and production had an academic interest. One of the very few letters Irving received was appreciative though critical:

> 69 *Broadhurst Gardens,*
> *Hampstead.*
> *May* 8*th*, 1903.

'Dear Sir,

Will you allow me to say that the Archbishop of Pisa walks on as an *Abbot merely*, in that he carries his crosier with the *crook* INWARDS; that the Grand Inquisitor and inquisitors would be *Dominicans*, shaven, white habits and black cloaks, not bearded *Capuchins* (who were not invented till the fifth day of the Nones of July *1528*); and that nuns sing their offices in the quire-stalls, not huddled on the floor. Nevertheless, I for one am deeply grateful to you for your Dante.

> Faithfully yours,
> Fred. Will. Rolfe.

Oh, and Cardinals were not "Eminence" and most "eminent" till 1630 (reign of Urban VIII). Prior to that date they were Most Illustrious Lord (Illustrissimo); or, in the case of the Cardinal-Dean and the Cardinal-Nephews, "Most Respectable" or "His Respectability" or "Most Worshipful" or "His Worship" (Osservantissimo) (Colendissimo).'

The prelates and their appropriate crosiers were illustrated in the margin. About this time Baron Corvo, who was labouring at his novel, *Dom Gheraldo*, in a wretched bed-sitting-room in Hampstead, was glad enough to tramp south and to feast his eyes for two or three hours on such a splendid glimpse of the Renaissance.

Dante was played eighty-two times and lasted out the season. One night very nearly all the Royal Family came to Drury Lane. Their loyal, humble and obliged servant saw them from the stage, ranged in the Royal Box. His sense of drama and his curiosity as to the succession prompted him to remark to Loveday: 'If somebody put a stick of dynamite under the box, who would be King?' Every favourable notice, the visits of royalty or of any distinguished patron, were cabled to New York in order to whet the appetites of the American public, to whom Irving would look, during the following winter, to redeem his losses. Constantly he spurred his press agent, Brereton, to advertise the success which he had persuaded himself it had achieved. 'Triumphant' was the word he used to his friends and to the press.

He gave a ' Dante' supper at the Criterion, though he can hardly have been blind to the artificiality of the occasion. It was a dangerous sign when Irving gave way to self-deception.

Before he left England, the Lyceum company went into liquidation. Bram Stoker stood loyally by his Chief. Having done his best to prevent him from having anything to do with the scheme, he now did all in his power to protect him during the winding-up of the proceedings from the recriminations of angry shareholders. He had only to tell the truth to prove to them that Irving had more than discharged his obligations to the company at a loss of money and of more precious time to himself; he told it so forcefully that he drew cheers from an audience whose £1 shares were worth sevenpence.

On the afternoon of July 14th at Drury Lane, Irving and Ellen Terry appeared together for the last time. *The Merchant of Venice* was played by an all-star cast in aid of the Actors' Benevolent Fund; it was the only occasion when Harry acted with his father—as Salerio, a part apparently invented for the occasion, and provided with a few lines filched from Salarino.

For the first time Irving was sailing for America without Ellen Terry. 'It will be strange and somewhat sad without Nell,' he wrote to Winter, 'but 'twas not to be and I shall not attempt to tell you anything 'til we meet,—Poor dear, she has been absolutely under the influence and spell of her two children—who have launched her on a sea of troubles . . . poor Toole . . . saw him a few days ago in Margate and read your message to him. His eyes brimmed over and he sent to you his best love. He is gradually growing worse but unfortunately his *trunk* is sound they say—and he endures a lingering and living death. His vitality is amazing.

My boys are both well. Laurence and his wife coming with me, Loveday and Stoker.'

Sad as Irving may have been at their parting, he had little right to reproach Ellen Terry for having an artistic fling. She was, perhaps, not so careless as he was. 'I have saved money for my old age,' she had written to Shaw, 'and in spite of my children pressing me to risk it, I cannot.' Her escape from the Lyceum had not brought her the opportunities she had been led to expect. She had enjoyed a personal triumph in *The Merry Wives of Windsor*. All that Shaw, the tempter, had to offer was her part in *Captain Brassbound's Conversion* at the Court Theatre in the autumn—' . . . Lady Cicely would get no salary, of course. £25 and find her own gowns is the sort of thing the Court runs to.' It was hardly surprising that the cascade of their correspondence had become an intermittent trickle and that now she determined to fend for herself and for her children. That autumn Ted and Edie finally persuaded her to finance a season at the Imperial Theatre, the purpose of which was to allow her son to show his talents as a designer and producer, using Ibsen's *Vikings* as the peg to hang them on. She lost her money or some of it. She had no regrets—it was a fulfilment of her love for Godwin. From that time forward no designer for the stage would be able to deny the debt he owed to the gospel of the inspired if unpractical prophet, the child of Godwin's genius, Gordon Craig.

2

The American public did not care for *Dante*. After playing it a few times in New York, Irving was forced to lay the vast production aside. The hurt to his pride was the more grievous, for he knew that it was the last great picture he could ever paint. This disappointment made the weary plodding from city to city—thirty-three in five months—with the old stock, harder than ever to endure. The usual receptions, the private hospitalities of a generous people and the courteous attention of their President, Theodore Roosevelt, helped to maintain the illusion, not of his own popularity, for that was never in question, but of a triumphal progress; indeed, in a sense it was one, for never before had an old actor of nearly sixty-six, playing the parts he had created thirty years ago, attracted an audience whose enthusiasm seemed to be as great as ever and whose capacity could be gauged from the half-million dollars that they subscribed to see him. If Irving had cared more about money, the profit of £32,000 which he brought back to England would have eased the bitterness of his disappointment over *Dante*, as it relieved the immediate needs of his exchequer.

It was fortunate that Irving, on returning from America, was kept in the provinces for a few weeks touring, once again, in *Becket*, for which new scenery had been prepared in his absence—so that he did not reach London until June. In March, the blow of the auctioneer's hammer rang through the empty Lyceum when, in the dusty twilight, a crowd of junk-merchants and souvenir-hunters bid for the last relics of the theatre's greatness. There was little to attract the eye except the thirty-eight yards of carpet—crimson powdered with gold fleurs-de-lis—which on great occasions had paved the way to the Royal Box—Lot 98—gone—£8. A dilapidated trunk lying half open with a soufflé of faded press-cuttings pouring over its edges, found no buyer. The cardboard models of a hundred splendid scenes lay unnoticed in a dark corner.

Lot 112 was an epitaph on the Beefsteak Room—indeed on the whole vanished glamour of the theatre—'Four Gothic doors and Gothic framing of alcove . . . and iron grid'. The mahogany table at which Irving had entertained a thousand guests fetched its value—or so they said—£9 15s. All the crowd were strangers to the place save two—Pinero and Bancroft, who had a simple love of funerals of any kind, flitted momentarily through the shadows and were gone. By the time Irving reached London, the house-breakers were already at work.

'Mm,' he muttered as from a cab he saw the signs of demolition, 'I suppose they'll—mm—turn it into a—boot factory?'

It was, in fact, being reconstructed as a music hall.

Irving, in these days, kept very much to himself. 'Now that we see so little of you,' wrote old Joe Knight, in congratulating Irving on Laurence's election to the Garrick Club, 'we must console ourselves as best we may with your boys.' He preferred to entertain his few friends at Stratton Street. Those who went there used to find on their place at the round table a small bunch of violets done up by a patently amateur hand. Hardly a day passed, when he was in London, that he did not call on the Baroness Burdett-Coutts at her house on the corner of the street. Their friendship had survived the years, and now they were able to recall a past which few remembered. In the summer he had a long and refreshing holiday in Cornwall. With Mrs. Aria and her daughter he wandered from Boscastle to Tintagel, Tintagel to St. Ives and so to Halsetown. The home of the Penberthys was now a grocer's shop and the village post-office. At the inn opposite, the tale was still told of his donkey ride. He lingered on the hillside above his old home, counting the derelict mine-shafts and looked into the Methodist Chapel where Mr. Wallington, the minister, had so confidently singled him out for the ministry. In Penzance they found his cousin, Kate Penberthy, living in a house overlooking the bay. She was now an old lady with 'some resemblance to Irving in the granite of her outlines'. At first Mrs. Aria bridled at hearing Irving called 'Johnnie'; but when Kate kissed him goodbye and made her promise to nurse him if he was ill and, if necessary, to become an actress in order to look after him in America, she was as touched as he was by his cousin's innocent concern. So back to Tintagel, where he spent a restful week or two wandering along the cliffs towards Boscastle or from the verandah of his room watching the rare and too-distant ships through his beloved telescope.

Perhaps when the sun set in peculiar glory he remembered with regret that it was no longer any use making a rough note of the effect to pass on to Hawes Craven for reproduction in the Lyceum painting-rooms.

With that thought came the one he tried to shut out—of his impending retirement, of the not-so-far-off day when even provincial water-bottles and tumblers would be beyond his reach. Then these rooms over-hanging the sea, with the gulls gliding ceaselessly beyond the windows, would be the place to come to. Here he might even assemble those scraps of anecdote and autobiography for which his friends and several publishers had importuned him.

No doubt these ruminations were induced by the word 'Farewell', which headed the note-paper he would be using during the autumn tour, and would soon be seen on the bills in many provincial cities. By tradition, the farewells of actors and opera-singers could be as pro-tracted as they pleased. He planned to take leisurely leave of his British and American public over a period of two years and to retire in 1906 when he and Ellen Terry together might celebrate their stage jubilees. Yet it seemed quite a short time ago that he had set out on his first tour under his own management—dependent on nobody but himself for its success or failure. Now, he had lost a little of that independence. . . .

Before the last American tour he had seen and thought well of a performance of Orlando by a young actor, Gerald Lawrence, who was playing in Manchester—the same young man who had so wisely hesitated to see him home after Tree's party. He was a well-set-up fellow and had a frank, unintimidated manner which reminded Irving of poor Terriss—though he was more richly endowed in the upper storey—whose parts he was engaged to play. Lawrence soon became a devoted disciple of his Chief. It was not long, however, before he realized that only by art and will power was Irving able to conceal his increasing weakness. In certain scenes they played together—par-ticularly in *Louis XI*—he had to fling Irving to the ground. When it became apparent that the old man had difficulty in rising to his feet, the young actor laid hold of his master in such a way that he could help him up and steady him without the audience being any the wiser. Neither of them ever referred to the matter; Lawrence was wise enough not to speak of it to others. Many years afterwards he was rewarded by hearing that Irving had said to one of his sons: 'Good fellow—Law-rence—does things for me and never lets anyone know about it.'

For this tour he had engaged Edith Wynne Matthison to play Ellen Terry's parts; she was a promising young actress, the niece of Arthur Matthison, who, in the old days, had played his double in *The Corsican Brothers*. She had been brought up in a family steeped in the Irving legend. At her first rehearsal her sense of awe and of her inadequacy as Ellen Terry's successor for a moment overcame her. Irving tactfully directed the company to another scene. As she stood, woefully gazing out of a window, a hand fell gently on her shoulder. After a word or two of praise and of discriminating criticism, Irving added: 'It's a difficult art, my child—but then we shouldn't love it so much if it weren't so difficult, would we?'

In the middle of September Irving wrote to Mrs. James: '. . . our tour begins on Monday at Cardiff. We have very many changes and the work has been hard to get everything harmoniously together, but I think we are shaping well.'

The tour began encouragingly. In Swansea, at the close of Irving's brief farewell speech, the whole audience rose to their feet and sang in their native tongue 'Lead Kindly Light' and 'Land of My Fathers'. It was a spontaneous and heartfelt salute, and it moved him deeply. As he might have expected, the leave-takings wherever he played were as emotional; almost every civic body honoured him with a reception or a banquet. The many speeches he made in acknowledgment of these public hospitalities were light-hearted and, for the most part, recalled his early struggles in each particular town. He played in Sunderland for the first time since his disastrous début. The Mayor and Corporation, perhaps with a desire to wipe out those unhappy memories, entertained him to luncheon and presented him with a handsome casket which contained the text of a most reconciliatory address.

During the previous week, at Middlesbrough, Lena Ashwell, who was touring with her own company, came over from a nearby town to visit him. She found him frail and very tired. Yet he talked to her earnestly and prophetically. The decay of the theatres in the provinces was inevitable. Already commercialism was threatening to debase a great art into a catch-penny industry; the theatre they loved would soon become a disputed field for avaricious speculators. He urged her to believe in the spiritual power of the theatre in a changing world to educate the hearts of men. In the course of that brief meeting, he so imbued her with a sense of mission that thereafter she devoted the greater part of her theatrical life to bringing the higher drama to the poor and hitherto neglected districts of London and to provincial towns where normally the theatre no longer thrived.

There was a break in the tour for four weeks at Christmas-time, which Irving spent at Bournemouth. Towards the end of January he took to the road again—or worse, to cold and draughty railway carriages and to suites of uniform dinginess in moribund hotels. At Bath, he unveiled a memorial to the actor, James Quin. The effort of addressing a large open-air audience on a bitter cold day proved too much for him. The three-hour journey from Bath to Wolverhampton was made in a snowstorm; his train arrived three-quarters of an hour late. The next morning it was evident that he had caught a severe chill, though during the day he wrote a buoyant letter to Burnand:

> Star and Garter Hotel,
> Wolverhampton.
> February 1905.

'My dear Burnand,

God bless you for all your good wishes. Coming from an old man to a young one they are doubly blessed. I don't know, all told, that you haven't had a better time than I have and that your old age shall not have more in it than mine. After all you can go on writing whilst the brain lasts even when the fingers give in you can dictate, but the poor old "ponger's" life is limited by his bodily activity.

By the way, you bury me a year before my time, whenever that time may be. I was born in '38, so, old friend, respect my pristine youth.

My love and greetings to Lady Burnand and to all with the best of all good wishes,

> Yours ever,
> Henry Irving.'

That night he managed to struggle through *The Bells* and *Waterloo* —but on returning to his hotel he fainted, though he seemed not to have realized it. The following morning he saw a doctor—Dr. Lloyd Davies—who reluctantly did what he could to enable Irving to play for the two remaining nights of his engagement. 'On Tuesday,' he wrote, 'and particularly on Wednesday the patient was practically in extremis . . . when I say that a hypodermic injection of strychnine and other potent measures were necessary, which are still done night and day, the gravity of the situation may to some extent reveal itself. The real nature of the mischief is emphysema of both lungs of long standing with an acute attack of bronchitis supervening this, together with a rapidly weakening heart . . . on Tuesday night I explained to Mr. Stoker the impossibility of Hanley on Thursday and I supplemented this on Wednesday by the fact that the tour must come to an end at once. . . .'

The company was disbanded. Nine disappointed mayors cancelled their banquets and laid aside their addresses of welcome. Dr. Lloyd Davies, to whom Irving owed his life, insisted on his patient having absolute quiet and receiving no visitors of any kind. At least, for the time being, Irving was spared the knowledge that his labour and suffering during these winter months had only resulted in a further loss of £2,000. Like a prehistoric herbivore unable to sustain its vast bulk in a withering world, the Irving troupe seemed unable to meet its ever-increasing expenditure from its receipts even though the theatres in which it played were still crammed to capacity.

3

In a few days, Irving's condition improved. The doctor's main task was to protect his patient from his friends—'he is best alone for the present—even from his own people—of course there are many things one could say which cannot be put in writing'. He referred, of course, to the faithful lieutenants, the family, and the female devotees who contended for the privilege of nursing him and, in some cases, their own interests.

Ellen Terry arrived from London to find him looking 'like some beautiful grey tree she had seen in Savannah'. Apparently he did not realize the gravity of his illness—or the cause of it. 'Fiddle,' he said, when she begged him to heed the doctor's warning. 'It's not my heart at all! It's my breath.'

They had not been alone together for several years. Very much moved and perhaps a little embarrassed, at first they exchanged the usual sickroom formalities. Then Ellen Terry, no doubt with an intuition that this moment of intimacy might never be repeated, said impulsively:

'What a wonderful life you've had, haven't you?'

'Oh yes,' he said quietly, 'a wonderful life of work.'

'And there's nothing better after all, is there?'

'Nothing.'

'What have you got out of it all . . .? You and I are "getting on", as they say. Do you ever think, as I do sometimes, what you have got out of life?'

'What have I got out of it?' said Irving, stroking his chin and smiling slightly. 'Let me see. . . . Well, a good cigar, a good glass of wine—good friends.'

He paused to kiss her hand with courtesy.

'That's not a bad summing up of it all,' she said. 'And the end . . . how would you like that to come?'

'How would I like that to come?' He was silent for some thirty seconds before he snapped his fingers—the action, as always, preceding his words. 'Like that!'

Mrs. Aria was close on Ellen Terry's heels. At first, she was regarded with even greater disapproval by the doctor, but he soon came to recognize her as an ally. Irving's sitting-room was embowered with flowers and deep in telegrams and letters of condolence; in his bedroom, Loveday and Stoker were striving to acknowledge them, but whenever they submitted a draft reply to the patient, he grunted: 'Very good—very good—but I should not say that.' She stayed no longer than to make arrangements for him to spend his convalescence with her at Torquay. The doctor had agreed that he might be well enough in April to fulfil an engagement to play for a short season at Drury Lane. They found Torquay cold and uncongenial and, moving on, spent most of their time at Tintagel.

4

It was very proper that, on this occasion, he played at the Theatre Royal. The illustrious procession of great English actors had graced its stage, and from it many of them had taken their farewell of the public. For the past thirty years the Lyceum, under Irving, had usurped the supremacy of the Theatre Royal; old Drury now claimed Irving to take his place in the line of its histrionic succession. The popular anxiety over his illness and the rejoicing over his recovery heightened the anticipation of old and young playgoers for his reappearance in London; many of them may have had an unspoken conviction that it was their last chance to submit themselves to his mesmerism, although there was no hint of farewell on the bills. On the opening night the theatre was crammed from gallery to pit. When the curtain rose upon Becket and Henry II playing their game of chess, there was a storm of cheering louder and more sustained than the oldest playgoers had ever experienced. Irving muttered impatiently to Gerald Lawrence: 'They're overdoing it—get on with your lines—me boy—get on—shout 'em down!'

'I won't do any such thing,' was the *sotto voce* reply of his insubordinate colleague. The ovation continued until Irving rose reluctantly and with bowed head stood for five minutes until the enthusiasm of the audience wore itself out.

Thus the season began and so it continued. Irving seemed to be lifted and inspired by his reception; age and infirmity seemed to fall from him, and he played the old parts with all the force and intensity of his youth. The incoherences which sickness had aggravated, the feebleness of gait and gesture vanished as he reacted to the only stimulant which, for an actor, never loses its potency from habit— the applause of a devoted and adoring public. He was once again the unregenerate actor-manager, impenitent of his artistic egotism, well content to be what Sickert, once a member of his company, called the 'lech' in the great picture framed by the proscenium. One night during *Becket*, as he came from his dressing-room—the ritual procession headed by Loveday bearing a light and little Walter, carrying the hand properties, elbowing aside loiterers in the narrow passage—he met the boy who had been newly-engaged to play Geoffrey, the king's bastard son. He stopped and asked him how he was getting on and what was his ambition. The lad replied that his ambition was to play Becket —adding on second thoughts that he would like to play Henry II as well. Irving bent over him and whispered confidentially: 'So should I—me boy—so should I.'

On the last night of the season he played Becket—and probably played it better than ever before. When the curtain fell the applause reached the crescendo to which it had been rising night by night. When it died down Irving was too moved to make any coherent acknowledgment. He was heard to say: '. . . Only my blood speaks to you in my veins.' And then, referring to some red roses which had been flung upon the stage and now were held against his brown monk's robe, he murmured that he could not congratulate himself that they were sweets to the sweet. During the play when the knights had rushed from the cathedral they had cried: 'King's Men, King's Men!' As he hesitated for words, a cry came from the gallery: 'Irving's Men. Irving's Men!' and was taken up by the whole house. He paused and, looking up with a smile, said: 'Good, good,' before he bade his audience goodbye. There were shouts of 'No, not goodbye!' 'Well— good night—then,' were his last words as the curtain fell. The audience refused to leave the theatre. Stoker plunged the auditorium into darkness, but with no effect. The pit and upper parts of the house, surging into the stalls, had occupied the orchestra where they beat the kettle-drums as an accompaniment to their shouting. Irving, having by this time changed, returned to the stage where the staff were assembled to present him with a loving-cup to which the stage-hands of every theatre throughout the kingdom had subscribed. Hearing the din beyond the curtain, he asked Gerald Lawrence what it was. 'They're still calling for you, sir,' he answered.

'Take the curtain up,' ordered Irving. When the shouting subsided, he said quietly to the silent throng: 'We were about to have a little festivity of our own, if any of you would like to join us—you are welcome to do so.'

The little ceremony was performed. After one more short, sharp cheer, the audience dispersed. It had been the perfect end to the season that Irving, his people and his public had been for a few moments united in friendly intimacy. A few days later, on June 15th, he played *Waterloo* at His Majesty's Theatre, in a performance organized for the benefit of old Lionel Brough, who had been with him in Toole's production of *Dearer Than Life*.

5

While Irving was enjoying his triumph, Harry was playing Hamlet for the first time at the Adelphi Theatre. When his father had heard that he was to do so he did not show the confidence in him which he had felt in Forbes-Robertson. In his notebook he wrote:

'. . . Poor little H. . . . he'll never make anything of Hamlet. He said: "I am rehearsing and I pick up the business that way." "What do you mean, pick it up?" "Learn the words, Sir"—he always calls me "Sir"—"The words! Why I knew them when I was fourteen."

I gave him a leg-up. I hope he'll read of it in the papers. I said something about his being an ornament to the English stage. No one applauded but someone said: "Ah—you're always very kind".'

On the first night he sent Harry a telegram, 'I am thy father's spirit brooding o'er ye'—a message which was not likely to allay the young actor's nervousness. Later, he went with Mrs. Aria to the Adelphi. At the outset he was irritated by a glowing brazier on the battlements which distracted attention from the actors. During the performance he sank lower and lower in his chair, a well-known sign of his disapproval. After the performance he saw his son—the meeting was as constrained as ever, the unspoken criticism as severe. At last, as he turned to go, he said: 'I see—me boy—the streets are up in Elsinore.'

Before he left for his holiday, he took the chair at a dinner given by the members of his profession in honour of the veteran critic, Joe Knight—Joe Knight who not long before had written to him: '. . . As the man and the artist I equally cherish you and your princely scorn of pelf, in worship of which others bow down, is but one of the many noble traits which endear you to me beyond measure. I am not in your or in any man's suite. If I could be before all it should be yours.'

Of late, Irving's after-dinner speeches had often been rambling and obscure, as though he was enjoying a private joke within himself. On one occasion he happened on the phrase 'Crummles and his pumps...' and he went on mumbling it to himself and chuckling over it rather to the embarrassment of his fellow-guests. That night his delivery was clear and his matter carefully prepared; the speech included a summary of his lifelong experience of dramatic criticism:

'. . . My own observation of dramatic criticism is pretty extensive, and it convinced me long ago that the critics do speak their minds, although they may not be all of the same mind. There is a cheerful diversity. Touching upon criticism, upon one occasion I ventured to use the phrase "Rapture of disagreement", to describe the effect produced sometimes by the reading of many notices. An eminent critic has been at pains more than once since then to explain to me on philosophical grounds why it is impossible for all the critics to take the same view and say the same thing. I am glad they do not. For sameness would be terrible. Even if they always said that we were all incomparable, that would cease to be stimulating after the first shock of surprise, and we should yearn for a discordant note. But there is one thing we do look for in criticism—the quality which Russell Lowell, himself a great literary critic, called the first essential—the quality of sympathy.'

Irving had an elephantine retention of memory for past kindnesses or grievances. In July he heard that Macmillans were publishing a collection of the late Canon Ainger's essays which had been prepared by his friend, Canon H. C. Beeching, and included the criticism of his Hamlet which had caused its author so much embarrassment. Irving's jaws snapped on this old bone. With the help of Austin, he drafted a letter to the publisher:

> 17 *Stratton Street,*
> *Piccadilly, W.*
> *July* 1905.

'Dear Frederick Macmillan,

I see your firm are about to publish a collection of articles contributed to *Macmillans Magazine* by Canon Ainger, including one entitled "Mr. Irving's Hamlet and Its Critics", written more than thirty years ago. In ordinary circumstances I should not dream of demurring to the republication of an article however severe upon myself—and this one is unmeasured in its hostility; but the fact is, to my certain knowledge, that the author regretted it and wished that it had never been written.

Some years ago I had a talk with Canon Ainger at Bristol. We had been on the most friendly terms for a long period, and he reminded me that we had first met in the house of Sir Theodore Martin. I said that I had known him before that in connection with his article on my Hamlet in Macmillans. "Ah!" he said, "that ought not to have been written. I am utterly ashamed of it."

I am sure he could never have desired that a criticism he felt so strongly to be so unjust should appear in any collection of his writings, more especially as the original publication was anonymous. I think it right to call your attention to the matter, lest later the republication, under the circumstances, should ever be deemed as an injury to the memory of the dead man.'

At first Canon Beeching showed fight, and threatened to ventilate in *The Times* Irving's attempt to suppress his friend's work. Irving, shifting his target, engaged Beeching with a telegraphic broadside:

> *Hotel Metropole,*
> *Whitby,*
> *August 3rd, 1905.*

'To the Reverend Canon Beeching,
Burford Vicarage,
Oxon.

I shall be sorry if I cause you any disappointment but not even terror of *The Times* can alter my resolution. I much appreciate the gracious courtesy of the Messrs. Macmillan and uphold the objection to commit a wrong to the loved memory of our mutual friend. H.I.'

Beeching hauled down his flag:

> *Burford Vicarage,*
> *Oxon.*
> *Thursday.*

'Dear Sir Henry Irving,
Macmillans have sent me a copy of your letter to them and I am only sorry that they did not take me into their confidence in the first instance; because I entirely agree that after a statement of that kind from Ainger, it would be, as you say, a wrong to his memory to reprint the article. I am sorry to have put you to the trouble of so much correspondence in the matter.

Believe me, with sincere respect,

> Yours very truly,
> H. C. Beeching.'

This successful and refreshing little skirmish cheered Irving's holiday at Whitby. Before he went on it, he had been to Margate to see Toole, whom he found completely crippled and utterly depressed. When Toole spoke to him of his approaching and now welcome death, Irving said: 'I shall not be long after you. I hope to die in harness, and if I should choose my epitaph it would be—The readiness is all'. Nevertheless he tried to cheer the dying man and promised that he would return to Margate when the company disbanded after the autumn tour, so that once again they could spend Christmas together.

From Whitby, Irving went with Mrs. Aria for a few days to Scarborough. There he found George Grossmith doing poor business at the Spa Theatre. George Grossmith had once boasted to him that in contrast to the enormous cavalcade which Irving took with him on tour, all he needed was a grand piano and a dress suit; to which Irving had replied: 'Ah, George—we don't all look so funny in a dress suit.' In order to help his friend, Irving promised to attend the Saturday matinée, against the advice of Stoker and Mrs. Aria, who saw that the reaction from his recent exhilaration was already setting in. When he entered the theatre, the audience rose respectfully from their seats and gave him an ovation, which he acknowledged. George Grossmith, at his piano, got his first laugh at this point by turning towards Irving and saying: 'I shall have to ask you to leave, sir.'

After the performance, Grossmith asked him which he would choose —to live ten years if he rested, or two if he continued to act. 'I should act,' answered Irving without a moment's hesitation. After his holiday he returned to London to conduct rehearsals for the provincial tour which was to start in October. He had decided to give up playing *Waterloo* before *The Bells*, and to substitute for it *King René's Daughter*, in which Gerald Lawrence and Edith Wynne Matthison would appear. They were appalled to hear that he was to undertake the production of a new piece. Loveday, however, reassured them. 'Let him do it,' he said; 'he's never happier than when rehearsing something new.' Irving applied himself to the task with his accustomed care and scrupulous attention to detail. Edith Wynne Matthison and her two fellow-actors found it terrible to watch the old man working so strenuously, though his mind seemed to lord it over material weakness. When they awoke from the spell of his direction, though spiritually refreshed, they seemed to be far more physically exhausted than their Chief.

But when Sam Elliott, an American friend, with Hatton and one or two others, dined with him at Stratton Street on the eve of his departure, they were shocked by his appearance. Though he made an effort to conceal it, he was much dispirited. A day or two earlier he had heard of Austin's sudden and unexpected death at Brighton. It was as though he had suffered the loss of a limb, for Austin, although he had become a very successful journalist, always found time to help and advise his old Chief and with him to hammer out the weapons of controversy. When his guests left him at eleven o'clock he was deadly pale and breathing with difficulty. Elliott, having told him that a very special dinner awaited him if he came to New York the following year, earnestly begged him to take care of himself.

'Oh yes,' replied Irving, 'yes—that will be all right, old friend.'

CHAPTER XXXV

Curtain : Westminster Abbey

———❦———

I

When the company assembled at Sheffield on Monday, October 2nd, they were alarmed by his evident frailty which courageous pretence could not conceal. His answer to enquiries after his health was invariably the same—'Quite well—thank you!' spoken with a quiet insistence. The Lord Mayor of Sheffield gave a luncheon in his honour. In his speech of thanks, Irving spoke of himself as of a man 'the sands of whose life are running fast'. That night, waiting for his cues, he sat in the wings, worn out and fighting for breath; but when they came he answered them like a battle-weary and disciplined soldier automatically obeying orders. Once upon the stage he wrought the old miracle. At Bradford, the following Monday night he played Shylock. When Gerald Lawrence came off the stage he found the Chief sitting in the wings waiting for his first entrance. Instead of his usual enquiry, 'Well—me boy, what are they like—cast iron?' Irving said meditatively: 'It's a pity—just as one is beginning to know a little about this work of ours—it's time to leave it.'

On Tuesday he played Becket. In the morning he had written a letter to Harry who had asked his advice about a contract he had been offered by Frohman. However feeble his body, his mind was as alert as ever to the business of the theatre:

Midland Hotel,
Bradford.
Tuesday, October 10th, 1905.

'My dear Harry,

The contract or agreement would be *no* agreement after the first month or two. It is full of pitfalls and I should not bind myself to anybody for five years. If you don't both agree, better to part and if you

666

do—well—all right and have fresh contract every year. Anyhow you are not entering into anything of the sort. As you say, they are all so mixed up and play into one another's hands that you cannot be too careful. Between ourselves—it has come to my knowledge that it needed the most influential interest to get Mrs. Pat's contract carried out after her accident in spite of clauses in black and white providing for such a contingency as hers.

I return the document, which is really impudent in its one-sidedness. There are really only seven good months in America and these people would send you almost at any time, North, South, E. and West—up and down and across the continent—one night stands and all such horrors and I see nothing at all about Sundays being excepted. Whichever way you went to America it would be well to have a representative of your own to look after your interest and save you worry and vexation.

By the way, I don't believe in your lawyer being Frohman's. I never found a man serve two masters properly and even such a friend as George Lewis fails at it.

God bless you,
With all love,

H. I.'

On Wednesday, when Stoker came to fetch him for a luncheon at which the Mayor of Bradford was to present him with an address, he seemed very feeble. As he climbed the steps in front of the Town Hall, he played the old comedy which hitherto had so successfully disguised his infirmity. He halted a moment, pointed to a local feature and made some enquiry about it. While he listened to the answer, he managed to regain his breath. At the lunch, though he looked desperately ill, he spoke well; his theme was the need for municipal theatres. 'It may be,' he concluded, 'that in years to come our countrymen will scarcely understand how in our times so potent an instrument for good or ill as the stage was left entirely outside the sphere of public administration.'

That night he played *The Bells*—a performance which the company had come to dread. They found it an agony to watch him. When the curtain fell, he collapsed and sat in the prompt entrance, fighting for breath for ten minutes before Loveday and Walter could help him to his dressing-room. At last he recognized partial defeat. He gave orders for *The Bells* to be sent back to London—it had made him and now it threatened to destroy him. Stoker had anticipated his order.

Theatre Royal, Bradford.

Lessee - - JOHN HART.

MONDAY, OCTOBER 9TH. 1905, FOR SIX NIGHTS.

FAREWELL TO HENRY IRVING

TUESDAY and FRIDAY NIGHTS, Oct. 10th and 13th at 7.30

❧ BECKET ❧

By ALFRED LORD TENNYSON.

ADAPTED FOR THE STAGE BY HENRY IRVING.

Thomas Becket { Chancellor of England, afterwards Archbishop }	**HENRY IRVING**
Henry II. (King of England)	Mr. GERALD LAWRENCE
King Louis of France	Mr. H. B. STANFORD
Gilbert Foliot (Bishop of London)	Mr. H. ASHETON TONGE
Roger (Archbishop of York)	Mr. WILLIAM LUGG
John of Salisbury } Friends of	Mr. MARK PATON
Herbert of Bosham } Becket {	Mr. JAMES HEARN
John of Oxford (Called the Swearer)	Mr. T. REYNOLDS
Sir Reginald Fitzurse } The Four Knights of	Mr. FRANK TYARS
Sir Richard de Brito } the King's Household,	Mr. G. GRAYSTONE
Sir William de Tracy } Enemies of	Mr. L. BELMORE
Sir Hugh de Morville } Becket	Mr. LESLIE PALMER
Richard de Hastings (Grand Prior of Templars)	Mr. J. ARCHER
The Youngest Knight Templar	Mr. STEVENS
Lord Leicester	Mr. VINCENT STERNROYD
Philip de Eleemosyna (The Pope's Almoner)	Mr. W. J. YELDMAN
Herald	Mr. H. R. COOK
Monk	Mr. A. GURNEY
Geoffrey (Son of Rosamund and Henry)	Master TONGE
Retainers {	Mr. A. FISHER / Mr. HAYES
Countrymen {	Mr. CHARLES DODSWORTH / Mr. R. BRENNAN
Servant	Mr. W. MARION
Eleanor of Aquataine { Queen of England, divorced from Louis of France }	Mrs. CECIL RALEIGH
Margery	Miss GRACE HAMPTON
Rosamund de Clifford (Fair Rosamund)	Miss EDITH WYNNE MATTHISON

Knights, Monks, Heralds, Soldiers, Retainers, &c.

Synopsis of Scenery

PROLOGUE.

Scene 1—A Castle in Normandy,   Scene 2—The Same:

ACT I.   Scene 1—Becket's House in London.   Scene 2—Street in Northampton leading to the Castle.   Scene 3—The Same: Scene 4—The Hall in Northampton Castle.

ACT II.   Scene—Rosamund's Bower.

ACT III.   Scene I—Montmirail, "The Meeting of the Kings,"   Scene 2—Outside the Wood, near Rosamund's Bower.   Scene 3—Rosamund's Bower.

" At Merton the Archbishop assumed the ordinary habit of the black canons of the Augustinian Rule, which dress he wore to the end of his life."—GRIM,

ACT IV.   Scene I—Castle in Normandy—King's Chamber.   2—A Room in Canterbury Monastery.   Scene 3—North Transept of Canterbury Cathedral.   Period—12th Century.

The Scenery has been Specially Painted by Mr. Joseph Harker.

The Overture and Incidental Music by Sir Charles Villiers Stanford.

The Costumes, &c., from designs by Mrs. Comyns Carr and Mr. Charles Cattermole, R.I., executed by Mrs. Nettleship, August et Cie, and Messrs. L. and H. Nathan. Wigs by W. Clarkson.

The following morning, Friday, October 13th, Irving seemed a little better, though Loveday and Stoker were alarmed by his too easy acquiescence to the abandonment of the projected American tour. 'A kindly continent to me,' he said, 'but I will not leave my bones there if I can help it.' In the evening he seemed stronger and was very serene. The curtain rose upon a performance of *Becket*, which left a deep impression on all those who saw it; those who played that night with Irving hovered on the borderland of supernature. It had seemed to them, during the past ten days, as though he was consciously dying— they had spoken openly of this to one another. The first inkling of approaching crisis was felt by Gerald Lawrence when Irving, stooping over his hand as Becket made obeisance to the king, brushed it with his lips. He had never done so before—normally his gestures never varied by a hair's breadth. At the end of the third act, after Becket had parted from Rosamund, his words were 'Poor soul! Poor soul!' Edith Wynne Matthison heard Irving repeat the words after she had left the stage. When the curtain rose and fell to thunders of applause, he kept repeating to himself 'Poor soul' as he was led away to his dressing-room— as though, she felt, he meant the human soul in general, as though it was a prayer for his own.

In the third and last act Rosamund leaves Becket with these words:

BECKET: '. . . Think not of the King: Farewell!'
ROSAMUND: 'My Lord, the city is full of armèd men.'
BECKET: 'Ev'n so: Farewell!'
ROSAMUND: 'I will but pass to Vespers
And breathe one word for my liege-lord the King,
His child and mine own soul, and so return.'
BECKET: 'Pray for me too; much need of prayer have I.'
(Rosamund kneels for his benediction and goes.)

On the second line, Edith Wynne Matthison made a rhythmic slip— pronouncing armed as a monosyllable. Her mistake did not pass unnoticed by Irving. With the ghost of a twinkle in his eye, he murmured: '. . . Armèd, my dear, armèd.' Disconcerted, she stumbled again, substituting his own words: 'And so farewell' for 'And so return'. The repetition of his earlier line seemed to strike a chord in his spirit. 'Pray for me too—much need of prayer have I,' he said, and then added, 'Farewell—farewell', as she left the stage, with such profundity of meaning that it seemed as though he was on the brink of eternity and was striving to tell her so.

During Becket's last scene with John Salisbury came these lines:

BECKET: 'My counsel is already taken, John.
        I am prepared to die.'
JOHN: 'We are sinners all,
        The best of all not all prepared to die.'
BECKET: 'God's will be done.'

Those standing in the wings and hanging breathlessly on his every word, heard him, in place of the last line say: 'God is my judge'.

When Fitzurse struck him, he did not grasp his adversary as was his habit, but gently laid his hand upon his arm. Those anxiously waiting in the wings heard him recite clearly and resonantly Becket's last words: 'Into thy Hands, O Lord, into thy Hands!' Then he fell, not as he usually did with his head downstage, but upstage towards the steps which led to the choir—another alarming departure from his meticulous practice.

The curtain fell. Loveday and Belmore, his assistant, helped Irving to his feet. He seemed dazed and bewildered. 'What now . . .?' he muttered, as though he hoped that the devoutly desired end had come and was ready to obey the supreme mandate. His people led him downstage to take the calls for which the audience was clamouring. The curtain rose and fell many times before he began a halting speech— losing himself a little and paying tribute to Shakespeare instead of to Tennyson. He rested for a minute or so in the wings before Loveday helped him to his dressing-room. While he was changing his clothes he seemed to rally. He chatted a little with Loveday and Stoker about the future of the tour and showed concern lest his advance agent, who had been kept needlessly at the theatre waiting to see him, might miss his supper if he was to catch the last train to Birmingham where they were due to play the following week. As Stoker was leaving to dismiss the man, Irving stretched out his hand to say good night. Stoker grasped it. They were too intimately associated normally to exchange such courtesies. This gesture and the pressure of Irving's hand were disturbing variations in the routine of their nightly parting.

'Muffle up your throat, old chap!' advised Irving, '—it is a bitterly cold night—you have a cold—take care of yourself. Good night. God bless you.'

After Stoker had gone, Irving was brought a charcoal study of himself drawn by a local boy; the young artist was waiting outside to have his work hallowed by his signature. He signed it and turned to wash his hands—very carefully and methodically as was his custom. Walter helped him into his heavy overcoat and, with Loveday, escorted him to his waiting cab. Shepherd, his assistant and messenger, was standing near and, as sometimes happened, Irving told him to get in with Walter.

'You ought to have a cab,' he said to Loveday. 'It's very cold. See you tomorrow—Good night.'

He himself got in and sat with his back to the driver to avoid the draught. He did not speak during the short journey. As he entered the hotel he stumbled, but Shepherd caught him and helped him to the inner hall. 'That chair. . . !' he gasped, pointing to the nearest one. He sat down to rest for a moment. His tired heart no longer sustained the fight for breath. Losing consciousness, he slipped from the chair to the ground.

A country doctor, who had been at the play and had missed his train, was having a drink in the manager's private room. Hearing someone call for a doctor, he went at once into the hall. An old gentleman, whom he did not recognize, lay unconscious on the floor; his head was supported by a frail little fellow who was quietly weeping. Somebody nearby told him that the prostrate man was Sir Henry Irving. He was too late. Irving and Brodribb had once again linked hands and were on their way.

2

The news of Irving's death was carried swiftly to his company in their scattered lodgings; shocked as they were, it seemed to be the climax to a tragedy long rehearsed. A porter brought the news to Tree as he sat with his friends at supper in the Garrick Club; in silence the message was passed round the table and in silence the members rose, and left the Club. His sons journeyed to Bradford through the night. The next day Toole, dazed and broken-hearted by the news of his friend's death, bade his servants recover from the waste-paper basket the last words which Irving had written to him—his address on a wrapper round a newspaper containing an account of the civic reception at Bradford. In Manchester, on the following night, Ellen Terry strove to keep faith with her public. She was playing *Alice Sit-By-the-Fire*. When she came to the lines: 'It's summer done, autumn begun . . . I had a beautiful husband once . . . black as raven was his hair . . .', she broke down. The curtain was lowered and in respectful silence the audience left the theatre. Mrs. Aria, hearing that the end had come as he desired, was content; she expended her grief in fashioning a pall of fresh laurel leaves such as she knew would have pleased him.

When the people heard of his death, the expression of their sorrow was akin to that inspired by Nelson, for, like the great sailor, Irving was honoured and respected for his actions and for his nature loved. The flags throughout the kingdom were flown at half mast. The pillars of the desecrated Lyceum were hung with crêpe and every London cab-driver tied a black bow upon his whip. The newspapers of the world published columns of eulogy and appreciation; the humble and the great subscribed their tributes. A few dissentient voices recapitulated the old contentions, but they were scarcely heard. Yet, while Irving's body lay in state in the house of the Baroness Burdett-Coutts, the controversy which had been the background of his life survived his death.

Ellen Terry once had asked him, half in jest, if he thought it possible that he might be buried in Westminster Abbey. 'I should like them to do their duty by me and they will—they will,' was his reply. His confidence in the people was not misplaced. Alexander and a few of Irving's close friends so gauged public feeling that they asked the Dean of St. Paul's if they might bury their dead leader in his cathedral. Their request was refused. They waited upon Dr. Armytage Robinson, the Dean of Westminster, with a memorial signed by the leaders of their profession and by the great men of literature, art and science and of a society whose intellectual recreation Irving had enriched. The Dean had been threatened with blindness and lay in a darkened upper room attended by his sister, in whom the old prejudices against players and playhouses lingered. When she heard the purpose of the petition she protested vehemently against the burial of any more actors in the Poet's Corner. The members of the deputation were still waiting for an answer when Sir Anderson Critchett, who had become the leading oculist in the country, passed through the room in which they sat, on his way to see his patient. Recognizing several of his friends, he asked what they were waiting for. When he heard the purpose of their mission, he promised that he would do all he could to help them. He reminded the Dean that, when he had saved his sight, he had asked what return he could make as a token of his gratitude. Now, said Critchett, was the time and opportunity to make that return by granting the request of the gentlemen waiting below. The Dean's sister repeated her protest—'No actors—no actors!' but in vain. The Dean honoured his debt.

On the eve of the funeral, Irving's cremated remains were carried

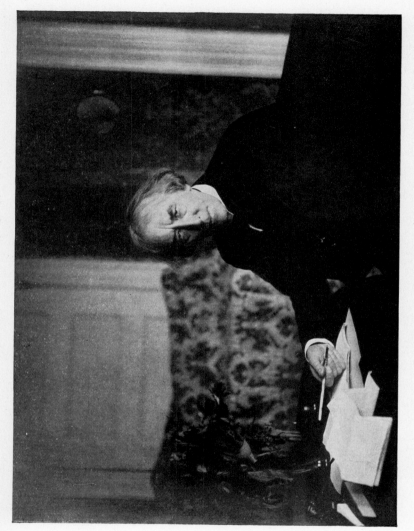

Irving on his last American tour

The Last Study of Irving by
Sir Bernard Partridge

Irving in 1905

The Death Mask of Henry Irving

through the streets lined with silent crowds. The people had finished their day's work and were grateful for this opportunity to pay their last tribute to the dead actor—for on the morrow there would be no room for them in the Abbey.

The actors and actresses whose working lives he had dignified, the craftsmen and handymen in the well-found theatres for which the Lyceum had been the model, the generations of patrons, humble and great, in whom he had created a hunger for the higher drama, the troops of friends he had known and those who had been but a blur of faces beyond the footlights—these Alexander and his helpers laboured to accommodate in the nave and transepts of the Abbey where in homage they would accord the great actor an ovation, silent but more eloquent than the applause that had so often thundered in his ears.

During the night, the coffin which contained the ashes of Irving lay in St. Faith's Chapel. On October 20th, shrouded with its laurel pall, it was borne upon the shoulders of his friends into the Abbey, where, in the presence of a vast congregation, it was laid at the feet of the statue of his beloved Shakespeare and at the side of his fellow-player, David Garrick.

Irving died penniless. On this account, there was no cause for tears, for pity or for disparagement. As he said, he had not been sent into the world to collect money. He may or may not have known that Toole and Mrs. James had, in their separate wills, left him ample provision for his old age had he survived them. The sale of his pictures, theatrical relics and the clothes and properties he had used in his most notable parts, which were contested for keenly by his friends and admirers, afforded enough to provide for his only dependant—his widow.

The Knight from Nowhere left no successor. The continuity of the Shakespearian succession was broken. The sceptre of the Globe Theatre had passed through only four hands before it reached his own. The brightest jewel in that sceptre was Hamlet, created first by Burbage. The second Hamlet, Joseph Taylor, an actor in the King's company at the Globe and Blackfriars theatres, was rehearsed by Burbage and succeeded him in the part. Betterton studied Hamlet with Sir William D'Avenant, who had seen Taylor. Garrick learnt his business from the veteran companions of Betterton. The survivors of Garrick's company communicated his method to Edmund Kean on whose interpretation—rehearsed by Kean's Polonius, Chippendale—Irving fashioned his own. The generation of actors who saw Irving in *Hamlet* passed away;

in that and in the next generation no supreme actor took the stage capable of transmitting the fiery message, through his genius—no actor of whom it might be said, as Théophile Silvestre wrote of Delacroix:

'There was a sun in his head and storms in his heart who for forty years had played upon the keyboard of human passions and whose brush grandiose, terrible and suave, passed from saints to warriors, from warriors to lovers, from lovers to tigers and from tigers to flowers.'

Such a man was Henry Irving.

Appendix A

ADDRESS

SESSIONAL OPENING
PHILOSOPHICAL INSTITUTION
EDINBURGH
NOVEMBER 9
1891

THE ART OF ACTING

I have chosen as the subject of the address with which I have the honour to inaugurate for the second time the Session of the Edinburgh Philosophical Institution, 'The Art of Acting.' I have done so, in the first instance, because I take it for granted that when you bestow on any man the honour of asking him to deliver the inaugural address, it is your wish to hear him speak of the subject with which he is best acquainted; and the Art of Acting is the subject to which my life has been devoted. I have another reason also which, though it may, so far as you are concerned, be personal to those of my calling, I think it well to put before you. It is that there may be, from the point of view of an actor distinguished by your favour, some sort of official utterance on the subject. There are some irresponsible writers who have of late tried to excite controversy by assertions, generally false and always misleading, as to the stage and those devoted to the arts connected with it. Some of these writers go so far as to assert that Acting is not an Art at all; and though we must not take such wild assertions quite seriously, I think it well to place on record at least a polite denial of their accuracy. It would not, of course, be seemly to merely take so grave an occasion as the present as an opportunity for such a controversy, but as I am dealing with the subject before you, I think it better to place you in full knowledge of the circumstances. It does not do, of course, to pay too much attention to ephemeral writings, any more than to the creatures of the mist and the swamp and the night. But even the buzzing of the midge, though the

675

insect may be harmless compared with its more poison-laden fellows, can divert the mind from more important things. To disregard entirely the world of ephemera, and their several actions and effects, were to deny the entirety of the scheme of creation.

I take it for granted that in addressing you on the subject of the Art of Acting I am not, *prima facie,* encountering set prejudices; for had you despised the Art which I represent I should not have had the honour of appearing before you to-day. You will, I trust on your part, bear this in mind, and I shall, on my part, never forget that you are members of a Philosophical Institution, the very root and basis of whose work it is to inquire into the heart of things with the purpose of discovering why such as come under your notice are thus or thus.

The subject of my address is a very vast one, and is, I assure you, worthy of a careful study. Writers such as Voltaire, Schlegel, Goethe, Lessing, Charles Lamb, Hazlitt, and Schiller, have not disdained to treat it with that seriousness which Art specially demands—which anything in life requires whose purpose is not immediate and imperative. For my own part, I can only bring you the experience of more than thirty years of hard and earnest work. Out of wide experience let me point out that there are many degrees of merit, both of aim, of endeavour, and of execution in acting, as in all things. I want you to think of acting at its best—as it may be, as it can be, as it has been, and is—and as it shall be, whilst it be followed by men and women of strong and earnest purpose. I do not for a moment wish you to believe that only Shakespeare and the great writers are worthy of being played, and that all those efforts that in centuries have gathered themselves round great names are worthy of your praise. In the House of Art are many mansions where men may strive worthily and live cleanly lives. All Art is worthy, and can be seriously considered, so long as the intention be good and the efforts to achieve success be conducted with seemliness. And let me here say, that of all the arts none requires greater intention than the art of acting. Throughout it is necessary to *do* something, and that something cannot fittingly be left to chance, or the unknown inspiration of a moment. I say 'unknown,' for if known, then the intention is to reproduce, and the success of the effort can be in no wise due to chance. It may be, of course, that in moments of passionate excitement the mind grasps some new idea, or the nervous tension suggests to the mechanical parts of the body some new form of expression; but such are accidents which belong to the great scheme of life, and not to this art, or any art, alone. You all know the story of the painter who, in despair at not being able to carry out the intention of his imagination, dashed his brush at the imperfect canvas, and with the scattering paint produced by chance the very effect which his brush, guided by his skill alone, had failed to achieve. The actor's business is primarily to reproduce the ideas of the author's brain, to give them form, and substance, and colour and life, so that those who behold the action of a play may, so far as can be effected, be lured into the fleeting belief that they behold reality. Macready, who was an earnest student, defined the art of the actor 'to fathom the depths of character, to trace its latent motives, to feel its finest quiverings of emotion, to comprehend the thoughts that are hidden under words, and thus possess one's-self of the actual mind of the individual man'; and Talma spoke of it as 'the union of grandeur without pomp, and nature without triviality'; whilst Shakespeare wrote, 'the purpose of playing, whose end, both at the first and now, was and is, to hold, as 'twere, the mirror up to nature; to show virtue her own feature, scorn her own image, and the very age and body of the time his form and pressure.'

This effort to reproduce man in his moods is no mere trick of fancy carried into execution. It is a part of the character of a strong nation, and has a wider bearing on national life than perhaps unthinking people are aware. Mr. Froude, in his survey of early England, gives it a special place; and I venture to quote his words, for they carry with them, not only their own lesson, but the authority of a great name in historical research.

'No genius can dispense with experience; the aberrations of power, unguided or ill-guided, are ever in proportion to its intensity, and life is not long enough to recover from inevitable mistakes. Noble conceptions already existing, and a noble school of execution which will launch mind and hand at once upon their true courses, are indispensible to transcendent excellence; and Shakespeare's plays were as much the offspring of the long generations who had pioneered his road for him, as the discoveries of Newton were the offspring of those of Copernicus.

'No great general ever arose out of a nation of cowards; no great statesman or philosopher out of a nation of fools; no great artist out of a nation of materialists; no great drama, except when the drama was the possession of the people. Acting was the especial amusement of the English, from the palace to the village green. It was the result and expression of their strong, tranquil possession of their lives, of their thorough power over themselves, and power over circumstances. They were troubled with no subjective speculations; no social problems vexed them with which they were unable to deal; and in the exuberance of vigour and spirit, they were able, in the strict and literal sense of the word, to play with the materials of life.' So says Mr. Froude.

In the face of this statement of fact set forth gravely in its place in the history of our land, what becomes of such bold assertions as are sometimes made regarding the place of the drama being but a poor one, since the efforts of the actor are but mimetic and ephemeral, that they pass away as a tale that is told? All art is mimetic; and even life itself, the highest and last gift of God to His people, is fleeting. Marble crumbles, and the very names of great cities become buried in the dust of ages. Who then would dare to arrogate to any art an unchanging place in the scheme of the world's development, or would condemn it because its efforts fade and pass? Nay, more; has even the tale that is told no significance in after years? Can such not stir, when it is worth the telling, the hearts of men, to whom it comes as an echo from the past? Have not those tales remained most vital and most widely known which are told and told again and again, face to face and heart to heart, when the teller and the listener are adding, down the ages, strength to the current of a mighty thought or a mighty deed and its record?

Surely the record that lives in the minds of men is still a record, though it be not graven on brass or wrought in marble. And it were a poor conception of the value of any art, if, in considering it, we were to keep our eyes fixed on some dark spot, some imperfection, and shut our eyes to its aim, its power, its beauty. It were a poor age indeed where such a state of things is possible; as poor as that of which Mrs. Browning's unhappy poet spoke in the bitterness of his soul:

> '*The age culls simples,*
> *With a broad clown's back turned broadly to the glory of the stars.*'

Let us lift our faces when we wish to judge truly of any earnest work of the hand or mind of man, and see it placed in the widest horizon that is given to us. Poetry, painting, sculpture, music, architecture, all have a bearing on their time, and beyond it; and the actor, though his knowledge may be, and must be, limited by the knowledge of his age, so long as he sounds the notes of human passion, has something which is common to all the ages. If he can smite water from the rock of one hardened human heart—if he can bring light to the eye or wholesome colour to the faded cheek—if he can bring or restore in ever so slight degree the sunshine of hope, of pleasure, of gaiety, surely he cannot have worked in vain? It would need but a small effort of imagination to believe that that great wave-theory, which the scientists have proved as ruling the manifestations of light and sound, applies also to the efforts of human emotion. And who shall tell us the ultimate bounds of these waves of light and sound? If these discernible waves can be traced till they fade into impalpable nothingness, may we not think that this other, impalpable at the beginning as they are at the end, can alone stretch into the dimness of memory? Sir Joshua's gallant compliment, that he achieved immortality by writing his name on the hem of Mrs. Siddons's garment, when he painted her as the Tragic Muse, had a deeper significance than its pretty fancy would at first imply.

Not for a moment is the position to be accepted that the theatre is merely a place of amusement. That it is primarily a place of amusement, and is regarded as such by its *habituées*, is of course apparent; but this is not its limitation. For authors, managers, and actors it is a serious employment, to be undertaken gravely, and of necessity to be adhered to rigidly. Thus far it may be considered from these different standpoints; but there is a larger view—that of the State. Here we have to consider a custom of natural growth specially suitable to the genius of the nation. It has advanced with the progress of each age, and multiplied with its material prosperity. It is a living power, to be used for good, or possibly for evil; and far-seeing men recognise in it, based though it be on the relaxation and pleasures of the people, an educational medium of no mean order. Its progress in the past century has been the means of teaching to millions of people a great number of facts which had perhaps otherwise been lost to them. How many are there who have had brought home to them in an understandable manner by stage-plays the costumes, habits, manners, and customs of countries and ages other than their own; what insight have they thus obtained into facts and vicissitudes of life—of passions and sorrows and ambitions outside the narrow scope of their own lives, and which yet may and do mould the destinies of men. All this is education—education in its widest sense, for it broadens the sympathies and enlarges the intellectual grasp. And beyond this again—for these are advantages on the material side— there is that higher education of the heart, which raises in the scale of creation all who are subject to its sweetening influences. To hold his place therefore amongst these progressing forces, the actor must at the start be well endowed with some special powers, and, by training, reading, and culture of many kinds, be equipped for the work before him. No amount of training can give to a dense understanding and a clumsy personality certain powers of quickness and spontaneity; and, on the other hand, no genius can find its fullest expression without some understanding of the principles and method of a craft. It is the actor's part to represent or interpret the ideas and emotions which the poet has created, and to do this he must at the first have a full knowledge and understanding of them. This is in itself no easy task. It requires much study and much labour of many kinds. Having then acquired an idea, his intention to work it out into reality must be put in force; and her new difficulties crop up at every further step taken in advance. Now and again it suffices the poet to think and write in abstractions; but the actor's work is absolutely concrete. He is brought in every phase of his work into direct comparison with existing things, and must be judged by the most exacting standards of criticism. Not only must his dress be suitable to the part which he assumes, but his bearing must not be in any way antagonistic to the spirit of the time in which the play is fixed. The free bearing of the sixteenth century is distinct from the artificial one of the seventeenth, the mannered one of the eighteenth, and the careless one of the nineteenth. And all this quite exclusive of the minute qualities and individualities of the character represented. The voice must be modulated to the vogue of the time. The habitual action of a rapier-bearing age is different from that of a mail-clad one—nay, the armour of a period ruled in real life the poise and bearing of the body; and all this must be reproduced on the stage, unless the intelligence of the audience, be they ever so little skilled in history, is to count as naught.

It cannot therefore be seriously put forward in the face of such manifold requirements that no Art is required for the representation of suitable action. Are we to imagine that inspiration or emotion of any kind is to supply the place of direct knowledge of facts—of skill in the very grammar of craftsmanship? Where a great result is arrived at much effort is required, whether the same be immediate or has been spread over a time of previous preparation. In this nineteenth century the spirit of education stalks abroad and influences men, directly and indirectly, by private generosity and national foresight, to accumulate as religiously as in former ages ecclesiastics and devotees gathered sacred relics, all that helps to give to the people a full understanding of lives and times and countries other than their own. Can it be that in such an age all that can help to aid the inspiration and to increase direct knowledge is of no account whatever, because, forsooth, it has a medium or method of its own? There are those who say that Shakespeare is better in the closet than on the stage; that dramatic beauty is more convincing when read in private than when spoken on the stage to the accompaniment of suitable action. And yet, if this be so, it is a strange thing that, with all the activity of the new-born printing-press Shakespeare's works were not known to the reading public till the fame of the writer had been made on the stage. And it is a stranger thing still, if the drama be a mere poetic form of words, that the writer who began with *Venus and Adonis*, when he found the true method of expression to suit his genius, ended with *Hamlet* and *The Tempest*.

How is it, I ask, if these responsible makers of statements be correct, that every great writer down from the days of Elizabeth, when the drama took practical shape from the wish of the poets to render human life in all its phases, have been desirous of seeing their works, when written in dramatic form, represented on the stage—and not only represented, but represented under the most favourable conditions obtainable, both as to the fitness of setting and the choice of the most skilled and excellent players? Are we to take it that the poet, with his eye 'in a fine phrenzy rolling,' sees all the minute details of form, colour, light, sound, and action which have to be rendered complete on the stage? Is there nothing in what the individual actor, who is gifted with fine sense and emotional power, can add to mere words, however grand and rolling in themselves, and whatsoever mighty image thay may convey? Can it be possible that there is any sane person who holds that there is no such thing as expression in music so long as the written notes are correctly rendered—that the musical expression of a Paganini or a Liszt, or that the voice of a Malibran or a Grisi, has no special charm—nay more, that there is not some special excellence in the instruments of Amati or Stradivarius? If there be, we can leave to him, whilst the rest of mankind marvel at his self-sufficient obtuseness, to hold that it was nothing but his own imagination which so much influenced Hazlitt when he was touched to the heart by Edmund Kean's rendering of the words of the remorseful Moor, 'Fool, fool, fool!' Why, the action of a player who knows how to convey to the audience that he is listening to another speaking, can not only help in the illusion of the general effect, but he himself can suggest a running commentary on what is spoken. In every moment in which he is on the stage, an actor accomplished in his craft can convey ideas to the mind.

It is in the representation of passion that the intention of the actor appears in its greatest force. He wishes to do a particular thing, and so far the wish is father to the thought that the brain begins to work in the required direction, and the emotional faculties and the whole nervous and muscular systems follow suit. A skilled actor can count on this development of power, if it be given to him to rise at all to the height of a passion; and the inspiration of such moments may, now and again, reveal to him some new force or beauty in the character which he represents. Thus he will gather in time a certain habitual strength in a particular representation of passion. Diderot laid down a theory that an actor never feels the part he is acting. It is of course true that the pain he suffers is not real pain, but I leave it to any one who has ever felt his own heart touched by the woes of another to say if he can even imagine a case where the man who follows in minutest detail the history of an emotion, from its inception onward, is the only one who cannot be stirred by it—more especially when his own individuality must perforce be merged in that of the archetypal sufferer. Talma knew that it was possible for an actor to feel to the full a simulated passion, and yet whilst being swept by it to retain his consciousness of his surroundings and his purpose. In his own words—'The intelligence accumulates and preserves all the creations of sensibility.' And this is what Shakespeare means when he makes Hamlet tell the players—'for in the very torrent, tempest, and (as I may say) whirlwind of your passion, you must beget a temperance that may give it smoothness.'

How can any one be temperate in the midst of his passion, lest it be that his consciousness and his purpose remain to him? Let me say that it is this very discretion which marks the ultimate boundary of an Art, which stands within the line of demarcation between Art and Nature. In Nature there is no such discretion. Passion rules supreme and alone; discretion ceases, and certain consequences cease to be any deterrent or to convey any warning. It must never be forgotten that all Art has the aim or object of seeming and not of being; and that to understate is as bad as to overstate the modesty of the efflorescence of nature. It is not possible to show within the scope of any Art the entire complexity and the myriad combining influences of Nature. The artist has to accept the conventional standard—the accepted significance— of many things, and confine himself to the exposition of that which is his immediate purpose. To produce the effect of reality it is necessary, therefore, that the efforts of an artist should be slightly different from the actions of real life. The perspective of the stage is not that of real life, and the result of seeming is achieved by means which, judged by themselves, would seem to be indirect. It is only the raw recruit who tries to hit the bull's-eye by point-blank firing, and who does not allow for elevation and windage. Are we to take it for a moment, that in the Art of Acting, of which elocution is an important part, nothing is to be left to the individual idea of the actor? That he is simply to declaim the words set down for him, without reference to the expression of his face, his bearing, or his action? It is in the union of all the powers—the harmony of gait and utterance and emotion—that conviction lies. Garrick, who was the most natural actor of his time, could not declaim so well as many of his own manifest inferiors in his art—nay, it was by this that he set aside the old false method, and soared to the heights in which, as an artist, he reigned supreme. Garrick personated and Kean personated. The one had all the grace and mastery of the powers of man for the conveyance of ideas, the other had a mighty spirit which could leap out in flame to awe and sweep the souls of those who saw and heard him. And the secret of both was that they best understood the poet—best impersonated the characters which he drew and the passions which he set forth.

In order to promote and preserve the idea of reality in the minds of the public, it is necessary that the action of the play be set in what the painters call the proper *milieu,* or atmosphere. To this belongs costume, scenery, and all that tends to set forth time and place other than our own. If this idea be not kept in view there must be, or at all events there may be, some disturbing cause to the mind of the onlooker. This is all —literally all—that dramatic Art imperatively demands from the paint room, the wardrobe, and the property shop; and it is because the public taste and knowledge in such matters have grown that the actor has to play his part with the surroundings and accessories which are sometimes pronounced to be a weight or drag on action. Suitability is demanded in all things; and it must, for instance, be apparent to all that the things suitable to a palace are different from those usual in a hovel. There is nothing unsuitable in Lear in kingly raiment in the hovel in the storm, because such is here demanded by the exigencies of the play; but if Lear were to be first shown in such guise in such a place with no explanation given of the cause, either the character or the stage-manager would simply be taken for a madman. This idea of suitability should always be borne in mind, for it is in itself a sufficient answer to any thoughtless allegation as to over-loading a play with scenery.

Finally, in the consideration of the Art of Acting, it must never be forgotten that its ultimate aim is beauty. Truth itself is only an element of beauty, and to merely reproduce things vile and squalid and mean is a debasement of Art. There is apt to be such a tendency in an age of peace, and men should carefully watch its manifestations. A morose and hopeless dissatisfaction is not a part of a true national life. This is hopeful and earnest, and, if need be, militant. It is a bad sign for any nation to yearn for, or even to tolerate, pessimism in its enjoyment; and how can pessimism be other than antagonistic to beauty? Life, with all its pains and sorrows, is a beautiful and a precious gift; and the actor's Art is to reproduce this beautiful thing, giving due emphasis to those royal virtues and those stormy passions which sway the destinies of men. Thus the lesson given by long experience—by the certain punishment of ill-doing—and by the rewards that follow on bravery, forbearance, and self-sacrifice, are on the mimic stage conveyed to men. And thus every actor who is more than a mere machine, and who has an ideal of any kind, has a duty which lies beyond the scope of his personal ambition. His art must be something to hold in reverence if he wishes others to hold it in esteem: There is nothing of chance about his work. All, actors and audience alike, must bear in mind that the whole scheme of the higher Drama is not to be regarded as a game in life which can be played with varying success. Its present intention may be to interest and amuse, but its deeper purpose is earnest, intense, sincere.

Appendix B

The author is much indebted to Mr. John Parker, the editor of *Who's Who in the Theatre*, for his permission to publish this comprehensive list which he has compiled of the parts played by Sir Henry Irving in the course of his career.

Parts played at Lyceum Theatre, Sunderland, Theatre Royal, Edinburgh, and Queen's Theatre and Operetta House, Edinburgh, from September 29th, 1856 to September 13th, 1859.

Advocate's Daughter, The	Herbert
All That Glitters IS Not Gold	Sir Arthur Lassel, Stephen Plum, Jasper Plum
Anchor of Hope, The	Richard Hargrave
An Hour at Seville	Peregrine Pyefinch
Artist's Wife, The	Lord Welford
Asmodeus	Ferdinand, Count Medora
As You Like It	Sylvius, Orlando
Avalanche, The	General Duclos
Balance of Comfort, The	Mr. Torrington
Barney the Baron	Augustus
Bashful Irishman, The	Pester
Bathing	John Beauchamp
Battle of the Inch, The	M'Kay, M'Intosh
Bay of Biscay, The	Tom Tunnell
Betsy Baker	Mr. Crummy
Beulah Spy, The	Beauchamp
Birthplace of Podgers, The	Edmund Earlybird
Black Eyed Susan	Seaweed, Lieutenant Pyke, Captain Crosstree
Blighted Being, A	Ned Spanker
Blind Boy, The	Prince Rodolph
Boarding School, The	Lieutenant Varley, Captain Harcourt
Bohemians, The	Paul Didier

Book III, Chap. I	Edmond de Mailly
Bonnie Fishwife, The	Wildoates Heartycheer
Boots at the Swan	Henry Higgins, Frank Friskly
Born to Good Luck	Count Manfredi
Bottle Imp, The	Albert
Bride of Lammermoor, The	Captain Craigengelt
Bright To-Morrow, A	Philip
British Legion, The	Colonel Davenport
Cabin Boy, The	Vincent
Cagot, The; or, Heart to Heart	Antoine
Carpenter of Rouen, The	De Saubigné
Castle Spectre, The	Earl Percy
Catching an Heiress	Captain Killingly, Captain Poodle
Catherine and Petruchio	Hortensio, Biondello
Charles XII	King Charles
Charming Polly, The	Nat Nowlan
Clari, The Maid of Milan	Duke Vivaldi
Conrad and Medora (Pantomime)	Yussuf
Corsican Brothers, The	Alfred Meynard, Baron de Montgiron
Cramond Brig	Tam Maxwell, James Birkie, King James
Creole, The	Alphonse de Nyon
Cricket on the Hearth, The	Gruff Tackleton
Critic, The	Dangle
Crown Prince, The	Frederick Storke, Francis
Custom of the Country, The	Frank
Cymbeline	Pisanio
Daddy Hardacre	Adolphus Jobling
Dancing Barber, The	Alfred Fitzfrolic, Lord Mincington
David Copperfield	David Copperfield
Day After the Wedding, The	Colonel Freelove, Lord Rivers
Deaf as a Post	Captain Templeton
Diamond Cut Diamond	Captain Seymour
Dombey and Son	Mr. Dombey
Dominique the Deserter	Count D'Anville
Don Caesar de Bazan	Don José
Don Giovanni (Extravaganza)	Octavio
Don't Judge by Appearances	Frank Topham

Double Dummy	John Timpkins
Douglas	Lord Randolph
Drapery Question, The	Mr. Ogler
Dream at Sea, The	Richard Penderell
Dred	Clayton
Drunkard's Doom, The	Rudolphus
Dumb Maid of Genoa, The	Count Corvenio, Antonio, Strapado
Dumb Man of Manchester, The	Mr. Palmerston
Ella Rosenberg	Colonel Mountfort
Enchanted Lake, The (Extravaganza)	A Cook
Esmeralda	Claude Frollo
Eton Boy, The	Captain Popham
Every Cloud Has a Silver Lining	Charles Digit
Evil Genius, The	Walmesley
Extremes	Frank Hawthorn
Fairy Circle, The	Philip Blake
Falls of Clyde, The	Kenmure
Fascinating Individual, A	Captain Thompson
Fazio	Philario
Fire Raiser, The	Piers Talbot
Flowers of the Forest, The	Linton, Leybourne, Captain Laverock, Alfred, Ishmael
Flying Dutchman, The	Lieutenant Mowbray, Toby Varnish
Fortunes of Nigel, The	Lord Dalgarno
Forty and Fifty	Altamont
Foundling of the Forest, The	Baron Longueville
Frankenstein	Prince of Piombino
Fraud and Its Victims	Count de Valmore, Alfred Seabourne
Frederick of Prussia	Captain Niddermannersteinchwanchoingen
French Before Breakfast (Ici on Parle Français—which see)	
French Spy, The	Didier
Gaberlunzie Man, The	The Organist
Gamester, The	Bates
Gentle Shepherd, The	Sir William Worthey
Gilderoy	Carbine, Sergeant Musqueton, Gilderoy

Gipsy Farmer, The	Luke Hatfield
Giralda	Don Manuel
Good for Nothing	Charley, Young Mr. Simpson, Harry Collier
Governor's Wife, The	The Governor of Surinam
Grandfather Whitehead	Langley
Green Bushes, The	Ned Keogh, George O'Kennedy
Green Hills of the Far West, The	Marston
Guy Mannering	Henry Bertram, Dirk Hatterick, Colonel Mannering
Gwynneth Vaughan	Evan Pritchard
Hamilton of Bothwellhaugh	Cyril Baliol
Hamlet	Guildenstern, Horatio, Claudius The Priest, The Ghost, Osric, Laertes
Happiest Day of My Life, The	Charles
Hard Struggle, A	Fergus Graham
Handy Andy	Mr. Furlong
Heart of Midlothian, The	Black Frank, Duke of Argyll, Reuben Butler
Helping Hands	Lord Quaverley
High Life Below Stairs	Philip
His Last Legs	Charles
Honesty is the Best Policy	Captain Lejoyeux
Honeymoon, The	Lampedo, Lopez
Hunchback, The	Lord Tinsel, Sir Thomas Clifford
Hunter of the Alps, The	Marco
Hunting a Turtle	Smatter
Ici on Parle Français	Victor Dubois
Ida May	Kelly
Idiot Witness, The	Earl of Sussex
Ingomar	Lykon, Myron
Invincibles, The	Captain Florville
Ireland As It Was	Connor, M. Voyage
Irish-A-Honey	Malden
Irish Assurance	Captain Herbert
Irish Emigrant, The	Henry Travers
Irish Lion, The	Mackenzie, Captain Dixon
Irish Post, The	George Lane
Irish Tiger, The	Sir Charles Lavender

Irish Tutor, The	Charles
Iron Chest, The	Armstrong, Orson
Isabelle	Coquin
Ivanhoe	Sir Reginald Frondebouef
Jack Robinson and His Monkey	José Rimiero
Jacobite, The	Sir Richard Wroughton
Jane Shore	Belmont
Janet Pride	George Heriot, Counsel for the prosecution
Jersey Girl, The	Dumouchard
Jessy Vere	Sigismund Fanshawe
Joan of Arc	Florine
John Overy	Baron Fitzjeffrey, Mayfly
Kenilworth (Burlesque)	Wayland Smith
King Henry VIII	Earl of Surrey
King John	Philip Faulconbridge, King of France
King Lear	Curan
King of the Peacocks, The (Extravaganza)	Franquille
King René's Daughter	Sir Almeric
King's Musketeers, The	Athos
King's Wager, The	Colonel Vane
Knight of Arva, The	Duc de Charbonnes
Ladies' Battle, The	Gustave de Grignon
Ladies' Club, The	Sir Charles Lavender, Mr. Bookly
Lady of Lyons, The	Second Officer, Gervais, Beauseant, Claude Melnotte
Lady of the Lake, The	Malcom Graeme
Lamplighter, The	Philip Arnold
La Somnambula (Burlesque)	Count Rodolpho
Last Man, The	Henry Wentworth
Laughing Hyena, The	Simon Hornblower
Like and Unlike	Louis
Little Bo-Peep (Pantomime)	Scruncher (The Wolf)
Little Dorrit	Sparkler
Little Treasure, The	Sir Charles Howard, Captain Walter Maydenblush
Loan of a Lover, The	Captain Amersfort
London Assurance	Charles Courtly, Dazzle

Lonely Man of the Ocean, The	Wyndham Bowyer
Lord Darnley	Lord Darnley, Earl Lumley, Will Eliott
Lost Husband, The	Lorain
Lost Ship, The	Ned Martin
Lottery Ticket, The	Charles
Louis XI	Tristan, Coitier
Love	Ulrick
Love Chase, The	Neville, Master Waller
Lucille	André
Luke the Labourer	Squire Chase, Charles Maydew
Macbeth	Seyton, Rosse, Banquo, Macduff
Maid and the Magpie, The (Burlesque)	Fernando, Villabella
Maid With the Milking Pail, The	Algernon
Man of the World, The	Egerton
Man With the Carpet Bag, The	Wrangle
Man With the Iron Mask, The	D'Aubigné
Marianne the Vivandière	Gaston de Montclar
Marie Antoinette	Count de Provence
Marie Ducange	Markland
Marble Heart, The	Frederick de Courcy
Marriage A Lottery	Herbert Manifest
Married Life	Frederick Younghusband, Lionel Lynx
Mary, Queen of Scots	Lord Lyndsay, Jasper Drysdale
Masaniello (Burlesque)	Selva
Masks and Faces	Snarl, Soaper
Matteo Falcone	Brozzo, Gianetto, Sampiero
May Queen, The	Secretary Sampson
Medea	Jason
Memoirs of the Devil	De Ferney
Memorandums in the Red Book	Count de Cerny
Mephistopheles (Extravaganza)	Marquis de Brancador
Merchant of Venice, The	Salarino, Bassanio
Michel Erle	Phillip D'Arville
Midas (Burlesque)	Jupiter
Middle Temple, The	Briefless
Middy Ashore, The	Mr. Tonnish
Midnight Watch, The	Antoine Deval
Miller of Whetstone, The	Fabian Leslie

Miller's Maid, The	George
Milliners' Holiday, The	Lieutenant Bowling
Mind Your Own Business	Mowbray
Mischief Making	Henri Desgrais
Momentous Question, The	James Greenfield
Money	Captain Dudley Smooth
Mother and Child are Doing Well	Maxwell
Mr. and Mrs. Pringle	John Brush
Muleteer of Toledo, The	Don Pedro
Music Hath Charms	Adrien
My Aunt's Husband	Captain Touchwood
My Poll and My Partner Joe	Oakheart
My Precious Betsy	Langford
Mysterious Stranger, The	Captain Gasconade
My Wife's Mother	Edward Waverley
Nervous Man, The	Captain Burnish
Nicholas Nickleby	Nicholas, Mantellini
No. 1 Round the Corner	Flipper
Norah Creina	Ned O'Grady
Not A Bad Judge	Marquis de Treval
Not To Be Done	Jonas Downeywag
Nothing Venture, Nothing Win	Duke of Vendome
Object of Interest, An	Sydenham Simmerton
Ocean of Life, The	Hal Harsfield
Old Gentleman, The	Charles Benedict
Old Joe and Young Joe	Frederick
Oliver Twist	Monks, Leeford
Orphan of Glencoe, The	Colonel Campbell
Othello	Messenger, Montano, Cassio
Our Gal	Henry Seymour
Our Mary Anne	Colonel Albert
Our Wife	The Marquis de Ligny
Paddy Miles's Boy	Henry
Padlock, The	Leander
Patrician's Daughter, The	Lister
Paul Pry	Harry Stanley
Perdita; or, The Royal Milkmaid (Burlesque)	Camillo
Perfection	Charles Paragon
Perourou, The Bellows Mender	Felix Raymond
Peter Bell, The Waggoner	Dubois

Pilot, The	Lieutenant Griffiths, Captain Manson, The Pilot
Pleasant Neighbour, A	Sir George
Plot and Passion	Berthier, M. de Cevennes
Pluto and Proserpine (Burlesque)	Minos
Poor Girl's Temptation, A	Walter Warren
Porter's Knot, The	Augustus Burr
P.P.; or The Man and the Tiger	Lieutenant Fusile, Mr. Somerhill
Prince Charles Edward Stuart	Prince Charles
Prince for an Hour, A	Colonel Pazzi
Puss in Boots (Pantomime)	An Ogre, A Demon
Quake, Shake and Simon	Bolding
Queen Mary's Bower	Lieutenant Wentworth
Raby Rattler	Frank Floss
Ragpicker of Paris, The	Count St. Fruilan, Baron Hoffman
Raymond and Agnes	Raymond, Jacques
Rendezvous, The	Bolding
Rent Day, The	Toby Heywood
Revenge, The	Carlos
Review, The	Captain Beaugard
Richard III	Catesby, Henry VI, Richmond
Richelieu	Duc d'Orleans, Louis XIII
Rifle Brigade, The	Captain Nugent
Rival Pages, The	Marquis de Preville
Rivals, The	Fag, Faulkland, Captain Absolute
Robert Macaire	Charles Dumont
Robert The Bruce	Comyn
Robinson Crusoe	Jack Wind
Rob Roy	Francis Osbaldiston, Rashleigh Osbaldiston, Rob Roy
Roland for an Oliver, A	The Gamekeeper, Alfred Highflyer
Romeo and Juliet	Paris, Tybalt
Rory O'More	De Lacy
Rule a Wife, and Have a Wife	Alonzo, The Duke
Rural Felicity	Unit
Saint Clair of the Isles	Roskelyn
St. Mary's Eve	Robert Vaughan
St. Patrick's Eve	Francis, Baron Trenck

Samuel in Search of Himself	Samuel
Sandy McDonald	Harry Frampton
Scholar, The	Frederick
School for Scandal, The	Careless
Secret, The	Dupuis
Self Accusation	Luke Brandon
Sentinel, The	Prince
Serious Family, The	Frank Vincent
She Stoops to Conquer	Jeremy
Shocking Events	Captain Spoff
Siamese Twins, The	Captain Vivid
Simpson and Co.	Mr. Bromley
Single Life	Charles Chester, Narcissus Boss
Sixteen String Jack	Horace Mordaunt
Slave, The	Somerdyke
Sleeping Beauty, The (Pantomime)	Venoma (a female part)
Soldier's Daughter, The	Young Malfort, Frank Heartall
Somebody Else	Hans Moritz
Somnambulist, The	M. de Rosembert
Son of the Night, The	Count D'Orbani
Spectre Bridegroom, The	Captain Vauntington, Mr. Nicodemus
Spitalfields Weaver, The	Darville
Spitfire, The	Captain Shortcut
Spoiled Child, The	Tagg
Spring Gardens	Lord Lovel
State Secrets	Calverton Hall
Still Waters Run Deep	Dunbilk
Stranger, The	Count Wintersen, Francis
Susan Hopley	Andrew Hopley
Sweethearts and Wives	Sandford, Charles Franklin
Taming of the Shrew, The	Hortensio, Biondello, Petruchio
Teddy the Tiler	Henry
Therese; or, The Orphan of Geneva	Fontaine
Time Tries All	Charles Clinton, Matthew Bates
Tom Cringle	Alfred, Mat Ironhand
Toodles, The	George Acorn, Fenton
Trumpeter's Daughter, The	Philliput
'Twas I	Delorme
Two Gregories, The	John Bull
Vagrant, The	Maillard

Victims	Herbert Fitzherbert
Victorine	Macaire
Virginia Mummy, The	Charles
Virginius	Appius Claudius, Soldier
Wallace: The Hero of Scotland	Monteith
Wandering Boys, The	Gregoire, Comte de Croissy, Roland
Wanted 1,000 Milliners	Tom Tipton
Warlock of the Glen	Clanronald
Water Witches, The	Charles Chester
Where There's a Will	Don Lopez, Don Scipio
Widow's Victim, The	Mr. Twitter
Wife, The: A Tale of Mantua	Count Florio, Leonardo Gonzago
William Tell	Michael, Gessler
Winter's Tale, The	Cleomenes, The Third Gentleman, Florizel
Woman Hater, The	Frederick
Wonder, The	Frederick
Wraith of the Lake, The	Charles Alison
Wreck Ashore, The	Walter Barnard
Writing on the Wall, The	Sir Philip Eaton, Richard Oliver
Young Mother, The	Frank Melrose
Young Scamp, The	Arthur
Your Life's in Danger	Krakwitz

First Appearance on London Stage
Princess's Theatre

September 24th, 1859	*Ivy Hall*	Johnson
October 10th, 1859	*The Two Polts*	Jack Bumpus
October 26th, 1859	*Hamlet*	Osric
November 16th, 1859	*A Wonderful Woman*	Rudolphe

Queen's Theatre and Opera House, Edinburgh, from November 23rd, 1859 to November 30th, 1859

Returned to London, December, 1859
Crosby Hall, Bishopsgate, London, E.C.

December 19th, 1859	*The Lady of Lyons*	Two dramatic
February 8th, 1860	*Virginius*	readings

Queen's Theatre, Dublin, from March 5th, 1860 to
March 31st, 1860

Boots at the Swan, The	Frank Friskly
British Legion, The; or, The Volunteers	Colonel Davenport
Castle Spectre, The	Earl Percy
Courier of Lyons, The	Didier
Critic, The	Dangle
Gissipus; or, The Forgotten Friend	Titus Quintus Fulvius
Hamlet	Laertes
Nicholas Nickleby	Nicholas Nickleby
Othello	Cassio
Pauline; or, A Night of Terror	Lucien de Nerval
Winter's Tale, The	Florizel

Theatre Royal, Glasgow (and Greenock), from
April 9th, 1860 to August 4th, 1860

Anchor of Hope, The	Captain Walton
Black Eyed Susan	Captain Crosstree
Bohemians of Paris, The	Paul Didier
Bottle Imp, The	Nicola
Buckle of Brilliants, The; or, The Crown Prince	Frederick Storke
Cool as a Cucumber	Sir Harry Lester
Corsican Brothers, The	Baron Giordino
Courier of Lyons, The	Courriol
Cramond Brig	King James V
Cross of Gold, The; or, The Maid of Croissey	Francis
Curious Case, A	Mr. Aubrey
Dowager, The	Sir Frederick Chasemore
El Hyder	El Hyder
Everybody's Friend	Mr. Icebrook
Every Cloud Has a Silver Lining	Charles Digit
Fair Maid of Perth, The	Captain M'Intosh
Frederick of Prussia	Adelbert
Gilderoy	Gilderoy
Gio, The Armourer of Tyre	Strato
Handsome Husband, A	Henry Fitzherbert
Hercules, King of Clubs	Captain Darling
Indian Revolt, The	Achmet, Prince Jung Bahadour

Jacobite, The	Sir Richard Wroughton
Lady of Lyons, The	Beauseant
Little Treasure, The	Sir Charles Howard
Maniac Lover, The	Philip Darville
Man o' Warsman, The	Ned Martin
Man With the Iron Mask, The	D'Aubignè
Marble Heart, The	Frederick De Courcy
Married Life	Frederick Younghusband
Memorandums in the Red Book	Count de Cerny
Merchant and the Mendicant, The	Henry Pelham
Midsummer Night's Dream, A	Demetrius
Naval Engagments	Lieut. Harry Kingston
Nick of the Woods	Roland Forrester
Paul Pry	Harry Stanley
Philip of France	Sir Lucien de Larrante
Pilot, The	The Pilot, Captain Manson
Porter's Knot, The	Augustus Burr
Pretty Piece of Business, A	Felix Merryweather
Ragpicker of Paris, The	Henri Berville
Rob Roy	Rashleigh Osbaldiston
Rough Diamond, A	Captain Blenheim
Time Tries All	Matthew Bates
Vagrant and His Wife, The	Maillard
Ways of the World, The	Charles Lovel
William Tell	Gessler
Warlock of the Glen	Clanronald
Witch of the Windermere, The	Captain Seymour

Theatre Royal, Manchester, September 29th, 1860

Spy, The	Adolphe

Theatre Royal, Liverpool, October 2nd, 1860

Faust and Marguerite	Faust
Maid and the Magpie, The	Fernando Villabella

Theatre Royal, Manchester, from October 1860 to April 1st, 1865

Adventures of a Love Letter, The	Arthur Clinton
Agnes de Vere	Edward Evelyn
All That Glitters Is Not Gold	Sir Arthur Lassel
Artist's Wife, The	Welford
As You Like It	Orlando

Aurora Floyd	Talbot Bulstrode
Bachelor of Arts, A	Adolphus Thornton
Belphegor	D'Arpinal
Betsy Baker	Mr. Crummy
Black Eyed Susan	Captain Crosstree
Blanche of Nevers	Prince Gonzagues
Brigand, The	Albert
Camilla's Husband	Maurice Warner
Charming Polly, The	Nat Nowlan
Cinderella (Pantomime)	Clorinda (ugly sister)
Colleen Bawn, The	Hardress Cregan
Comedy of Errors, The	Antipholus of Syracuse
Contested Election, The	Mr. Wapshott
Cool As A Cucumber	Frederick Barkins
Corsican Brothers, The	Montgiron
Courier of Lyons, The	Courriol
Cramond Brig	King James V
Critic, The	Earl of Leicester
Curious Case, A	Charles
Dark Cloud, The	Philip Austin
David Copperfield	David Copperfield
Dead Letter, The	Cornelius Nepos
Deaf As A Post	Captain Templeton
Deborah	Joseph
Diamond Cut Diamond	Captain Seymour
Doing the Hansom	Mr. Everton
Dombey and Son	Mr. Dombey
Douglas	Young Norval
Dowager, The	Sir Frederick Chasemore
Everybody's Friend	Mr. Icebrook
Family Secret, The	Frederick Crawford
Faust and Marguerite	Faust
Flies in the Web	Paul Weldon
Flowers of the Forest, The	Alfred
Fool's Revenge, The	Serafino Dell'Aquila, Galeotto Manfredi
Fortune's Frolic	Rattle
Game of Speculation, The	Sir Harry Lester
George Barnwell	George Barnwell
Guy Faux	Walter Tresham
Guy Mannering	Colonel Mannering

Hamlet	Laertes, Hamlet
Handsome Husband, A	Henry Fitzherbert
Handy Andy	Mr. Furlong
Hansom Driver, The	Felix Pottinger
Hard Struggle, A	Fergus Graham
Heart of Midlothian, The	Duke of Argyle
Henry IV (Part I)	Prince of Wales
His Last Legs	Charles
Hunchback, The	Sir Thomas Clifford
Husband To Order, A	Pierre Marceau
Irish Assurance	Mr. Clifton
Irish Emigrant, The	Henry Travers
Irish Lion, The	Captain Dixon
Iron Chest, The	Wilford
Island Home, The	Charles Darrell
Jacob's Truck	John Slipton Stasher
King John	Philip of France
King Lear	Edmund
Kiss in the Dark, A	Frank Fathom
Knight of Arva, The	Duke of Chabonnes
Knotting'em Brothers, The	Joe Smith
Ladies' Club, The	Sir Charles Lavender
Lady of Lyons, The	Claude Melnotte
Little Toddlekins	Captain Littlepop
Little Treasure, The	Captain Walter Maydenblush
Lord Flannigan	Henri la Carge
Love and Lucre	Horace Cheeryhale
Love's Sacrifice	Eugene de Lorme
Macbeth	Malcolm, Banquo
Manchester Wives	Mr. Easy
Married Daughters and Young Husbands	Digby Spooner
Masks and Faces	Ernest Vane
Medea	Jason
Merchant of Venice, The	Bassanio
Merry Wives of Windsor, The	Mr. Page
Midnight Watch, The	Marquis de Merville
Miller and His Men, The	Lothair
Miriam's Crime	Bernard Reynolds
Money	Captain Dudley Smooth
Mr. and Mrs. White	Frank Brown

Much Ado About Nothing	Claudio
Music Hath Charms	Adrien de Beauval
My Aunt's Advice	Charles Arundel
New Way To Pay Old Debts, A	Wellborn
Nice Firm, A	Ryder
Nicholas Nickleby	Nicholas Nickleby
Nine Points of the Law	Rodomont Rollingstone
No. 1 Round the Corner	Flipper
Not a Bad Judge	Marquis de Treval
Othello	Cassio
Out of Sight, Out of Mind	Captain Prettyman
Overland Route, The	Captain Clavering
Paddy Miles' Boy	Henry Coates
Paul Pry	Harry Stanley
Payable on Demand	Marquis de St. Cast
Peep O' Day	Captain Howard
Perfection	Charles Paragon
Playing With Fire	Herbert Waverley
Poor Gentleman, A	Edmund Stubbs
Poor of Manchester, The	Oliver Random
Porter's Knot, The	Stephen Scatter
Raising the Wind	Jeremy Diddler
Rendezvous, The	Captain Bolding
Retained for the Defence	Mr. Whitewash
Returned to Life	Arthur Aubrey
Richard III	Richmond, Duke of Buckingham
Richelieu	De Mauprat
Rival Pages, The	Marquis de Preville
Rivals, The	Captain Absolute
Rob Roy	Rashleigh Osbaldiston
Roland for an Oliver, A	Alfred Highflyer
Romance and Reality	Frank Meredith
Romeo and Juliet	Benvolio, Mercutio
Rose of Amiens, The	Count de Brissac
Rural Felicity	Singleton Unit
Scholar, The	Frederick
School for Scandal, The	Sir Benjamin Backbite
Secret, The	M. Dupuis
Serious Family, The	Charles Torrens
She Stoops To Conquer	Young Marlow
Signal Engagement, A	Count Theodore

Simpson and Co.	Mr. Bromley
Single Life	Narcissus Boss
Slowtop's Engagements	Clarence Greyleaf
Soft Sex, The	Frank Goodenough
Soldier's Daughter, The	Frank Heartall
Spectre Bridegroom, The	Mr. Nicodemus
Spitalfields Weaver, The	Mr. Brown
Still Waters Run Deep	Captain Hawksley
Stranger, The	Count Wintersen, Francis
Sweethearts and Wives	Charles Franklin
Temptation	Henry Travers
Ticket of Leave Man, The	Bob Brierly, Jem Dalton
Tit for Tat	Don Carlos
Too Late for Dinner	Frank Poppleton
Trumpeter's Daughter, The	Phillipot
Unequal Match, An	Henry Arncliffe
Used Up	Ironbrace
Wandering Boys, The	Count de Croissy
Wanted 1,000 Spirited Young Mil-liners	Tom Tipton
Where There's A Will There's A Way	Don Scipio de Pompolino
Who Speaks First?	Captain Charles
Wife, The	Leonardo Gonzaga
Wonderful Woman, A	Marquis de Frontignac
Word in Your Ear, A	Sir Hubert Denzil
Ye Merchant's Storye	Paul Falconer
Young Widow, The	Mandeville

Theatre Royal, Oxford, from August 8th, 1864 to
September 17th, 1864 (Summer vacation)

As You Like It	Orlando
Betsy Baker	Mr. Crummy
Flowers of the Forest	Ishmael
Green Bushes, The	Connor O'Kennedy
Hamlet	Hamlet
Hunchback, The	Sir Thomas Clifford
Lady of Lyons, The	Claude Melnotte
Love's Sacrifice	Eugene de Lorme
Macbeth	Macduff
Miriam's Crime	Bernard Reynolds

Ticket of Leave Man, The	Bob Brierly
Wonderful Woman, The	Marquis de Frontignac
Wife, The	Julian St. Pierre

Manchester Athenaeum, February 25th, 1865

Exposure of the Davenport Brothers, The	The Doctor (Doctor Ferguson)

Prince's Theatre, Manchester, April 5th, 1865

Louis XI	Duc de Nemours

Free Trade Hall, Manchester, April 12th, 1865
(his benefit)

Exposure of the Davenport Brothers, The	Doctor Ferguson
Raising the Wind	Jeremy Diddler
Who Speaks First?	Captain Charles

Prince of Wales Operetta House, Edinburgh, from May 8th, 1865 to May 20th, 1865

Dark Cloud, The	Philip Austin
George Barnwell	George Barnwell
Raising the Wind	Jeremy Diddler
Robert Macaire	Robert Macaire
Ticket of Leave Man, The	Bob Brierly

Prince's Theatre, Manchester, from May 30th, 1865 to June 8th, 1865

Extremes	Frank Hawthorn
King Lear	Edmund
Much Ado About Nothing	Claudio
My Wife's Dentist	Dick Hazard

Athenaeum, Bury, June 23rd, 1865

Hamlet	Hamlet
My Wife's Dentist	Dick Hazard

Victoria Hall, Douglas, Isle of Man, July 10th, 1865

Ladies' Club, The	Major Mortar
Wonderful Woman, A	Marquis de Frontignac

Appendix B

Theatre Royal, Oxford, from July 31st, 1865 to August 31st, 1865

Flowers of the Forest, The	Ishmael
Fool's Revenge, The	Manfredi
London Assurance	Dazzle
Macbeth	Macduff
Othello	Iago
Robert Macaire	Robert Macaire
School for Scandal, The	Charles Surface
Ticket of Leave Man, The	Bob Brierly
Woodcock's Little Game	Woodcock

Prince of Wales's Theatre, Birmingham, from September 11th, 1865 to October 28th, 1865

Dearest Mamma	Nettle Croker
East Lynne	Archibald Carlyle
Hamlet	Laertes
Medea	Jason
My Aunt's Advice	Charles Arundel
Scrap of Paper, The	Anatole
Ticket of Leave Man, The	Bob Brierly
Used Up	Ironbrace
War to the Knife	John Blunt

St. James's Hall, Liverpool, from October 30th, 1865 to November 18th, 1865

All That Glitters Is Not Gold	Stephen Plum
Bonnie Fishwife, The	Wildoates Heartycheer
Dark Cloud, The	Philip Austin
Married Daughters	Digby Spooner
Tom Noddy's Secret	Captain Ormond
Woodcock's Little Game	Woodcock
Who Speaks First?	Captain Charles

Victoria Hall, Douglas, Isle of Man, from December 6th, 1865 to December 8th, 1865

Prince of Wales's, Liverpool, from December 11th, 1865 to July 28th, 1866

Dark Cloud, The	Philip Austin
Done on Both Sides	John Brownjohn

East Lynne	Archibald Carlyle
Ernani (Burlesque)	Scampa
Fairy Circle, The	Phillip Blake
Favourite of Fortune, The	Fox Bromley
Game of Speculation, A	Sir Harry Lester
Lesson in Love, A	Captain Freeman
Naval Engagements	Lieutenant Kingston
Needful, The	Captain Feargus Daly
Nine Points of the Law	Rolingstone
Only A Clod	Harry Thorncote
Paris; or, *Vive Lempriere* (Burlesque)	Oenone (Female)
Raising the Wind	Jeremy Diddler
Robert Macaire	Robert Macaire
Silver Lining, The	Arthur Merivale
Used Up	Ironbrace

Prince's Theatre, Manchester, from July 30th, 1866 to
August 25th, 1866

July 30th, 1866	*Two Lives of Mary Leigh*	Rawdon Scudamore
Aug. 17th, 1866	*Plot and Passion*	Joseph Fouché
Aug. 20th, 1866	*Hamlet*	Ghost
Aug. 22nd, 1866	{ *Raising the Wind*	Jeremy Diddler
	Ticket of Leave Man, The	Bob Brierly
Aug. 24th, 1866	{ *Much Ado About Nothing*	Claudio
	Sheep in Wolf's Clothing, A	Colonel Kirke

St. James's Theatre, London

Oct. 6th, 1866	*Belle's Stratagem, The*	Doricourt
Nov. 5th, 1866	*Hunted Down* [*Two Lives of Mary Leigh*]	Rawdon Scudamore
Feb. 9th, 1867	*Road to Ruin, The*	Harry Dornton
Mar. 2nd, 1867	*Rapid Thaw, A*	O'Hooligan
Mar. 19th, 1867	*School for Scandal, The*	Joseph Surface
Mar. 30th, 1867	*Robert Macaire*	Robert Macaire
April 22nd, 1867	*Idalia*	Count Falcon
May 27th, 1867	*My Aunt's Advice*	Charles Arundel
June 1st, 1867	*Lady Audley's Secret*	Robert Audley
June 8th, 1867	*Serious Family, The*	Charles Torrens

Theatre Des Italiens, Paris, from July 8th, 1867
to August 4th, 1867

July 8th, 1867	*Our American Cousin*	Abel Murcott

Appendix B

On Tour with St. James's Co. (Additional parts), August to October, 1867

	Liar, The	Young Wilding
	Rivals, The	Captain Absolute
	She Stoops To Conquer	Young Marlow

Prince of Wales's, Liverpool

Sept. 30th, 1867	Meg's Diversion	Sir Ashley Merton
Oct. 7th, 1867	Nine Points of the Law	Rolingstone

St. James's Theatre, London

Oct. 16th, 1867	{ Only A Clod	Harry Thorncote
	{ Widow Hunt, The	Felix Featherly
Nov. 4th, 1867	Story of Procida, A	Charles Mowbray
Nov. 20th, 1867	School for Reform, The	Ferment

Queen's Theatre

Dec. 26th, 1867	Katherine and Petruchio	Petruchio
Jan. 8th, 1868	Dearer Than Life	Bob Gassitt
April 11th, 1868	Oliver Twist	Bill Sykes
June 1st, 1868	School for Scandal, The	Charles Surface

Haymarket Theatre

June 5th, 1868	London Assurance (Benefit matinée)	Cool

Queen's Theatre

July 8th, 1868	Rivals, The	Faulkland
July 24th, 1868	Lancashire Lass, The	Robert Redburn
Feb. 13th, 1869	Not Guilty	Robert Arnold

Drury Lane Theatre

Mar. 11th, 1869	Spitalfields Weaver, The (Benefit matinée)	Brown

Queen's Theatre

Mar. 15th, 1869	She Stoops To Conquer	Young Marlow
Mar. 19th, 1869	{ Plot and Passion	De Neuville
	{ Spitalfields Weaver, The	Brown

704

Appendix B

Standard Theatre (with John L. Toole)

Apr. 16th, 1869	{ *Içi on Parle Français*	Victor Dubois
	Doing for the Best	Harry
Apr. 22nd, 1869	*Dot*; or, *The Cricket on the Hearth*	Tackleton
May 4th, 1869	*Black Eyed Susan*	Captain Crosstree
May 7th, 1869	*Paul Pry*	Harry Stanley

Theatre Royal, Croydon (with John L. Toole)

May 11th, 1869	*Steeplechase, The*	Doctor Clipper

Tour (with John L. Toole)
May 10th, 1869 to May 29th, 1869
Croydon, Newcastle-on-Tyne, Glasgow, Birmingham etc.

Surrey Theatre (with John L. Toole)
June 14th, 1869 to July 3rd, 1869

June 28th, 1869	*Dot*; or, *The Cricket on the Hearth*	John Peerybingle

Haymarket Theatre

July 12th, 1869	*All For Money*	Captain Robert Fitz-herbert

Drury Lane Theatre

August 5th, 1869	*Formosa*	Compton Kerr

Gaiety Theatre

Dec. 13th, 1869	*Uncle Dick's Darling*	Mr. Reginald Chevenix

Vaudeville Theatre

April 16th, 1870	*For Love Or Money*	Alfred Skimmington
June 4th, 1870	*Two Roses*	Digby Grant
March 23rd, 1871	*Boots at the Swan*	Frank Friskly
April 5th, 1871	*Sheep in Wolf's Clothing, A*	Colonel Percy Kirke

Lyceum Theatre (under Bateman management)

Sep. 11th, 1871	*Fanchette*	Landry Barbeau
Oct. 23rd, 1871	*Pickwick*	Alfred Jingle
Nov. 25th, 1871	*Bells, The*	Mathias
Mar. 30th, 1872	*Raising the Wind*	Jeremy Diddler

Sep. 28th, 1872	*King Charles I*	Charles I
April 19th, 1873	*Eugene Aram*	Eugene Aram
Sep. 27th, 1873	*Richelieu*	Cardinal Richelieu
Feb. 7th, 1874	*Philip*	Philip of Miraflore
Oct. 31st, 1874	*Hamlet*	Hamlet

(under Mrs. H. L. Bateman)

Sep. 25th, 1875	*Macbeth*	Macbeth
Feb. 14th, 1876	*Othello*	Othello
April 18th, 1876	*Queen Mary*	King Philip
June 12th, 1876	*Belle's Stratagem, The*	Doricourt
June 23rd, 1876	*King René's Daughter*	Count Tristan
Jan. 29th, 1877	*Richard III*	Duke of Glo'ster
May 19th, 1877	*Lyons Mail, The*	Dubosc and Lesurques
Mar. 9th, 1878	*Louis XI*	Louis XI
June 8th, 1878	*Vanderdecken*	Vanderdecken
July 8th, 1878	*Jingle*	Alfred Jingle

(under own management)

Dec. 30th, 1878	*Hamlet*	Hamlet
April 17th, 1879	*Lady of Lyons*	Claude Melnotte
June 6th, 1879	*Eugene Aram*	Eugene Aram
June 13th, 1879	*Richelieu*	Cardinal Richelieu
June 20th, 1879	*Louis XI*	Louis XI
June 27th, 1879	*Charles I*	Charles I
July 4th, 1879	*Lyons Mail, The*	Dubosc and Lesurques
July 11th, 1879	*Bells, The*	Mathias
July 25th, 1879	{ *Richard III* (1st act)	Glo'ster
	{ *Raising the Wind*	Jeremy Diddler
Sep. 27th, 1879	*Iron Chest, The*	Sir Edward Mortimer
Nov. 1st, 1879	*Merchant of Venice, The*	Shylock
Dec. 10th, 1879	*Two Roses* (W. R. Belford	Digby Grant
May 20th, 1880	*Iolanthe*　　　　[Matinée)	Count Tristan
Sep. 18th, 1880	*Corsican Brothers, The*	Fabien and Louis dei Franchi
Jan 3rd, 1881	*Cup, The*	Synorix
April 16th, 1881	*Belle's Stratagem, The*	Doricourt
May 2nd, 1881	*Othello* with Edwin }	Iago
May 9th, 1881	*Othello* Booth　　 }	Othello

July 23rd, 1881	*Hunchback, The* (Scene from)	Modus
Dec. 26th, 1881	*Two Roses*	Digby Grant
Mar. 8th, 1882	*Romeo and Juliet*	Romeo
Oct. 11th, 1882	*Much Ado About Nothing*	Benedick
June 14th, 1883	*Robert Macaire* (Royal College of Music Matinée)	Robert Macaire
July 8th, 1884	*Twelfth Night*	Malvolio
May 27th, 1885	*Olivia*	Dr. Primrose
Dec. 19th, 1885	*Faust*	Mephistopheles
June 1st, 1887	*Werner* (Westland Marston Matinée)	Werner
Dec. 29th, 1888	*Macbeth*	Macbeth
Sep. 28th, 1889	*Dead Heart, The*	Robert Landry
Sep. 20th, 1890	*Ravenswood*	Edgar of Ravenswood
Jan. 5th, 1892	*King Henry VIII*	Cardinal Wolsey
Nov. 10th, 1892	*King Lear*	King Lear
Feb. 6th, 1893	*Becket*	Thomas Becket

Prince's Theatre, Bristol

Sep. 21st, 1894	*Story of Waterloo, A*	Corporal Gregory Brewster

Garrick Theatre, London (Charity Matinée)

Dec. 17th, 1894	*Story of Waterloo, A*	Corporal Gregory Brewster

Lyceum Theatre

Jan. 12th, 1895	*King Arthur*	King Arthur
May 4th, 1895	*Don Quixote*	Don Quixote
	Story of Waterloo, A	Corporal Gregory Brewster
Sep. 22nd, 1896	*Cymbeline*	Iachimo
Dec. 19th, 1896	*Richard III*	Duke of Glo'ster
April 10th, 1897	*Madame Sans-Gêne*	Napoleon
Jan. 1st, 1898	*Peter the Great*	Peter the Great
May 4th, 1898	*Medicine Man, The*	Dr. Tregenna

Under the management of the Lyceum Ltd.

April 5th, 1899	*Robespierre*	Robespierre
April 15th, 1901	*Coriolanus*	Coriolanus

Appendix B

708

Oct. 11th, 1905 *Louis XI*	Louis XI
Oct. 12th, 1905 *Bells, The*	Mathias
Oct. 13th, 1905 *Becket*	Thomas Becket

NOTE.—It was customary towards the end of each season for a number of plays from the repertory to be performed and which were mostly included in the numerous provincial and transatlantic tours which followed.

American and Canadian Tours

1st.   Opened at Star Theatre, New York, October 29th, 1883
Bells, The

2nd.   Opened at Academy of Music, Quebec, September 30th, 1884
Merchant of Venice, The

3rd.   Opened at Star Theatre, New York, November 7th, 1887
Faust

4th.   Opened at Grand Opera House, San Francisco, September 4th, 1893
Bells, The

5th.   Opened at Academy of Music, Montreal, September 16th, 1895
Faust

6th.   Opened at Knickerbocker Theatre, New York, October 30th, 1899
Robespierre

7th.   Opened at Knickerbocker Theatre, New York, October 21st, 1901
King Charles I

8th.   Opened at Broadway Theatre, New York, October 26th, 1903
Dante

Final performance in America
Harlem Opera House, New York, March 25th, 1904 *Louis XI*

Bibliography

While it would be purposeless to specify all the books, newspapers and articles to which the author has referred, his argument rests primarily on the following publications from which, with the kind permission of the publishers and of the authors or their executors, quotations have been made:

The Personal Reminiscences of Henry Irving by Bram Stoker.
(Macmillan & Co. Ltd.)
The Life of Henry Irving by Austin Brereton.
(Longmans, Green & Co. Ltd.)
Henry Irving by Edward Gordon Craig.
(J. M. Dent & Sons, Ltd.)
Impressions of Henry Irving by W. H. Pollock.
(Longmans, Green & Co. Ltd.)
Ellen Terry and her Secret Self by Edward Gordon Craig.
(Sampson Low, Marston & Co. Ltd.)
Ellen Terry's Memoirs. Edited by Edith Craig and Christopher St. John.
(Gollancz)
Ellen Terry and Bernard Shaw: A Correspondence. Edited by Christopher St. John.
(Constable & Co. Ltd.)
Sir George Alexander and the St. James's Theatre by A. E. W. Mason.
(Macmillan & Co. Ltd.)
My Memories by Frank Benson.
(Ernest Benn Ltd.)
Around Theatres by Max Beerbohm.
Dramatic Opinions & Essays by Bernard Shaw.
(Archibald Constable & Co. Ltd.)
The Theatrical World, 1893–1897 by William Archer.
(Walter Scott Ltd.)

Bibliography

The Scenic Art by Henry James. Edited by Allan Wade.
  (Rupert Hart Davis Ltd.)
Time Was by W. Graham Robertson.
  (Hamish Hamilton Ltd.)
Reminiscences by Mrs. J. Comyns Carr.
  (Hutchinson & Co. Ltd.)
The Dramatic Works of James Albery. Edited by Wyndham Albery.
  (Peter Davies)
Studio and Stage by Joseph Harker.
  (Nisbet & Co. Ltd.)
The Life of Augustin Daly by Joseph Francis Daly.
  (Macmillan & Co. Ltd.)

Other books and pamphlets to which reference has been made:

Henry Irving: A Record and Review by Charles Hiatt.
Sir Henry Irving by Percy Fitzgerald.
Sir Henry Irving by Haldane Macfall.
Henry Irving by Frederic Daly. (L. F. Austin.)
The Shadow of Henry Irving by Henry Arthur Jones.
Henry Irving's Impressions of America by Joseph Hatton.
The Fashionable Tragedian: A Criticism.
Henry Irving: Actor and Manager by An Irvingite.
Henry Irving, Actor and Manager: A Critical Study by William Archer.
The Drama: Addresses by Henry Irving.
Macbeth at the Lyceum: Mr. Irving and His Critics by Two Amateurs.
Irving as Hamlet by Edward R. Russell.
King Lear at the Lyceum: Some Extracts from the Press. Chiswick
  Press 1893.
From "The Bells" to "King Arthur" by Clement Scott.
Theatrical Notes 1874–1879 by Joseph Knight.
Dramatic Values by C. E. Montague.
The Life of William Hazlitt by P. P. Howe.
The Life of Edmund Kean by F. W. Hawkins.
Memoirs of Samuel Phelps by John Coleman.
The Diaries of William Charles Macready edited by William Toynbee.
Pascoe's Dramatic List, 1880.
H. B. and Laurence Irving by Austin Brereton.
A Player Under Three Reigns by Johnston Forbes Robertson.
Reminiscences of J. L. Toole. Edited by Joseph Hatton.
The Bancrofts: Recollections of Sixty Years by Squire Bancroft.
W. G. Wills, Dramatist and Painter by F. Wills.

Bibliography

The Life and Achievements of E. H. Palmer by Walter Besant.

Alfred Tennyson by Charles Tennyson.

Browning: Background and Conflict by F. G. R. Duckworth.

William Archer by C. Archer.

My Sentimental Self by Mrs. Aria.

Myself and Others by Jessie Millward.

Between Ourselves by Seymour Hicks.

The Conscious Stone: The Life of Edward William Godwin by Dudley Harbron.

Charles Reade by John Coleman.

An Actor's Notebook by Frank Archer.

J. H. Friswell: A Memoir by Laura Hain Friswell.

The Life of Oscar Wilde by Hesketh Pearson.

The Life and Adventures of G. A. Sala by Himself.

That Reminds Me by Edward Russell.

The Life and Art of Edwin Booth by William Winter.

Other Days by William Winter.

The Annals of the Edinburgh Stage by J. C. Dibdin.

The History of the American Theatre by Arthur Hornblow.

Index

Index

Index

Index

Index

Index

Index